Naunton 2000

A brief look at both ends of the last two millennia –
set within a timelessly beautiful Cotswold landscape

*Featuring
a village of families
nestling amongst a family of villages*

*Neville
with thanks and I also
enjoyed your own work.*

© David Hanks, 2004

*Best wishes
David
18-9-04.*

Alden Press Ltd

To all who have made this place what it is today

In appreciation of the forbearance of my wife Ann

Dedicated to the memory of two special
Nauntonians - my parents, Harold and Sheila

Front Cover:
(Above) An impression of ancient Niwetone, as it may have looked some 2000 years ago, where the first settlement is popularly thought to have been established. Painted by Robert Juggins of Naunton.
(Below) A modern view – the west end of Naunton. Painted by Peter Hodge of Evesham in 2000AD.

Rear Cover:
(Above) An earlier ploughman (at virtually anytime) harnessing horse-power; used here well into the c20.
(Centre) A modern ploughman - Mr Jim Organ, Farm Manager, Roundhill Farm, Naunton, c21.
   Jim is driving a New Holland TM150 tractor pulling a Kverneland EG85 four-furrow reversible plough. The tractor's 7.5 litre engine is the equivalent of some 140 horses.
(Below) Aerial photograph capturing this area of outstanding natural beauty (AONB) by Philip Juggins c21.

ISBN: 0-9546850-0-8

Typing, design and digital restoration:
David Hanks, 35 King William Drive
Cheltenham, Glos. GL53 7RP. UK
email: enquiries@old-england.com

Printing: The Alden Group Ltd
Osney Mead, OXFORD OX2 0EF, UK

Published By David Hanks

Contents

Rough-Guide Timeline	iv
Forward by Joan Johnson (author & historian)	vii
Author's Introduction	viii
Chapter One, Late Iron Age (56BC)	1
Chapter One, Early Roman (79AD)	31
Chapter Two, More Recent Times (Waterloo Farm 1920s-1977)	60
Chapter Two, Growing up in Naunton (1950s -1965)	131
Chapter Three, Naunton 2000 (Index of residents)	155
Chapter Three, Naunton 2000 (Pen-pictures of residents)	158
Chapter Three, Naunton 2000 (Photographs of residents)	194
Chapter Four, Naunton Pictures (mono 1 – 234)	217
Chapter Four, Naunton Pictures (colour 236 – 310)	248
Maps (6) & 'The Dixton Harvesters' painting	261

Appendices

1.	What's In A Name!	269
2.	Norman Domesday (1086)	273
3.	Sir Robert Atkyns (1712)	277
4.	Samuel Rudder (1779)	280
5.	Dissenters' Document (1779)	285
6.	Trade Directories (1856-1939)	287
7.	School Memorandum & Staff (1864 -1969)	305
8.	School Register No 1 (1865-1923)	307
9.	School Register No 2 (1924-2000)	341
10.	Census (1901)	359
11.	Financial Domesday (1914)	367
12.	Victoria County History (1965)	376
13.	The Lost Dialect (1952)	389
14.	War Service & Epilogue	393

Bibliography	395
Thanks and Acknowledgements	396

Rough-Guide Timeline

The two grey areas, each representing approximately 100 years, are the main two periods of this storyline. In reality they are only slightly less grey than all the other periods!

10000 BC	After the retreat of the last Ice Age, Hunter Gatherers, using primitive stone tools moved into and foraged through this area and country.
8300 – 750 BC	Hunting and gathering people (Neolithic/New Stone Age) continue visiting here. Numerous flint arrowheads and scrapers used and lost locally. Commencement of the metal ages with the smelting and use of bronze.
2000 BC	First permanent farmsteads established in this area. Further advances in use of bronze-metals, skilfully used for tools, weaponry and adornment.
751BC – AD42	Iron Age. Fortified settlements e.g. Salmonsbury & Stow; development of iron industry in the Forest of Dean, beginning of trade and early market centres, e.g. Salmonsbury & Stow; more farming settlements established.
55/54 BC	Present day Gloucestershire now part of the tribal kingdom of the Belgic Dobunni. Roman reconnaissance expeditions, preparatory to full invasion (not followed through) British Celtic tribal culture survived. First permanent farmstead(s) probably established in 'Niwetone' (Naunton).
43 AD	Roman Offensive resumed. Gloucestershire settled peaceably, Roman way of life assumed; Cirencester & Gloucester important centres; Fosse Way a major military and trade route, possibly upgrading an earlier track way.
410 AD	Roman rule subsides and is then withdrawn. Replaced by Anglo-Saxon invaders. Introduction of Christianity. Farming continues throughout all periods. Gloucestershire, east of the Severn now in kingdom of Hwicce.
850-950 AD	Viking Invasions. Gloucestershire not seriously affected.
939-1065 AD	King Athelstan dies at Gloucester in 939. Saxon Charter for Harford drawn up in 963. King Aethelred crowned at Gloucester 1014. Edward the Confessor holds his Courts at Gloucester.
C11 1066	Norman Invasion. Establishment of feudal society; Norman dominance secured through building of castles, monasteries and market towns. Gloucester chosen for Christmas meeting of the Royal Court.
1086-89 C12	Niwetone included in the Norman Domesday Survey A Norman nobleman, Roger de Olgi, is believed to have built first stone church in Naunton. Rector of Naunton, Hugh de Wallingford, given licence to undertake a pilgrimage to the Holy Land in 1286 AD.
1348/9	Black Death decimates population of country – local effect unknown.

C12 –C15	Middle Ages. Gloucestershire achieved fame nationally and internationally as a result of its flourishing wool trade. The wealth of the sheep farmers and merchants accounted for many stone-built town houses, charitable undertakings and magnificent churches (e.g. Cirencester & Campden).
C15 1485-1603	The Tudor Age. Royal visits to Gloucestershire. Expansion of inland and overseas trade; County provided soldiers for wars in Ireland and defence against Spanish Armada (1588). Re-allocation of land following dissolution of monasteries. First Atlas made, including (Saxton's) first map of Gloucestershire.
1500	St. Andrew's Church rebuilt by the Aylworth Family.
C17 1642-1660	Civil Wars and Commonwealth. Temporary importance of the Aylworth family as supporters of Parliament. Captain Richard Aylworth's troop stopped the King's Army at Stow-on-the-Wold in 1644. Much military activity in the Cotswolds after which the surviving Aylworths escaped to Canada. Last Battle of the Civil War fought at Stow in March 1646.
C18	In 1700 there were some 140 people living in 34 houses in Naunton. By 1767 this had increased to 257 people in 52 houses. Enclosure Movement leading to agricultural improvements. Turnpike Trusts increasing road transport. Re-emergence of one of the greatest trading commodities of all times - wool, now created new wealth in Gloucestershire. Cheltenham established itself as fashionable Spa after 1788 visit of King George III.
1719	End of Aylwortyh dynasty – having been here since *c.*1066.
1778	Naunton Enclosure Act – Parish's great open fields superseded by enclosed fields and farms. 433 inhabitants in Naunton by 1801.
1779	Naunton Dissenters document drawn up as some local people broke with the Church.
C1800	'Top Road' built south side of village, replacing the ancient 'Winchcombe Way' on north side as the main east/west route from Stow to Winchcombe.
1819 & 1853	Bridges at each end of village built by Rev. John Hurd. (Vicar 1807-1860).
C19	Victorian Age; continuation of progress in farming and industry. King George IV stops for meal at Naunton Inn on way back to London in 1821.
1850	Building of Naunton Baptist Chapel. 1300 people attend its opening.
1851	Population of parish now 568.
1864	Building of School.
1898	Parish Council formed.
1899	Major restoration of Church with box pews and gallery removed, font and pulpit repositioned.

C20 1914-18	WW1 and loss of local men, names memorialised. First tractor on local (Manor) farm working alongside farm horses.
1920s	Radio broadcasts received. Huntsmans Quarry business established 1926 after several centuries of ad hoc stone extraction.
1927	Pulham's first motor-bus gets to Cheltenham from Naunton, replacing the horse-bus operating out of Naunton since 1885.
1928	'Naunton Upon Cotswold' published by Rev. E F Eales MA(Camb).
1930s	First telephones installed. More tractors to local farms, Village Hall built.
1938	Closure of 17c Water Corn Mill, which had replaced earlier mills.
1939-1945	WW2: Home Guard formed. On 4 January 1941 Luftwaffe drops HE bomb on Harford. Loss of more local men in war, names memorialised. First pair of 'agricultural cottages' built by the Council during WW2 in 1943.
1945-50	Tail end of draft animal usage on local farms; Electricity installed in 1948. First Bed & Breakfast Services offered by one or two local households.
1950s	Street lighting installed, and population falls to 340 (only anecdotal evidence links the two!). Mains water installed 1953; continued unacceptable black and white television transmissions received, wartime rationing ends.
1961	Mains sewerage installed replacing cess pits and long-drop privies; quality of life improving steadily all the time. North Cotswold RDC draws up plans for eight flats to replace the last of the sub-standard dwellings known as The Yard, behind the Church.
1970s	Small compact farms in decline; trend continues.
1980s	First acceptable television transmissions received in Naunton Vale.
1990s	Last shop closes, computer and mobile telephone usage increases.
2000	Naunton 2000 Millennium Survey undertaken by D R Hanks.
2004	After three fruitless years of applications for grant money to print the book, manuscript taken direct to Alden Press (same printer as Eales' book) Costs met by pre-publication sales and support from Naunton Social Committee.
C21	The Twentieth Century saw significant changes taking place with unprecedented speed. Throughout the ages, mankind has experienced advances and reversals with little certainty of what was to come; so, even primed with knowledge of past history, we can but wait to see what the technical sophistication of the C21 will bring forth. Will civilisation ever come to mean exactly what the word implies? Only time will tell.

Foreword

For some time now, local history has been so popular a study as to have achieved the dimensions of an industry. The wealth of source material in the County Record Office has undoubtedly encouraged this enthusiasm in Gloucestershire, and the history of many villages and towns, stately homes, notable families and individuals has now been recorded in written studies of varying depth and detail. Hitherto, Naunton has not received much attention, but now David Hanks has redressed the balance, seeking to gain recognition and appreciation for the place where he grew up and first became aware of evidence in his surroundings that linked present day Naunton with its past.

Almost invisible in its steep sided valley, unless passing by, and perhaps because of this, a settlement has existed here for centuries. Only indirectly affected by events in the surrounding countryside, yet never completely cut off from them, the inhabitants of Naunton, self-sufficient to a large extent, nevertheless needed contact with and knowledge of developments that were taking place along the Fosse Way which for centuries was the main channel of news and trade in this part of Gloucestershire. Unlike places whose features have been determined by the presence or influence of a notable family, Naunton's history has essentially been that of its inhabitants; and it is his interest in and concern for ordinary folk that has inspired the author to produce this book. Reversing the more usual way of writing history, he began with a detailed survey of the people of Naunton and their homes in 2000AD; he then travelled back in his imagination (2000 years or so) and on a foundation of known facts, built up a fictitious account of the village as it was before and after the Roman occupation of Gloucestershire. The centuries in between have been left in the hope that others may be inspired to fill the gap; and as signposts to help them on their way, the author has listed some potentially useful sources such as 18th century descriptions of Naunton, Census Returns and School Registers.

Like most students of the past, David Hanks has found research addictive and he has ranged widely in search of material. This book contains only a fraction of what he has discovered about Naunton and its past – a fact which should encourage others to follow in his footsteps. I hope that he and the people of Naunton who have supported him in this project will not only take pleasure in the finished work but also feel satisfied that they have brought the village and its history to the notice of a wider public.

With all good wishes to the success of <u>Naunton 2000</u>.

Joan Johnson

Author's Introduction

Someone once said,

*'you can take the boy out of the village
but you cannot take the village out of the boy'*

In **Chapter One** I will attempt a two-in-one, slightly novel approach, to illustrate how the proto-farmstead of *Niwetone* (new farmstead) may have established itself here some 2000 years ago; dropping in during the first century before the birth of Christ, to take a closer look at this part of the *Windrush Vale* in the late *Iron Age*. Rather than refer dryly to various inanimate objects in our museums, I will try and put a little flesh back onto the bones of the people living around here at the time. In doing this I have relied on some of the very real artefacts that have since been found again, having once been lost, concealed or casually discarded. This combination of accepted facts and fictional detail is blended together to offer a 'factional' account of how things may have been. It should not be read as an authoritative account of how things really were.

In **Chapter Two** I have included some information about Naunton's more recent farming heritage. This includes a few details of my paternal family's experiences on Waterloo Farm, from the 1920s to 1977 when the farm was sold; they having followed on from numerous earlier generations who had farmed around the parish since at least the 16th century. This is intended to give a flavour of what family farming comprised of here, well into the 20th century, with some of the old farming practices and routines changing very little over the past two thousand years. It should also ensure that just a little of all that farming, as it was so determinedly undertaken here, is recorded at least once during the last 2000 years. Around this I have wrapped a few of my own childhood reminiscences, formed whilst growing up in Naunton (1948-65) before overlaying them with a few personal observations from my later life.

In **Chapter Three** most of the current residents of Naunton have 'fleshed-out' their own very real presence here in writing and photographs. This moves us away from the quasi-fictional content of Chapter One, and surpasses the interesting but mainly anonymous old village photographs in Chapter Four, allowing us to see for the first time ever the true makeup of the village in 2000AD. It also supports the intended dual meaning behind the title **'Naunton 2000'**; by taking us from an imaginary look at things here some 2000 years ago, to a factual look at Naunton and its people today.

In **Chapter Four** you will find a selection of images from the twentieth century, and mostly from the first half of it. They include many of Naunton's earliest photographs and continue the theme of the slide shows that spawned the book, whilst giving you far more time to look at them than was ever possible on a projector screen. Unfortunately, page space and knowledge of who they all were does not permit more than the briefest details to accompany these photographs, though frustratingly, most of the people's names will be contained somewhere within the appendices.

The **Appendices** introduce some additional sources of information about Naunton that may be of use to anyone pursuing other periods of its history, which scarcity, time and space have forced me to overlook. I have included some fairly recent records, such as the School Registers from 1865 to 2000, the latter adding some more 'living history' to our record, and of potential use to family researchers. The oldest known written record of *Naunton* is the incredible Norman 'Domesday' taxation survey, compiled for King William in 1086, and this too is included. The complete package offers a unique cross section of some, but I emphasise, only some, of the village's written records and imagery, drawn together at one significant point on Naunton's endless timeline, as it now forges its way gently and unstoppably into the 21st century.

Pictures that confirm long-term human activity in this valley

From these hunter-gatherer type implements of pre-historic times, to the camera recording them today, we have just two examples of cutting-edge technology from each period.

Unfortunately, it is what occurred here during the intervening time-span that we know so little about.

1.

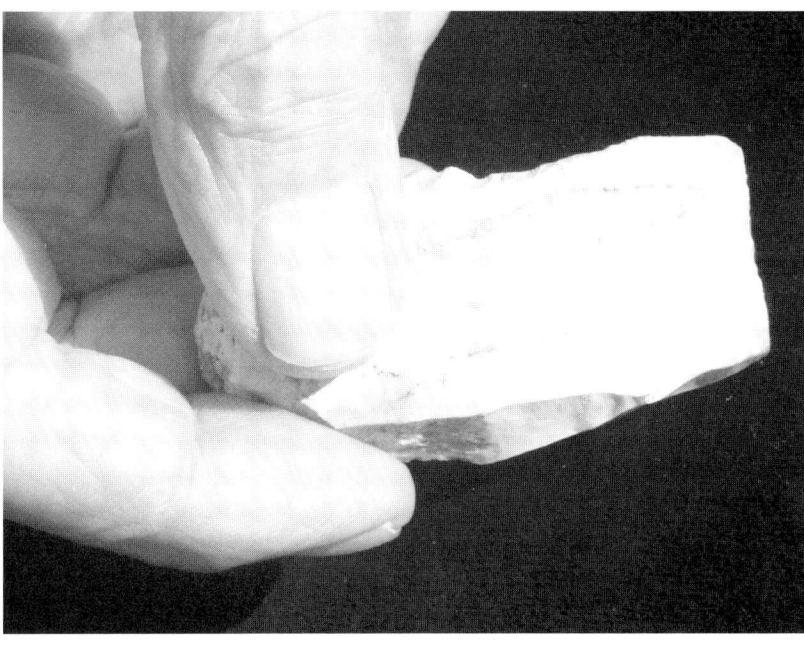

2.

(1) Flint arrowhead with tang and barb. (2) Flint scraper.
Both once used and lost in this valley. Both are now safely preserved here.

Modern Naunton, in at least one respect, is an extremely deprived community. This is because most of its inhabitants, from pre-historic until more recent times, had no written language. Even when all the children had the opportunity to become literate in the late 19th century, very few of them seem to have had very much incentive to extend their newly taught skills beyond the classroom. After chalking their slates or dipping their pens into the old inkwells and scratchily practising their letters, from whatever it may subsequently have encouraged them to write, precious little of it survives until today. This was probably due to the limited demand for writing skills amongst rural people, whose working lives were then spent mostly behind a plough, a slate-hammer, a horse and cart, a loom, an anvil, and rarely, if ever, any other kind of desktop. So it appears that until comparatively recently, local people have been unable, or unwilling, to leave behind a retrievable account of what occurred here. Unwittingly or otherwise, this has deprived us of a wealth of fascinating detail of who they all were and what they all did in old *Niwetone*, and even in the much more modern Naunton, throughout too much of the past 2000 years[1] *(bookmark endnotes on page 151).*

Although situated within an accessible and thriving part of the Cotswolds and within easy reach of the many tracks that criss-cross the higher wolds of this area, my limited research suggests it is unlikely that Naunton was ever a leading settlement, or any great hub of activity, other than in the field of farming. It is my firm belief that it established itself as a satellite of ancient *Salmonsbury*, (modern Bourton-on-the-Water) sometime during the period in which *Salmonsbury* was a thriving *Iron Age* fortified encampment, before itself becoming an even larger Romano-British settlement, some 2000 years ago, having already been settled and farmed since Neolithic times. From the dawn of human existence, people have progressed along major waterways, and smaller tributaries, whilst seeking new territory to forage or settle upon. So to me, it seems highly likely that it was from *Salmonsbury*, following the lush winding valley of the Windrush, that the earliest settlers may have come from to the place we now call Naunton, finding here in the midst of safe and pleasant surroundings, all the necessary elements for their existence and survival.

Between the natural landscape and the more enduring landmarks representing the handiwork of earlier farmers and artisans, such as buildings, walls, fields, gardens, orchards, coppices and track ways, are thousands of other lost fragments of human presence here. The loss or destruction of so much local history has without doubt occurred on many occasions before our own time due to illiteracy, oppression, fear and disasters, whether natural or manmade. But sadly, it has also occurred on a few occasions during our time. By way of example is the self-immolation of Cyril Tims in 1988. Cyril's demise probably mirrors similar tragedies stretching back across the two millennia, even though it is no longer possible to identify earlier victims [2], where local lives and historical treasures were lost forever. This is precisely what happened in the fire that destroyed Cyril, his cottage and countless irreplaceable village artefacts. But little gems do still surface occasionally [3], either in private hands or in public records. I hope they continue to do so, each adding another tiny piece to Naunton's hopelessly incomplete historical jigsaw puzzle.

So without the benefit of more recent Public Records, such as Trade Directories, Parish Council Minutes, 'Naunton News', the Press and other similar sources, we have to accept that most of the historic minutiae of village life, as it was lived out here over some two millennia has all passed by totally unrecorded. Consequently we can only guess at the number and variety of things that have taken place here from pre-historic (pre-Roman) times to the present.

Creating a scene.......

Those of you who have seen our Village Hall slide presentations during the 1980/90s may acknowledge that some emphasis was placed on trying to 'set the scene'. This was done using dual 35mm dissolve slide-projectors, with some evocative music accompanying various themes, taking us on an east-west, audio-visual trip along Naunton's memory lane. Such is the pace of change today that the hardware side of this alone now struggles to keep up with modern digital projectors. Valuable as these old pictures are and regardless of the technology presenting them to you, we have to remember that they only record a few scenes from the beginning of the last century (early 1900s). Studio photography may well have arrived in the towns soon after the 1860s, but it was another 30 or 40 years before the Victorian and Edwardian photographers began to haul their comparatively bulky, full and half-plate cameras out into the villages. Their fine work, together with family 'snapshots' captured on smaller Kodak Brownies, anytime after 1900, now enable us to take a real look at old Naunton, as opposed to an imaginary one, but only during this most recent century.

Within the confines of a book, an 'audio-visual' experience is of course considerably more difficult to achieve. Nevertheless, I would like to preserve something of it by encouraging you to use a little 'image-ination' to embrace the idea again here. It seems to be the only way to step back into the vast chasm of pre-photographic time prior to the 1900s, from which few, if any, surviving images are available. If I were to project this story and these pictures onto the screen, I would, as previously, accompany them with music, and have selected two albums for the purpose. You may choose to listen to your own music, or to that which I would use, [4] or simply read on in silence. The slide shows may then be remembered as the precursor to the book and this is my way of passing Naunton's oldest pictures on for everyone else to see and enjoy, rather than have them secreted away in numerous less accessible places. And if nothing else, I feel sure that an hour or two sitting in your own armchair will prove considerably more comfortable than an evening sitting in the Village Hall.

Celtic Tribes Of Ancient Britain c2000 years ago

David Hanks - 2000AD

Chapter 1

It is worth commencing with what Julius Caesar wrote after leading his two exploratory expeditions to southern Britain from Gaul in 55 and 54 BC. Accepting that it gives a rather one sided account, it still offers us the first ever picture to emerge from that vast unwritten period of British pre-history, and of the Celtic farming people who were living here and making it. Caesar is painting an overall picture, because as far as we know he did not visit this particular area. His thoughts would still have reflected a little of the character of the *Belgic Dobunni*, who by this time had moved into, and ruled the higher wolds of what is now Gloucestershire and just beyond. It should also be remembered that Caesar was describing a country as one might describe a hornet's nest after provoking its occupants with a stick. It was not necessarily how the natives, as physically strong, relatively agreeable farmer-warriors may have chosen to impress themselves upon more peaceable visitors arriving from abroad with less sinister motives:

"In chariot fighting the Britons begin by driving all over the field hurling javelins, and generally the terror inspired by the horses and the noise of the wheels are sufficient to throw their opponents' ranks into disorder. Then, after making their way between the squadrons of their own cavalry, they jump down from the chariots and engage on foot……They combine the mobility of cavalry with the staying-power of infantry".

Neither does Caesar restrict his observations to purely military activities, as he further describes the British countryside and its people:-

"The interior of Britain is inhabited by people who claim, on the strength of oral tradition, to be aboriginal; the coast, by Belgic immigrants who came to plunder and make war – nearly all of them retaining the names of the tribes from which they originated – and later settled down to till the soil. The population is exceedingly large, the ground thickly studded with homesteads, closely resembling those of the Gauls, and the cattle very numerous.

For money they use either bronze, or gold coins, or iron ingots of fixed weight. Tin is found inland and small quantities of iron near the coast; copper that they use is imported. There is timber of every kind, as in Gaul, except beech and fir. Hares, fowl and geese they think it unlawful to eat, but rear them for pleasure and amusement. The climate is more temperate than in Gaul, the cold being less severe. The island is triangular, with one side facing Gaul……

So here we have possibly the earliest recorded 'snapshot' of Britain, to help create the opening scene of our story. Add to this the thousands of artefacts in our local museums, which provide even more substance to what follows, together with historical features remaining in the landscape, some of which have been excavated, many of which have been destroyed, and some, I hope, are just waiting to be found. We then begin to see how rich the area is in history, if not particularly in the precious metals that the Romans originally appear to have come to Britain to exploit. We have to accept that just about everything of any historical significance occurring in *Niwetone* was influenced by people and events from beyond this valley. We can see this by keeping the bigger picture in our mind's eye, as well as the local one. This was particularly so in the formative years of the settlement, as we are about to discover.

A business trip through the Cotswolds in the late Iron Age. (56BC)

At this early time, a little under six decades before the birth of Christ, the Naunton valley finds itself empty of men, women and children, though there are traces of several abandoned round houses indicating earlier attempts to settle here for a season or two. Leading up to the people who will arrive and settle here permanently, we will transport ourselves further north to the ancient salt manufacturing settlement of Droitwich, finding ourselves near the busy salt pools. Here, great cauldrons of subterranean brine are constantly on the boil, from which the salt is scraped and packed. From Droitwich, traders move off to trade amongst the various warring tribes of Britain, some more disagreeable than others, and all living haphazardly across the thriving, corn, cloth and hide producing landscape, studded with numerous small farmsteads and settlements. Traders and merchants of the time usually had a string of pack-horses, and Bodrun was no exception. He is of the *Coritani* people, whose territory stretches from the midlands to the east coast. His forefathers tried farming but diversified after the land became barren through overuse, a constant problem facing early farmers who overworked the precious soil without putting something back. Bod and his youngest son, Hatha, now have ten horses, each with a double wicker container strapped over their backs. Some of these strong baskets contain a 'weigh' or what would later be known as a *briquetage* (a rough fired clay container) of seven stone of salt, hanging on either side of the horse. Others carry baskets full of contemporary merchandise including pottery, iron, (trading bars) and some bronze ware. Further down the route, several of them will have additional bundles of skins and sacks of wool added to what is already straddling their sturdy backs.

Bod and Hatha are preparing to leave their midlands home today and travel south along a favourite route, used by traders and others for as long as anyone can remember. They are following the track-way down to the Cotswolds, and onwards to one of the two busiest south coast ports. These are Poole, then the largest natural port in the known world; the other is Hengistbury Head nearby, in the territory of the *Durotriges*, both situated in what later became Dorsetshire. On the final leg, it is usually possible to learn which port is expecting, or already has a foreign ship tied-up. Father and son will then make for one or the other, to trade with British and foreign merchants. The visiting traders arrive in small wooden sailing ships from as far as Italy, after plying the Mediterranean ports of southern Gaul, then around the Iberian Peninsula to north-west Gaul. When the weather is favourable, as it now is, some make the short northerly hop to trade with the Britons on this side of the channel separating Britain from Gaul.

As they follow the well worn dusty track south, Bod and his son do modest business at several small farming settlements where they lay off salt and acquire more local goods to trade along the route. This is often challenging, because of the various tribal dialects. But by pointing, smiling and nodding, together with several hand and finger gestures to quantify or agree things, they have over the years established a trader's jargon and some common gesturing. Finally, at the port, they do much the same thing with the exotic mix of people there and the fact that trade has flourished proves that folk will always communicate in the marketplace. The Gauls usually arrive with a selection of spices, wines, olives and jewellery, items of ironware, copperware, glass and pottery. Hatha has worked with his father since he was a boy. He now has 19 annual notches cut on his 'birth-stick', and half of the ten horses in the train are his, together with several items stowed about them for the trip. But Hatha's heart is set upon one particular settlement further down the route, where one particular young woman has previously managed to quicken it.

Bod is a 42 year old widower who has almost had enough of this itinerant wayfaring lifestyle. Besides Hatha, he has two older sons who work out of the Droitwich salt pools. They are Bryn and Aled, who prefer to journey slightly eastward towards Lechlade, a thriving new settlement on the Thames River, where a busy trading port has developed on the back of steady ship-borne commerce. To those who know him he is referred to as 'Bod the salt', a trustworthy merchant, whose word is his bond.

It takes Bod and Hatha three days to reach the Cotswold ridge-way where they make one final stop to refresh themselves and the horses at the small round-house near *Salter's pool*. They have arrived here after a couple of one night stops, including Alcester last night. This safe drinking water is just off *Winchcombe Way*, and they soon press on towards the edge of the broad escarpment overlooking the beautiful vale of *Salmonsbury*. At this late stage in its lengthy development, the busy *Salmonsbury* trading settlement is expanding considerably beyond its old earthen banks. The magnificent vista that now opens up before them as they look down onto the broad well watered vale is topped with clear blue sky to the furthest horizons. The almost vertical smoke curls rising from the settlement indicate to Bod and his son that the weather will probably remain good for the rest of the journey to the coast. Like anyone else, they have no concept of the shape of the island as a whole, relying on their intimate knowledge of the tracks, and by mentally mapping great stretches of terrain ahead of them, especially when standing on higher vantage points such as this.

As they paused to look down into the vale that afternoon, the ten horses sensed another opportunity to graze the *Salt Way* [5] grass. Whilst Hatha peered ahead, hand on brow, he realised the settlement had grown further beyond its substantial berms since he stood here earlier in the year. He saw a slightly extended mass of squat wooden round houses, surrounded by a distinctive patchwork fields with lynchet boundaries, low stone walls and withy fences fanning outwards from the old fortification. The sun was passing its highest point as they took it all in again, refreshing their earlier mental pictures with this newer one. It was not easy because noonday shadows were almost non existent, making it difficult to see exactly where the banking of the old fort lay amongst the growing cluster of houses. The flies were troubling both them and the horses as they moved on towards the lower slopes, where they crossed the old *Stow-Bagendon Way*, and then the *West Fields* to approach the north-west gateway in *Salmonsbury's* great banks. Now they had a partial view of the pointed roofs behind the double-banked earthworks, as they passed between the newer houses outside.

This industrious and very large settlement was situated between the Windrush and the Dikler, or '*tweenbrooks*', and possession of it now lay almost entirely in the hands of the *Belgic Dobunni*, which we shall call the Cotswold *Dobunni*. The village chief was Edrig [6] of the *Dobunni.*, an archetypal community leader of these times. As they approached *Salmonsbury* that afternoon, the scent of wood smoke and faint cooking smells reached their nostrils, followed by the shrill and happy cries of free-range children, well in advance of the entranceway, adding to the enthusiastic welcome these two men received. They had already passed a number of workers in outlying fields, whose shouts and waves of recognition simultaneously alerted everyone that the men approaching were non-threatening visitors.

The tall wooden gate within *Salmonsbury's* stone walled entrance was open and they passed through without let or hindrance, watched by an all-seeing straw chewing old man within. They exchanged a friendly greeting and walked on through two high stone-lined embankments into the heart of the settlement. This was the oldest part of *Salmonsbury*, where the current occupants, Edrig's family, together with his long-term workers and closest allies, had built and re-built their sturdy houses, with conical thatched roofs, some decorated with distinctive swirling designs on daub covered under-walls. To the west of the encampment, beyond the old earth and timber banked palisade, and between the fields, newcomers had built even more houses in a piecemeal fashion, and Hatha saw men thatching two of them that afternoon. This expansionism and the desire for betterment was nothing new, but entirely dependent on the whims of Chief Edrig of *Salmonsbury*. But even his undisputed seniority within the unwritten power structure of the *Dobunnic* tribal area occasionally required him to defer to the most senior man at Bagendon, Chief Bodvoc, who was the rarely disputed and supreme leader of the entire Cotswold *Dobunni*.

The salt merchant and his son were regarded as old friends around here and no sword or dagger had ever been unsheathed on their approach. The welcome they were about to receive was as genuinely given as they experienced anywhere. It was almost two seasons since they last visited *Salmonsbury*, and in the absence of any other means of communication, Bod had calculated remarkably well that Chief Edrig's people needed a salt delivery to preserve butchered and unsmoked meat during the remainder of the mild weather and through the winter. Edrig, and his up and coming warrior son, Comux, were working behind Edrig's fine round house, wedge-cleaving another felled oak trunk for the ongoing programme of house-building and refurbishment. Some of the more slender cuts would be seasoned for Edrig's new chariot, to replace the older one he had been driving around in for several years, but which had seen little of the combat they were famed for. When armed action was required these days, it tended to be Edrig's elder son Comux who led the men and not his weary father. Comux's blonde dyed warrior locks, shaved front-of-head and huge moustache were visible badges of the gradual patriarchal handover of power, in much the same way as the triple-plaited horse's tail struck onto local coins still bore symbolic witness to Edrig's overall authority. When informed that Bod the Salt and his son had arrived, Edrig had willingly taken the opportunity to break off from the tiring work.

Chief Edrig of Salmonsbury with his customary gift of an iron bar.

The Cotswold villagers loved the traders, especially the children, who soaked up as many stories as they could tease out of them. They particularly enjoyed it when Bod and Hatha regaled them with tales of flat bottomed trading boats from foreign lands, of men with turbans, and seafarers with curved glistening blades hanging from their midriff, and with even fiercer stares than Bodvoc, their esteemed leader from the *Dobunnic* capital settlement. Though once admired for his prowess in battle, as were many of these seasoned warrior-farmers, Bodvoc was now increasingly despised for the tax burden he was imposing on the farmsteads and small settlements on the higher wolds of the *Dobunnic* tribal area. His grain tithes had increased disproportionately with the yield from the land and this was said to be because he now desired to increase his iron making capacity. He was developing a new, more efficient heating process in his bellows-driven furnace, intending to attract the best blade-smiths in the land to produce superior weaponry for his armoury. Some of these men had come perilously close to carbonising the iron and producing steel, without yet realising it.

Whilst this might add to the wealth and prestige of Bodvoc and the *Dobunni*, a few shrewd village headmen, such as Edrig, recognised that Bodvoc's coveted iron manufactory would inevitably lead to more sword rattling, or worse, towards the *Catuvellauni*, the easterly people with expansionist tendencies. One thing they all agreed on was that after this neighbouring clan had reaped a good harvest, some form of madness seemed to descend on their young men, especially after they over-indulged on the new barley brew. Bands of them were now in the habit of ravaging and pillaging the border settlements, grabbing women, cattle and anything else they could cart off. The *Dobunni* were heartily sick of this because it was sucking many of their best men, including Edrig and his sons, into more unnecessary skirmishes to repel attacks and recover possessions, occasionally with loss of life. Edrig, once a formidable warrior himself, had begun to hope that men from the farmsteads would one day be left alone, no longer called upon to take up arms against other men. But his detailed knowledge of the histories and his own life experiences now caused him to fear such peaceful coexistence might not be achieved in his lifetime, or beyond it.

Edrig knew that the line between legitimate defence and pre-emptive attack was a blurred one. He also knew that in a less anarchic world, a few good men were still just able to preserve order by the use of firm but carefully chosen words, at least within their own tribal settlements. But in these more modern times, Edrig had to accept the fact that men from times long before his own, when molten bronze first left the crucibles, had effectively ended unarmed peace and unity forever. The old bronze smiths had taken weaponry into a new dimension, casting metal that could be cold-forged into sharp edged bronze celts (ancestor of the axe), swords, spears and numerous other killing tools. He and other more peaceable leaders now had to live, and occasionally die, by the legacy of the bronze men. The cruel twist of fate bestowed on mankind by the bronze smiths had since corrupted that most ancient and trusted method of human interaction, 'the word'. A few self assured men like Edrig could still just rule by the 'word' alone, it being recognised as the oldest means of exchanging news and settling differences – or the way intelligent men interacted with one another, even if they did not always understand or agree with each other. But since the bronze times, a new and permanent twist of emphasis had been added to the commands of 'sure-worded' men, leaving them with 'swords' as well as 'words'. The world was now caught up in an arms race, dominated by the men with the finest blades. This regrettable situation had been unwittingly forged by the skilful 'smiths' and their power-hungry paymasters and more men were now dying by the swords of ruthless men than living by the conciliatory words of wiser ones. But even so, some wise men were known to be ruthless so there was no going back, and almost everyone was now armed.

Blade-smiths with the level of expertise that Bodvoc now sought were still few and far between, and commanded high reward, taking many days to forge a single battle blade of the quality he desired, these days using superior iron, whilst keeping the secret of how they did it all securely in their heads. The best blade-smiths were now part of an elite group of father-son travelling armourers who oversaw the complete process from beginning to end, carefully screened behind hanging skins. If the ore was pure enough, they could present tribal leaders such as Bodvoc with blades of hitherto unsurpassed quality. Weaponry of this calibre seemed to elevate such men to almost kingly status; or the kind of grandeur he and a number of leaders now aspired to, and with varying degrees of justification. Trained and proficient use of these keen edged blades caused braver men with spears alone to cower; to risk losing their head at a stroke if they were lucky, or disembowelment if they were not.

Today, wherever you sat within the powerful *Dobunnic* tribal structure, you were valued and protected after foreswearing to take up the sword, spear or bow behind your Chieftain; and all able-bodied men sought to hone their skill-at-arms through hunting, training and local contests. The leadership were as dependent on the virtually enslaved peasantry, as the latter were on fair and effective leadership. Each family enjoyed the protection of their Chief providing they cultivated their allotted strips of land, reaped and sowed the fields prepared by the skilled ard-man [7] and contributed to the communal granary, meat house and the ever-boiling pot. There were stockmen, woodsmen and shepherds of both sexes and many of them were multi-skilled, engaging in land-work as well roles of carpenter, slaughter-man, butcher, thatcher, potter, wright, weaver, and of course the essential smiths, who wrought crude pre-formed lumps of iron into whatever was needed on the farmsteads, from iron mattocks to iron wheel bands. Whatever your role, you were trained to cut off the heads of enemies in times of conflict and of corn in times of peace. If you proved dependable in this way, the spoils of war were as sweet as the times of peace, when fair minded Chiefs like Edrig treated you as an important spoke in his commercial wheel, enabling his increasingly popular market to flourish and his chests of valuable iron trading bars to fill. Simultaneously, the increasingly powerful, up-and-coming druidic priesthood, who made the laws and adjudicated upon them, encouraged Bodvoc and his leadership to extract maximum taxes from the peasantry. Understandably, they were regularly cursed for this by the working people.

During this more peaceful period, the success of Edrig's expanding market here in *Salmonsbury* was due in no small part to his entrepreneurial flair, and it now drew in more and more people from local settlements to buy and sell animals, hides, fruit, vegetables and a variety of other produce. Whether your handiwork was made in *Salmonsbury* or beyond mattered little. For the payment of a nominal fee in *Dobunnic* coin or metal, which invariably ended up in Edrig's oak chest, you were permitted to display and sell your wares in his flourishing marketplace. All this commerce simply enabled Edrig to acquire more iron bars, which further increased his wealth, status and influence in and around the vale. There was little doubt that he planned to do even greater things over the coming years, possibly even surpassing some of Bodvoc's bold commercial schemes.

As he tethered the horses to a rail that afternoon, Hatha was thankful that his name was not amongst those whom powerful men like Bodvoc could enslave to the land and call upon to bear arms, whatever the quality of the iron blade he may been given to wield. He was a freeman and a peaceable trader, allowed to travel unhindered with his own kind throughout most tribal areas. As he lowered the last of the *briquetage* salt containers and other wicker baskets to the ground that afternoon, all he had to pay to anyone was a single bronze coin to the willing lad who dragged them into the hut nearby. The boy was tasked with taking six containers of salt to Edrig's house, four of which would be sold on Bod's behalf in the village market and two traded with Edrig, for salting his own meat, probably in exchange for corn, providing Bod could see no mould and smell no damp in it. The boy would keep an eye on the remainder until Hatha and his father re-packed the horses and departed.

Hatha had already concluded that Edrig must be nearby having noticed his distinctive white horse tethered near his house. It was one of the finest animals Hatha had ever seen, instantly recognisable by the triple-plaited tail, so favoured by the Dobunnic leadership that they even depicted it on their coins. This form of equine insignia was something no sensible man, owning a lesser animal, would ever dare to copy. The strong lines of the horse had been recorded in chalk hillsides across the land since the times when the first bronze was cast. That was when the noble species first attained its near deity status, allowing man to rise above the ground, transporting himself at inhuman speeds for the first time in history; ferociously wielding a bronze blade and rightly regarding himself as superior to any foot warrior. In centuries to come, others may evencome to describe these times as being the 'age of the horse', that is if something more durable such as metal did not become the predominant time-label of the past. He now looked admiringly at the resting animal for some time before locating two pails with which to fill the trough for their own well lathered team of work-horse. Bod was un-strapping a personal bag from his own mount, which of late he was obliged to ride more as the gout increased his lameness. Most people were still out in the fields and the relative peace was disturbed by little more than Celtic women's small talk, the barking of dogs, baying of numerous cattle and the intermittent ring of the anvil at the open-air smithy nearby. Suddenly, even that resonant sound was drowned by Chief Edrig's raucous, curse-filled greeting, as he emerged from behind his house, a splendid structure some 26 feet in diameter, and well befitting the great man who occupied it.

Edrig was in his forties, and about the same age as Bod, but swarthier and courser in manner, characteristic of the warrior-farmers. He also appeared to be as strong as one of his numerous oxen and any sensible man would do well to have him as a friend as opposed to their foe. In his younger days it was said that Edrig's arms had been capable of guiding an ard to the point where some claimed to have seen the swingle-tree between ard and ox slacken, as he thrust it effortlessly through the sod.

Edrig loped down the dusty track from the house, flinging aside a large wooden mallet as he grinned towards Bod and his son. He then expended a fair bit of his still formidable strength in an unrestrained embrace of his old friend Bod, who was holding the customary gift of an iron bar, which he knew Edrig valued above all other gifts. Hatha, though several paces behind, clearly heard the wheeze of exhalation from his father's lungs as he was hug-lifted from the ground, as Edrig graciously received the gift and his old friend with equal enthusiasm. Within seconds Edrig turned his friendly gaze towards Hatha, clasping his hand so firmly that the bones within it cracked audibly, partly because Edrig still had the iron bar in his hand. Bod-the-salt and his son, stinking as they might be from a hot journey and the unloading work were clearly more than welcome here. All young Hatha could do as he winced and met the stare of the burly Cotswold farmer, with his fetid breath and iron grip, was smile and regard it as a great honour to be so well met.

'My house is your house' bellowed Edrig, as he gestured proudly towards the largest of the old, sagging straw-roofed, oak framed round-houses within the massive earth-banked enclosure surrounding them. Hatha quietly mentioned that there was one additional house within the enclosure since they passed through in the spring and Edrig was clearly impressed with this astute observation, knowing that they visited so many settlements. He explained that the third of his three sons had since married, and with a half hearted laugh, added ruefully that only the youngest of the three daughters was now left with him and Hilda. He said one of his two married daughters was expecting her first child any day now, making him a grandfather for the fifth time, appearing to revel in the fertility of both his land and his offspring. The comment about Erin was not lost on Hatha, who glowed inwardly the moment he learned she was still owned by no one but her proud father.

Edrig, in his unsubtle but entirely *Dobunnic* way, went on to say that there was plenty of river reed and straw around this year for another roof, adding light-heartedly that there was no shortage of wood with which to build it, daub for the walls, thresh to go behind the threshold, wool for blankets and horse-hair for mattresses. He emphasised the last item even more bawdily, gesticulating clearly as he did so and pointing towards the equally productive land on all sides of the enclosure, which no one could actually see over the banks. Hatha visualised them nevertheless, knowing they were delineated by tough thicket fences to keep the animals in one from the crops in another, one of which was being scythed by a dozen stooped workers as they arrived.

Another nearby field was being ploughed by ard and oxen, and there were other fenced fields beyond in which countless cattle and sheep grazed contentedly and escaped from occasionally, sometimes eating the low roofs of the houses when grass or hay was in short supply. Edrig confirmed what Bod and Hatha already knew; that it had been a good summer, pointing towards two open pits nearby where women were busy winnowing grain, confidently announcing that they would soon be full, sealed and covered for the winter. Not only could they afford *Bodvoc's* tithe payment this year, but the arrival of these two old friends coincided with a time of the moon, justifying a spontaneous decision on Edrig's part to hold the usual autumn feast. He insisted they stay as his guests, saying so in a way that was as hospitable as it was compelling, and any plans they had of moving on that day were forgotten. This was after all, a time when clocks and calendars ruled no ones lives; simply the rising and setting of the sun. The sacred solstices drove the farming year and the worshipful sun and moon were the only dependable calculators of time beyond day and night.

Salmonsbury encampment or fortified village consisted of some 56 acres of enclosed fertile meadowland with a spring, all contained within the old double grassy banks and ditches. The wattle fence or palisade that topped the inner part of the enclosure's banks was more to help retain the livestock at night than to exclude potential marauders. In ancient times the earthworks were said to have been constructed by the farmers as a moderately defensible settlement, for the protection of its human occupants and their valuable livestock, when inter-tribal disputes were more intense. In those days men and women wore little more than paint on their bodies when fighting, but things had progressed a little since then. The most recent occupation of *Salmonsbury* had come about only three or four generations ago, after Edrig's *Belgic* ancestors had followed the Thames and then one of its tributaries into the *Salmonsbury* Vale, and quite understandably, decided to go no further.

Edrig's clannish forebears remained at *Salmonsbury,* whereas Bodvoc's larger group of kinfolk had moved further west to occupy and refurbish a similarly fortified settlement at *Bagendon*. From *Bagendon,* Bodvoc's ancestors and the accompanying priestly caste carved up the territory amongst the first waves of Belgic immigrants. A bench of elders, including Edrig's great ancestors had convened the first Council at *Bagendon,* where they had negotiated tenancy agreements with Bodvoc's forebears. Edrig's people followed on and secured a good few tracts of land here in the *Salmonsbury* Vale, but like everyone else, ended up paying a tenth of their harvest to Bodvoc, risking sequestration of land and stock in default, such was the power now exercised by Bagendon's priestly hierarchy. Edrig's family had now farmed here, as part of the larger Cotswold *Dobunni* for almost 100 years.

The substantial territory now occupied and controlled by the *Dobbuni* was still completely unmapped, even in these more progressive times. Their area of influence was roughly enclosed between the Severn and the Thames. The boundaries took the form of visual landscape features, including the edge of a wood or field, marker stones, track ways and smaller rivers. The tribal area contained within these bounds now incorporated some of the oldest upland farmsteads, with the re-occupation of numerous older earth-banked enclosures on the hilltops and smaller settlements nearby. Land acquisition, from the earliest times until Edrig's time, had never arisen from a purchase and rarely from a consensual transfer. It had simply been a land-grab by the most powerful newcomers, including earlier hordes of Edrig's and Bodvoc's people. By sheer strength of numbers they had forcefully taken whatever land they could from less powerful occupiers, in the usual 'winner-takes-all' type acquisitions that vanquished folk simply had to live or die with.

This last takeover had arisen after the local farming people were faced with the formidable *Belgic Dobunni*. Several waves of them had arrived here in less than conciliatory mood after being displaced from northern Gaul by the Romans. Once here they made it clear they intended to stay. They forced themselves into the old fortified settlement, squatting amongst the powerless few farmers who then occupied it and refused to move. The locals either accepted them or were driven out like cattle if they resisted. There was a certain melding of cultures but it had been more of a takeover than a merger, as Bodvoc and his people vowed they would never be uprooted again from 'their' land, regardless of how they may have acquired it. Up until now this resolve had been firmly conveyed to other newcomers harbouring similar intentions, and they either knuckled down or moved on. So far, the *Dobunni* had held on to most of what they claimed was within their bounds, because they could usually muster enough manpower to do so. The current boundaries were now stabilised after hand-clasping agreements between neighbouring chiefs, and roughly as marked on Bodvoc's calf skin map of the borders, where Edrig and other local elders had since added their personal marks. In this apparently indisputable way, the *Dobunni* had now staked what they thought was a right and proper claim to land that had previously been mostly cleared, common pastureland, open to almost anyone who chose to settle on its wolds and vales, before relinquishing it, as and when a more powerful newcomer appeared over the horizon.

Edrig's *Dobbunic* ancestors had continued to farm this area, much as countless earlier smaller groups of farming families had done, since the first land clearances. Like previous occupiers, the *Dobunni* had cleared and cultivated more land over the past century. They were said to be the most organised settlers, building their more substantial Gallic style round houses, grow crops, rest and dung the fields and graze livestock. They were now living on semi-peaceable, almost commercially beneficial terms with their neighbours. In this area, Edrig, with his kinsman and workers carried on cutting the old woodlands and coppicing new ones. They tackled the overgrown corners of the vale whenever they could with bill hooks and axes, and recovered pastureland from marshland by digging ditches here and building banks there. They cultivated the arable land by breaking it up with their ards, before sowing, cropping, resting and dunging the same fields all over again. They grazed livestock steadily along the vale, accompanied by a stockman, armed with bow and sword when animals were taken further away; tended by little more than children when grazing near the homesteads. The 'milkers' were kept close to home during daylight and herded in twice a day for milking. Cattle were brought in at dusk and sheep tended by a shepherd at night. All this had brought them sufficient prosperity to pay the detested tithes to Bodvoc, knowing at the same time that the despised priestly caste was exempt from such payments, but responsible for the lore that imposed it on them.

Busy farming people like Edrig and Bodvoc knew little of priestly powers but acknowledged they were somehow based on ancient stories that only the learned few were taught before handing it down to their chosen acolytes, and no one else. In these stories it was said that the ancient priests of the bronze times had once communicated with the gods through the sky disc. This was said to be at Nebra, somewhere in the great southlands, or where the *Dobunnic* people's great ancestors lived before they were forced north, but Edrig was still far from convinced about these stories. Though no one had ever seen a real one, most people understood that when a priest held a platter shaped object up to the heavens in both hands and called out to the gods, it was a symbolic representation of the disc from this ancient but eternally unwritten story.

The rump of the *Dobunnic* people were proud, intelligent, hard working folk with more down to earth skills, borne from much trial and a good deal of error. These skills were passed down orally from father to son, mother to daughter, which generally enabled them to steer a wavering path between the extremes of starvation and the joy of plenty. By these times, Chief Edrig and his group of about 115 people had gained almost complete mastery of all known methods of cultivation and animal husbandry in the Windrush Vale. Such was their confidence and skill base that they knew the only things likely to inflict starvation upon them were crop failures, disease, defeat in the face of further inter-tribal warfare, or complete annihilation by some insuperable force. Much had been learnt along the way of course, ensuring that they survived the near starvation of poorer years as a result of prudently storing a proportion of their surplus grain, meat, fruit and roots from better ones. The grain was skilfully clay-sealed in pits, some under the floors of the houses, some outside under open sided conical roofs of straw. The meat was either smoked gently up in the roof space of the smoke-house or preserved as a result of what the women did to it with Bod's salt. And because no one wished to live by bread alone, his visits were greatly valued, avoiding the times when mild weather occasionally left them with putrid carrion.

To help ward off known risks, they were content to pay lip service to paganism by worshiping the druidic shrines and revering the spirits of their ancestors, with due deference to the mystics who preached to them, and to toil on the land for their own survival and to fill Bodvoc's coffers. They respected him as regional overlord and pledged to take up arms to follow his shield of bronze and gold, as and when faced with attack. But none of them seemed to have the slightest inclination that the threat of overwhelming force might ever come from further away than the tribal borders surrounding them.

Chief Edrig was an intelligent and contented leader who believed that life was pretty good for him and his people these days. From his productive part of the territory he and his kinfolk were now reaping the benefits of proven farming techniques, accompanied by a sound understanding of the seasons, the sun and the moon which controlled it all, and which they were obliged to worship with varying degrees of enthusiasm. Much of the higher ground was dotted with numerous small stone pens for the sheep known as *cots*, a topographical feature that would one day lend its name to several of the surrounding settlements and eventually to the entire upland area lying between the wolds and vales of Severn and Thames. Two of his lowland fields had been enlarged last year and this necessitated the building of a new raised wooden granary and several more ricks of straw to preserve what was gathered in before the winter rains. The village smithy was now fired up regularly to forge and beat iron bars into a whole variety of items needed locally.

Several additional enclosures of wattle construction, for segregating and milking sheep, goats and cows had been constructed outside *Salmonbury's* banked enclosure, retaining the inside pens for the fattened animals, awaiting market or slaughter. A thriving trade now took place here including much barter, due partly to a shortage of local coinage. But as time went by Edrig was able to purchase even more of the precious iron bars he so loved to hoard. There were fenced gardens where herbs and vegetables grew in patches separated into numerous small family strips. His wife brought wild flowers in from the meadows and planted them around the house and other women did the same. There was a small clay furnace that had so far only been used to fire *Salmonsbury* pottery. Edrig had plans to build a better one, leading to a successful bloomery where stout leather bellows would be used to infuse the charcoal with the breath of great fire, increasing the temperature to the point where a smelt of iron ore might be possible. Increasing amounts of ore were passing through the area from Clearwell, in the great forest to the west and Edrig could now afford to buy enough for his future test productions, having a modest heap of ore lying nearby already. When this happened Edrig planned to use his own smiths to shape some of it into *Salmonsbury's* first iron bars, instead of having to obtain them from elsewhere, as he did at present. He hoped this might eventually give him the edge over Bodvoc who had cornered the local market, producing his own precious iron, swords and coinage, for which Edrig had to pay him, in addition to a finger's worth of all they produced, known as the tithe.

Everyone who knew Edrig and his sons understood they were straightforward hardworking men, willing to help genuine and peaceable new settlers get established. These days they encouraged newcomers to build their homesteads beyond the old enclosure, particularly in the outlying reaches of the river valley or higher up the vale's gentle slopes. New families, whether passing through or wishing to settle here, were welcome providing they did not cross swords with Edrig and his people. Only recently they sold a cow and loaned a wagon, an ard and two oxen to a young farmer and his family, after he successfully negotiated with Edrig for the tenancy of two abandoned yardlands further up the valley. It all added to the strength of the local economy by putting more grain through his querns and granaries. Edrig knew there were still several promising locations for settlement upstream, but had not yet been able to persuade people to take them on permanently, preferring as they did, for no good reason, to remain within sight and protection of old *Salmonsbury*.

Most of this productive scene had been recalled and taken in again by Hatha during several admiring panoramic glances across the vale, before they descended into it that afternoon. After more banter had been exchanged, Edrig, with his arm still firmly round Bod's shoulder, walked slowly towards the house, reminiscing noisily as they did so. Edrig's wife, Hilda emerged from the entrance, accompanied by Erin, the youngest of their three daughters. As Hatha finished settling the horses, he noticed Hilda and Erin approaching and saw that Erin was carrying a jug of cider. Though slightly unsure of himself, he could see from their smiles that his presence pleased them, a fact that was confirmed when Hilda threw her ample arms around him, Erin standing forlornly nearby. After thanking them, Hatha slaked his thirst on the fine brew, the like of which he believed was unmatched anywhere else in Britain.

After thanking Erin, he tried to engage her further as they walked to her house, but his courting ineptitude and her shyness resulted in prolonged silence. As he dropped his bag onto the mattress he asked about her sisters and Erin confirmed that Boudicca was heavy with child, before they emerged from the smoky interior, squinting in the afternoon sun. She reluctantly excused herself for the food preparations and Hatha decided to clear his journey-worn head down at the Windrush with a much needed wash, upstream from where contented cattle were muddying and drinking the same waters and downstream of where several boys were successfully spearing trout.

By the time he returned from the river a flautist was playing a familiar but forever unwritten piece, accompanied by a woman with such a beautiful voice that Hatha paused momentarily to listen to her. The joint rendition emanated from the vicinity of a small throng of folk assembling by several oak trestle tables. Next to them a huge fire was being stoked up at the foot of the north embankment. Hatha found himself captivated as he took in this wonderful scene, with the sun sinking to his left, in a magical moment he could not adequately put into words. In this brief interlude he felt all his senses were suddenly stimulated by everything he could see, hear and smell in this wonderful place. It seemed to epitomise the very essence and magic of *Salmonsbury* and its hospitable occupiers. Most of the day's work was over; indeed the summer's work was almost finished, with nearly all the corn now in the pits. The distinctive sound of the smith's anvil was also silent, the livestock settled for the night, as the day gently drew to this magical closure around him.

As he walked back through the entrance he saw more people gathering near the fire, with the prospect of a joyous evening and full bellies ahead. Whilst this further stimulated his senses, the vision of Erin entered his head again, with her inimitable sweet smile, mellifluous Cotswold tongue, bright blue eyes and that amazing shock of red hair, trussed up with a bronze pin; hair he wanted to release and see flow over her shoulders. In those few moments Hatha knew that he would give almost anything to live amongst these industriously contented folk, and if it was ever to be, he wanted Erin to be at his side.

As he approached the gathering he thought most of *Salmonsbury's* inhabitants were present around the huge log fire, but they were not. At least two shepherds and several boy cowherds would arrive later, once their stock was settled for the night, and even then they would have to return to rudimentary shelters for what remained of it. Upon getting closer to the fire Hatha recognised the procedure unfolding before him. He saw six men, responding effortlessly to the guidance of Coldrin the swineherd, manhandling a butchered carcase towards the red hot embers. He knew they had just lifted it from huge iron flesh-hooks in the butchery hut and quietly watched them expertly skewer it throat to tail on the pole-spit. They carried the disembowelled beast towards the sturdy iron fire-dogs; one planted firmly into the ground either side of the fire. The two ends of the blackened oak spit were carefully lowered into the cleaved iron dogs, upon which the whole dripping mass was soon rotating under Coldrin's expert gaze, turned by lads who would wait for his nod before each gave it a few revolutions, earning their own appetizing portions in the process. This steady, self-greasing rotation continued until Coldrin's eyes and nose told him it had reached the wonderful state whereby it was 'done to a turn'. More spitting fat would then ooze on to the hot stones surrounding the glowing pyre, hissing and vaporising as it did so, adding to the salivating aroma that pervaded this expectant scene at feasting time. He would then remove a sliver with his keen iron blade, sink the last of his rotting teeth into the succulent morsel, before giving a gentle nod of approval towards Edrig.

As Hatha remained absorbed by these ancient practices, a jug of ale was offered to him and he glanced down to see Erin holding it. Both now looked longingly at each other, finding it much easier to converse in the relaxed and heady atmosphere that filled this convivial scene. As the light faded further the intensity of the music and singing increased and Hatha was now convinced the oldest and the youngest *Salmonsbury* residents must be present to eat and drink their way through the night. Eager children pestered the young trader, much as they ever did, but this time he was too preoccupied to respond, talking and laughing with the beautiful Erin.

After what seemed like only minutes to Hatha, but which in reality was an hour, even though he had no concept of such time, Shep, the wizened old herdsman who had been guiding the boys on the spit, assisted Coldrin by deftly removing slices of golden brown meat from the sizzling rump with his sharp and trusty bone handled knife. Coldrin proffered a morsel towards Edrig's wife Hilda, for her expert opinion. After carefully chewing it between what few remaining teeth she had, accompanied by much appreciative sucking, Hilda's expression conveyed unmistakable culinary satisfaction to the grinning Coldrin, and the horn player and flautist struck up with renewed enthusiasm. The appetising smells of carefully cooked meat had by now tantalised everyone's nostrils for too long. The increased fervour of the Celtic music and the beautiful singing voice added to the communal pleasure, all eerily contained within the old earthen banks. The whole atmosphere enveloping *Salmonsbury* on this glorious occasion seemed to release primordial urges within men and women alike, and Hatha truly believed he had never experienced anything quite like it before.

Every man, woman and child were more visibly excited as the musical cue signalled the prospect of satiating their hunger and various other urges, a privilege that sat so well with the individual parts they had played in rearing the sizzling, ungainly mass of steak that now reposed motionless before them. A loose queue of smiling chattering folk formed up so naturally that it appeared the trait was almost innate within them, each holding a wooden platter and personal bone handled knife to receive the generous portions all had bent their backs to enjoy this fine night. Only when each felt that no more would safely sit on the platter, or when old Shep, the carver of these succulent portions indicated they should move on, did they depart the edge of his fire. Most sat or stood around the trestle tables, where flattish loaves of bread and plentiful amounts of cider and ale in black stoneware jugs and beakers awaited them for this, the annual *'drowning of the harvest'* festivity.

Hatha and Erin moved towards the short queue by the spit. He found his gaze drawn towards her again and the sight thrilled him, almost overwhelmingly. She offered him a platter and knife and the skin of her soft white face was momentarily lit from one side by the flickering tongues of fire, the other by the last rays of the evening sun, as it struggled to reach in over the top edge of the palisade. Erin's wide smile beamed up at him, with her face illuminated by these two opposing, but entirely complementary light sources. Her sun pierced red hair was now trailing down over a plain white flaxen dress, with leather thong tied loosely around her waist. He found himself almost speechless for the second time that day, as he took the items from her and felt her warmth press gently against him in a queue he wished might last forever.

None of the food that Bod and his son were so generously served that night had the salty tang their palates were so familiar with. As far as these people were concerned, such adulteration was required only for preserve meats, to feed them into to the following year. The meat they ate that evening was freshly butchered, like nothing Hatha had experienced beyond the *Cotswolds,* and he assumed it must be due to the lush vale grass. Looking round the table he tried to locate the face of the man whose skills had helped reduce the animal to such a delicious state, but with no success whatsoever, because Coldrin the swineherd, stockman and butcher was now flat on his back in the damp grass, snoring loudly. Hatha's thoughts soon returned to the sweet smelling girl next to him, and only the magical singing voice of the Celtic woman was able to momentarily distract him from her.

Towards midnight and after more jugs of ale were downed, several *Salmonsbury* folk, who salted their meat, and had eagerly tried to converse with Hatha earlier on, now extended hands of friendship to him by clasping his in theirs, wishing him a safe onward journey next morning, before sensibly departing for their beds. Some, who had never travelled beyond the vale made light hearted reference to the dangers of being waylaid, a risk which journeymen always faced from brigands and spirits within the forests, once away from the safety of the vale. Hatha preferred to believe it was well meant but slightly exaggerated talk, reassured by the presence of his own keen edged sword which he kept concealed within easy reach upon the lead horse.

As the night fell silent Hatha could not remember whose arm it was that slipped gently around his waist and guided him to his bed, where he was soon asleep. But not for long, because almost everyone was up and about, doing their various chores when he emerged groggily from the house of Edrig to dunk his sore head in the trough from which his father had just led the last horse. At that particular moment, no words were exchanged, or needed to be, between father and son, just a knowing smile from the older man. Hatha sank down against the trough to reflect on things, trying to clear his head and collect his thoughts for the day ahead. As he did so, his reluctant lack of attention to detail was mercifully interrupted by Erin's arrival as she brought him a mixture of crushed elm bark in warm milk and a lump of bread.

Erin had older brothers, and knew exactly what was needed to clear throbbing skulls such as the one Hatha now held. Despite his lack of enthusiasm for the concoction, she easily persuaded him to down it in one and he was pleasantly surprised as the latest mixture to reach his belly maintained a respectful distance from his mouth again. Bod, with his wiser head, had already harnessed the horses and fed them some hay and oats and the boy who had watched over the baskets now helped reload them. The end result of all this early-day efficiency was silently transmitted to Hatha, leaving him in no doubt that he was delaying their departure. As Bod said his farewells to Edrig and his wife, Hatha attempted to do likewise towards them all, but realised he was clumsily directing most of his attention towards Erin, who looked as fresh and bright as a dew covered daisy in the morning sunlight. He clasped all their hands, but found himself holding hers a moment longer; something that was apparent to several of the women who had gathered to see them off with swathed bundles of foodstuffs that would feed to Gaul and back, had they been going that far.

They left towards Clapton and waved to the villagers who were out in the south fields, where an ard drawn by two oxen had already scored a good few furrows this fine morning. Bod looked at his son, who was walking quietly ahead of him, correctly assessing that his demeanour was the result of over enthusiastic consumption of ale. He knew that each of his sons were very different, but in Hatha he recognised a strong minded, adventurous young man, who may not desire to wander the trade routes of Britain very much longer.

He knew from the way Hatha had previously spoken with traders and sailors in Poole harbour that he had a yearning for knowledge, accompanied by a spirit of adventure. Bod sensed that one day soon their partnership may well come to an end. It would not have surprised Bod if Hatha decided to join the crew of a ship bound for some exotic place beyond the horizon. Shrewd as Bod and Edrig might be in their respective fields of farmer and trader, what neither had noticed during one convivial evening around the table was any hint of that unstoppable flame of human attraction flickering right under their noses. How could something which might impact so greatly on both their lives and prove so essential to the continuity of their bloodlines have been completely missed in this way?

So, at this particular moment in time, Bod was unable to comprehend how several hours intermittent eye contact, and some quietly spoken words between his son and Edrig's daughter during one sumptuous evening, were about to change all their lives. On the other hand, Hatha, the itinerant salt trader's son from Droitwich, had tentatively concluded that his future could now only get better. Hatha had served his father with unquestioned devotion since boyhood. He and his brothers had helped build up the business from two horses, to several teams of horse. They were all reasonably contented men, each with their own stake in a family business that somehow seemed to place Bodrun and Chief Edrig on an almost equal footing, whenever they met. At least, this was how it appeared to Hatha, from the way the two men always greeted each other, talking incessantly and bawdily, like long lost friends.

Hatha was well aware that when they visited the likes of Chief Edrig at *Salmonsbury,* in the *Cotswolds*, they were performing a vital dual role. The growers of meat were as dependent on people like Bod, as he was on them, and it was one of those successful business arrangements that had grown up since the first settled farmers discovered the curative and preservative qualities of salt on butchered flesh. Shrewd tribal elders, who had come to lead local communities like Edrig of *Salmonsbury,* relied heavily on traders, not only for the goods they transported, but equally, for the news they brought in from beyond tribal boundaries, and occasionally from across the seas. Edrig could rely upon plenty of eyes and ears to tell him what was going on locally, but one of the many things that set him apart from others, with more parochial minds, was his unquenchable thirst for information about things beyond his own immediate sphere of influence and understanding. His considerable knowledge and wise counsel equated with the old truism of knowledge equalling power. In difficult times and on more than one occasion, Edrig had somehow avoided, or managed to ward off trouble by learning of it and tackling it in advance of the point when rumour became reality. Sometimes he had neutralised it with tactful words or firm diplomacy, instead of engaging in the use of peremptory force, as had so many of his ancestors.

The criss-crossing of the Cotswolds by traders, journeyman-craftsmen, vagabonds and entertainers, resulted in many of them passing through *Salmonsbury*. Edrig and his sons constantly tapped this news-source, enabling them to build a broader picture of the tribal kingdoms and the politicking taking place within them. Edrig was particularly adept at gleaning both gossip and fact, which he then drew together and forged into as accurate a picture as was possessed by almost anyone. He did this by listening to stories from a whole variety of travellers, carefully weighing up their view of things, balancing the veracity of one against the exaggeration of another. All this news-mongering and banter may also have contributed to the fact that *Salmonsbury* was rapidly developing into one of the busiest local markets. Over the years people like Edrig and Bodvoc had successfully nurtured their local economy, and to a lesser extent understood the state of the island economy as a whole, even though they still had no real concept of its size, population or shape.

Besides staking their claim to the ancient *Salmonsbury* encampment, including the eleven houses inside the old earth-banked enclosure, and almost twice as many beyond it now, together with livestock and several working ards, Edrig controlled the river, all the fenced fields and most of the fenced woodland. He also held the extended river valley for several miles upstream and down, but only paid taxes on those parts of his fiefdom that were bordered, cultivated and crop-yielding. Hatha was now beginning to better understand the complex structure of *Dobunnic* economy together with Edrig's delicate power-structure and the genuine respect afforded to him by his people. This included the oppressed peasantry, who despite having few rights and being virtually enslaved to the land, in order to enjoy his protection and other benefits, were still grateful, despite their pitiable servitude. The sum total of all this gave chief Edrig considerable standing and authority within the Cotswold farming community and he had no desire to reduce his acknowledged influence and authority in the slightest.

In the course of the 12 years Hatha had spent roving the track-ways of Britain; his eyes had gradually been opened to all of this and more. He had willingly exposed himself to the great school of life. It was after all the only form of learning available outside the pagan priesthood. The expanding commerce of the country now depended upon traders like Bod and Hatha, and intelligent farmers like Edrig. If you were inclined towards the world of the priests then a young man could educate himself in the words of the gods and even learn some letters. But Hatha despised most of the priests he had met, believing he could see through their sorcery and having no desire to engage in their dubious ways, even though he tried to be curious and open minded about all facets of life. He now understood that the term 'Headman' or 'Chief', which tended to vary from one settlement to another, was not always synonymous with the wisest man in each community. Insofar as *Salmonsbury* was concerned, Hatha had no doubt that Edrig deserved this dual accolade. He also believed that he regarded Edrig in this way because he enjoyed the natural respect of his people, and not because he now had designs on marrying his youngest daughter. Hatha concluded, maybe a little simplistically, but almost correctly, that Edrig's powerbase was dependent on a combination of factors. These included who he knew, what he knew, how many bars of iron, working ards, oxen, and other livestock he possessed; and more importantly, how strong others perceived him to be.

After Hatha's mother died, Bod and his sons had adjusted their approach to life. They decided to see a bit more of the island and that is when they commenced plying their essential salt and other goods up and down Britain's long established packhorse routes. No longer would they subject themselves to the gang-masters of the salt-yards, crack their skin, or suffer the drudgery of preparing, drying and packing salt. They had been fortunate in that Bod had some modest savings, and after a little horse trading with a retired merchant they purchased several more animals for a fair price. Arising directly from the sadness of his wife's death, a whole new world had opened up for Bodrun and his sons. He believed that their investment in those first ponies was only the beginning, but the prospect of spending the rest of his days plying the track-ways of Britain was not one he particularly relished.

Hatha was an ambitious young man. Despite the customary British un-schooled approach to life, he now desired to improve his lot by learning more about the settled life of farming, as an alternative to wandering the deep trodden byways forever. He knew that his own forebears had once been forced to give up farming but was convinced he could now make a success of it. These past years had shown him the wider countryside, which he had grown to love, particularly the Cotswolds. But he regretted the situation whereby he stayed amongst its capable farming folk and then departed, just as he was beginning to know them better and realise his true potential. He had known for some time that he wanted to become a farmer, and not just any farmer. His plan now encompassed the very real prospect of joining the Cotswold people at *Salmonsbury*; if he could only persuade Edrig he was the right man to marry his strong and beautiful young daughter, Erin. As soon as he finished this trip he would learn how to build one of these beautiful round houses, how to thatch it himself and top it with a simple corn dolly. He would keep his two horses; buy a yoke of oxen, make an ard, plant his corn and quietly trust to the gods that everything else would follow from there.

The final details of his plan had germinated in his mind the previous afternoon down by the river. He now knew that he had arrived at a defining moment in his life, when nothing would stop him. He did not think he was being overly hasty, having mulled over the details many times, particularly, during the earlier, more lucid parts of the evening. He remembered times when he and Bod stayed at farmsteads in other parts of the land. They had, traded a little salt for shelter when the weather was poor, some hay to sleep on when it was good, imbibed a little, received breakfast and exchanged news on the down-route, doing much the same, with some iron, pottery, trinkets and wine on the return journey. But it was only amongst the Cotswold people that he had been made to feel this welcome. And so it was that he now decided what he wanted to do – marry Erin, settle down and build a new house and a new life with her.

Another significant incident occurred the previous summer, when he joined them for a few days in *Salmonsbury's* fields, to help gather in the last of the harvest, an occasion that always needed many extra hands. This was when he discovered how cheerfully tough and resilient these people were. He admired them persevering against the elements, and their tenacious and unhurried approach to life, but above all, their complete understanding and mastery of the land and livestock. Their patience was legion, unless faced with gathering in a crop if a storm was brewing, when they seemed to become possessed, as if their very lives depended upon it. He had seen them work feverishly until all the grain was in the granaries, or in clay sealed pits, and though he still did not fully appreciate the difference between the two, he knew he would. After all this they became totally relaxed again, celebrating in the traditional way; putting as much energy into feasting and revelry as they did into work.

Hatha now found himself wanting to learn his farming skills from Edrig and his people. He wanted to understand their mastery of the soil from which they carefully sowed everything that grew from it, whether einkhorn or emmer wheat, barley or flax. Whilst he had a basic idea of these things, his insatiable appetite for learning now extended to how they fed, bred, lambed, reared, crossed, sheared, plucked, butchered and finally cooked their beef, pork, mutton, lamb, venison, boar, fish and wild fowl; how they knew which cattle to milk and which ones to breed from; which ones to slaughter; or having milked them, how they made butter and cheese, or a tasty milk pudding or one of those delicious flour cakes topped with honey from the woods, the same honey as they put on cuts and wounds, with almost magical healing powers.

He now wanted to learn how things he had traded for in the past were made, and to make them himself. He knew how wheat was ground into flour but wanted to know how it was planted, raised, harvested winnowed and stored. He wanted to know how to turn apples into mead and malting barley into ale, and all manner of nuts, berries, fungi and plants into foods and some into curative potions. How they fired clay into pots; skins, pelts, wool and leather into tough studded footwear, durable smocks, trousers and jerkins. He had always marvelled at how the women, including his own mother, weaved fine cloth after rooing the fleece of the hardy Moufflon and Soay sheep, before expertly twisting the strands around drop spindle-whorls, hooking the wool onto the anchor notch, teasing it out, pinching and pulling it through the warp-weighted looms. The end result of this skilful work provided everyone with woollen cloth for blankets, or to be sewn together to make warm clothes, some of which was light enough for summer use, some with fleeces left on the skin, greased and worn inside out and capable of keeping out the worst of the wet and cold.

He studied the plain but rugged construction of their impressive round houses, held together with stout pegged timbers, supporting tight thatched roofs, impervious to wind and rain, yet somehow able to release the smoke they all reeked of. There were a thousand other things he wanted to learn to become an efficient farmer, and he wanted the peaceable Cotswold folk to be his mentors; the kindly tribal people who had secured and now held sway on these uplands, whose talents enabled them to feed and clothe themselves, and thrive as a result. In good times they were able to create a surplus to sell at their markets and occasionally to share with less fortunate neighbours. Who could fail to be other than impressed by the Cotswold farmers?

At the port – 56BC

Trade was slow at Poole, where Hatha and his father arrived without incident, finding lodgings in an old thatched ale-house with stabling. No ship was berthed when they reached the port and although no one quite knew when one might appear, the locals somehow knew one was due here at this, the oldest British cross-channel port, and not at Hengistbury, a short distance to the east. The weather was favourable, which meant that a Gallic sail might appear on the horizon at any time. Two days later it was the Poole beacon that blazed on the nearby hilltop, as a cry went up from the east wooden jetty, for the medium sized, friendly vessel that was approaching the landside jetty, and not one of the outlying islands, as occasionally happened. The seafront soon swarmed with merchant adventurers, local traders and various other people.

Bod and Hatha had already sold most of the remainder of their salt between *Salmonsbury* and Poole, parting with the last two weighs at the inn before the ship arrived. Both men were journey-wise traders, realising that they needed to be extremely careful, possessing as they now did, an additional 12 gold and 15 silver stater coins, and more quarter-staters between them. These were concealed about their bodies in several small leather purses that would attract the attention of any cutthroats aware of the fact. This age-old dilemma forced them to carry their savings with them or risk concealing them around the countryside, something they had never favoured doing, lest they could not return to recover them.

Hatha and Bod had already filled the baskets on two of the horses with various items of home-ware and a few seashells from the beach; aware that inland the women adored them for decorative purposes. These baskets were left in the care of the innkeeper. By the time they reached the wooden quay with the remaining nine horses, carrying grain, pottery, skins and wool, the ship had tied up. The scene on the busy quay included much scurrying about, preparatory to loading and unloading, taking place amidst what was spoken so fast as to be unintelligible to most of the Britons, it being the neighbourly language of the Celtic Gauls but annoyingly dissimilar to their own tongue. Two rough planks were placed against the port gunwales, the ship-side being lashed by sailors with knives in their belts who clearly regarded the deck as their territory.

As the gangplanks were secured the quayside gathering grew, including merchants, traders and other rustics, some surging forward as though about to board the vessel. A swarthy individual, a retired seaman from Poole was now attempting to restore order in his role as harbourmaster, ringing a bronze bell which momentarily halted them; some risking drowning as the complete land lubbers they were. Calling in a strong southern drawl which they understood, more by its authoritative deliverance than its oral clarity, they grudgingly moved back. Unbeknown to the old seadog, his words were silently backed up by the unspoken, menacing looks of a dozen Gallic sailors at the ship's side, some holding longish curved blades quite unlike the Briton's straighter ones. It appeared to Hatha, who was still wisely standing in the wings, that only a combination of the two convinced many of those present it was wiser to retreat than to risk a blade, a dunking, or both.

After things settled down Hatha learned from a fellow trader that earlier in the year a ship from Gaul had been completely overrun by armed cutthroats and two of the crew had suffered badly as goods were seized and carted off into the depths of the forest. Three local chiefs offered sizable rewards for the capture of the thieves and recovery of the goods but the dense arboreal blackness swallowed them up, and as usual, no one was talking. Bod, Hatha and other midlanders now kept westward when travelling to and from these ports, through quieter areas, away from the busier southeast track ways. The greater number of traders using them tended to attract unwanted attention, especially within the largest forests where the spirits made men's blood run cold, even if it was not actually spilled. That such people might now be in the crowd or skulking along their northward route made Hatha uneasy. He could perhaps understand them not robbing a salt train as it headed south but it would be obvious that more attractive goods would soon be heading north.

Bod stayed back a little with the horses, which were restless from the noisy crowd milling around them. Hatha mingled amongst the seething mass of Celtic traders, many of whom he had not seen for a good while, a few he had never seen at all, and some he did not particularly want to see again. They were a mixture of roughnecks, reputable traders, dubious entrepreneurs and a few Gauls of similar ilk. Some were on friendly nodding terms with one another, whilst the cold stare of others was met more cautiously, hoping it was the last eye contact made. Such was the crush that the predominant noise became the scrape and clash of weaponry as men tangled swords and garments, defusing things with good natured banter, amidst the noise of yapping dogs, pushy peddlers and fulsome fishwives. Some Britons wanted to see this exciting European market open up even more but the political situation in Gaul, now firmly under Roman occupation made trade erratic, sometimes with no ship venturing across for weeks. The minor public order problems on this side could have been resolved if the traders banded together, but none had so far been willing to pay the port tax to secure a small militia to protect their interests. These and related problems of security would not be properly addressed for years, and until then, each man had to look out for himself.

A much more orderly state of affairs began to descend on the quayside and Hatha concluded it had not so much been an attempt to board the ship; more an overenthusiastic surge to see what market bargains could be had; reinforcing another endemic trait that would endure amongst these proud islanders. By now, men, women and children were preparing to display a whole variety of goods, which Hatha saw included bundles of leather, sacks of wool, rolls of flax linen, colourful fabrics and quantities of delicious but perishable foodstuffs. The Britons were acquiring amphorae of wine at knock-down prices because a good grain harvest on this side of the channel seemed to have offset the value of the grape harvest on the other, ensuring that the exchange rate currently favoured the Britons.

All manner of exotic spices, fruit, fish, fabrics, Samian-ware, glass, colourful birds and even a monkey could be bought from the foreign merchants who had hired this vessel and its wiry crew. Eventually, Hatha saw a man disembark with a tray of merchandise of exactly the kind he was looking for. He was an olive skinned man from the Orient, wearing traditional long flowing garb. Abdul had set off from a port in the Levant some years before, telling his father that he wanted to see what lay beyond their own flattish land, venturing out into the wider world that some still feared an incautious captain might sail over the edge of. Abdul had since visited most of the ports around the Mediterranean without such mishap, encouraging him to further broaden his horizons, visiting ports in Iberia and then Gaul. Earlier this year he had crossed the Channel, selling so much of his jewellery to the Britons that he had re-stocked and returned twice before today. Abdul was a trader who enjoyed hopping from port to port on virtually any ship going his way. Hatha pushed through the crowd, finding him at the edge of the wooden jetty, so close that a step backwards would have put him into the shallows. Abdul always did this so that he could only be approached from the front where a gaggle of men and women, unable to understand his native tongue, were struggling to understand the poor man's attempt to speak a little of theirs.

A few would-be customers were shouting ever louder as they realised he was failing to understand them. The joint failure to comprehend one another resulted in Abdul gently wringing his hands over the jewellery tray, supported by a leather strap around his neck. The more the islanders raised their voices, the more benignly he smiled at them. By this fourth trip, he was beginning to appreciate that this was a character trait of the Britons, and knowing several languages, he realised that you needed a smattering of their tongue, as they would have no truck with yours. Hatha eased his way towards Abdul's fine selection of gold and silver jewellery, including brooches, pins, chains, buckles, necklaces of coloured glass beads, bangles and rings, many of which were set with bright coloured stones, the likes of which he had never seen before. He saw that Abdul had two swarthy, keen eyed ship's crew standing beside him and realised he had wisely invested in a little personal protection. Hatha moved closer to the display tray and his eye was caught by a thick gold ring with delicate engraving. He looked up to make businesslike eye contact with the harassed but ever smiling trader from abroad, proffered one gold stater and pointed towards the ring, hoping as he did so that one might equal the value of the other.

Abdul's expression and head movement instantly conveyed to Hatha that that it was insufficient for a sale to take place. With a hint of the universally understood smile and regardless of tongues, Hatha picked up a necklace of fine glass beads, together with the ring and with two gold coins he pressed all four items into Abdul's hand. Abdul gestured negatively again, but more firmly, whereupon Hatha retrieved his two coins and made to leave. As he did so he felt Abdul's hand on his arm, and turned to see the same two items of jewellery being thrust towards him. Abdul was saying something like 'like you' or 'you like'. Hatha quickly gave him the two gold coins and received both pieces of jewellery. Neither man really knew who had profited from the transaction but both laughed, each believing they must have gained something.

But even after the exchange, Abdul maintained a light grip on Hatha's sleeve, looking rapidly to his right and left and scanning the crowd over Hatha's shoulders before meeting his gaze once more. Speaking in a lower, more earnest tone, he said "I see you at the alehouse when the sun at noon, you meet me there, yes!" Hatha's instinct told him to decline, the transaction being complete and hoping to be some ten miles north before sunset. But something in the young Arab's voice made him hesitate and he nodded affirmatively. Abdul immediately continued shouting his wares as though nothing but a sale had taken place, and Hatha, somewhat bemused, made his way cautiously back through the crush on the jetty to where his father was; discreetly placing his new jewellery in a calf skin pouch around his neck on the way.

A little further along the beach it appeared that half of the traders had gone to Bod as he sold all his skins, wool and most of the pottery to people from Britain and Gaul. Bod had also crossed off most of the items symbolised on Edrig's birch-bark list, and was packing these purchases onto the horses, including some fine table ware and two amphorae of red wine. Hatha helped him strap the basket lids down, before asking his father to wait with the horses as he still had things to do. Bod laughed and assured his son that he was amongst many friends and acquaintances here, all of whom looked out for each other in the busy cross-Channel market, surrounded by a hundred eyes, some looking for opportunities, others keen to thwart the opportunists.

Hatha made his way to where the wooden jetty met the beach, having seen several men there with strong hunting dogs. They were always to be found when a ship was tied up because trained British dogs sold so well abroad. He looked the remaining three animals over and made an offer that was much too low for a sleek two year old dog. Understanding each other perfectly this time he raised the offer slightly and as it was now late morning, with people drifting away, his offer was accepted. On the way back he found a Gaulish metal dealer and paused to check his prices. He was doing brisk business with several local traders, who unusually, were not haggling with him. By the time Hatha reached the metal dealer there were just ten black greased iron bars left in his box. His prices were so reasonable that Hatha believed he was fortunate to find any left, having seen the same weights at twice the price inland. He quickly bought all ten bars, paying with most of the gold staters he had in one purse. The Gaul tested and accepted the coins and Hatha believed he had struck his best deal that day. He returned to his father with the bars on his shoulder, together with one disconsolate dog on a length of flax rope and slipped five bars into rawhide sheaths on each side of his horse. Bod was not so much surprised about the dog as he was by his son's eagerness to return to the inn before they headed north again, having half feared he might hand him the reins and head off to sea one day soon.

They made their final purchases and filled the remaining baskets and containers. Bod had sold the 12 bushels of corn Edrig had given to him and the proceeds of this sale would be set against four salt *briquetage* containers supplied to Edrig. They now sought out the remainder of items Edrig and Hilda had listed. Bod had already crossed off symbols representing two containers of wine, a bag of iron nails, pot of wool dye, two new pots and a cauldron for Hilda. For the first time since leaving Droitwich two weeks earlier, Bod was able to mentally calculate profit and loss for the down trip. The initial outlay for the salt, plus expenditure and barter along the route for lodgings, less port sales was now weighed against what they had purchased, less Edrig's corn sale and purchases. So far he was reasonably happy and believed that the wine and exotic cloth would bring a tidy profit inland. It needed to because two weeks of their time had also been invested in the journey.

Hatha, on the other hand, had a portion of the salt sales and had paid the innkeeper with part of the profit from the portage and sale of Edrig's corn. He was now personally down in coinage terms but felt he had begun to invest soundly in his future with the ring and a shale necklace. He was not yet sure about the dog with its tail still tucked between its legs. But with the iron bars, he believed he was about to invest even more wisely in his future, and would have thanked the gods for such good fortune had he felt so inclined. All in all Hatha was an extremely happy man, and it was he who had arranged to travel north as far as Salisbury with four other merchants, reassuring himself, as they faced a perilous passage through the dark forests of old Dorsetshire.

But before doing this, he had given his word that he would meet Abdul at the ale house. They made their way their way there with the horses through the reducing crowd on the seafront, Bod with the lead horse and Hatha at the rear so that he could see them all at a glance, this being the way they did things until back in the open countryside. Once in the rear yard of the old wooden alehouse they joined other traders who were loading and strapping down for their inland journeys. Hatha left Bod amongst them and entered the building where he soon spotted Abdul at the far side of its dimly lit interior, where men were eating and drinking near a hearth. He beckoned Hatha to join him at a table nearby, where ale was served, which Abdul politely declined. Abdul seemed genuinely pleased he had come and carefully enquired if Hatha was the son of a chief or a trader, basing his assumption on his easy going style and shrewd manner in which he had transacted the quayside business. Hatha said he was a trader, with no obvious reaction from the man opposite.

Abdul knew instinctively that Celtic traders were the roving ambassadors of Britain, well connected with tribal chiefs and others of influence. After glancing once more around the gloomy interior Abdul went on to quietly tell Hatha that a man from Italy, one Julius Caesar, was at this moment in northern Gaul drawing up plans to invade the island some time soon, stabbing his finger onto the table as he said it. Abdul saw Hatha's jaw drop but continued, saying that in the port on the opposite coastline, only the day before they sailed, he and other traders had been drinking with a Roman and had gained his confidence. The Roman had a good command of the Celtic tongue and whilst in drink had let slip that *Britannia* was about to experience the same kind of treatment that had already befallen the Germanic and Gallic tribes. Abdul's eyes widened as he informed Hatha that the same Roman, now entirely sober, was here in the port today posing as a metal dealer. He said that he did not know he had boarded the ship until they had left port, and having spoken with him again on the way across he had given the Roman the impression that he disliked the Britons. There was now no doubt in his mind that the Roman was here to spy and meet with one or two tribal chiefs who were sympathetic with the ambitions of Rome. Abdul went on to say the Roman was also here to assess the level of resistance that might be expected from the southern tribes. All this left Hatha completely speechless as he stared at Abdul and recalling the man who just sold him the bars, wishing that his father had come along as well because he was more worldly-wise and would know what needed to be done.

All kinds of thoughts now raced through Hatha's troubled mind, and he found his eyes darting around the faces of men in the ale house; the main one being what he would like to do to the treacherous Roman somewhere here in the port. They included running him through with his sword, to dragging him back to Bagendon where Chief Bodvoc and the ruthless priests would surely know what had to be done, probably torturing every last detail from him to thwart whatever plans were being hatched. An irrational patriotism now washed over him as he hastily convinced himself of the need to stop the scheming arrogant Romans, who already ruled over most of the known world and had been kept from this beautiful isle by little more than its protective moat. He realised the naiveté of his thoughts, before they had left his head because trading ships had been arriving for hundreds of years and they could just as easily carry men and armour as they could wine and pottery. But what really shocked Hatha, who until now believed he was reasonably well informed about tribal politicking, was the realisation that some British chiefs might be prepared to fall in with Caesar's plan to extend his northern frontier. Abdul could see from the look on Hatha's face that he had thrown his new friend into a state of turmoil and though he knew the nefarious Roman was not at the inn, he placed a cautionary hand on Hatha's arm, imploring him not to act rashly, pointing out that the Roman was unlikely to be alone and that others would follow, even if this one were killed.

Abdul was travelled enough to know what these proudly independent island people thought of the Romans but believed they had become complacent, and that in Britain, as elsewhere in Europe and the Mediterranean, some influential men would always be opportunists, or willing to be bought, welcoming any benefits that might flow from such an alliance. Others would simply believe it could never happen and others would remain ignorant of the gathering storm until it was rolling unstoppably over them. Hatha was aware of Roman conquests elsewhere, but until now, he knew nothing of the preparations being finalised across the channel for the invasion of his land.

Abdul quietly told him of all he had seen as he sold his jewellery from port to port on the opposite coastline, assimilating all that was underway there in the form of ship building, horse breeding, requisitioning, weapons manufacture and the preparation of what was probably the largest baggage train the imperial army had put together in his lifetime. Abdul had to agree that he had done quite well from trading with the Romans but he hated and despised them for the way they had treated his family, dispossessing them of their Levantine property. He told Hatha all this and more, before advising him to tell the tribal chiefs he felt he could trust exactly what they were up against in the shape of the massive war machine, preparing to flex its muscles again, crushing everything that resisted it. Abdul, though no military tactician, felt that with sufficient forewarning and preparation, a seaborne invasion might just be repelled on the beaches, the Romans perishing in the waves under the weight of their armour. He tried to convince Hatha that once ashore, mounted and grouped for set-piece fighting, they would prove unassailable. Abdul said he would spread the word to as many trustworthy people as he met before his ship sailed again.

Hatha felt indebted to his new friend for the risks he had obviously taken to inform him but immensely burdened by what he now knew; almost wishing they had never met. But met they had, and nothing could now undo that. He thanked him and they wished each other safe journeys back into their respective unknowns, though Abdul seemed to have a greater appreciation of what lay in store for Hatha and his people than Hatha did himself that day. They parted company with a firm handshake and comments about meeting again some day, a parting gesture both men meant quite sincerely. In doing this Hatha forgot Droitwich and proudly imparted the name of *'Salmonsbury'* in the kingdom of the *Dobunni* to his new friend, instantly affording himself a greater sense of belonging there than was actually the case, and simultaneously reassuring himself of some realistic prospect of doing so.

Thankfully, the journey northwards proved as uneventful as the trip south in relation to unwanted surprises. This served to reinforce the 'strength in numbers' arrangement, offering a cluster of traders much greater protection along intimidating forest trails, where swift strong hands were never far from keen edged swords. Hatha's greatest fear was an arrow in the back but Bod always insisted each man walk closely ahead of one horse and just behind another, offering smaller targets to would be assailants. Setting out from Shaftsbury at daybreak, they emerged unscathed from *Gillingham Forest* by midday, out onto *Salisbury Plain,* where the traders bade each other farewell near the ancient stones, before heading off their separate ways.

Hatha had chosen to remain silent about his meeting with Abdul whilst in the company of the other men, but now told his father with blurted urgency. Bod listened intently, asking occasional questions, including when and where such an invasion might take place, all of which were complete unknowns to his anguished son. Hatha was amazed to discover that his father was less than surprised. Bod explained that Edrig had discussed the threatened invasion at the feasting table, when he indicated that the *Dobunnic* council would strike the best deal they could with Rome – when it happened. *Bodvoc* was not prepared to see his people annihilated, especially after what he had learned of the Germanic slaughter. Edrig sat on the council of elders and most were reassured that the *Dobunni* were cushioned from the first wave of any attack by the *Durotriges*, the *Atrebates* and the *Cantiaci* in the South. Edrig had said that by the time any Romans reached the Cotswolds, *Bodvoc* and his council would have decided whether to join with others to make a stand, in which they might be annihilated, or to capitulate, surviving to trade and maybe even fight another day.

Bod outlined to his son that if it ever got to this point, and more elders believed it would than those who did not; Bodvoc planned to negotiate beneficial supply contracts with the Romans, and carry on farming and trading, concealing their swords in the thatch and bide their time. The one thing they had all been agreed upon was that no Briton, regardless of tribal differences, would ever willingly become a slave to Rome and they would do all within their power to avoid this outcome. Hatha was slightly reassured upon hearing all this and realised just how much Erin must have distracted him that night, missing this conversation completely. He tried to convince himself that his future plans might not after all have been completely crushed by the alarming but well intentioned words of the Levantine trader. They stayed at three more villages on the journey north, seeing much the same people and making one or two new acquaintances. The prospect of returning to *Salmonsbury* after one more stop at Cricklade was once more beginning to raise the spirits of the young salt trader.

From thinking he was the sole bearer of grave news, to having the burden lifted from his shoulders overnight, Hatha now believed he could relax and concentrate on his future plans again. He told himself he would ask Erin to marry him, his instincts telling him that she would accept, so that part was almost settled. The other matter concerned his own dowry contribution to Edrig's family. He mused on this a while longer before making his over generous decision. He could not afford to insult Edrig by offering him the hunting dog alone and his revised plan was to overwhelm him with generosity. He knew two things that would gladden the old man's heart; one being horses, knowing he would soon need more for his new chariot. Hatha felt he would not need all six himself after this trip, and could breed more if he did. The other area which he knew Edrig was expanding into involved his metal working enterprises. He would give him some of the iron bars upon arrival, to add to the great hoard that was already in his wealth chest. He believed this might be regarded as adequate reward for his beautiful daughter, and had no idea that any one of the three would have sufficed. Finally, in what he hoped would be a joyous evening of celebration, he would present Hilda with the glass beaded necklace and shale bracelet, and the other women with some sea shells and announce that he too intended to become a farmer. But before any of this could happen, one other thing remained to be resolved, as they completed the final leg of the return journey to *Salmonsbury Vale* on that fine clear morning during the late summer of 56BC. Hatha knew he must outline the plan to his father, to discover how he felt about it all and what he might do with his future life.

Bod listened intently, without saying a single word. As Hatha continued, he believed more and more that what he was saying was having a very bad effect on his tired father. He tried to draw it to some kind of tidy conclusion by explaining how he planned to build a fine wooden round house for himself and Erin somewhere near *Salmonsbury* and how Bod would be welcome to live with them, as there

Hatha returning to Salmonsbury, prior to handing Chief Edrig more iron bars

was sure to be plenty of work on the new farmstead. He explained that he wanted his brothers to bring the salt down and stay with them, that he wanted his sister to visit them, and then decided he had said more than enough, desperately wanting to hear his father speak. The palpable silence that followed troubled Hatha almost as much as Abdul's news. He now regretted not telling Bod before, to get the unpleasantness over and done with long before they reached *Salmonsbury*. They were both mounted as he gently drew alongside his father's horse and looked across at him, trying to read his thoughts whilst remaining compassionate and committed to his plan.

Bod looked thoughtfully at his son as the two horses' flanks rubbed together, bringing both to a gentle halt in the sunshine, apparently sensing the importance of the moment as they bore their owners northwards along the dusty route. Bod's grizzled but expressionless face began to contort; his jaw relaxed and then opened out into a broad smile as he said, *'son, a while ago I thought you were going to tell me you'd had enough of all this and wanted to spread you wings and be away. What you've just told me is more than I could ever have wished for and I hope she'll accept you as her husband. I know Edrig is fond of you so there'll be no problem there, and you'll not have to give him your horses if you intend being a farmer'*. Both men reached across and embraced for the first time ever. Bod still had to decide what he was going to do with the rest of his life, but was a contented man regardless. They spent that night at Cricklade before setting off on the final leg of the journey.

As they approached *Salmonsbury* both men sensed something was amiss. They passed several people in the fields, who glanced their way, but when Hatha raised his hand to them, the response lacked enthusiasm. After reaching the entrance Hatha dismounted, removed several iron bars from his horse and walked proudly ahead with them, ready to make his more than generous offering to Chief Edrig. Although several children ran towards him, the place was quieter than usual and the mood difficult to gauge, adding to his bewilderment. He walked on towards Edrig's house where it was Erin who saw him approach and she ran towards him from the entrance. He could see her eyes were red as she explained that Boudicca went into labour a few days earlier. The birth was long and difficult, her beloved sister dying soon after the stillborn child.

The family and communal grief was palpable and overwhelming, though entirely natural as the anticipated joy of new life, together with well loved one had been cruelly snatched from their midst, leaving a great void in this family based settlement. They were now struggling as one large family, in an effort to come to terms with the double tragedy that gripped them. Though familiar with such losses, it was always a terrible blow and even the toughest of men could not hide their emotions. The only way they knew of dealing with such things was by pulling each other through it together. Hatha and Bod now attempted to console Hilda and her two daughters, whose wailing pierced the air less frequently with the passing of several long sad days. The woman who sang so beautifully at the recent feast could occasionally be heard offering a Celtic dirge that pierced the autumn air, causing Edrig and his distraught son-in-law to retreat to fieldwork as a way of coping and distancing themselves from it. As with several other recent bereavements, Edrig had not called the priest from Bagendon to officiate. This would have resulted in the bodies being burned in sack cloth, amidst much chanting to the pagan gods. Hilda had insisted they bury them both quietly nearby because of her young age and Edrig had not argued with her. The bodies had been lovingly wrapped in wool and interred in a disused grain pit on grazing land west of the old embankments, forever undisturbed by the ard. The whole village and people from outlying farmsteads had been present two days earlier for the wake and burial, which accompanied the traditional send-offs from Celtic timber-fuelled conflagrations, overseen by a High Priest.

Bod and Hatha remained at *Salmonsbury* during the traditional grieving period. Several days later, as the lamentations subsided, Edrig announced that a feast would be held to greet the autumn and celebrate the happier times they all fondly remembered, when Boudicca was with them in body. He hoped it might lift the spirits of the family and the settlement as a whole. Several animals were butchered and the following evening everyone gathered near the great fire for this less than happy occasion, without the music and jollity that would normally have accompanied such feasting. Food and drink were consumed moderately amidst many reflective thoughts. Comments were heard about why the gods had chosen to punish them in this way again and at the end of the meal Edrig rose to address his assembled clan, sitting respectfully before him. He made a short speech in genuine appreciation of the help and consideration everyone had shown to him and his family over these difficult days.

As Hatha listened it became even more evident to him why this great man held the undivided attention of his people, all of whom were feeling the pain, as though the loss was their own. Edrig faltered slightly as he looked at the empty place they had left for Boudicca, but quickly regained his composure as he outlined stories from her childhood. He reminded those who had not heard the tale before of how she had once taken two frail lambs to bed with her, the bleating keeping them awake all night. He reminded them that although she had been weak as a child, she had gained her strength upon reaching womanhood, becoming an accomplished horsewoman, even surpassing her brothers. He told them of her excitement about the approach of motherhood and giving them another grandchild before he noticed that his wife Hilda was smiling and weeping at the same time. He told them of her love for her husband and her horse and tried to make them laugh, adding that he did not really know which came first, but both were missing her badly. He told them of a more recent time when she had joined them on a boar hunt, and though several spears found their mark, it was Boudicca's that brought it down. As these last few words trailed from his lips they seemed to sum up how life and death were such close bedfellows in the Celtic world of hunter-farmers. Edrig concluded by saying they must now all move on, and that something good would soon come into their lives, though no one seemed to know how, no one spoke or seemed able to offer him and his family a single crumb of comfort in the long sombre moment that followed his trailing words.

Then the completely unexpected happened, as all heads turned to see Hatha rise nervously to his feet and face Edrig. After a silent pause Hatha coughed to clear his dry throat, suddenly becoming unsure of what he was doing. He fixed a nervous stare directly at Edrig, whose gold torc appeared to be constricting his strong neck muscles, making his eyes bulge, he too being unsure of what was to follow other than perhaps a few well meant words from this likeable young man. Bod also looked uncomfortable as his son's faltering voice raised slightly to utter some heartfelt words in front of the assembled village as he said, *'Chief Edrig, I too share in your family's grief but I would like your permission to ask your daughter Erin if she will be my wife'*.

There was a collective gasp from everyone present and the two men stood facing one another, both rocking slightly on their heels. Hatha seemed to realise the folly of what he had just done. The poor man had just mourned the loss of one daughter, and here he was, an outsider, suggesting he take his third and youngest away from them. Convinced that his timing was completely wrong he felt sick in the pit of his belly. But the collective intake of breath, drawn by the assembled gathering barely a moment before was now exhaled as a raucous cheer which became a chant of approval, the likes of which he had never heard them utter in unison before.

Hatha glanced back towards Edrig who was now hugging his still tearful wife. Erin quickly crossed the space between them and slipped her arm around his waist in a way he thought was slightly familiar, but for the life of him was unable to recall precisely when it had happened before. She kissed him fully on the lips, which simply resulted in the crescendo of communal delight drowning all else, with knives now banging on platters, amounting to a kind of public betrothal that surely no one would now undo. It was as though a black cloud had suddenly been lifted from them all. Old Shep's bone flute soon had spittle leaving its lower end as he roused the gathering into almost dance mood for the first time in weeks and celebratory drinks were now poured with almost indecent haste.

People were still whooping and clapping and several clasped Hatha's hand, including Erin's brothers. Hilda was still wiping tears from her eyes but the emotion behind them had changed completely. Bod was in conversation with Edrig, who slowly stood up again, prompting those present to become hushed once more, as if by some kind of silent command, several believing he was about to say 'no' to young Hatha. Even Edrig was seen to quickly wipe a hand surreptitiously across his glistening eyes, as if mimicking the removal of some imaginary cobweb to preserve his dignity. Before addressing everyone he fixed a steady and unnerving gaze on a now trembling Hatha. A smile slowly appeared as he said, *'Well young man, I wasn't expecting that and it seems you've got my answer from everyone else, including my dear daughter, so I can hardly object now that the village has given you my permission, can I?'* Both men stood there beaming at each other. After a murmur of approval had subsided, Edrig continued, *'I am also informed, by my good friend Bod that you wish to compete with me as a farmer'*, which put that way, visibly embarrassed Hatha. Edrig immediately relieved the tension by adding, *'and there's nothing wrong with a bit of healthy competition young Hatha, just let me know where you intend to build your house and raise your children'*, resulting in more cheering, and visibly easing Hatha's obvious discomfiture in the same breath.

Looking round the now joyous faces, Edrig added, "*I suppose I'll have to hire a priest*", and once again it was Hatha's totally unrehearsed response that caused Edrig to tilt on his heels, as he parried the second verbal blow from the young trader's fistful of announcements that evening. Hatha continued by saying, *'Chief Edrig, I would be honoured if you would marry us instead of the man from Bagendon'*, without going on to say what he really felt about pagan sorcerers. Edrig, still slightly off guard, looked quizzically towards several of the village elders who sat on 'Salmonbury's' ruling council. You could have heard a bronze pin drop as they furrowed their brows and exchanged non-committal nods and glances. Receiving no guidance, Edrig waved a powerful hand of indifference towards them, as he so often did after such useless consultations, some men always preferring to sit on wattle fences when faced with difficult decisions. Without wavering Edrig replied firmly with, *'Let the Romans have the nay-sayers young Hatha, I shall consider it an honour to give you my dear Erin, and I don't need a priest to do it for me'*. In that one euphoric moment, those few words conveyed more to Hatha than Edrig could have known. Old Shep's bone flute played again at just the right moment. Before anyone else could say a word, a hearty tune pierced the cold night air, through a chill that no one was the slightest bit aware of.

On a crisp autumn afternoon soon after, everyone from Salmonsbury was present outside Edrig's decorated and garlanded house. Invited friends from Bagendon and many other villages and farmsteads were present to see him walk proudly out with his youngest daughter, Erin. She was dressed in a simple white flaxen dress made by her mother; a thin white cord tied around her waist and the finest bronze brooch pinned over her left breast. A garland of fresh ivy sat lightly on her head. Her long hair was plaited and her blue eyes transfixed themselves adoringly on the young man standing nervously before the House of Edrig, waiting to marry her. His brothers Bryn and Aled, sister Isla and of course Bod, were also present.

What followed was a little unorthodox within the conventional style of Pagan Celtic wedding ceremonies, and Edrig realised that when word of it reached Bagendon he would probably be accused of heathenism, or worse. But Edrig was a free-thinker with scant regard for the haughty priesthood and knew it was high time someone took a stand against them, this day being as good as any he could think of to do so. He knew Bodvoc would chuckle to himself when he heard of the sacral snub, and that he would not take sides, as long as his tax was paid. And as for the lowly *Salmonsbury* folk, they were as irreverently delighted to shake a stick at shamanism as they were overjoyed at seeing their respected elder proudly hand his youngest girl to Hatha.

Erin's face turned from her father to the young man before them, positively glowing on this, the happiest day of her life. Hatha looked back at her just as adoringly, their love now apparent to everyone. Edrig seemed to know the appropriate words well enough, and as could be expected, the women knew them perfectly, whispering prompts several times from motionlessly smiling lips. The unwritten but entirely traditional ceremony that followed included a series of hand-clasping promises of love until death, the creation and the raising of children, and respect for each another. This was followed by some Celtic chants, and throughout, only the briefest reference was made to the gods. Although Edrig publicly failed to revere them, he commanded that the most important gods of the locality, including Aine, Tamesis, Nodens, Cernunnos and Cucullus, all look favourably on the young couple, their house, offspring, land and livestock. Hardly anyone noticed as Aled quietly passed something that glistened to his younger brother, but all eyes were focussed as Hatha gently slipped the magnificent gold ring onto Erin's finger. It represented a tangible and symbolic joining of two lives in the Celtic world and would probably be the only lasting evidence of the union, there being no other record to prove the ceremony ever took place, even if a priest had been disposed to try and create one later.

Although no one in pre-historic, pre-literate Britain could know it, not even the wisest of the pagan soothsayers; this was to be the long bitter winter of 56/55 BC. It was also the winter during which Hatha, together with his young wife, her parents and Bod, all lived together under Edrig's old roof, sagging even more under the weight of snow. It was the winter in which Bod and Hatha learned as much as they could about Cotswold farming and hunting. It was the winter in which Hatha and Erin's first child was conceived. It was the winter during which Rome's preparations slowed slightly, but never veered from its irreversible and expansionist military timetable, intended to finally subdue and enslave these proud people. Whenever the weather permitted, these plans were further drawn towards finality at several known locations along Gaul's north coast; a place that most *Salmonsbury* folk thought was as distant as the moon.

As winter released its frozen grip on the *Salmonsbury* vale, allowing the rebirth of the precious all-giving soil, the numerous small hay ricks built at the end of the last harvest proved inadequate to sustain all of the livestock until the next harvest. A selective cull now put so much meat on the butcher's block that the salt was soon exhausted, and what could not be eaten was smoked. Bod was keen to forget his old trade as he immersed himself in his new Cotswold life, having arranged for his other sons to re-supply Salmonsbury, increasing their own business in the process. The way-worn trader was now proving himself a proficient carpenter, having acquired new tools to make first a stool, and then a chest. The womenfolk kept the looms busy in the houses, making garments and bedding. They made new pottery using their skills with clay, kiln and paint. They also ground more corn on the great saddle quern, baked their daily bread, cooked meats and boiled broths in large hanging cauldrons. As the ground softened and warmed a new carpet of greenery spread out on all sides of the great settlement. This was followed by a variety of blossoms bursting forth after which the bleating of lambs added to the cacophony of cattle, sheep, pigs and goats. Hatha now saw the vale in a newborn light to the arid one of summertime. As the landscape and the people were released from winter's torpor a new vitality crept through the pallid, smoke-stained community. They emerged from their steaming dwellings each day to shake off the last of winter's downbeat mood, and greet the springtime with yet another great feast.

Bod was now completely at ease with his decision to cease trudging around the country's track-ways and took to carpentry with a fervour that threatened the livelihood of Grad the carpenter. With his tools and a sharp bladed knife he whittled and sawed an increasing number of rudimentary but presentable items of furniture. He was now looking towards the first spring market to discover if others might convince him a living could be made from it. Hatha had also learned all he could about the winter side of farming in a practical hands-on sense, from Edrig and his family, and other workers around the settlement. He soon realised that it was very hard work and occasionally wondered if he was cut out for it. Any lingering doubts were dispelled the day he helped Erin deliver a calf and the sense of elation he received from bringing a new life into the world convinced him it was the second best decision he had made in his life, especially as Erin and their future child were there with him.

Hatha and Erin began riding out from *Salmonsbury* together, visiting many neighbouring settlements and farmsteads, where she introduced him to more local people, some of whom he had met fleetingly before and who would now become lifelong friends. One morning Erin took him several miles upstream to a location known as *Harford*. It had been worked many times in the past and abandoned by struggling families. It was now supporting just one family who had almost a yardland under cultivation, but hardly enough surviving livestock to sustain them after the hard winter. Hatha and Erin stopped there and were offered customary refreshment. In the course of the visit Hatha mentioned that they were looking to start out on their own soon but had not yet found what they were looking for. Most people knew that Erin's brothers were now running things at *Salmonsbury* and Hatha did not wish to encroach on their land. Edrig had indicated that there was no hurry for them to leave his house, there being ample room. There was also plenty of work around the place for Hatha and enough meat, vegetables and grain to last until the summer. At the same time Edrig gently hinted they should look at a vacant holding in the Slaughters and another further up the river valley beyond Harford, which is where they now headed for.

After leaving Harford Hatha spotted two dilapidated houses nearby and concluded that although someone had started there before, it looked unproductive so they rode gently on along the meadowland track alongside the *Windrush*. Eventually they arrived at a spot where the thaw had caused the river to spill out across both sides of the central meadowland. Hatha and Erin dismounted and sat in the sun on the north bank for some time, viewing it all in silence. Erin had been here before and could see Hatha was captivated by the place. He saw the abandoned remains of several round houses at the edge of floodwater on the south side of the river. Edrig had mentioned that this place had been occupied in the past, before being deserted again after winter thaws swelled the river, flooding houses and grain pits alike. Hatha guessed correctly that people must have come here in the spring when the floodwater had subsided, building too close to the river, which after a severe thaw had easily submerged grain, ricks and houses alike. He had seen it all before in other parts of the country and knew that people just had to be prepared to walk further for their water, if they were to keep their houses dry.

Hatha moved purposefully around, wading through the river twice to assess ground levels before returning to Erin. They walked the horses further along the riverside until the ground rose a little higher and where the remains of two more buildings were visible. Hatha realised that this was the top end of the valley, the place where the ground appeared high enough to escape most flooding and flat enough to build upon without having to dig platforms in the bank for houses. Like the other locations downstream, Erin only knew that people had been here and moved on again for as long as anyone could remember. They both agreed that this west end of the valley was the safest and most sheltered of all the locations they had seen along the way. After looking around a few more times they decided it was as good, if not better, than anything they had seen so far and stood there hugging one another for finding it.

Hatha was still thinking ahead, concluding that even downstream, it was really only a matter of building further back, banking the river in a few places and maybe stilt-building a granary instead of using the old pit storage, now understanding the difference between the two. Erin knew her husband had learned a lot during the winter and said nothing about the several skilled men who had come here before and given up. Whilst she did not want to dampen his enthusiasm, neither did she yet fully appreciate her husband's determination to succeed where others had failed. They rode back down the valley past where its north bank touched the river to the more central location where one or two roofless houses sat pathetically in the mud and both were convinced that the end where the sun set was the best to build on, near to the river, without being too threatened by it. A good bit of clearance and cultivation had been attempted in the past, with several broken down sheep *Cots* now completely overgrown by wild grass, returning previously cleared ground to scrub. The neighbouring woodland was in need of considerable work but the potential was there and Hatha was enthused enough to want to discuss the location with Edrig that night.

As they rode back downstream to *Salmonsbury* he further outlined his plans to Erin and she could tell that he had virtually made his mind up about this beautiful part of the upper river valley. His enthusiasm was infectious and she soon found herself as keen as her husband to head west from *Salmonsbury* and make a go of it. That evening Hatha outlined his plan to the rest of the family and Edrig quickly realised Hatha had found what he was looking for. He listened carefully as he explained about banking the river up, where he proposed to build the first house and how much land he needed to sow this year. By the end of the meal it was agreed that half a dozen men would travel up with Hatha and Erin over the next few days, taking Belgun with them because he had been the last man to build a house in this unnamed place, before giving it up after the flooding. They would take two oxen and the old wagon, and anything else that could be spared by way of tools and materials.

Edrig said they could have the old thatch from the last three ricks for their first roof. They would fell and shape local timbers to build the first house. Grad the carpenter would knock them up the two next essentials of life, an ard and a bed frame, if Bod did not beat him to it with his new pole lathe. Hilda, Erin and some other women would make a horse hair mattress, blankets and swaddling for the baby. Edrig said they could have two oxen, one in-calf cow, six sheep and as many pigs, as a gift for their new farmstead. He had shrewdly realized this could eventually relieve a little of the pressure on *Salmonsbury*, which was becoming too attractive for its own good. He knew that if Hatha and Erin made a success of it they would need extra workers and he could direct some of those arriving at *Salmonsbury*, further upstream. Edrig had known for some time that things were becoming unbalanced, with more newcomers squatting on his land and building more permanent houses, leaving him with little alternative but to drive them out as they arrived and burn the flimsy structures down; something he never enjoyed doing. He had declared that from now on house building must be approved by him if his community was not to be swamped with an unsustainable number of mouths to feed.

Hatha thanked Edrig for his generosity but Edrig had said he had done the same when his sons and daughters left home and took pleasure in seeing his bloodline flourish, with that wicked glint in his eye again. Everyone who could be spared mucked in over the next few weeks, the result being a solid new round house built in a better location than any of the earlier ones. Several of the ruins were converted by leaving the old base, tidying them up at waist height to become animal pens. Bod added a platform to another and extended it upwards to make a stilted granary; pit storage in this location now being considered unwise.

Two weeks later the daily riverside trek to and from *Salmonsbury* was over because the new house, several outbuildings, boundary fences and livestock pens were completed. All who had helped Hatha and Erin build their new farmstead were now keen to see them settled there. The day arrived when Edrig's family, together with a good few workers, rode and walked upstream from *Salmonsbury* to celebrate the occasion. Edrig and Hilda proudly rode up in their new gig, which everyone was genuinely pleased to see their esteemed leader and his wife travel in, as it added a certain prestige to *Salmonsbury* as a whole.

Hilda brought cold meats, bread and her usual honey-cakes together with re-used amphorae of her best cider and another of ale. She and Erin fussed around all morning laying it out on Bod's oak trestle table. Finally, as the sun's shadow past the high point, Edrig called everyone to join him in front of the house. When each had a drink in their hand, Edrig raised his beautiful wooden tankard with its fine bronze handles skyward and called out to the gods to protect the new house. He then threw part of its contents over the thatch and proclaimed, *'To Hatha and Erin's new house'*. Everyone present raised their drinks and repeated the same words before imbibing heartily. Turning to Hatha and Erin, Edrig then raised his re-filled tankard and through his still dripping beard, called out to the gods Cernunnos and Cucullus, for there to be an abundance of everything in their lives. Edrig then proclaimed to the assembled group of family and workers *'I name this place Niwetone'*. Several people tried to repeat the new name, which at this point rolled off no one's tongue easily. They quaffed their drinks and soon found their vessels refilled from a large earthenware jug. Many more were downed and much good food consumed that afternoon and the only mouths drinking from the river that day were the small number of ever contented animals. And had there been someone present with sufficient artistic ability, the most precious image ever of this embryonic settlement might have been created.

Over the next quarter-century Hatha and Erin rebuilt their house, re-thatching it several times. They had three sons and three daughters, calling the eldest boy Hatha, in the customary way. They and a handful of loyal workers, who had arrived and settled with their families nearby, gradually enlarged the farmstead, pushing back the tree line and ploughing more ground north and south of the river with teams of oxen. They reared many more cattle and a good number of sheep. The small settlement slowly expanded further down the valley, adding more round houses as several more families arrived, having been directed upstream from *Salmonsbury* to *Niwetone,* and elsewhere along the various tributaries of the Windrush. *Niwetone* was never abandoned again and many more generations of Hatha's descendants were raised in the valley, most of the male line remaining to carry on the great farming way of life, it still being what they were destined to do - whenever peace reigned over war.

☐

Throughout this time elsewhere, flourishing cross-channel commerce was maintained, with British traders bringing an increasing amount of goods and news from the ports. Foreign exchange remained buoyant as local traders and drovers took more livestock and more British goods to the coast for export, including cattle, horses, grain, hides, wool and leather for tents and sails. By 55BC trade improved again, the Romans needing more British commodities; especially gold and silver. Rome had now set its sights on the resources of this highly productive tribal culture with its 33 small kingdoms, controlled from numerous old fortified settlements. The immense food producing capability on this side of the Channel had remained frustratingly beyond the grasp of its ever hungry, marching legions for too long. During his Gallic Wars, Caesar systematically slaughtered about one million Gauls, whilst enslaving a similar number of others from the Celtic tribes of Germania and Gaul, after they dared to oppose his ruthless legions. More confident than ever of his military prowess and statesmanship, in 55BC he sent the first of two expeditionary forces of about 10,000 men to Southern Britain, returning the following year with twice as many. Tribal leaders were always in possession of considerable intelligence from the ports, from agents and spies across the water, and of course from the alert traders. Consequently they knew of the large build-up of ships; they knew parts of Caesar's invasion plan and they knew of several likely places he might try and land. Some, but not all of the internecine struggles at 'home' were put on hold, as convenient inter-tribal, but still totally unholy alliances were formed, in a determined attempt to thwart Caesar.

Despite reaching the Medway, Caesar's ambitious plans, expeditionary or otherwise were repelled, as much by the weather as any ongoing hit and run tactics used by the British farmer-warriors, as they cunningly avoided set-piece battles along the south coast and kept him in the water. Militarily, Caesar was overstretched and only good fortune avoided these expeditions turning into his disaster. The close run events, many details of which are now lost in antiquity, earned the British the reputation of being a fierce and clever adversary; one which Rome would treat with due respect in future. Rome consolidated her northern border along the channel coast of Gaul for almost another 100 years, with no political or military ambition to follow through Caesar's two forays. Even so, the tribal leaders of Britain could never have failed to appreciate their tenuous situation, now firmly in the shadow of this militarily superior neighbour. They were no longer complacent about Britain's protective moat, few now believing it would always be their saviour, as it just proved to be in 55BC.

The tribes who witnessed this first attempt to subjugate them all, continued to live out their lives without being ruled by Rome, some even profiting from the ongoing cross channel trade with the Empire. A few suspected that some kind of alliance had already been struck as a period of mutual commercial activity followed Caesar's expeditions and the markets opened up further. More goods than ever were traded through Britain's *Iron Age* ports, with luxury items such as wine, fine pottery, jewellery and glassware exchanged for metals, grain and animal by-products. This may have increased the wealth of certain tribal leaders during the next century, but some must have wondered what fate awaited their descendants; for it was them who were going to reap the whirlwind of this relatively peaceful interlude. Whilst Britain remained beyond Roman control for a further 98 years, various emperors, and senior military planners continued to set their eye this way, nurturing ambitions that would soon include most of this productive isle within the Roman Empire.

Much political upheaval took place during this period of respite for the British, resulting in a bitter (Roman) civil war, as the Roman Empire moved from a republic to a dictatorship. Augustus proclaimed on his death bed that the Empire was already large enough and his wishes were maintained under his successor Tiberius, but the excesses of Caligula again threw the State into turmoil. Following his assassination, the elderly Claudius found himself pushed into a power vacuum. Now needing a victory somewhere to exert his authority, Britain seemed the natural target. As the year 43AD approached, having settled tribal uprisings in Germania, he calculated there was spare military capacity on the Rhine. Wily old Claudius understood only too well that inactive legions could create serious political and public order problems, judging the time was now right to bring Britain into the Roman orbit. He directed that four legions and their auxiliaries be despatched from Germania to northern Gaul to prepare for the invasion. By the summer of 43AD a massive fleet, together with some 40,000 men were ready to cross the channel, with no expeditionary intentions this time, but as a full scale invasion force. The inter-tribal bickering on this side still ensured a fragmentary political situation in Britain, with no central parliament or dominant tribal group emerging as ruling elite. Britain was still unable to galvanize itself into one fearsome unified force to repel what it was about to receive.

Under the command of Aulus Plautius, a distinguished General, the Romans landed on the Kent coast and fanned out across the countryside. Advance scouts moved quickly ahead to sound out the opposition, and although they met it in a number of places, by the time the Second Augusta Legion [8] under the command of Vespasian arrived in the territory of the *Dobunni*, his 10,000 infantrymen felt no real threat and the worst was over. Meetings were no doubt quickly arranged by senior officers and terms of surrender discussed, after which a treaty was probably drawn up under Roman terms. The lives and farming routines of people like Hatha the 4th and his sons, in centrally isolated locations such as *Niwetone* probably carried on much as before, though they would have been aware within days of the vast upheavals taking place elsewhere. The 2nd Augusta Legion established an advance base on the banks of the River Severn; in an area we now call Kingsholm (King's Home) near to where they would build the civitas of *Glevum* (Gloucester).

Within a year or two of 43AD Roman officials were probably escorted on visits to most of the local settlements, including *Niwetone*, where Hatha's land would have been assessed for tax purposes. No longer would it be paid to the tribal, kingly type hierarchy at Bagendon. The new tax *(Anona)* would now be paid into the Imperial coffers of the newly installed administration within the expanding Roman town of *Corinium* (Cirencester).

Naunton, Corinium Dobunnorum, Britannia. 79AD (approx 135 years later)

Antonius Maximus, was a twenty year old Roman Officer of Engineers attached to the Garrison of Prima al Thracum (1st Thracian Horse) at Corinium. The Regional Tribune is a firm believer in his younger, more versatile officers becoming multi-skilled, which explains why Antonius now finds himself deputising for his good friend Gracchus, who is on leave. Antonius's task this week is to meet with the Elders in some 12 North Cotswold settlements to collect the *Anona*. This is assessed by the number of ards, oxen, and sheep in each settlement, together with the amount of cultivable yardlands running under the ard. It is the subject of constant bickering and wrangling with the Roman authorities. Last night was the third spent at the busy Mansio (Posting Station) next to a new Fosse Bridge at *Salmonsbury*, rebuilt for the first time with stout wooden planking on stone plinths. Antonius helped draw up the plans for what became the first stone based bridge at this location. Although he had since crossed it many times, he had done little more than glance into the small farming settlements alongside, as he rode his fine horse along the Fosse. This latest bridge on the Fosse had been built over the Windrush, just west of the old fortified settlement of *Salmonsbury,* (at a much later time the bridge would still take its name from the nearby village and become known as *Burton Bridge* and finally Bourton Bridge). The previous wooden construction had rotted at water level and Antonius had designed the stone replacement with two superb 'keyed' arches. Placed laterally across these and rising slightly towards the centre were some 15 easily replaceable squared tree trunks, seated well above normal water level. Across these stout timbers were numerous smaller sturdy planks, making the whole construction strong enough to carry the heaviest wagons, or even a two-by-two Legion without breaking step.

Antonius had conversed briefly with the headman, Edrig, whilst engaged on the bridge. He was recognised as the local chief and elder son of a number of similarly named chiefs and he had ridden majestically back and forth across it several times on his fine horse, with its triple-plaited tail. He did so to emphasise his importance within the client-king arrangement Rome had actively encouraged, but which in reality left proud men like Edrig almost powerless. On one occasion, with his slightly nervous horse stepping high-footedly, hooves clattering on the unfamiliar slatted timbers, Edrig had deigned to look as dignified as possible as he closely inspected the new structure. He had even dismounted and sought out the young engineer to commend him on the fine quality of its construction. As if to test the water on that memorable day, Edrig had then famously pointed out to Antonius that as the bridge was adjacent to his village, on his land, it must still fall under his control. A few tense moments had followed during which Antonius recalled having to stifle his laughter, whilst several of his cocky guard had been completely unable to do likewise.

Antonius had then tactfully but authoritatively touched chief Edrig's elbow and taken him aside. What followed had been one of his most testing man-to-man exchanges during his brief time here amongst the belligerent Britons. Antonius pointed out to Chief Edrig that 35 years ago, this might well have been true. He had looked him straight in the eye, admiring the fine gold torc, which forever encircled his bullish neck, worn purely to impress others with his status. Antonius had hoped, in the fevered standoff that followed that chief Edrig would remain unaware of the palpitations he felt growing within his own chest as he pointed out, with a perfectly straight face, that the bridge, like the highway, was now the property of Imperial Rome, with the highly important military road passing over it. He went on to tell Edrig that he and his people should consider themselves fortunate they were allowed to use it at all and that its primary purpose was to ensure the swift movement of troops around Britain to suppress any insurrection. He had stressed the word 'insurrection' very strongly, just stopping himself from adding the words 'efficiently' and 'ruthlessly', which he tactfully omitted in these more conciliatory times.

Antonius had then paused, realising that all this must be more than obvious to Edrig and any other village elders living around here. The construction work had, after all, cut straight through many of their fields, and across old tribal boundaries, as efficiently as any sword blade, totally regardless of local sensibilities. In the heat of the moment, he almost told Edrig that he should think himself lucky he had not been required to pay tolls for crossing it on his noble horse that historic afternoon. The sharpness of the exchange had resulted in Edrig taking a step backwards in apparent amazement at the boldness of the self-assured young Roman, and he had almost fallen off the bridge. Antonius's sword hand had then swiftly reached out and grasped Edrig's hand, saving him from a Windrush dunking. Almost as quickly as the two men found themselves clasping each others hands, they found themselves laughing uncontrollably, probably to release the tension of the moment, as much as to acknowledge each other's undoubted authority. This confrontation resulted in both men developing a healthy respect, even a liking for one another thereafter.

It was not that Edrig was unaware of any of these things, having been as dismayed as anyone when he first observed the engineers crossing his father's *Salmonsbury* fields years before, driving wooden stakes into the ground to set down the line and the levels of their new road and demolishing two houses in the process. He knew the road was never intended for their convenience and that this arrogant intrusion had been a statement of power as much as the creation of an efficient military highway.

Last night Antonius had invited Edrig to join him for a meal at the busy hostel next to the bridge, both to renew their acquaintance and build upon the slightly shaky bilateral relationship, as well as collecting the tax under the most favourable circumstances. Edrig now grudgingly accepted the road as Roman property, even though it had scythed through the Dobunnic heartland. During this convivial evening both men exchanged many anecdotes as Edrig imbibed on the Roman wine he had now acquired a taste for. Antonius learned that Edrig's forefathers had adopted the shortened version of the old name *'Antedrig'*. He also understood that in the past they had used the further truncated version of *'Ted'* on local coinage, which used to be struck for Edrig at the Bagendon mint. Antonius learned that his influential family had controlled things along the *Salmonsbury* vale for almost two centuries, but only after helping Edrig to understand what was meant by the word 'century', using his own fingers and sandaled toes to do so.

Whilst Edrig's father had been more resentful of some of the changes made by the first Tribune at Corinium, this Edrig, and his kinsfolk, appeared more relaxed towards their colonial overlords, and not particularly displeased that Bodvoc's ancestors and the zealous priests had been brought to heel. They now lived in the Vicus, just outside the Roman fort at Corinium, with little influence beyond it. Discussing such tribal politicking with farmer-chiefs like Edrig and getting the other side of the story for the first time was a refreshing experience for Antonius. As an Officer of Engineers, who for the past year had been engaged on several major construction projects beyond Corinium, he had had very little social contact with the Dobunnic hierarchy on the higher wolds. Antonius was now prepared to judge them as he found them and not as others described them. Applying these criteria, he had found Chief Edrig to be a fair, hard-working and reasonably sophisticated man, even if he was completely illiterate.

This morning Antonius had despatched the previous day's triple collection of *Anona,* with his personal seal on the hasp of the chest. It was now in the charge of a small contingent of Fosse Guard who would deliver it to the Exchequer's vault at *Corinium* Fort later that day, collectors not being permitted to carry more than three lots at any one time due to earlier attacks by Dobunnic renegades along the Fosse. The balance, usually in corn, wool or hides, generally followed when the farmers visited the forum at Corinium. After bidding farewell to the staff, Antonius set out from the Fosse Posting Station at *Salmonsbury*, this time to introduce himself to the final three village elders for the same purpose. By early afternoon he and his guard of six Thracian mercenaries were leaving the Slaughter settlement and heading for Naunton, it being the last of the week's visits, situated several miles upriver from *Salmonsbury*. As usual, the journey gave him ample time to reflect on his knowledge of the histories he had been taught, and his personal experiences, adjusting pre-formed ideas slightly after each new day's encounters, against the exaggerated stories he had heard and re-heard over the past two years in the mess at Corinium and beyond.

Antonius realised of course that it was now some 36 years since Rome had extended its northern boundary beyond the coast of Gaul and imposed its rule over Britannia, mindful that the campaign had occurred some 16 years before he was even born. His father had initially been of the opinion that this particular piece of expansionism, crossing the British Channel, had been excessive, disapproving of it strongly at the time. He believed that the Emperor was becoming despotic and would eventually over-extend the capabilities of the army and even lose the Empire, though he didn't voice such thoughts beyond his fine Pompeian villa. As the years went by he had moderated his views a little, surprising both his wife, and Antonius, by raising no objection as their son announced his intention to join the army after completing his course at the Naples Civil Engineering Academy.

The conquest of Britannia had actually been less costly than certain Senate doom-mongers had anticipated. The future for an ambitious young officer in the new province offered great prospects, particularly for qualified engineers, with the reducing threat of serious force directed towards the military. Whilst military force would still be required to suppress sporadic uprisings, and to push the boundary further northward, almost everything else would depend on the skill of men with engineering and building expertise. This would ensure that the culture, civilisation and technical infrastructure of Rome was properly extended into what the Emperor saw as the furthest and most backward reaches of the empire. Whether building new road systems, bridges, viaducts, aqueducts, mills or houses, Antonius now believed his future was secure. But what he did not yet know was how this particular week was about to impact upon it.

Antonius now understood that the Cotswold Dobunni felt more secure under the Romans, having once been surrounded by other fractious tribes, some they suspected might attack them at any time, carving up the Cotswolds between them, and with much unnecessary bloodshed in the process. When, in 43AD, the feared incursion finally came, it was not from their tribal neighbours, but from beyond the southerly seas. By this time they had learned, from numerous sources, that it would be futile to offer resistance against Rome's formidable military might. The old tribal leadership had apparently gleaned so much useful information prior to the first attempt, more than 130 years ago now, by keeping their fingers firmly on the trading pulse. Antonius acknowledged that some of the Briton's intelligence had been obtained at great risk, by sending brave Gallic speaking men across the water to infiltrate the civilian shipbuilding workforce. But disinformation had also been fed back to British chiefs, by Roman agents on this side of the water, to help instil a degree of shock and awe amongst the Celts as a whole, and the southern tribes in particular.

Many alert British traders, moving to and from the south coast ports kept the tribal leadership informed, particularly Commius, the self appointed king of the *Atrebates*, and leaders of the *Belgae, Durotriges, Regnensis* and the *Cantiaci*, of the impending invasion plans being finalised on the opposite coast. There was still no British king of kings, only a succession of undeniably brave, ambitious and relatively undisciplined regional leaders, many of whom aspired to sit at the pinnacle of the ancient and power-hungry tribal network. But mainly due to the prevailing illiteracy, the resultant lack of written orders, clear communication channels and old rivalries, no kind of unified resistance was ever properly coordinated. All of this was now simply a matter of oral history on the British side, with many exaggerated stories being swapped on both sides. This was especially so when good ale or wine flowed at meetings such as the previous evening at the *Salmonsbury* Posting House. Here, Edrig related to Antonius details of what his father had told him about the difficult but necessary decisions made back in 43. He told him how brave Celtic men either had to capitulate or try to unite themselves in the face of the first wave of the awesome Praetorian Guard whose advance landing parties commenced the now historic cross-channel assault. Everyone now accepted that the prospect of facing this military incursion should have galvanised the Britons into some kind of concerted reaction; but alas, history records that it did not do so.

Amongst the verbal intelligence available to the Celts, was a whole variety of confusing facts and figures, much of which became totally exaggerated. The overall picture that emerged still presented the various chiefs with a fairly accurate one of Rome's incredible ultra-modern army and its equally powerful weaponry. They were well aware that Rome's sophisticated armoury contained state of the art, long-range sling-ballistas and field catapults, including the formidable *'scorpion'*, which was feared by everyone who had seen it. These armaments meant the legions were capable of hurling huge boulders that would pulverise earthen banks and wooden palisades, crushing flimsy round houses and showering missiles of fire down on them from the sky, regardless of collateral damage to women, children and livestock. All of this and more equally alarming reports had reached the attuned ears of the old leadership. Their bravery in the face of such opposition was beyond doubt to Rome but tribal enmities had created a situation in which many of them would now fall divided rather than stand united; a course of action that had been cleverly exploited by Rome.

Antonius concluded once again that to individual tribal leaders such as Bodvoc, here in the *Dobunnic* midlands, the futility of resisting such a powerful and highly trained army must have been obvious. Antonius now learned that Bodvoc and his warriors knew of the bloodbath suffered by their Germanic cousins, after they had bravely tried to resist and harass Rome's superior forces. Not only that, in the back of all their minds was the inescapable fact that their own Celtic forefathers had once taken this land by force, and the only impediment to its future retention appeared to be the arrival of this highly mechanised Roman military machine. The shrewdly calculated Dobbunic capitulation that followed was inevitable if their best men, including skilled archers, swordsmen and charioteers were to survive, being quickly followed by cooperation. As a result they began to integrate fairly painlessly with their new Roman masters and trade actually increased under Graeus Julius, as he cleverly allowed them to prosper through the marketplace, only to impose swingeing taxes upon their well known agrarian productivity.

This had created considerable resentment amongst many young men who had been persuaded to hide their weapons and direct their energy towards the land, commerce and the marketplace, rather than against their new masters. The local Governor was well aware that quite a few of the hot-headed young men and women of the Dobunni were now gathering secretly to swear allegiance to equally hot-headed self-appointed agitators, saying they would rather spill their blood than pay homage and tax to Rome. It was only the firm control exercised by more cautious local elders like Edrig that had since prevented several pointless ambushes on soldiers and other Roman officials travelling on the Fosse. Edrig understood that such depredations would be dealt with swiftly and ruthlessly by the Romans, realising that they were at their most deadly when faced with insurrection. Antonius now realised that it was the trader's accounts of things, from as far away as the Iceni, as well as from Gaul and Armenia, that had brought home these inescapably hard facts of unwritten history to the Dobunnic leadership.

Antonius had heard all of these stories so many times now in the mess during raucous bacchanalian nights at Corinium, but in the past week he was hearing the other side of the same stories. Some of the old guard, many the sons of men in the original invasion force still described the Celts in contemptuous terms, as though they themselves had defeated them single-handedly back in 43. Having this past week been closer to these fair-haired and occasionally red-haired folk, Antonius realised that many were comparable to any gladiator in courage, resolve and stature. He also felt that he may also have rashly pre-judged them. This was certainly so with a number of his older comrades, who still openly despised and pitied the vanquished upland farmers.

The truth was that during the past week, Antonius had been able to balance many of his preformed views of the Dobbuni, even though he still had little understanding of the other tribes on the island. He was thankful that those round here were mostly friendly towards him, knowing that this was not the case further north, where the Picts and Caledonians would sever your head, given half a chance. Several engineering colleagues had suggested that a wall should be built from coast to coast to keep the northerly barbarians out. Antoinius thought that local roads and bridges were a greater priority at the present time, approving as he did of the long-term action-plan to build ten thousand miles of good quality highway throughout the colony, together with many more forts. He had to acknowledge though that if anyone ever achieved the seemingly impossible task of a coast-to-coast wall, it would rank as one of the greatest engineering feats in the whole Empire and something he would like to be associated with. During this particular week though, he would satisfy himself in other ways, by trying to interact socially with the Cotswold clan. He now found that he understood them better and liked them more each day.

As they rode away from the Slaughters that afternoon, Antonius removed a scroll-map from a leather tube behind his saddle to remind himself of the final visit they were about to make. He read the name *'Oppidum Novum'* [*Naunton, or New Farmstead*] and saw the name *'Hatha'* scrawled beneath, together with the amount of tax due. After climbing the hill they descended into the Windrush valley once again, joining the riverside track that led into the east end of this small settlement. As they approached the first two round houses, Antonius thought it was probably the most pleasant ride he had made all week. Somewhat poetically he found himself reflecting upon its attractiveness, feeling it was due to the undulating countryside that was neither monotonously flat nor threateningly steep, with clumps of trees providing a balance of sunlight and shade, where his men and horses could rest easy by the river.

Like his faithful Thracian posse, he also naively believed they may even have arrived unexpectedly, as they reached a second, slightly larger cluster of round houses which formed the main settlement at the west end of Naunton. A number of youngsters ran out to meet them and a little further on a woman appeared carrying a pitcher of water. Antonius became aware of a man walking out from the grandest of the circular timber and thatch dwellings and quickly gauged he was about thirty years old. He had immensely strong arms and an easy, self-assured way about him, but no swagger. Hatha was of course more than expecting them, having received the traditional overnight warning from the Slaughters, enabling them to drive the usual half dozen cattle up into the woods until the taxman had gone. Antonius and his men dismounted and after the customary hail-fellow-well-met greetings were exchanged, Hatha invited him towards the larger house to meet his wife and daughter, briefly mentioning that his three sons were busy in the fields rather than tell the young Roman the truth. They had much better things to do than entertain tax officials and were quietly grazing a few prized animals amongst the trees, north of the valley, intending as they did so to keep both the tax and the cattle noise to an absolute minimum, until the 'all-clear' horn was blown. The fact was that Hatha had been briefed to listen out for the horn after departing each village. The Romans laughed at this novelty; the only real evasive action the Celts could take these days, and indulged them by ignoring it.

Beer was served generously by Hatha's girl, Livia, who poured her father's into his fine wooden tankard; the guest being offered his in a traditional heavy black beaker. Hatha knew this was quite different to the fine Samian ware the young officer would use in the Corinium mess and sought to put him in his place from the outset. As each man took their first gulps, the canny farmer and the fast learning Roman sat a few feet apart outside the house. Hatha began with some friendly verbal jousting and small-talk as each sought to get the measure of the other. Beside the obvious cultural differences, both soon realised the other was quite human and became more relaxed after each mouthful of ale. Before long they were happily comparing details of their very different backgrounds, describing work, families and future plans. In reality Hatha was relying almost entirely on the young Roman's understanding of the Celtic tongue, with its additional tongue-twisting Cotswold dialect, both of which Antonius had mastered over the past two years, conversing with Dobbunic road workers on construction work along the Fosse and Ermin Street. Antonius quickly realised that Hatha was a shrewd *'Dobi'*; this being the dismissive term many of his less enlightened colleagues used when describing and deriding the locals. He also discovered Hatha had a fairly detailed knowledge of agrarian law and a smattering of Latin phrases used in the forum at Corinium, concluding correctly that he had spent some time there after the monthly markets, listening to the Tribune's notices and decrees as they were read out by the crier. This impressed Antonius and it was apparent that the man was keen to learn, ruthlessly picking the brains of others as he did so. Maybe it was because he had been denied the opportunity of any kind of classical education that now drove his quest for raw knowledge!

Hatha fully appreciated that his beloved land in *Naunton* was situated within the district of Corinium, and that this was now the second largest town in Britain, with *Londinium* the largest. He fully understood how his land had been assessed by an official from Corinium for the tax, which farmers were now required to pay quarterly, in animals, corn, wool, hides or coin, so long as the corn was dry and the coin not counterfeit. He acknowledged that his land was still private and had not been seized by Rome, as it would have been if conquered forcibly, instead of by wise Dobunnic capitulation. Knowing all of this and more, Hatha good naturedly tried to draw Antonius further into the tricky area of Agrarian Tax Law. It was obvious that Hatha was unhappy about the rate being levied upon his productivity, livestock and few possessions and that he was forever trying to get it reduced.

Throughout all of this good-natured Romano-British banter, Livia attentively served more beer to her father and their good looking young visitor. Antonius soon found he could not take his eyes off the girl. One moment his mind was wrestling with some obscure question directed his way about what was public land or belonged to the state and what was private land belonging to Hatha. The next he found his eyes and thoughts diverted towards the girl as she tantalisingly tended to minor jobs near the house. She glanced his way increasingly, with a smile that conveyed either sympathy for his predicament or something else, he was not yet sure what. Hatha belched, grabbing his attention once more, as Antonius found himself struggling for an answer to the intricacies of Anona and then another concerning 'landed' property of the state. He fumbled through explanations about this being either consecrated to the gods or allotted to men like Hatha, to sow and crop for the benefit of Rome. This was followed by another query slipped in as to who now owned the river and its banks and who had dipping rights to it and whether the river was public or private. By now Antonius's thoughts and emotions were more than a little confused. He had had enough of this legal nonsense, but at the same time he was forced to remind himself that it was Imperial Rome that had heaped these legal and bureaucratic complexities upon this haplessly inquisitive Celtic farmer, if not on his beautiful daughter.

If only Hatha had wanted to talk about local bridges, or road construction, or even the almost completed Coliseum back in Rome, Antonius would have been able to hold his own. He realised in the same instant that a man who was still living in a small thatched hut was probably unable to comprehend structures as enormous as the Coliseum, and that he would probably be unable to convince him that it existed anyway. So he unashamedly steered the conversation round to the *Via Fosse*, this being something he was proudly involved with and which all the local farmers were happy to use. The ploy was successful because like so many other new things around here, Hatha was actually impressed by the new road and bridge, certainly more so than he was with legal dictates, ideology and the several other 'improvements' Rome had forced upon his proudly independent kinfolk.

As soon as he got his wagon over the hill from Naunton and down the other side to *Salmonsbury* Bridge, Hatha, with most other local farmers, could now safely and more speedily transport their goods to Corinium forum. They could now travel from *Salmonsbury* to Corinium without sustaining a broken spoke or axle. The problem was that the horses preferred softer ground, often having to complete the journey lame and with worn out hooves. Another problem facing outlying farmers like Hatha, was hauling laden wagons to the Fosse. To get that far meant having to negotiate the old rutted tracks for several miles between Naunton and the new road, especially along the potholed Salt Way. Antonius felt that for the first time during their meeting he might just be able to offer some constructive, even placatory news to his new farmer friend at Naunton.

He knew full well that the old beaten paths and tracks in and around settlements like this were likely to stay much as they were. But when it came to the wider tracks worn by men, animals and wagon wheels that joined the Fosse, at places like *Salmonsbury* Bridge, a plan to upgrade them had now been authorised by the Tribune, with the work due to commence next year. He explained that this upgrade would probably see five miles of all the feeder roads, such as Salt Way having their surface repaired and strengthened. These side roads were now classified as *'economic roads'*, it being uneconomic to delay the transit of goods to the marketplace, with breakdowns and spilled loads clogging up the feeder roads. The surface would be levelled and hardened with wagonloads of compacted gravel and a layer of close-fit paving stone laid on top at a slight gradient. Though not as good as the straighter, multi-layered Fosse, it would be a great improvement on the current rutted state of these old back-roads.

Antonius went on to explain that he was currently checking the measurements of some 45 mile-stones along the new Fosse from Corinium to *Salmonsbury* and on past *Dorn*, which had been incorrectly spaced. This would be followed by the requisition of even more horses and wagons from the settlements to haul the gravel from the numerous local deposits, with the *'economic-road'* upgrade commencing in the spring. Hatha groaned loudly on hearing this but listened intently as Antonius outlined the grand plan fluently and confidently. Antonius went on to say that this might increase hoof-wear on their unshod horses, suggesting he try some Roman 'hippo sandals', or loose iron horseshoes, secured with leather straps, adding that he would bring some over for him to try. All this surprised Hatha, who said he would not hold his breath in anticipation of it ever happening, adding cynically that if it did, it would be more to speed up the collection of tax than to improve his trips to market. Both men looked at each other quizzically for a few moments before throwing their heads back and releasing the heartiest laughs heard in Naunton that particular day.

The conversation was now more relaxed as Antonius found himself exchanging more furtive, even lustful glances with Livia as she sat seductively on a small milking stool nearby. He then learned that Hatha was born in Naunton, as was his father and grandfather, who had all successfully farmed the open fields along this stretch of the Windrush, three miles west of *Salmonsbury*. Hatha proudly touched the modest bronze torc around his neck and explained that it was passed down from father to son in each family. He learned from Hatha's wife Bessie that Hatha's great grandfather, once a nomadic salt trader, had married one of Edrig's daughters. Antonius knew of the old *Salmonsbury* Chieftain called Edrig, having hosted one of his descendants the previous evening. He had also seen the name *'Ted'*, on the old Dobunnic coins. Although banned from circulation, some Romans regarded these cruder coins as local curios, often keeping them as souvenirs.

Hatha's wife, Bessie said that the first generation of her husband's people to farm here started out with just a few animals and several of the good hunting dogs they loved breeding. She said it was here, towards the top of the central meadowland that they had built the first houses, raised a family, cropped the fields and reared their animals. Despite occasional flooding, they had never moved away again. She described how the settlement had grown steadily with Hatha's great grand-father taking on more workers, as he and his sons cleared more woodland, extending their fields higher up both sides of this most pleasant valley.

Some of the current workers could also now claim to be third and fourth generation Naunton families. Almost four generations on, the settlement had more roundhouses of varying sizes, in two main clusters. At the westerly end, Hatha and his wife and daughter lived in the largest and their three sons with their women and children lived a little further downstream, in the houses Antonius had ridden past as they arrived from Slaughter. Their eldest son was now thinking of moving again, taking on some land a mile downstream, where the track crossed the river at the lower ford. Antonius had not seen this location as they approached; which was known as Harford, and Hatha told him it was round the bend from where they would have joined the track, almost as though he had seen them do so. He said the location had been abandoned years before, but was now rested and ripe for cropping and grazing again, once the scrub was cut back. Antonius had gleaned all this information, and more, in an hour spent talking to Hatha and his wife, after which his head was reeling slightly from the grilling and the strong ale. Throughout this time, Livia had poured the ale generously, whilst standing much closer to him than was necessary as she did so. The combined effect was something Antonius could not have anticipated when he arrived that afternoon, and it had whetted his appetite in a number of ways. Livia had been an attentive servant and although she had not said much, an unmistakable frisson of excitement had been transmitted between the farmer's daughter and the bold young Latin visitor, the intensity of which he was unable to ignore. Her simple fawning Celtic beauty and bright blue eyes, forever darting towards him through a shock of red hair, had enamoured the young man from Corinium and he realised he would not easily forget this visit to Naunton, even if he tried to.

At some point during the concluding moments of conversation, Hatha handed six denarius to Antonius, which he must later have put into his saddlebag with other similar coin. Antonius then spoke briefly to his men, but soon found himself distracted again, later having pangs of guilt about the whole episode. Neither did he recall entering this part-payment on his record, nor asking Hatha when the balance in skins, animals or corn might be paid, further confirming the wiliness of the older man whom Antonius found himself liking even more.

Some two hours after they arrived at the Naunton farmstead, Antonius and his men climbed back onto their horses where he checked his map again, unsure whether to head east or west, before waving and turning his horse towards the setting sun. As they reached what Antonius recognised as the foot of a gentle incline taking them up out of Naunton, his still befuddled mind wandered once more, this time triggering subconscious thoughts of his own precious land. As was common with all true Romans, Antonius retained a homeland image in his mind in the shape of a human foot. As yet he had no such concept of the true shape of Britannia, beyond a crude triangular island, because it had still not been fully surveyed. To Antonius, home now seemed a million miles away from the green and pleasant valley he was now leaving, with a part bag of coin, an incomplete payment list and a head full of emotions, after one of the most memorable afternoons yet spent in Britannia.

But the image of his homeland was still troubling him, as it inexplicably transformed into two smiling faces; being almost ethereal masks of his mother and father. They appeared to be reaching out to him over their beloved Bay of Naples. Antonius found himself momentarily disturbed by the vision, which faded almost as quickly as it appeared, disappearing into a swirling cloud, as his mind cleared slightly, returning him to the journey he was now on and the very real smiling faces he had just left behind.

He assumed that the image must have been triggered by the homely and friendly atmosphere of Hatha's farmstead that afternoon. Only last week his brain had been hard-set on measurements, gradients and calculations relating to a new stretch of the Fosse, beyond Corinium towards Illchester, together with the 'miliaria' (milestone) relocation work from Corinium to *Dorn* (Moreton). At the end of that particular week he had looked forward more than usual to the day he might receive a posting to more southerly climes, well away from Britannia, one of the northernmost and least hospitable places to spend a winter in the whole Empire. Then, just a week later, having been given this temporary fiscal detail, he had seen a very human, even emotional side of the Cotswolds and its people. This recent encounter was now opening his mind to greater possibilities, for he had now done that most human of all things; he had fraternized with the Dobunni.

He slipped further back into his thoughts, recalling how today he had met three more village headmen for the first time, in the Slaughters and then at Naunton. He had visited twelve settlements and almost as many houses, conversing with twelve influential men upon the local scene this week. As a result he had now seen the proud Dobbuni from a very different perspective to the one formed supervising a truculent gang of construction workers. In that role, other than snatches of conversation and shouted instructions to gang-masters, he had been entirely focussed on building the impressively straight, multi-layered eighteen foot wide highway, past settlements just like this. But he had not previously ventured into them as engineer, tax official or tourist, the latter being considered an unwise move, especially when alone. This past week, in his role as tax official, he had been forced to interact with them, man to man, and man to woman. Despite this duty, he had now experienced first-hand an uncompromising combination of hardiness, friendliness, sincerity and passion amongst them on their own territory. He now found himself wanting to know them more and exploit them less. He also thought he had a better understanding of what Marcus Gracchus had meant when he once said to him, *'If truth be told young Antonius; the Northern Dobunni surrendered willingly to Aulus Plautius and most of them see us as their liberators, not as their conquerors.'*

Whatever a few of his seasoned colleagues might say about them, the Cotswold Dobunni had quickly adapted to the demands of their new rulers, and in the main they appeared to be as content with their lot under the yoke of the Roman Empire as ever they did under their old despotic leadership. The more blinkered Romans who failed to get to know them as well as Antonius believed he now did, would continue to regard them as small-minded, parochial farmer-warriors, tied to equally small fields, with no great ambition or desire to divide and conquer neighbouring lands. The latter, after all, was a disciplined and skilful calling that came so naturally to trained men such as Antonius Maximus, Marcus Gracchus and their campaign hardened cohorts. Having interacted with them these past few days, more so than he would have believed possible a week ago, he now realised that their desires and aspirations were much the same as those of people anywhere, whether Briton, Gaul or Roman.

As an engineer, he also appreciated, more so than some of his less enlightened colleagues, that Brittania was no barbarian backwater. As a student he had learned that the really ancient Britons, those living here a thousand or more years before these modern times had somehow developed, and then lost, engineering skills that enabled them to build the great henges, particularly the one a day's ride south of Corinium. To this day his tutors and more thoughtful colleagues gave due credit to the brilliance of men who in bronze times, or earlier, with no classical schooling, or the kind of engineering equipment he had access to, had somehow hauled, and then erected, 162 massive standing-stones to create such a magnificent shrine to their gods. No, whatever might be said about the people of this land, at the height of their unwritten power they were an enlightened and skilful race, and still one to be reckoned with, especially when roused. The fact that they made little use of written language or other known means of performing calculations to build or record their old shrines, and that a thousand years later, were still mostly illiterate, living in thatched huts, was even more incredible. But it had not prevented them from creating an extremely productive farming, mining and manufacturing base, resulting in Rome's acquisitive eye being cast this way on many occasions. Rome acknowledged that the conquest had been no walkover and it was only the second invasion that had finally subdued them, or so everyone now hoped.

It was true that the invasion had met some fierce pockets of resistance early on, but once the more enlightened chiefs knew they faced annihilation, they had been won over and their people had carried on with life much as before, and been encouraged to do so. After all, the Roman war machine needed feeding and the local horses, together with cereals, wool, leather goods and livestock were much in demand in these northern climes where wheat grew so well, but the olive and grapevine less so. It was also true that part of the next ten-year plan saw Rome showing a much more conciliatory face towards the Britons. Rome had learned to be less authoritarian in its approach to the southern tribes and only last week he read some political comment in the *Despatch* of a Roman Senator who had argued that the strength of Rome now lay in reason and not oppression.

He had also learned that Pax-Britannia would only succeed as a result of the enlightened and fair approach of young officers like him winning the hearts and minds of villagers such as Edrig at *Salmonsbury* and Hatha at Naunton. He and his colleagues knew full well that several years of steady progress were capable of being undone in an instant if the local garrison were heavy handed. Whilst these hardy folk would generally listen to reason, he knew they had no qualms about verbally challenging their rulers if they thought imperial dictates were unreasonable or actions too harsh. Antonius understood that this dictum had been ignored at great cost some 20 years before in the easterly part of the island, formerly controlled by the Iceni. Their strong leader, Queen Boudicca, had risen up almost successfully, killing many of the 9th Legion who struggled valiantly and at great cost to quell the revolt. Both sides had of course learned a lot about each other over the following years, and this was now beginning to show in a number of mutually beneficial ways.

Antonius now found these thoughts interrupted as they passed the last conical thatched round house on the right, built well above the river; a spot that would one day be known as Hunts Green. The scent of wood smoke reached his nostrils again on the early evening air, whilst the sound of a solitary cockerel and several hunting dogs grew fainter in his ears, overridden by the snorting of the horses, creaking of leather saddlebags, and constant chink of metal. His mind was abruptly returned to reality as he picked up some ribald comments between the men concerning the best maidens seen that week, making him flinch in the saddle as he heard the words. He considered the possibility of the six Thracian hard-nuts riding slightly ahead of him, now laughing loudly, knowing what had happened earlier in this small settlement, and how he might become the butt of jokes in the mess at Corinium for months to come.

He was also being slightly naive in thinking that his battle hardened, well travelled, extremely astute guard did not know exactly what had occurred that afternoon. But Antonius was too distracted to care very much, as his still intoxicated mind slipped back into reflective mode again, allowing his thoughts to race through the most stimulating of his recent, if not entirely sober experiences, discarding the mundane parts and constantly replaying the pleasurable ones………

'Just to think, my own mother told me that I was generous to a fault after buying her that farewell trinket. What was it she used to say to me; 'A fool and his money are soon parted' I think it was. And my father warned me not to let my heart rule my head as we all embraced that day, two whole years ago now, just before he pressed that precious gold coin into my palm and we parted company, not knowing if we would see each other again.

What point remembering such gems of advice now, if only to ignore them in moments of weakness. I shouldn't have done it. I should not have given her that precious gold aurius. Almost a month's pay, what a fool I've been. Passion dulls the brain as surely as it stirs the blood! My sole purpose in going there was to collect the tax from her father, Hatha. But I cannot forget his beautiful daughter, Livia; barely 16 years old, and so alluring. I knew about her of course from my friend Gracchus, who normally collects the tax. He had been sorely tempted on more than one occasion, saying he had resisted, whereas I had succumbed on my first visit. He did of course tell me it was only because his wife Julia was with him at Corinium that he didn't fall for her wiles. 'Julia would have known' he said. How clever these modern women are!

Thank the gods I'm single, but to think, Gracchus actually warned me she was out for all she could get, to make something of herself, 'determined to improve her fortune' he had told me. She had certainly caught my eye enough during the hour or so I enjoyed sipping that strong beer with her father as he quizzed me for free legal advice, arguing with good humour about being taxed to the hilt, and the requisition of even more of his horses and then proudly telling me about his family. He was a shrewd man, of that there is no doubt, and whilst he may have been a bit belligerent, he was certainly no fool. But Hatha was more than a little naive to think that a busy man like Graeus Julius could be implored to make local tax dispensations, just because he is in charge of the colony. He can complain until his cows come home, however many he has got hidden out there, but his horses won't be returned just yet and the tax rate won't be reduced either, because Rome is due what Rome is due. Of course we knew their harvest was not as good as last year, with half of it germinating in their damp granaries before it could be bought; but he also knows we are paying fair prices for their produce, their livestock and the woollen cloaks they are contracted to make for us up here in this god forsaken place.

But sweet Venus, Livia was beautiful. I have never known anyone like her since being posted here from Germanica in 77.'

To the laughter of his men Antonius then exclaimed, 'Come on horse, it's me that is half-drunk and half-witted. You've climbed hills like this before without so much as pausing'. Finding himself half way up the hill out of *Naunton*, he belched, then spoke with his guard before his thoughts took over again……..

'Yes, we will definitely call in at the Centurion Mansio on the Fosse again tonight. The men and horses are tired and the cook there is good. They will appreciate his roast pork. We have collected from 12 villages this week; not bad considering it has been so soft underfoot. Pull yourself together man or you'll be off at the [Aylworth] ditch and nightfall will be upon us.

Livia was beautiful though, with her long red hair and those amazing blue eyes. That simple smock which showed her curves so well as she left their house to go and milk the cow; but I do wish that I hadn't given her my one gold coin…………...

But hold on a minute; of course………… it's becoming clearer to my befuddled brain now. Did her father, Hatha not actually suggest to her that she leave us to go and do her milking? How else would I have known she was in that stall? After rejoining my men at the ford and instructing them to rest awhile longer as they had ridden well today, hadn't I deliberately strolled towards it? Of course, that's how I knew where to find her. Hatha had as good as told me hadn't he! And that smile when he waived us off; was it not more of a smirk, or maybe a last laugh? Did they set it up together perhaps, intending to make me look stupid? Did she shake those coins from my pocket deliberately when all I thought she was doing was shaking my toga after that glorious session in the hay, brushing it down before handing it back to me, or am I just imagining it all?

She certainly mentioned how difficult it had been for them this year, virtually having to give their sheep away at market, which I found hard to believe. I know our quarter- master is paying a fare price for their livestock and produce, so someone is making a tidy denarius somewhere along the line. But I could have just given her a silver coin or two, instead of saying 'keep it' as she had looked admiringly at my single gold aureus with its precious portrait of Nero.

Of course it would be just too embarrassing to mention this hour in the hay to my good friend Gracchus. He would roar with laughter at my stupidity, having given her three times what we collected in tax from her father; and my foolish extravagance would be scoffed at in the mess for months to come.

That she was beautiful is undeniable. I could perhaps buy her a piece of fine Roman jewellery for my next visit.............. or maybe even a ring!

I wonder if Flavius will have me collect the Emperor's dues again next time!'

His train of thought was suddenly interrupted again by a shout from one of the Thracians who enquired gruffly where they might be stabling and eating that night.

Antonius replied, 'We'll make the Happy Centurion if we get a move on,' as if the tardiness of the climb out of Naunton had somehow been their fault. Although the weather was good by British standards, he added, 'Come on my fine horse, we must make the Fosse before this damnable northern weather closes in on us.'

Six months later, after a number of weekend visits to Naunton, Antonius Maximus obtained special permission from his commanding officer to marry Livia. The small civil ceremony took place at Corinium and was attended by Hatha and his wife and two of their three sons. Hatha was particularly pleased to see his daughter marrying into what he regarded as the ruling elite, believing that it might soon benefit him in relation to the payment of taxes - if he got to know the right people! Before his marriage, Antonius sent a lovingly written letter back to his parents, proudly telling them of his plans and promising to bring his wife to meet them one day. The chain of despatch was famously unreliable once mail reached Gaul and Germania, and he never received a reply. Several of his colleagues with family in the same area were similarly perplexed by the silence from home and one actually deserted to make his way back to Italy, once rumours of the disaster finally began to reach Britannia. When the facts were fully known, there was almost insurrection in some regiments, as it became apparent that the authorities had deliberately suppressed the awful truth to avoid desertions. Antonius gradually resigned himself to the fact that his parents were dead and buried beneath the ash of Vesuvius. It was only his dear wife, Livia, who persuaded him not to resign his commission and make his way across Gaul to the ashen landscape that now entombed them.

Antonius and Livia, together with their two sons and a daughter lived at Corinium, where as children of a Roman officer they received a free education in Latin. For the next 22 years Antonius did his best to keep away from matters fiscal, as it never endeared him to his wife's aged father, or his brothers-in-(Roman)-law, who received no dispensation whatsoever. Now in his 50s Hatha was leaving much of the running of his Naunton fields to his three sons. Two of whom got on well with Antonius, one always keeping him at arm's length, for no good reason, other than he was not yet considered a 'local'. Antonius retired after 25 years with the rank of Engineer Centurion having attained two laurel leaves in recognition of his work on the rebuilding of the original Fosse and the construction of the first completely stone bridge next to the Posting Station at *Salmonsbury*. It also recognised the massive northerly push of the road-system he had worked on, which now enabled the efficient movement of the legions. *Salmonsbury* Bridge proved so strong that it did not need rebuilding for another 150 years. The pattern was repeated in the same local stone once more before finally falling into disrepair in the 5th century anno-domini.

Antonius could have retired to a modest villa almost anywhere in the Empire, but Livia had always said that she wanted to be near to her blood family in the Cotswolds. With two of their own sons now in the army, and their daughter Flavia, still living with them at Corinium, they felt they were ready to move back into the countryside. Antonius accepted that the Naunton and *Salmonsbury* areas of the Cotswolds were as attractive as any he had ever seen in the province. Having ridden out and examined the high ground all round Naunton on visits to Livia's family, they eventually settled on a midway location on high ground at the east end of Naunton. With his savings and pension, he now planned to build a modest stone house where they and their daughter Flavia would all live. It was the first stone house in Naunton, and amongst the first stone-built houses in the locality. They chose a location just off the track that Antonius had ridden along when he first visited to collect tax, over twenty years ago, when the westward approach along the river valley had inspired him poetically. He could have built a larger house but had no real desire to upstage the fine round-house his father-in-law still lived in. He also wanted the local people to see how they too could benefit from using the easily extracted freestone in the opencast delves nearby, from where road stone had already been removed. He could have purchased fired *Tegulas* (roof tiles) from Corinium, but felt that local men would appreciate an order for split-stone tiles, even though they did not last anything like as long as the harder kiln-fired variety.

The three of them stayed in rooms at the Posting House for the two months it took to build their seven roomed, single storey, three sided house on the hill at Naunton. Antonius rode up there each day to supervise several hired men from *Salmonsbury*, together with his two masons, to ensure that his plans were interpreted correctly. The masons dressed the stone from a new delve which they opened nearby. Antonius surveyed the site, measured out the pegs, set the lines and carried out or directed many tasks, ranging from boundary marking, sinking a well and rechecking levels, as the walls grew steadily from their solid foundations.

During these two months he hardly needed to encourage anyone from several miles around to come and marvel, as the beautiful honey coloured stone grew higher than anything previously seen locally. Invited or otherwise, people just came, and they were impressed by what they saw. Several locals actually brought them small gifts of precious seeds, some woollen blankets and local ornaments, which clearly touched Antonius and Livia. Not only did he believe it was a gesture of welcome, but more importantly, he considered it was tacit acceptance, before he had even moved in. The people living in several of the nearby settlements seemed genuinely pleased that he had married a local girl and chosen to live amongst them, when he could so easily have stayed in Corinium, moved to *Londinium*, or even returned to the country of his birth. They were of course underestimating the influence of a Cotswold girl upon her man, or the attractiveness of the Naunton neighbourhood, over either Corinium or *Londinium* upon her husband. Regardless, the canny locals were well aware that he was now going to bring them the benefit of his expertise, and that he usually made no charge for doing so, being content to receive a little local produce and their friendship in return.

When completed, their fine stone house set a new standard on the wolds. Antonius felt honoured each time a village elder rode up to inspect it or when others occasionally walked past to do so from afar. After walking round the building and running their hands over golden chunks of dressed limestone, they appeared almost in awe of its transformation from the nearby hole in the field. But what seemed to impress them most was the fact that a simple mixture of sand, or stone-dust and lime mortar, became so solid a jointing compound that individual pieces of dressed stone now sat firmly together, taking on the appearance of the nearby stone-face from which it had been hewn.

Impressed as they might be, the majority could still not be persuaded to make the leap from their circular wooden houses in which they had reassuringly rested their heads since birth. Antonius also appreciated that round houses could be built far more cheaply and in a fraction of the time it had taken for the masons to quarry and dress the stone for his new house, though everyone acknowledged it would outlast wooden houses many times over. This point further intrigued Antonius, who occasionally wondered how long the house might survive after he was gone, and if anyone else might ever be inclined to rebuild it. The concept of affordable stone housing for local people was not something he had much experience of yet, as he began to realise that many people simply did not want or need things to change.

If the gods gave him time in retirement, Antonius planned to try and persuade at least two of his brothers-in-law to build themselves a stone house down in the valley. He proposed to offer them the benefit of his undoubted building skills, expecting no more in return than to learn some of their farming skills, having always recognised that the one occupation was highly dependent on the other. He bought some sheep because of Livia's expertise on the loom and somehow believed that producing home grown and home spun garments might further convince her eldest brother that this was no mere dalliance with farming but a serious enterprise. Neither did he want them to treat him as a representative of Rome, who simply bought or commandeered whatever was required. He wanted them all to be on an equal footing as neighbouring farmers and knew that if it worked out they would all benefit. He would offer them the use of his own comprehensive selection of tools and measuring devices and the services of his two retired, but still eagerly employable masons from Corinium, who now relished getting out of the city, having spent most of their working lives in its dusty workshops.

Antonius had seen these two Corinium trained masons dress the local stone like no others, and it had been them who some years back had produced the keystones for the fine new bridge at *Salmonsbury*. The stones had fitted so perfectly that despite his insistence lime-mortar be applied, none was really needed, and once the wooden supports were removed its perfect arched symmetry and stability was apparent to all, acting as a salutary lesson to the young engineer for doubting the professionalism of the masons. Similar keystones were now being used above local doorways and even the most skilled Cotswold carpenters were forced to accept that a new *stone age* seemed to have returned to the area, cleverly using the abundant material which had always lain underfoot.

The difference was that the Romans had charts, templates, callipers and measuring devices, enabling them to cut and chisel the stone to finer tolerances, accompanied by an open-minded approach to change. Antonius now believed this was the way to spread more progressive building methods within the villages, and one of the first families to request his services were Edrig's descendants, who still lived within the crumbling earthworks of old-Salmonsbury. They too were showing themselves to be forward looking men who wanted to depart this redundant fortification, moving beyond its earthen banks into a stone house that would elevate them above the local peasantry. Modern *Salmonsbury* had long ago spread west beyond the embankments to the extent that it now bordered the Fosse at *Salmonsbury* bridge. Here the farmers did brisk business with the Romans and other travellers at the increasingly busy and impressive Posting House and the growing number of ancillary brick and stone outbuildings being built on both sides of the busy road. Whilst Antonius always had great respect for these productive farmers and their quaint arboreal dwellings, he could not help feeling that most of them had remained firmly locked into the old British construction methods for far too long now.

That the men of *Salmonsbury* had finally come to him in retirement, requesting a building-plan for a house of rectilinear design, to be erected beyond the old settlement, was something approaching an honour. It was also a definite, if not somewhat overdue indication of progress from certain scions of the old ruling families. He recognised it as a great opportunity to modernise their housing stock on a wider scale, but knew that many of them would never be persuaded to change from the utility housing the majority were so comfortable with. In trying to understand this unwillingness to change, Antonius had branded them traditionalists to their Celtic bones. But the failure to understand was partly on his part, in not yet realising that most grass-roots Britons simply dug their heels in, resenting any form of change or control being thrust upon them from Europe. Let them think the idea was theirs and he would be busy for the rest of his days. He had been wondering for some time now how best to persuade them to move away from their trusted timber and thatch, without the usual accusation of being another patronizing Roman, but recognised that however good your motives, some would always choose to misinterpret them.

He also recognised that wood was such a natural resource for the Dobunni; being a material as readily available to them as wool or hide. They had simply always used it, cutting and coppicing it with an expertise that even he would have to learn from scratch. He now understood that either the timber would have to run out, or he would have to engineer a change of heart by encouraging the use wood for roof supports and floors, and maybe thresh for their floors, if flag stones or boards proved too expensive. He also appreciated that mosaic flooring and fired *tegulas* for roofing was well beyond the means of the local folk.

The latter point had been demonstrated at Corinium, where a number of the old Bagendon people still insisted on thatching their houses with the cheaper read or straw, arguing that complex hypocaust heating systems were no match for a central fire beneath a well thatched roof. In addition, there were still a number of master-thatchers who did not intend to see their traditional skills replaced overnight by a hod-carrier casually placing baked oven tiles on the roofs. He acknowledged that some were now prepared to use the local freestone construction method for building the circular base of the biggest round-houses instead of the traditional interwoven wattle and daub. But this stonework never seemed to extend beyond the lower edge of the overhanging roof, or some four feet above the ground, being the maximum height they appeared confident to take dry-stone walling to. He would show how, using lime mortar they could build using weatherstone and ragstone, from a sunken foundation, to almost any height, with no risk of it collapsing in on them. He knew it would no longer be difficult to convince them of the practical possibilities because most had now visited Corinium, or the Mansio at Salmonsbury, or seen his own fine house on the hill at Naunton. As none had yet fallen down, he knew it was only a matter of time before more of the leading families followed suit.

But this would only be the start of his ambitious local improvement plan. Commencing at Naunton, Slaughter and *Salmonsbury*, Antonius intended to show the farmers how a wooden water wheel could benefit them, using the free power of the Windrush, Eye and Dickler. He would instruct the local carpenters and have them create the first wheels to sit over these rivers. The wheels, once geared, would then miraculously drive a shaft of solid oak that would in turn transmit the free power of the river through a pegged gear-wheel to the great spur wheel that in turn would power the millstones, relieving countless women from the drudgery of their saddle and quern stones. Antonius felt that the use of wood instead of iron would also sit more comfortably with men famous for their skills in felling, splitting, cutting and turning local timber. He also knew that the flow of these rivers was sufficient all year round to turn the wheels as well as replacing any number of treadle lathes, which would appeal to the carpenters as well as the farmers.

If they could be persuaded to do this, he would build an open sided wooden structure over it one day, turning it into an all-weather, water powered workshop. He felt sure that after Naunton's mill was up and running, *Salmonsbury* men would soon follow them. This would enable the several skilled men who had helped build the first mill to take their skills elsewhere. If necessary he would request the latest plans from *Londinium* where he knew numerous water wheels were now running on tributaries leading into the great *Tamesis* River, but would have to scale it down for the local rivers. Once the first wheels were revolving he knew that other settlements would want to harness the free and untapped power running through their midst.

As a joint mark of respect for Hatha, and as a memorial to his own parents he told him that he would design and build a wooden *columbarium* [dove house] somewhere near to Hatha's house in Naunton. He wanted it to be one of the best in the area, and knowing they would probably insist on a wooden construction, he was still confident that in time, if he left them with a design for something grand enough, a future family might be inspired enough to rebuild it using local stone. He knew his parents always had a *columbarium* in Italy, and thought of his Naunton plan as a kind of lasting memorial to them, even if the original intentions behind its construction became lost over the centuries ahead. Knowing that tradition featured strongly in the lives of the Britons, he believed that others might build, rebuild and cherish it for as long as these things were important to them, though he had absolutely no idea how long that might be. He hoped to leave the names of his parents on a stone within this *columbarium*, and even if they became lost, he hoped that their spirit might one day inspire others to take up the baton and perhaps remember their own loved ones in this way.

If he could achieve all, or just some of this, Antonius hoped he might be remembered as someone who came to this place and made a positive contribution to it, as opposed to being just another opportunist, one of a conquering force who sought to enrich themselves at the expense of the hard working farming folk that the empire had so unashamedly subjugated. As far as he was concerned, what was now done could not easily be undone, and many things were indeed now set in stone. He was nevertheless an enlightened and educated man who wished to show his adopted homeland that the imperial apparatus had a much more human side, by trying to redress the balance in this small way.

Antonius also knew that after some three generations of rule, many of the up and coming citizens of Romano-Britannia saw things differently to how their newly conquered fore-fathers had. Several of his military colleagues who had stayed on after marrying local women were also enjoying levels of acceptance and success within this broader minded, multi-racial colony than could ever have been imagined only fifty years earlier, and the Celtic and Roman gods appeared to be propitious towards them as they genuinely sought to improve the technological backwardness of the country. Locally, he felt that it might now be possible to convince the remaining *Dobunnic* hard-liners, that with a little Roman guidance and expertise, they could prosper even more. If all this could be achieved Antonius felt that they would finally have won the hearts and minds of these proud people; who once again would be able to hold their heads up high. This cultural shift could only come about if the Dobunni as a whole wanted it to, and he was realistic enough to know that some would find it impossible to shake off the ingrained resentments he had seen exhibited by hard nosed provincials, regardless of any improvements introduced by outsiders like him.

Over the next few years Antonius achieved most of what he set out to do in Naunton and several surrounding villages. Although he and Livia had started a smallholding of their own on the eastern hill soon after occupying their fine new stone house, he soon found that he did not need to grow very much for himself in the form of crops. Such was the gratitude of local elders for his help with the construction of the many new water wheels that were now effortlessly grinding their flour, as well as powering lathes and wood saws that he found himself granted almost weekly gifts of flour, meat and other produce in return. The women were particularly grateful as it was releasing more and more of them from the drudgery of the quern stones, and relieving the wearing out of countless knee and ankle joints. Several of the local farmers had also asked him to oversee the layout of their first stone house, and at least three now lived in such dwellings, though each still had a thatched roof as they were preferred over the famously expensive baked tiles from *Corinium*. The nearest stone built house to Antonius, was just down the hill at Harford, where Hatha's youngest son was the first of the family to depart from the traditional style. He had given the old wooden one a new lease of life by turning it into a granary.

One summer's afternoon Antonius was sitting in front of his villa admiring the westerly view across Naunton, towards a glorious sunset when he saw old Hatha riding slowly up the track from the valley.

He dismounted and hugged Livia and his grand-daughter Flavia and shook his son-in-law's hand warmly. They all sat outside and Livia brought wine and a bowl of fruit for herself and the men and a fruit drink for Flavia. They remained there, talking in front of the villa for several hours, reminiscing about so many things, including an afternoon many years before when Antonius, as a young tax official, had first visited them. To some laughter, they recalled that day as being just another when the beer may have flowed too freely. Then Hatha made a light hearted reference to the fact that Livia had been late milking their cow that afternoon, adding that for the life of him he never knew why, with a twinkle in his eye, as he looked so fondly at them all. They all laughed heartily again, including Flavia, though she knew not why at that moment.

They sat there almost until the sun had set, when old Hatha made to leave, saying he did not wish his horse to stumble on the track after dark. As they parted Hatha casually imparted to his only son-in-law, almost as an afterthought, that he and a number of other the local elders wished to express their gratitude to him for the way he had moved things forward for them all in the nearby villages in the three years since he had retired from the Army. He asked Antonius if he would ride out with him the next morning as he wished to visit his old friend Gould, at Slaughter.

Hatha arrived the following morning and the two men left on the rear track that joined the *Salt Way*, known locally as *Buckle Way*, where, to Antonius's surprise, Hatha turned his horse left, when Slaughter was to the right. They passed the Salter's Pool and the nearby round house where Dorgan was tending his field, with his children playing nearby. They dropped down into the hollow and up onto the higher ground on the far side where Antonius had never been before. They left the cover of the trees and suddenly a clearing opened up before them and the stumpy bases of a several very old wooden houses were just visible in the undergrowth. As they passed through them, Hatha pointed to a number of small humps in the long grass, which Antonius would probably have completely missed if his attention had not been drawn to them. The two men sat there on their horses surveying the deathly quiet of the place.

Hatha explained that these were the sacred burial grounds of the old Celts who lived here long before his own Dobunnic ancestors arrived uninvited, much as the Romans did later. The occupiers of this settlement had apparently abandoned the place, like so many others, fleeing westward when Hatha's ancestors rolled into the area, countless generations before. Hatha said there were a number of these old burial grounds strewn across the Wolds and began to explain to his son-in-law that this ritual landscape was highly respected within the modern Celtic Chiefdoms. He went on to explain that part of this respect for the dead involved the mid-summer and the mid-winter festivals when they implored the ancestors to give them back the sun the following year, to permit their crops to grow, lambs to be born and all the other cyclical events that naturally followed the thaw. Antonius listened thoughtfully and began to appreciate the true significance of these things to the older Britons, in much the same way as he knew their own gods were important to them. Antonius also recognised the degree of trust now being bestowed upon him as a result of what old Hatha was revealing to him, being well aware that the initial invasion force had ridden roughshod over many similar burial grounds, deliberately offending British sensibilities by desecrating them. Rome had even driven roads straight through many of them, as an arrogant statement of superiority over the indigenous population.

Because of this despicable behaviour on the part of the invaders, tribal chiefs had concealed as many of the burial grounds as possible, to prevent further destruction and avoid what could have resulted in the complete dissolution of the Celtic spirit world. For Hatha to now take him, a Roman, albeit an integrated and retired one, and show him one of these undisturbed and sacred places was unheard of and indicated the kind of acceptance he had earned here. As this realisation sank in, Antonius felt even more honoured by the gesture of trust, something akin to offering him a form of honorary Dobunnic citizenship. Rome had only ever sought to offer certain Britons Roman citizenship and in its arrogance had never stopped to consider there may have been any kudos in the reversal of such an honour; as Antonius now found himself accepting with some humility. They both stared down at the neglected and overgrown graves a little longer before both men turned their horses and began to retrace their steps in silence along the old *Salt Way,* towards the nearest Slaughter settlement, where Hatha's old friend Gould was expecting them. Antonius had learned so much more in the last hour, and without having to say very much in the course of doing so.

Gould welcomed them both into his fine old round house. Drinks were served, after which he explained to Antonius that he wished to enlist the skills he was now famed for by having him plan and oversee the building of a water wheel next to his house on the River Eye, being a mile upstream from the one he designed and helped build the year before. The nether mill was working well and could cope with as much grain as local farmers could offer to its stones. This was something the miller was now benefiting from financially and Gould wished to remove his monopoly and have his own source of power, maybe even undercutting his charges, laughing, as he used an old phrase about there being nothing wrong with a bit of healthy competition. Antonius was, as usual, more than willing to help design and build the mill and the size of the wheel was dependent on his calculations of the flow-rate, as this reduced further upstream, and more so again in a dry spell. Gould then lifted a blanket covering something nearby, revealing a fine leather saddle, complete with stirrups, which he then presented to Antonius. Stirrups were something that traditionally the Romans never used, but Antonius prided himself on recognising the need to adapt and the phrase, 'when in Britain, don't do as the Britons do' was recalled, and he graciously accepted Gould's gift. This visibly pleased both men and for the second time that day Antonius realised that he was being further welcomed into the Dobbunic heartland, this being more than enough reward for any help he gave them.

As they rode back up the hill towards Naunton that afternoon, Hatha imparted to Antonius that he was now a tired old man and knew he would soon be passing into the spirit world. He referred to the burial ground they had seen earlier and joked about not wanting his last resting place cut through by some Roman road construction gang, as plenty of others had been. Antonius assured him that such a thing would never happen as long as he was around. He said that he could never see it happening again because the relationship between Rome and southern Britannia had improved to the point that such antagonistic behaviour would not be tolerated, by the Governor, any more than it would by local elders. Fair minded governance was to be the new order of things.

Antonius asked Hatha if he had decided on his final resting place, or if he preferred the conflagration method of reaching the afterlife. The old man laughed and said he had told his family where to put him, but did not know if they would ever remember. After they dismounted by the stables at the side of Antonius's villa, Hatha pointed west, towards Naunton and the high ground to the south of the small settlement, saying that up on the top of the East Upper Field was his chosen spot, so he could forever watch over the village and his people. Antonius asked if he meant by his stone built corn drier they had built a few years earlier and Hatha confirmed that it was, adding that no more crops would rot if he was there to keep an eye on things. Both men laughed and that was the end of the conversation, having seen Livia approaching them, announcing as she did so that the meal was almost ready. Antonius proudly carried his new saddle into the house and from that day forward he used the stirrups like any other good Briton.

When Hatha died in 104AD, he was buried in accordance with his wishes in the East Upper Field, well below the depth of any ploughman who might pass over him. Before the interment there were two days of mourning during which most of his old farming friends rode to Naunton to pay their respects. Hatha's last trip saw him shrouded in a fine woollen blanket, [9] and borne upon one of his two wagons, pulled by his white steed, assisted by two additional working horses. Hatha's three sons led the cortege up the ancient 'Swilleys' track-way, followed by his widow and other family members including Antonius.

Behind them were many friends and workers from Naunton, and neighbouring farmsteads. When they reached the highest point on the southern side of the valley, everyone gathered around the grave, leaving a natural gap through which the three sons carried the body to the graveside. They lay him at the edge of the pre-dug, stone lined grave, before realising another man, on the fourth corner of the blanket, would greatly ease the burden of lowering him into the ground. Without a word being said Antonius joined them and the four men lowered Hatha to his last resting place; a few yards away from the circular corn drier and its two stone-lined flues. Each man stood and looked down fondly at the shrouded form of the old man for the last time. Each understood that his life had played another short but significant part in the history of the valley and that his spirit would now watch over them forever. In the wind-blown silence that followed, the thoughts of everyone recalled a few things about Hatha's life. Each understood that a wise and capable friend had passed, mourning the fact in their personal ways. Bryn then raised his head and his voice to compete with the wind said a few thoughtful words about his father, most of which were lost in the air.

Quite unexpectedly, Antonius then turned towards those assembled on this bleak windswept spot. He looked towards his wife Livia, and then to her elderly mother, both of whom were weeping and consoling each other. He said how proud he was to have known Hatha and his wife, and to have had the good fortune to marry their daughter, finding he had joined a proud and noble family. He said he could think of no better place than the Cotswolds to raise their children and was only saddened by the fact that his parents could not have known them all. He added that he and Livia intended to remain at Naunton. He said that much progress had been achieved locally with the help and support of the good man they had just laid to rest. Antonius described how Hatha had now crossed his beloved Windrush for the last time, in much the same way as his own parents had entered their spirit world by crossing the River Styx. He concluded by saying that as he spoke these words, at this sad moment in their lives, standing here on this windswept hillside, he had become more convinced than ever before that there was no real difference between people, wherever they came from. He said that whatever their individual beliefs might be; in facing this thing called death they were as one before the gods. He finished by saying that regardless of individual strengths and weaknesses, rights and wrongs, all went back to Mother Earth, taking nothing more than they had entered the world with. After saying his few words Antonius better realised what his countrymen had done to these proud people and the fact that even after defeat, they had mostly welcomed him into their midst and part of him almost wanted to apologise on behalf of Rome.

Hatha's sons showed no sign of disapproval at what they had just heard and actually seemed to appreciate his genuinely spoken words. Although they came from someone they had always regarded as a representative of Rome, a little of the old enmity faded on that windswept ridge. In life Hatha had demonstrated acceptance of his son-in-law, especially to his stubbornly resentful third son Lucco on many occasions, but outwardly at least, their intransigence remained undiminished, and whether it was a form of cultural intolerance, xenophobia or plain old jealousy, Antonius was never sure. But in death Hatha had somehow achieved what he had singularly failed to achieve in life. They all fell silent once more with only the sound of the wind and the stomping of the horses, as Bessie knelt at the graveside to place two pots next to Hatha, one containing food and the other drink for his journey to the next world.

After helping her to her feet her sons set about covering their father's resting place with two heavy protective slabs of local stone. The earth was shovelled back before Bessie and Livia placed a corn dolly on the fresh mound and turned away to lead the wagon and horses back down the hill, with everyone following quietly behind. When part way down the 'Swilleys' track, Hatha's eldest son Lucco placed a hand on Antonius's shoulder and almost thanked him for his words. In that single moment during the journey of life and death, Antonius believed he had begun to close the rift that his three brothers-in-law had chosen to maintain between them these past years. He thought to himself that the keystone in one of the most challenging bits of bridge-building he had so far been engaged in may just have slipped quietly into place.

Hatha's death resulted in Livia and Antonius inheriting two more oxen, and some sheep and pigs to add to their modest smallholding on the eastern hill, and with no rancour from anyone else within the family. Livia continued to weave her wool with her faithful servants, for she preferred to call them this, rather than slaves, tend the animals, milk two cows and grow a few crops and vegetables. For much of the time Antonius remained pre-occupied with various projects in the surrounding villages, his horse knowing most of the local tracks. On the way home from the Fosse, Antonius could usually do his mental calculations for the next day's work on the hoof, hardly needing to command his horse at the last few deviations along the way. The family continued to prosper, with Antonius advising numerous people within at least a ten-mile radius on construction plans and water related engineering projects. Many of these now combined the use of both traditional wood-working methods, with an ever increasing use of the local limestone.

Soon after Hatha's funeral, Antonius set out one morning to visit *Castlett*, a little further up the Windrush valley; the brook being known locally as *Gytingbroc*, where the farmer wanted to build a mill. This was largely as a result of word reaching him that the two Slaughter mills were now working well on one stretch of the *Eye*. On the way he detoured slightly from the *Winchcombe Way* a short distance along *Salt Way*, towards the old hunting and burial ground a mile from his house. He did so to call at Dorgan's house, just past *Salter's Pool*. He soon spotted Dorgan and his wife, as both were out tilling their patch of gently rising ground behind their round house. They were struggling to do this with hand tools and he saw the ard lying uselessly next to their house. A clutch of scrawny children were running around nearby and Antonius could not help but recall the old saying about children being a poor man's riches. Dorgan's old steer had died recently and word of this reached Antonius through Livia. She had told him that they were now experiencing some difficulty in breaking up their patch of ground, which really needed preparing before the autumn. Realising that he was their nearest neighbour, and now having two additional under-worked oxen of his own, Antonius thought he would make a neighbourly gesture by offering the use of his oxen to this struggling family. Dorgan had seen Antonius many times over recent years riding by alone, and once with old Hatha, putting them on nodding terms as neighbours.

Dorgan was a poor but proud man, never likely to call upon Antonius for his professional skills, though he knew well enough what amazing things his Roman neighbour had designed and built in the locality, and of course everyone knew he had married Hatha's girl after calling to collect the tax many years before. They bade each other an uneasy greeting and Antonius could see they were scratching a very meagre living from the sparsely covered ground, and that the children were a lean but happy bunch as they ran around his horse. Dorgan's dogs now tried to snap at the rear quarters of the fine animal, on their territory, where the horse's eyes had the greatest difficulty following their darting shapes and vicious teeth, even though it could hear them well enough. Dorgan shouted and kicked out at the dogs, lifting one yelping bitch from the ground with his foot, before they all skulked into the undergrowth.

Antonius considered it was now safe enough to dismount, allowing the two men to greet each other with due deference. He was still wary of the mean looking creatures cowering in the scrub nearby and Dorgan was equally wary as to the reason for this visit. His wife was also unsure as to why their important neighbour had dropped in and offered him some refreshment from the old black pitcher nearby; as she might any thirsty trader passing by, before suddenly realising that he had only ridden a short distance along the track from his fine house. Antonius knew that it would be easy to insult them by offering these poor but proud folk his unwanted charity, so he tactfully enquired if Dorgan might be able to find the time to do some ploughing for him in the top field. Dorgan hesitated, and then almost agreed, before drawing back slightly as Antonius went on to say that when the work was done he could use his two oxen and plough to turn his own ground. He pointed out that his new iron plough share would cut through twice as much ground in a day as the ard would, inclined as they were to break in this thin stony soil.

Dorgan and his wife were solitary people, quite content with their lot up here and when things were difficult for them they somehow always made ends meet, filling their children's bellies before their own. A passing trader would invariably recognise their plight and leave them a coin or a small bag of produce after refreshing themselves at Dorgan's house, and their horses at the nearby pool, before setting off again along *Salt Way*. Although things were difficult for them at present, Dorgan still didn't jump at the offer and seemed to be weighing it all up before mumbling something to his wife about last years tax.

Antonius' astute mind quickly interpreted what was troubling Dorgan, the rate of tax being entirely dependent on the amount of ground each smallholder had under the plough, many of them declaring a lesser area than was the case. Antonius laughed loudly as he called to mind what many people still remembered him for, attempting to reassure Dorgan that he was not remotely interested in how much ground he cultivated, had no intention of pacing it out and had only been involved in local taxation for one week in his whole life, with no interest in such things now. Dorgan relaxed visibly upon hearing this and seemed to accept that his good neighbour was being just that. He even allowed a slight smile to cross his wizened face, as an indication that the ground between them was now more level, even if it was still hard. Antonius went on to say he had bought too much seed corn last year and rather than see it rot he would be glad if Dorgan could use some of it. He said he had too much dung for his fields and Dorgan could collect some if he wanted it. The faces of Dorgan and his wife visibly lightened again, which was reward enough for Antonius, who was not the kind of man to stand by and see a family go under.

It was agreed that the ploughing work would start the next morning and Antonius remounted his horse. As he turned back towards the track, still conscious of the prostrate and keen eyed dogs nearby, he paused to compliment them on the quality of the newly thatched roof on their beautiful little round house. They were clearly proud of their house, having just topped it off with a traditional corn dolly that sat precariously on the conical straw point. Dorgan confirmed it was the latest in a long line of similar houses on the same spot, the previous one being built by his wife's father. Antonius gestured towards Dorgan's small field and pointed out that if his corn grew well enough to give him a surplus he could sell some to the local miller. He went on to say that this might increase his income sufficiently to employ a Mason to dress some of the plentiful stone nearby, to build a house that would last a lot longer than this one would. Dorgan laughed loudly as he pointed out that such money did not interest him, as long as he had enough for him and his family to survive. He added that there was nothing wrong with the house they had already and even if he had enough money to afford a fine woollen shroud one day, he would have no need for any pockets in it. Antonius laughed now because Dorgan had taught him another simple lesson in life; that he and many of the other Britons were quite satisfied with what they already had in life; being happy to survive it and then depart with nothing more than they entered with – providing no one rode roughshod over their spirits!

Following some two thousand years of occupation in and around Naunton, coins of almost every period have been found, confirming human presence throughout two millennia. This connecting picture shows some local British (Dobunnic) gold and silver staters and a QEII One Pound coin, representing both ends of this storyline.

Some factional bi-millennial bridging notes (in no particular order)

❉ The *Fosse Way* and *Salmonsbury Bridge* were kept in a good state of repair over the next few centuries. Ostensibly, this early super-highway was built for the Roman Army, but all kinds of people continued to use it, and still do. They included some of the earliest Christian missionaries and countless others, from kinglets to travelling entertainers, horse dealers, vagabonds and peddlers, to modern commercial travellers, commuters, tourists, parents on school-runs and various others. But the most frequent users over the 20 centuries were always the farmers, taking their animals and wagonloads of produce to market. Within 50 years of the Roman withdrawal from Britain in 405AD, the bridge began to sag under the unregulated weight of overloaded wagons, before finally collapsing into the Windrush. What remained of the stone bridge was cleverly rebuilt to utilise just one side of its old stone base, providing a solid footbridge. The many Roman buildings adjacent to the bridge, including the Posting House [Mansio], stabling and workshops and the buildings along the road into Salmonsbury eventually became dilapidated, much of the stone being used for later, post-Roman buildings. The next vehicular, stone-built Bourton Bridge did not appear for more than six centuries, until after the Norman French invasion of 1066.

❉ The old Fosse-Way eventually deteriorated beyond repair, its surface becoming rutted and potholed and with insufficient funding or expertise to refurbish and maintain it, it remained the most impressive superhighway in this area for the next twenty centuries. Not until the 20th century (1969AD) did anything comparable scythe its way through the fields of Gloucestershire. Although the modern farmers were still unable to do much about it, they were at least compensated for the loss of their land. Over the following centuries several more footbridges were built, with the ford coming back into use for the passage of horses and wagons. The road surface remained in a poor and rutted state until John McAdam invented a revolutionary new bitumen surface c1850AD. The last stone bridge to be constructed at this important location on the Fosse was c1850 [10] being widened to accommodate today's heavier transport in 1958. Although no one knows how long the latest bridge will last, larger and faster wagons, of a completely different type are now contributing to its downfall. A few of these modern wagon drivers also come from old Gaul. Some people believe that they should now be paying tax to the Britons for its upkeep, but so far they have neatly avoided doing so. The old Salt Way route from the Fosse, across the top to Naunton was never metalled by the Romans who planned to upgrade all 'economic' roads leading to and from the Fosse. It remained in a rutted, parlous state until about 1937AD when it was first tarmaced. Today, its users can understandably be forgiven for thinking that parts of it have not been resurfaced since then!

❋ Fragments of Edrig's ancient Salmonsbury encampment, together with its overspill, were unearthed by archaeologists twenty centuries later. Amongst the many discoveries were the skeletal remains of his daughter, found in one of the ancient pits. Such was the modern interest in it all that a National Television Company monitored the dig in 1998 and a reconstruction was made of her skull. Her facial features were rebuilt in clay and although it no longer conveys the verve and spontaneity of her true being, something of her Celtic beauty undoubtedly reaches through to us. Now known as 'Bourton Betty', she occupies a glass case in Bourton Primary School where today's highly literate, historically aware pupils watch over her; fully appreciating that their school occupies the site of her family's pre-historic farmstead. They are also conversant with the housing design of her time because a modern reconstruction is located in their playground [11]. Only 146 of Edrig's great hoard of precious iron currency bars have so far been recovered from the north-east bank of Salmonsbury during modern excavations. He concealed them there when this was the only kind of bank in which to place his wealth. He died, taking the secret of their location with him; lost and forgotten until people armed with little more than trowels and brushes located them some two thousand years later. A range of other artefacts were recovered from the few remaining accessible bits of old Salmonsbury, representing but a fraction of the material wealth that this vibrant and thriving community once generated along the Windrush Vale. Edrig's descendants, also unaware of where he had carefully hidden his hoard, were probably driven out after further disagreements within the tribal hierarchy, as well as the inbred reluctance to submit to their Roman masters.

❋ By the end of the 4th century AD, only the wisest of the old Salmonsbury and Naunton widows could vaguely recall tiny fragments of ancient stories, once so well known in the days before their ancestors were obliged to submit to Rome. Countless new stories had of course since overlaid the old ones, many of them created within the four centuries of post-conquest life and the undeniable improvements that flowed from it, all generating thousands of new stories. But somehow, certain small threads of the old, pre-Roman lore, customs, traditions and superstitions managed to leach through from pre-historic times, when people carefully kept everything in their wise heads. Regardless of who subsequently arrived here, whether they did so forcefully or peacefully, minute traces of this Celtic ancestry was mysteriously, maybe even mystically, passed on and survived. It was carefully transmitted along thousands of completely unrecorded bloodlines and through numerous intermarrying generations of people who followed on. It has since become an intrinsic part of the modern gene pool and psyche, intertwined amongst a welter of modern beliefs; confused as to its true origins and unable to be separated from more recent influences that have been introduced or imposed upon the great mix of peoples that occupy this land.

✤ Hatha's descendants, the eldest male in each new family generally being given the same name, continued farming in and around Naunton; occasionally opening up more ground with their efficient new (Roman) iron plough shares. They and all the other farmers who followed continued to grow and mill their corn in the two local water corn mills, one of which survived until the mid 20th century. They sold their surplus grain; flour, meat, wool, leather and other produce at nearby markets, generation after generation, and century after century, until cheaper imports undercut them in the 20th century. It became the only way of life that local people knew of or could relate to, with little real understanding of what life was like in pre-historic times. The Celts, subsequently assisted by Roman technology, imposed an early farming and industrial revolution upon the old Cotswold farmscape. Thereafter it was inherited and carried forward by thousands more farming families. Whether they were landowners, tenants, freeholders, common holders or landless men, they lived on and from the same land, in much the same way as the men who originally tamed and tilled it.

✤ During the opening centuries of the first millennium and under the stewardship of more new people, adopting more personal names, Naunton continued to put additional acreage under an increasing number of ploughs each year [12]. The increased productivity drew in more workers who built more of their functional little cottages, some round and some square, using both wood and stone. The people continued to build, rebuild and refurbish the important buildings such as the Mill and the Dove House. When a Saxon Christian missionary eventually reached Naunton and preached to the community, they were sufficiently enthused by his teachings to build themselves a small wooden church at the west end. Further visits by monks and other itinerant preachers reinforced the Christian message, bringing an entirely new spiritual dimension into their lives, eventually forcing out most of the old pagan practices and superstitions forever.

✤ The arrival of the Normans after 1066 is believed to have resulted in the building of the first small stone church in Naunton by the local Overlord, Roger de Olgi. His church was maintained for some 300 years before it was rebuilt by John Aylworth in about 1500; building a house for the preacher at about the same time. Less than a thousand years after the first Roman presence in Naunton, almost all trace of them had disappeared, other than possibly rebuilding places such as the dovecote and the mill, or finding their plentiful coins, a few bits of masonry, some villa remnants and a burial ground. Whilst many of their technological improvements lived on, from concrete to corn driers, almost everything else appears to have slipped permanently below the ground, to join so much else of Naunton's lost and ancient past. Most of it has remained there ever since, patiently awaiting either destruction from the plough and modern earth moving equipment, or perhaps gentler discovery by trowel and brush. Today, even more sophisticated methods of subterranean detection are available to us, and maybe, some day soon, a little more of Naunton's topsoil will be carefully scraped back to reveal a few of its oldest secrets.

✤ Over following centuries more of the traditional round-houses in Naunton and nearby were gradually replaced by small rectangular wood-framed cottages, and finally by many small stone cottages, and a lesser number of substantial stone-built houses. But who is to say that all of the little round houses were replaced like this? It depended on personal preference, affordability and availability of materials. Whilst individuality was the byword of the working people, some no doubt achieved it by adding their own personal touches to the traditional housing stock. During the early centuries this probably resulted in some people building the lower walls (below the thatch) with stone and covering them with daub or lime mortar to keep the weather out. Some people may have continued decorating the lower walls with pebbling or bright coloured paints and swirling scrollwork for the relatively few years these houses stood. But round houses could have remained popular for centuries, especially during the Roman period, when a few Britons may have characteristically delighted in showing contempt for the foreign designs built around them. It was after all one of the few ways open to a proud but conquered people to brazenly cock-a-snoot at the Italian School of *rectilinear* design and rule. But gradually house design did change. Assisted by Roman lime mortar, rather than daub, houses began to incorporate walls of ashlar stone, rubble stone, timber framing, chiselled stone, buttered stone, rendered walling, and fired bricks, the latter becoming the most popular of all building materials.

❋ No one really knows how long those little bastions of Britain's early housing stock endured across the centuries, because there are no pictures. It is reasonable to assume that after the Roman withdrawal, they may even have enjoyed some resurgence. In post-Roman times, the retention of former British designs and values would have depended largely on the willingness of the people to retain past traditions. Some were indifferent to the loss of tradition, whilst others may have been keen to preserve a little of their proud and increasingly diluted heritage. At this early point on the timeline, it was quite impossible to know who would win, the traditionalists or the modernisers. Only people living in some unimaginably far-off time, such as the late 20th century AD, could possibly answer the question of what survived, and even then, such a person might be unable to convince anyone else of its probity. It is similar to us asking if an existing house, dovecote or church might still be around in 3500AD. Only people living here one and a half millennia from now will know the answer to the question, possibly aided by some of these notes and pictures to help them decide. By that time the world will again be a vastly different place, even though its people will be biologically the same as their distant Celtic forbears.

❋ This brings us to the final and possibly most controversial linkage point, and if it generates nothing more than a little thoughtful argument, it will have been worthwhile. To do this we will move away from the unknown and fictitious personalities who may or may not have occupied the ancient round houses and villas in and around Naunton during the first few centuries AD, to take a closer look at their houses. It is my contention, revealed to no one before keying it on to these pages that the ancient British or local Dobbunic round-houses that we know were once extremely common around here, due to the ongoing downstream excavations at Salmonsbury, may not have completely fallen into disuse after the Romans arrived, or indeed after they left. We accept that they introduced the ancient Britons to *rectilinear* stone-built houses or villas and that some Britons began to adopt that style thereafter, including all of us today. But I believe a few of the beautiful little *curvilinear* houses of the ancient Britons may have lived defiantly alongside the all the others, right up to the twentieth century, before finally petering out in the 1900s.

Naunton's last occupied round-house was recorded in writing in 1901. It was lived in by Abel Tom Smith [13] whose forebears had lived and worked around here for more centuries than we yet know, and whose descendants, as you will soon discover, are included with photographs, beside their *rectilinear* houses [14] in this book. Abel Tom would have been proud to know that his great-great grandson, Robert, was living here today, to paint a picture for the front of this book. On the 8th of April 1901, when Census enumerator John Buffin knocked on his door, he recorded that 30 year 'Abel Tom' was a Farm Bailiff, who we know had previously moved out of the village for farm work; returning later. He lived in the last round house with his 28 year old wife Sarah and their three children, William 4yrs, Elsie, 2yrs and baby Matilda 7 months [15]. It would be disingenuous of me to assume that Abel Tom never contemplated the possibility that he represented the last of some two millennia of people occupying this style of house; a style designed and constructed by skilled artisans in both wood and stone, living way back amongst the tribes of ancient Britain. Another reason why I am inclined to suggest this is because some small acknowledgement of its importance lingered vaguely on through oral tradition amongst more modern Nauntonians for another fifty years, to when I was a boy here in the 1950s.

I was privileged to know about this little house because as children we explored most of the interesting places dotted around our 3000 acre rural playground, and its location, tucked quietly away amongst the trees, was no secret to Naunton boys and girls. Local people who knew of it always referred to it as the 'Round-House,' in a similar way to the little 'Flour House' (the former schoolroom known as the Academy at Waterloo), hinting at human occupancy in earlier times. I have spoken to two of the oldest surviving Nauntonians about the 'Round House,' but neither have any memory whatsoever of it being occupied, which is hardly surprising. Within their memories and mine it had been little more than a semi-derelict shell, used as a lowly cattle bower. But like me, they acknowledged that some greater historical significance was apparently attached to it, without knowing exactly what that was. I did not appreciate how significant it might be until 2001, when the 1901 census was opened to the public. The census contains factual information, previously closed to us for 100 years. But the information recorded in the census was no secret to the people who knew these things first-hand in the late 19th and early 20th century, when its occupants routinely imparted their names to the census enumerator.

We must remember that matters of common knowledge around Naunton a century ago were soon to be crushed beneath tragic and weightier events when two World Wars and the economic depression of the 1930s, indelibly marked many local people's memories. As these modern calamities bore down on the parish, it is hardly surprising that such titbits of local history became obscured. By the time that I and my contemporaries picked up on their receding echoes in the 1950s, conditions had eased again considerably. But by then, this little building had become derelict and just one more trifling detail of fading parish antiquity, of the type that played a very insignificant part in the modern rebuilding of post-war lives. The structure, as I recall it, had almost round stone walls, a wooden door, broken glass windows, central hearth, flagstone floor and the remains of a conical roof that was collapsing inwards. Its roof may have been tiled, as others before it probably were, situated as it was next to the village's centuries-old stone quarry and in keeping with the traditional, non-thatched roofs that are now pre-eminent in this part of Britain. It was however still a round house, based on the oldest style of housing, and not exactly as it appears today after a rebuild and change of use. Its latest makeover has turned it into a rustic shelter for shooting parties, which thankfully has saved it from the final one of razing it to the ground, leaving little more than fading memories and possibly a few soil stains to acquaint us with its past. Despite having no pictures of our old buildings before the 20th century, it is not unreasonable to suggest that this quaint structure was not the only round-house left in Naunton during more recent centuries; though it is fair to say it is the last surviving one.

The fact that stone eventually subsumed timber as the main construction material around here was due to a combination of factors, and in my opinion, two in particular seem to override the others. Firstly, there were external influences, as the Romans showed the more influential Britons how to increase their status by building themselves grander houses in stone, with higher walls and square corners. It gave the locals an 'upstairs' view of things for the first time, and just imagine the vertiginous novelty of that! Then there was the over consumption of local timber, which was used indiscriminately for house building, fuel, charcoal clamps, hurdles, fences, gates, tools, wagons, weapons, baskets and much more. Local carpenters were eventually faced with having to seek alternative materials as the once plentiful supply of timber became exhausted. The proof of this lack of timber, at least during the central part of our 2000 year storyline, is clearly recorded in the Domesday record. This tells us that by 1086AD, 3060 of Naunton's 3106 acres was under the plough and that there were no woods or meadows left.

A situation such as this would not have come about overnight of course. It is vaguely similar to the much earlier extinction of certain animals through over-intensive hunting. Local people now seem to have done much the same thing to the woodlands by over intensive felling, with little or no resource management. Though now denuded of timber, the area was not sitting on hard-won granite or crumbling gravel, but on readily accessible and easily dressed limestone, bedded down between 100 and 170 million years ago and largely ignored as a building material until a little after two thousand years ago. Local people were then shown how to use it by the Romans and the walls and roofs of houses were increasingly built using this cheap alternative material which had always been underfoot, and which would then have been extracted from 'delves' [16]. At the same time, upper floors, joists and roof timbers had to be constructed with timber, as most still are today. In earlier times, until sufficient trees were grown and coppiced again, the village's demand for timber probably resulted in the wagoner being busier than the woodsman, having to haul it in from beyond Naunton's boundaries for years. We are fortunate that there is still an abundance of these natural materials today; enabling us to continue building in both wood and stone, even if like some of our food, more of it is now imported.

You are of course at liberty to take issue with anything I have said about the continuity of these circular houses generally, or about this one in particular. The locals may once have said that a single swallow does not make a summer. Conversely, the departure of the last swallow does not mean that summer did not precede it! A similar rule I was once taught was that the absence of evidence is not evidence of absence. If you are still unconvinced, let me conclude by saying this: If houses of circular design had disappeared completely somewhere down through the ages, being overtaken by houses of rectangular design, consider the learning curve (pun intended) required to regain the necessary skills just to make and assemble the purlins, laths, beams and other roof timbers, if all the building expertise was now being channelled into rectangular houses. And why would they bother to resurrect them if they had all been replaced by rectangular houses? Lest you think it was some kind of Victorian folly, why build one in such an isolated location, with no views over the surrounding countryside? And is there a precedent for a Victorian folly changing into a humble dwelling? I now rest my case, leaving it for others to decide the context, chronology and significance of this particularly intriguing local building plot.

❋ But this part of the debate has focussed on a solitary round house. What about finding some small trace of a house belonging to Roman or Romano-British people who lived here, in retirement or otherwise? Roman coins have always been more plentiful in Naunton's fields than *Dobunnic* coins, but until you find traces of Roman dwellings, the scatter of their coins across the landscape can be attributed to the fact that the locals were trading heavily with the Romans over some four centuries. The *Dobunnic* coinage was only in circulation for 100 years or so before the Romans arrived, after which they outlawed its further manufacture and use.

To extend the debate, a Roman house is what we need and the likes of our fictional *Antonius*, marrying into Celtic stock, would not have become *'Britonised'*, or lived here in a modest 1st century *Niwetone* round-house. Integration was the other way round, with Britons becoming 'Romanised', occasionally to the point of gaining Roman Citizenship. Someone with *Antonius's* construction and engineering background could easily have built himself a modest farmhouse or *Villa*. The sceptics amongst us are perfectly entitled to say that whilst Naunton had a Romano-British farmstead and burial ground (in the field called Well Ground) at Summer Hill, no villa has yet been found amongst the more modern buildings situated there today, possibly because it lies beneath them. We know that Gloucestershire, with more than thirty known Roman Villas, probably has more than any other county and that some of the finest were at places like Chedworth, Withington, Wycomb, Witcombe and Woodchester. But these rank amongst the grandest villas that have been discovered locally, built at later times during the 350 year period of occupation and by wealthier Romano-British families. A middle ranking chap such as *Antonius*, marrying into a local family, or just a successful and well connected local farmer, might well have built the first stone house in Naunton, even though this particular building has not survived.

I believe it is reasonable to suggest that someone like Antonius may have proudly occupied a modest farmhouse or villa, like the one that must have been at Summerhill. Alternatively, as this story suggests, he might have laid out his villa estate on the Eastern Hill, a mile to the south-east of Summerhill, in a location we can be more certain of. His farmstead might have been the one situated almost literally in Mike and Jane Arnold's back yard at Brockhill, close to where their own modern house or villa of this name now stands; carrying on the name of former farm buildings there. Modern 'Brockhill' commands the same kind of imposing presence and views over Naunton and the Cotswolds, as its neighbouring Roman house once did. Its name is now lost and if you see **'New Court Ground Roman Villa'** on maps of this location; this is likely to be a more modern description. Like so much else around here, the Roman *villa* was eventually abandoned before becoming dilapidated, it's stone probably reused in other buildings, all trace of it eventually becoming 'ploughed-out' during almost two thousand years of cultivation that followed its construction. By the time the first recorded excavation was undertaken to relocate it in the 1930s, the few bits of archaeology remaining represented a tiny fraction of what must once have been there, following its abandonment. [17]

The 1930s excavation was undertaken by Helen O'Neill, an extremely competent archaeologist from Bourton-on-the-Water. Although countless people would have seen the villa in much earlier times, her excavation appears to be only the second time anyone bothered to record it. Archaeologists tell us today that whilst such sites have always been destroyed by ploughing (with the exception of some of the better known ones mentioned), since 1945 alone this activity has continued to destroy our precious archaeology at the appalling rate of one site per day. Today, any farmers that are still fortunate enough to be ploughing fields, may claim to be the guardians of our countryside, but they might also reflect, particularly when 'sub-soiling' deeper down, whether such ploughing activity is causing irreparable damage to these priceless antiquities! Bill Bryson [18] said that our (English) heritage is suffering death by a thousand cuts, and he is quite right when it comes to ploughing up treasures like this.

I did say the second time it was recorded because some ten centuries before Helen O'Neill tried to relocate the 'New Court' *villa,* it had been a much more prominent feature on the local landscape. Like so much else around here, it was unable to be recorded by non-literate people at just about every other time during the two millennia. It appears that the first occasion was about a thousand years earlier, during a Saxon land survey. This was in 963 AD and the Saxon scribe who walked the bounds that day recorded what he saw on a modern parchment. Thankfully this particular document was not lost or destroyed, providing us with what is now an extremely ancient document known as the 'Harford Charter'. Having said that, the Saxons were famous for reusing Roman stone, and this is probably where it all went.

The following is taken from the Harford Charter, published in 'Saxon Charters and Field Names of Gloucestershire' by G.B. Grundy, 1935/6. Helen O'Neill may well have read this before going out to try and re-locate the completely obliterated site.

Quote '*This synd tha land gemaero thaere hidae into Heortforda;* 'These are the bounds of the one hide at Harford'.

1. '*Of Stan Forda up on Maeres Slaed;* 'From Stone Ford up to the Slade on the Boundary'. The ford was where Harford Bridge now stands, i.e. where the track that became the Stow to Cheltenham road now crosses the Windrush. The *Maeres Slaed* is the valley up which the Naunton boundary runs N.E. from the ford.

2. *Of* etc. *up on tha Caestello* [19] easteweardre; 'From Slade on the Boundary up to the (Roman Villa?) in a general easterly direction.

This ruined building or *villa* must have been on the north boundary, and judging from the next landmark, in the slade towards its head.' End quote.

Grundy believed that the only 10th century buildings on the landscape built of stone were old *Roman Villas*, suggesting that all the other [British] houses were built using other materials, and of course it is reasonable to assume that they were made of timber and maybe some stone as well. Grundy cannot say whether the British houses were square or round because the Saxon chronicler did not record this particular detail back in 963. It is reasonable to assume that there may have been a proportion of *rectilinear* and *curvilinear* houses by this time, it being at roughly the half-way point on our 2000 year timeline and its inseparable storyline.

◻

Iron Age Hunting and Harvesting

Naunton's last surviving Round House near Salter's Pool – rebuilt as a shelter for shooting parties
NB It is on private property which is why the photograph has been included.

The field in which the 'New Court' Roman Villa was once situated – now completely ploughed out.

Chapter Two

More Recent Times

A picture representing the centuries-old, pre-mechanised, labour intensive harvest scene (1800s).

Today, or some 2000 years further on from the point at which we started our story, these fascinating rearward glimpses are directed with some difficulty towards the people who once lived here, as we strain to see how they lived and worked, leaving us hungry for more information. Whether looking at ancient ruins, skeletons, artefacts, old field systems, track-ways or what is possibly the last round-house near Salter's Pool, each can barely hint to us today as to how things really were here during the great tracts of time that have since rolled, mist-like, over the parish during the intervening periods of occupation, which after the Romans departed were aptly labelled the *'dark ages'*. This is when some of the Romano-British are believed to have returned to the old hill-forts and round houses, resuming the Celtic way of life, though after 400 years of occupation, their lifestyle must have been somewhat different to pre-Roman times.

The absence of pre-twentieth-century photographs as well as the absence of any personal stories and histories, (no 'herstories' either I'm afraid) means that we really do not have an inkling of the lifestyles, values, the strife, the joy and the other life experiences of the ordinary men and women who created and maintained it all, through sweat and toil, grief and pain, faith and happiness, starvation or plenty. But despite this enforced ignorance of our rich past, I believe that what little we do have, tends to confirm that people were always here, from at least 2000 years ago, and that *Niwetone* was never one of the 3000 odd villages in Britain that became abandoned throughout this lengthy period [20]. Population fluctuations certainly occurred, and for a variety of reasons, probably including the plague and other diseases, in both humans and animals, together with flooding, crop failures, famine and emigration. But I do not believe people ever had sufficient reason to leave this particular golden vale, *en masse,* for very long, if at all, with its glistening *'white strand'* water course that supplied both them and their livestock, and once powered at least two waterside mills within the parish [21].

I believe that most past Nauntonians would willingly have left us a little more than these impersonal and fleeting glimpses into their lives, before they finally slipped away, had they only realised that others, like ourselves, arriving here anything up to two thousand years later would be remotely interested. Today, many of us are extremely interested in what occurred before our time but so little is left to satiate our curiosity. As for archaeology, as far as I am aware, no professional excavations have ever taken place down in the village, but some have taken place on the ancient burial grounds on the north edge of the parish. This means that there could still be plenty of potential round house stains waiting silently below the ground to add a little more to Naunton's hopelessly incomplete storyline. The danger is that when modern development has occasionally been permitted, in the form of new house-builds such as the east end Council Houses (1943 and 1950s), Springfield/Northfield (1963), Village Avenue (1968), Lower Grange Hill (1969), Longford Yard/North Street (1974) and Windrush View (1987), heavy plant machinery operating on tight schedules move in. Several thousand years of whatever delicate traces may have been lying there are then indelicately scoured out, adding to the kind of losses I need to describe here.

Learning to do better….

Other than the traditional father to son, mother to daughter, handing on of vocational skills that have always taken place in family oriented settlements like this, formal teaching did not become available much before the 19th century, as State Education sought to bring literacy to all of Naunton's children in 1865 [22]. There is mention of a 'village school' in the first (1856) Trade Directory, and this may refer to the schooling of a few children in rooms connected with the Church or Chapel. Earlier than this, some select tutelage was probably undertaken by the Parish Priests and other benevolent individuals, such as small dame schools in private houses.

The Trade Directories also mention the 'academy' at Waterloo and this refers to the little building that later became known as the 'Flour House' where some kind of instruction seems to have taken place. Whenever and wherever it was that teaching was first offered to some or all of the local children, why-oh-why did one or two of those early scholars not leave us a small account of themselves and their village as they grew older and wiser? We can ponder that question forever of course, but in doing so we might perhaps ask ourselves why a few more of us are not doing so today - or perhaps you are, in which case you are to be congratulated. It must also be true that their priorities were very different to ours, and I guess that having sufficient foresight to satisfy the curiosity of later generations by handing down stories and village artefacts just did not enter most people's minds.

The opening of the new village school in 1865 must have presented some problems on the farms, being a way of life that necessitated a seven-day working week. Each day essential jobs had to be done and quite often all able hands were needed in the fields. Compulsory education simply drained the village's strong young labour pool, taking boys and girls away from this work. Our present day school summer holidays, still inordinately long, are a throwback to the compromise that must have been reached in the 19th century to ensure sufficient hand-labour was available to gather in the all important harvest before it spoiled in the fields. In a pre-supermarket society, no harvest (including hay, straw, root crops, wheat, barley, fruit and vegetables) could so easily result in there being less than enough food for the people and the animals during winter, or until the next successful crop was harvested, simple as that. In the more desperate of those early times people were occasionally known to steal a sheep or a pig in desperation. When the law caught up with them, Gloucestershire's transportation records show that even a few Naunton men were not immune from embarking upon involuntary spells of banishment to the southern hemisphere.

So in times long past, it was not so easy and it was certainly no priority to hand down stories and other ephemeral details much beyond the immediate two or three generations living here. Word of mouth generally proved adequate for this and if nothing else, it kept the village gossips busy. Stories and good story tellers may well have abounded but village scribes were few, and alas, memories such transient things.

Some families seem to have lived and worked within the village over many centuries. Occasionally local people would travel to a neighbouring parish or farm for work or to provide help when planting out or gathering-in the harvest and such labour-loans were reciprocated into the 20th century. Transport, as we know it today, just did not exist, forcing workers, who would almost certainly not have owned a horse, to walk a considerable distance to do a day's work, and men were still walking to and from Huntsmans Quarry and outlying farms when I was a boy. The advent of the railways in the 19th century, particularly the Cheltenham-Kingham branch line, with local stations at Notgrove and Bourton (1875-1962) further opened up the North Cotswolds enabling farm-workers and their families to move greater distances for work.

But the Parish fields, fertile as they might be when properly managed and rotated [23] could only comfortably sustain a finite number of people. When the population swelled beyond an unsustainable level, or during frequent downturns in agriculture, the pioneering spirit of the time no doubt encouraged or compelled some people to depart, seeking better prospects in the New World as it opened up beyond Britain's shores from the 16th century onwards. But as some left, others would still have come here, in hope more than expectation, and so it ever was I believe. An optimum population level would generally have been arrived at, creating a kind of natural balance, this being a keyword in past times, just as it is today. A sustainable balance would depend on such things as the need for new labour and skills, the fertility of the land, the avoidance of farming crises, coupled with the willingness and ability of landowners and tenants to hire and fire workers. But perhaps more importantly, it would also depend upon the availability of those ever precious little wood and stone cottages, however basic and of whatever size, shape or design.

As the centuries passed, this two-way flow of humanity, and the accompanying advances in building design, agriculture, transport and supporting trades, appear to have shaped Naunton into what it is today, with population expansion in good times and the laying-off of workers in harder ones. Thinking of when I grew up here in the 1950s and 60s, the noise of metal wheel rims on the last horse drawn vehicles in the village street can have missed my ears by only a few years. My early recollections of transport involved many people walking around the parish; including workers to and from places like Huntsmans Quarry, Aylworth Farm and the railway. After that came the ubiquitous bicycle, Pulham's bus and the few people who owned motor cycles or cars. The latter were Austin-Seven, Ford Popular, Morris Oxford, Morris Minor, Vauxhall Wyvern and several 'shooting-brake' models. But whatever make they were, even as recently the 1950s, they were exclusively British makes. This rearward glance into a 1950s childhood naturally saw me as one of the smallest parts within this mutually supportive, close-knit, hard working, team oriented, easy going post-war community. Local employment was still mainly farming, quarrying, tiling, roads, or the railway. These occupations were accompanied by a few other vibrant trades and professions, happily coexisting alongside the primary one of farming. I seem to recall that altogether they included farm workers, builders, a blacksmith/metal worker, carpenter, undertaker, haulier, baker, publicans, and shopkeepers, a post woman, several office workers (Comeleys and Huntsmans) road workers, railway workers, several 'jacks-of-all-trades' and a teacher or two. The remainder mostly fell into the categories of mothers and housewives, retired folk and of course children.

But significant changes were afoot, and I now believe that amongst the older generation of folk around me, especially those still running the seven or eight family farms here, some were beginning to see the writing on the wall. In retrospect, I believe that my own immediate family were facing up to the fact that they represented the last generation of their family-line to work the land here; as part of a wider family cluster that had collectively farmed substantial portions of the Parish throughout recent centuries. The surviving bits of the Parish Register record that my namesakes were here in the 1500s, as were one or two other surviving families, and if we could only locate the missing register [24] we might find some of them were here earlier than that. As far as I know most of my ancestors were mainly, if not exclusively involved in farming and some no doubt had a hand in building a few of the oldest surviving houses and cottages, both for themselves and their workers.

To me a few of the things I saw happening around me as a youngster seemed to presage the period of change that has since taken place. This included the end of the line, not only for the local railway, but also for a number of the fairly small, family-run mixed farms. In the last quarter of the 20th century many of the Parish's productive 3,210 acres were to undergo a sea change from their lengthy and traditional usage, similar to how many of the old buildings had already slipped away and how a number of others, including barns, farmhouses, mills, bakery, forges, shops, cottages and one of two pubs were to go in the near future. Some of this change was radical because it represented a departure from the primal and historic use of the buildings and the tilth that surrounded them, reaching back over centuries.

Towards the close of the 20th century the process of decline in the farming economy was well underway, and involved a number of factors. It included the slimming down, slowing down and eventual stoppage on the part of the small farms. Some were broken up, allowing expansion on the part of contiguous farms. Others were taken out of production or 'set-aside' as pastureland under a Government sponsored run-down of British agriculture that began to rely more on imports to feed the nation. Some land underwent diversification away from farming altogether, to meet the burgeoning demands of the leisure, pleasure and tourist industries that were making greater inroads into the Cotswolds, whilst at least providing a little new employment as it did so. Conversely, the demand for the ever popular Cotswold Jurassic limestone saw a new stonemason become established together with an additional field or two being opened up at Brockhill Quarry. It also saw many of the redundant farm buildings converted into modern dwellings.

But whatever the causes were, their sad effects obliged a number of traditional farms and farm workers to bow out gracefully, one by one slipping quietly into retirement and then the kind of obscurity that I hope to prevent here. This is particularly sad when you consider all that has been achieved and all that they nurtured and managed here so carefully over the centuries, much of which has apparently become surplus to the requirements of modern Britons. As I grew up, the people doing all this around me were indigenous country folk who displayed a quiet and sage-like knowledge of what could and could not be done in the precious soil. The culmination of what they had learned in this 'hands-on' continuum of rural life had been handed down from generation to generation for as long as anyone could remember, and a lot longer than that. Many of the old villagers appeared to be descended from people who held an unshakeable belief in the Almighty, in themselves and in their individual talents or ability to survive, come what may, and some of the worst things did indeed come their way. By fortuitous timing of birth, my own generation were spared the traumas of living and dying through one, and in some cases two World Wars. My village mentors had not been so fortunate and I imagine that in experiencing it they had become inured or hardened to most of life's other little adversities, or the kind of things we are more readily inclined to regard as difficulties today.

By survive, I also mean that most of the people living here before I was born were conditioned to a working life with basic forms of housing and farm mechanisation and primitive transport. With no

Welfare State or National Health Service, early Nauntonians had to manage entirely on what was produced by their own hand-labour out in the fields, gardens and orchards; at a pace which had been dictated for centuries by the horse. They had carefully harnessed the productivity of the land with their innate skills of commerce and trade within a fairly localised farming economy that made them virtually self-sufficient. If someone fell on hard times (fell on the parish as it was once known) examples of how others would step in and help get them back on to their feet were commonplace. Those who could afford it, often under the auspices and anonymity of the Church, made donations knowing it would be apportioned to others according to need. In doing this they had in effect created their own in-house 'welfare system' and 'social workers'.

Some Parish Register entries are included here to demonstrate this point:

PR Dec 5 1727, *'Church paid Henry Hancks 15s 8d on account of 10 yards of cloth for clothing four boys, and 6 buttons as by Mr Boswell's bill and Henry Hancks receipt upon same. To Henry Hancks likewise for making the four boys coats and for Bukrum 3 shillings. The four boys clothed this year are Tho' Smith, Jack James, Giles Berry, Wm Kilminster.'*

PR. Dec 29 1734, *'There was 1s 6d left over from the sacrament on Christmas day which was given to 6 poor communicants at 3d each, but there being two more poor communicants, & the clerk, Mr Churchwarden Henry Hancks and I thought proper to give 9d of the Christmas Day overplus to them three, so y thus the 2s 4d set down falls short by nine pence which must be allowed me.'*

PR. 1735. *'The Mercers bill for garments for 3 boys & 2 girls this year is as follows: Fourteen yards of Brown Linsy at 14d yd. (16s) Three quarters of a yard of coloured Linen at 10d (7½d) One Dozen and a half of Metal Buttons (6d) Two ounces of thred (3½d) Canvas & Tape (4d) Making of garments at 9d each (17s 9d) The children who had garments this year (3s 9d).'*

To me, these were the people who formed the core of this place, with Naunton eventually becoming an integral part of them; almost their very being. They were confident and competent enough to roll up their sleeves and toil here in family run shops, workshops, fields, orchards and gardens, making do with what they had, or had not, as a result. In the early part of our two millennia, these people would have been descended from Celtic & Roman stock, whose ancestors could also have lived here for centuries. Then others arrived, settling and intermarrying amongst the indigenous people, strengthening the stock with the essential genetic diversity as they did so. Subsequent newcomers no doubt included forerunners of the next two waves of conquering peoples to cross our shorelines, as they sought to fill the power vacuum created after the Roman withdrawal, as the parish began to absorb people of Viking and Saxon origin in the process. As some arrived in victory a few others no doubt left in disgust, but before long that ever essential balance was regained and life carried on.

Whether the impact of all these forceful and resourceful migrations of people, as they arrived this far up the relatively inaccessible Windrush Valley, could be described as a ripple or a wave is unknown, and it will probably remain so forever. But there is no reason to doubt that some of all these people did arrive here from time to time, integrate here and carry on farming here, because this kind of human absorption and integration has always been a feature of life here; suffered, tolerated or accepted, as the case may be. Though others have since tried, the final hostile incursion to have any significant and lasting impact upon *Niwetone* appears to have been the Norman French, almost a thousand years ago. They certainly made their presence felt as they dispossessed the 11th century 'English' of their lands, perhaps more ruthlessly than even the Romans did one millennia before. The Normans however left us an incredible legacy in that they created a written record of what they found in places like *Niwetone,* whereas for some reason the equally literate Romans appear not to have done so.

So, whoever our farming forebears are, as they lived, toiled and occasionally fought around here, most of them just seem to have got on with cultivating the land, mostly by hand and with teams of oxen, and later with oxen and horses, in much the same way as people always have, just to survive. Using a more modern, or maybe it is not such a modern metaphor; 'if it ain't broke, don't fix it', all most newcomers ever really needed to do, once settled, and having an essential roof over their heads, was add their own refinements and ideas to tried and tested methods of animal husbandry and cultivation; methods that were well and truly established by the *Iron-Age* and *Roman* period. Methods of assarting, (woodland clearance to provide more tillage) tilling the soil, scattering the seed, cutting the corn, gathering it in and grinding the flour, simply stood the test of time; with, as yet few alternative methods available to ease the physical burden of it all, until the earliest forms of farm mechanisation.

Away from the actual fields, one of the early technological advances coming to their aid would have been in the shape of revolving mill stones, powered by water and introduced by the Romans, who copied the same technology from ancient Egypt. Whenever it was that they first arrived here, that great leap forward meant that women no longer needed to distort their toes and bend their backs kneeling over saddle querns, or with rotary querns to grind their precious flour, enabling more flour to be ground and traded. Other parts of the old agrarian infrastructure also seem to have remained relatively unchanged, until early forms of field mechanisation became available during the 17th and 18th century Industrial and Agricultural Revolutions, and such improvements have of course continued at an incredible pace ever since.

The increased farm mechanisation that flowed from the inventiveness of people during the more recent centuries did at least bring a reduction in the very labour intensive practises of old, which is so well captured in the 'The Dixton Harvesters' painting and the above engraving. The continuing demand for skilled workers in the New World also meant that struggling or redundant farm workers could see another way out of the agricultural downturns, and mechanisation of their hand-labour. People were still leaving like this in the 20th century, being just the same confident and competent folk as had been desperate or adventurous enough to board outward-bound ships during the previous two or three centuries. Innovative Nauntonians were amongst the many who exported themselves with one-way tickets into that brave new world, where their skills were such that they succeeded from a base of practically nothing, turning great tracts of virgin land into even greater countries, further confirming my opinion about the calibre of these people. My own ancestors are recorded as leaving for America in 1672 and 1676 and other times thereafter until the 1920s but their stories are all now lost forever.

One little anecdote I will include here about pre-mechanised farming concerns the occasional problem of getting obstinate oxen to move, despite the customary prodding and cursing. Practical as ever, one local ox-driver (William Herbert senior) used an ingeniously simple device with sound results. This comprised nothing more than a matchbox, an elastic band and a button. The button was threaded onto the elastic band which was stretched round the inner part of the matchbox. After winding the button on the elastic it was squeezed firmly within the box to keep the button still. When placed behind the ear of a stubborn beast and the pressure released, the freed button 'buzzed' around inside, sounding sufficiently like a bee to goad it into movement again! There must be thousands of similar little ox-tales like this which unfortunately we are now deprived of forever. The arrival of more modern alternatives to ox and horse-power in the shape of the majestic steam engines provided a more predictable, if at times less popular source of traction or turning power, initially supplementing the animals but inevitably replacing them. Whilst the animals may have welcomed this burdensome release, the poor farm workers who fed, harnessed and handled them all did not, relying on this work for their very existence. Furthermore, the impact of all this new steam technology on the 19th century chattering classes was also something to behold.

Whilst a single hired steam engine could now be contracted for threshing the corn at harvest time, it required two of these great machines to undertake the heavier work of the 'balance' plough. Usually hired because of their cost, the engines were positioned on opposite sides of a field, with a taut steel hawser running between them. The plough was then attached to the cable, which pulled it to and fro across the field, first towards one steam engine, and after tilting or turning the opposite end of the plough into the soil, back towards the other, the two trundling imperceptibly in parallel along the two headlands. The skills involved in this first ever mechanised version of 'God speed the plough' were considerable, and no small part of that skill involved keeping the cable taut and the great engines as close as possible to the edge of the field, which occasionally bordered a road, in order to minimise the unproductive headlands.

From this kind of rural background, my own farming forbears seem to have evolved within the local farming scene, adapting and moving on as and when necessary.

Taking a rest from their labours.

Waterloo Farm

Continuing with the centuries old custom of using oxen and horses and with the occasional assistance of steam power, but still with no tractors on any Naunton farms, the twentieth century seems to have dawned on the village at yet another difficult time in the agricultural world. In the aftermath of just one more farming crisis, in 1912 my grandfather, Horace Leslie Hanks, (1892-1969) together with his older brother Bert, left their family home at Naunton Mill to embark on a new life, farming in Canada. As a son of the miller and farmer I imagine Horace was destined to carry on farming wherever he found himself. The two brothers settled near the small town of Crystal City, Manitoba, and about a year later Hilda Griffin (1894-1976) who lived with her parents next to Naunton Mill at Waterloo Farm, left Naunton, age 18, to join Horace in Canada where they married and started their family. It must have been soon after photograph 20 was taken (1913) where Hilda is on the right in the white dress. Their first two sons, Edward (b1916) and my father Harold, (b1917) were born in Canada.

In his teens Horace had served three years in the Royal Gloucestershire Yeomanry, riding his horse from Naunton to Chatcombe Pitch Training Camp, near Seven Springs (the source of the Thames) where young men practised their soldiery skills. As a good shot, a keen village cricketer and accomplished horseman, he was a man of action, engaging in various inter-village sporting contests, from tug-o-war to wrestling on horseback. The latter involved the skilful removal of your opponent from his horse before being unhorsed yourself; a kind of jousting without the impaling pole. From this kind of background, aged 19, he no doubt felt he was equipped to take on the world as he started out on this adventurous new life, farming on the Canadian prairies. Under different circumstances, I believe that after a few more years Horace and Hilda would have become firmly established in Canada, their lives being as good, if not better than before, raising their as yet, incomplete family in that great new land of opportunity, where virgin land was still anyone's opportunity. Had that happened, a full two generations before my own generation was anything more than an occasional fleeting thought in their busy pioneering minds, this story would of course have ended before it began insofar as my presence was concerned. But fate was about to introduce a predictably cruel twist, which at least ensured that their story continued back here in the Cotswolds, through my eyes, and not in Canada, through, well, we will never know the answer to conundrums like that will we!

Like so many other young men's life-plans in the first half of the twentieth-century, Horace's were about to be cruelly dashed by war, in his case, the Great War; being the same terrifying spectacle that throughout so much of the past two thousand years seems to have consistently taught mankind, that it has taught him absolutely nothing. When WW1 broke out, like many other expatriates, he volunteered, and in 1916 he found himself in the Canadian Expeditionary Force, one of the armies of the British Commonwealth [25]. The following year, after more skill-at-arms training and with thousands of other young men, he returned via England (Liverpool) to join the allies in the costly struggle against Germany, where he saw action in Belgium and France. His generation represented the very pinnacle of modern fighting men, who across several millennia had entered war on horseback and whatever their training afforded them, it did not protect Horace and his brothers-in-arms from being 'gassed' on the Ypres salient, on the France/Belgium border in 1918. Horace was duly shipped back to a British hospital on the south coast to commence a lengthy convalescence, having one lung removed under much baser medical procedures than today. But at least he got out of it alive, unlike so many of his brothers in arms.

Army medical staff advised him that his health was too frail to permit his survival in the harsh climate of northern Canada. Consequently Hilda was compelled to pack-up and repatriate herself and the two young boys (Edward and Harold) back to England. Hilda's parents were still living at Waterloo Farm (as tenants) where they appear to have had a cow and a couple of fields [26]. Horace joined them there when his health improved and apparently bought a small Ford car with his discharge money from the Canadian Army, which I am told was the first, or one of the first cars in Naunton. His parents were still living nearby at the Mill, where his father, William Bullock Hanks died in 1921, and his mother Clara in 1928. Horace and Hilda remained at Waterloo after Hilda's parents died, grazing a few cows in the two nearby fields called Waterloo Field and Mill Field (Hobb's Hill and Ploughed Field on 1838 map) and milking them in a small 'dairy' (shed) in front of Waterloo house. (Picture W6)

Sadly, I am not aware of how they fared during the 1920s when Waterloo Farm comprised little more than the house and these two adjoining fields, but by the early 1930s the three younger children were born, completing the family of five [27]. After my father finished his secondary schooling at Northleach in the 1930s he went to agricultural college and in 1937 at the age of 19, continued working for his parents, Horace and Hilda at Waterloo Farm. His younger brother John was still at Naunton School and would join them later. The eldest of the three brothers, Edward (1915-1985) did not choose farming and had now left Naunton to work in Torquay. After Harold returned from college he began to keep a brief 'scribbling-diary' of daily events on Waterloo Farm, opening a tiny window on their farming activities, but on very little else. The routine, one-line pencilled entries of feeding stock, checking their condition and moving them around the farm daily, and the many other small but essential tasks, are humdrum and highly repetitive to say the least and will only be mentioned occasionally to help build the whole picture. By the mid 50s Harold kept this diary in the Nissen hut [28] on the footpath south of the main road, no doubt because childish hands like mine were inclined to scribble in them at 2 Millview!

The diaries were of course kept as a reminder of what had been done on the farm and are little more than lists of daily and less frequent routines, ranging from ear-tagging cattle to changing a wheel on a horse drawn trap or thatching a hayrick. I do not believe he would ever have envisaged they might one day fall into the category of farming history, never mind social history, or be of any interest whatsoever to anyone else. What follows (1937-1977) is extrapolated from this mass of farming detail. If it does not interest you please pass it by. My fear is that if I do not include a little of it here, there is a very real possibility that some 2000 years of farming activity will have passed through Naunton completely unrecorded, leaving nothing for future generations, living in a largely non-farming environment to gain some small understanding of what once underpinned everything else here. I am only touching upon a fraction of the day to day work but believe it gives a brief (40 year) overview of Cotswold dairy farming in the mid-twentieth century, at the end of some 2000 progressive years of animal husbandry and cultivation.

Harold's forebears appear to have been disinclined to write anything down. In that respect they were simply mirroring a long tradition of unwritten history by mimicking the reticence of their own ancestors. They could even be likened to the mindset of the Iceni, and their formidable leader Boudicca, who some 2000 years ago allegedly said: *'we didn't write about it, we just lived it'*. Today, a few people might prefer to see these things consigned to Naunton's bulging dustbin of lost history instead of giving it some illumination here, regarding it as of little interest to anyone else. Others may acknowledge that intertwined amongst the mass of farming detail is a smattering of village and social history. Such is the regularity and repetitiveness of certain daily and less frequent farming tasks that they are not mentioned in the diaries, e.g. the first thing done every morning was the milking and the last thing, shutting the chickens safely away as darkness fell, after milking the cows for the second time. I know this, but these and other regular jobs were simply taken for granted by all concerned, even though they were an essential part of the business. Because the end of my family's farming coincides roughly with the end of the second millennium, I believe it would be remiss of me not to include a few cryptic details of it now. In the 1920s, The Rev. Eales chose not to elaborate on the main occupation being carried on in every field around him. I am simply including a little of what Mr Eales chose to leave out.

1937

This is the earliest diary we have and although I now regret not asking Harold more about these things when he was alive, it is still possible to draw certain conclusions from the scant details we have. From the 'Notes' column in 'The 1914 Financial Domesday Record of Naunton Properties',[29] it will be seen that in 1935 Horace bought Waterloo House, adding some more fields over the next year. It is reasonable to assume that Harold's return from Cannington Agricultural College at about this time coincided with his parents plan to expand the farm, and with his help improve the family's station in life, after the setbacks in Canada during WW1. Horace and Hilda appear to have bought up to 20 more fields south of the main road, which today is mostly Naunton Downs Golf Course. This additional acreage had previously been known as 'Hill Farm' or 'Lodges Farm' [30] and appears to have been held in trust by, amongst others, Reginald Graham Hanks (1877-1948) of Charlton Abbots, near Cheltenham [31]. Horace and his son Harold then began to work-up this newly enlarged acreage into a mixed, arable and dairy farm. The homestead and several fields north of the main road (village side) continued to be known as Waterloo Farm and the larger portion, south of the main road (from Harford

Bridge Meadow westward to Naunton Inn) as Lodges Farm, though all had now effectively been consolidated into one single unit known as 'Waterloo Farm'[32].

To get the essential water supply to the top (west) end of 'Lodges', in 1936 they obtained a water extraction licence and contracted Godwins of Quenington to erect a metal-framed windmill at Harford Bridge Meadow, some 200 metres from the river. A gang of Godwin's men spent many weeks manually digging a trench across Harford Meadow and up through eight fields to a concrete reservoir at 'Cox's' Barn, (North Oat Ground)[33] to the windmill's pump and then up to the Aylworth Road end of 'Lodges'. The water was gravity-fed back down through a series of concrete cattle troughs, supplied by Bences of Cheltenham, built into the dry-stone walls between each field, as well as to the Piggery/Dutch Barn and Lodges Barn [34].

With the still small dairy herd, a few sheep and some poultry, which were almost akin to family pets, Horace, Hilda and Harold were initially doing most, if not all of the work around the farm themselves, assisted by casually employing local men and youths. As they became old enough, the three younger members of the family also helped more, and eventually even the grandchildren, including myself, 'mucked-in' for half-a-crown (12½p) a week, especially when 'mucking-out', and at harvest time. In the 1920/30s they had no tractor and all pulling, or 'draft' work, was initially undertaken by two horses called Colonel and Blackbird, though by 1937 a local man (Sid Roberts), was contracted to use his small tractor to do some ploughing. The old Mill House and the Water Corn Mill behind Waterloo House was by now owned by Mrs Ballantyne and rented by Miss Donisthorpe. The commercial or Water Corn Mill side of the property functioned until 1937/38, with Horace and my father two of the last men to operate its incredible, mostly wooden apparatus.

At the other end of the village the Cider Mill (now tastefully restored as 4/5 The Quadrangle) and the Bakery (part of The Bakehouse) under George Reynolds, and pretty much everything else in between, as can be seen in the Trade Directories, seem to have survived reasonably well during the depression years of the 1930s. Horace and Hilda were now milking seven Friesian and one Jersey cow by hand each morning and evening in the original small dairy in front of Waterloo House, where they sat on small three legged stools, hand-milking into pails. This dairy was upgraded slightly in 1937 when a boiler and a sterilizer were installed, still well before mains water or electricity came to Naunton. The water supply for washing the cows' udders and other dairy equipment, including the milk-cooler, came from the sunken concrete reservoir higher up in the adjacent 'Waterloo field' [35]. A small 1½hp Lister petrol engine was used to pump water from the river to this reservoir and gravity-fed back down through a filter into the dairy. Drinking water for the house was obtained from a standpipe in the road outside the Mill House. One of the men would take two empty buckets, suspended by chains on a wooden yoke carried across their shoulders, fill the buckets and bring them back up to Waterloo House kitchen, where they stood until emptied. The original dairy was about the same size as a single garage [36] and by the 1950s that is just what it became, for Horace's three-gear Vauxhall-Velox motor car. This was after the more modern six-abreast dairy unit was built 'round the corner' in 1954, where Nicholas & Katherine Wheeler's house and outbuildings are situated today, still called 'Waterloo Farm' [37].

In the 1940s they delivered the milk and eggs around the village in the 'milk-float' pulled by a horse called Kitty, milk being jugged from churns into containers brought out of cottages along the street, at a cost of 3d a pint and 6d a quart [38]. At this time, the small dairy herd appear to have yielded barely enough milk to supply the village and occasionally they had to buy some in from elsewhere. Hilda's Jersey cow provided milk for the family and she also kept turkeys, geese, chickens and ducks. She reared the lambs and calves as well as supplying 'pats' of butter and 'cones' of honey, the latter coming from hives in the 'Bee-Pen', a small fenced enclosure at the east end of Waterloo field [39] Sheep were sheared by hand and if one died it was skinned for its fleece, the carcass being buried or collected by the hunt kennels. The cattle ate grass during the summer and were fed on hay and straw from the ricks, together with ground-oats, kale and root-crops such as swedes and mangolds from a straw covered mangold-bury during the winter months.

A Friesian bull called 'Butts Cumbermere' was kept in a bowsing [40] in the field called 'Bowsing Ground' [41] (sometimes pronounced and written 'Bowsen' Ground) above Harford Bridge Meadow [42]. The bull served the cows as and when necessary, when they were 'bulling'. Heifer calves were reared for milking or sold at market; bull calves were reared and fattened for markets in Bourton, Andoversford, Gloucester, Kingham and elsewhere. They had two rams to serve some 51 ewes and when doing so, the 'Southdown' ram had its belly blue-dyed and the 'Hampshire Down' ram's belly was red-dyed, as visual confirmation that they had 'covered' the ewes. To enlarge the embryonic dairy herd in the 1930s entailed buying the occasional cow or calf and one such purchase costing £30 from Stratford market gave four gallons of milk the next day, indicating a very sound acquisition.

Winter fodder in the form of hay and straw for the cattle and sheep was frequently carried down from 'ricks' on Lodges [43] to Waterloo and to the barn opposite the Mill House called 'Mill Barn' (references to the Mill or Mill Stable or Mill Buildings from now on refer this run of buildings, where the house called 'Mill Barn' now stands) [44]. Ricks were generally built and thatched close to where the hay or straw was cut, but some was 'carted' to the 'rick-yard' in Waterloo Field, bringing bulk fodder and corn closer to the homestead for feeding or threshing. A constant problem with wheat ricks was damp from below and infestation by rats which ate the grain stored within them, it being common to kill as many as a hundred at a time as they scattered when threshing the rick, using ferrets, farm dogs and sticks. This is why ricks were once built on top of the staddle-stones that now adorn many Cotswold gardens, though today the tops are invariably reversed, quaintly resembling stone mushrooms [45]. Root crops such as mangolds and swedes were hauled round the farm in two splendid old Cotswold Box Wagons [46], as was almost everything else. Farm buildings containing animals or poultry needed cleaning out regularly and the manure was forked onto wagons, trolleys and later into manure-distributors and tractor drawn muck-spreaders, to be broadcast across the fields as an essential but natural fertiliser to prevent the soil becoming barren. This was a smelly job described as 'muck-cart' or 'dung-cart', though some nitrogen based fertilisers were also being used by the 1930s.

Occasional farm sales enabled them to acquire the many bits and pieces they needed and in 1937 this included an essential plough, a horse and harness, another cow, their first four pigs, a seed-drill, horse-hoe, manure-distributor, sack-cart, two wooden chicken-houses, a root-pulper, a side-rake, a cattle-crib, a dung-cart and a chest of drawers. Tommy James and his lorry were regularly employed to carry these items back to Waterloo, and his services were also used to take animals to and from the markets. In the case of the horse-hoe and rake, Harold and Norman Willis took two horses down to Bourton and pulled them back, 17 year old Norman being paid a shilling (5p) for his help.

Ploughing, sowing [47], rolling, harrowing and horse-hoeing all continued with many other cyclical tasks, with Blackbird and Colonel drawing the various implements, but they were still short of essential items to work the enlarged farm. To overcome these shortcomings, until they could be bought, farmers invariably helped one another by loaning labour and equipment on a reciprocal basis, and in 1937 this happened when Clem Timms leant them his seed-drill. A grey horse was also trialled from George Williams but was returned a few days later, described as 'useless!' The 66 sheep they owned in 1937 were sheered by hand, 'dipped' in Longford's sheep-dip near the Mill Coppice [48] and washed in the 'Washpool' opposite Taterbury Row (now Sunny Cottages) to clean the fleeces after they had been on root crops, ready for shearing [49].

Every single day was extremely busy, involving milking at 6.30am and again at about 4pm, week-in, week-out, throughout the next 40 years. In between these two main fixed tasks all manner of other jobs were fitted in. Many were weather dependent, but still had to be done even when postponed. They included moving and feeding stock, carrying almost daily 'trolley' loads [50] of hay and straw from one part of the farm to another, muck-spreading, stone-cart, ploughing and disking the soil prior to planting or sowing (also known as drilling), harrowing, rolling and hoeing the crops. This was followed by the main summer events of haymaking and then harvesting, the two sometimes overlapping. Building and repairing walls and fences, cutting back trees, hedges, thistles, nettles and weeds, washing and white-washing cattle sheds and the dairy, and amongst this and a whole load more they still managed to attend dances and whist-drives at the village hall, harvest festivals at the Church and Chapel and 'Young Farmers' meetings at Stow. Only war or a broken leg was ever likely to interfere with a Saturday afternoon game of cricket, and even then the milking still had to be done. They occasionally rounded the week off by seeing a Saturday night film at Moreton Cinema or the 'pictures' as it was known locally.

Newly born calves were caringly weaned before moving them to sheds and barns around the farm, to be reared over the next few years until they were either ready for milking or sufficiently fattened for market. Horace employed local men at haymaking time and in 1937 they were paid 6d an hour for casual work, e.g. for 24 hours overtime, paid 12 shillings (60p) for work such as harvesting, including hay-making, threshing, bale-cart and building ricks of hay and straw.

In the 1930s Waterloo did not have its own threshing machine (colloquially referred to as a 'drum' because they contained two bearers or rotating drums) to separate the grain from the husk and they were still hiring the services of Ernie Bartlett from Lower Slaughter [51]. Ernie trundled around many North Cotswold farms with his own men and a complete threshing outfit. Before Ernie visited Waterloo, Horace had to purchase 1½ tons of coal from Finch's of Andoversford, which Tommy James then carried to Waterloo as fuel for Ernie's traction engine. The wheat, oats or barley had been cut by Harold using a horse drawn mower attached to the reaper/binder and over the following days it was all threshed by him and several other men, the grain going into strong Hessian sacks and then the Mill for grinding into flour, or storage in nearby barns or the 'Flour House, because Waterloo did not have a granary as such, as the Manor did. The straw 'boltings' [52] coming from another small machine behind the threshing machine, were then used for thatching ricks of hay or straw.

By the end of this first year of steady expansionism they had one bull, 29 heifers (five in-calf) eight calves, three steers, eight milking cows, two rams, 29 tegs, 51 ewes, three horses, one pony, four gilts [53], 22 Christmas turkeys, numerous chickens and ten ducks. They also had several pear trees but no partridge as far as I am aware!

The year was rounded off with the family eating one of their free-range turkeys on Christmas day. They milked the cows and tended to the needs of all the animals that day, just as on any other day of the year. No one seems to have had more than half a day off during the whole year, which was how it was and how it would remain for Harold from 1936 until 1964, when I was 16, and legally able to help John with the milking (though I had been helping in this way for some time) permitting my father to take his first week off since he married in 1947. But even so he went to stay with his cousin Edward in Kent – on a farm; something I could have understood better if he had been working for Pulhams Coaches; if you know what I mean!

1938 (the year before the outbreak of WW2)

On 1 January they sold 'Fillpail' and her calf at Gloucester Market for £21 15s getting them off to quite a good start, but on 3 January another beast strayed onto the nearby railway line and was killed, no doubt reminding everyone of the fine line between profit and loss and the constant need for 'gapping' (repairing dry-stone walls) and mending fences. Daily tasks continued as usual, fitting in the occasional Young Farmers Club at Bourton, as the children were entertained by a pantomime in the new (1937) Village Hall.

On 1 February Ernie Bartlett's traction engine and threshing tackle arrived, more sacks were hired, more coal was purchased, more oats were threshed and taken to Longford for crushing in their small tractor-driven corn mill and 24 sacks were sold to Bloodworths [54] for 27 shillings (£1.35) each. Horace attended his regular British Legion meeting, and this one was held at Guiting; as a whist-drive and dance was held at Naunton. The Heythrop Hunt crossed the farm and George Williams was paid six shillings (30p) for a day's threshing, suggesting a 12 hour day at 6d (2½p) an hour.

Some mischievous individual turned the windmill off preventing water from being pumped to the water troughs in the fields above, which may have prompted the shrewd placement of the bull, 'Butts Cumbermere' in Harford Meadow for a few days, accompanied by six heifers to double up on his duties! A spring stock-check listed: 63 cattle, four gilts, four horses, 50 Ewes with 84 lambs and 29 Tegs with 13 lambs and two rams.

Harold celebrated his 21st birthday on 19 March, noting that he received £1 from his mother, five shillings from Eddie, his older brother, 20 cigarettes and a holder from Auntie Janet, a telegram from Auntie Mable and allegedly only a card from a girlfriend, Joan Howman of Stow. He walked there to see her that evening, and clearly, whatever it was, it didn't last, because my mother's name was Sheila!

Milk samples sent to Bristol by the County Vet passed the accreditation test; Horace and Hilda went to the Heythrop Races; Captain Dewinton's boar was borrowed and put in with four gilts; Harold ploughed the Barn Ground using three horses on a double plough; planted half an acre of Yellow Globe mangolds; carried Sainfoin grass to the Dutch Barn and a load of wood from Harford meadow to home. Planted more potatoes and paid Binky Bowles seven shillings and sixpence for taking a cow (Crystal) to Gloucester Market. A Leicester ewe died and rats killed 5 turkeys. The sheep shearing commenced in May. John was on holiday from Naunton School and helped his older brother erect a new barbed wire fence around the Ewe Pen Ground. They rolled the cricket pitch in Mill Hayes that evening, prior to playing on Saturday 4 June (Naunton 102; Dowdeswell 58). To round that off, on the BH Monday, 6 June, they played a team from Birmingham (Naunton 105; Birmingham 84).

The cow called Pansy 'slipped' her calf and another, 'Bluey' was sold at Gloucester market for £22 but they brought her heifer calf back unsold. The following Saturday, 11 June they played cricket against Stow (Naunton 100; Stow 33). Ted Temple helped 'drench' all the ewes and lambs; they brought yet another trap-load of hay from Harford meadow to Waterloo; Clem Timms root drill was returned to him; cricket (Naunton 106; Andoversford 40). A 'Summer-Gathering' was held in the village; cricket (Naunton 145; Bourton 105 for 7). The mare, 'Peggy' died and was collected by Dan Perkins from the Cotswold Kennels at Burford; Horace and Harold dipped 96 lambs at Aylworth and thatched ricks at Waterloo and by the Dutch Barn and by the Windmill. In July there was an abundance of mushrooms on the farm. Charlie Hawker and Bill Dean continued hoeing and singling mangolds. Cricket again (Naunton 145, Billings Sports Club 32). One evening they played a team of artists (Artists, 60 for 6 declared, Naunton 110 for 8). The wool dealer called and purchased bagged-up wool and Tommy James took 81 fleeces to Notgrove Railway Station. They played cricket at Cheltenham, won, and the August Bank Holiday game was much the same, (Naunton 89; Withington 70). They started cutting wheat and oats on 15 August and finished stooking it up on the 19th. The ever supportive Mr R.G. Hanks of Charlton Abbotts helped them sort and select the sheep: two Ewes and 74 lambs and 19 sheaves for sale; 20 lambs, 46 ewes and ten sheaves kept for breeding.

A ewe died and was skinned for its fleece, Marina the cow was 'blown-out' on new grass but treated successfully with soda and water; Mr R.G. Hanks bought a Friesian bull calf for five guineas *(£5 5 shillings or £5.25p, and we are still not into Euros!)* Cricket (Naunton 125; Bourton 33) and again the following Saturday, (Naunton 101; Dowdeswell 21) and the following week (Naunton 80; St. Gregory's Cheltenham 41), with land work, honey gathering, animal feeding, milking, delivering it and everything else fitted in before the next game (Naunton 111; St. Phillips 45). On 18 September they all attended the burial of Frank Bayliss.

Horace went to Cheltenham to see a pony but with 'nothing settled'. Charlie Parsons and Bert Gleed were involved in a motorcycle crash at Stow in which Charlie died and Bert was seriously injured. A sale of the property of the late Jim Hooper took place [55]. Ernie Bartlett delivered his threshing tackle on 27 September and Harold and several men finished the job two days later filling 77 sacks (38½ qts) with Little-Joss wheat. Ernie was paid six shillings for the hire of his machine. Con Taylor was paid six shillings, Edgar Caldicote £1, Albert Dean 12 shillings, old man Dean 12 shillings and George Williams five shillings for their labours; Total £3 1/- (three pounds and one shilling). 69 sacks of the wheat were sold to West Midland Farmers Association (WMFA) at 27/- 9d each (£1.38) and four to George Hanks at the Manor for 30/- each (£1.50).

Harold shot three rabbits, selling one to his auntie Janet for 8d (3p) and the others to Cromwell House. He continued drilling wheat with Mr Habgood's drill from Grange Hill and then helped Clem Timms (no relation to Cyril) do his threshing and bag up the chaff. Horace and Hilda went to Gloucester Market selling 14 little pigs for a total of £2 12/- (£2.60). Horace paid George Williams £8 for a pony. The Hampshire ram was marked blue and put in with 72 ewes, as was the Southdown with 21 tegs, marked red. 'Great Scot' potatoes were lifted (dug up) and sorted, the ram's bellies were re-painted after it mysteriously rubbed off; a bumper crop of mushrooms was picked and on 26 October Mr Gerald Hanks got married. On the 28th October John (14) left school to start work with his brother Harold and their father Horace. Tommy James took more wheat and oats to Bourton Mill to be ground, as Naunton Mill had now ground to a halt for want of expensive maintenance. The 'red' ram had now 'marked' 70 of the 72 ewes after two exceedingly productive weeks!

A cricket dance was held in the Village hall, fences were repaired around the farm, cow sheds cleaned and whitewashed, dung carted and spread over the fields, and Harold pledged not to buy any more cigarettes! Horace took ten dozen eggs and some mushrooms to Cheltenham, and on Saturday 26 November Harold went to Cheltenham on the bus to watch Cheltenham Town play Cardiff City. Horace went to Andoversford and bought two wooden 'folders' (moveable poultry houses), Harold repaired the thatched roof on the cart-shed and John creosoted four poultry folders. Whilst Kath played hockey at Cheltenham, Horace and Hilda went to a sale at Bourton and Hilda bought a double barrelled 12-bore shot gun!

As Christmas approached, amongst the usual round of daily jobs, three turkeys were plucked and dressed, and one eleven-pounder taken to Cromwell House. It was freezing hard and snowed all day on the 22nd with no mail, no telephones and no papers as a result. Christmas saw the same jobs listed as at any other time with milking and feeding all stock on freezing cold days.

The cricket club whist drive and dance took place on the 27th and they no doubt hoped for another unassailable season to follow, but more poignantly, the final entry for 1938 read 'the end of a worrying year for this country'.

1939

The new year opened with snow and rain. Repairs were carried out in stables and cattle sheds and the meadow ditches were cleaned out. Harold's own Roan Heifer went 'to profit' with Butts Cumbermere, and there was more snow and frost each night. The cattle were fed hay and mangolds. Horace went to Cheltenham with Bert Bayliss on Pulhams bus. 48 eggs were collected from four chicken folders; the 'engine' was taken onto Lodges to drive the chaff cutting machine; Henry and Terry Muller did more repair work in the farm buildings, hanging a new manger and putting several new hanging-posts into gateways and other similar jobs that they did regularly. Horace took more eggs to Cheltenham market and went to Stratford in Mrs Walker's car (apparently not owning one himself at this stage) to sell one stock turkey and three drakes, before buying one stag and three hen turkeys.

On January 20 the North Cotswold Hunt met at Naunton and the Cotswold Hunt at Puesdown, the latter running a fox to a kill in Guiting Brake. A 'trolley' load of seed-hay was brought down from the rick in Ewe Pen Ground to the Mill for the horses. Tegs were given a new hitch on the roots and 1½ tons of Cotton Cake and ½ ton of linseed was delivered by WMFA. Horace shot two more rabbits for the pot and a 'tiddler' pig from a litter of 10 was taken into the house for rearing. One hundredwieght [56] of 'Layers Mask' was brought by Pulhams bus from Bloodworths in Cheltenham; Horace took a bull calf to Andoversford market, getting a lift with the commercial traveller, selling the calf for 46/- and came home on the bus, *(it being just as well he sold the calf!)* More rabbits were shot and skinned, more cows taken to the bull; more horse ploughing; four pesky foxes were seen near the chicken folders; a stag turkey was sold to Sam Hughes for £1; Mr Habgood visited on his horse and Hilda bought 102 chicks. The ever helpful and clearly much loved Mr R.G. Hanks paid his weekly visit and must have been saddened to learn that a fourth Ewe had died. The annual cricket dance was held in the Village Hall on 8 March; Horace bought two Roan calves at Andoversford market, and went to the Heythrop races with Kathleen, as Harold and Hilda went to a sale at Fox Farm and bought a dung cart.

Mr Bint, the Thorleys traveller, made the usual delivery of cow-cake and pig food and John continued working with the horses in Little Barn Ground. Harold had his 22nd birthday and fetched the muck-cart from Fox Farm with a horse. Eddie came home from Torquay; Harold, John and Terry Muller went to the Cotswold Hunt Luncheon; eight pigs were castrated; the Heythrop Hunt crossed the farm; Harold buried two dead sheep as Auntie Janet Griffin, Hilda's teacher sister came home for Easter, by which time 96 lambs had been born. They sent nine pigs to Andoversford with Tommy James, selling them for 30/- each; sent a sow to the boar at Longford; carted stones off the newly planted oats in the Barn Ground; bought two-cwt of 'wheatings' from Mr Reynolds at the bakery. Mr Sell, the Farm Manager from Roundhill 'tailed' 109 lambs; Pansy had a bull calf; hens were sitting on ducks, geese and turkey's eggs; five rows of potatoes were planted in Roundhill Road Ground and three new valves were fitted to Waterloo's 'wireless' (radio). By May 1939, 88 ewes had given birth to 110 lambs; ten Hudsons sacks were returned by Young's bus; two little pigs from 12 were taken to the Misses Bedwell; Mr Dartnell the County Vet from Cheltenham inspected the cows; 24 little ducks were sold at 9d each; 15 dozen chicken eggs were taken to Cheltenham and Harold bought himself a new pair of cricket trousers from The Famous. On the way back he collected a cream-separator from Andoversford Police Station where it had been left by his cousin, Harold Hanks from Withington. He later skinned a bull calf; 70 eggs were collected from the chicken folders and they started to prepare a tennis court at the bottom of Mill Field. A cockhorn heifer was sold for £24 10/- and Eddie returned from Torquay on May 28 prior to starting his new job with Shirers & Lances Department Store in Cheltenham.

Horace went to the Three Counties Show at Worcester; cricket was played (Naunton 105, St. Gregory's 40) but they lost to Bourton the following week! The following week it was Naunton 48, Temple Guiting 64! The next two games were cancelled, followed by a game against Bourton, with another win for Naunton. Haymaking commenced as their cricket continued to improve, Naunton; 125, Cheltenham Shop Fitting Company 88. The following week it was Naunton, 45 for 4 against Stow – rain stopped play. 193 sheep were dipped at Aylworth; bountiful mushrooms were picked and the bull, Butts Cumbermere, was sold for £16. Another ewe died, 'blown' and much thatching; horse-hoeing and side-raking was now underway. A 'Show' of some kind was held at Bourton and Mr R.G. Hanks came to help sort the sheep and trim the lambs. 11 ewes and 99 lambs were identified for market, keeping 72 ewes and 11 lambs for breeding. Cricket; (Naunton 70; Withington 52). On 9 August Dr Bibby's funeral was held at Naunton. 195 sheep were dipped at Aylworth and Horace went to Shurdington on the bus to pick plums. On 14 August Harold went to Cheltenham Cricket Festival to see England v. West Indies and the following Saturday Naunton beat Andoversford. Eighty-eight fleeces and a bag of loose wool were sold to the wool buyer. On 24 August everyone was issued with a gas mask at the Village Hall, *and this must have been a very poignant moment for Horace!* On 26 August Naunton beat Temple Guiting, winning the Cheltenham Challenge Cup again and noting that a photograph was taken of the team [57].

On 3 September he wrote 'England and France declared war upon Germany, who are already at war with Poland', but work continued as usual and on 15 Sept, it was recorded that 'Russia invaded Poland'. On 23 September Ernie Bartlett's threshing outfit arrived on Lodges and Tommy James brought three tons of best coal from Andoversford for the traction engine; Billy Herbert (then working at Aylworth) came to help and 43 sacks of oats, followed by 90 sacks of best wheat and five of tail-wheat were threshed in $1\frac{1}{2}$ days from 12 acres; 90 sacks being collected by WMFA. Aylworth were then helped with their threshing whilst Aubrey Richards from Hawling started ploughing on Lodges. Blackbird broke her leg and Mr Parsons put her down. Because Blackbird had been in a field with Mr Walker's chestnut horse and Dan Perkins said she had been kicked, Mr Walker (from Aylworth) loaned them his chestnut. The rent was paid to Mr R. G. Hanks *(this being the first indication that they were buying or renting fields from him)* and two working horses were purchased from Clem Timms before returning Mr Walker's chestnut. The rams were turned out, painted black this time! Harold borrowed Bert Bayliss' shotgun and went shooting with Mr Walker and others, and together they shot 17 hares, 70 rabbits and 2 pheasants.

Using the two new horses and a double plough, the results were pleasing and Mervyn Benfield from Dale Street helped with the ploughing; Harold took a trap load of potatoes to the barn; carting and clamping more mangolds; WMFA delivered 12 sacks of Victor seed wheat as apple picking got underway. Arthur Dean was given two rabbits and two baskets of apples as a tip. John went 'ferreting' with Mr Sell; Auntie Irene was paid the rent for the Mill Field and the whole family had their hair cut for 2/6d ($12\frac{1}{2}$p). On 30 November, 'Russia invaded Finland'. Nine pigs were sold to Victor Hayward for £2 each and Mr Pexton (headmaster) paid £1 19/- $11\frac{1}{2}$d for 'school milk'. Mr Richards was contracted to plough the 17 acre South Oat Ground at 13/ 3d an acre and Mr Charles' (Roundhill) Alvis car and caravan were fetched from the Dutch Barn to be sold. A horse was bought from George Williams to pull the trap and he then bought ten pigs for 35/s each. Mr Forth killed a pig for Christmas and seven pigs were castrated and moved to Mrs Bedwell's 'Grays Orchard' and Doreen had her 8th birthday on 8 December. 42 turkeys and 15 dozen eggs were sold in Stratford. Horace and Hilda took a turkey to Mr R.G. Hanks; Mrs Bedwell was paid rent for having pigs in her orchard; an application was made for more 25 gallon 'agri-petrol' coupons, making a total of 259 gallons for the year.

1940

The winter was particularly hard with frosts described as the worst for years, the ground everywhere being like a 'sheet of glass'. Concrete water-troughs froze solid and cracked despite being well covered with dung and straw. When it thawed the Mill House flooded for a week, as did the village street, followed by more snow and yet another freeze-up with no water at the dairy or in Waterloo House for many days because the extreme cold had cracked the pump's inlet valve in the river. No travel was possible and the village's few telephones were inoperable; Waterloo's 'phone (Guiting Power 70) being out of use for six weeks. Urgently needed animal feedstuffs finally got through in February from Oldacres and wartime fuel rationing allowed them just 25 gallons of petrol each month. Nevertheless a sow gave birth to eight piglets; a teg to dead lambs and calves were born in the relentless, age-old conflict of nature versus the elements.

As conditions eased Mr Davidson-Smith's tractor and disc-harrows got to work in the North Oat

Ground after which the two farm horses were used to do the harrowing. Mr Dale's winnowing machine was borrowed from Roundhill and Clem Timms corn drill was borrowed to plant the prepared fields, as the usual range of spring tasks got underway and eventually caught up. More calves, pigs and sheep were born, but sadly some were stillborn and some failed to survive for long. Turkey, geese, duck and chicken eggs were laid and collected. Cattle were 'warbled' [58], some were taken to market and 20 young cattle were taken to graze on Mr R.G. Hanks's fields near Winchcombe, being herded along the lanes by family members. Nine of the cattle were returned to Waterloo several weeks later in Tommy James' lorry and the remainder were herded back through the lanes by family members in the way cattle-drovers had moved livestock around the countryside for the past 2000 years. Even after the first steam trains pulled cattle trucks into Notgrove Railway Station in the 1880s, or early lorries hauled livestock around after the Great War, many local farmers continued the traditional droving of livestock for short distances, and probably still do today, in places where there is a reduced possibility of a speeding car approaching them.

Wartime bureaucracy entailed filling out even more forms to obtain a little more petrol from Central Hall in Bristol. The farming routines continued with ninety-five lambs being 'tailed' and 83 sheep going to the Wash Pool and then 'drenched' for worms. Potatoes were planted in the 'Up Street' Garden, situated behind Yew Tree Cottages [59]; seed barley was collected from the Manor and Mr Habgood's seed drill borrowed from Grange Hill. Half a ton of sulphate of ammonia was put on $8\frac{1}{2}$ acres of barley in the Ewe Pen Ground and five-cwt of Nitro Chalk on wheat in the North Oat Ground as Naunton continued to play its small but essential part in the desperate struggle to feed an increasingly blockaded and starving nation during WW2.

Sheep were sheared by hand and later 'dipped' at Aylworth. The Longford boar was put with the sow at the piggery and returned the next day, the diary was endorsed; 'One Sow to Profit', to justify his visit and the subsequent farrowing of seven piglets confirmed the fertility of all involved. Mowing was commenced, followed by hay-raking, cocking and carrying it for a week or two, with hay ricks built at the Waterloo rick-yard and the horses, the farm wagons and everyone else were immensely busy throughout.

A 50 gallon petrol voucher was received and Tommy James lorry was used to take six loads of manure from Waterloo to Roundhill Road Ground which Mr Richards then tackled with his tractor and four-furrow plough. The little Massey Harris reaper-binder was repaired again, ready for the wheat harvest which commenced in August, in between which 178 sheep were dipped at Aylworth and the cutting of the oats began. Harold and Horace continued cutting and binding the wheat, whilst John was horse-hoeing turnips and mangolds. Their brother Eddie came home for a week before leaving to join the RAF, 'somewhere in England' and Harold's Home Guard unit were called out at night yet again on 'General Alert'.

U.S. Army personnel were now billeted at the Mill and at Mrs Bibby's house ('Hatters' cottage). The Mill Orchard was crammed full of U.S. Military vehicles. Harold continued with his uniformed LDV duties (Local Defence Volunteers or Home Guard) in the evenings, with occasional practice at Longford, the Village Hall and on the cricket ground, where Guiting LDV men sometimes joined them. On 14 November 1940 he wrote, "Coventry bombed terribly, Cathedral hit" and today we only have a small idea of the awful destruction inflicted there as a result of seeing the magnificent new Cathedral that rose from the ruins. On 9 December he wrote, 'heavy air-raids on Birmingham and some bombs dropped on Cheltenham'. The same evening he attended a Home Guard meeting at Snowshill House with a lecture and film by the RAF which must have had added impact.

Harold took the pony and trap to Westfield and returned from a sale, how safely is anyone's guess, with a gate, trough, ladder and some fence posts on board. He and Eddie Higgins (15yrs) went to Aylworth for several days to help them with their threshing before returning to continue harvesting on

Lodges, now with several Aylworth men helping them; hiring another 100 Hessian sacks from Bourton Mill to bag the corn. The oats and barley then went with Tommy James to Bourton Mill to be ground and returned to Waterloo. The harvest was now in full swing with the war effort requiring greater productivity and as many men and youths as could be spared were now working on Waterloo and neighbouring farms [60] to complete the harvest. They were also winnowing and dressing wheat, bagging sheared wool, taking it to Notgrove Railway Station, building ricks and a variety of other jobs. Some of the men went to Lower Harford Farm to help Stan Clifford with his threshing for a week before wet weather brought things to a halt in November. At the same time the dairy side carried on running under Hilda, daughter Kathleen, and her friend, occasionally having to buy in five gallons of milk from Moreton Mutual Dairy to supplement what they were producing at Waterloo with their few cows.

Horace and Hilda went to a farm sale at Bourton and bought a Jersey and a Friesian heifer, then to a sale at Roel Farm, near Guiting Power and bought five chairs. Maurice Hanks's root drill was borrowed from Longford to plant 1½ acres of swedes and they bought a pony-trap, a separator and another cow. On 19 December ten turkeys, eight geese, eight ducks and ten cockerels were sent to Cheltenham market but the ground was now too hard for ploughing.

In 1940, as part of the war effort they had ploughed up an additional 45 acres of grassland that had lain as pasture for at least the previous seven years, they planted 16 acres of wheat, eight of barley, 35 of oats, and four of mangolds and mowed 29 acres of grass for hay. They now had a total of 79 cattle, four sows in pig and nine young pigs, 86 ewes in lamb and 260 young fowls.

1941

The year started well with 'Puffy' giving birth to a bull calf and on 3 January they purchased their first tractor, a little iron-wheeled Fordson Standard from Meats of Cheltenham, and ordered a new plough. On Sunday 5 January Harold wrote, *'a big bomb dropped near Mr Clifford's house'* (Lower Harford), and it blasted a large crater in the bank behind the house. But it would take more than this to disrupt local farming routines and work continued, regardless of the Luftwaffe's attempt to break the will of the people. The next morning a load of cut wood was delivered to the Rector to keep the home fires burning, noting in the diary that he did not actually pay, probably because he became distracted talking about the bomb! 'Puffy' and her bull calf were sold at Gloucester market for £37, they had a practice drive on the new tractor and Harold did Home Guard drill in the evening. He took three hares to Cheltenham and sold them for five shillings and sixpence (27½p) each – fresh meat being in short supply. Wood sawing was followed by more Home Guard drill and John joined the Home Guard on 31 January (age 16). The new Ransomes three-furrow plough arrived and Horace and Hilda went to Cheltenham on the bus and saw the 'The Great Dictator' at the cinema. On 8 February they tried to start ploughing with the new tractor and plough but did not get on too well with this new fangled mechanization and gave up! Words like 'Bring back the horses' were probably heard at Waterloo that day but the march of progress had commenced and to get over it they all went to the Gaumont cinema in Cheltenham that evening.

On 10 February they helped Stan Clifford with his threshing at Lower Harford for three days before doing exactly the same at Aylworth. A man from Meats of Cheltenham came to, *'show us how to get on with the tractor and plough'*, probably without realising that between them all that day they had sealed one of the great farming advances ever on these fields! This was followed by more chaff cutting at Lodges Barn and they settled up with Stan Clifford for the men exchanged for threshing. Harold now seems to have mastered the new art of 'tractor-ploughing' in Roundhill Road Ground, referring to it more confidently thereafter as 'tractor-ploughing', but whether he spoke as affectionately to the plough as he would have done the horses I do not know! On 1 March Harold took his own heifer to Gloucester market, sold it for £27 10/- (£27.50) and whilst there bought the farm's first milk bottles from the market-shop run by Listers of Dursley [61].

The Petroleum Board delivered 50 gallons of agri-paraffin for the tractor; all the usual jobs and Home Guard lectures continued and Tommy James took a ton of mixed barley and oats to Bourton Mill for grinding. They collected a 'tractor cultivator' and disc-harrows from Rissington belonging to the War Agricultural Committee and Ernie Bartlett's threshing tackle arrived for two days. An Aylworth man together with Cyril Timms and Arthur helped with the threshing. The reservoir at Cox's was found to be empty, the windmill having stopped and a gallon of oil was put into the windmill gearbox to help get things running again. 111 eggs were collected; more cereal coupons were obtained from Gloucester for the cattle and horses and the Home Guard lecture this week was on 'Gas'. The 'War-Ag' cultivator was tried out; all the animals fed, as on every other day of the year and the usual Home Guard duties carried out in the evenings. Horace went to a farm sale at Bourton-on-the-Hill and bought a dung cart and root drill which Harold and Arthur pulled home next day with three horses. They planted a mixture of one-cwt of oats, half a cwt of barley and 28lbs of peas per acre in Ewe Pen Ground and Tommy James brought two tons of ground oats and barley back from Bourton Mill.

They bought six gallons of petrol and 20 gallons of paraffin from Pulham's pump in the village [62] and 100 gallons of paraffin from the Petroleum Board. Chris Bryning, a serviceman from Liverpool, customarily stationed 'somewhere in England' came to The Mill to rest for a few weeks; more land was expertly 'tractor ploughed' and then sown with barley and wheat; 'cooch' grass was burned; Home Guard duty was from 8pm to 6am; Mr R.G. Hanks walked over Lodges with Horace; the stock of hay was just holding out for the animals; chicken folders were moved from one field to another and 14 store cattle were taken by Mr W Rose in three lorries to Gloucester market. 'King Edward', 'Doon Star' and 'British Queen' potatoes were planted using Mr Walker's potato banting-plough and the first, twice-weekly ten gallon churns of bulk milk were supplied to United Dairies. Tommy took 15 yearling heifers to Gloucester; Horace and Maurice Hanks together with a Mr Fisher, from the 'War-Agri' Department, walked over Lodges to discuss ploughing up another field. Terry Muller's wood-splitting wedges were returned and Mrs Bedwell's rat cages were borrowed. More dry-stone walls were repaired and more fencing erected and Harold did the milk-round because Kathleen was unwell. A cat and four kittens were taken to the barn to control the rats; more loads of wood brought home from Roundhill Hollow; horse-hoeing the mangolds with cow-cabbages planted amongst them; turning hay in the meadow; topping hay ricks; broadcasting turnip and kale seed; the Home Guard were issued with Service Respirators and John, age 18, was made Lance Corporal due to his leadership qualities and shooting proficiency. Bought some new metal grips for the tractor wheels, and Harry Revers (local lorry driver) delivered a load of chippings and filament from Slade Quarry.

Terry Muller repaired a wagon wheel, and Mr Davidson-Smith's two tractors ploughed the North Clay, it being too heavy for the little Fordson tractor. Horace bought another trolley from a sale at Burford and later fetched 170 bundles of straw from Hawling Lodge and they thatched a hayrick at Waterloo. Harvesting was now in full swing; stooking oats and barley; threshing and building more ricks with the help of Norman Hughes, Peter Davis, Mervyn Benfield and others. They moved all the poultry houses again so the chickens had fresh ground to scratch around on; Bob (the horse) was lame so the milk was delivered using Norman Hughes' car for several days. Hilda was extracting and bottling honey and on 18 September Ray Comeley was buried. The plough got stuck in boggy ground in Drapers Field and on 22 October Norman Hughes went to Gloucester to join the Air Force. Leslie Lockey shod the four horses, Bob, Sharper, Colonel and Dolly. Harold and John finished thatching the fourth rick on the footpath and 28 dozen eggs were sent to the packing station as 15 cattle were brought back from Winchcombe along the lanes. The Home Guard lecture at Temple Guiting this week was on unarmed-combat; Bert Bayliss finished the middle room and hallway of the house before putting a concrete path alongside the 'Flour House', using ten-cwt (half a ton) of cement delivered by Sharpe & Fisher. Dolly the mare died and was collected by Ben Bedford (the knacker man) from Burford Kennels, and in December they started threshing another corn rick on the footpath. They bought more milk bottles and a butter churn from Listers in Gloucester and Sharpe & Fisher delivered a cooking and heating stove which Bert Bayliss fitted in the kitchen.

In May 1941 Harold (24yrs) listed the total acreage of the farm as: 236 acres (grassland 92½). Arable 118a (wheat 37a; barley 21½a; oats 12a; mixed corn 36½a). Potatoes 4a; roots 8a. Rough grazing 25½a. Horses, 4 (2 teams). Cows, 15; other cattle 48. Breeding Ewes, and sheep - none. Breeding sows 2. Other pigs 16. Poultry 450. Tractors 1.

Other Staff: Kathleen, 19yrs – Dairy and milk-round. John, 16yrs – cowman & farm. Arthur Dean, 16yrs – Farm-hand. Eddie Higgins, 15yrs – Farm-hand.

On 31 December, referring approvingly to the Prime Minister he wrote, 'Mr Churchill in Ottawa – speech alright' before carrying on with manure-cart and several other routine jobs.

1942

On 1 January, as the New Year opened, so too did the thatched mangold-bury to help feed the ever hungry cattle. Tommy took 2½ tons of corn to Bourton Mill and brought 2½ tons of grist back the following week. A dance was held in the village hall for the benefit of 'Mr Churchill's Aid to Russia Fund'. John fell out of a cart and hurt his leg; 18 inches of snow fell and travel became almost impossible. Horace attended a sale at Bourton and bought a trailer for the tractor, a cattle crib and a roll of barbed wire. Another trolley load of hay was taken to Waterloo from the meadow; double egg-ration coupons came allowing people, 'one each' (per week) and on 18 January the roads were cleared to permit Ernie Bartlett's threshing tackle to reach Lodges. They all spent several days threshing a mixed rick for animal feed and a barley rick, in the open air, in raw weather he noted as being 'very cold indeed - the coldest winter for 56 years, Ernie (Bartlett) had to put fire under the engine to prevent it freezing'! After that they then helped with the threshing on Mr J. Bayliss's farm.

The bull, 'Butts Active' put the cow Bluebird 'to profit' as a sheep gave birth to a dead lamb. Tommy took 24 sacks of barley (making 80 altogether) to Cheltenham Original Brewery and 2½ tons of corn to Bourton Mill, bringing the same amount back crushed, together with five cases of tinned milk from Gilberts Store. Brother Eddie came home on leave from Doncaster; the snow and frosts continued; 30 dozen eggs went to Moreton and 'tractor ploughing' started on 12 March. Harold had his 25th birthday and fed all the stock as usual before Home Guard duty in the evening. Horace went to a sale at Great Rissington and bought two horses, as Harold continued 'tractor ploughing' on Lodges, before chain-harrowing Waterloo & Mill Fields with the new horses, who 'worked well'. The 'War-Ag' combine corn drill was passed on from Longford; they started planting a mixture of corn on Lodges and there was an air-raid alarm between 4am and 5am! Horace bought a new pair of harness and a pair of clogs for the horses [63]; planting, rolling, harrowing and yet more ploughing continued almost every day.

There was a fire at the potato-bury which destroyed 160 bags of potatoes and the weighing scales and two mischievous evacuees were suspected! One ton of King Edward and one ton of Great Scot potatoes had to be bought, delivered later by Crafts of Stow, borrowing Roundhill's scales to weigh them. Potatoes were planted in Ewe Pen Ground. Home Guard shooting practice was at Rissington Aerodrome. Eddie and his wife Ethel arrived from Doncaster for his leave on 1 June and Ted Temple took them for a ride in 'Pulham's car'. Gerty Bayliss started part-time work on the farm, hoeing mangolds. Hay was cut, turned, baled and lifted; 32 sheep went to the Longford dip and Kathleen was admitted to Bourton Hospital for a month with Rheumatic Fever. Two land girls started on 6 July, cabbages were planted, and the old bull sold at Gloucester. A hayrick was thatched at Waterloo and more forms filled out, this time to obtain 38cwt of Phosphoric Acid and 3½cwt of Potash. The WAEC or 'War-Ag' [64] potato banting-plough was now on loan, cattle were taken to Aubrey Richards rented field at Hawling (Harold cycled) and John broadcast Sulphate of Ammonia on the mangolds with the International Broadcaster. The tractor received its regular oil change, 200 gallons of TVO was delivered and Eddie Higgins and the land girls were cutting swedes and turnips out of the ground all week.

285 bales of hay made using Mr Richard's tractor and baler; 120 of them to the Mill barn and the rest into a rick at the Dutch barn. Arthur Wheeler brought his 'Ford 8' motor car over for Horace to look at and he bought it! Tommy took 21 fleeces to Taylors Skinyard at Cheltenham, returning with the repaired binder and they started cutting and binding 16 acres of corn next day. Wheat and barley was cut over the next few weeks and two boys (evacuees) were caught, having knocked all the stooked wheat down in Parson's Close [65], all of it having to be re-stooked over following days to dry it! The horse-drawn 'Lees' trolley came back from Terry Muller with new floor boards, ladders, brake blocks and a repaired wheel. Harvest continued with Lionel Beames and Harry Revers helping out and 75 pullets were put in folders in the North Clay stubble *(young chickens in wooden houses to eat the spilled corn)*. Ben Bedford fetched 'Colonel' the horse away; *(I assume Colonel must have died to attract Ben's services!)* Potatoes were lifted; 'Duke' and the 'trolley' were loaned to Harwoods for picking-up their harvest at Church Farm and fruit picking started. During the week commencing Monday 5 October, the little Fordson tractor and the horses were both working the North Clay down for wheat at the same time. This casual note is possibly one of the most historically significant entries, being the only written record I have seen of the ancient and the modern technology working side-by-side in the same field. Two young soldiers spent their leave on the farm; they helped thresh 303 sacks of wheat from the ricks, (290 of which were collected by Bloodworths), this time using Longford's threshing drum; potatoes were lifted, sorted and 100 sacks were filled, helped by Edward Beames and Dennis Herbert; eight tons of potatoes being taken by Tommy to Hintons of Cheltenham. They built and thatched more ricks and clamped more mangolds. Kathleen Gibling and Winnie White, the land-girls, finished work; Ministry of Information films were watched in the village hall with a collection made for the Red Cross; the Home Guard held a parade; more dredge corn to Bourton Mill and more flour came back; Terry Muller fitted a new twin-seat on Waterloo's outside lavatory and on 21 December the turkeys and chickens were killed and dressed for Christmas - and the war continued as another year ended.

1943

The year opened by feeding roots, hay and straw to the animals, buying a heifer calf at Andoversford market and both brothers now went on Home Guard exercise with men from Hawling, Notgrove and the Slaughters. The regular trip was made to Bourton Mill with 25cwt of mixed corn, bringing the same amount of flour back. Harry Revers brought eight apple trees and two pear trees from Fuller & Maylam in Charlton Kings which Kathleen and Joan Evans (land girl) planted on Mill Orchard Bank. Tommy took four fat pigs to Bourton market; the two 'greys' (Blossom & Duke) were taken to Mr Lockey to be shod with used horseshoes; 120 straw boltings were fetched from Summer Hill; Victory Garage supplied a pulley-wheel for the Fordson tractor and Longford's 'drum' was taken to Lodges and the march of progress meant they could now thresh using a drive-belt on their tractor's new pulley-wheel to drive Longford's threshing machine, no longer needing to hire Ernie Bartlett's services. A Bamford 'No 2' Corn-Brushing Mill was bought at Hyde Farm sale. The almost daily 'trolley' load of hay rumbled from Harford Meadow hayrick to Waterloo; they rolled six acres of beans with the two 'greys'; a new part for the tractor was sent up from Victory Garage in Cheltenham on Young's bus; more work was done on the tractor and eventually it ran well; a Ministry of Food Officer visited [66];

Mr Dale's winnowing machine was borrowed from Naunton Downs and nearly had a mishap, coming down the hill with the machine trying to overtake the horse! The 'War-Ag' combine seed drill continued on its way around numerous local farms. Dressing was mixed in with seed corn and seed barley, ready for drilling; grass seed was purchased from Comeley's; they borrowed Mr Walker's 'seed-barrow' and a set of grass 'seed-harrows'. Horace bought a 410 shotgun at a farm sale; Kathleen fetched a horse from Pegglesworth; they bought two tons of Majestic seed potatoes and five cwt of peas.

Lionel, Harold and John went to the theatre; did more Home Guard shooting practice, and on 8 June Horace and Hilda went to Cheltenham where they bought a milk float, pony and harness which Harold rode home the next day for it to do its first delivery of milk in the village on 10 June. Harold went to Cheltenham General Hospital about his leg; Horace & Hilda took the pony & trap to Clapton to pick strawberries and on 27 June Norman Hughes got married. Jack Smith, John and Harold went to Moreton in the pony & float; Home Guard training continued – this time using a machine gun, *and I trust everyone else kept their heads down!* Threshing the ricks was described as being at 'full steam' *(and thankfully, modern propulsion methods have not completely replaced that lovely old saying)* as they went on to produce a total of 354 sacks of best wheat from this harvest. The broken plough was repaired, and Olive Lawley horse-ploughed the South Clay. Cattle were put on Dale House bank; Henry Muller took the engine out of the Ford car and reconditioned it; July 31 was said to be the hottest day since 19 August 1932! Ploughing and wheat cutting overlapped in August and two Cardiff school boys helped on the farm. Dennis Benfield helped cut six acres of beans, and from September onwards up to five Italian Prisoners of War came to Waterloo from the Northleach Hostel each day to help with the harvesting, carrying and threshing, after which they dug holes and put new fence posts and barbed wire up the Swilleys *(it is worth remembering that this was to contain the cattle and not the prisoners as they enjoyed the British summer and local hospitality)* after which they did some fruit picking.

☐

Probably without knowing it Naunton had now reached a notable watershed on its two thousand year timeline of farmer-warriors. The seemingly insignificant event whereby history now appeared to be repeating itself was the arrival in the valley of these five young but relatively happy Italian soldiers who were about to work for Naunton's modern farmers. If perchance they had ridden in from the east-end, who am I to say that the *deja vu* of the occasion was not lost upon one or more of them on that fine summer's day in 1943AD. Although these men had come here against their will, they were granted the kind of Cotswold hospitality that other young men from their homeland had been afforded soon after 43AD. The difference this time was that the locals were firmly in control and their horses could no longer be commandeered by the men from Italy. Although almost everyone was now literate, and a few hearts would still have fluttered on both sides, characteristically no one thought to record any of these amazing things beyond the brief diary entry I now rely upon to confirm it really happened. The local population were no doubt as distracted by the exigencies of war as the Italians were lamenting their freedom and the lack of a good local wine!

☐

More honey was 'taken' from the hives in the Bee Pen; Eileen Hammond, with several other women using the tractor and potato spinner started lifting 'Majestic' potatoes and 100 Gopsill sacks were collected from Notgrove Railway Station. The sacks were repaired, potatoes sorted and filled for Tommy and his lorry to take five tons of 'eaters' to Hintons of Cheltenham as part of the relentless struggle to feed the war torn nation. Thatching of ricks commenced; the wheat drilling got underway again as the usual round of weather dependent farming tasks rolled on. Mr Dartnall the vet did his annual testing of all cattle over six months old for TB or Bovine Tuberculosis [67]; mangolds were pulled and clamped; tractor ploughing commenced and the Longford 'drum;' brought to Cox's for the harvest.

The threshing of wheat continued at full steam and an elevator was borrowed to top out the ricks [68]. Tommy took barley to be dried by Carro of Hawling; the two 'greys' were shod by Les Lockey as Horace made a phone call to stop the five Italian prisoners from coming today because it was too wet for outside work. Hilda was admitted to Bourton Cottage Hospital for treatment to veins and leg ulcers; 'tractor ploughing' continued, cattle were fed turnips and kale; Home Guard training was followed by the Home Guard Social. After almost three weeks Hilda came home and carried on sorting potatoes in the Mill garage and the following day the rest of the family became ill with flu [69]. Attended a 'Young Farmers' meeting at Cheltenham Grammar School on 'Improved Breeding for Milk'. The 22 cows were ear-marked; more potatoes were taken to Cheltenham, more fruit trees purchased (six apple, three pear, and two plum), more firewood was cut and more cows sent to market. Two rabbits were shot in the kale; chickens and turkeys were killed, plucked and dressed for Christmas and so another year ended.

1944

In January Longford's threshing 'drum' was taken to Bowsen Ground with the help of four land-girls from Mickleton, producing 11 trolley loads of corn as a result of their labours; two new mould-boards for the plough and a bucket of grease are bought from Hartwells; 50cwt of slag put on the meadow; more tractor ploughing, cross-ploughing and muck-cart each day. A shorter bull calf is sold for £35 at market as a 'side delivery rake' is bought at Chasleton sale; the bull is sold at Andoversford market; more potatoes are planted than ever before and Home Guard training is at Rissington with rifles and Browning machine gun. On 29 May a Sports Day was held at Naunton in aid of 'Salute the Soldier' week and on 6 June the Allies invaded German occupied France. In June they started mowing the hay-grass and using Longford's baler, with Freddie Porter and Edgar Coldicott, they bale and carry 301 bales of hay from Parson's Close and 235 from the North Oat Ground. Les Lockey put the same loose horseshoe back on Duke and Mr Kennard borrowed Blossom, as the horse-hoeing of potatoes and mangolds continued. Fred Worrell and George Miffling moved into 'Agri-Cottages' [70] and both men started working at Waterloo; new hay ricks were thatched; a Prisoner of War Fete was held at Moreton and a Horse Show was held at Bourton; Home Guard at Notgrove Station this week and the cabbage plants were repeatedly watered in July; 'Holdfast' and 'Leyton 21' wheat was cut until the platform canvas roller on the binder broke. They tried to replace it with the roller from Geoffrey Hanks' old 'Massey Harris' binder but it was not the same length and a new roller was bought from Meats of Cheltenham. Stooking the wheat was followed by more rick-building; followed by shooting 12 rabbits; moving the chicken folders again; erecting a 'sectional' shed in front of the 'Flour House'; John and George Miffling thatched the roof of the Cart Shed; cutting more wheat; getting a load of walling stone from Huntsmans Quarry; sending three bull calves to Kingham market; with more cows served, more cows calved and more cows sold. Longford 'drum' to Lodges footpath again and threshing more dredge corn and wheat ricks, helped by the five Italian POWs.

Mr R.G. Hanks came to see the Cart Shed to discuss its repair and PC Perry from Guiting Police Station 'phoned to say Foot & Mouth had broken out near Tewkesbury. Scandia seed wheat arrived from Oldacres who then took 35 two-cwt bags of milling wheat to Notgrove Station; two 'bulling' heifers were turned-out with the bull; George Miffling and John thatched two barley ricks at Bowsen ground and Harold's tonsils were causing him as much grief as mine always have! Tractor to Lower Harford to help Stan Clifford move his 'drum'; Buttercup had a heifer calf and Doreen's puppy died. George Miffling was harrowing wheat with 'the greys' in South Clay and on 8 November it started snowing. Being too wet for threshing today the four Italian POWs spent the time basket making; Loads more potatoes were bagged and sent to Hintons; a Whist-Drive and dance raised £104 for the Red Cross; caught five rabbits on Mill Bank with a ferret and a pear tree was cut up into logs in Mill Orchard, and so ended another year.

1945

The daily tasks continued, from a trolley load of hay to the Mill stable and cutting even more fire wood. On Saturday went to Cheltenham races with the Scudamores; cleaned the brook out in the Meadow; grinding (milling) of corn; Harold had tonsils out age 22 at Cheltenham and came home on the bus; to Bourton YFC and pushed the Ford 8 car home; an ill-wind damaged the windmill and Godwins dismantled it for repair, the four Italian POWs helped with the threshing in February and the Russians were now only 110 miles from Berlin. Bought two new grinding-plates for the Bamford-Mill from 'Meats of Cheltenham' and eight more bags of flour were ground. The WAEC manure distributor arrived from Mr Oughton of Swell; Slade quarries delivered a 12' length of timber for a new whipple-tree [71]. Duke was shod, Mr Temple killed a pig for meat; Terry Muller hung two new gates at the mill buildings; planted 30cwt of 'Gladstone' and 30 cwt of 'Majestic' and some 'King Edward' potatoes; Threshing barley-rick with their own tractor and used Longford's tractor on the baler with the four Italian POWs and the next day (8 May) the war ended with the surrender of Germany to GB, the USA & USSR. The 8th and 9th of May were declared a National Holiday with an Up Street v. Down Street cricket match in Mill Barn Orchard and a street party in Dale Street for the children; a bonfire was lit, the Church bells were rung with vigour and what a wonderful celebratory time it must have been for everyone!

With the country almost on its knees, work continued unabated, threshing 128 sacks of best barley with the help of the captured Italians who were by now treated almost as honorary farmers. Topsy had a calf; a trolley load of litter-straw was brought down to Waterloo and on the Bank Holiday (21 May) a cricket match was held between 'up street' and 'down street', and 'down street' won. Longford's manure distributor was borrowed; the Lees trolley was broken and repaired; faggots of wood were collected from Stan Clifford's orchard. At the end of May, Hilda (51yrs) was admitted to Cheltenham Hospital with a 'stroke' and remained there until 16 July. Mr Howman called and 'finished the business up re the Mill property' [72], planted three acres of swedes and six of mangolds; a Whist-Drive and dance were held in aid of the 'Welcome Home Fund'. To Gloucester market in the car and Mr W Rose took Bluebell and her calf in the lorry. Only Bluebell sold and the calf was brought back in the car and finished horse-hoeing the potatoes (the same day). Blossom was loaned to Mr Townsend at Church Farm and Shep' Parsons brought Church Farm's tractor-mower to Lodges. Mr Dartnell the vet injected the turkeys for 'black leg'; hay was horse-raked and cocked up in Little Dutch Barn Ground; a new wagon-rope arrived, and it became too wet for hay-making in June. Hay-making recommenced and Church Farm borrowed Duke, bringing their tractor-mower to Bowsen Ground. Rain stopped things again and Mr Walker's potato-banting plough was borrowed. Potatoes and mangolds were horse-hoed for the third time; Duke had his hind-feet shod; horse-raking continued in Parson's Close.

Instead of the Italians, five Austrian displaced persons now arrived to help on the farm for several weeks by hoeing and moulding the potatoes in Roundhill Road Ground followed by a slightly amusing note of their next task, describing it as, 'Austrians singling Swedes' before they singled mangolds, (wartime diary entries did not have to preclude a little humour)! Longford finished baling the Bowsen Ground; carrying the last of Drapers hay to the rick so that George could start thatching it as Bill Dean cut the thistles in Waterloo Field. Eddie Higgins continued putting Sulphate of Ammonia on the mangolds and more ricks were built and thatched and ploughing started a couple of weeks before cutting the first barley in the South Oat Ground. As they were cutting 18 acres of wheat in Parson's Close the war against Japan ended (15 August) but the ceaseless work carried on regardless through two more days of 'National Holiday'. Harvesting and ploughing proceeded together, carrying wheat and barley from the fields helped by the 'four camp boys from Temple Guiting'. GWAEC brought some disc-harrows before taking the manure distributor away and a Farm Sale was held at Castlett, Guiting Power. In September two German POWs were borrowed from Church Farm to help get the potatoes up; wheat drilling was started; Longford 'drum' was borrowed again and its protruding pulley wheel hit the Black Horse wall, damaging it, though I have no idea whether the driver had just come from the nearby barn or bar! In October the horses and the tractor were 'dragging' together in 'Drapers' for winter oats; ploughing in the South Clay and five POWs helped clamp and cover the mangolds.

Binky Bowles took 'Millie' and her calf to Gloucester and Aubrey Richards' threshing outfit arrived but the weather was too rough to start work for several more days and the POWs cleaned out a ditch in the Meadow. There was a 'mishap' with the pony and float on the bank and the barley threshing started. November was ushered in with more threshing of barley and wheat and after keeping 18cwt of best barley for seed; 137 sacks of barley were sold to Bloodworths. Two new tyres on the 'Ford Eight' car; a load of walling stone from Huntsmans; 18cwt of seed barley to Church Farm to store until the spring; George Miffling and John thatched a clover-rick, before they thatched the mangold-bury at Cox's; John set some rabbit snares and caught four rabbits. Someone decided to take the old bull, 'Waterloo Winston' by the horns and he found himself leaving the Mill 'Bull Shed' and sold at Gloucester market, being replaced by a new and younger bull who was ensconced at Cox's. According to the diary, on his first day there (20 November 1945) he was given a bag of oats! Whether this was written to suggest that he 'got his oats' on day one I know not, but knowing my father, it probably was! Gloucester Produce Co delivered 300 potato bags and collected seven tons of Majestics and four tons of Gladstones which the five POWs helped to bag up. More bales of hay were moved to the Mill stable; six old hens, together with some cockerels, ducks and turkeys were plucked for Christmas and taken to Cheltenham by Horace and Hilda; shot a hare and a rabbit; Blossom went to the blacksmith and another farming year ended.

In 1945 Waterloo Farm had:

Milking cows & heifers in milk 18: Cows in calf, four: Heifers in calf, 14: Bulls in service, one: Bulls being reared for service, one: Cattle, over one year old but under two, 25; under one year old, 30: calves, nine.

Pigs, two: Poultry, 120: Horses, three.

Hay, 25 tons: Wheat straw, 8 tons: Oat straw, $2\frac{1}{2}$ tons: Mixed corn, $3\frac{1}{2}$ tons: Wheat, 12 tons: Oats, 12 tons. Labour; four male and one female.

1946

On 1 and 2 January, ploughing in Parson's Close; Kitty was shod at the front only; water troughs covered with straw due to heavy frosts; Helen Wheatley, Land Army girl started work, and the snow continued; five POWs did the muck spreading and a 'shed' made of bales was built on the Footpath Field (called Roundhill Road Ground on 1838 map) to protect the tractor and the paraffin tank from freezing up (where a WW2 Nissen hut would later be erected). Four POWs borrowed from Longford to help with wheat threshing. Cut four old pear trees down and sawed them up for firewood; planted six Bramley seedling apple trees in Mill Orchard and two in Waterloo garden; milling more flour at Lodges with seven bags to Waterloo; Mr Temple killed and butchered a pig; two sides of bacon and two hams taken to Collins of Broadway to be smoked; three 'drifts' of wood bought in sale at Upper Slaughter; Heifer taken to Gloucester Market, sold for £30 5/-. Two Huntmans lorries and drivers for muck cart from Waterloo field to Lodges. On 26 March Kathleen married John Young from Stow-on-the-Wold at Naunton Church. 100 gallons of TVO were delivered from Stow Sack Depot.

George Miffling drilled six acres of oats with the two 'greys' before rolling the winter oats and taking a trolley load of hay to the Mill stable with the same horses. Planting barley with Mr Wood's seed dresser 'set' (positioned) by the clover rick. On 17 April borrowed two German POWs from Stan

Clifford and shot a fox. Bloodworths delivered seed corn and foodstuffs and Oldacres delivered two tons of granular manure, three tons of Nitro Chalk and one ton of Sulphate of Ammonia and took eleven cwt of red clover seed away. Meats of Cheltenham delivered a Bamlett finger-bar tractor mower; cleaned three heifers up ready for market; 'chitting' the eating potatoes; white-washing more cattle sheds; played cricket for 'old boys' against present day Westwoods Grammar School *(curiously the diary is silent about the result – perhaps it was just too embarrassing)!* Celebrated Victory Day on 8 June; continued the threshing of wheat and horse-hoeing of potatoes; On 3 July Dennis Benfield joined the Army. On 14 July Government bureaucracy caught up with them when a curt Ministry Of Food (Potato and Carrot Division) note arrived pointing out that when they completed their previous return they omitted to state the type of seed used!

Heavy storms in July hampered the thatching of ricks. A new Lister Cockshut plough was fetched from Notgrove Station by a Huntsmans lorry; Horace, Hilda and Harold went to Cheltenham Cricket Festival to see 'Glos v. India'. Started cutting spring oats, barley and wheat in August; Hartwells (of Bourton) delivered a new Martins Cultivator and five-cwt of binder twine. Caught up with the stooking and thatching after the rain; On 5 September went to Cheltenham on bus and met Sheila and bought an engagement ring *(the first mention of my mother)*. 'Helen' (John's Guernsey cow) had a bull calf which went to Bourton market and just three weeks later Helen 'went to profit' again with the bull. Longford's 'drum' was moved to two oat ricks in North Clay and all corn taken to the barn. They now shared the purchase of a threshing machine from Maugersbury with Mr Wheeler of Church Farm, to use between the two farms, having it repaired at Lower Slaughter on the way. A new 'milking machine' was collected from Bourton Station, an Alfa Laval (Swedish dairy equipment) engineer called to fit it in the dairy and Listers of Dursley delivered a $1\frac{1}{2}$ horsepower engine to power it.

The first ever mechanised milking to take place in Naunton after several thousand years of milking cows by hand was undertaken by Harold (after each of them received instruction by the Alfa Laval engineer) on Thursday 31 October 1946 and was watched by all of the family and several other people, including two POWs.

Harold and Henry Muller fitted new piston-rings to the Fordson tractor and continued milling with it in the afternoon. On 28 October Cousin Maurice was buried at Naunton Chapel. The Ford Eight went to Victory Garage in Cheltenham to have the headlamps fixed; shot two hares and a partridge; used the Lister engine to drive the root-pulper; six British Friesian cattle were taken from Lodges to the Mill and readied for market, 'having too many to winter' but only four sold. Went to a party at the Cheltenham Nurses Home; 'Poppy' is overdue for calving and needs watching; sawed wood with Longford saw-bench and put four cart loads of blocks into the Mill stable; Tommy James brought Mr W.H. Butler's potato sorter from Temple Guiting and the three POWs helped bag up $16\frac{1}{2}$ tons of Gladstone and Majestic potatoes for Gloucester Produce Co. to collect, keeping 33cwt for ourselves. On 14 October Sheila (author's mother) finished nursing at Cheltenham General Hospital and transferred to Oxford; started using 'our' threshing drum and did the footpath wheat rick bringing five-cwt of flour to the 'Flour House' at Waterloo; Alfa-Laval engineer called to fix the sterilising unit in the sterilising shed behind the dairy; turned windmill off to do small repair job on it.

POWs coming almost every day now; on 23 December turkeys and chickens were plucked and dressed for Christmas and Harold went to Evesham on Christmas day to have tea with his fiancée Sheila and again on Boxing Day! On 27 December borrowed two ferrets from Tommy James and got 17 rabbits on the Mill Bank. On 31st took the 'truck' to County Electric Co for work on the dynamo and another year ended.

1947

Started with threshing dredge corn at Cox's Barn; hauling swedes around to feed the cattle every day; selling a Guernsey and Jersey heifer at Gloucester market for 67 guineas (a guinea was a former gold coin, last minted in 1813, worth £1 1/- or twenty one shillings, or £1.05p in decimal currency). On 10 January Auntie Janet Griffin was buried at Naunton Church; Dennis Benfield was home on leave and helped thresh small oat rick until the threshing drum broke down; Horace and Bert Bayliss to Guiting Grange to look at Army Nissen huts that are now for sale; the regular trolley load of wheat straw taken to the Mill; one-way traffic to Andoversford with the snow plough struggling to keep the road open and then no traffic to Cheltenham for many days with very high winds causing drifting; Fordson tractor refused to start; no busses running; trying to milk and thaw water pipes at Waterloo; snow still drifting badly; dug gate at bottom of the Swilleys to get cattle to Lodges; dug across main road; cattle must be fed; got two loads of hay from rick on footpath to Waterloo; all roads to Cheltenham, Bourton and Stow still blocked on 7 March; got water to house and dairy after eight days; digging up Swilleys again; then a hurricane on 16 March leaving much damage and the thaw commenced.

Church Farm brought the 'drum' back to Cox's Barn and three bags of wheat they had 'borrowed' *(a frequent practice between the farms);* with mother and father to Barrington to see a sire and dam of a year old bull and purchased them; Mr Temple killed a pig for us; two POWs were 'walling', three helping with threshing in April; another 'drift' of wood from Slaughter Wood; No POWs available today so we borrowed five from Church Farm and paid for them, ordering five POWs for Friday; Mr Bloodworth called to see about 58 sacks of barley; to Heythrop Hunt point-to-point races at Burford on 22 April; continued drilling dredge-corn and barley with the horses - too wet for the tractor; one year old British Friesian Bull called 'Windrush Zyder Zee' delivered by Mr W. Rose; GWAEC Combine Drill moved on to Church Farm; Horace bought a manure distributor from sale at Temple Guiting and Binky Bowles brought it; fetched Church Farm's Ferguson tractor for the weekend and worked South Clay with two tractors; Mr John Tippett called for the annual valuation of the stock; planting potatoes with Mr Marsden's tractor and potato planter.

Cricket practice in the evening; on May B.H. played cricket, Up Street v. Down Street; Up Street won by two runs! John, Harold, Eddie Higgins & George Miffling to Bath & West Show in Cheltenham; Misty slipped her calf and we buried the calf; 50 pullet and 50 cockerel chicks from Broadway; one POW was now helping with the threshing in June and July and after that there is no further mention of them so most had now gone home, but a few stayed in England. On 9 July the North Cotswold Rural District Council allocated Harold a couple of rooms in Kiftsgate House as the two 'agri-cottages' (Council houses) were occupied and on 14 July he married Sheila Hill at Evesham. They went to Weston-Super-Mare for a week and moved into Kiftsgate on 22 July.

Farm work continued with the harvesting starting in August; threshing and rick building, milking twice daily, delivering it through the village each morning in a Hillman, canvas backed pick-up truck of WW2 vintage [73]; stock movements, breeding plans and sales and all the other tasks continued. In October Horace was thinking of installing electric lighting and went to Cirencester to look at an Electric Light Plant. He bought one and they installed it but with a total output of 250 watts it struggled to light the several bulbs connected to it. Within weeks they were looking around for a more powerful electricity generating plant and brought one home on approval that would light the dairy-sheds as well as the house. He then bought an 'elevator' from Mr Witts of Upper Slaughter to help raise bales, or loose hay and straw to the top of ricks and into the barn. 30 cwt of apples were picked in the Mill Orchard and on 12 October the Harvest Festival was held at the Church.

As the autumn approached all the other now well documented tasks were repeated around the farm. Christmas arrived with cockerels and geese being killed, plucked and dressed; firewood was cut and it snowed on Christmas day and so ended another year with a scribbled note showing:

Cows in milk 17; Cows in calf (dry) 5; Heifers in calf 17; Bulls used for service 2; other cattle 54. Horses 3; Gilts in pig 2; Fowls 160; Ducks 9.

Stocks of (tons) Wheat 1; Autumn sown Wheat 17; Barley 4; Oats 3; Mixed corn 5; Hay 12; Straw 8. Regular workers: Male 4; Female 1.

1948

John (23) now appears to take over the diary with only sporadic entries until Harold resumed keeping it in 1954. Whether Harold's marriage in 1947 or the departure of extra hands in the form of the POWs had anything to do with the pencil changing hands is unknown.

Foot and Mouth restrictions were imposed and police permits required for stock movements. Ploughing got underway; the Dutch Barn was painted red; coupons were still required to obtain petrol; Dennis and John planted eight Norwegian spruce (four in each top corner) and 40 larch trees in Mill coppice and two apple trees on the bank and Dennis returned to his unit; ten ducks and ten chicks were hatched; Sir Charles Hambro sent two men over and bought a Guernsey and Jersey cow, both being in-calf, together with two hogs and one gilt pig; 40 gallons of petrol and four gallons of gear oil from Pulhams; the bull 'Penticroyd Leopold' had pneumonia and was taken away after the vet was called. Wire netting was put around the Mill coppice to stop the pigs getting out. On Monday 8 March Victory Motors in Cheltenham delivered a new Fordson Major tractor and took the old one back for service. Duke was fetched away by Ben Bedford. Mr R. G. Hanks died on 9 March.

On the day of the author's birth (31.05.48) the entry reads, 'started digging silo pit; hoeing mangolds' indicating that the arrival of his brother's first child was of little consequence to busy farmers! Haymaking continued and ricks were built and thatched and a boar pig was purchased from Peterborough, arriving by train at Bourton.

The remainder of the year saw only some of the daily, weekly and seasonal tasks being recorded. As Christmas approached a pig was killed and the customary cockerels and geese prepared and on Christmas day 13 sat down for dinner and 14 for tea when Dennis joined them.

They now had 18 cows in milk; 4 in calf; 18 heifers in calf; 1 bull; 53 other cattle; 2 sows in pig; 8 young pigs; 2 horses 246 poultry; 18 ducks. There were four regular workers, with two women and girls. The previous 235 acres was now 241 and included six more for grazing on the Mill Bank.

1949

Doreen was now keeping a diary of her own and only mentions the daily milk round using the utility truck. A sow called 'Naunton Dainty' had 15 piglets and the Hunt met at Bourton Bridge. Other than this Doreen makes little mention of the farm events, which must have carried on in a similar way to other years.

1950

They sold 8 pigs at market; four at £6 each, four at £5 12/- 6d each. Threshed dredge corn and Black oats on Lodges and applied for more Ration Coupons. A sow farrowed in the Mill shed (16 piglets).

They took ten weaned pigs to market in the trailer and sold them for £5 each; erected scaffolding at the Dutch barn for Bert Bayliss to repair the roof; sold a sow for £22, a fat pig for £22 10/- and six store pigs for £7 12/- 6d each and 12 weaned pigs for £5 5/- each. They planted more dredge corn; chickens were moved from Longford Meadow to the Barn Ground; Ivor James brought two loads of larch poles from Snowshill for fence posts; a sow farrowed with 16 piglets. Up Street and Down Street played cricket on 29 May, a drawn game; Dennis Benfield was 'demobbed' and started working at Waterloo.

Beatle dust was put on Ewe Pen Ground; 200 gallons of TVO purchased for £12 5/- 10d; horse-hoeing commenced and so did the filling of the silage pit. Cockerels and Muscovy ducks were sold at Castle Market; Mr Walker brought two sows to the boar at Waterloo; the large white gilt farrowed with 18 piglets and a bull calf was sold to the Ministry at Bourton for £28; 23 hens were taken to Castle Market; haymaking got underway in the South Clay, and the diary fell silent until October.

The harvest was complete; mangolds were raised and clamped; potatoes lifted and sorted; more National Health Stamps were purchased from Bourton GPO; straw was put on a wheat-rick on the footpath; Harold repaired the 'drum'; the river was cleaned out by the Washpool and the following week a man called from Gloucester to inspect the brook from the Mill to the Bridge at the bottom of The Lane. They bought a disc-harrow from a sale at Bishops Cleeve Aerodrome; Mr E Hughes was paid £4 for the services of his Landrace Boar and another hard but scantily recorded year had passed by.

1951

Amid light snow the year commenced cutting up an old apple tree and walnut tree; cleaning out the ditches in the Meadow; Alan Wheeler measured up for four new windows in Waterloo House; 13 weaner pigs were sold at Gloucester for £7 2/- 6d each; a Nissen hut was bought from Mr Finch's Farm at Chedworth, dismantled and brought home; a sow farrowed 14 pigs in the Mill Tool Shed and 12 survived on a bitterly cold night; the Hillman truck was painted green (*I now wonder if seeing this may have sown an idea in impressionable young boy's minds – the likely answer will be revealed later*)

The diary is blank until 4 June when Cyril Tims sow was brought to the boar at Waterloo and Longford's digger was used to clear the ground on the footpath for the Nissen hut, the remainder of the year passing by unrecorded.

1952

Young calves were moved round at Waterloo and the Mill; one hare and three rabbits were shot; 'Fillpail II' to 'AI' (Dutch Bull); five tons of Artificial Manure No 5 ordered from Crafts; a sow farrowed with 15 piglets at Lodges piggery; threshing dredge-corn on the footpath and storing it in the Nissen hut; nine strong store-pigs to Gloucester market, selling for £7 6/- each. On 10 March ploughing the North Oat Ground; Horace went to a 'potato-meeting' at Stow; two bull calves to Andoversford market and they bought a Denning Combine Drill at Icombe sale.

Drilling oats in Ewe Pen Ground and grass seed in Bowsen Ground; sold six store-pigs, ten weaned pigs and two cows at Gloucester market; Foot & Mouth at Crudwell, Wilts; thatching a bale rick in South Oat Ground; cutting wheat in North Oat Ground on 31 July; killed and picked two cockerels; busy keeping birds off the wheat; Foot & Mouth now at Lower Slaughter, all cows kept at Waterloo with nothing crossing the main road; wheat cart in North Oat Ground; application made a week later to Guiting Police Station to move cows from Waterloo to Lodges; threshing wheat at Dutch Barn; three heifers to Gloucester Market selling for a total of £245; sold 40 sacks of wheat to WMFA at 31/- per bushel; cut two walnut trees down and sold the trunks for £10, cutting the rest for firewood.

On 14 November the 'drum' and elevator were stored in the Dutch Barn; thatched Cox's shed and by 25 November were having to thaw out the water troughs. After converting the old Bull Shed at the Mill, the poultry in Harford Meadow were transferred there, no doubt with due deference to Reynard! The cost of 2129 bales supplied by Mr Maurice Hanks in 1951/52 came to £85 and this was offset against the cost of £216 worth of milk supplied over the same period.

The quarterly Ministry of Agriculture And Fisheries (MAF) Return for Waterloo and Lodges for June 1952 indicates (in acres) Wheat 16; Barley 6; Oats 4; Mixed corn 34; Kale 11; Temporary grasses for mowing 56 (including clover and sainfoin), for grazing 33; rough grazing 37; permanent grass for mowing 5; for grazing 39.

Stock was: Cows 47 (24 in milk); Bulls 1; other cattle 37 (Total cattle and calves 85); Horses, one mare; Total pigs 30; Total poultry 203; Male workers 3; Female workers 2.

1953

'Shirley' gave birth to a heifer calf (Dutch sire, Alaridus) but it died; they cleaned out the brook in the Meadow; 400 chicks were purchased from Hawkins; monthly bills were paid to Listers, Pulhams and Mullers; oil, mash and fertiliser bought from WMFA. A Massey Harris Baler was delivered by Hartwells and used in Roundhill Road Ground to make 1850 bales of hay. This was followed by baling for Mr Wheeler at Church Farm and at Grange Hill Farm before doing the rest of the haymaking.

The quarterly MAF return for June indicates (in acres): Wheat 12; Barley 6; Oats 4; Mixed corn 28; Kale 12; Temporary grasses for mowing 73, for grazing 54; permanent grass for mowing 5; for grazing 12; for rough grazing 37.

Stock: Cows 38; Bulls none; other cattle 55 (Total cattle and calves 85); Horses, one mare; Total pigs 24; Total poultry 510; Male workers 3; Female workers 2.

More cattle and pigs went to market at Gloucester and Andoversford; more calves were born; in August NCRDC connected the mains water to North Bank (variously called Hanks' Bank, Bayliss' Bank North Bank and now Adams' bank) the nine acre grazing field being bought by Waterloo Farm in 1953. The harvesting was finished on 10 September with little more of note being recorded. The ongoing records of cattle breeding such as 'F43 (Dimple Horn II) AI today' and 'Queenie calved today, a heifer calf by Montgomery Marks Superb', are prolific throughout this and every diary.

In October they were 'drilling' the Barn Ground with 'Oats 172' from WMFA and mains water was connected to the Mill Buildings for the first time, after all the houses in the village had been connected. Horace went to Northleach to buy a boar pig; the Bowsen Ground shed was prepared to take Pullets (raising Reynard's hopes again!) and they sold 6 live chickens for 15/- (75p) each. The NCRDC Water Account for 6 months (April – Sept 1953); Waterloo 86,000 gallons; £9 13/- 6d, North Bank 1000 gallons; 2/- 3d, The Mill Buildings; Nil. With rental for three meters this came to £10 19/- 11d or one old penny short of £20. Lodges farm (non-mains) was still being supplied by water pumped from the Windrush by the windmill in Harford Bridge Meadow.

On 18 November the Heythrop Hounds met at Harford Bridge Meadow; they started threshing a wheat rick at Dutch Barn; an application form was submitted to licence the boar pig; more gilts were served; more cows to 'AI'. Although the year passed by with chunks of the diary left blank, a thousand other jobs would still have been well done.

1954 Harold resumes keeping the diary.

A 'Ministry Return of Agricultural Machinery' for January 1954 indicates they now had: two tractors; one 200 gallon liquid fuel storage tank; one corn drill; one combined seed and fertilizer drill; one fertilizer distributor; one mower; two side rake and swathe turners; one hay rake; one buck rake; one elevator; one binder; one portable threshing machine; one hay and straw baler; one grinding mill; one dairy milking machine; one sterilising installation; one milk cooler (non refrigerated); two wagons and carts; two electric fence units; two tractor trailers. They ticked a box to indicate that they did some contract work using their machinery elsewhere and that the main residence as well as some outbuildings was now connected to electricity from the Public Mains.

A gilt farrowed at Mill Barn, having 15 piglets and they were moved to the piggery at the Dutch Barn on Lodges; they bought a Nissen hut from Staverton and erected it on a double layer of breeze-blocks on the footpath (*I was then 6 and well remember being tasked with handing the bolts from a bucket to the men using the spanners*); the baler went to Hartwells for repair; more oats were ground for animal feed; baled a rick of dredge-corn (397 bales); a fox killed at least five hens at Harford Meadow; the Victory engineer came to fix both tractors, Ivor James took 18cwt barley and 15cwt oats to Bourton Mill to be dressed for seed; Fisons 31 fertiliser was applied at two-cwt per acre, the 'AI' [74] man called again and Spring Hill Point-to-Point races were held.

Hay making, side-raking and baling got underway, with a total of 4,310 bales of hay by 21 July, each one being loaded onto a trailer using a pitchfork, requiring very fit and strong men to do it. There was lots of 'bale cart' and several ricks were built and thatched as a result. A few days later another 350 hay bales went into a rick in Harford Meadow from the perfect meadow-grass growing next to the river.

In August Bert Bayliss and Les Gorton commenced building Waterloo's the new milking parlour, helped occasionally by Harold, John and Eddie Higgins. There was no earth moving equipment and as usual, they all dug the foundations by hand [75].

Harvesting commenced using a combine on the barley; several loads of Cotswold walling stones were delivered by Huntsmans Quarry; 100 new chicks were reared under heat-lamps; there was a serious accident on the top road between Kearseys bus and a Fina Petrol Tanker (*most of us boys visited this scene on 27 October, but luckily there was no explosion or you may not be reading this. I was given a 'Fina' lapel-badge by someone and treasured it, as might any six year old*).

Eight 'bacon' [76] pigs went to Andoversford market; the cows were being 'hitched' on the kale by advancing the electric fence forward a little each day as they ate it down; 300 bales made from a rick of wheat straw; the Heythrop Hunt were hosted by Horace in Harford Meadow (*where he proudly offered the customary port 'stirrup-cup' to all present*) and soon after they found a fox in the kale; three litters of pigs were castrated at the Mill (*how well I remember their squealing*); the Alfa-Laval engineer installed the new piping and equipment in the new dairy, which was partitioned for six cows to be milked simultaneously. On 21 December the MEB connected the power to the dairy and the changeover from the historic old dairy to the modern new one took place. The last day of the year was spent ploughing the Barn Ground (*where Hatha was buried some 2000 years before and where his remains were about to be unceremoniously exhumed. Unfortunately, Harold did not record this event in the diary!*).

1955

The dairy herd were taken up the track called The Swilleys and across the main road and back every day and even in the 1950s and 60s, this was hazardous as they lumbered across the road. Once on Lodges they were herded towards fresh fields of grass or to where root crops such as mangolds, swedes and kale grew in the winter; hay was also fed to them in various fields.

340 oat straw bales were made; Pork and bacon pigs sent to Cirencester and Andoversford markets; daily grinding of oats for cattle feed; changing engine oil in tractors every few weeks; fly warbling the cattle. On 7 June for the first time, a ten-gallon milk churn was returned from Moreton Dairy; 'of poor keeping quality'! Threshing of more wheat and the commencement of hay-making; borrowed a horse from Longford to horse-hoe between the mangolds; cutting charlock in the kale; 'gapping' walls; cutting thistles with a scythe on banks or with the tractor mower on flatter ground.

On 24 August a combine was hired from Longford and dredge-corn harvested; thatched wheat and straw ricks by the Dutch Barn; Bert Bayliss, assisted by Harold, John and Eddie to dig out the foundations commenced building the lean-to shed against the dairy for storing animal feedstuffs; electric fence moved forward daily in the kale giving the cows a new 'hitch' each time; a pig went to Longford's boar; the Fordson Standard tractor had rubber tyres fitted in place of its metal wheels; apple picking commenced in October; breeding yet more bacon and pork pigs for market; a sow had no milk and seven piglets were taken into the house for hand feeding; set the 'drum' by a wheat rick and started to thresh and bale the straw; bought a saw-bench in November, power-take-off from the tractor to drive a circular blade and wood cut up as winter fuel; castrated three steers at Lodges Barn; 110 bags of dredge-corn and 70 of barley taken to Summer Hill for drying and several ricks were thatched. Ploughing done and land prepared once more for drilling, this time with a Denning Chard seed drill.

The annual meet of the Heythrop hounds took place at Harford Bridge Meadow in November; wood was cut from Mill Coppice to make ash fence posts and poles, bean sticks also being cut from this coppice; Hillman truck to Stow for service; finished threshing and the 'drum' put back into Dutch Barn. A total of 5000 bales of hay had been stored for winter use and if all went well there would be no need to buy any in the spring.

On Christmas Eve John married Sylvia (nee Miffling) at Moreton-in-Marsh.

The year ended with six pigs being weighed ready for collection by FMC and a sow that was 'ranting' had two rings put in her nose!

1956

Started with 'Mary' for 'AI' and the vet calling to see a heifer with a bad eye, prescribing cream to be applied twice daily; all water troughs heavily covered to prevent them freezing; 'ditching' (cleaning out ditches) in Cow Bank Hollow; Ministry official ear-punching Aberdeen Angus cattle; another 200 gallons of TVO delivered to the tank; Hartwells returned the baler engine; Mr Hamblett's boar pig from Guiting Power to serve the gilts; finished threshing at Oat Ground by 16 March; all straw baled and all corn to the Nissen hut storage bins; a fox entered the Bowsen through the thatched roof and killed all the fowls. On 18 March a Ferguson TE20 tractor (petrol/TVO) was bought at Church Farm sale and two days later Church Farm borrowed it back from Waterloo! *The wonderful thing about this amazing little tractor was the amount of optional extras you could attach to it, the most useful being the hydraulic 'bucket' on the front that was so useful for lifting things that were a bit too heavy for 'manpower'.* Disking and dragging underway, planting of grass seed, oats, wheat and rye grass completed.

Planting potatoes in 'up street garden'; the banting-plough was readied for potatoes and John learned a hard lesson, that it was extremely unwise to check a tractor's petrol tank with a cigarette in your mouth - if you wished to retain you eye-brows! Vet castrated a steer and Doreen's horse; kale and mangolds planted, more horse hoeing of potatoes and mangolds; ricks of baled hay were thatched with straw; in July, Harford Meadow was mowed, turned and yielded 180 bales of best quality hay. 100 pullets into deep litter at Waterloo; porch built onto left of Waterloo House; finished cutting Drapers and stooking it up; castrated litter of pigs at the Mill; mending dozens of hessian sacks using Copydex,™ and 'patches' cut from old sacks; five trips round North Clay dredge corn and stopped because it was unfit for harvesting; corn to Hawling for drying; Vicky (cow) died after she was 'blown' and was later fetched by Dan Perkins.

De-horning and warbling cattle; pick-up tines on the baler were replaced by Hartwells engineer; Pearl (cow) became 'blown' eating too much kale. She had to be 'stuck', and survived as a result [77]. Pulling, hauling and clamping of mangolds. On Christmas Eve, four 'heavy-in-pig' sows were moved from the piggery near the Dutch barn to the Mill Barn pig-sty and it snowed on Christmas day. On 27 December as Harold emptied the water troughs, covering them up for the rest of the winter and milled more flour for animal feed, an additional entry in the diary in childishly joined-up writing reads: 'and David Hanks watched'. Twinkle had a bull calf and one of the farrowing sows had 12 pigs as the year ended.

1957

The year opened with the other two sows having nine pigs each. Foot and Mouth restrictions were imposed after a confirmed outbreak at Sherborne and cattle remained confined, fed where they stood, until the all-clear was given two weeks later. A new hanging post and gate was fitted at the Mill Barn, three pork pigs were moved to the Mill for collection by FMC; faggots were made from dead wood in the Mill Coppice; the weather was hopeless for threshing and wheat was purchased from Comeley's; four litters of pigs were castrated; an oat rick was threshed; frequent muck-spreading took place; bagging and sorting of potatoes at Bowsen Ground, some as 'eaters' some for 'seed' and 17 cwts of 'eaters' were taken to Gilberts at Bourton. More 'bulling' heifers were separated to await the 'AI' man (*with that green-stained rubber glove reaching to his arm-pit)!* The North Clay was hopelessly wet for ploughing as per usual; Mr Hamblett's boar was brought over by Ivor James and dutifully served four sows the following day.

Harrison's emptied the milking parlour sceptic tank; five-cwt of salt was put on one and a half acres of mangolds; the Ferguson's parking brake mysteriously 'failed' causing the little grey tractor to run down the bank and embed itself firmly into Lodges Barn; the ridiculously high-revving Allison engine on the Massey Harris 701 baler broke down yet again and Hartwells' engineer, Bill Corbett fixed it. On 12 May Bert Bayliss commenced building the calving-shed against the new dairy and the job was completed 12 weeks later.

Hired Mr Davidson-Smiths' small combine and harvested nine acres of oats before it was taken to Westfield Farm for drying. Thatching more ricks of wheat and rye and bales of straw; a water blockage in Waterloo House perplexed them for days until a dead mouse was finally removed from the outlet pipe on the attic tank; made new wooden calf mangers and hay racks at the Mill barn. The Heythrop Hunt met in Harford Meadow in November and five not so crafty foxes were quickly chased from the nearby kale. The 'Denny' drill was used to plant 'Bersee' and 'Sword' wheat and 'Proctor' barley. There was more engine trouble with the old Hillman Tilley-Truck (used for the village's 'milk round'); more cleaning of cow sheds and deep litter houses at Waterloo, and ever more ploughing on Lodges.

The last day of the year was spent ploughing and grinding corn, cleaning out poultry houses, sending a bull calf to market with Ivor James and of course moving and feeding the other stock and poultry. In addition to all this, the dairy herd was milked first thing each morning and at the end of each afternoon, every day of every year.

1958

On 1 January the Heythrop met in Naunton, confidently making for the Ewe Pen Ground kale, but there were no pesky foxes there this time, leaving the hounds and men in green outsmarted; for the time being at least!

On 22 March a fox or foxes got into the Bowsen again (next to Harford Meadow) through the thatched roof and killed all the hens, (*an incident I remember so well. Aged 9, I was with Harold when he discovered this scene of utter carnage that morning, which by then seemed almost peaceful, or as quiet as the grave. It was almost trivialised by the site of thousands of feathers still blowing gently across the fields. We later saw a fox up a tree in Roundhill hollow and if my father had had the 12 bore shot gun with him that morning it would not have sat there leering at us for long*). About a hundred hens were killed, many being buried across the fields, (the fox's larder) later being unearthed by the tines of the cultivator. Some of the dead hens that 'Reynard' left behind in the Bowsen were sold on the milk-round over the next few days, with one customer buying several as they were such good value!

After severe storms in May a total of 27 loads of beech, oak and larch was bought from Guiting Grange; borrowed Don Walker's potato planter; bought a 'hatch' of ducklings; Hartwells took the troublesome baler engine away again; moulding potatoes and making silage; 3236 hay bales by July and at end of July they bought a second-hand 'Allis-Chalmers' combine harvester from Bemborough Farm (now the Cotswold Farm Park). 340 bales of hay from Harford Meadow; yet another magneto fitted to the baler and then the binder broke down!

Wheat harvested and taken to Summer Hill for drying; two wagon loads of wheat sheaves to Dutch Barn; 100 cockerels from Waterloo to Parson's Close; four sows out on the stubble; bought a 61' x 24' Nissen hut from Stowell Park which was dismantled and brought to Lodges by the men to be erected near the Dutch Barn. A cow had to be 'stuck' and survived but a sow died; apple picking completed and baled 1400 oat straw bales at Aylworth and 1150 Barley straw at Roundhill for Lodges Barn after Don Walker said he did not need them, leaving him just 200 at Aylworth;

Total hay bales for 1958; 4763 and total straw 4647 (2097 Lodges; 2550 from Aylworth and Roundhill). 'Cynthia' (a cow) gave $6\frac{1}{2}$ gallons of milk in one day; started delivering Channel Island milk in the village.

The final entry for 1958 was made by 15 year old Richard Collett as he started work at Waterloo, adding a useful note for forgetful employees: 'Richard and Eddie Higgins live in Dale Terrace; Horace at Waterloo, Harold at 2 Mill View and John at Sunny Cottages'. On 31 December they milked the cows and bottled the milk as on every other day of the year; did 'muck-cart at the Mill; built a breeze-block wall as a base for the Nissen hut on Lodges; Polly had a heifer calf and a sow farrowed with three pigs. On the 31st 'it rained all morning but was fine later' and so ended another busy farming year.

1959

The base for the Nissen hut was finished and erection of curved girders continued over many weeks; in March the cows were still on silage, mangolds and hay; 'Koga II' spring wheat and 'Proctor' barley planted and Fisons-45 added to assist its growth. On 22 April, 87 gallons of wholesale milk were sent off to Moreton. In May Aylworth and Roundhill farms were sold for £88,000. Borrowed Geoff Hanks' tractor when the Ferguson's hydraulics failed and on 20 May, 120 gallons or 12 churns of wholesale milk, were now collected by lorry from Moreton Dairy each day. Tried to finish threshing wheat and oats but the 'drum' broke down and carried on bagging chaff. Doreen's horse 'June' had a foal (filly);

the Ferguson came back from Hartwells at Bourton; thistles, charlock and ragwort control commenced; a new drive-rod for the Bambett mower; a power failure resulted in all the milking being done by hand and acted as a wake-up call for the installation of back-up power in the form of a small Lister engine and generator in the 'engine-house' next to the dairy. By July they were putting curved sheets of corrugated tin roofing on the Nissen hut and painting them.

They ground (milled) the last of the 1958 corn; built new bases for additional corn-bins in the Nissen hut; collected the 'new' (second-hand) pick-up truck from a sale at Bemborough Farm. 83 cockerels were 'caponised' [78]; baling and carting oat straw at Aylworth; borrowed Bert Bayliss's long ladder to thatch a rick of wheat and oat straw. Mr Masters boar from Rissington to serve one sow; grinding more flour, creosoting gates and posts; potato spinner to lift crop in Parson's Close; bought a banting plough at Aylworth farm sale; put huge canvas sheet and netting on straw bale rick at Cox's; bought a Ransome (three-furrow) mounted plough and a Bamford (five-foot cut) trailer-mower from sale at Broadway.

Apple picking in October; six sows now at the 'Lodges' piggery; the ongoing repair of gates and fences and 'gapping' fallen down dry-stone walls to try and contain the stock; stone-picking on the fields; and in October they filled in the now redundant concrete reservoir in Waterloo field. The muddy deposit (silt) from the old Mill drain (once part of the Mill race) was cleaned out and spread in the Mill orchard over the road; potato sorting for 'eaters' and seed crop; painting of various agricultural implements with anti-rust paint; 100 cattle routinely tested for tuberculosis; Cynthia lost her calf at six months; Godwins taking windmill down for repair; Mr Wyatt's man helping with the ploughing as Harold filled in the open end of the Nissen hut 'wind tunnel' with bales! Six tons of slag put on 20 acres of young seeds in North Oat Ground; five tons of Huntsmans lime dust spread on 16 acres of Roundhill Road Ground. The annual meet of the Heythrop in Harford Meadow; built a new partition in the Mill Stable for Doreen's horse; Gloucester Market closed due to F&M outbreak in the Forest of Dean.

Rick of hay bales moved from Cox's yard into nearby shed after gales tore the covering sheet and netting to shreds. On 17 December plucked 44 cockerels with Mr Harker's plucking machine; 'Cynthia' *(a barren cow and not a local lass)* went to Cirencester market!

On 31 December the Bowsen Ground mangold-land was ploughed and 50 barley bales moved from Bowsen to the Mill Barn for litter. Two bacon pigs were entered at market and the usual milking, feeding and cleaning out tasks completed. Susan Hanks aged five wrote her name impressively several times on the last page of the diary and the same page recorded that 3139 bales of hay (500 from Rosemore and 300 from Roundabout field at Aylworth) and 2400 bales of straw (1600 from Aylworth) were produced this year.

1960

Two bacon pigs were collected; broke the circular saw blade and the pick-up truck broke down again; a bull calf died. In heavy snow, gateways were being dug out to get around the farm and to feed the animals hay from a trailer and by 16 January they had used all 800 bales of hay from Aylworth and started feeding the Aylworth wheat straw bales. Bought 50 ash poles from Slaughter Wood and built hay-racks at the Mill stable to minimise floor wastage; fitted hardboard under calving-shed roof at Waterloo in vain attempt to reduce condensation; moved three loads of barley from the big Nissen hut to the smaller one for grinding, for weighing and some for seed.

Bought five tons of hay from Martins of Buckland; seven tons of hay at £11 per ton from Whitmore of Upper Slaughter and three tons from F.J. Ruck, Cirencester. Bought 200 pullet chicks and ten cockerels from Sweetings; Wood sale at Guiting Grange, buying rails and a gate. Now feeding hay and mangolds to cows; two sows served by Mr Masters' boar; creosoting poultry houses; walling at

Washpool; the 'scrap-metal' man took the old Ford car, and bought the Standard Fordson tractor (£6) and the binder (30 shillings). Hillman truck to Youngs garage in June for service; 333 hay bales from Harford Meadow; one ton of 'Nitra-Shell 23' was spread on ten acres of kale; six nearly bacon-weight pigs from the Mill to Lodges piggery; John Alcock, Smiths engineer still working on the combine; Bill Corbett, Hartwells engineer working on the baler magneto; loose straw now 'tied' on a rick of straw bales, not thatched!

Bought two grain storage bins from Stan Clifford (Lower Harford Farm); apple picking started in Mill orchard in October; took four tons of wheat to the Manor and ran it over the cleaner; John Cooper collected his Aberdeen Angus bull which had been with 12 heifers for three weeks. On 16 November the Heythrop Hunt were hosted as usual at Harford Bridge Meadow and killed four foxes nearby. Root pulper used to pulp potatoes and apples for the pigs; collected a permit from Guiting Police Station for stock to cross the main road; the little Lister engine taken to Waterloo for emergency milking power.

In December they bought a new Commer Cob van from Young's garage; gave a cockerel to the Cheery-Club raffle; the Milk Recorder man called as usual; Mr Wyatt finished ploughing; a Germination Report was received from Comeley's; Harold was home for one day with flu. By the years end 45 tons of corn had been to Summer Hill for drying; 4290 bales of hay proved inadequate, but 3585 bales of straw seemed to suffice.

1961

An inauspicious start when the Fordson Major tractor broke down with 'serious problems' and Hartwells returned it to Waterloo as 'non-reparable'! After realising that a new tractor was required, a couple of weeks later Victory Motor Co (Cheltenham) delivered a Fordson Super Major (four cylinder, 52hp), which was a big blue tractor, though compared with the modern New-Holland on the rear cover, was puny and never had a cab. A new 250 gallon diesel tank was supplied by Burgess Fuels and installed on the footpath, next to the first Nissen hut because TVO was not for this new machine! They then used it to plough for the first time with a mounted plough and all went well.

The latest little Hillman pick-up truck has now done 117,000 miles and also appears to be on borrowed time! The usual round of seasonal tasks began to overlay the daily feeding and milking tasks together with the preparation of animal-feed with the Bamford Mill grinding oats and barley, belt-driven by the new tractor, as was the saw bench. Crops planted included 'Koga II' spring wheat, 'Rika' barley, 'Marrow Stem' kale and grass seeds from WMFA. A new wooden bed was put on the old trailer; wheat and barley was sprayed with 'Bexone Plus'. Parson's close was mowed and the side-rake turned the new hay.

The installation of the village's new sewerage system commenced in June and was completed before the end of the year; potatoes were horse-hoed; 270 bales of meadow-hay from Harford Meadow; *(probably one of the sweetest of all farm smells, at the opposite end of the scale to muck-cart or cleaning out animal sheds)* wholesale (bulk) milk now averaging between 110 and 120 gallons each day; Smiths of Andoversford repaired the combine harvester which continued working in South Oat Ground where $5\frac{1}{2}$ tons a day was the average yield, going straight into sacks hired from Bourton Mill. Ricks of straw were now covered with loose straw and the time-consuming thatching of yesteryear appears to have become one more historical fact.

On 18 September the Weights & Measures people were in the Village Hall and anyone from shopkeepers to farmers could take their weights there and have them calibrated. They bought Bill Pulham's Steerage Hoe at his sale at Wales Barn Farm and Albert Williams from Church Farm borrowed his own combine drill! The Hillman truck went to Young's garage at Stow for repairs and service; they dug a trench by hand from Waterloo bridge to the back door for 80 sewerage pipes and two inspection covers, the pipe being previously laid by the Council as far as the bridge to await connection; Richard Collett left on 11 November and by now all cattle were being fed hay and straw. The pigeons were destructive on the newly planted seeds; the vet de-horned two calves; all water troughs were covered again as the freezing weather set in. The Heythrop Hunt met at Harford Bridge and ran a fox across Lodges and then past the Village Hall. The year ended with snow-blocked roads and burning thorns in Drapers, probably as much to keep warm as to keep the farm tidy!

1962

The year opened with relieved comments about the water running again on Lodges Farm and with no burst pipes! Cinderella had a Friesian calf, Queenie a Hereford calf and a sow farrowed. 50 bales of essential hay were moved from the Dutch barn to the Mill Barn. A calf disappeared and they failed to find it; 16 cattle were put on the kale each day; much 'gapping' of walls, repairing of gates, cleaning out of sheds. The 'Flour House' was prepared for 200 chicks under lamps; more ploughing, a bacon pig died, and second one that was off its food died the following day; reconditioned engine fitted in Ferguson tractor by Hartwells and then they painted it (grey, of course!).

Crafts delivered six tons of Fisons 41 fertiliser; rolled 18 acres of turf-ploughing in the snow and rain; moved load of barley between Nissen huts for grinding; bought tree-tops from Guiting Grange and cut them up; Terry Muller & Sons building new poultry house at Waterloo; drilled and harrowed Ewe Pen Ground with barley; feeding and grinding more feed each day; Hereford and Friesian fat heifers to Gloucester market with Ivor James; Heythrop Hunt staff 'gapping' and 'hurdling' walls on Clays and Drapers; calf died and vet cut it open – inconclusive. The Council put a 'Cattle Crossing' sign on main road; two loads of stones taken off barley in Bowsen Ground; Top-dressed Dutch barn ground; $2\frac{1}{2}$ cwt per acre of Fisons 42 on young seeds in South Clay; 'warbled' 21 calves; sawing and sharpening fencing stakes with circular saw.

On 8 May put 110 of the February hatched chicks into the new poultry house at Waterloo; went to Stow fair and bought a two-wheeled tractor trailer and brought it home with a poultry-folder from Kathleen Young's; after some work got the baler engine going again and yes, it failed and went to Hartwells for an engine overhaul! Vet called to a cow with 'wooden tongue'; rented Mrs Bayliss' bank for the summer and put eight cattle on it; getting mower ready for haymaking; Ministry man visited to advise re fertiliser use; Hartwells fitting new axle to trailer; mowing South Clay; new tines fitted to baler and side-rake; treated cattle for ring-worm; 'Betty' (barren) to Gloucester market; 1205 hay bales stacked up in South Clay; ten-cwt of Nitro Chalk on Meadow; bale cart from South Clay into Dutch barn; two cows for 'AI' and 'Fiona' calved; 1460 bales of hay from Roundhill Road Ground and 1310 bales from Parson's Close.

In July Terry Muller connected Waterloo to the mains sewerage and the outdoor privy became redundant after 140 years, as did the quaint double-seat he made for it 20 years ago! Steerage hoeing swedes and kale with the Ferguson; de-beaked 200 pullets; painted large Nissen hut and put new tin on Dutch barn lean-to; cutting and trimming bushes on Mill bank; Mr Wyatt tried to plough North Clay in July but it was impossibly hard.

In August, maintenance was done on combine harvester but the Smiths engineer had to be called to sort the engine out and after eight days the required parts came; bought a ton of barley from Aylworth for £19 to tide them over and on 25 August they started combining Drapers, bagging four tons of barley (about 80 sacks) that day and grinding some of it the following morning; Smiths engineer was soon back again and changed the magneto on the combine. By 29 August they had 390 straw bales out of Drapers and moved on to Bowsen Ground; milking the dairy herd twice a day; moving cattle from North Oat Ground to the Meadow and several other jobs in between. A calf died and was collected by the Cotswold Hunt Kennels; 500 bales of straw baled in Bowsen Ground.

Mr Stanley from Roundhill offered them ten acres of barley straw at £1 per acre (better than burning it) and it produced 552 bales. Winter wheat was combined and the straw baled and all was safely gathered in by the end of September when they stored as much as they could in the barns before making several barley bale ricks and covered them with straw boltings or trusses from Roundhill; apparently distrusting the modern plastic sheets but unwilling to revert to full thatching!

Ploughing and planting started over again; apple and pear picking at Waterloo and the Mill Orchards into October; potato picking and sorting; the Heythrop met at Naunton Green and took a fox from Longford Brake; four down-calver cattle to Waterloo for feeding and three 'bulling' heifers for 'AI'. Two beef cattle (Friesian steers) and one barren heifer to Gloucester; an ambulance hit a cow crossing the main road at 3.30pm; Heythrop met in Harford Meadow in November and killed a fox in the kale and took another one away; lagged all water troughs and pipes around farm and at Waterloo; Guernsey cow hit by a car on main road; an Aberdeen Angus calf was born on Christmas day and as the year ended drifting snow stopped traffic getting to Cheltenham and Bourton; and this time they had 4095 bales of hay to try and see them through the winter!

1963

The year opened during this severe winter with snow blocked roads, no post and very little else moving, but on 1 January Polly gave birth to a calf at the Mill stable as the snow continued to wind-drift across the high wolds plateaux of the North Cotswolds. The Trinity Road to Guiting was filled with snow for weeks. All the water troughs on Lodges Farm had to be thawed out daily with burning straw to enable the animals to drink and then covered again until next day. Gateways were dug out almost daily by hand to get a trailer load of hay to the animals; more hay and feed straw was brought down to Waterloo and the Windrush froze over. The mains water to Waterloo House froze where it crossed over the bridge and the North Cotswold Water Board were informed. Calves were carried down to Waterloo to feed them and to ensure their survival as water was now not running anywhere on Lodges, believed frozen somewhere by the old cart shed and piggery. The water pipe at Waterloo was exposed on the bridge with pick-axes and blow-lamps were used to try and thaw it out but digging proved too difficult as they tried to extend the trench in rock-hard ground. Pauline had a dead calf and the Cotswold Kennels collected the carcase; three Water Board men were now trying to restore the essential water supply to Waterloo but gave up after two days. Gateways were dug out again on Lodges and cattle led to Aylworth ditch where water was running beneath the ice. On 31 January 'Snow Flake' was appropriately presented to the 'AI' man as they all expectantly awaited the big thaw and the Water Board men returned with plastic piping to run water above ground from the Mill House to Waterloo each day, bringing the first water to the milking parlour in 11 days. A power failure was then overcome thanks to the little Lister standby engine.

In February, to get two heavily in-pig sows from Lodges piggery to the Mill meant digging the route ahead of them as they made there way down the Swilleys and two days later they farrowed with seven and nine healthy piglets. On 10 February 11 bacon and pork pigs and two fat cattle were taken to Gloucester despite the snow. Ice and frozen muck was constantly being removed from the parlour yard as the cows had difficulty standing and by 4 March they got the Ferguson tractor going and dug the snow away around the Nissen huts, from the gateways and then created a four-foot wide corridor down the Swilleys and into Waterloo field to enable the dairy herd to get up to the Barn Ground for the first time since 29 December! On 12 March the Water Board thawed the underground pipe between the road and Waterloo and the Heythrop Hounds met in the village. On 18 March they bought 3½ tons of hay from Mr Bowles at Ford.

Ploughing commenced; new tines were fitted to the Martin Cultivator; bought 50 sleepers from Toddington Goods Yard; bagged more barley from the storage bins for grinding. Then after I had worked some barley land on Good Friday (12 March) Harold inserted a comment that read: 'David knocked off early – too cold', *which indicates I was rebelling slightly by showing my unwillingness to spend all day on an open tractor on my day off from my indoor job at Little Rissington!* Two tons of hay bought from the Trafalgar Estate; new parts were fitted to the Denning Drill; harrowing, rolling and drilling more land; Robinsons delivered two tons of Sulphate of Ammonia; ten big calves moved from the Mill to North Oat Ground; bought two trailer loads of wood from Eyford Park; cleaned big poultry house out at Waterloo.

In June they installed a Cold Room in the dairy and this ended the practice of carrying full ten-gallon milk churns down to the Windrush each evening in the hottest weather, to sit them on a platform in the river below the bridge to keep the milk cool until the lorry collected it the following morning. Amazingly, the baler engine appears to have started without a problem and the tractor mower was readied for haymaking in June; 1470 hay bales from South Clay. Started new four-strand barbed wire fence along Aylworth Road using sawn up sleepers as posts; bale cart at Bowsen Gd; the periodic milk sample was taken from Waterloo; manure spreader to Hartwells for repair and the new Vicon Lely mounted Swathe Turner was delivered; 1220 hay bales from Parson's Close and 1470 bales of hay from South Clay; 555 bales from Harford Meadow, 155 in Little Dutch Barn Ground.

Cutting thistles and pulling ragwort on Mill bank; cleaning ditch out at Meadow; cutting thorn bushes and getting combine ready for harvest by greasing, changing oil and filters and starting engine, then combining undersown-barley in South Oat Ground; Smiths engineer to the combine – parts awaited! Baled 12 acres barley straw at Roundhill bridge and 410 bales at Lodges, all bales 'ricked'. Combining resumed; 65 bags of wheat to Church Farm for drying; Ministry-man ear-clipped 11 beef cattle; lambs to Gloucester market; Lupin aborted her calf; 900 bales of wheat straw from South Clay; 505 bales from field of surplus straw opposite Hunstmans Quarry belonging to Mr Brian Hanks; lifting potatoes in Ewe Pen Ground; planted six acres of 'Cappelle' wheat (eight-cwt of wheat with ten-cwt of '8.20.16' fertiliser) and harrowed it in; covered barley ricks with straw trusses from Roundhill;

On 30 October all the implements were put in the large Nissen hut for the winter; thatching continued; beef cattle moved to new grass; potatoes sorted; Caroline had twin bull calves and Cinderella had repeat 'AI'. Meadow hay from Dutch barn to Mill and on 27 November the Heythrop met at Harford Bridge Meadow and found three foxes in Ewe Pen ground kale, killing one and taking two away to Aston Farm, bringing one back and killing it near Roundhill Farm. 'Pamela' (a cow) died after being 'blown' and was collected by Ormond Eeles. Water troughs covered up for the winter; 'picked' 30 cockerels with Mr Harker's machine-plucker; repaired corn mill for grinding and the year ended cleaning out calf sheds and repairing gates and fences and apparently without a breakdown on the baler!

1964

Commenced with the breaking up the remainder of the old threshing 'drum' for scrap and a general tidy up around the Nissen hut and Dutch barn; cutting ash trees down for fencing stakes and making pea-sticks; cross-ploughing, grinding and lagging water pipes; sold scrap metal from threshing drum *(or what was left of it!)* FMC collected five pork pigs; poultry houses cleared out ready for new chicks from Sweetings; report from Bourton Mill – 'Proctor' barley 94% germination; report from Comeley's – Rika barley 97% germination. The Heythrop met at Bourton Bridge and North Cotswold met at

Temple Guiting bringing a fox on to Lodges; cultivating, disking and harrowing the fields; $2\frac{1}{2}$ tons of barley cleaned and dressed at Summer Hill ready for sowing.

In April I am recorded as harrowing the North Oat Ground; disking the Ewe Pen Ground and 'trying' Drapers but it was too wet so we cleaned the seed drill. Still feeding hay to the stock; engine oil changed in Fordson Major again (2979 hours on clock); filled in the old septic tank next to Waterloo House with earth and stone from Mill House; 'Pat' calved, dead bull calf collected by Cotswold Hunt kennels; planted 'Proctor' barley, 'Marrow Stem' kale, potatoes and winter wheat; stock moved around farm, 56 non-dairy cattle in four fields; sprayed winter wheat and barley; re-concreted part of dairy floor; built a milk-churn stand outside dairy for easier loading of the lorry, only to have the lorry back into and knock it over soon after! The vet treated several pigs for enteritis; cutting thistles in Mill Orchard and on 11 June started mowing young seed-grass for hay. Prepared swathe turner and baler for haymaking; to sale at Notgrove Station with tractor and trailer, bought 20 good railway sleepers at 6 shillings each and 40 rough ones for firewood at 1 shilling; using the good ones for fencing posts. On Sunday 21 June, my 13 year old sister Pat endorsed the diary very tidily by writing: 'brought Nigel (5yrs) and Janet (7yrs) to haymaking with daddy at 4-o-clock for a picnic. We went home at 6-o-clock and heard the Church bells ringing', thereby capturing a little of the magic of growing up here, though she does not say where our nine year old sister Susan was that fine day.

Mowing continued and after another 950 bales the baler broke down again and they bought a field of baled hay from Albert Williams. After repairing the baler, the turning, baling and carrying of hay continued, with extra turning needed after more rain. 1450 bales from North Clay and after building a rick with them, this time they covered it with sheets of curved tin and placed railway sleepers on top to hold it all down! The tractor and trailer were also repaired; walling and fencing; moving stock, cutting thistles; weighing pigs and a host of other jobs done. After buying seven telegraph poles and 20 more sleepers from the newly redundant railway line, they somehow brought them all home on the trailer! They took the straw and gorse roof off Cox's bowsen and after removing the cross-bars from the telegraph poles, spliced and bolted them together into 25' lengths to act as roof supports for a new asbestos roof, the asbestos sheets being cut and handled in a way that would bring most organisations to a complete halt today! John Alcock, Smiths engineer came to the combine and on 13 August, three journeys were made around North Oat Ground but the barley was not yet fit enough so they carried on fixing Cox's barn roof. Combining of wheat and barley and baling the straw and carting it to barns and ricks continued on Lodges and Church Farm, needing lots of baler and binder twine from WMFA to complete it all by 15 September, or 'Battle of Britain Day', Harold took his first holiday since getting married in 1947.

On his return a week later they sent two more cattle to Gloucester; surprisingly, still thatching a bale-rick at Cox's barn with wheat straw trusses from Roundhill Farm and covered another straw bale-rick with tin and sleepers. The refurbishment of Cox's was completed with a new breeze-block wall, replacing the old railway sleeper floor and installing a new breeze-block manger. After buying six new plough-shares ploughing started on 13 acres of barley stubble. Apple picking commenced on 10 October and on 17 October, Cousin Edward from Kent stayed at Waterloo for the weekend; two sows were taken to Mr Mead's boar; Heythrop Hounds met at Harford Bridge Meadow, putting four foxes out of the kale, running one up a drain at Lodges barn and prompting Harold to record: 'now we know where the drain goes'!

On 18 November 1964 Harold wrote: 'to Speech Day at Bourton School'. *(As I read this entry I reached for my old (1960) 'Concise Oxford Dictionary' next to my computer keyboard and the endorsement inside the cover reminded me that it was presented to me on that very date. I recall my parents attending, a full year after I had left school. But I am more curious about what the thinking of the school may have been, after failing my 'O' level English and leaving in 1963. The school can rest assured that the dictionary became a trusty well-thumbed friend thereafter).*

Vet called to 'Flossie' who had milk fever and by November there were 62 non-dairy cattle spread around eight locations on the farm. Lagging of troughs and water pipes began as the first frosts were felt; 70 bales of meadow hay from Dutch barn to Mill; more cattle to market; Comeleys collected 68 Greenock sacks of spring wheat and on 23 December ground some extra barley to last over Christmas. A cow had a Friesian calf on Christmas day, followed by three more over the next three days, one going to Cheltenham abattoir with 'navel trouble'! At the end of the year they again built a wall of straw bales inside the open end of the big Nissen hut to stop snow and fog blowing in, another dead calf was born and the year closed with my sister Janet writing out her multiplication tables inside the back cover of the diary!

1965

Over one week the bushes at the top of the Mill Bank were all cut back and tidied, ash trees in the Mill coppice thinned out, the wood taken to the saw bench. The Fordson Super Major was returned from Hartwells fully serviced (3850 hours on the clock). Cattle moved from the Meadow to the Mill and two in-calf heifers back to the meadow. A man from Taylor & Fletcher accompanied Horace to the Bell Acre [79] in Parson's Close; on 3 February the Heythrop met on The Green and Mr Wyatt ploughed Parson's Close grass. Waterloo garden, Mill View garden and Up Street gardens were all dug; more cattle to Gloucester market. Another 200 gallons of diesel and 100 gallons of TVO were delivered to the tanks on Lodges footpath and on 14 February the customary annual cycle of cultivation commenced in Ewe Pen Ground. A sow farrowed with eight pigs; more barley was cleaned, dressed and sown and the Cotswold Hounds met at Roundhill Farm for the first time ever.

Mr Harrison, the vet, tested a total of 114 cattle; 70 more bales of litter straw taken down to the Mill; cleaning calf sheds out then mud and muck cart at Waterloo and the Mill; six tons of ICI No 2 fertiliser and nine-cwt 'Rika' seed barley from WMFA; new standing platform fitted to seed drill; water supply to top reservoir now being pumped again; chain harrowing Waterloo and Mill fields, and several others; Ministry Man ear-clipped 18 cattle; put new topping stones on wall at old quarry with concrete *(now Golf Club car park)*. Hartwells to Ferguson and baler engines and took baler engine away *(no surprises here)*; cutting thistles and nettles in several fields; new metal gate fitted at Up Street garden; looked at Mr Thorpe's combine harvester which he wants to sell. On 14 June started haymaking; 1320 bales of hay from Bowsen Ground, 1100 from South Clay; lost an Ayrshire heifer from Harford Meadow! 127 gallons of wholesale milk on 6 July; borrowed Albert Williams bale-elevator; fetched Mr Thorpe's combine from Harford Farm; Mr Albert Hathaway from Canada visited Horace and Hilda for a week - an old friend from the past [80].

On 10 August they broke up the two old Cotswold Wagons for firewood and burnt the roof of the cart shed. The old Allis Chalmers and the slightly newer Ransomes 'PTO' [81] combine harvesters were then prepared for the harvest. In between the twice-daily milking and moving stock around, treating cattle for ring-worm, hiring 800 sacks from Robinsons, grinding barley, doing dung-cart on the fields, they somehow managed to start combining in the Ewe Pen Ground. Amongst the problems facing farmers were everyday events that could cause unscheduled stoppages, particularly mechanical breakdowns, Mother Nature or ill-health of staff and stock. A simple example here was a puncture on the Fordson Super Major which had to be repaired, without a spare wheel, before harvesting could continue. Then, after sorting that out rain stopped the harvest resuming anyway, adding more frustration to the situation. Godwins managed to sort the windmill out in the meadow where mud had blocked the inlet of the riverside well. They built a half-end on to the Nissen hut on the footpath field; Hartwells did the same welding job on the combine as before and it moved onto the winter wheat, where by 6 October, although the equipment was now functioning, combining proved very difficult because of fog, with

Ivor James taking lorry loads of wheat to Mr Thomas of Hawling for drying before they finished and put the implements away on 22 October, many days behind schedule.

The Heythrop met at Harford Bridge at 11.45 on 17 November and on the Village Green on 1 December. The various daily routines of milking, cleaning out, grinding corn, feeding and moving stock and feedstuffs and everything else continued unabated. On 21 December they picked cockerels, no longer keeping turkeys but that evening Harold won a 23lb turkey at the Village Hall Christmas bingo! A Friesian cow had a bull calf on Christmas Day and another a heifer calf on Boxing Day and the year closed with the Fordson now showing 4900 operating hours on its Smiths clock.

1966

Yet another calf was born on 5 January, as three barren cows were sent to Gloucester market and the time honoured and relentless cycle of animal husbandry continued. They de-beaked hens, milked the cows twice a day; more calves were born; cut back hedges and repaired walls. Serviced the Bamford Roller Mill; sent more cattle to market; cut more ash trees down for posts and rails and called the vet to a cow with 'foot trouble'. More germination tests on the barley by Comeleys of Church House; cleaning out sheds and stables and spreading muck on fields; received six tons of 20-14-14 compound fertilizer from WMFA; carried more bales to the Mill and used the last telegraph pole from the railway sale to carry a power line to the poultry house at Waterloo. By March cultivating started again and they bought a Twose Vibratiller (cultivator) from Stow Fair, having its wheel repaired by Hartwells before bringing it home and attaching it to the Ferguson T20.

On 16 March the Heythrop met on The Village Green; the old kale land was ploughed; bought a Massey Harris combine corn drill from Meats and used it for planting 'Rika' seed barley in Parson's Close before harrowing and rolling it. On 31 March Labour won the General Election with a massive majority and it was too wet to plant grass seed in North Oat Ground. They bought two tons of hay from Mr C. Davidson-Smith of Westfield; sent four fat cattle to Gloucester; top-dressed 13 acres of young grass with nitro chalk and on 27 April the BBC spent four days in the village filming 'Softly Softly' [82]. Kale and potatoes were planted; Eddie Higgins took his twice-yearly one-week holiday; all water troughs were emptied and scrubbed out and the poultry houses cleaned.

On 6 June the mower, baler and sledge were readied; grass was cut and turned and hay-making was underway in Ewe Pen Ground; they hoed the kale; bagged more barley from the storage bins; and after more rain the river flowed out over the Harford Meadow and all efforts to stop it failed. A new fence was put on Dale House Bank and 15 cattle moved there; the old elevator was broken up for scrap and Albert Williams elevator was borrowed; 1560 bales of hay in Ewe Pen Ground, 1500 in Bowsen Ground before the baler's overworked 'knotter' failed. Hartwells engineer came, bringing ten more rolls of bale twine; 1200 bales from Barn Ground; 950 from South Clay and by 28 July hay making was finished with 6260 bales of good hay going into the barns and ricks, covered with tin and old railway sleepers. A fox was seen around Mill-field chicken houses; they cleaned the river out at the Meadow; Hartwells fitted safety guards on the Super-Major and Ferguson tractors to comply with the latest regulations; ploughing was underway again and on 18 August harvesting started on the barley, using 500 hired sacks.

The manure spreader was repaired and working almost daily; straw bales were stood up to dry after heavy rain; carting bales to the ricks and covering them with tin and burning the unwanted barley straw in the fields. Drilling 'Champlain' winter wheat and lifting 'Majestic' potatoes. On 3 October I took a week's leave to stand in for Harold again, for a much needed holiday with his cousin in Kent. Jobs the 'hired hand' helped with that week included milking, morning and evening, bottling the milk, grinding flour, moving stock around the farm, repairing a water trough, covering broken windows in the Nissen hut, feeding the cattle with flour and hay, taking the tractor to Bourton for two new tyres and generally appreciating how busy my father was and looking forward to his return. The plough was repaired and several fields were ploughed. On 19 October Harold went to see a ploughing contest at Moreton, and carried on doing it himself on Lodges the following day. Several loads of wood were sawn for the winter, then a lovely little error indicates that the Council are working on the 'Bridal Road' down the Swilleys, conjuring up images of newly-weds trying to negotiate this muddy track where I once lost my Wellington boots in the quagmires which cattle created there in wet weather!

By November they were emptying and covering the troughs; sending more cattle to market; spreading more muck on the fields, hanging and repairing more gates. On 12 November he was not best pleased after the Cotswold hounds met at the nearby Fox Inn, brought a fox to Lodges kale where they killed it and took another out, endorsing the diary; 'very annoying in view of the Wednesday meet at Naunton'! The following Wednesday the Heythrop duly met at Naunton, came up to the kale and predictably - no fox; The 'Cotswold' being held responsible for spoiling that particular day's hunting!

They put the little Ferguson in the lean-to garage at Waterloo that backed on to the 'Flour House' for the winter; treated 29 cattle for warbles with Bells Warpax concentrate; winter-proofed the open end of the Nissen hut with straw bales again and on 3 December he recorded that I had sent a postcard from Weymouth as I was about to board the topsail schooner, Sir Winston Churchill, as one more farming year ended.

1967

The new-year opened with crisp clear weather; some fattened cattle being sent to Gloucester market. A calculation indicated that the number of 'grass-hitches' on the kale were sufficient to feed the dairy herd until the end of the month. Milking, cleaning out and muck spreading continued unabated and the Heythrop met at Naunton Green on 25 January. Horace Bayliss fitted a kissing-gate [83] on the Swilleys 'bridal' road for the Council! Repairs to walling in Bowsen Ground; 'Sybil' for 'AI'; a fence erected around Waterloo garden using stakes made from railway sleepers and covered with netting; started using the outside hay from under the tin; ploughing and cross-ploughing fields; Huntsmans Quarry filled in the silage pit; the windmill was not pumping again because an elver (young eel) had entered the well at the side of the Windrush before growing too big to escape through the inlet pipe, partially blocking it when attempting to exit. 70 bales of best hay to the Mill loft; nine tons of ICI No.2 fertiliser from WMFA and 75 bags of 'Rika' barley taken to Bourton to be cleaned and dressed for planting on Lodges, returning with nine-cwt of 'Zephyr' seed barley and three tons of nitro-chalk; Changed oil in Fordson Major which now has an incredible 6262 hours on the clock, averaging 1000 hrs per annum.

MEB fitted new Hunts Electric Rolling Mill at Waterloo; three cattle sent to Gloucester (Aberdeen Angus heifer, Friesian steer and a Guernsey bull calf); more field work each day, working Parson's Close with the two tractors; dairy herd grazing new grass; vet to 'Sybil' (unable to get in-calf); dressing Barn Ground grass with nitro-chalk and North Oat Ground with ICI No.2; and on 15 April Hartwells delivered a new Massey Ferguson Model 15, P.T.O. drive baler. Planting, harrowing and rolling 'Rika' barley and on 30 April, Dowdeswell Railway Viaduct was blown-up! They sold the old Massey Harris 701 baler and Allis-Chalmers Allcrop 60 combine harvester at Stow Fair on 11 May; cleaned out all water troughs; put new posts and rails around the parlour yard and the regular tuberculosis tests proved clear. Making pea and bean sticks; cleaning out poultry runs and houses; planted potatoes in Ewe Pen Ground; sent poor old 'Sybil' to Gloucester market (barren) and on 11 June started haymaking by mowing the Barn Ground, using the new baler a few days later to produce 1280 bales there before a part broke and Hartwells engineer was called to the new machine! Ewe Pen Ground 1175 bales, North Oat Ground 2500 bales, Meadow 488 bales, Drapers 710 bales; the final total 6153. They filled the barns, built some ricks and covered them with tin and sleepers. The next job on the list entailed moving many loads of soil to the side of the Windrush to try and prevent the Meadow from flooding again.

All the usual cleaning jobs continued and cattle went to market most Monday mornings. 12 new plough-shares saw ploughing commence on 11 August in 13 acres of Ewe Pen Ground which had been 'down for two years'. The combine was readied to commence the barley harvest in Bowsen Ground on 16 August, bagging the grain and baling 2435 straw bales before burning the rest. Hartwells were soon called, replacing belts and doing welding work before carrying on again until sunset each day. Aylworth's bull got onto Lodges and served at least one Ayrshire before it was returned; ploughing was continued; trees were cut back against the main road and on 8 September combining resumed in the North Clay but progress was slowed because of 'canvas' trouble and an excess of clover! They carried on in South Clay and put two foxes out of the winter wheat. The moisture content was 20%+ and it was sent to Thomas of Hawling for drying and two plastic sheets were tightly lashed over two straw ricks and tin placed over another.

On 30 September Moreton Dairies made their last wholesale milk collection from Waterloo and it now went to Mr Norman at Bourton. Comeleys collected 130 sacks of wheat and WMFA had 51. On 16 October, excluding the dairy cows they had 16 cattle on South Oat Ground, 5 on Cow Bank, 5 in the Meadow, 12 on North Bank and 7 at the Mill, all of which were moved around frequently. Wheat drilling continued; potatoes were lifted; new field gates fitted; walls and fences repaired and on 8 November the Heythrop met at Harford Meadow but there was no fox in the kale! A F&M restriction notice was imposed on all animal movements on 18 November and a licence enabling them to cross the main road was not granted until 14 December and so another trying year ended.

1968

On 1 January Gloucester Market reopened after F&M restrictions were lifted, enabling two fat cattle and a barren cow to leave Waterloo. Work continued throughout spring and on 6 March the Heythrop met in the village. They bought a used Morris Oxford car; planted 'Zephyr' barley, grass-seeds, swedes, kale and potatoes and sent another barren Friesian cow to Gloucester, selling for £85; bought a new Bamford R4 mounted mower from Hartwells and haymaking progressed as usual. They borrowed Albert's elevator, serviced it, used it and returned it.

On 8 June he noted that with my mother (Sheila) and my wife to be (Ann), I went to Buckingham Palace to collect the Duke of Edinburgh's Gold Award but that he could not go himself being too busy with the haymaking. By 27 July they took 520 bales from the Meadow, adding to 2140 from North Clay, 1330 Barn Ground, 2400 North Oat Ground and 400 from part South Oat Ground, totalling 6830, but would even this get them through a really hard winter?

On 14 August they were preparing the Ransomes MST combine harvester again and started on the barley soon after, before rain hampered their progress. 13 yearling calves were moved from Drapers to North Oat Ground, this being another token entry here for the continuous pattern of animal movements around the farm. On 5 September they were combining barley in Parson's Close again and got three trailer loads of corn in the dry that day using hired sacks from Bourton Sack Depot at Little Rissington, followed by 330 straw bales.

Mr Humphreys of Bourton bought all the old hens from the Mill; 1750 straw bales were made and the rest was burned; the trees behind Waterloo House were thinned out with the help of Mr Ball from the Mill House. In October they started combining winter wheat in Ewe Pen Ground, taking it to Hawling for drying; after which WMFA sampled it and offered £22 5/- (£22.25p) per ton. CAT [84] then offered

£23 per ton and duly bought it, collecting 126 sacks (9 tons 18cwts) from Mr Thomas's yard at Hawling and 125 sacks from Lodges; a total of £426.

The open end of the Nissen hut (left like this to get the combine and other implements in and out) was sealed with straw bales again for the winter; ricks were covered with two new heavy-duty plastic sheets as well as the old tin and sleepers. Potatoes were lifted, sorted and bagged. On 13 November the Heythrop met at Harford Bridge Meadow and a press clipping found inside the diary reads:

'Mr Horace Hanks and his family had their customary meet at Harford Bridge on November 13 and the large field that came were not disappointed. Killing one fox in the kale the bitch pack crossed the Cheltenham road to Naunton village and checked on the plough but hit it off to go by Hill Barn to Brockhill Clump, over the road to Bunker Hill, Harford Mill and down the water to Redesdales and on to Aston Mill. Came away left handed to go down by Upper Slaughter and across to Swiss Farm where the leading hounds turned short back through Cressbeds and ran hard by Copse Hill to the Slaughter Copses. Fresh foxes now got afoot after a run of 1 hour 50 minutes and a 4½ mile point. From Gashouse hounds ran back to Slaughter Copses and accounted for a fox which had done some work. Mr Strutt's Brickyard Covert held but the start over Slaughter Farm was unpromising. However Mr Maurice Shaw viewed the fox into Aston Bottom and after a turn round Manor Farm the pack ran well by Severn Springs, Bunker Hill, over the road to the right of Brockhill Barn to Naunton Church, up over the Cheltenham road and caught their fox on Mr. Hanks's bank after a very nice hunt of 65 minutes and 4 mile point'.

Sadly, this was to be the last time Horace so proudly hosted his beloved Heythrop Hunt.

Muck-cart continued on the wheat stubble in the exhaustive cycle of extracting the goodness from the soil through the crops and the need to constantly replenish it again with that smelly stuff. The diary ends in a surprising way with Harold writing the following recipe: 8 ozs self-raising flour; 4 ozs margarine; 4 ozs sugar; 4 ozs of dried fruit; 1 egg; 1 desert spoon vinegar; 3 table spoons water, 7" cake tin. I have absolutely no idea why he wrote this as he never had the time or the inclination to do any baking but I am mildly curious to know what it might have turned out like.

1969

On 8 January the Heythrop crossed Lodges after meeting at Bourton Hill Farm and on 15 January Horace (77yrs) was admitted to Cheltenham General Hospital. All the work on the farm continued and he returned to Waterloo on the 29th as the ploughing commenced. On 5 March the Heythrop met in the village. On 19 March, (Harold's 52nd birthday), he was ill with flu and wrote, 'gave up smoking today'. *He made this pledge thirty-one years before in 1938 but this time he meant it and never smoked again!* Bought a set of chain harrows from Hartwells; carried on harrowing and drilling and planting the fields; 'Nancy' had twin calves; mended the plastic water pipe at water trough on Holly Bank; making fencing stakes with circular saw; John Tippett did the annual stock valuation; 12 new nozzles and strainers were fitted to the sprayer boom and 13 acres of barley in Ewe Pen Ground was sprayed. On 7 June he wrote 'David Married Cheltenham' *somehow managing to take the day off to attend my wedding and accepting that I was unable to stand in for him!*

Haymaking started on 13 June; 2180 bales from Parson's Close; 1900 North Oat Ground; 405 Harford Meadow. The Commer van and the Morris car went to Young's Garage at Stow for servicing; and Heythrop Hunt staff repaired several hunt-jumps on Lodges.

On 14 August he wrote, 'my dear dad died at 3.10am'. The cows still had to be milked at 6.30am and Horace would have understood this perfectly well. I received a 'phone call during an early shift on the streets of Gloucester and on the 18th we attended his funeral at St. Andrew's Church. The two brothers prepared to start the harvest the next day because despite Horace's death the relentless farming cycle had to continue. The inevitable repairs were carried out on the combine and they commenced on the barley in Ewe Pen Ground, needing more new machine parts within days. Albert's elevator was borrowed, the straw baled and put into barns and ricks. They bought a fertiliser-spinner from Jess Wheeler's sale at Wood House Farm; ploughed the fields, bought 'Capelle' seed wheat, drilled it in and then bought another plough from Mr Cutts at Aylworth for £30.

The routines of milking, feeding, and cleaning-out, inspection and movements of livestock continued with the invaluable assistance of their ever loyal sole employee, Eddie Higgins. The combine and baler were jacked up in the large Nissen hut ready for cleaning, oiling and winter storage and on 22 November the Heythrop met at Harford Bridge Meadow and found two foxes in the nearby kale, killing one and taking the other away. The Farm Safety Officer visited for an impromptu inspection of equipment and everything was satisfactory as a sad year for the whole family ended.

1970

The usual cattle left for Gloucester market on Monday mornings and they milked and fed the dairy herd morning and evening, together with repair work, cleaning out, stock feeding, stock movement and a welter of other daily jobs. Amongst all this Hilda and her adult family of five now had to apply their minds to necessary but equally unfamiliar matters, including paying Horace's death-duties and the future of Waterloo Farm which was a Limited Company comprising Hilda, her three sons and two daughters. It was agreed that the farm should carry on much as before, for the time being at least, with Harold and John running it, helped by their one invaluable full-time employee, Eddie Higgins. On 25 May Uncle Bert died, drawing to a close the life-stories of two ambitious young Naunton men who had set off for Canada with such great plans back in 1912.

The usual spring work commenced with 37 acres of 'Sultan' barley planted and the fertiliser spinner used to apply Fisons High Nitrogen fertiliser to the land. By April they had to buy-in three tons of hay from Manor Farm and one from Longford. Drilling continued by planting their own 'Zephyr' barley and more work was done to keep the windmill working to try and maintain the essential water supply to Lodges troughs for the livestock. On 13 May a thunderstorm flooded the village street and washed stone, silt and tarmac down Summer Hill Lane (North Street), as it had done on various occasions in the past and as it would undoubtedly do in the future!

On Sunday 7 June the last ten journeys with the mower around Parson's Close resulted in all the grass being cut. In between turning it and baling it they delivered an Ayrshire calf, did the milking, greased the baler a few times each day when in use, ordered ten balls of bale twine from Broughton & Wilkes (formerly Hartwells) in Bourton, shut the chickens away at night, milked and despatched the wholesale milk in the morning and did several other routine but equally essential jobs. Only then did they bale Parson's Close whilst trying to remember they had wives and families at home, an ageing mother at Waterloo, whilst trying to keep the whole show on the road before it rained and put everything back once again.

The Meadow mowing was next on the list and it was still only Monday, with bale cart from Parson's close hardly finished and the calf sheds cleaned out at Waterloo, turning hay in the Barn Ground before the rain once more brought everything to an unscheduled stop. But by the weekend they had produced and carted 420 hay bales from the Meadow, finished baling the Barn Ground, mowed the North Clay and started mowing Drapers in a race against unpredictable weather. 16 Cattle were moved from the Cow Bank to North Bank where the grass had re-grown, 1060 bales were lifted from the North Clay and by the following weekend they had cut thistles in Waterloo field, cleaned the sheds out at Lodges Barn and were putting the dairy herd onto Manor Farm bank each morning.

16 beef cattle were moved to Harford Meadow, 19 to Drapers and some walling done in Parson's Close. Harold was cleaning out calf sheds at Waterloo on 17 July when he recorded that David and Ann visited *(but David did not grab a fork and join in this particular activity any more)!* Two Aberdeen Angus cattle went to Gloucester market; ploughing Roundhill Road Ground and on 16 August the windmill blew down after 34 years, apparently due to a 'flaw in the spindle'. Harold later visited the Water Board in Cirencester to discuss the feasibility of installing mains water on Lodges.

In August Combining of barley and wheat was underway again amidst all the other daily routines. The inevitable repairs and welding jobs cropped-up as machinery was driven beyond its normal limits for 5% of the time, only to remain idle for the rest of the year. The rain then stopped everything and after resuming once more a quick brown fox exited the wheat and the harvest was eventually completed on 8 September. The machines were cleaned and put back into hibernation on blocks; corn dried and ricks of straw bales covered with tin and sleepers. A few days later 16 acres of 'Capelle' seed wheat was planted to start the whole cycle all over again. Apple picking started on 2 October; my brother Nigel helped plough the Ewe Pen Ground; the dairy yard was extended with rubble and concrete to try and defeat the regular quagmire the dairy herd created as they left the milking parlour each day; 'Maris Piper' potatoes were lifted, sorted and stored; wheat samples sent off and a total of 324 bags of wheat sold to CAT and newly sown wheat had not germinated because the weather was now too dry! They repaired the old bull shed at the Mill for calves and on 28 November the Heythrop Hunt met at Harford Bridge Meadow, leaving up the hollow towards Harford Hill Farm. Enquiries were made and forms filled out for tapping into the water supply at Harford Bridge and Alan Bayliss and Stan Lane submitted estimates for the cost of digging a trench for water installation to Lodges. On 5 December the 'Beagles' met at Harford Bridge and then crossed Lodges despite being asked not to!

At the end of this year's diary, my 17 year old sister Susan waxed poetic by penning the following inside the rear cover and I am pleased to include it here:

One long street without a name
The village of Naunton owns.
One greengrocer, one Post Office,
And one public telephone.

The River Windrush along its path
Flows with elegance each day,
Until whereupon the clouds burst their seams,
then to the road, the river comes to play.

It enters the houses, in fact any place it can get,
without anyone's consent.
as days pass by, sometimes even weeks,
and you still can't see where it went

The sound of the hunt is often heard,
And the folk come out to watch,
Cursing and swearing at Wallace and his men,
For chasing the poor sweet fox.

Through the kale they pass of Waterloo Farm,
with varying amounts of success,
As from the crop come three fox or more,
Moving with the speed of a small express.

But the Master's temper was soon to rise,
As the field all realise with much surprise,
the foxes had won the day,
And were safely home, no longer prey.
The moral of this little verse;
Harold Hanks forgot to stop the earths.

1971

The top, or 'Lodges' part of the farm is still without water in the New Year and a lot of manual digging was done to locate the pipe under the footpath to install an inspection cover and stop-cock. Ploughing and all the other jobs continued alongside a Postal strike. By March they were buying more hay to feed the cattle. Also at this time they heard from the Ministry of Agriculture Fisheries and Food at Elmbridge Court, Gloucester, that the estimate submitted, Mr S Lane had been accepted for the purpose of a 40% grant for the water installation. Mr Lane started work at Harford Bridge in March, digging a trench up Stan Clifford's field towards the water main. He finished a week later and a cheque for £21 was sent to the Water Board to connect Lodges to mains water. When they started crop spraying in March it was apparent that the new water supply, especially at the Nissen hut, was of immense value.

In April a scrap metal dealer arrived to cut up the two old pick-up trucks. They rented Geoffrey Hanks' bank for summer grazing for £16 (the one which once had his TV aerial at the top); 'stone-cart' on 'Bowsen' Ground before planting barley; more cattle treated for warble fly; the 'MAFF' inspection of the dairy and parlour took place; hay making started in June, mowing Parsons Close and continued as planned. Harvesting with the Ransomes combine harvester started on 18 August and was finished by 17 September and Mr Wyatt's (Temple Guiting) two tractors commenced the ploughing. The Capelle wheat was sown as usual; more cattle taken to the Mill for fattening up and four fat cattle sent to market; The Cotswold Hunt and the Beagles crossed the farm; all equipment was cleaned and put away for the winter. On 10 November the Heythrop met at Harford Meadow, found a fox in Waddingham's Wood at Roundhill Farm, led them all a merry dance to Westfield and back to Waddingham's Wood and escaped.

All the other routines from ear-tagging to milking the cows continued like any other day, week or month and another year ended.

1972

The Cotswold Hounds ran a fox to ground in a drain on the top road (above the sewage treatment plant): Comeleys delivered 12 tons of 20-10-10 fertilizer; the MEB re-wired the 'Flour House'; hedging was done in the Mill Field against the road. On 5 February the Heythrop hounds met at Broadwell, ran through Lodges Farm and knocked some gaps in the walls. The same day the Cotswold hounds met at the Fox Hill Inn, with the fox pursued down through Lodges Farm, creating more gaps in the walls and on 7 February – Cotswold Hunt sent their man to repair some gaps in the walls! On 2 March the Heythrop Hounds met at Cold Aston and the same day Harold noted that David and Ann had there first child, Mark Edward Hanks, in Cheltenham.

By 8 March they had to buy 1½ tons of hay from Geoff Hanks', collecting it from Brockhill, New Buildings. On 25 March went to Bristol Street Motors, Winchcombe Street, Cheltenham to buy a second-hand Ford Cortina 1600 Estate and part-exchanged the Morris Oxford. Taxing it 'Private and Goods', at £25 for 12 months. This time they planted 'Vada' seed barley from WMFA on 16 acres of Roundhill Road Ground with Fisons 20-10-10. On 26 April Harold went to Andoversford Point-to-Point races; the vet did Brucellosis tests on 49 cattle (tested clear); collected three five-gallon drums of Agroxone spray from WMFA and Lucy & Nephew delivered three more tons of 20-10-10 fertilizer. Successfully 'stuck' a blown cow; 26 cattle broke out of a field and were eventually recovered – 14 at Kirkham Farm and 12 at Rockliffe, Eyford.

More maintenance was carried out on machinery preparatory to haymaking which started on 16 June; borrowed Albert's elevator and sent the engine to Broughton & Wilkes for servicing and then filled just about every available space with bales before building a hayrick in the corner of Parsons Close and another one in Drapers, covering them with plastic sheeting, with another layer of bales on top. The dairy was cleaned and painted; bush, thistle, thorn and nettle-cutting around the farm; ploughing and preparing the combine for harvesting which commenced 28 August on the new 'Vada' barley, until a breakdown necessitated welding an old part back on from six years previously! In between breakages, rain and other tasks, the barley and 'Capelle' winter wheat harvest continued and in one field a fox stayed in the wheat until the last few yards were cut behind its brush! The straw was baled and ricked on Roundhill Road Ground; the stable door was probably heard closing as the Ministry machinery safety inspector visited after everything had already been used for the harvest; more land work with plough and Vibratiller and then they caught up with de-horning and warbling cattle and cleaning out sheds before the equipment was stored away in the bale-sealed Nissen hut for the winter.

Drilling of 'Capelle' wheat and harrowing continued; more ballast was put in rear tyres of Fordson Super Major; 346 sacks of wheat collected by Comeleys and 250 sacks returned to Aldsworth Depot. Eight-cwt of 'Malta' seed barley and 1½ tons of 8-20-20 fertiliser delivered by WMFA; Captain Ronnie Wallace 'phoned to confirm the Heythrop Hunt meeting in Harford Meadow on 18 November; more cattle moved and more sent to market; Harold & Sheila went to watch the wrestling at Cheltenham Town Hall and so another year ended.

1973

Four calves were moved from Waterloo to the Mill buildings where a 'drinking bowl' had now been fixed in the calf shed (old dog kennel). On 6 January the Heythrop met at Harford Bridge, found a fox up a tree, running it to ground under buildings at Aylworth. They pursued another from the same tree into 'Cotswold country'. Five days later the fox was seen back in his same tree in the 'pig paddock' on Lodges, this time having 'beaten Wallace and his men', Harold showing a kind of grudging respect for their quarry on this occasion! On 11 January PC Geoffrey Sindrey from Guiting Police Station called to say someone local had complained about mud on the top road and it was duly cleaned. The Heythrop met at Naunton on 24 February and found a fox in Longford Brake but it too escaped. They have now started the last hay rick at Drapers Ground, moving a load to the Mill loft and it is too wet for any work on the land, having tried to start cultivating the North Oat Ground three times. Ploughing, disking and harrowing re-started and a weather measuring device on a parachute from Bracknell in Berkshire landed in a field, being sent back to them when a 'returns' box arrived.

Harold saw some fox cubs at Bowsen Ground and took some photographs; more ploughing and bagging of barley from the bins to go to Waterloo. John Tippett valued all live and dead stock; 14 calves moved from Mill to Longford Meadow; crop spraying with the Super Major and yard cleaning with the Ferguson tractor and loader and patching the old 'Flour House' roof at Waterloo. On 14 June haymaking commenced and Chris' Curtis was paid £5 for ploughing the South Clay with Aylworth's tractor and plough. On 2 July Concorde flew over Naunton and Janet and Harold had a good view of it. Combining started on 10 August before they finished haymaking and the two overlapped for a week with the usual stress-breakages on both machines. On 25 August Joy Muller was married; the combining of winter wheat continued and most of the wheat straw was baled, the rest burned and Albert Williams' elevator returned. On 4 September the Mill Buildings and Orchard, which had been part of Waterloo since 1945 were apparently sold to a Mr Jackson from London for £17,000. A Friesian cow died after becoming 'blown' and was collected by Cheltenham abattoir and an Atcost building representative came to Waterloo to discuss supplying a new building to allow for the possible expansion of the herd and replace the older buildings that were lost due to the sale. On 25 October a hot air balloon landed nearby after a 6 hour flight from Bristol; more 'Malta' barley was planted. On 17 November the Heythrop met at Harford Meadow, found three foxes in Roundhill Hollow, hunted over Lodges and Captain Ronnie Wallace was thrown from his horse, bringing his bruising year to an end.

1974

In early January gales tore the roofs off the Dutch barn and the Nissen hut. At 11am on 16 January David and Ann had a daughter, Emma Kate Hanks, in Cheltenham. On 4 March it was necessary to purchase $4\frac{1}{2}$ tons of hay from Geoff Hanks at Brockhill New Buildings. They bought a second-hand Lister Elevator from WMFA and a second-hand Nuffield Tractor from Burgess (formerly Broughton & Wilkes); worked the fields and started drilling 'Julia' seed barley on 3 April; Nigel (16yrs) was planting grass seed on North Oat Ground before harrowing and rolling it all and they installed a new (polythene) pipe from the mains to the Pig Paddock trough. On 27 April the 'Golden Horse Shoe' rode over Lodges! Burlinghams sent a man to estimate a new galvanised tin roof on the Dutch barn; sprayed undersown-barley in several fields; pulled bushes out of ground with the tractor to tidy up the Hollow and on 12 June Stan Clifford sold Lower Harford Farm and 69 acres for £126,000.

Haymaking started on 18 June and on 23 June to cricket at Moreton; Glos v. Sussex with Pat and Paul (Sussex won); haymaking continued and they were notified that a partial grant had been approved towards the cost of the proposed new Atcost building at Waterloo. Sharpe & Fisher delivered new timber and corrugated sheeting to repair the Dutch Barn; haymaking was now done alongside fixing the new roof, in between all the other work. Harvesting started on 6 August on the Bowsen Ground spring barley, continuing through to 27 August after which the baler broke down and was taken to Burgess's for repair. 1000 sacks in total were received from Aldsworth Depot; more fencing and walling done to prevent stock escaping from fields whenever they could and on 7 September went to the Moreton Agricultural Show.

Ploughing the Bowsen Ground barley stubble; baling straw at North Oat Ground; drilling and harrowing grass seed in Ewe Pen Ground; combining barley in Drapers Ground; moved 22 steers from Parsons Close to Cow Bank; hydraulics on Fordson Super Major failed and tractor taken to Bourton; finished combining South Clay and baled Drapers. Wheat samples taken by Lucy & Nephew; moisture content was 22% and they offered £53 per ton after it was dried, as rain stopped the harvesting.

In October Stan Lane levelled the newly approved building site in the Mill Field at Waterloo, preparatory to the footings going in. He dug the post holes and Atcost commenced to erect their new building with a crane hired from Gloucester. At the same time all harvesting machinery was cleaned and jacked up for the winter; One ton of Fertilizer (8-20-20) one-cwt of slug pellets, a ton of 'Capelle' wheat and 24cwt of 'Malta' seed barley was ordered and planted; another cow was sent to Gloucester market; the vet caught up with the de-horning and castration of stock and the Milk Board man discussed the installation of a vat for bulk-milk storage.

The Heythrop met as usual at Harford Meadow in November, running a fox to ground on the railway line. A November stock dispersal list (non dairy) indicated 19 cattle on Cow Bank; 17 on Parsons Close; eight on North Bank; 13 on North Clay; ten on Holly Bank and four at the Mill barn. A fox was found in the piggery next to the Dutch barn and chased out and all the many routines continued. Harold fell off the trailer whilst feeding the stock and probably cracked some ribs on 27 December, being unable to resume until 3 January *(when there was no one to help him he was obliged to ignore the luxury of 'Health and Safety at Work' when forced to distribute bales of hay across fields to the dairy herd on his own before crossing the draw-bar and back onto a moving tractor, it being small wonder that my mother worried about him so much when he was at work)* and so ended another bruising year on the farm!

1975

He was back on the open tractor in January ploughing Drapers Ground; 'hitching cattle on kale on Bridal [sic] road' *(had we known of this lovely little 'grammatical' at the time this track-way could have been renamed the 'wedding route' and I'm sure enough of my own mistakes will be found between these covers).* 14 calves moved from Waterloo to Lodges Barn; two Simmental cattle from Parsons Close to Waterloo; one for fattening and one for 'AI'. Cotswold Hounds met at Naunton Downs; North Cotswold at Guiting Power and with both packs in full pursuit they got mixed up in Parsons Close, perhaps confirming the craftiness of the foxes after all! The vet 'TT' tested all 149 cattle, with a clear result; Milking parlour inspected by Alfa Laval engineer and estimate obtained for new piping, bulk tank, milking machines, and all given the go-ahead, thus ending the use of ten-gallon milk churns. Bill Davis wired the new Atcost building at Waterloo; land-work continued when weather permitted; The 'Maris Huntsman' wheat planted in the South Clay last autumn was very poor and now has to be re-planted in March! 'Julia' barley planted on 13 acres of Ewe Pen Ground; bulk milk collected by tanker for the first time on the 1st of April; cleaning out more sheds, four steers sold at Gloucester market at £163 each.

On 9 June they were mowing first-year seeds on North Oat Ground; turning and baling until the Fordson Super Major broke down and was collected by Burgess; baling with the Nuffield, and yes, the baler broke down again and was taken to Burgess! Resumed haymaking later amidst other welding jobs on the equipment and on 8 July the drought ended as the clutch failed on the overworked Nuffield! The combine was then prepared for harvesting with some new blades and one more welding job and on 24 July two journeys around the South Oat Ground winter barley went well. Nigel ceased his part-time work at Waterloo to work at Huntsmans Quarries on 28 July; Bill Davis re-wired Waterloo House; Harold and Sheila went to Cheltenham Cricket Festival. Combining and straw baling continued on the footpath; the ploughing was started and six acres of Rye corn planted for cattle feed the following spring. Norman Hughes delivered four loads of rubble to the new Atcost building and Alan Bayliss levelled it before it was covered with 3½ loads of ready mixed concrete and the sides built up with concrete blocks.

On 22 November the Heythrop met at Harford Bridge Meadow; the usual tidying away of farm equipment took place; milking of cows twice every day; stock feeding and movement of food and animals, many of which were about to winter in the new Atcost building at Waterloo, as a host of other jobs ended one more busy year.

1976

Five beef cattle left for Gloucester market; as others remained in their new shelter at Waterloo as opposed to being rotated around the several old farm barns or fed in the open fields. Their more comfortable lifestyle was however on borrowed time because things was about to change forever.

On 20 February, with heavy heart, Harold wrote in his diary, 'my dear Mother died', thus drawing to a close the final farming generation of his many forebears; the last of the folk who had helped to set agricultural standards around here over several centuries. Despite the hard lessons they had been forced to learn, and the setbacks they had suffered earlier on in their lives, his parents had still somehow managed to realise their farming dream, albeit back here in the Cotswolds and not in Canada. Harold would now have to convince himself that he was as resilient as they had been because his plan to work on until he was able to draw his pension at the age of 65 was about to be curtailed as the democratic processes of a family run Limited Company were set in motion.

The cultivation of the land, caring for the animals and maintenance of the machinery all continued, no doubt amidst much reflection on the past and no little anticipation about what the future now held for the two brothers, Harold, (59yrs) and John (52yrs).

The Heythrop met at Harford Bridge Meadow on 17 March and they were buying barley straw from Geoff Hanks; planting Julia seed barley in South Clay; cleaning out sheds and of course milking the dairy herd each morning and evening. They dug the floor up in Lodges barn to repair a leak in the old pipe; took the Ferguson tractor, steerage hoe and muck-fork to Stow Fair where it sold for £125; sent two fat cattle to Gloucester and arranged for Robin Hughes from Haselton to spray Gramoxone on six acres of old rye before planting it with kale. They replaced the fence behind Dale House and had to throw 159 gallons of milk away due to a problem with the dairy cooler. On 8 June they started mowing the hay grass as the weather got steadily hotter, reaching 91 degrees in the shade as they sweated at bale-cart. They finished haymaking on 24 July, essential maintenance work was carried out on the tractors and the harvesting commenced with Mike Wood combining winter wheat in the Bowsen Ground and Brian Cullimore baling the straw behind him.

During a year of uncertainty they persevered doggedly with all they knew. Lucy & Nephew delivered two tons of fertilizer, ten-cwt of rye seed corn, some stubble turnips and collected a load of wheat. The two brothers continued to milk the dairy herd and supply the village with milk and eggs. Another new hanging post and gate were installed; several fields were ploughed, cultivated, harrowed and rolled; wheat stubble was burned and 34 cattle were moved from the Oat Ground to Waterloo so that the vet could catch up with de-horning, castration and removal of spare teats. On 2 October my sister Janet married Brian Cullimore at St. Andrew's Church at Naunton; three more fat cattle went to Gloucester market; the cattle crush was moved to Waterloo for the vet to take blood samples; straw bales were transferred from a rick into the new Atcost building; spring wheat was planted in Bowsen Ground and $2\frac{1}{2}$ cwt of fertilizer per acre was added with the 'spinner'. On 27 November the Heythrop Hounds met at Harford Meadow but they found no foxes nearby. The vet delivered a calf by Caesarean section and a fat steer was sent to Kingham market with James Transport, as the penultimate year drew to a close.

1977

The first calf was still-born; two fat cattle and a barren cow went to Gloucester market; the barley corn bale-rick was opened and the Cotswold hounds ran through Waterloo. Roundhill Road Ground was ploughed and 'Aramir' seed barley sown and harrowed; Mr and Mrs Griffiths (Accountants) called regarding the farm accounts; the dairy wall was repaired at Waterloo after it got in the way of Ivor James' lorry; more hay was bought from Geoff Hanks and more straw from Albert Williams.

On 5 April Mr Gannicott and Mr Griffiths (Solicitor and Accountant) attended a meeting of the five siblings regarding the future of the company (H.L. Hanks Ltd) and farm work continued in the afternoon for Harold and John. Aylworth's cultivator was taken back and Waterloo's hay making side-rake collected. Spraying of the wheat, rolling the barley and top-dressing the fields carried on alongside cleaning out sheds, warbling cattle and maintaining equipment; fencing and walling; cutting bushes back and celebrating The Queen's Silver Jubilee on 7 May.

On 17 June mowing was commenced in North Clay, essential maintenance done on the Vicon Lely Hay Turner and haymaking got underway for the last time, even if they did not wish to accept the fact at the time. They rolled the swedes and kale in Ewe Pen Ground; put new fencing up the Swilleys and on 1 June another Company meeting was held at Waterloo before bale-cart resumed. 41 cattle were moved from the Meadow to Waterloo; on 9 August new parts were fitted to the baler and on 10 August Bloss Tippett & Taylor personnel toured Waterloo Farm regarding the proposed sale of same. On 19 August the first prospective purchasers were arriving to view the farm and on 20 August, Burgess delivered a safety cab for the Nuffield tractor, as one was now required by Health & Safety Regulations, another exercise almost as pointless as closing the old Mill Stable door this late in the day!

On 29 August they started combining Roundhill Road Ground; Mike Wood combined the Bowsen Ground and some prospective purchasers from Scotland found themselves looking around a working farm. They burnt some wheat straw and continued generally tidying up around the place as Mike Wood was chisel-ploughing several fields. They also carried on milking the dairy herd and delivering the milk throughout the village to the bitter end. On 5 October Waterloo Farm was offered for sale by auction at the New Inn, Bourton-on-the-Water. Only the North Bank, Waterloo Bank, The Washpool and the Up-Street Garden sold that day, the remainder (approx 225 acres) was withdrawn from sale having failed to reach the reserve price of £190,000, being sold two days later and becoming part of the neighbouring Aylworth Farm. The sale of Stock and Equipment took place at Waterloo on 9 November. Although a painful wrench for Harold and John, it was probably a blessing for my father. I doubt if he could have continued working at this pace for the next five years, or until he was 65.

Harold and Sheila were then able to purchase '2 Millview' and remained there for the rest of their lives. They now had time to enjoy their grandchildren. Sheila died in 1996 and Harold in 1998 or I would have proudly included them both in Naunton's Millennium project.

Waterloo Farm - The End Game

The sale of 'Waterloo Farm' not only represented the end of the line for one long-term farming family; it also represented the end of an era in relation to the land they and countless others had prepared, sown and cultivated. For two or more millennia men, women and children had carried on the great tradition of tilling this soil in a variety of productive ways. During the first half of the 20th century these particular fields became a 236 acre mixed dairy farm. Whatever it had been called prior to 'Lodges', and finally 'Waterloo Farm', there is little doubt that its acreage was always ploughed and sown with corn and other crops; or grazed by livestock, set out as meadows, orchards and gardens, or simply maintained as pastureland or coppice. Regardless of which foreign power, monastery, abbey church, college, manor, baronial overlord or Cotswold farmers had once tamed, seized, owned or tenanted it, most of it has now been discarded from the traditional practices of old. Some of its last farming custodians saw hockey, tennis and cricket balls touch its surface in their leisure time but I doubt if they ever envisaged most of it would become permanently fallow, with many of its once highly productive fields touched by little more than golf balls.

The following fell under the auctioneer's hammer in the public sale catalogue:

By Direction of H.L. Hanks Limited
Waterloo Farm
Naunton, Cheltenham, Gloucestershire

Highly important and genuine dispersal sale of live and dead farming stock comprising
151 CHOICE ACCREDITED CATTLE
VIZ: 48 Dairy Cows – Mainly Friesian, 9 Served Heifers, 7 Bulling Heifers, 8 Fat/Fattening Cattle, 30 Forward Outlying Stores 1¼-2¼ years old, 49 Other Cattle from young calves to 1¼ years old, and the
Dairy Equipment, Implements, Machinery & Effects
Which will sell by auction on

Wednesday 9th November 1977

Comencing with the Cattle (to be sold under cover) at 11am sharp.

Light Refreshments available   On View day of Sale

Catalogues from- Bloss, Tippett & Taylor, Chartered Surveyors, 11 High Street, Winchcombe, Tel. 602267 & Bourton-on-the-Water, Tel. 20536

Cattle (all dehorned) The Dairy Herd was founded in 1936 and in the last twenty years all replacements have been home bred using A.I. All females over 5 months of age have been vaccinated with S.19 and there has been no reaction or abortion. The Friesian cows are in calf to a Friesian bull, Friesian heifers to polled Hereford, Simmental to Simmental and Ayshires to Charolais. The nine served heifers are a particularly fine selection of cattle and there are 7 healthy bulling heifers. Of the 8 strong cattle some are in forward condition suitable for the butcher and the remainder capable of early finishing. The 30 outlying Stores are fresh from this healthy hill farm and the young stock, being well bred, are worthy of attention. The older cattle in this group are also outlyers.

The catalogue gives individual stock details which are condensed here as: 43 dairy cows (40 Friesians & 3 Ayrshire); 5 Beef Cows (Simmental, Ayrshire & Hereford); 11 Dairy Followers (Friesian & Simmental Served Heifers); 5 Bulling Heifers; 7 Butchers/Fattening Cattle; 78 Store & Other Cattle (Hereford, Ayrshire, Simmental, Charolais heifers, steers and calves).

Dairy Equipment
Lister 1½ H.P. Petrol Engine	£10
Belt Driven Vacuum Pump	£2
Brook Motors Single Phase 1 H.P. Electric Motor & Vacuum Pump	£32
Alfa Laval Pipeline Milking System	£115
Cold Cabinet about 6' x 4' x 6'	£5

Farming Tools & Sundries
12 4"x4" sawn larch fencing stakes	£11
Approx 100 hollow concrete blocks	£26
Set of Platform Scales	£2
Bamford Mill	£5
Metal Sack Truck on Pneumatics	£19
Galvanised Wheelbarrow on Pneumatic Tyre	£5
Brenton Sawbench	£24
250 Gallon Diesel Tank	£11
250 Gallon Water Tank	£3
Circular Galvanised Water Tank and tap	£0.50
2 Cast Iron Water Troughs	£3
Quantity Big 6 Corrugated Asbestos Sheeting	£0.50
Quantity Everclad solid & Ventilated Sheeting	£10
32 & 16 Round Extending Wooden Ladders with Aluminium Rungs	£31 & £9
2 Ransomes 3F Mounted Ploughs	£9 & £44
Set 9' Trailed Tandem Disc Harrows	£17
Single Furrow Potato Plough	£21
2 Horse Hoes	£4

Double Chain Harrows, approx 14' wide	£25
Gascoignes Pig Weighing Scales (Imperial)	£30
Simplex Tubular & Galvanised Cattle Crush	£55
Two 2 Wheeled Flat Bed Trailers on Pneumatics	£11 £ £16
International F.Y.M. Spreader & old muck spreader	£30
9' Mounted Vibrotiller with Pneumatic Land Wheels	£46
Vicon Mark 2 Mounted Fertiliser Spinner	£50
R.Hunt & Co B.M.O. Corn Crushing Mill & 3-phase Electric Motor	£150
Massey-Harris 728 15 Coulter Combine Drill	£3
Denning Chard 12 Coulter Combine Drill	£3
Set of Seed Harrows	£5
Single Cambridge Roll	£42
Mounted Sprayer with 15' Boom	£1
Bamford's Mounted PTO Mower with 5' Cutter Bar	£50
Vicon Acrobat Side Rake	£67
Massey Ferguson 15-8 Pick-up Bailer PTO Drive	£280
Perry Bale Collector	£20
Lister G.P. Elevator with Villiers Petrol Engine	£150
Ransomes 5' Cut Trailed Bagger Combine PTO Drive	£15
1969 Nuffield 4/65 Diesel Tractor, Reg. No. RDG222G with Lights, Hydraulics, PTO Drive, Cab fitted, Roll-bar on order – 7,100 hours	£700
1961 Fordson Super Major Diesel Tractor, Reg. No. 7879AD, PTO Drive, Hydraulics, Pulley Wheel and Roll Bar Fitted	£475
Poultry Houses	£2
Oak Table 4'6" x 3'6 & 5 Oak Dining Chairs	£30
2 bar Electric Fire	£3
2 Old Dressers & 1 Cupboard	£2.25

Livestock: £27,795.   Implements, Machinery Etc: £2,813.75.   Total: £30,608.75

Waterloo Farm
For Sale by Auction in 4 lots
At The Old New Inn, Bourton-on-the-Water
on Wednesday 5th October 1977 at 3pm
LOT 1
A valuable Arable and Accredited Stock Farm in the Heythrop Hunt.
Cotswold Farmhouse, Modern Covered Yard, Dairy and Milking Parlour,
Excellent Block of Arable Land
About 236 Acres in all with some frontage to River Windrush
LOT 2
A Valuable block of Accommodation Land, Approximately 9 Acres
LOT 3
Garden and Pasture Orcharding, Approximately 1 Acre
LOT 4
Garden Land, Approximately .103 Acre

Lot 1. **The Farmhouse.** This bears the date stone **1822** and is constructed of Cotswold stone under a stone slate roof. It requires some improvement, although modern services are connected and re-wiring has recently been carried out. The property possesses a pleasant south westerly aspect and is approached over a tar macadam drive and forecourt bounded by a dwarf stone wall.
On the ground floor: Porch entrance, with door leading to **hall** with flag stone floor, telephone point, stairs to first floor and door with stone steps down to **cellar** with electric light.
Sitting Room: 12' x 11' with modern tiled fireplace and window seat.
Living Room: 12' x 10'8" with modern tiled fireplace having built-in cupboards to one side, window seat, flag stone floor, door to
Kitchen: 12' x 11'3" with flag stone floor, oil-fired Rayburn cooker having built-in cupboards to either side, cooker control panel, deep glazed sink (h&c) secondary staircase to first floor having storage cupboard under, door to
Rear Porch/Conservatory: with quarry tiled floor and glazed roof, door to

Cloaks Area: with washbasin (h&c) coat hanging rail and door to
Separate W.C. with low flush symphonic suite.
On the First Floor: Landing with stairs to second floor. **Bedroom 1,** 12'3" x 11'3" with washbasin (h&c). **Bedroom 2,** 12'3" x 10'9" with washbasin (h&c) and built-in cupboard, door to **Bathroom** fitted with panelled bath (h&c) washbasin (h&c) having a mirror and infra red heater over towel rail, door to **Rear Landing** out of which the bathroom is partitioned, with stairs to second floor and airing cupboard enclosing lagged hot water cylinder and immersion heater, built-in storage cupboards.
On the Second Floor: Two Attic Areas approached from the main landing and measuring 20' x 12'6" including stairs and 12'6" x 10' **Additional Attic Area** 12' 4" x 12'4" housing cold water storage tank approached from rear landing.
Outside: Timber and Galvanised Iron Lean-to Garage 21'9" x 8'9" with electric light and water tap, door to small hen house of similar construction. A door leads from the forecourt to a Cotswold stone and stone slated outbuilding affording
Two Stores: approximately 12'9" x 12'9" average and 14'6" x 8'6" average. Also approached from the forecourt is a stone and stone-slated building comprising a 20'3" x 13'3" workshop or store with electric light. Pleasant secluded garden of good size laid mainly to lawns with a number of mature fruit and evergreen trees, various staddle stones.
Greenhouse 10'7" x 7' Good sized vegetable garden.
The Farm Buildings:
At the Homestead: these comprise open fronted **Garage/Implement Store** 21' x 18' in concrete block with an asbestos roof, electric light and 10amp power outlet.
Modern Four-Bay Pre-cast Concrete covered Yard by Atcost 60' x 30' with concrete block walling Everclad cladding and asbestos roof with lean-to on two bays approximately 10' wide, and 2 Halogen lights. This building connects with concrete block and asbestos building incorporating **Dairy** 12' x 13' with electric light, power and water connected. **Door to Six-Abreast Milking Parlour:** 22' x 18' with door from concrete Collecting Yard, electric light and water connected. **Engine House** with switchgear and electric light. **Feed and Mixing Store** 17' x 13' with electric light and door to **Isolation Box** 17' x 13' with electric light and door to field. Off the Collecting Yard there is a **Concrete Block and Galvanised Iron Shed** incorporating **Two Calf Boxes.** Adjacent there is a **Lean-to Shed** of similar construction forming two calf boxes, timber and corrugated iron chicken house, 31'9" x 16'9" with water and electricity connected.
Timber and Asbestos Calf Shed 21'3" x 14' with electric light and water connected.
In OS.109 Four Concrete Block & Asbestos Pigsties with timber, galvanised iron and asbestos **Meal Store** leading off small Cotswold stone walled Yard.
In OS.108pt. Three-Bay Steel Framed Dutch Barn 45' x 18' with 12' lean-to at each end and **Nissen Hut** 54' x 24' with water supply.
In OS.107 Cotswold Stone and Stone Slated Barn about 30' x 21' with a feeding box having a loft over each end, and leading into a cattle yard with **Open Fronted Cattle Shelter, Two Loose Boxes** and water trough.
In OS.90 Two Loose Boxes and stone walled yard with water connected.

The Land

The main block of the land lies to the south of the A436 road and is largely arable being good easy working typical Cotswold limestone brash and having to the southern boundary some sheltered stock valleys. Most of the arable land is at present in long leys affording a purchaser exceptional opportunity for corn entry. Only one enclosure is un-watered, the majority have troughs from the metered supply and the remainder watered by brook. The whole extends to about
236.472 Acres

Lot 1 Waterloo Farm

OS. No	Name	Arable	Permanent Pasture	Houses Buildings Roads & Yards
259	Waterloo Farm			.418 acres
250A	Waterloo Bank pt.		.244 acres	
240	Long Orchard		.768	
241	Mill Field		3.336	
242	Waterloo Field	7.418 acres		
99	The Meadow		5.840	
101	Bowsing Field	17.000	1.135	
102	Drapers Ground	12.000	2.356	
104	North Clay	17.038		
105	South Clay	13.881		
105A	South Clay Bank		4.288	
106	Barn Paddock		1.954	
107	Lodge's Barn			.169
108	Little Dutch Barn Ground	5.298		

109	Barn Ground	18.080		
169	Cow Bank		14.641	
193	Foot Path Field	22.308		
192	Ewe Pen Ground	18.703		
191	Old Buildings			.081
192A	Ewe Pen Bank		3.226	
170	South Oat Ground	17.000	4.539	
190	North Oat Ground	21.794		
172	Parson's Close	19.744		
		188.179	47.625	0.668 Total 236.472 acres

LOT 2

Approx 9 acres of Accommodation Land. Situated at the western end of the village and lying between the A.436 and the village road and having frontages to both, the land comprises a permanent pasture bank and has a separated metered water supply. It forms an ideal opportunity to acquire a small area of land for horses, ponies or livestock and is made up as follows:

OS. No	Name	Area	
OS.324pt	North Bank	6.951 acres	
OS.325	North Bank	2.479 acres	Total 9.430 acres

LOT 3

Approx 1 acre of Garden and Accommodation Land. This is situated in the centre of the village and consists of a garden plot having a frontage of approx 93' to the main village street and running back to the bank of the River Windrush. The area is cultivated in part and planted with roses, a prunus and two horse-chestnut trees, and there is a footbridge leading from it into a small paddock laid to permanent pasture. The purchaser of this Lot will be required to erect and maintain a permanent stock-proof fence down the easterly boundary marked C.D. on the plan. It comprises:

OS.No	Name	Garden	Pasture	Total	
OS.249pt	Washpool	.086		.086 acres	
OS.250Apt	Waterloo Bank pt		.921	.921 acres.	Total: 1.007 acres

LOT 4

Approx .103 acres of Garden Land which measures approx 81' x 55.9" is situated in the centre of the village on the north side of the village street and is approached via a 6' right of way on foot or with wheelbarrows, between points A and B on the plan. It is contained with Cotswold dry stone walls. It has more recently been cultivated but is stocked with apple, plum, pear and spruce trees and has a light but productive soil. The sale netted approximately £139,000 for the five siblings.

Farm Sale Maps – 1977

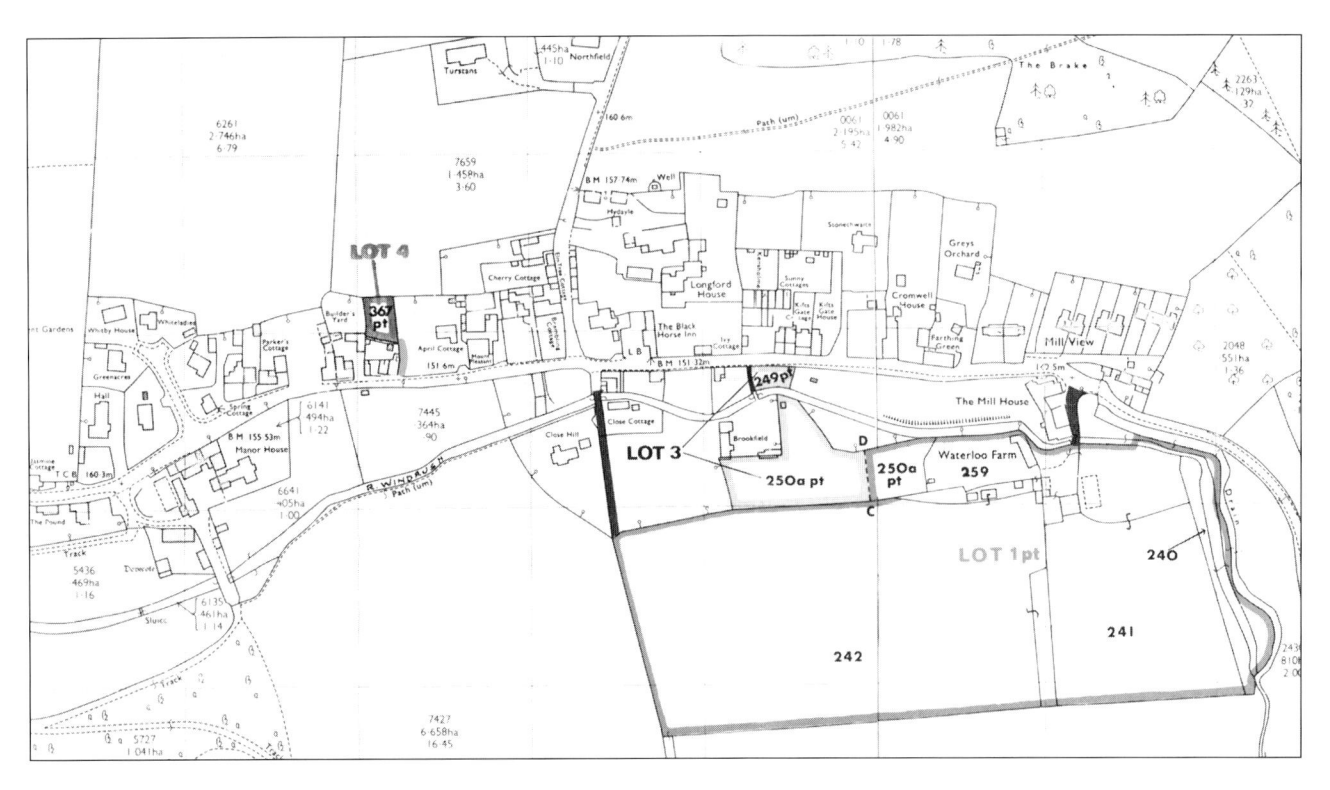

Waterloo Farm north of the main road and related parcels of land in the village.

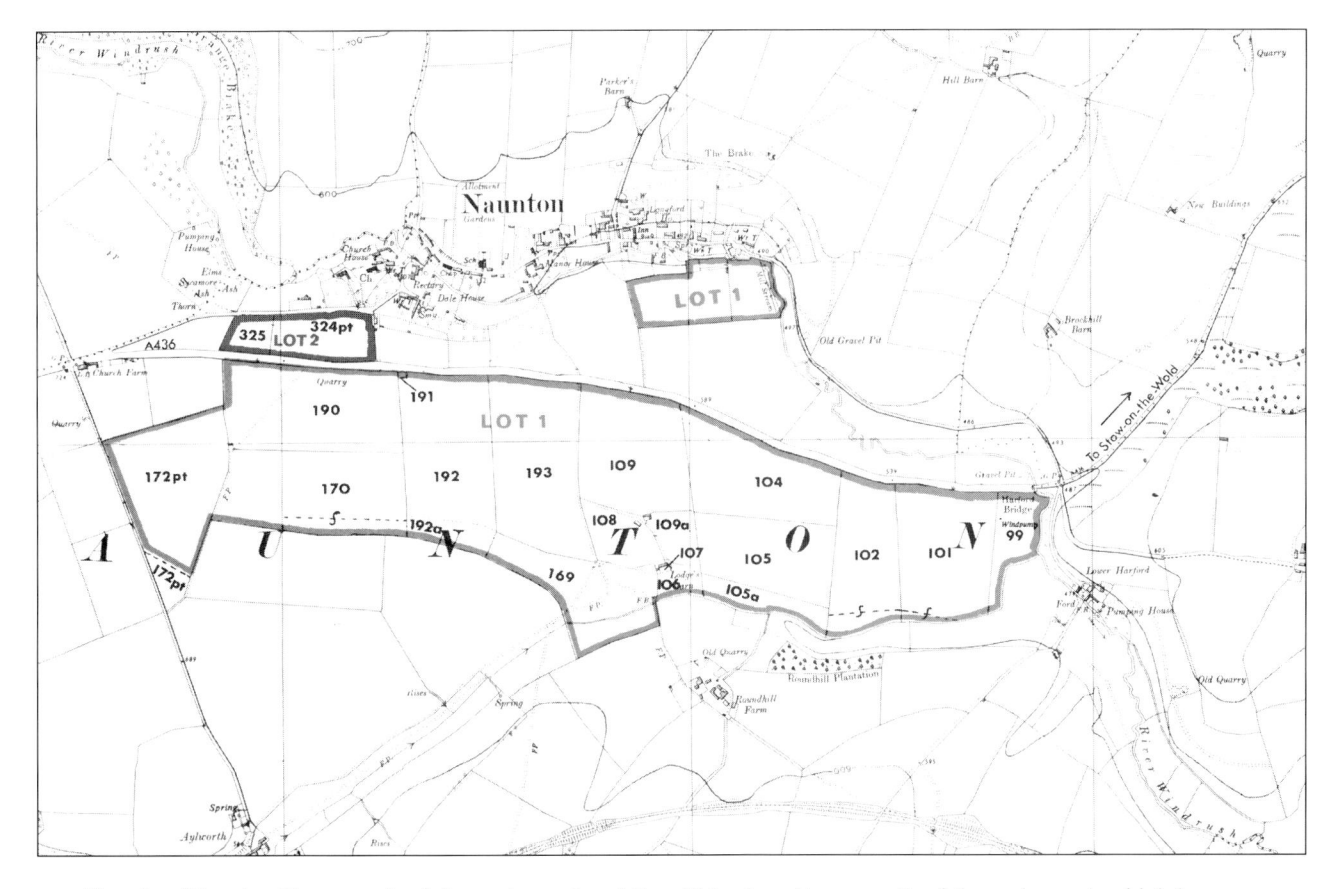

Showing Waterloo Farm north of the main road and the old Lodges Farm, south of the main road, which became incorporated into Waterloo Farm in the 1930s.

The dairy, diary and diarist now stand silent (1980s)

W01 Horace Hanks, Royal Glos Hussars (1910)

W02 Horace and Bert about to leave for Canada (1912)

W03 Horace Hanks, Canadian Army (1917)

W04 Hilda, Eddie and Harold in Canada (1919)

W05 Hilda feeding poultry, Waterloo field (20s)

W06 Hilda and turkeys, next to the old dairy (30s)

120   *Naunton 2000*

W07 Hilda and four children at Waterloo (20s)

W08 Eddie, Harold, John, Doreen and Kathleen at Waterloo Farm (30s)

W09 Waterloo field, (reservoir on horizon) (40s)

W10 Waterloo from the Bee Pen (30s)

W11 Waterloo from the Mill Field (30s)

W12 Horace and gig by the old dairy (40s)

W13 Horace and his horse (40s)

W14 Farm note paper (40s)

W15 Young dairymen; Eddie & Harold (30s)

W16 Young cricketers; Eddie & Harold (30s)

W17 Young farmers; Harold & John (30s)

W18 Waterloo House and Ford Eight car (40s)

W19 Doreen by cart shed on Lodges (40s)

W20 Another load to the Dutch barn (40s)

W21 Horse and trolley on Lodges (30s/40s)

W22 Horse drawn reaper-binder (30s/40s)

W23 Horse drawn reaper-binder (30s/40s)

W24 The work horses (30s/40s)

W25 Collecting sheaves in Barn Ground (40s/50s)

W26 Footpath Ground & Nissen hut (50s)

W27 Harold & Horace harvesting (40s/50s)

W28 Fordson 'N' and side-rake (40s/50s)

W29 Horace with Fordson; side-rake & elevator (50s)

W30 John, the Fordson and a load of bales (50s)

124   *Naunton 2000*

W31 Steam powered threshing on Lodges (30s)

W32 Ernie Bartlett's steam threshing outfit (30s)

W33 Harold & others, threshing on Lodges (50s)

W34 Tractor driven threshing on Lodges (40s)

W35 Harold threshing on Lodges (40s)

W36 Eddie & Hilda lend a hand (40s)

W37 Rick building on Lodges (40s)

W38 Horace and others rick building (40s)

W39 Thatched ricks on Lodges (20s-50s)

W40 John with Fordson (40s)

W41 John, Eddie and Harold (40s)

W42 John & Kathleen deliver milk & eggs (40s)

W43 John on milk-round with Hillman truck (50s)

W44 Waterloo field, before the new dairy (40s/50s)

W45 Harold on Lodges with chicken folders (40s)

W46 Harold, Fordson Major & reaper-binder (50s)

W47 Horace and 'weaners' by Flour House (50s)

W48 Ferguson T20 and side-rake (50s)

W49 Fordson Major and seed drill; Harold & John (50s)

W50 Threshing drum, Dutch barn, Doreen & Harold (50s)

W51 Horace by the cherry tree, Waterloo House (50s)

W52 Unemployed car painters & John, bailing (50s)

W53 Installing sewerage pipes at Waterloo (1961)

W54 Sow and litter, Mill Barn & Cousin Robert (50s)

W55 Heythrop Hunt at Harford Bridge Meadow (50s)

W56 Harold milking in the new dairy (60s)

W57 Harold bringing the herd in for milking (70s)

W58 Dairy herd grazing on Lodges (50s/60s)

W59 Dairy herd in Waterloo Field (50s/60s)

W60 John and Bert Bayliss, extending the dairy (50s)

W61 Distant harvesting in Bowsing Ground (50s)

W62 Doreen at top of 'The Swilleys' (50s)

W63 Eddie Higgins by the Flour House (60s)

W64 Waterloo Dairy (50s)

W65 Mr Wyatt and Harold (70s)

W66 Harford Meadow and remains of windmill (80s)

W67 Waterloo House (1977)

130 *Naunton 2000*

W68 Mill Barn (70s)

W69 Lodges Barn (70s)

By direction of the Trustees of Mr. H. L. Hanks, deceased.

"MILL BUILDINGS", NAUNTON, Gloucestershire

A Small Period
COTSWOLD BARN
and other Buildings
(with planning permission for residential conversion)

together with

Pasture Land, Orcharding and
Small Coppice

IN ALL OVER 3½ ACRES

For Sale by Public Auction
at The Old New Inn, Bourton-on-the-Water, on
THURSDAY, 4th OCTOBER, 1973
at 6 p.m.

Vendors' Solicitor:
D. G. COX-HOWMAN, Esq.
Vine House
BOURTON-ON-THE-WATER
(Tel. 20265 - STD 0451)
And at Stow-on-the-Wold

Auctioneers:
Messrs. TAYLER & FLETCHER
The Square
STOW-ON-THE-WOLD
(Tel. 30383 - STD 0451)
And at Bourton-on-the-Water

A peek at tomorrow's archaeology. Not an ancient coin or token but a Mid twentieth-century bottle top!

Recently unearthed, its crushed lettering reads:
**Tuberculin Tested Milk
Farm Bottled
H.L. HANKS Ltd
Waterloo Farm
NAUNTON**

Growing up in Naunton (1950s – 1965)

My father Harold met my mother Sheila in 1946, whilst she was nursing in Cheltenham Hospital, after he was admitted there for an operation and they married the following year. My first two years (1948/49) were spent in a couple of rooms at Kiftsgate House, which my parents rented from Miss Townsend. Its 17th century walls would have absorbed the shriek of infantile lungs many times before mine touched them, but this is when I believe I must have begun to fall under the spell of this magical place. In 1949 we moved slightly eastward, to the much more modern (1943) dwelling, or 'Number 2 Council House' (only two at this time) the address changing to '2 Millview' after the others were built in the 1950s [85]. Most of my childhood was spent with my father and other family members on Waterloo farm and this was when I absorbed something of the old Cotswold farming scene. On reflection, I believe that living here as a child in the 1950s and 60s, and remaining in touch with the village after leaving in 1965, enabled me to catch the tail-end of a very long tradition of village life and family farming in Naunton.

Machinery has always fascinated me, and Harold and his father Horace were still using an old wooden threshing machine in the 1950s (photos W31-36). It was no longer steam powered but belt-driven by a Fordson tractor. These same machines had been powered by steam engines during my father's and Horace's younger days, and throughout the whole of his father's (William's) life [86]. To me, this grand old machine was the most amazing of them all because its cavernous wooden frame, containing a mass of whirring and gyrating internals that somehow consumed the tall stalks of corn sheaves and thrashed them to pieces, separating the grain from the chaff, which even I understood was a vital commodity for feeding both ourselves and the animals. Although small boys were no longer pushed inside threshing machines, like Dickensian chimney boys, to clamber across the bearers and straw-walkers and clear blockages of chaff from the 'drums', there were still a number of lighter jobs boys could be given to introduce us to the traditional farming life. The age-old social scene of large rural families working together in the fields (See 'Dixton Harvesters' painting on p268) is probably as good as any within which to debate the nature-nurture theory, influencing and developing numerous generations of kids here throughout as many centuries, and to me at least, a little of both appears to have contributed towards our comparatively healthy upbringing.

One amusing incident I recall involving this majestic old threshing machine involved a rat running from the nearby pile of straw, desperately seeking another bolt-hole for its escape. At harvest time farm workers usually wore their trousers with a bit of bale-twine tied around the bottom of each leg to avoid the hazard. On this particular occasion my father had not bothered to tie his trousers and the rat ran straight up the inside of his trouser leg. Harold instinctively grabbed at the rapidly ascending rodent, probably looking pretty shocked in the split second his brain calculated he might be rendered incapable of completing his family of five! Apparently he coolly strangled it, shook it from his trousers and carried on threshing; reflecting on the gnawing pain he would have suffered if his reactions had been that fraction of a second slower.

Harvesting hiccups, more usually in the form of breakdowns and blockages had accompanied the use of these lovely old machines since the 19th century, or when my great grandfather (William Bullock Hanks) was using a steam driven threshing machine at Naunton Mill. This is confirmed by a Press report in 1893: *"At Stow-on-the-Wold Petty Sessions, William Bullock Hanks, farmer of Naunton, was summoned for erecting a steam engine within 25 yards of the highway at Naunton on 17 July. PC Hunt stated the facts; Defendant pleaded guilty and said it had been the custom to do so in the same spot at Naunton for many years. The Chairman said that as it was the first case of the kind that had been before the Bench for a long time they would dismiss it on the understanding that the offence was not repeated"* [87].

In the 1950s, the old static threshing machine, now belt driven from a tractor, was finally replaced by an ageing combine harvester and left to decay rather sadly near the Dutch barn in 'Little Dutch Barn Ground', as were several other decrepit pieces of farm equipment. This included a WW2 Hillman utility truck (W43) replacing the pony and trap that previously delivered milk and eggs in the village (W42). But the old threshing machine had some hidden value as it stood there with grass growing around its axles. My father had mentioned that it did not have the usual type of wheel bearings on the drive shafts, but phosphor-bronze bush-bearings. As no one else was interested, aged twelve, I set about dismantling the machine to retrieve the numerous half-circular chunks of bronze. To a youth earning two shilling and sixpence (12½p) a week, only after I reminded my grandfather that last week's milk-bottling money was still owing to me, this was pure treasure trove. My next trip to Cheltenham on Pulham's bus from Harford Bridge saw me laden with a boxful of those weighty objects. I took them to Burke Bros, Scrap Metal Dealers and received the going rate. The proceeds bought me a much needed pair of stylish (non-school) trousers, which thereafter my father referred to as my 'bronze trousers' and perhaps I wore them as my initiation into the modern Bronze Age.

In the 1950s Horace and his two sons were still using their first tractor, a 1942 'Fordson Standard' (W27-W30). Without pneumatic tyres, it had metal spade-lugs protruding from iron wheel rims, giving it excellent traction on wetter ground around the farm, and there was plenty of that! Later there was the magical 'Ferguson T20' tractor, known affectionately as 'the little grey Fergy' (W48). Everyone, especially us boys, enjoyed driving the 'Fergy' and using its hydraulic bucket, which lightened many tasks that were previously done by strong hands holding a pitch-fork, muck-fork or shovel. At one time there were up to three tractors as well as a Massey Ferguson 702 bailer and in 1958 they bought a not so new American made Allis-Chalmers combine-harvester.

The 'baler' and the 'combine' had bolt-on engines that drove their workings but did not propel them, having to be towed behind a tractor. The combine was purchased from a sale at Bemborough Farm (now Cotswold Farm Park) and when it could not be fixed by my father or his brother John, an engineer was called. It now seems to me that there was a connection between the familiarity of the engineer's faces and the serviceability of these hard-worked machines, which, weather permitting, continued almost non-stop at harvest time. I and others spent many hot and dusty days standing on the combine's sack platform, with its roaring engine close by. We hooked sacks under grain chutes, filled them, tied them off and slid them down a well polished slide into the stubble to be manually lifted onto trailers. The noise was deafening and left me with temporarily impaired hearing after a day's work. This and the dust you breathed in must have been the opposite to the glass-sealed air-conditioned cabs of the modern self-propelled combine harvesters, which were never to be part of our farming experience. These older self powered (not self-propelled) machines, though a great leap forward from the pre-mechanised days of scythes, as in the Dixton Harvesters, must also have contributed to the end of the great social scenes that harvesting once gave rise to. This was not only because there were now less people in the fields to interact with but also because you could no longer hear yourself speak as you did the work!

In my youth on Waterloo Farm no tractor ever had the luxury of a cab and all-weather farming meant just that to my father and the rest of us, as we all spent days ploughing, chain-harrowing, disking and rolling fields south of the main road, now part of Naunton Downs Golf Course. But Harold spent most of his working life out on these fields exposed to all weathers. In his early farming days he was walking behind horse drawn implements, before progressing to an early tractor in front of identical implements. The comparative luxury of sitting atop an open tractor, as opposed to walking with cloddy feet behind a team of equally tired horses may have had something to do with Horace never over indulging his sons by including the luxury of a tractor cab. Despite this, I believe Harold usually enjoyed, but more often endured the traditional 1950/60s al-fresco method of working the land, with nothing more than a porous hessian sack across his shoulders and legs in the foulest of weather. I suppose his earlier experience of walking behind horses at least kept him warm, though not exactly dry.

And so throughout almost all their tractor owning years, my grandfather, or 'boss' as he was affectionately known to his sons, seems to have decided a cab was an unaffordable luxury we could manage without. This was despite the fact that by the 1960s such improvements could be seen on some of the neighbouring farms. This observation quickly taught me that you could only subject employees to these kinds of working conditions if they were family, as they were less likely to rock the boat by complaining to the National Farmers Union. I cannot imagine anyone working the land under such stark conditions today, other than when participating in a ploughing contest for old time's sake.

Although I had not lived through the trauma and privations of two World Wars and had little experience of the pre-mechanised farming era myself; traces of it all lingered in the farmscape I found myself wandering through during my childhood. In the 1950s there were two redundant, heavy-duty wooden Cotswold wagons decaying in an old thatch-roofed bowsing on the Barn Ground [88]. These magnificent horse drawn wagons had optional end-ladders to support higher loads of hay or straw. In their day they must have been used to haul just about everything, including goods to and from Notgrove Station, timber from the woods, various crops from the fields or sacks of corn and flour to and from the Mill, Bakery and Brewery. Like many other old implements lying around the farm, they were once pulled by working horses called Blackbird and Colonel, Duke and Blossom, Dolly and Sharper, until about the time I was born. After the first tractor was purchased in the 1940s, the horses continued working alongside them for about ten years, before they were eventually put out to grass, and the wagons parked in this old thatched shed (W19), 'just in case' they were needed again some day. They never were of course and both wagons, together with the roof that collapsed in on them, became just one more heap of farm detritus that was eventually burned.

Other than periodic design improvements to horse drawn vehicles over the centuries, this type of transport can have changed little throughout the two millennia. From the popular two wheeled, pre-historic Celtic chariots to the two wheeled horse drawn buggies, traps, gigs, dog-carts and hansoms, et al, being used here until about 1950, the underlying design principle, remained much the same. from lynchpin to wheel, I feel privileged to have seen the last remnants of it all, as this lengthy period of horse-powered transport and draft animals drew to a silent close around us. Another wonderful little machine I saw working on the 1950s farming cusp included the Lister 'reaper-binder', which until then had also been horse drawn, but by the 1940/50s was towed behind a tractor. This quaint machine had flimsy wooden bar 'sails' that revolved as it moved, folding the wheat and barley down onto lethal mower blades, driven by its forward motion. The machine's ribbed canvas internals swathed and bound the corn into sheaves which were deposited across the field behind it. Farm workers collected the sheaves together, standing them up into 'shocks' or 'stooks' of six or eight sheaves, ready for easier 'pitching' onto a wagon or trailer with a 'pitchfork', after which they were taken to the threshing machine or 'drum'.

It is worth taking another step back here to recall that the horse drawn binder was the first pieces of 18th century farm machinery to replace the reaper with his scythe, during the early stages of the industrial and agricultural revolutions. We do not know if a Roman *'Vallus'*, a kind of early wooden combine harvester, ever worked the fields of old *Niwetone*, tearing corn from the stalks and depositing it into a wooden bin. Assuming it did not, then lines of workers with scythes would have been the only means of garnering grain crops until these early horse-drawn binders arrived, cutting the stalks with mechanically driven blades and binding it into sheaves for easier handling and setting the standard for almost all future farm mechanisation. I believe that one of the oldest and finest depictions of the pre-mechanised Cotswold landscape is the famous c1715 oil painting called 'The Dixton Harvesters' [89]. This beautiful oil painting shows how Cotswold fields were then laid out, capturing the extremely labour intensive harvest scene on a large farm three miles west of Winchcombe, during the busiest and most important period of the agricultural year. Such a scene would have been an annual occurrence on the fields of this Parish, and it takes very little imagination to transpose the oil painting onto Naunton's landscape, which sadly, is unrecorded in this way.

Also in the 1950s it was common to see a selection of different sized ricks of hay and straw around the farm, built and thatched each summer by my grandfather, his sons Harold and John, Eddie Higgins and other casually employed men. When the old stone-built Lodges and Mill barns and smaller bowsings were full, ricks were built. Some ricks were round and some rectangular, vaguely similar you might agree, to the oldest houses, and no doubt just as ancient a feature on the landscape. Twentieth century farming practices and pressures now resulted in less time for thatching. Ricks were increasingly covered with strong plastic sheeting and some netting, invariably exposed to the elements again after the next storm. Hand built ricks of loose hay and straw also disappeared from the farmscape after machine-made bales of hay and straw began to replace them. Bales were more easily raised by 'elevators' for higher and drier storage in rectangular ricks, or under permanently roofed and more accessible 'Dutch' barns, covered with corrugated metal sheets, or in relocated and recycled WW2 'Nissen' huts. In today's larger scale, highly mechanised, intensive agri-businesses, the bales have again been transformed into massively less friendly spherical objects wrapped in polythene, or equally large rectangular ones, weighing so much that only machines can lift them. The bales of old were designed to be man-handled from the field onto a trailer with a pitchfork, and unlike me in my youth; my strong-armed father could raise them to the top of the highest trailer loads in this way.

The end of the traditional bale-cart and rick-building were just a few more indicators of the changes taking place on the farms. Was I perhaps seeing some of the last moments, maybe even the dying embers of the older methods, as agriculture slowly dragged itself into a machine dominated, prefabricated era, now employing bigger machines and fewer hands to do the same, or more work, with greater efficiency! But even this was not the end of the rolling programme of change that was now impacting on the smaller farms as they found themselves heading inexorably towards just one more 'farming crisis'. The combined effect of all this was sounding the death knell for several small farmers who were desperately hanging on, much like the contents of their old store sheds, in the vain hope that they might just be needed again one day.

During my early years in Naunton, I found myself amongst the modern end of an old and fairly large farming clan and even though many of them had the same surname, they seemed a fairly disparate bunch of folk to me. Outside my immediate family, I would describe those who condescended to talk to me as being old-style country farmers, one or two of whom displayed distinct leanings toward the squirearchy. Nevertheless, they had a clear understanding of what farming, hunting, cricket and several other country pursuits were about, but to comment further would be unjust because I simply did not know them well enough. With the exception of Maurice Hanks of Longford (1877–1946), I am not aware of anyone having much interest in recording details of their family history, if indeed they ever knew much about it, or presumably they would have written a little more of it down for us to see today.

From this rather blinkered, 1950s childhood perspective there seemed to me to be other quite natural variations amongst them, ranging from those who worked at the sharp end as farm workers, as my father and his brother did, to those enjoying a somewhat more comfortable existence, which I have hinted at already, employing others to do much of the donkeywork for them. The more fortunate ones inherited farms and fields from their forefathers and had not necessarily experienced great setbacks in their lives by going over the top of deadly trenches in the killing-fields of Europe, as my grandfather did. But even so, Horace never mentioned any of his war experiences during the remainder of his lifetime, not even to his sons, and it appears that it may only be my generation who are now commenting on the absence of his name from the WW1 Veterans Roll of Honour in St. Andrew's Church, due of course to the fact that he was serving in the Canadian and not the British Army.

During the 1950s and 60s several other entirely welcome changes were occurring around us that would lead to improvements in the quality of life and living standards generally. A few of the more basic dwellings, particularly those in 'The Yard' (no direct photographs available) behind the Church, and one or two others in the village were condemned as unfit for human habitation. Several could fairly be described as hovels, before being demolished or converted to meet more modern housing standards. I visited these humbler dwellings with milk and eggs in my youth and even to me they seemed grim. We were living in fairly basic utility-housing ourselves and I imagine it must have been harsh for the occupants, though of course they had no choice at the time, until more Council Houses were built in the 1950s, simply having to make the best of the situation at the time.

These old village cottages may have been built of stone, with tiled roofs, but like the rest of the village they had waited a long time for connection to modern services, such as mains water, electricity and sewerage, which by now was normal in the towns. Our own 1943 Council house was a completely non-insulated, draft ridden place, with a semi-outside toilet, a cess-pit under the lawn and a recently installed electricity supply. Courtesy of what must have been a cash-strapped Council, 'Millview' somehow seemed to resist the kind of improvements that crept in elsewhere and remained a fairly basic, cold, utility type dwelling until well after I left in 1965.

The post WW2 climb back to prosperity was also overshadowed by the Cold War threat of a nuclear holocaust. To a child of the 1950s, the Royal Observer Corp's network of Cotswold underground observation posts and the ongoing programme of Civil Defence that ran alongside it all was boyishly exciting. Occasionally, brick built ovens or 'soup kitchens' were constructed in front of the Village Hall in which food would be prepared in the event of a nuclear attack taking-out the National Grid, which no doubt introduced some of us to barbecuing. I recall the unconvincing reassurances of visiting 'experts' that Naunton was very fortunate, tucked safely away down in the vale and almost immune to a whole variety of harmful external influences, ranging, as we knew only too well, from television signals that could entertain us in the evenings to nuclear pulses that could melt us in seconds. What they never told us of course was that after London, Cheltenham was the second most likely target on the Soviet ICBM hit list, a chillingly cold-war fact that is a matter of public record today.

Thankfully the same Village Hall was a more reassuring and entertaining focal point in other respects, much as it still is today. In June 1953, aged five, I found myself there dressed up in green stockings and a feathered hat as Robin Hood, during Queen Elizabeth's Coronation celebrations, without really understanding the relevance of it all at the time. The hall was also the venue for a weekly Doctor's surgery. This found us queuing there occasionally for the usual childhood inoculations and ailments, and the kindly doctors from Bourton became almost family friends. I remember the hall so well for shows that held us all spellbound, and several of the younger performers from the 1950s are still pounding the boards today, deserving awards for lifelong devotion to amateur entertainment on the village stage. I also fondly remember Village Hall whist-drives where as youngsters we would occasionally find ourselves paired against senior ladies, whose penetrating stares, I thought, enabled them to see through my cards, such was their skill at disposing of us lesser mortals.

But whether it was being soundly whipped at whist, dabbling at cricket in the summertime or skating (in my case, sliding around unshod of ice skates) across a frozen Mill Hayes in wintertime, or simply being enveloped by the farming ethos, the whole thing seems to have had an edifying affect upon more than a few generations of youngsters here. Whatever the ingredients were of the age-old rural mix we were fed copious amounts of during childhood, the end result seems to have served most of us fairly well thereafter. It seems to have provided us with a sense of caring, of communal ownership and of belonging. We respected our elders and all they had painstakingly created and maintained here. We understood, without being told, that it was the adults around us who really were this place and that without them there would be nothing to bind it all together. It was they who contributed the most important ingredients to this community and we were simply the follow-on act in this completely unrehearsed, self-sufficient series of everyday village life.

On my way to and from the village primary school other humdrum things began to stick in my mind. I had to walk past the village's petrol and paraffin pumps and recall the price of petrol being more constant then than ever it was in my adult life as a motorist. Somehow it seemed to remain at one shilling and 10½d a gallon for many years (just under 10p a gallon at today's prices). In 1937 the price at the village pump was one shilling and 4d a gallon, so it had only increased by about 6d (under 3p) in twenty years [90]. These petrol pumps were initially installed to serve Pulham's coach business after WW1, remaining there after the family business moved to Bourton-on-the-Water in 1937. I wonder if 70% of the pump price was government tax then, as today! At the time of writing (Sep 2000) a gallon of petrol (4.5 litres) costs some £3.90 [91] with the prospect of a £4-5 gallon somewhere round the next sharp bend.

On the way to school I also had to pass 'Vine House Yard', where Henry and Terry Muller's business was situated. They ran a builder's yard (where John Stevens Stonemasonry business is now situated), containing a workshop and forge. Terry was a wheel-wright, carpenter and undertaker and did repairs to horse drawn wagons and farm vehicles, using the forge for heating and forming metal. This was a spectacular sight, once the leather hand-bellows had the coke glowing red-hot, accompanied by the skilful hammering and dousing of glowing iron to produce a variety of items from farm gate-hooks to wheel rims. They had a wheel plate in the yard for assembling the metal rims, or 'tyres', that were until recently fitted to wooden wagon and carriage wheels. The workshop was also used for making coffins, though thankfully Terry was generally busier with the other side of his business. Henry was an engineer, trained by Victory Motors in Cheltenham on Ford Model 'T' cars, but was now doing mostly tractor repair work on the local farms. Theirs was the last anvil that I heard ring in Naunton because the Forge in Dale Street had ceased operating by this time.

Although I had seen the aerials in the old village photographs (tall poles with a wire attached) I was not old enough to remember the 'crystal' radios that were apparently connected to them in the 1920s. However, I fondly recall our own valve radio in the 1950s which was eventually replaced by a more modern transistor model, both of which held my undivided attention when programmes like 'Journey into Space' were broadcast; the concept of space travel still being entirely fictional, though not totally beyond belief. The Archers was however entirely believable and Ambridge could so easily have been Naunton!

After the arrival of the first few television sets in the 1950s, it is appropriate to amplify the problems that viewers then encountered. By some fluke or other, the early VHF (405 line) transmissions were occasionally known to lightly touch the aerials [92] down in Naunton, giving the few people owning those small-screen receivers a frustrating, highly variable and extremely snowy picture. The sound side was almost good enough to justify paying for the Radio Licence that everyone still had to have. But the quality of those black and white pictures was diabolical because the Oxford transmissions went straight over the top of Naunton, much as we all hoped the feared nuclear blast might do. Interestingly, when an aircraft flew over, which was a frequent occurrence with the RAF Central Flying School at Little Rissington, the picture would improve fleetingly as some extra signal was deflected down onto the aerials. The only person who successfully resolved this long term dilemma was Geoffrey Hanks, who installed an aerial on a tall mast at the top of the bank against the main road, with a lengthy cable-run down to the Manor.

When UHF (625 line) colour transmissions commenced in 1969, most Nauntonians saw an improvement in their reception. They now received enough 'colour' signal to give them a half-decent black and white picture, with the sort of quality they should have been enjoying throughout the previous 20 years! An insipid colour picture now flickered on a few screens in higher parts of the village. The rub was that people now had to pay the colour T.V. licence fee to get a better monochrome picture! In 1981 the local UHF repeater was installed at the west end of the village, to beam the Icomb transmitter's signal into the valley, enabling all those who were still alive to receive their first acceptable colour pictures. And of course there was no dispensation whatsoever in the licence fee during all those years of sub-standard reception, in which Nauntonians became more familiar with the 'horizontal-holds' than they were with the on/off switch. 1969 was doubly exciting because many people saw man land on the moon, in colour, or at least I smugly did at Gloucester Central Police Station!

Beyond the actual roof over our heads and these other little distractions now appearing below it, I believe that the three generations of people still living around me in the 1950s were witnessing the winding down of a lifestyle with deep historical roots here. The two older generations may have regarded this as being the very foundations of the community. I am again referring to the part they played on the rural scene by upholding its farming inheritance, passed down from generation to generation, throughout some two thousand years. Even at this late stage it was still the village's balanced and, God willing, unfaltering ability to cultivate the land and support its people from its own three thousand plus acres. As we now know, more and more of the fertile fields that permitted this self-reliance have since been abandoned (set-aside) and the market price of local produce, including crops, milk and livestock have slowly rendered their production unprofitable, for the time being at least.

The changes impacting on the old agrarian way of life here have since turned what used to be an almost completely self-sufficient community into one with an ever-increasing reliance upon external supplies. The closure of Mr Morris's chip making enterprise was followed by the arrival of a mobile Fish & Chip van every Tuesday evening in my childhood. Though a welcome treat, it was a harbinger of things to come, as the community began to rely more and more on external sustenance. If the 'chip-van' represented the thin end of the wedge, the blunt end was the subsequent loss of small farms, allotments, orchards and much else, including the bakery, dairy, shops, and Post Office. This is not a derogatory comment, merely an observation based on what seems to have happened to a greater or lesser extent in many rural communities. It seems to have been linked to the post-war improvements in the quality of life coupled with global markets undercutting what was once produced locally. A modest fight-back seems to be emerging through 'farmer's markets,' some held in the towns, but the bell has already tolled for far too many rural traders, farmers and growers.

Sadly, at the time of writing this in 2000, Nauntonians find themselves recently deprived of a Post Office, probably for the first time since 1870 [93] and without shops for the first time in more centuries than I would care to guess at. Nauntonians are now forced to buy their provisions where they can, perhaps as a result of having shopped where they liked, even if they did not fully appreciate the long term consequences of what it might lead to.

Of course those with a car, so long as they are able to drive it, will overcome most of the resultant difficulties in obtaining provisions, many of which could once be found literally on the doorstep. Those who have no car, or lose their mobility, will become more dependent on the declining public transport, or on help from others for their shopping and, reassuringly, this kind of mutual assistance is more than evident today, showing that such qualities and values will always live on. The lure of the rural idyll has begun to present some people with difficulties, of a kind that were not necessarily envisaged when they moved to Naunton. As fossil fuels decline, or as health deteriorates, some people may be compelled to migrate back towards the towns and cities where the various shops, services and other facilities may still be on the doorstep, and there are small signs of this happening already.

A situation such as this would probably have been unbelievable to villagers just half a century ago and once again, to me at least, it seems that life here over the past 2000 years may never have changed quite as drastically, or as rapidly as it has during the second half of the 20th century. I also accept that

I may be wrong about this because I only have personal experience of one fortieth of the past two thousand years.

As a child I spent most of my time around Waterloo Farm which was then owned by my grandparents, Horace & Hilda. They supplied milk, eggs and other produce (once including honey, butter, poultry and various meats) to the village, cattle to local markets and grain to local mills. Horace's father, W.B. Hanks, had farmed at Lower Harford, Aylworth, The Manor and The Mill.

As children we all ran freely and happily across this vast playground, fit as butcher's dogs and having no great interest in things beyond Naunton, and one or two adjacent villages. As youngsters, details of village or family history were of scant regard and as for the immediate future, well, it just came and it went. Life was at times difficult but at other times it could be idyllic, in a simple and predictable sort of way. This was happening in a period when the Country as a whole was still trying to regain its stature after the Second World War. Naunton, like most other villages lost men in this war, as it had in WW1, and the aftermath of any war sees people pulling together, trying to re-establish and rebuild their lives after hardships and the loss of loved ones. Post-war austerity meant that money was never plentiful and the main priority for most families was simply to get by. Finding enough food, fuel and clothing to sustain them through bitterly cold winters in pre-centrally heated, single-glazed, non-insulated houses was challenge enough for most people. The aftermath of wartime rationing, which persisted until about 1954 could still be felt. There was a great deal of make do and mend and I recall times when the Council 'rent-man' called, only to leave empty handed, because the money just was not there for him in days when a farm-worker's weekly wage of £7-8 a week could only stretch so far. I cherished the first old bicycle I had until I started my first job; it was a ladies model, had no gears and cost my dear mother £1, but I was at least mobile, and extremely grateful for that.

I recall the mains water being connected to the village in 1953, which meant that my mother no longer needed to carry bucketfuls from the standpipe tap outside the Mill opposite [94]. The mains electricity had only recently been connected and the old oil-lamps were still at 2 Millview, being just one more example of the kind of technology that reached right back to the *Iron Age* part of our story. This was followed by the installation of electric street lamps to lighten the total darkness that enveloped the village on nights when the oldest of village lanterns was obscured by cloud. I also recall the ubiquitous 'privies', either in cottage gardens or tacked on to the side of cottages, especially the stone built annex at Waterloo, containing a splendid two-hole *'garderobe'* [95] which my grandparents used, though not necessarily at the same time. Like everywhere else, this archaic facility reached back to medieval times, replaced only when they built a modern toilet against the side of the house and connected it to the mains sewerage in 1961. I once recall peering into the old double-aperture 'long-drop' with my cousin one day, lest you think I had a solo boyhood fixation for such things. It was an 'Izal' (a more modern chemical than lime) scented pit, which as a boy I believed was a bottomless black hole, but which in reality was only 'bottomless' whilst we stood blinking into its inky blackness! Longford House had a five-seat version and I can only imagine such multiple-use may once have been a kind of family gathering, by way of explaining these unusual multi-seated lavatory structures.

Many wives and mothers were still enduring what might be termed post-war domestic drudgery. By the late 1950s at '2 Millview', I saw my own dear mother progress from washing in a steam tub in the 'wash-house' to become the proud owner of a Hotpoint top-loading washing machine. She willingly stood next to this in her kitchen because they were still non-programmable machines; the green van from Bourton being the first importer of any chips into Naunton. She most definitely deserved this bit of modernity, as she struggled to pay for it over the next few years on the 'never-never', and though basic by modern standards, it was essential for the mother of five children. As for a fridge, the nearest these houses ever got to such a luxury then was the concrete 'cold-slab' in the pantry, which was a poor substitute. I cannot recall exactly when the immersion heater was fitted, putting an end to heating the water from a boiler behind the fireplace, and the occasional tin bath on the floor in front of the fire in the winter, but even that particular Council improvement never extended to the fitting of a proper indoor toilet. To use the freezing bathroom during the winter my father hung a poultry hothouse lamp above us to reduce chattering teeth below.

The more modest little brick privies adjacent to most cottages, complete with green painted doors and torn up portions of post-war tabloids, were gradually made redundant after the Council navvies dug their trench along the village street in the summer of 1961, piping everything nicely away to the new plant at the east (down-wind) end of the village. After the road was resurfaced, it was rolled flat by the Council's lovely old Aveling Porter steam-roller, which trundled back and forth along the street for weeks, without ever squashing any of us inquisitive children as far as I recall. The newly redundant privies like the old ovens and pig-stys next to many cottages, did not vanish overnight though, some being utilized, as was so often the case after the war, for another decade or so as garden tool-sheds, which would surely be 'grade-one' listed buildings today, but I do not think any have survived. The new sewerage treatment plant created just one more adventure playground for us boys beyond the village, where I recall its unfenced mechanical delights intrigued us, without any of us causing any problems there. We also marvelled at the prize-winning tomatoes that grew on the slurry heaps, but I could never bring myself to eat the enormous red fruit, the seeds of which I later learned were one of the few to pass intact through the human digestive tract.

But uppermost amongst my early memories are those of so many happy times spent on Waterloo Farm. Amongst them is one that became indelibly imprinted on my infantile mind. It is now completely healed under the tiniest of psychological scars and I will share it here for the benefit of today's children, hoping it might give them a little room for manoeuvre after similar transgressions. On a summer's day in the 1950s my cousin Robert Young, from Stow-on-the-Wold, came down to our grandparents at Waterloo Farm for the day. Although we were well under ten years of age, we believed we were almost employable by the relatively unconcerned farming standards of the time; even though we had never actually been pushed into the threshing machines to clean them out ourselves. In reality our pathetic lack of muscle meant we were near useless when it came to real work, such as humping bales of hay or straw. But we all know who makes work for idle hands! Consequently we were tempted to find our own that fine summer's day and commenced to explore farmyard store sheds for something useful to apply our limited talents to.

Always a favourite place to rummage was the lean-to garage near Waterloo House which backed onto the east wall of the little 'Flour House' [96] where all sorts of farmyard clutter had accumulated over the years, leaving just enough space to park two farm vehicles. Farmers rarely throw anything away and this trait has lived on with me throughout my life, resulting in a town garage becoming full of everything but the car it was intended for.

Amongst the 'might be useful again one day' selection of old horse tack, gate hooks, barbed wire, empty sacks, obsolete tools, rusty nails, screws, bail twine, fence posts, electric fence units, a scythe, a beetle (sledge hammer) and the odd bill hook were numerous part-used tins of substances ranging from relatively safe 'Copydex' to less than safe Creosote, paints, fuel and worse. From amongst this noxious selection Robert and I chose we knew would be useful again, that very day. And in addition to that part-used tin of paint we even found some old paint brushes nearby.

Our granddad Horace kept his little black 'Ford 8' car (they were all black then) in this lean-to garage. Robert and I easily convinced ourselves that if we were to paint his car a different colour, it would not only give him a very pleasant surprise but he would also be exceedingly pleased with us into the bargain. I certainly do not recall that we intended to charge him for the work, or set a new standard for the Ford Motor Company, or do anything else that might incur displeasure.

Our expertise at prizing lids off old tins meant that we were soon dipping our brushes into a very pleasant shade of green gloss-paint. We set about the job with some enthusiasm, painting not only the bodywork but also the windows, the tyres and the chrome. I imagine that given time we would have painted the interior! You know how it is when a good DIY job is almost completed, just before you stand back and admire your handiwork! Well we were cruelly deprived of that moment when our Auntie Doreen came round the corner from Waterloo House and spotted the devil's own handiwork. I believe that momentarily we mistook her shocked stare for one of admiration, as we awaited some never to be heard words of praise. To our complete surprise some much stronger words fell from her lips, delivered in anything but an appreciative tone. Although neither of us seemed to fully comprehend their meaning at the time, we did very soon after.

Robert and I were already in a mess simply from doing this creative painting without protective clothing, and now, curiously enough we found ourselves in an even greater mess as a result of its discovery! Perhaps fear is a good teacher because we quickly learned that our survival was not exactly at the top of granddad's priority list that fine day, and interpreted various adult throw-away comments such as, 'he'll kill you if he sees it', quite literally.

Nevertheless, our auntie Doreen had a wide streak of humanity, especially for animals and lesser creatures like us, and I believe this is what ensured our survival. In order that we might continue living, she decided it was prudent to place some distance between us boys and our ungrateful 'grampy'. It was alright for Robert because he was whisked off to the safety of Stow. But I lived just over the road at Millview, and knowing granddad kept what we used to refer to as his 'elephant gun' in Waterloo house, I felt it was much too dangerous to risk being seen by him for some time to come. The difficulty was, knowing just how long I needed to evade him. I can confirm that to a child, fear does indeed breed fear, and as far as I recall no one sought to reduce the level of it for me.

Much effort was apparently expended by several adults during the remainder of the day trying to restore the car to its original condition and Eddie Higgins recently told me that valuable harvesting time was lost as a result. Being fairly adept at making myself scarce around the parish when necessary, some days passed before 'grampy' actually caught sight of me, and even then that was all he caught, as I heard his soft spoken words grow fainter behind me.

Whether he mellowed with time I do not know, but I can still point to the spot I found myself rooted to some weeks later, as he came round the corner from Waterloo House, from where I stared up at him and he back at me for several seconds. As we looked into the whites of each others eyes, I chokingly tried to say, as innocently as possible, 'hello grampy'.

I felt particularly lucky because even my impish brain grasped the fact he did not have a gun in his hands. I do not recall him being too severe with me over this episode and life carried on much as before. I rarely exercised such initiative again though, being content to receive instructions and occasionally small reward in the form of a few pennies for jobs I was actually asked to do. Anyway, it was Robert's idea in the first place!

We were less likely to get into this kind of mischief when out in the fields and another particularly fond memory I have relates to nocturnal expeditions when Doreen took us kids out 'lamping'. This involved the use of an old spot-light from a car connected to a six-volt electric-fence battery carried in a backpack. On a moonlit, frosty or snow covered night we would set off across the farm and locate foxes eyes in the powerful beam. They were so mesmerised that we could get really close before they detected a human presence and darted off before we pursued them again. It was a kind of hunting without any gathering and it is was great fun.

We did other things under the guidance of Auntie Doreen including Cray-fishing at night when wire-mesh basket traps would be set in the Windrush between Waterloo and Harford Bridge during the early evening. Later the same night we harvested them, ending up with bucketfuls of crayfish. They resembled a small lobster and my grandmother had recipes which involved boiling them alive, removing the meat and serving it with a dollop of butter and some pepper, though I do not recall ever eating such delicacies myself.

The river must always have been a magical attraction for children in this vale and we had the added feature of mechanical flood-gates or sluices in at least two locations. The one by the Mill was out of sight and the frustration of fishing for trout with a bent pin attached to button-thread was occasionally alleviated by lowering the floodgate. Paul Staite and I knew from experience that after the river-bed below the gates drained to a trickle we had ten minutes or so to gather up floundering trout before the water came over the top and we had to raise the gate again. Things like bully-heads were ignored, being thought of as small-fry by young hunter-gatherers. The dovecote also had a floodgate but the risk of being caught by Geoffrey Hanks from the Manor was usually sufficient deterrent so we directed this particular activity to the less visible Mill floodgate. Our Manorial expeditions were usually restricted to the excellent all-weather and slightly 'greasy' climbing wall within the Dovecote, where I imagine boys had secretly traversed the rows of pigeon holes up to the roof timbers for a century or two before we ever did. Elsewhere at the Manor there were hay barns and corn driers where we played just as stealthily, and without mishap.

One of my earliest personal experiences of inter-parish travel occurred in 1954 when I was six years old. It was a Saturday and I became aware that some of my young friends and their parents were off to a fete in Guiting Power that afternoon but my father was unable to take us. I set off on a small scooter, being obliged to stop for the first time as I entered Guiting. This was when the Naunton Baptist minister pulled his car up in front of me. Together with the scooter I was bundled in and driven the last few hundred yards to the fete because Mr Ferris thought it a safer option for me. He delivered me home later and I do not recall anything too severe being said as a result. Understandably such junior excursions are discouraged these days, though they were not exactly encouraged then. It was just that we lived in slower, safer times when parents worried less about where their offspring were at any particular moment of the day. Mrs Ferris was my first Sunday school teacher and between the ages of about five and ten Sunday mornings were spent in the happy environment of her Chapel room where the teaching of the scriptures had some small influence upon my easily distracted mind.

The old water corn mill, opposite where I grew up was redundant but completely intact in the 1950s and the adjoining house against the road was occupied by someone who did not seem to emerge very often. I may well have been one of the last boys to clamber amongst its incredible elm-wood frame and workings, walk along the drive shaft, touching the beautiful pegged and bevelled cogs on the crown wheel and winding shaft, climb through the huge metal overshot waterwheel (twice as powerful as an undershot wheel) in the stone-lined wheel chamber, with mill-race orifice on river side and the mill-leat or mill-tail orifice on the exit side. This was before it was all tragically ripped out by Mr Groves, a London barrister, in the 1960s, when this particular bit of gentrification turned the whole building into the one large house you see there today. Being fond of playing with the wheels and cogs of Meccano™ I had a reasonable understanding of how it all worked when the water was sluiced over the last Victorian wheel, before flowing out the far side of the yard, opposite what is today called Mill Barn. Unlike the floodgates, the mill wheel was never thought of as an easy challenge by us boys, or with a bit of tinkering we would doubtless have brought it to life again. So whilst the sight of it all is still quite clear in my mind, the sounds were to elude me forever. From a safety point of view it was probably just as well or I could have found myself hoist by an ankle up through the sack-flaps and dumped in an ungainly heap somewhere amongst its workings.

I have fond memories of the traditional old-style funfair that visited each summer during the 1950s, setting up its magical swing-boats, roundabout, hurdy-gurdy and other stalls in the small central meadow between the Manor and El Hogar (Hatters cottage). The noise and thrill of it all was enjoyed by adults and children alike and we were always a little sad when these travelling folk moved on again. Before WW2 the funfairs were set up in 'Maggits' or Magets' Hays'[97], depending on where you read it, the field opposite the Mill. After the first two Council houses were built there in 1943 the funfair moved to the other more central location.

In the early 1950s when I was three or four years old, my uncle John was ploughing in Barn Piece when a plough-share snagged against a large piece of stone just under the surface of the high ground. When the stone slab was lifted it was found to be part of the cap stone over a grave, and a full sized skeleton lay beneath. I recall visiting it with my father and grandfather and looking in before it was taken away by someone Horace had called to inspect it. All my father ever knew about the find was being told that it was a typical Romano-British cist grave, but no trace can now be found of it in any archaeological records that I have pursued over recent years. The 'gentleman from Cheltenham' apparently failed to record the details and it is does not therefore appear in the Sites and Monuments Record. This field has since been landscaped to accommodate tiny modern holes. They are numbers 15 and 16 on Naunton Downs Golf Course. This archaeological oversight resulted in 'The Elbow' and 'Bridleway' replacing what might fittingly have been called 'The Grave' [98]. Near to the grave was a stone lined construction with two flues that I am told could have been a vented Roman corn drier, but all has now been lost forever to the less ancient game of golf.

By the time I was about twelve I had several regular jobs around the farm, one of which was to bottle the milk each evening after school in the new dairy. After flowing over a stainless steel cooler and through filter pads the bulk-milk went straight into ten gallon milk churns which were collected by Moreton Dairy next morning. Non-bulk milk was put into a tank from where I jugged it into glass milk bottles (quarts, pints, third and half-pints, the latter being for the school children) for delivery throughout the village the next morning, together with eggs. Each bottle was 'capped' using a hand held crimping tool that secured silver and gold foil caps, depending on the cream content of the milk. Everything was highly sterilised and the smell of this clung to your hands each evening. Most of the milk came from the herd of Friesian cows with a small amount coming from Jersey and Guernsey cows to increase the butter-fat content. There was no messing about with skimmed or semi-skimmed milk then! A steady hand was also needed for another job. After a cow had calved I was occasionally tasked with carrying a jug of cherry-curds from one end of the village to the other without spilling it. The Misses Bedwell were keen consumers of this rich dairy by-product, using it for puddings. I usually got a few pence for delivering it to the Post Office which these two charming ladies ran in the 1950s (now Littons) [99].

Ray Davis, the local roadman also cut boy's hair and one particular visit to the 'village barber' sticks in my mind, almost literally. I was about eight, and having arrived on his doorstep in Dale Street one Sunday morning, clutching my shilling (5p) Mrs Davis sent me off to find him at the bee hives in Sheepwell Lane (Grange Hill). Bill had obviously upset the bees considerably by removing the fruits of their busy labours. Unable to exact their revenge on his own hooded head and gloved hands must have angered them further, but they were not to be completely disappointed and soon re-directed their venomous attention to this witless head coming up the Lane. They descended on my scalp en-masse and despite my screams and Ray shouting at me to stand still, I ran off, clawing at stinging head and bees alike, straight back to Dale Street. Ray and his wife rubbed raw onion into my throbbing scalp with beneficial effect, but my haircut was postponed. I returned, as arranged, the following Sunday for a free basin-cut and whether my unspent shilling was compensation for the stings or for the unstylish cut Bill was famous for I do not know.

At this age my parochially juvenile belief systems had me thinking that certain patches of grass might actually be greener in the towns, where our contemporaries seemed to enjoy amenities we did not have in Naunton. For starters they could go to the cinema and had better shops. They could also join clubs and organisations such as Scouts and Guides. Despite not being able to join cubs or scouts, I occasionally mimicked their activities on 'survival' type exercises, sleeping out on the farm in improvised but leaky tents, or in the barns, completely unperturbed by mice running over me during the night. This partly arose from seeing better-equipped and well organised scout troops from the towns encamped in the lovely meadows above and below the village each summer, where they would light fires and cook delicious smelling food.

I and pals would watch enviously from the trees at the edge of these encampments until some observant leader spotted the harmless, salivating natives. And if they did not spot us, we made sure that they did, after which we were invited to join the camp activities around the fire in the evening, no doubt being recognised as culturally deprived members of the same species. This was pure magic to us and in a poor sort of exchange we joined them on walks, imparting all manner of exaggerated local knowledge to the 'townies', thus adding a little more variety to all our lives. On one such walk through Lower Harford meadows I remember matter-of-factly pointing out where the WW2 bomb had exploded, and although entirely true I was never able to convince the town boys that it was, it being just an overgrown crater in the grassy bank behind Harford House. To street-wise boys from the towns this was about as far removed as you could get from the usual kind of strategic or industrial targets they knew were chosen by the Lufwaffe. It was an unlikely example of where seeing is believing, involving as it did, savvy kids who had probably played on real bomb sites.

I later recognised certain other inherent differences, between the village community and our urban counterparts. Unlike the town boys who could go to youth clubs and do other town oriented activities, we did actually know, for what it was worth, the names, not only of our neighbours, but also of every other inhabitant in the village, and accepted that this had always been so in similar sized, close-knit communities. They of course all knew us, which has the beneficial effect of damping down the more boisterous antics of youngsters in any community. I was even deprived of that childhood pleasure of 'scrumping' someone else's apples, simply because my granddad's Mill Orchard (next to Mill Barn) usually had sufficient, where we climbed rickety wooden ladders to fill the apple baskets. Upon first moving to town and city I immediately discovered that life could be much more insular and that some people did not know, and did not even want to know or interact with their neighbours.

As a youngster, although I knew all of the people in the village, together with some of the fields and even a few of my grandfather's cows by name, I also had a basic understanding of the seasons and of our dependence on the land. But I was complete novice compared with the level of knowledge displayed by a few old sages who pontificated on matters rural. If and when one of these erudite countrymen talked to you, their sentences, uttered in the then much more pronounced local dialect, usually ended with the customary *'bwai,'* (if you were a boy) which served to remind us kids where we stood in the rural pecking order. This particular sentence tag-ending seemed to change to *'youw'* (you) as adulthood approached. These and numerous other fragments of the old vernacular, have alas, almost completely faded from the village-voice, as heard at the close of the 20th century. It seems to have been overtaken by more refined and affected utterances; *'an I beunt sure if this be a sort o' dummin-down, o' dummin-up- youw'*! To me the local dialect, as spoken by the last of these dear *ole bwais,* was another priceless bit of historic Naunton, fading away almost as quietly as it was spoken, and which I had the privilege to hear the tail end of. If only we had had the foresight and wherewithal to tape-record a few of them!

When I was about seven I remember one of these stalwarts stopping me on the way to school one morning with something like, *'cum yer bwai, you got egg on yer face'*. My mother had apparently missed the fact I had left the house with egg yolk on my mouth and more the pity for that, because this gentleman pulled out his truly grubby handkerchief. He then spat generously upon it before wiping my mouth clean, as I stood silently grimacing, lips tightly pursed to prevent goodness knows what from entering. Funny how that little experience taught me to check my face was good and clean each morning thereafter! His actions may have been based on some kind of village pride, not wanting dirty-faced *'slommacks'* on *Nat'uns* clean Street [100].

My fondness for Naunton and its people remained undiminished, despite such experiences, or maybe because of them. I knew nothing about the really old Naunton of course and at the village school, where we could and should have been taught something about it, we were told nothing, as far I remember, about our rich and fascinating local history. We were however told rather too much about far flung places on old maps of pink, upon which the word 'Empire' still featured prominently. By then, it was probably more to do with tight Local Education Authority budgets, than our diminishing global influence.

It seems to me that shortcomings in the curriculum, or shortages in budgets were somehow connected with people who felt that what we had possessed abroad for a few centuries and were now losing our grip on, was somehow of greater importance than what had been achieved locally over some two thousand years, much of which we still had! The priorities were also skewed in other areas because we seemed to do an inordinate amount of 'nature walks' and related field studies! I believe that our teacher was fonder of strolling through these pleasant (and safer) lanes than in instructing us with the 'three Rs,' and who could really blame her for that! The fact that no one seems to have done so may be connected with the next black mark in our development, when aged ten, together with my peers we all managed to maintain the fairly low standards we had been set up until that time, failing our 11-plus examinations with no trouble at all. You may observe that the School Register was routinely endorsed 'Transferred to Bourton'. I am surprised that the Local Education Authority did not provide a rubber stamp for such frequent endorsements. We all found ourselves pushed unceremoniously into round two of the divisive state system, a failure I was not allowed to forget for several years.

A few Naunton children, whose parents could afford it, were occasionally whisked away to receive their education elsewhere in the lottery of birth, ability, finances and parental aspirations. Of course the rest of us could not fail to notice when one of our peers, who may already have been given a disproportionate amount of the teacher's time (kids do not miss much and generally tell it as it is) were spirited from our midst, even though we knew they still lived in the village. We would soon discover, as kids do, that they now attended some posh school elsewhere. And there were one or two others living here who were spared ever having to scuff their shoes in our rough playground. That of course was only the beginning of the void that opens up so effortlessly between children who may have started off the same but end up with vastly different life experiences in this much trumpeted land of equal opportunities.

So there were no distant dormitories or hallowed halls ahead for us lot, only the lesser privilege of a bog-standard secondary-modern education that soon spewed us out on to the great treadmill of life. If anyone thinks this is a slightly exaggerated version of events, you need only take a look at the 'remarks' column in the School Register, to make your own judgment as to how many Naunton children progressed to Westwoods Grammar School at Northleach during the 1950s and 1960s. The Register may be a crude alternative to modern performance tables, but it is revealing enough for this simple assessment. Any educationists (I hope I spelt that right) reading this may accept that there is no statistical fluke here; simply a consistent pattern of underachievement on the part of the school, as opposed to all of its pupils. I imagine an OFSTED inspection would soon identify such a pattern of failure today, but it appears to have been overlooked or tolerated in our time. The situation we were exposed to is epitomised in an unscheduled but revealing classroom photograph taken by Stu' Russell in 1954 [101], where children aged five to eleven appear to be vying for teacher's attention; another bit of photographic evidence which speaks volumes.

We might also remember that church sponsored education for poor children started in Naunton during the 1700s, but more than 200 years later it was still unable to compete adequately in the equality of opportunity stakes being espoused within this county and country. Surprisingly, I have few regrets about my schooldays as they were exceedingly happy ones but now realise that you only got one chance when you are ten and I am therefore slightly happier that such a divisive system no longer exists for most of today's children. The beneficiaries and proponents of Grammar School education will no doubt continue to fight their corner in this ongoing debate of selection versus rejection. At the same time they might try and see the other side of the coin, or as it fell for most of Naunton's children, and I am certainly not alone in thinking that it let us down.

I remember being sent out from school once with some maps of the fields to record all the different crops growing within the parish. It was of little or no academic benefit to us because we knew what was growing in them. I had insufficient political awareness or cynicism at that age to realise we were simply being used by the State to undertake a national crop survey, and of course in those pre-satellite days this was how the Government got their statistics without it costing them a penny. We were also sent out to collect rose hips every summer that were crushed to make nutritional syrup for undernourished babies. This was slightly more worthwhile and we did actually get a few pennies for that chore, even though a good few were used for producing another effective by-product; itching powder; but I doubt such extraneous activities were imposed on children in private schools.

The commencement of five years bussing to and from Bourton was in reality a happy time and if you shone academically, which I did not particularly, I suppose you stood a reasonable chance of doing almost as well as the kids who went to Westwoods. I was more practically inclined at school, enjoying art, and working with metal and wood more than I ever did with maths, possibly because I had been brought up that way, seeing and doing practical jobs on the farm. This is of course just another way of saying that I found maths academically challenging. Nevertheless, I was always willing to board that wonderful old Bedford Duple 39-seat bus from Guiting Power every morning, with its bull nose, crunching gear box, and whining transmission that I can still hear today. I do not recall there being any truanting or bullying at Naunton or Bourton schools and we had considerable respect for the teachers. And this was not simply because corporal punishment was still permissible, administered as and when necessary, and with beneficial results all round. But that is all I will say on that subject, restricting myself to just one area of educational controversy.

When my generation left Bourton Vale School, it was taken as read that no really permanent jobs existed in Naunton, but many unskilled and semi-skilled jobs lay just beyond it. Any prospective employers that I now managed to secure an interview with were about to be underwhelmed with my two GCE 'O' levels (pre-GCSE), one for Woodwork, the other for Art, plus the risk of quickly discovering my failed one for English when they enquired. Despite this, aged 15, I somehow convinced a Squadron Leader and two NCOs at RAF Little Rissington, that I was ready for the high flying world beyond Naunton by securing a low-level job in the aircraft stores. Even though it was 20 years before the politician Norman Tebbit proffered his helpful 'on your bike' advice for jobseekers, I had progressed from scooting between the villages, and in 1963 began peddling determinedly to Little Rissington and back each day. I was now the proud owner of a £28 Raleigh bicycle, paid for at £1 a week from a weekly wage of £7. It was equipped with a Sturmy-Archer 'three-speed' hub-gear and carried me there without dismounting on that testing climb beyond Bourton. I have to admit that the severe winter of 1963 was a bit of a challenge, but it was never going to prevent a determined Nauntonian from reaching work, even carrying a bicycle through snowdrifts; and thus it ever was out in the countryside, or so I believed at the time.

A year later, redundancy forced a change and I took a job at Smiths Industries (Clock & Watch) at Cheltenham. This was a bit too much for the bicycle and I commuted there with John Ridge in his

Mini, before redundancy reared its head again. This time it was more to my convenience because as 1965 approached, some longer term plans were nearing fruition. I worked for Geoffrey Hanks on Manor Farm for the remainder of that summer. Even though there was no such thing as a 'minimum wage' in those days I have to say that Geoffrey paid me a fair hourly rate of five shillings (25p) enabling me to spend some, save a little and pay mother for my keep. Having by then attained the appropriate entry qualifications, in 1965 I entered the Gloucestershire Constabulary Cadet Corps to embark on an extremely interesting police career, retiring in 1995. Since then I have developed a former hobby into a small business involving old pictures of the Cotswolds, and latterly beyond the Cotswolds [102]. A slide-show of village and family photographs in the Village Hall for my father's 70th birthday in 1987 was the catalyst for the village slide-shows. Those presentations duly spawned the Millennium photographic project, which now results in my writing this.

But it is only later in life that I began to realise there was so much more we could all have learnt about the old, and the not so old, but equally fascinating things surrounding us in Naunton. I do not recall any village history being taught at school (perhaps I was not listening) but now recognise that so much of it was wrapped all around us, almost taken for granted, like a comfortable old coat! If only the teachers of the past (1865 to 1969) had thought to send pupils out to ask a few selected questions of the village people. Most villagers had memories like elephants and were just waiting to be asked. What a fascinating account we might now have of them all, including who they were, where they came from, what they did here and what stories they may have heard of really old Naunton.

It is ironic that in more recent times this awareness of the loss of local history has finally been recognised and the modern curriculum has begun to incorporate projects in which teachers can initiate the gathering of local information by pupils. What I find even more ironic than my enforced schooldays ignorance of Naunton's Stone-Age arrowheads, is learning about the more recent traces of Iron-Age *'Salmonsbury'*, that most impressive local Iron-Age settlement, which I have briefly touched upon in this book. Unbeknown to my headmaster and his staff, the outlying traces of *Salmonsbury* were hidden silently under their feet all the time. The more recent finds, in the shape of even more round-house post-holes and contemporary artefacts were unearthed in 2002 next to the school, during far more careful digging than appears to have taken place when the school's foundations were gouged out in the 1950s. Significantly, our history classroom was situated right next to the most recent excavations, which explains why they never knew of or imparted any details of this amazing place and its people to us! I am still unable to understand why modern Bourton-on-the-Water fails to capitalize on its incredible Celtic roots, in addition to the thin commercial veneer that it currently relies upon, which appears to exploit little more than 'Brum', a few bridges and bus loads of Brummies! To confirm this view, regrettably I can only refer you to Bourton's sole museum at: www.cotswold-motor-museum.com. In relation to the school you can look at: www.cotswold.gloucs.sch.uk.

Whilst playing, and later working in Naunton fields, it was possible to find many spent brass shell cases (·303), being evidence of conflict in much more recent times. My father was able to satisfy my curiosity this time, telling me that many thousands were expended as training rounds in WW2, fired from fighter aircraft at target 'drones', towed by other aircraft over the Cotswolds. This may have been from the RAF Central Flying School at Little Rissington (1938 to 1976), now called Upper Rissington, and other local WW2 airfields. He also showed me the bomb crater at Lower Harford. In between the use of these items of weaponry (the Stone Age arrowheads and the 20th century bomb and shell cases) so many other historic items must have slipped under the ground here, leaving no lasting trace.

As mentioned, rightly or wrongly we thought that the kids living around the smaller but greener patches of urban grass had other joyous opportunities denied to many of us. They could learn to swim in heated Municipal swimming pools. We were mostly healthy non-swimmers, using a damned-up and extremely dangerous 'fish-pond' at the east end of the village, next to Harford Bridge. In this old gravel pit we would make a raft of reeds and other natural flotsam, and try to keep our heads above water. Looking back now, with no competent supervision and absolutely no sense of danger, it could all so easily have ended in a Coroner's report on each occasion [103]. With my peers at Bourton School we had worked for several years to raise the funds for the school's first swimming pool, leaving just before it was completed, so we all remained healthy non-swimmers just like all the previous generations.

During the 1930s, continuing after WW2 into the 1950s and 60s, some people were becoming more mobile; car ownership was slowly establishing itself as the successor to horse drawn transport. Although I can only describe the 1950s, through to 1965, it was apparent to me that post-war prosperity was encouraging a few more people to visit or revisit Naunton by car, motorcycle and bicycle. The village was spared the coach loads and train loads of visitors now descending on the touristy Bourton. Increasing numbers of people from the towns and cities, and even from as far as America, were venturing into the Cotswolds for weekends and holidays. Those who came to Naunton of course found friendly natives in their natural habitat, and they seemed to like what they saw and found here. We certainly liked what we saw because such interaction introduced us to boys and girls from elsewhere, and some town-girls were more enthused about certain aspects of life, in a hands-on context, than us boys had ever imagined, even in our juvenile fantasies. We did our best to catch up though! Hay barns have always leant themselves to multiple uses and I was simply one of numerous boys and girls to have rolled amorously in Cotswold hay, recalling that my father was less than pleased with me one day when I missed helping him in the dairy. I used to delude myself that he knew not why on that particular summer afternoon, when a boy and girl's fancy got the better of them.

In the 1950s I recall an American family camping in the meadow at the east end of the village and they were washed-out in a downpour. Dejected and bedraggled they walked into the village and knocked on the first occupied door they found, which at that time happened to be ours [104]. My mother would help anyone in distress and soon had them and their belongings dried out. Before long it was as though we had always known each other and we became good friends for the remainder of their holiday. After returning to the US a letter arrived with a twenty dollar bill in it. It was worth far more than my father's weekly wage as a farm worker and such generosity amazed us. But it was simply the kind of interaction generated when visitors and locals got to know each other properly, and genuine friendships were made.

One person who appears to have seen the early potential for tourism in Naunton was Maurice Hanks from Longford. He placed an old 'caravan' at the lower edge of the wood known as 'The Brake' (a wood or thicket) in the 1930s [105]. In reality it was an ageing, iron-wheeled, roadman's living-van, but it had bunks, a table, seating, a wood burning stove and of course that beautiful view across the valley, attracting visitors from far and wide. Occasionally, when it was not occupied in the 1960s, I would sleep in it with pals. This was another little adventure on long summer evenings, when we eventually fell asleep to the undulating distant tones of Radio Luxembourg.

But it was still reasonably early days for 'Bed and Breakfast' in Cotswold villages like Naunton and the tourism industry was still developing. Post-war austerity meant that motoring visits were beyond the reach of many people, and those who did get out here by car usually preferred to return to some creature-comforts by nightfall. The fact was that until some of the basic living improvements I have already touched upon began to permeate the countryside, post-war holiday destinations generally saw people making for coastal resorts, holiday camps and National Parks, still shying away from rural backwaters. At this time, as I recall, the clean air, hospitable folk and good ale attracted visitors, including seasoned campers and walkers, but very few overnight stays. Not that I recall there being 'B&B' advertisements for these visitors, any potential Naunton landladies seeking to honestly advertise their services in the early 1950s might have had to couch them in terms like this:

'Single or double-seated privy, pre-torn tabloids; tin bath in front of the fireplace, drinking water nearby; intermittent electricity, plenty of candles; forget the T.V for a while, no heating beyond the living room, Public Telephone in village. Smoking encouraged; no charge made for pets but they may be shot if they look sideways at livestock; full English breakfast and full cream milk no problem; petrol pump; but a four-star rating cannot be guaranteed, or only on a clear night'!

Seriously though, under those fairly austere post-war conditions, was it surprising that city folk still preferred to leave their country-cousins to our own devices and take their holidays elsewhere, particularly at coastal resorts or abroad? But gradually, the beautiful summers and increasing mobility did entice a few more people out into the countryside and the occasional family discovered, then rented or even bought a cottage, becoming part of a new, semi-rural breed known as 'weekenders'. We all made new friends and had many exceedingly enjoyable times together as our fairly isolated situation was further eroded. This led to more visitors deciding they and their offspring had enjoyed it all so much that they would return. Many did so, and some decided to stay permanently, by purchasing a property. Fleeting visits to the heart of the real Cotswolds led to an increasing demand for accommodation here, especially in retirement. Quite naturally this resulted in the provision of several more cottages for rent or sale, and some new-builds and conversions, as owners renovated properties and sold or developed parcels of land, to meet this perfectly understandable, ever increasing, but still satiable demand for a place in the country.

Either way, our best kept rural secret was bound to slip out eventually as more urban folk discovered where the real quality of life was to be found, coupled with the more reliable means of reaching it within an hour or two. The most recent Census (2001), although denied to us in its entirety for a century, already confirms my own thoughts on various demographic matters by revealing some current trends. It verifies that London's tentacles continue to reach relentlessly outwards, increasing their grasp on properties in attractive places like Gloucestershire, which is now described as being just another leafy suburb of the Metropolis! I am sure people in several hundred other similarly attractive Cotswold villages saw the same trend developing around them. Although it probably happened on a smaller and slower scale before the war (WW2), the main influx has taken place subsequent to the introduction of the several improvements already mentioned. These include the basic utility services, more efficient heating and insulation, coupled with the ongoing advances in the fields of Information Technology and Television. Top that off with some fairly good shopping facilities nearby and you have analluring modern mix that continues to entice and almost painlessly transfer city folk to the more tranquil life-style of the countryside during the second half of the twentieth century.

The ensuing change from the old and mainly indigenous farming community has had some benefits. It has brought in new blood, new money and fresh ideas to reinvigorate certain aspects of village life. It has brought in people with technical, managerial and boardroom skills, many with retirement time on their hands and a few with the wherewithal and flair to offer a more dynamic approach to fund-raising and problem solving. I am not saying that this was not happening before, just that it was in a lower gear, once even a single gear dictated by equine power and speed. That particular form of low-octane drive had quite naturally dictated the pace of life for people in the countryside for centuries, much as it did so in the towns, until trams, trains and buses arrived. The easiest way to demonstrate this point visually is to look at a few of our pictures, maybe starting with W12 (my grandfather's gig) and village pictures 18, 119, 167, 213, 215, 230, 245 and 246. This progressive range of transport exemplifies how one kind rapidly overtook the next, during the 20th century alone. So whilst life may have operated here less hectically and for longer than it did in the towns, it does not mean that life was any easier or less efficient. The people who were tied to the land at that gentler pace of life needed to be as tough and resilient as anyone I can think of today and more so in the physical sense, just to survive the rigours of hard winters, and hard work, with more basic housing and working conditions.

But we need to remain positive about the irreversible change that has, and continues to take place here and perhaps regard the migratory part of it as reversionary human behaviour. Most of the people moving here today, or on the waiting lists of those wanting to do so, are the descendants of people who once left the countryside in centuries past to find work in the towns. Their descendants are simply recognising the attractiveness of the countryside over so many of our towns and cities. Anyone can now see that the quality of life, scenery and local amenities has as much, if not more to offer than inner city life does. As long as people integrate (and are integrated) and support the rural community and its modern aims, all will be well. The fact that most people do so is evident from what is going on here today, and through what has been achieved recently. The modern village community has contributed towards a more focused approach to things such as fund raising. Witness the Church roof, Church bells, the Village Hall and Chapel refurbishments of the 1990s, and various other projects, including the ongoing the laudable objectives of Naunton Dovecote Conservation Society, to name but a few. I doubt all this would have been achieved so easily within the framework of the old rural economy alone, and several such projects may have withered on the vine, going the same way as some of the farms.

Modern Nauntonians have shown themselves just as willing to pull together to achieve communal objectives as those here before them. The majority continue to be highly motivated when it comes to investing in the future of their village, acknowledging that they are building on largely unspoilt foundations, laid down by the toil of countless previous generations. After all, whoever we are, we are only custodians of the place for its future occupiers. I believe that most of what anyone could ever possibly want to say about Naunton would reflect a highly developed and civilised community, hardly justifying any adverse comment. Just occasionally, as in any community, a few residents have disagreed with or failed to interact quite as well as they might. But hey, such things are a well known part of the human condition, and if they were not we would be living in utopia, instead of the very real world we are privileged to occupy. The reasons for such minor differences are varied, invariably trifling and possibly symptomatic of perceived class, educational, financial and other similar but inconsequential matters, some real, some exaggerated, some imagined. Summarising the comments of the many people I have spoken to over the past few years indicates, unsurprisingly, that providing people respect you and your property, together with your right to privacy and some quietude (without killing the cockerels, etc), all is generally well and good.

My own thoughts about such things are that newcomers, whether they spoke in different tongues or accents, displayed different values, lifestyles or beliefs, were probably always absorbed fairly painlessly and without too much animosity, so long as they were willing to contribute something to the community, its economy and its values. If people came in friendship, prepared to settle, to work together, play together and take no more than they could give, that was acceptable. But we might remember that this was not always the case. Our histories record that less friendly outsiders once arrived here speaking different languages, forcibly enslaving the locals and dispossessing them of their land. The feelings and emotions stirred up amongst the indigenous population on those occasions must have been acrimonious to say the least. But even then, after the new masters had subjugated them and employed them, I believe the people may have concluded, more often than not, that little could be done to change the new situation and simply got on with their hard lives, much as before.

Villages like Naunton have always absorbed newcomers, for two thousand years or so and always will, as of course have the towns and cities that developed from many similar villages. The ability and willingness to do this is another enduring trait that has seen the people of Britain accommodate wave after wave of migratory peoples over vast periods of time. Consequently the psyche of the people as a whole seems to have developed a long standing tolerance to newcomers and this is unlikely to change, although there will always be one or two exceptions to the rule.

You are now reading these last few lines towards the end of Naunton's lengthy and largely unrecorded timeline, at a point upon it that is neither in its past nor its future. At such moments, some of us may occasionally hear the faint ethereal cries of our ancient ancestors, who lie buried somewhere within the unwritten periods of Naunton's lengthy past, assured of anonymity and denied the kind of immortality Naunton folk were offered within this book. Perhaps this could serve as a lesson to those who follow us, as they may be fairly criticised if they too obscure the parts they come to play here from those who later inherit this amazing place, again and again. So says the scribe!

I think we can safely conclude that Naunton's south bank has formed a natural balcony for sightseers from the earliest of times. In recent times it appears that more artists and photographers have stood there and been inspired to try and capture the village's signature image, than have writers. From this natural vantage point, people have created numerous pictures, ranging from television commercials, to sketches and photographs appearing in books, brochures, reports, newspapers, calendars, the front cover of what you are now holding and even a few modern but less-inspiring postcards. But one written description that I believe captures the essence of the place as succinctly as any I have seen was in a book lying on someone's coffee table in Cheltenham. It was *'The Complete Illustrated Guide to Feng Shui'* by Lillian Too. The centre pages were a colour picture of this familiar and quintessentially Cotswold view. Lilian Too could quite easily have chosen a picture of a hundred or more Cotswold villages, but of course she did not. Her picture-caption read: *'This pleasant English Landscape offers good Feng Shui. The undulating countryside is not monotonously flat or too threateningly steep; the clumps of trees provide a balance of sunlight and shade'*. The second part of her sentiment could have been written by a visitor arriving here at almost any time in the past 2000 years. And I believe it actually may have been once, though to be realistic, like so much else, it probably remained in the young Roman officer's emotionally charged thoughts that particular afternoon, never quite making it into his official chronicle - and for reasons that are entirely understandable!

So much
There is to catch,
And the years
So short,
That there is
Scarce time to
Snatch
Pen, palette,
Or ought,
And to seize
Some shape
We can see,
That others
May keep
Its moment of
Mystery,
Then go to
our sleep.   Edward Plunkett (Lord Dunsany) 1878-1957

End-notes for Chapters 1 and 2

1. One exception was James 'Jimmy' Mattock, the 'Pigman Poet'. See Bibliography at rear for details.

2. An early example was a Roman Villa near the Fosse at Bourton, apparently destroyed by fire during the Roman occupation. It was excavated by Helen O'Neil. Blackened Roman coins were found in the ashes there, as were many similar coins in Cyril's Naunton collection in 1988. [BGAS Vol 56, 1934]

3. See appendix 5, the 'Dissenters' document of 1779. Under the Toleration Act of 1689 some men broke with the Church and obtained the Bishop's authority to worship in the house of Robert Taylor, prior to the building of the original Baptist Chapel. It surfaced again in 1998 when Billy Herbert passed it to Fiona Milton, after he had safely looked after it for many years. It is included here to represent other similarly precious Naunton documents that must have been created and lost over the centuries.

4. The selected music is: 1) Music from Gladiator by Hans Zimmer & Lisa Gerrard and 2) The Armed Man: A Mass for Peace by Karl Jenkins; produced to commemorate the millennium.

5. At various times known as Buggilde Street, Limekiln Road and Buckle Street. Today it is just one more unnamed 'Class Three' potholed road on the higher wolds around Naunton. It crosses the 'new' road (former A436) that runs south of Naunton (c1800) before crossing the ancient Winchcombe Way, north of Summerhill. See Rudder's 1779 map, page 265 which shows Winchcombe Way as the only EW route, north of Naunton

6. Full name 'Antedrig'. Factional version, 'Edrig'; engraved on his coins was the shorter version; 'Ted' (see Dobbunic stater coins in the link picture, page 52).

7. The ard was a light wooden device (an early plough). Initially using a stone and later an iron 'share' for breaking the soil, but having no coulter or mould board it could not turn a furrow.

8. The Legio II *Augusta* which had previously served in Spain & Germany

9. This very old practice would eventually become enshrined in law. The Wool Burial Act of 1666 required that everyone be buried in wool under penalty of a fine, the object being to benefit agriculture and the wool trade generally.

10. Other recorded stone-arched bridges were built in Bourton village in 1654, 1756 and 1776

11. Those unfamiliar with this house design can view it at www.bbc.co.uk/history/games/iron_age_build

12. See appendix 2. By 1086 Naunton had 25½ Plough Teams, (8 oxen to the plough) working upon the great open fields of the parish. See also page 266 (pre-enclosure field system).

13. Photo 37 shows Abel Tom Smith (1871-1958) standing in front of Ivy Cottage. His daughter Elsie was Lionel Beames' mother. His great-great grandson, Robert, painted a cover picture for this book.

14. See current families of Beames and Juggins in 'Naunton 2000'. Pen picture & photo's 13 and 70.

15. See 1901 Census at appendix 10 - house No 51. Before the Smith family occupied the 'Roundhouse', William Miffling from Cutsdean and his family lived in it. Prior to that no record exists to indicate when it was built or who occupied it but it is reasonable to assume it is as old, or older than most other dwellings here.

16. A pit or depression in the surface of the ground where 'delvers' extracted stone or gravel. Overgrown ones can still be found around Naunton. The west end of the car park at Naunton Downs Golf Club was an old stone delve. Another one, for stone or gravel can be seen some 300 meters from the east end of the village on north side of the road. The extant local quarries would have started off in much the same way.

17. Sites & Monuments Record (SMR) 93; just north-east of today's Brockhill Barn – see photo p59 (bottom)

18. American author of 'Mother Tongue' and other titles and a Commissioner for English Heritage

19. From 'Saxon Charters & Field Names of Gloucestershire' by GB Grundy, BGAS 1935/6:
    '*Caestello* is an unusual form – perhaps a Hwiccian form – of the Saxon *ceastel*. In various cases in the charters this term is applied to the remains of a Roman Villa. The Saxons applied *ceaster* (Latin, castrum, castra) to enclosures surrounded by walls of stone or brick, which under the circumstances of the time would be of Roman origin'

20. This assertion accepts that what are thought to have been medieval settlements at Aylworth and Lower Harford (both once being within the Salmonsbury hundred) may have been even earlier Celtic or Romano-British farmsteads. Only an English Heritage authorised excavation may finally settle this point.

21. Appendix 1 'What's in a Name' for meaning of '*Windrush*'. The second Water Mill was somewhere at Harford (Rudder 1779, appendix 4)

22. Appendix 7 - Naunton Board School memorandum & staff

23. During the Agricultural Revolution and the advent of smaller enclosed fields the rotation of nitrogen-fixing and cereal crops reduced the old custom of leaving up to half of the land fallow after each planting

24. No chance of this happening. Mr Eales had custody of the Parish chest during his incumbency and could not find it and Rudder records in 1779 that the old Parish Register was lost by then (appendix 4)

152 *Naunton 2000*

25. See Waterloo Farm photo 3, (page 19) c1917 (photographs prefixed with a 'W' are Waterloo Farm photo's)
26. Waterloo Field & Mill Field; see 241 and 242 on farm sale map, page 117.
27. Edward 1915-1985. Harold 1917-1998, Kathleen (m.Young) 1921-2004. John b.1924. Doreen (m.Eddlestone) 1931-1987. Waterloo photo's numbers 7 & 8 show them next to Waterloo House c1929 and late 1930s.
28. A pre-fabricated hut of corrugated iron, having a semicircular cross section; an army or field hut. The one on the footpath is in Waterloo photo 26. The later one was built NW of Lodges Dutch Barn.
29. Appendix 11 page 367 (Financial Domesday) Properties 31/33/35/49/50/51
30. Believed once owned by Edmund Lodge. See 1856/66 Trade Directories; appendix 6.
31. Reginald G. Hanks's father was William Wood Hanks (1839-1900) of Aylworth. William Wood Hanks's father was John Hanks (1810-1884) of Charlton Abbotts and Roel Farms. John's brother William (1812-1871) of Naunton had five children, one being William Bullock Hanks (1852-1921) latterly of The Mill; - father of Horace and great-grandfather of the author.
32. See Farm Sale Map at page 117 for visual interpretation of the fields referred to.
33. This small building is now a store shed on the Naunton Downs Golf Course. The concrete reservoir was just behind it, in the lower left corner of field 190 on the farm sale map. The windmill was in Harford Meadow; field number 99.
34. Lodges Barn (since razed to the ground and the stone reused) is at 107 on the farm sale map.
35. Waterloo Field, No 242 on sale map. The reservoir is at the top right brow of the field in photo W9
36. Photo's W6, W12, W18, being where the west-wing extension of Waterloo House now stands
37. Photo W66 and rear cover - aerial photo.
38. Photo W42 shows Kathleen & John Hanks delivering milk and eggs from the milk float (a pony and trap is another way of describing the gig) during the 1940s.
39. The strip of land at the east side of Waterloo Field (number 242 on the sale map). The bee hives are where the photographer was standing in W10
40. Variant of old Gloucestershire/Somersetshire name, 'Bowsin' meaning stone built cattle shed or stall
41. On the 1838 map this field was called Harford Bridge Ground (page 267). By the 1930s it had long since been split into the Bowsing Field and Drapers Ground as shown on the farm sale map (fields 101 & 102)
42. Harford Meadow is field 99 on farm sale map
43. Photo 7 (though difficult to see at this size) shows at least seven ricks on the Footpath Field, (now on the golf course, see field 193 on farm sale map) long before the Nissen hut was erected there. Similar ricks appear in other old pictures, such as Waterloo farm photo's W10, 24, 29, 37, 38, 39 and at Manor Farm.
44. Photo W54 and W68 and village pictures 25, 26 and 304
45. Rare glimpses of staddle-stones, as they were originally used to support the wooden platform upon which ricks were built can be seen in pictures 29, 63 and 244
46. These rugged four-wheeled, horse-drawn wagons, with optional end-ladders for higher loads, were similar to those in photo's 209, 215, 216, 217 and 218
47. Spring wheats: Little Joss, Red Marvel & A1. Spring Barley: Plumage Archer and Spratt Archer. Later sowing: Victory & Danish barleys. Spring Oats: Victory, Eagle, Star and Golden Rain are all in the diary.
48. Photo 6 shows the sheep dip below Mill Coppice; next to Mill Barn and the Mill Orchard
49. Photo's 34 & 35 and part of Lot 3 - 249 on farm sale map.
50. They had two small horse-drawn 'trolleys', calling one the 'Lees' Trolley and the other the 'Burford' trolley (probably denoting where or who they bought them from). See photo' W 21. Both were lightly sprung horse-drawn road vehicles, sometimes fitted with optional end-ladders, to carry about 18 bales.
51. Photo W32
52. Manageable bundles of straw, approx 4' long with two ties round them.
53. A teg is last years lamb that has been kept for breeding, or to be sold on at one year or so old. A gilt is a young female pig, before she was used for breeding.
54. Bloodworth & Son, Grain Merchants, Millers, etc, then in Albion Street, Cheltenham
55. Photo 63 is Mr Jim Hooper
56. One hundredweight (or 'Cwt') was one twentieth of a ton in those wonderful pre-metric days.

57. Photo 207 in which the author's father Harold is 2nd from the right (standing)
58. Treating them for the fly-blown larvae that hatched under the animal's skin.
59. Plot 367 or Lot 4 on farm sale map
60. Men listed here include Mr Reginald.G.Hanks (who generally dealt with the sheep), Horace Hanks and his two sons, Harold and John, together with Eddie Higgins, Arthur Dean, George Williams, Fred Miffling, Edward Miffling, Mr Richards and two Aylworth men.
61. The last known surviving milk bottle is included within picture 238; courtesy of John & Sylvia Hanks
62. See (aerial) photo 77. The two fuel pumps are in front of Pulhams' coach in the lay-by
63. Clogs were the lengths of chain between the shafts on the machine/implement and the horse-harness
64. War Agricultural Executive Committee. Some of the decisions of the 'War Ag' were resented, particularly the calculation of ploughing targets for individual farms and fields, with the farmer's opinion frequently at odds with that of the 'War Ag'. If the committee felt that land was not being farmed correctly they had statutory powers to commandeer the farm and evict the farmer with little or no compensation. Nationally, some 15,000 farms were seized in this way, often with the farmer and his family never regaining the land after the war. Understandably, members of the local committee were often less than popular during the war years, but the role of the 'War Ag' was vital to increasing food production. By late 1942 home production of food had increased by 70% compared to that of 1939.
65. Field 172 or Parson's Close on the farm sale map, with the historic 'Bell Acre' at the southern tip
66. MOF, Albion Chambers, Kings Square, Gloucester.
67. During the 1930s a large proportion of dairy cows were infected with *M. bovis*. Many were kept near large cities to provide urban dwellers with fresh milk. Most were closely confined, in poorly ventilated cowsheds, ideal conditions for the disease to spread. Many cows developed infection in the udders and because most milk was then drunk raw (untreated), *M. bovis* spread easily to humans and was the major source of tuberculosis in humans. During this time, over 50,000 new human cases of TB infection were recorded each year, with over 2,500 deaths. (info' courtesy DEFRA website)
68. See photo W29 (behind Horace) and representational picture number 238 for elevators in use
69. The 1918/19 Spanish Influenze pandemic killed up to 50 million people and this was within living memory of many people. Flu was therefore treated seriously and no inoculations were yet available.
70. The initial name for the first pair of Council Houses, built for farm workers during WW2 in 1943. Later the address changed to 1 and 2 Council Houses and then to 'Mill View', where the author grew up.
71. This is another word for a 'swingle-tree', the stout horizontal crossbar(s) behind the horse(s) or oxen, to the ends of which the traces of a harness were attached; also called a 'whiffletree' or 'single-tree'.
72. We have to assume this means they purchased the Mill Orchard and the bank above, but it was sold in 1973 and does not appear on this sale map, (see page 130 for sale particulars).
73. Photo W43 shows John Hanks with the Hillman utility truck in Dale Street (1950s)
74. Artificial Insemination: either they no longer owned a bull or when another breed was required.
75. Plans drawn up in 1954 by Miss Townsend of Kiftsgate Cottage (with an office in London) based on a sales drawing of Alfa-Laval's 'Combine Installation No 2'. Designed for farmers to build their own sheds to match the drawing. Once built, a standard dairy kit was installed; this one being a six unit dairy.
76. Bacon Pigs were generally 24-26 weeks old and Pork Pigs were generally 16-18 weeks old before going to market. Earlier on almost everyone kept their own pig in a nearby paddock or orchard.
77. The stainless steel penetrating device and its stainless steel sheath were always kept ready to hand and if a beast needed to be 'stuck' (stabbed) this was skilfully done to deflate the gastric inflation which would otherwise distend the animal's gut and cause its death. Farmers had to know exactly where to puncture the animal or they simply hastened its death.
78. A rooster gelded to improve the flesh for eating.
79. Bell Acre was the lowest point of Parsons Close (172pt on sale map) which was rented from the Church for the upkeep of the bells, once delineated by a stone in the wall at the edge of the field.
80. Albert (born 1899) left Naunton for Manitoba in 1920, as a 20 year old, as Horace had 8 years earlier. He probably met Hilda and her boys (Eddie 5yrs and Harold 3yrs) out there, before she returned to Naunton and he may even have helped her to pack up and leave. See School Register No 1, (Albert Hathaway).
81. 'Power Take Off' from the rear of the tractor; this particular combine having no engine of its own.
82. A police drama series that ran between 1966 and 1969.
83. This kissing-gate is now situated in The Lane (North Street) at entrance to track leading to the Brake

84. Cheltenham Agricultural Traders, 268 High Street & 66 Winchcombe Street, Cheltenham.

85. 1 & 2 Agricultural Cottages when built in 1943; then 1 & 2 Council Houses; finally 1 to 9 Millview.

86. Village photos 14 & 16 capture the busy steam-powered threshing scene at The Mill.

87. Photo 14 shows the steam threshing outfit. The steam engine (with tall chimney stack) is perilously close to the road – or as far as the law was concerned it was!

88. 108/109a on farm sale map or *'Barn Piece'* on the 1838 field map. Wagon in photo W20.

89. Courtesy Cheltenham Art Gallery & Museum a small black & white version is included at the rear. One tenet of this book is the need to try and view the bigger picture. On this occasion you are encouraged to do this by visiting the Gallery (or its website where sections can be seen). The painting is behind glass and the original really needs to be seen to appreciate the superb detail that it contains.

90. Doris Stratford's pen-picture, No 117, page 187.

91. The equivalent of about £3. 19 shillings, or 79 shillings (£3.95p) a gallon in 2000 compared with an increase of less than two shillings (10p) a gallon from the 1930s to the 1950s.

92. For those who do not know what the larger (and already historic) 'X' and 'H' VHF aerials looked like, a 'H' shaped aerial is just visible behind my mother's left shoulder in photo' 121.

93. Based on the appearance of a Post Office in the Trade Directories at appendix 6.

94. Supplied, like the earlier village pumps, from a stone tank near Humphries Barn and its nearby spring.

95. Before the modern sewerage system was installed, these were a common type of outdoor toilet in either a small wooden shed or stone outbuilding (aka privy), consisting of a bench with seat holes in it above a pit. From 14th century, Old French, *garder* "to keep" + robe.

96. The small building to left of Waterloo House in photo's 7, 8, 9, 10 and in W63, W47.

97. Possibly once Margaret's Hay or Hayes, from Saxon *'hecge'*, hedge or fence. Photos 7 and 23 show the old enclosure wall separating Maggits Hays from Sidland, as does the 1838 Field Map.

98. The location of the cist grave was roughly the centre of Barn Ground, or field 109 on the farm sale map, almost exactly where the number '109' is. This is to the right of the tractor in photo W25 or near left edge of photo W26. All is now lost under the golf course - see www.nauntondowns.fs.net.co.uk.

99. Photo's 164/5/6/8 and 245/7/8.

100. See The Lost Dialect, appendix 13.

101. Photo' 275 was taken by Stu Russell and shows the author learning to read. Stu, an American, was living in Naunton in the 1950s (at El Hogar, now 'Hatters' cottage; see his photo at 253). Before moving to Germany in 1955 he took a number of local photographs. Those dated '1954' in this book were kindly contributed by Stu from Florida. See also School Register No 2. His sons Gregg and Scott were at school with the author before the family left for Germany.

102. From 1998 www.cotswold-images.co.uk, in future changing gradually into www.old-england.com.

103. It would not have been the first drowning at Naunton as surviving bits of the Parish Register record at least two others in past centuries; one child in the river and one in a water butt. (Gloucester Record Office, Alvin Street, Gloucester).

104. At this time Mill Barn was still a farm building; numbers 3 to 9 Millview were not yet built and the occupants of The Mill House opposite were often away.

105. The caravan is visible at top right of photo 30. Also visible in photo 30 is an old bowsing to its left in the lower corner of the Brake and an old (Pulham's?) bus that slowly rotted away in the orchard below.

Chapter 3

Naunton 2000

Index of people living in the Parish in 2000AD

The number corresponds with the Pen-Picture and Photograph following on

Name	Address	No.	Name	Address	No.
Adams Carole	Upper Dale Cottage	2	Cooper Erica (non-res)	Kingston, Jamaica	27
Adams Christopher	Upper Dale Cottage	2	Cooper Paul (non-res)	Kingston, Jamaica	27
Adams Simon	Upper Dale Cottage	2	Cowan Joan	Hatters Cottage	28
Adcock Ian	Farm House, Dale St	3	Crystal Licia	Kiftsgate House	29
Anderson Alfred	The Mill House	4	Crystal Michael	Kiftsgate House	29
Anderson Zosha	The Mill House	4	Davies Henry	Summerhill Farm Hse	30
Arnold Jane	Brockhill	5	Davies Jane	Summerhill Farm Hse	30
Arnold Joanna	Brockhill	5	Davies Joe	Summerhill Farm Hse	30
Arnold Michael	Brockhill	5	Davies Meghan	Summerhill Farm Hse	30
Ash Inga	Stonegate	6	Davies Robin	Summerhill Farm Hse	30
Ash Richard	Stonegate	6	Davies Christian	Sunnydale	31
Bacon Jean	Hilltop	7	Davies Jayne	Sunnydale	31
Baker Camilla	Brockhill	5	Davies William	Sunnydale	31
Baker Emma	Brockhill	5	Davis Oliver	1 Ashtree Cottage	32
Barber Christine	10 Windrush View	9	Davis Theresa	1 Ashtree Cottage	32
Barber Leslie	10 Windrush View	9	Dearman Constance	1 Mill View	33
Barber Andrew	3 Mill View	8	Donoghue Jeanette	4 Mill View	34
Barber Helen	3 Mill View	8	Donoghue Thomas	4 Mill View	34
Barber Kevin	3 Mill View	8	Duval Alexander	The Pound	35
Barber Mandy	3 Mill View	8	Duval Jonny	The Pound	35
Barton Enid	Spring Cottage	10	Duval Julia	The Pound	35
Barton Neville	Spring Cottage	10	Duval Katie	The Pound	35
Barwood Andrew	Rock Cottage	11	Duval Tom	The Pound	35
Barwood Judith	Rock Cottage	11	Dyer Jeffrey	5 Mill View	36
Bayliss Alan	Summerhill Cottage	12	Dyer Karen	5 Mill View	36
Bayliss Edna	Summerhill Cottage	12	Dyer Rachel	5 Mill View	36
Bayliss Marcella	Summerhill Cottage	12	Dyer Robert	5 Mill View	36
Bayliss Neil	Summerhill Cottage	12	Dyer Ryan	5 Mill View	36
Beames Lionel	Elm Tree Cottage	13	Egan Joan	Lavender Hill Stud	37
Bedford Cecilia	Dale House	14	Egan John	Lavender Hill Stud	37
Bedford David	Dale House	14	Elliott John	Greenacres	38
Beer James	1 Jasmine Cottage	15	Elliott Marion	Greenacres	38
Beer Jeanne	1 Jasmine Cottage	15	Evans John	10 Dale Street	39
Bond John	Old Well Cottage	16	Evans Maria	10 Dale Street	39
Bond Lillian	Old Well Cottage	16	Ewart-Perks George	Aylworth House	40
Bond Stephen	Old Well Cottage	16	Ewart-Perks Jane	Aylworth House	40
Boult Patricia	2 Mill View	17	Ewart-Perks Lucy	Aylworth House	40
Boult Ralph	2 Mill View	17	Ewart-Perks Simon	Aylworth House	40
Bowen-Jones Benjamin	Rosemary Cottage	18	Ewart-Perks Stephen	Aylworth House	40
Bowen-Jones Edward	Rosemary Cottage	18	Ewart-Perks Victoria	Aylworth House	40
Bowen-Jones Rowley	Rosemary Cottage	18	Fellowes Lyn	3 Littlesworth	41
Bowen-Jones Victoria	Rosemary Cottage	18	Fellowes Rory	3 Littlesworth	41
Bowen-Jones Jonathan	Rounhill Farm Cottage	19	Fieldgate John (non-res)	Slaughter Vicarage	1
Brett Nora	Church Farm House	20	Fiveash Martin	Brambling Cottage	42
Bruening Elmar	The Old Rectory	21	Fiveash Mary	Brambling Cottage	42
Cameron Jonathan	Riverside Cottage	22	Ford Jane	Grays Orchard	51
Cameron Vanessa	Riverside Cottage	22	Foster John	4/5 The Quadrangle	43
Chalmers David	Upland Hse, U-Harford	68	Foster Mary	4/5 The Quadrangle	43
Chalmers Elizabeth	Upland Hse, U-Harford	68	Foulkes Sarah	Waterstone Cottage	128
Chudleigh Charlotte	2 Littlesworth	23	Gatford Vanessa	Farm House, Dale St	3
Chudleigh Marie-Louise	2 Littlesworth	23	Goldman Forbes	Parkers Barn	44
Clifford Natasha	5 Windrush View	24	Goldman Richard	Parkers Barn	44
Collett Clara	11 Windrush View	57	Goldman Sophia	Parkers Barn	44
Collier Agnes	Overbrook	25	Gullen Olivia	The Old Forge	71
Collier Dominic	Overbrook	25	Gullen Tamsin	The Old Forge	71
Collier Karen	Overbrook	25	Gullen Zoe	The Old Forge	71
Collier Rufus	Overbrook	25	Hallsworth David	Staddlestones	45
Collins Alex	Cromwell House	26	Hallsworth Fiona	Staddlestones	45
Collins Charles	Cromwell House	26	Hanks Ian	Dale Cottage	48
Collins Fiona	Cromwell House	26	Hanks Tracey	Dale Cottage	48
Collins Matthew	Cromwell House	26	Hanks William	Dale Cottage	48
Collins Robert	Cromwell House	26	Hanks Joyce	Longford	49
Collins William	Cromwell House	26	Hanks Geoffrey	Manor House	47

Name	Address	No.	Name	Address	No.
Hanks Charles	Spring Barn	46	Manley Katherine	Ash Piece, Aylworth	78
Hanks Douglas	Spring Barn	46	Manley Pippa	Ash Piece, Aylworth	78
Hanks Gerard	Spring Barn	46	Manley William	Ash Piece, Aylworth	78
Hanks Penelope	Spring Barn	46	Marston Susan	Foxhill	79
Harding Gail	4 Sunny Cottages	50	Maughan Mollie	Boundary House	80
Harding Jordan	4 Sunny Cottages	50	Meyer Atalanti	The Bakehouse	81
Harding Kevin	4 Sunny Cottages	50	Milton Fiona	The Manse	82
Harding Luke	4 Sunny Cottages	50	Milton James	The Manse	82
Harman David	Grays Orchard	51	Mitchell Beryl	8 Mill View	84
Harper Robert	The Cottages, U-Harford	68	Mitchell Douglas	8 Mill View	84
Harper Barbara	The Cottages, U-Harford	68	Mitchell Arthur	9 Mill View	83
Hartley Gladys	The Flat, Longford	64	Mitchell Joan	9 Mill View	83
Harvey Kathleen	Ivy Cottage	52	Morton Barnaby	Lower Dale Terrace	85
Hayward Angus	1 Aylworth Cottages	53	Morton Eleanor	Lower Dale Terrace	85
Hayward Archie	1 Aylworth Cottages	53	Morton Janet	Lower Dale Terrace	85
Hayward Harriet	1 Aylworth Cottages	53	Morton Peter	Lower Dale Terrace	85
Hayward Megan	1 Aylworth Cottages	53	Murphy Judy	6 Windrush View	86
Hayward Nicholas	1 Aylworth Cottages	53	Murphy Oliver	6 Windrush View	86
Hayward Theo	1 Aylworth Cottages	53	Newton Carol	Brambles	87
Hendry Polly	2 The Quadrangle	104	Newton Robert	Brambles	87
Herbert William	2 Ash Tree Cottage	54	O'Brien Fergal	7 Windrush View	88
Hickman Christopher	Barnhill	55	Ogilvie Angus	2 Dale Street	89
Hickman Daphne	Barnhill	55	Ogilvie Hannah	2 Dale Street	89
Hicks Caroline	Hill Farm, Aylworth	56	Ogilvie Kenneth	2 Dale Street	89
Hicks Robert	Hill Farm, Aylworth	56	Ogilvie Sara	2 Dale Street	89
Hicks Sam	Hill Farm, Aylworth	56	O'Malley Austin	Windrush Cottage	90
Higgins Edward	11 Windrush View	57	O'Malley Jane	Windrush Cottage	90
Hill Elizabeth	Windrush Vale Ctg	58	Outhwaite John	Sheepwell Cottage	91
Hill John	Windrush Vale Ctg	58	Outhwaite Rose	Sheepwell Cottage	91
Hindley Madeleine	Mill Barn	59	Owens Graham	Cromwell Cottage	92
Hindley William	Mill Barn	59	Palmar Derek	Church Farm	93
Hoult Anne	Northcote	60	Palmar Shuna	Church Farm	93
Hoult Graham	Northcote	60	Parry Michael	Roundhill Farm	94
Hoult Richard	Northcote	60	Pickup David	Farthing Green	95
Hoult Robin	Northcote	60	Pickup George	Farthing Green	95
Hoult Sophie	Northcote	60	Pickup James	Farthing Green	95
Hull Jean	2 Jasmine Cottage	61	Pickup Jane	Farthing Green	95
Hunter Graham	Springfield	62	Porter Abigail	The Gables	96
Hunter Margaret	Springfield	62	Porter Ben	The Gables	96
James Derrick	1 Littlesworth	63	Porter David	The Gables	96
James Mary	1 Littlesworth	63	Porter Lesley	The Gables	96
James Peter	c/o 1 Littlesworth	63	Porter Matthew	The Gables	96
Janssen Harry	The Flat, Longford	64	Powell Corrine	Kiftsgate Cottage	97
Janssen Lesley	The Flat, Longford	64	Powell Graham	Kiftsgate Cottage	97
Johnson Paul	Cotswold Cottage	65	Quaranto Len	Glebe House	98
Johnson Juliet	Waterloo House	66	Quaranto Nancy	Glebe House	98
Johnson Katy	Waterloo House	66	Quaranto Paul	Glebe House	98
Johnson Lucy	Waterloo House	66	Quinn Patricia	Lower Harford Farm	99
Johnson Robert	Waterloo House	66	Renney David	Parkers Cottage	100
Johnson Timothy	Waterloo House	66	Renney Donna	Parkers Cottage	100
Jones Adrian	11 Dale Street	67	Ridge David	Ferndale, Dale St	101
Jones Hannah	11 Dale Street	67	Ridge James	Ferndale, Dale St	101
Jones Heather	11 Dale Street	67	Ridge John	Ferndale, Dale St	101
Jones Lara	11 Dale Street	67	Ridge Paul	Ferndale, Dale St	101
Jones Anne	3 Sunny Cottages	69	Ridge Valerie	Ferndale, Dale St	101
Jones Michael	Upper Harford House	68	Robinson Paul	Pooh Corner, U-Harford	68
Jones Janet	Upper Harford House	68	Robinson Helen	Pooh Corner, U-Harford	68
Jones Philip	3 Sunny Cottages	69	Roome Audrey	2 Yew Tree Cottages	102
Juggins Beverley	2 Rose Cottage	13	Rugge-Price Edward	5 Sunny Cottages	103
Juggins Philip	2 Rose Cottage	70	Rugge-Price Sophie	5 Sunny Cottages	103
Juggins Robert	2 Rose Cottage	70	Rugge-Price Thomas	5 Sunny Cottages	103
Kelleher Kevin	The Old Forge	71	Samuels Christopher	2 The Quadrangle	104
Kelleher Susan	The Old Forge	71	Scudamore Maralyn	Grange Hill Farm	105
Kelly Julia	Upper Dale Terrace	72	Scudamore Michael	Grange Hill Farm	105
Langley Kevin	Greystones	73	Scudamore Peter	Grange Hill Farm	105
Langley Robert	Greystones	73	Scudamore Tom	Grange Hill Farm	105
Langley Valerie	Greystones	73	Scudamore Michael	Mucky Cottage	105
Langley Vicki	Greystones	73	Seal Emily	Brockhill Farm	106
Loker Adrian	Lower Harford Farm Ctg	74	Seal Jack	Brockhill Farm	106
Macklin Helen	1 Village Avenue	76	Seal Lotte	Brockhill Farm	106
Macklin James	1 Village Avenue	76	Seal Nicholas	Brockhill Farm	106
Macklin Martin	1 Village Avenue	76	Seligman Lincoln	Aylworth Barn	107
Macklin Bill	Close Hill	75	Seligman Patricia	Aylworth Barn	107
Macklin Mary	Close Hill	75	Seymour Andrea	1 Church Farm Barn	108
Mangan Isabelle	Summerhill House	77	Seymour Ben	1 Church Farm Barn	108
Mangan Julia	Summerhill House	77	Seymour Mark	1 Church Farm Barn	108
Mangan Melissa	Summerhill House	77	Seymour Samantha	1 Church Farm Barn	108
Manley Annabel	Ash Piece, Aylworth	78	Seymour Tom	1 Church Farm Barn	108

Name	Address	No.	Name	Address	No.
Smith Ella	1 Sunny Bank	109	Turton David	Bakehouse Cottage	122
Smith Jack	1 Sunny Bank	109	Vincent Lois	Valley View	123
Smith Jayne	1 Sunny Bank	109	Vincent Neil	Valley View	123
Smith Theresa	Honeyman's Cottage	110	Virgin Cedric	Cotswold House	124
Smith William	Honeyman's Cottage	110	Walker Claire	5 Dale Street	112
Smith Eileen	Summerhill House	77	Warbrick Paul	Sunny House	119
Smyth David	Sidelands	111	Wardrop Frederick	Old School House flat	125
Smyth Louise	Sidelands	111	Webb Adam	2 Hillcrest Cottages	126
Steele Philip	5 Dale Street	112	Webb Daniel	2 Hillcrest Cottages	126
Steiner Barbara	Shepherds, Aylworth	113	Webb Lorraine	2 Hillcrest Cottages	126
Steiner Lolly	Shepherds, Aylworth	113	Webb Mark	2 Hillcrest Cottages	126
Steiner Richard	Shepherds, Aylworth	113	Webb Simon	2 Hillcrest Cottages	126
Steiner Robert	Shepherds, Aylworth	113	Wells Glenda	Close Cottage	127
Stevens Brian	Conifers	114	Wells Michael	Close Cottage	127
Stevens Mary	Conifers	114	Westall David	Waterstone Cottage	128
Stevens Elizabeth	Vine House	115	Wheeler Elizabeth	Waterloo Farm	129
Stevens Freya	Vine House	115	Wheeler Kathryn	Waterloo Farm	129
Stevens Harriet	Vine House	115	Wheeler Nicholas	Waterloo Farm	129
Stevens John	Vine House	115	Wheeler Victoria	Waterloo Farm	129
Stevenson Pamela	Cotswold Cottage	65	White Frank	Naunton Downs Ctg	130
Stonehewer Kenneth	Foxways	116	White Jennifer	Naunton Downs Ctg	130
Stratford Doris	2 Sunny Bank	117	White Jill	Naunton Downs Ctg	130
Stutowicz Laura	2 Sunny Cottages	118	White Katherine	Naunton Downs Ctg	130
Tilbrook Richard	Sunny House	119	White Susan	Naunton Downs Ctg	130
Timmins Beth	Littons	120	Wilkie Gillian	1 Harford Hill	131
Timmins Hannah	Littons	120	Williams Vera	The Gatehouse	132
Timmins Joan	Littons	120	Wintle David	Foxhill	79
Tucker Claire	Sunnyside	121	Wood Marion	Eastern Hill Farm	133
Tucker Derek	Sunnyside	121	Wood Michael	Eastern Hill Farm	133
Tucker Margaret	Sunnyside	121	Woolley Diana	Humphries Barn	134
Turton Catherine	Bakehouse Cottage	122			

Total included 342 or approx 93%. (excluding the 3 non-residents)

Whilst disappointing, the decision by a few residents not to participate in this project and leave a small trace of themselves does not detract from the fact that the overall majority of residents were not so reticent. Those who appear above can be proud of the fact that they made an enlightened, forward lookind decision and I believe that in the fullness of time future generations may endorse that fact.

Naunton 2000: in village but not included in the book (DTP = declined to participate. NR = no response to letter)

Name	Address			Name	Address		
Abraham (1)	9 Windrush View	NR	11	Hanks (2)	Brookfield	DTP	9
Allan (1)	4 Windrush View	NR	9	Loughscott (1)	3 Windrush View	NR	14
Bond (2)	6 Mill View	DTP	8	Padgham (1)	Church House	NR	11
Burroughes (5)	Naunton Downs Farm	DTP	14	Russell (2)	Church House	DTP	11
Edgeworth (2)	7 Mill View	DTP	13	Small (1)	5 Village Avenue	DTP	9
Gaston-Nash (4)	Huntsmans House	DTP	15	Smith (1)	1 Windrush View	NR	9
Greenaway (1)	12 Windrush View	DTP	13	Taylor (1)	8 Windrush View	DTP	10
Halford (2)	Stonecroft	DTP	11				
Hone (2)	Fox Hill, Dale Street	DTP	8				

Total not included approx 29 – or 7% of total population of 371

Naunton 2000 Pen Pictures

The Reverend John Fieldgate

1. 'There has probably been a church in Naunton from the late 12th century and certainly from the 14th century, which means that the people of Naunton have worshipped God here for at least 700 years. Over the years so many children must have been baptised at the fifteenth century font, so many couples must have stood before the altar to be married and the number of headstones in the churchyard are witness to just some of the many, who have been buried in the churchyard over the years.

The church is part of the community of Naunton and having been the Priest in Charge of Naunton at the time of the Millennium, one prays that both priest and people will have passed on the torch of faith not only to a new generation, but also to the people, who live in Naunton in the new Millennium.

We should pray that our stewardship has been faithful in passing on the church building in good repair and that our worship, Sunday by Sunday, will encourage a new generation to continue to work to living God.

God bless Naunton and all who live within her parish bounds'

John Fieldgate, Priest in Charge, 1992 – 2001

---

2. Chris and Carole Adams are in their 40s and have one son, Simon (18yrs). They have lived in Naunton for 20yrs, both being brought up in Gloucestershire. They are all keen on Field Sports (Hunting and Fishing). Chris who has his own design business in Cheltenhamm, is joint secretary of the Cotswold Hounds and Carole is secretary. This occupies them in the winter. In the summer Chris fishes a variety of local rivers and Carole pursues her horse interests. They have two dogs and a few sheep.

Adams: from the Hebrew personal name *Adam,* which was borne, according to Genesis, by the first man. Of uncertain etymology, it is often said to be from Hebrew *adama,* earth; the Greek legend that Zeus fashioned the first human beings from earth. It was a very popular given name among non-Jews throughout Europe in the Middle Ages.

---

3. Ian Adcock and Vanessa Gatford, 49 and 50yrs respectively, moved to Naunton 4 years ago from Norfolk, with their Bernese MountainDog, Digby. Ian is a full-time freelance motoring journalist and photographer writing for publications in 10 countries, plus the U.K. where his work has regularly appeared in 'The Times'. Vanessa has a business making home furnishings when not helping Ian out with administration. Both have immersed themselves in village life - Ian on the Village Hall Committee and Chairman of the Millennium Fund. Vanessa is a member of that too, and the Village Shop Association. Both also support the N.D.C.S. "Who said country life is quiet!"

Adcock - (variant of **Adams**)

---

4. Andy and Zosha Anderson bought The Mill House from Mrs Grove in August 1978. They have four children, Zo (34), Hilary (33), Jean (29), and Alfred R (27). Andy was financial director for Gulf Oil (Great Britain) before becoming an American diplomat, posted in Saudi Arabia and South Africa, renting out the Mill House for a number of years before they returned around 1998. Zosha was employed by the BBC, producing radio packages and organising interviews with important foreign leaders. Their main activity today is caring for their elderly parents who often visit. They also own a second home in Middlebury, Vermont and divide their time, according to the seasons, between Naunton and Middlebury. All of their children went to school in Cheltenham (Berkhamstead, Ladies College and Boys' College). Zo, the eldest daughter, is married and works as a freelance artist. Hilary, second daughter, is a BBC foreign correspondent, currently based in Johannesburg after having been posted 3 years in both Jerusalem and Lagos. Jean, third daughter, is enrolled in medical school in Vermont and married this year. Alfred R, the youngest, also married, is a pilot for Delta.

Anderson: variant of **Andrew**: English: from the Greek *Andreas,* (from *andros,* man, male) by which the first of Jesus Christ's disciples is known, in various local forms, throughout Christendom. The disciple is the patron saint of Scotland and legend has it his relics were brought to Scotland in 4th century. Also patron saint of Russia and a popular name in Eastern Europe.

---

5. Michael and Jane Arnold, aged 65 and 51 respectively, together with Emma Baker (23) and Camilla Baker (19), (Jane's daughters) and Joanna (19) (Michael's daughter) moved into Brockhill in 1996. Michael and

Jane fought the Planners for five years before obtaining permission, on Appeal, to build the property on 100 acres which Michael purchased in three lots, in 1985, 1989 and 1992.

Michael, together with Joanna, first came to Naunton in 1981 when they lived at Harford Farm House. He also had a house in London where he worked as a Chartered Accountant with one of the major firms and where he was head of Corporate Recovery and Insolvency. Michael remembers with considerable gratitude how in 1984-85, when he was the Court Appointed Receiver of the National Union of Mineworkers, and subject to considerable media attention, Nauntonians preserved his local privacy. Michael continues to work, although he has given up his Insolvency Licence, and is Chairman of two public companies and director of another as well as having other business interests. Jane has been involved with horses all her life. When she married Michael in 1989 she was working with racehorses, this being the "mutual connection", and living in Findon, West Sussex. Shortly after their marriage they moved to Nether Wescote, although the London house was not sold until 1993. At Brockhill there is considerable stabling and Jane and Emma bring on National Hunt horses and point-to-pointers. They also have their own "retired" racehorses who are given another "life" in the hunting field. Camilla is at Greenwich University studying Media and Joanna is at Edinburgh reading Philosophy and Modern Languages. The three Labradors in the picture have been bred by Jane from a long line in her family and consist of grandmother, mother and daughter!

Arnold: 1) English: from a Norman personal name composed of the Germanic elements *arn* eagle + *wald* rule.
2) Habitation name from one of two places, in Notts. and Humberside. The name of both places has been assimilated to the given name from earlier *Ernehale, Arnhale.* 3) Jewish (Ashkenazic): of uncertain origin.

6. Inger and Richard Ash moved from nearby Evenlode to live in Naunton in 1985. They know the Cotswolds well, having first come to the area from Northumberland in 1964. Inger comes from Oslo, Norway and since they married in the 1950s have always lived in villages, several smaller than Naunton. Both their children are married - their daughter and family living in Norwich; their son in London and New York. Richard's work in the construction industry entailed a great deal of travelling worldwide. He vowed on retirement to pursue his hobbies of oil painting, woodwork, D.I.Y. and golf in a quiet and peaceful environment. Inger actively pursues her many interests which include the arts, needlework and bridge. They both enjoy gardening. The face of Naunton has changed in recent years with an increase in the number of weekend homes but despite this it still retains a lively and active community spirit.

Ash: 1) English: topographic name for someone who lived near a prominent ash tree or a habitation name from some minor place so named. 2) Jewish (Askenazic) acronym from Yiddish, *AltSHul.*

7. Jean Bacon moved to Naunton from Guiting Power in 1989. She is a librarian, working for the Countryside Commission (now the Countryside Agency) in Cheltenham, for the past 20 years. Hew spare time is mainly spent on her house and garden, with frequent but much appreciated visits to her brother, sister-in-law and teenage nieces in Kincardineshire; nearer family are her parents in Guiting Power. Jean enjoys living in Naunton for the village itself and as a base for using local bridle paths to appreciate the Cotswolds.

Bacon; 1) English: metonymic occupational name for a preparer and seller of cured pork. 2) English: from Germanic personal name *Bac(c)o, Bahho,* from the root *bag-* to fight. It was a relatively common name among the Normans in the form *Bacus,* of which the oblique case was *Bacon.*

8. Mandy and Andy Barber, 41yrs and 49yrs old. Mandy has lived in Naunton all her life. Andy moved to Slaughter Farm in 1967 and moved into the village when they married in 1980. They have two children, Kevin, 15yrs and Helen, 13yrs. They both attend the Cotswold School at Bourton-on-the-Water. Andy is a self-employed window cleaner. Mandy prints compact discs at Bourton-on-the-Water. Andy's mother and father live at 10 Windrush View, at the other end of the village and Mandy's mother, Connie, lives at 1 Millview.

Barber: 1) English: occupational name for a barber (derivative of *barba* beard) who in the Middle Ages was a person who not only cut hair and shaved beards, but also practised surgery and pulled teeth.

9. Leslie and Christine Barber, 88yrs and 80yrs originally come from the Forest of Dean. Leslie started work at the age of 14yrs in the mines for 2 shillings and a penny a day (about 10p) where he was driving a horse to the coal face. After 20 years in the mines Leslie was made redundant and in 1957 he and Christine left Blakeney and moved to Lower Slaughter to take up agricultural work, retiring in 1973. They have 2 daughters and 3 sons (Andy lives in Naunton) and 11 grandchildren. Leslie and Christine enjoy their small garden, growing fuscias and geraniums to the point where there is now little room left for their vegetables. Having such a large extended family means they are never short of visitors and they are very happy with their bungalow, enjoying their retirement years in Naunton. **(Christine passed away in 2002)**

10. Neville 'Bart' and Ethel 'Niddy' Barton, 72 and 70yrs, live at Spring Cottage. Neville comes from a farming family in Cheshire and Niddy comes from Warwickshire. 'Bart' was a Captain in the Royal Tank Regiment, leaving in 1950 to spend 12 years in Industry, then Management Consultancy, before joining a Merchant Bank in the City for about 10 years. After this he went to America, forming a television company involved with scientific work and interactive postgraduate training courses, finishing with this in 1997. Neville met 'Niddy' in Broadway and after marrying in 1989 they moved to Spring Cottage, Niddy having previously visited and fallen love with the village. Neville has three daughters from a previous marriage, Caroline Louise, Victoria Jane and Nicola Dale (deceased) and two grandchildren, Holly and Jamie. His daughters live in Cheshire and Reading. In 2000 Neville formed a new company with an office in the village. It has a web presence and is best described by looking at www.classichouses-countryestates.com. Neville was Church Warden for 12 years and plays the organ in the church and the chapel. Niddy is involved with many church events and is an accomplished flower arranger. They believe that Naunton is as close to being a classless community as they have previously found anywhere – everyone being kind and generous whilst respecting your privacy at the same time. They hope to spend the rest of their days in this beautiful place.

Barton: 1) English: habitation name from any of the numerous places so called from Old English *bere* or *bœr* barley + *tun* enclosure, settlement, i.e. an outlying grange. 2) U.S.: Anglicization of Czech *Barton*, a form of BARTHOLOMEW.

---

11. Andrew and Judith Barwood moved to Naunton in 1997 from the West Midlands. Andrew is a Director of a Manufacturing Company based in Witney, whilst Judith works part-time for the National Health Service in Cheltenham. They have 2 sons. Jonathon is 29 and lives in Jersey and Stephen is 25 and is currently based in Cheltenham. The family have had many house moves with Andrew's job and now Andrew and Judith hope to stay in Naunton for a good many years to enjoy the unspoilt nature of the village and beautiful surroundings throughout their future retirement years.

Barwood: Not in dictionary but Andrew says: "Barwood appears to have originated in Berwickshire on the Scottish/English border. The family name "Barwood" is believed to be descended originally from the Boernicians, who were an ancient founding race of the North around 1000 A.D. comprising Scottish Picts and Angles, with the name itself surfacing around mid 16th century".

---

12. Alan and Edna Bayliss, 60 and 55yrs, and their two children, Marcella (31) and Neil (22) have lived at Summerhill for 17 years. Alan was born in Naunton (Taterbury Row) and his family were engaged in building and slating work here, with their roots firmly in the village for the past two centuries at least. Edna was born in Winchcombe and met Alan at the Farmer's Arms in Guiting Power, when her parents ran the pub. Alan is a self employed Plant Hire Contractor, using a number of JCB machines (3CX, 4CX, JS130 and JS200). He was a keen village cricketer in his younger days. Neil and Marcella attended the Cotswold School in Bourton. Neil works for his father and plays cricket for Naunton and Bourton Vale. He also plays rugby for Cheltenham Firsts and Gloucestershire County Seniors. For the past 10 years Marcella has been travelling-head-girl with the Nigel Twiston-Davies/Peter Scudamore Racing Partnership, nearby. Her training successes include the formidable 'Earth Summit', who won the English Grand National, together with the Scottish and Welsh Nationals in 1998, the first horse to win all 3 races. The family are currently in the throes of purchasing Hill Barn, just south of Summerhill, where they intend to move and build an equestrian centre for Marcella to run - subject of course to the usual vicissitudes of the planning authorities. Alan and Edna are Cotswold people who love the area and its people. Alan is concerned about some of the great changes that have taken place in the make-up of the village community during his lifetime, and has strong feelings about some aspects of this change. He says that as more and more people from the towns and the city have moved out here, or bought properties here to use occasionally, property prices have increased disproportionately and are now beyond the reach of many country folk, with some of those who were born here becoming displaced citizens. He agrees that it is not all negative, as most of the newcomers integrate well and add something to the community, but he believes that a minority of newcomers remain too isolated and just occupy a portion of the precious housing stock without contributing anything very much to the village in the way that his forbears did.

Bayliss is a variant of **Bailey:** English: 1) Occupational name for a steward or official. From Middle English *bail(l)l*, Old French *baillis*, oblique case *bailiff* from Late Latin baiulivus, a derivative of *baiulus* carrier, porter. In Scotland, name survives as *bailie* the title of a municipal magistrate, and elsewhere as *bailiff*, which in England denotes an officer who serves writs and summonses. 2) Topographic name for someone who lived in a district by the outermost wall of a castle which sometimes became a place name in its own right; some bearers of the name undoubtedly derive it from the Old Bailey in London which formed part of the early medieval outer wall of the city. 3) Habitation name from *Bailey* in Lancs.

13. Lionel Beames with Meg (dog) and daughter Bev' and her stallion "Magic" now 20 yrs old (Magic, that is). The Beames family came to Naunton in 1880 living at Summerhill. Lionel's mother, Elsie was from a long established Naunton family, the 'Smiths'. Elsie's father Abel Tom Smith (Lionel's Grandfather) is mentioned in E. Eales book, 'Naunton Upon Cotswold'. Recent research has traced the Smith family back to the early 1600s in the Parish. Many old Deeds in the village will show the names of George Smith or his brother John. Lionel followed in his father's footsteps as a farm worker, something that has now passed down to daughter! Bev' keeps and breeds sheep and Welsh cobs. Bev' is also Vice Chair of the Parish Council.
Beames is a variant of **Beamish,** English and Irish (Norman): habitation name from *Beaumais*-sur-Dire in Calvados, Normandy, or *Beaumetz* in Somme and Pas-de-Calais; in the last *departement* there are three different places of the same name. From Old French *beu* fair, lovely + *mes* dwelling. Beamish in Co. Durham is a Norman French place-name of the same origin, first mentioned in the 13th century; it is possible that a few bearers take their name from this place.

14. Cecilia Bedford, or Cecilia Leigh as she then was, moved to Naunton in 1983 from Stoneleigh Abbey in Warwickshire. She married David in 1986, who for over thirty years worked for Victoria Wine as a Director and Master of Wine. They each have two children, Christopher Leigh who is married and has two children, lives at Adlestrop, and Camilla, a barrister, now doing overseas charity work. Simon Bedford, who is married with two children, is a major in the Royal Green Jackets and Nicola, who is also married, has triplet boys and lives near Tetbury. David's main interests apart from wine are shooting and fishing and he is a regular 'picker-up' with several local Shoots. Cecilia also enjoys salmon fishing, tennis and music.
Bedford; English: habitation name from the county town of Beds., or a smaller place of the same name in Lancs. Both are so called from the Old English personal name *Beda* (apparently a derivative of *bed* prayer) + Old English *ford* Ford. The name is now very common in Yorks. as well as Beds.
Leigh: English habitation name from any of the numerous places (in at least 16 counties) but especially Leigh in Lancs. So called from the nominative case of Old English *leah* wood, clearing. (In this instance Cecilia has almost certainly identified the locality from where her name originates)

15. James and Jeanne Beer have been married for 29 years and have lived in Harrow, just outside London for 22 years. They bought Jasmine Cottage in 1985 and they and their family and friends have spent many enjoyable times there. They have made lots of friends in Naunton and take part in many of the village's activities and consider it a privilege to be classed as 'honorary Nauntonians'.
Beer: English (W Country): habitation name from any of the forty or so places in SW England called *Beer(e)* and *Bear(e)*. Most of these derive their names from the West Saxon dative case , *beara,* of Old English *Beara* grove, wood (the standard Old English dative *bearwe* being preserved in BARROW). Some may be from Old English *boer* swine pasture.

16. John and Lilian Bond together with their son Stephen say they have always felt more at home in a country environment. This is probably due to Lilian having spent her young childhood as a wartime evacuee in a village in Somerset., and my own childhood in what was then a very rural part of Essex, so it was all part of the game plan that at some point before retirement, we both felt that we would like to escape to a less stressful location than our had then become. As fairly regular visitors to relations in Cheltenham, we were quite familiar with this area, so having closed my business as an electrical contractor in 1980 we began looking for a property in this area. We finally agreed on Naunton after staying at one point in the 'Black Horse', and when Old Well Cottage became available in October 1981, Lilian and I together with our unmarried son made the move. The first "Local" we had contact with was on moving day when we collected the keys from the nicest person possible, Billy Herbert. A good start to a very happy time in Naunton!
Bond; English: status name for a peasant farmer or husbandman. Middle English *bonde* (Old English *bonda, bunda,* reinforced by Old Norse *bonnde, bondi).* The Old Norse word was also in use as a personal name and this has given rise to other English and Scandinavian surnames alongside those originating as status names. The status of the peasant farmer fluctuated considerably during the Middle Ages. It is likely that the word is akin to *bindan* to bind: the Proto-Germanic word *bonda* probably signified a member of a band or tribe bound together by loyalty to their chief. *A number of English bearers of this name come from a Dorset family traceable back to Robert Bond of Hache Beauchamp, whose name is found in records dating from 1431. The surname is however extremely common in N as well as S England, and several genealogically separate origins are probable.*

17. Pat Boult (50) returned to Naunton with her second husband, Ralph (53) in September 1997 to give full time care to her father Harold Hanks. She is a 4th generation Hanks, growing up in Naunton with brothers David and Nigel, and sisters, Sue and Janet who all still live close by. Childhood was spent on Waterloo Farm, which then belonged to their grandparents, Horace and Hilda Hanks. Their great grandparents were William Bullock and Clara Hanks who resided at The Mill, opposite the family home at 2 Millview. After leaving Westwoods Grammar School (now a housing development) at Northleach, Pat moved to London to work. She married and raised two children there, Phillip (31) and Catherine (28) but often visited Naunton with the children to visit her parents at Millview and her sister Sue, who was then living at 'Farmhouse' Dale Street, to give the children a taste of the beautiful countryside and an insight into farming life. Pat and Ralph regularly visited Naunton from London to take part in the many events going on here, even if just for the day. Since the death of her mother Sheila in 1996 they came more often and after the death of her father Harold in 1998, they decided to buy No. 2 and retire here. They are now visited by their own grandchildren - Daisy (7yrs) and Poppy (4yrs), who live in Somerset with Phillip and Clare. Catherine lives near Chichester. Ralph's daughter Melissa (29) and son Sam (25) still live in London. Even though 'retired' there is always plenty to do. They belong to a walking group and take an active part in village events. Pat is a member of the W.I. and Secretary to the Dovecote Conservation Society. Ralph is on the Buildings Committee. They both envisage a long and happy retirement in a very special village.

Boult variant of **Bolt**: English (chiefly W Country) 1) occupational name for a bolter or sifter of flower, from Middle English verb *bo(u)lt* (Old French *beluter*, of Germanic origin). 2) From Middle English *bolt* bolt, bar (OE *bolt* arrow; the bolt shot from a crossbow). In part this may have originated as a nickname or byname for a short but powerfully built person, in part as a metonymic occupational name for a maker of bolts.

---

18. Edward and Victoria Bowen-Jones live at Rosemary Cottage with their 2 children, Rowley, 4yrs and Benjamin, 2yrs. Edward was born in Northleach where his grandfather was the local GP. He moved to Naunton with his parents in 1977 when they took on the tenancy of the Black Horse Inn, which he helped run when he left school until his father's retirement and death in 1996. Edward now works in Cirencester for Mitsubishi. Victoria moved to the Cotswolds in 1989 and to Naunton in 1990 to work for local National Hunt Trainer, Nigel Twiston-Davies. Since the birth of the children she still rides out regularly but is no longer full-time. Naunton still has a strong nucleus of people who work locally which prevents the village becoming a dormitory. It has access to good schools, towns and is within easy reach of motorways. Its great community spirit makes us feel lucky to live here.

Bowen: 1) Welsh: patronymic from the given name **Owen** with fusion of the patronymic element. 2) Irish: Anglicized form of Gaelic **O'Buadhachain.**
A Welsh family called Bowen trace their ancestry to Llewelyn ap Owen, living in Pembrokes. in 1364. One of the sons was recorded with the surname Bowen in 1424.
Jones: English and Welsh: patronymic from the Middle English given name *Jon(e)* JOHN. The surname is especially common in Wales.

---

19. Jonathon Bowen-Jones, 30yrs, grew up in Northleach with his brother Edward and their parents, Jenny and Adrian. The family moved to Naunton when Jonathon was 9, when Adrian and Jenny took over the Black Horse pub. After leaving Cold Aston Primary School, Jonathon went to the Cotswold School at Bourton and when he was 16 he commenced a course at the Hartpury Agricultural College. After college he obtained a position as Farm Manager at Roundhill Farm. In this capacity he was responsible for the day-to-day running of the arable farm on which he and Mr Parry grow wheat, Winter and Spring barley, oil seed rape and occasionally, peas and linseed, a small part of the farm being left for grazing by local livestock An annual pheasant shoot is another feature of the farm and when the full-time gamekeeper left Roundhill Jonathon moved into Keepers Cottage and took over the rearing of some 4500 pheasants each year, about 1500 of them being sold and the remainder being released in July for the 'shoots' that take place between November and January. Since Mr Parry bought Roundhill they have planted some 70,000 (seventy thousand) trees; being native oak, ash, beech, cherry, larch and rowan. Jonathon enjoyed his childhood in Naunton but amongst the changes that he has seen take place the one that disturbs him most is how many local youngsters will be able to stay here. He believes the influx of people from the towns and cities has been the direct cause of property prices spiralling so high that he and other young people like him are finding it difficult, if not impossible to get onto the property ladder in the very place where they grew up and where they would like to remain.

---

20. Nora Brett, her husband James and their three children moved to Church Farm House as a family of 5 in 1976. James retired early and because he was born in the Cotswolds, he had always looked forward to the day he could come back here. Within three years of doing so the children were all married and left the district. James and Nora lived here happily together until his death in 1996, aged 82. Nora continues to live in a house of good memories and hopes to stay here until her time is up!

Brett: English and French: ethnic name for a Breton. The Bretons were Celt., speakers driven from S.W. England to NW France in the 6th cent. AD by Anglo Saxon invaders; some of them reinvaded England in the 11th cent. as part of the army of William the Conqueror. In France and among Normans, Bretons had a reputation for stupidity, and in some cases the name and its variants may have originated as derogatory nicknames. The English surname is most common in E. Anglia where many Bretons settled after the Conquest.

21. Elmar Bruening, 72yrs, has lived at the Rectory since 1991 when he purchased it from the late Nicholas Ridley M.P. The purchase price in 1991 was £725,000*. Elmar was born in Germany but left to live in South Africa in 1952, spending much of his life in South Africa after that where he was engaged in the export of minerals from S.A. to other parts of the world. For the past 3 or 4 years he has been involved in the export of S.A. wine to the Seychelles, Mauritius, Singapore and Kenya. Elmar has 4 children and 7 grandchildren from his first marriage and they all live in S.A. In 1990, seeking a home in even more beautiful surroundings than South Africa, Elmar received a sale brochure from Knight-Frank for the Rectory. He visited Naunton to view the Rectory and fell in love with it immediately, saying 'I virtually bought it having only seen it from the outside, and have never regretted doing so; and within a very short time we moved in'. Elmar soon found himself drawn into various village activities and committees, and he was on the PCC in about 1995 when some £30,000 was raised to repair the roof on the church.' Of the part of the world, where he currently finds himself, Elmar says, 'The Cotswolds are a very special part of England but Naunton is certainly a very special part of the Cotswolds'.
Bruening: not listed - of Germanic origin.
*The Rectory was valued at £1,575 in 1914. It was sold for £11,000 in 1960 and £725,000 in 1991. It was sold again in 2002.

22. Jonathan and Vanessa Cameron 47 and 48yrs, moved to Riverside Cottage on 4 July 1997, having previously rented the Old Forge in Dale Street some 5 years earlier. Jonathan is an intellectual property and new media solicitor practising in the city. Vanessa is the Chief Executive of the Royal College of Psychiatrists. They love their life in Naunton and are keen walkers, cyclists and gardeners. They have two miniature schnauzers, Rumpus and Rollo. They think they are particularly lucky living next to a working farm run by their next door neighbours, Sylvia and John Hanks. They are active participants in the music societies of Naunton, Guiting Power and the opera festival in Longborough.
Cameron: Scots: 1) as a Highland clan name it represents a nickname from Gaelic *Cam* crooked, bent + *sron* nose. 2) in the Lowlands it is normally a habitation name from any of the various places so called, all of which show early forms such as *Cambrun,* and seem to be named from Gaelic *cam* crooked, bent + *brun* hill

23. Marie-Louise Chudleigh, 32yrs, and her 8 year old daughter Charlotte are living at No 2 Littlesworth on a short-term rental agreement at a cost of £475 per month; the cottage being owned by Derrick and Mary James. Marie works in a boutique in Stow-on-the-Wold and Charlotte attends school at Temple Guiting. Marie-Louise comes from Oxfordshire and is currently the manager of a bookshop known as 'The France Shop' in Stow-on-Wold.
Chudleigh: Not listed because insufficient names are clustered anywhere in the country: it is however likely to be a habitation name originating from two villages bearing that name in Devon.

24. Natasha Clifford moved from Cheltenham six years ago and she works in the village, looking after children. Her mother (Helen Macklin) and her step-dad (Martin Macklin) run the Black Horse Pub and a Guest House. "I am a member of the Naunton Players and we put on a show in the village hall every year. I was baptised in the Chapel after moving to Naunton."
Clifford: English: habitation name from any of the various places, for example in Devon, Gloucs., and Herefords., and W Yorks., so called from Old English *Clif* slope + *ford* ford.
A family of this name trace their descent from Walter de Clifford, eldest son of Richard FitzPons, living in the reign of Henry II (1154-89). He adopted the surname from Clifford Castle near Hay-on-Wye, which was acquired on his marriage to the daughter of Ralph de Toeni. The present Lord Clifford of Chudleigh descends directly from Walter de Clifford in the male line; the hereditary title was acquired by Thomas Clifford (1630-73), a leading minister of Charles II. The present Clifford family of Frampton-on-Severn, Gloucs., descends through the female line, but deliberately resumed the name in 1801 and again in 1943.

25. Dominic and Karen Collier, 45 and 40yrs, with their two children, Rufus (7) and Agnes (5) moved into Overbrook in August 2000, (The house being the former home of Lord Grey of Naunton). Dominic, originally from Stafford, is a director in a Venture Capital firm in The City of London. Karen, originally from Buckinghamshire, is a self-employed Corporate Identity Consultant. Both have lived in London for the past 20 years and have visited the Cotswolds over recent years, being attracted to the area for fairly obvious reasons. They fell in love with Overbrook as soon as they saw it, immediately thinking that it would make a fine family home. "We have no regrets whatsoever about moving here. The garden is fantastic for produce and for the children to play in and we are just beginning to feel our way into the local community." The children attend Cheltenham Junior College.

Collier: English: occupational name for the burner of charcoal or a gatherer or seller of coal, from Middle English *cole* (char)coal.

26. Matthew and Fiona Collins, both aged 40, and their four sons, Will, aged 11, Charles, 9, and seven-year-old twins, Alex and Robert, bought Cromwell House shortly before Christmas 1998. Although their main home is in London, where Matthew works for an investment bank in the City, they spend as much time as possible at weekends and during school holidays, enjoying the peaceful surroundings of Naunton and the Cotswolds and making the most of the opportunities for walking, cycling and exploring this beautiful area.

Collins: 1) English patronymic from Middle English *Col(l)in* a diminutive of **Coll**, itself a pet form of NICHOLAS. 2) Irish: Anglicized form of Gaelic *O Coileain* and *Mac Coileain*.

A visitor's perspective...............

27. Paul and Erica Cooper, 54 and 53yrs, live in Kingston, Jamaica. They have two children, Joseph (28) and Carina (24).

"We first discovered Naunton in 1995. Paul, whose grandfather was an Englishman by birth, feels he is one too. He has always loved the countryside and anything to do with farming and after our first visit to Naunton he felt like a true 'native'. In fact we both felt really accepted here, which is one of the reasons for our numerous visits. We found the cottage through English Country Cottages and it was exactly what we had been looking for. The first people we met were Brian and Molly Ganniclift (then living next door). We enjoyed their company very much and have fond memories of them. The next was Joan Mitchell who is our landlady's agent. We have grown very fond of Joan and her entire family. The first 'little' and true friend I met here was Freya Stevens. I had gone to the Post Office shop to get some supplies and this red-cheeked little girl was sitting under an umbrella, dressed in blue and selling courgettes at the gate of Vine House. How could I resist! She won my heart as all children do and I have made good and solid friends of John and Lizzie Stevens and through them many other friends. The first person Paul met was old Mr Harold Hanks (who died in 1998). He told Paul many things about the village and about his farming family who have lived here for a few years. In fact he suggested Paul look at some of their names on the Chapel and Church gravestones, and he did. We have been back to Naunton every year since, with one exception when we stayed at Longborough - a pretty village, but NOT Naunton. We even brought our son, our daughter, son-in-law and my sister Sandra here, to meet our friends and see our home-from-home, for that is what Naunton means to us now. I once recall going to the 'open gardens' here and oh, I was just so thrilled with all the flowers and vegetables. I bought honey from someone called the 'Honey Lady'. I gave her nutmeg and became the 'Nutmeg Lady'. Knowing Paul's interest in horses, some friends told us about Peter Scudamore. I recall our meeting him one day - quite by chance, through our son Joe. We were sitting outside the Black Horse when Peter drove up and walked into the pub, dropping a £5 note on the way in. Joe picked it up, followed him in and gave it to him. I think that must have proved us Jamaicans to be 'OK' folks! This brings me to Jenny and Adrian Bowen-Jones, who were then running the Black Horse, and their son Edward. We enjoyed meeting them and Adrian would talk to Joe to try and persuade him to stop smoking. I'm pleased to say that he has since stopped smoking but we were sorry to learn of Adrian's death.

We have met so many other nice people here, including Mary and Martin Fiveash, David and Jane Pickup and their boys, and a number of others.

Last but by no means least, we know David and Ann Hanks and have even met their two year old granddaughter, Georgia. David has taken us out and shown us all over Cheltenham where he now lives, together with a number of the surrounding villages.

The people we have met here are just nice people; they are all real people who together, make Naunton what it is today - our home away from home." (Paul is an attorney-at-law in Kingston but is also registered in the UK. Erica teaches children up to the age of 9 years).

Cooper: English occupational name for a maker and repairer of wooden vessels such as barrels, tubs, buckets, casks and vats.

28. Joan Cowan, 85 yrs, moved to Naunton from Aylesbury in 1980 after being widowed. Her late husband was a retired Brigadier. She enjoys living here in retirement, liking the village and its people very much, whilst lamenting the closure of the village shop. She has a daughter living nearby (Donnington) and a grand-daughter is an assistant trainer in one of the local riding stables. The house was built in the 1700s and was originally 3 small cottages for local farm workers, and a barn at one end next to the river. It boasts a modest outdoor swimming pool which is now stocked with fish and plants. The name 'Hatters' cottage has nothing to do with any previous work there but derives from the tiny room which once sat on the apex of the roof and which was likened to a hat. (Joan passed away in 2003).

Cowan: Scots: 1) common Lowland surname of uncertain origin. None of the explanations put forward is very convincing. The name is not recorded before the middle of the 16th cent. *(James Cowhen, Berwicks. 1560).* 2) Highland surname of Gaelic origin.

29. Michael and Licia Crystal, are 52 and 54 respectively. They lived in St John's Wood, London when they discovered Naunton and bought Kiftsgate House as a country retreat. They have two children, Ben, age 22, has come down from Oxford and is starting work in the City and Sarah, age 19, is at Kings College, London. Michael is a QC working in London. Licia is a retired solicitor involved in charity work. Michael and Licia are passionate supporters of the Royal Shakespeare Company, Stratford on Avon.

Crystal: variant of **Cristal:** Scots: from a Scots pet form of the given name CHRISTOPHER.

30. Robin and Jane Davies, aged 45 and 47, moved to Naunton on New Years Eve 1993 from Cheshire. Robin had recently taken up a new job with Westbury in Cheltenham. They have three children, Meghan (18), Joe (14) and Henry (12). Meghan has just completed her A-level exams and is currently taking a "gap" year and is working at Waterstones bookshop before travelling around the world and taking a place at Manchester University to read German and Italian. Joe and Henry both attend St Edwards School in Charlton Kings and enjoy playing rugby, football and cricket. Jane is very active in the village as a member of the Social Committee. She is a regular bell-ringer, enjoys yoga and can often be seen walking the family's four dogs (Ella, Millie, Poppy and Jessie) in the fields around Naunton. Robin keeps four hives of bees and is the Chairman of the Naunton Dovecote Conservation Society and a trustee of the Naunton Village Trust. The family enjoys a full and varied social life in the village and get involved in helping to organise a wide range of community activities.

Davies: one of the numerous variants of **David:** Welsh, Scots, English, French, Portuguese, Czech and Jewish: from the Hebrew male name *David* 'Beloved'. The given name has been perennially popular and this popularity was increased in Britain, firstly by virtue of its being the name of the patron saint of Wales (believed to have been a 6th cent. monk or bishop) and secondly because it was borne by two kings of Scotland.

31. William, Jayne and Christian Davies, aged 54, 47 and 12 years, moved to the village with Jayne's daughter Danielle, 24yrs, in December 1979. William has his own manufacturing company, LSC Ltd, (Incorporated in 1979) in Bourton-on-the-Water. Jayne is an accountant and works both for the company and on a freelance consultancy basis. Danielle moved from the village in 1998 with her partner in Farmington but she still remains a "villager". Christian is at boarding school (Dean Close Prep' in Cheltenham) but regards Robert Juggins as his best friend. William was born and bred close to Naunton and loves village life. He is captain of the cricket, he is on the Parochial Church Council and until recently was Chairman of the Parish Council. Jayne, after finding it difficult initially to settle to life in a small village, now adores Naunton and would hate to live elsewhere. She finds the kindness, generosity and neighbourliness unrivalled.

32. Terri (nee Herbert) and Oliver Davis, 36 and 44yrs, live with their 10-year-old cat Tigger. They moved to Ash Tree Cottage in 1993, following eighteen months of renovation work. Terri's family on both sides has lived in Naunton for several generations and she herself, grew up in this very house.

Oliver was born in London and spent his formative years in Sussex before moving to Cheltenham in the 1980s. Ash Tree Cottage was formerly two dwellings dating from around 1790, one of which was once lived in by Terri's paternal grandfather's grandmother - Jane Higgins, and converted into one house by her father Robert in the 1950s. Oliver is a qualified surveyor and teacher of Economics and Business Studies. He currently renovates and develops property whilst also working as a Consultant for a health food company. Terri is a qualified therapist in several fields and currently works as a nutritional advisor for the same health food Company. Their work takes both of them away for most of the week, so Naunton is a quiet and peaceful retreat from an otherwise hectic life.

They were married in Naunton Baptist Chapel in May 1999 and have been together for almost 12 years. Terri's grandfather, 'Billy' Herbert lives next door.

Davis: another variant of **David**. See **Davies**.

33. Connie Dearman was born in Naunton (at Overbrook House) in 1928. Christened and married in St. Andrew's Church, Naunton. "Apart from two years living in Gloucester, I have lived here all my life. My parents moved from Overbrook to a small cottage behind the Black Horse and Mrs Fletcher lived next door. We later moved to 1 Rose Cottage. When my husband Bill and I returned from Gloucester we lived in the Quadrangle, then Ashtree Cottage and finally, 1 Millview. I have 3 children, Paul, Roger and Mandy, who each have 2 children. I worked at Thomas Comely and Sons Ltd, Church House, Naunton (Corn Merchants) from 1961 to 1994 when the Company moved to Shipston on Stour. The village has altered considerably since I was a child with new houses being built here and there. Village Avenue was an apple orchard and the cricket pitch and play area was the allotments. I had many happy years at the village school (now offices for Huntsmans Quarries) when Miss Longford was the Infant's Teacher and Mr Proctor Pexton the Headmaster. All my children started at this school. Paul and Mandy moved on to Bourton Secondary and Roger to Westwoods Grammar at Northleach. Many happy days were spent by the children of Naunton paddling in the river, playing by the dovecote and on the ice when the 'Millaize' was flooded and froze over in the winter. They used to play cricket on the 'Millaize' once, before it moved up to Summer Hill. Unfortunately those days are gone (but not forgotten) and Naunton has changed. Today I don't know half of the residents and even house names have changed, i.e, El Hogar is now Hatters; Brookside is Waterside. I remember when we had a dairy, a bake house, a paper shop, 3 grocery shops, a post office, a green grocers and a garage with 2 petrol pumps. Now we have NOTHING"! (Connie passed away in 2003).

Dearman: variant of **Dear:** English: 1) from the Middle English personal name *Dere*, Old English *Deora*, in part a short form of various compound names with the first element *deor* dear, in part a byname meaning 'Beloved'. 2) Nickname from Middle English *dere*, Old English *deor* wild animal, or from the adjective of the same form meaning 'wild', 'fierce'. By the ME period the adj. was beginning to be restricted to the sense of modern English *deer*, so that this may be the sense of the surname in some cases.

---

34. Thomas and Jeanette Donoghue (Tom and Jean) have lived in Naunton for 3 years having previously lived in Cheltenham. Tom works for Smiths Industries at Cheltenham and Jean works at Cheltenham General Hospital. Both have been in their present employment for the past 14 years. Prior to this they were publicans for Whitbreads but changed from that lifestyle when their grandchildren came along. They have three children. Kelvin and his wife Julie have three daughters; Karen and her husband Jeff (who live next door) have twin boys and a daughter; Kim and Mark have two sons and a daughter. "We enjoy walking, DIY, gardening and reading. We spend our holidays walking on Dartmoor with our dog and we also keep canaries and exotic finches in an outside aviary".

Donoghue is one of many variants of **Donohue:** Irish: Anglicized form of Gaelic **O Donnchadha** 'descendant of *Donnchadh*', a personal name composed of the elements *donn* brown + *cath* battle.

---

35. Jonny and Julia Duval have three children, Alexander, Katie and Tom. They came to Naunton some 4 years ago and are very happy in the 'Pound' which the previous owner, Mrs Evelyn Day, described as a "friendly house". The Duval family consider they are extremely fortunate to be in Naunton and to have met some delightful and helpful people in the village. The river and the Dovecote in the valley are both overlooked by the "Pound". The animals (both tame and wild) living nearby are like 'old friends'. These all help to form a refuge from the tribulations of maritime law which Jonny practises and which Julia, a trained biochemist and toxicologist, is also now studying.

Duval is a variant of **Vale:** English: (chiefly S England and Midlands) topographic name for someone who lived in a valley, Middle English *vale* (Old French *val*, from Latin *vallis*). The surname is now also common in Ireland, where it has been Gaelicized as **de Bhal.**

---

36. Jeff Dyer, originally from Stroud, and his wife Karen, originally from Cheltenham, moved to 5 Millview in 1994. Jeff is a satellite engineer and Karen a hairdresser. Married in Naunton Chapel, they have 3 children. Twins, Ryan and Robert are 13yrs old and Rachel, 2yrs on this date in October 2000. Jeff is a keen metal detectorist and Karen loves horse riding. She likes life in Naunton, especially since her parents moved in next door at No 4 Millview in 1998. They enjoy the various social functions in the village and fundraising events.

Dyer: 1) English: occupational name for a dyer of cloth, Middle English *dyer* (from Old English *deag* dye; the verb is a back-formation from the agent noun). 2) Irish: variant of DWYER.

---

37. John and Joan Egan purchased the estate in 1998 where they operate the Lavender Hill Stud and racing yard on the ridge above Naunton Village. John's business is based in London and the U.S. They began visiting the area in 1995, having a mare in training with Nigel Twiston-Davis and Peter Scudamore. When racing at Cheltenham they stopped at Fox Hill BandB. Through their friendship with Sue Marston, they eventually purchased the James Barn Farm Estate where Joan has begun breeding flat and National Hunt horses. D.J. Wintle is their head trainer. They farm lavender, oats and wheat. They have spent the last two years renovating the house, building new horseboxes and barns, and hope to remain in Naunton indefinitely. Their four children live in California and Chicago but came to celebrate the Millennium in Naunton with their 5 grandkids.

Egan is a variant of **Higgins:** 1) English: patronymic from the medieval given name *Higgin* a diminutive of HICK. 2) Irish: Anglicized form of Gaelic O hUiginn 'descendant of '*Uiginn*', a byname meaning 'Viking', 'Sea-rover' (from Old Norse *vikingr*).
3) Irish: Anglicized form of Gaelic **O hAodhagain** 'descendant of *Aodhagan*' a personal name representing 'Fire'.
Francis Higginson (1586-1630) was a Leics. Puritan who emigrated to New England in 1629 as first minister of the Massachusetts Bay Company. Most of his descendants were merchants including his grandson Nathaniel, who returned to England in 1694. As an employee of the E India Company he became Lieutenant-General of India.
The Irish adventurer Don Ambrosio O'Higgins (1721-1801) rose to become Viceroy of Peru under the Spaniards, but his fame was exceeded by that of his own son Bernardo O'Higgins (1780-1846), remembered today as the 'Liberator of Chile' where O'Higgins province is named after him.

38. Marion and John Elliott (both 60) moved to Naunton from St. Albans, Hertfordshire in 1992. John was a civil servant with the Department of Employment and Marion was a primary teacher until their daughter, Judith, was born. They have one daughter, Judith (aged 34) who is married with two sons and lives in Kent.

Marion is a member of Naunton WI and arranges the flowers in Naunton Chapel. John works part-time for the North Cotswold Voluntary Help Centre (based in Moreton-in-Marsh). He was treasurer of Naunton and Guiting Power Baptist Chapels for 7 years until April 2000. He became treasurer of Naunton Village Hall in 1994.

They both enjoy their garden and walking in the area that they discovered when travelling to Wales on holiday. They enjoy supporting village activities and welcomed the opportunity to escape the rat-race of urban living.

Elliott: English and Scots: from Middle English given name *Elyat, Elyt,* This represents at least two OE names that have fallen together. In Scotland, Anglicized form of the originally distinct Gaelic surname **Elloch, Eloth,** a topographic name from Gaelic *eileach* dam, mound, bank.
A major family spelling their name Eliot *is found in the border region of Scotland. They can be traced back to Robert* Elwald *(d. 1497) of Redheugh, Roxburghs, who was squire to the Earl of Angus.*
Andrew Eliot, a shoemaker of East Coker, Somerset, who emigrated to Boston, Mass., in 1670, was the founder of a distinguished American family which included the poet T.S.Eliot (1888-1965), who was born in St Louis, Missouri. However, the earliest Eliot *recorded in N America was John Eliot (1604-90), a Puritan missionary known as the 'Indian Apostle', who was born in Herts. and sailed to Boston in 1631. He then settled in Roxbury, Mass. His father was a yeoman who owned a considerable amount of land, some in Essex, and claimed Norman descent.*

39. John and Maria Evans, 43 and 51yrs, moved from London to Dale Street in May 1998. They had lived in the Dordogne for a couple of years and had moved back to Ealing, knowing they wanted to sell their house and recreate the country life they had enjoyed in France. They have their own computer software company and work from home. Naunton's central location and ease of motorway access make it a good base from which to see their clients who are as far a field as Dorking and Hartlepool. They were pleasantly surprised to find a thriving community spirit which they fully participate in. They enjoy their family and friends coming to stay to share in the beauty, peace and quiet of their idyllic surroundings.

Evans: variant of **Evan:** 1) Welsh: from the given name *Ifan, Evan,* JOHN. 2) Scots: variant of EWAN.

40. Stephen and Jayne Ewart-Perks moved to Aylworth House in 1996 from Shipton Solers. Stephen is a Land Agent and Jayne an entrepreneur. They have four children, Simon, training to be a Land Agent. Lucy graduated from Camberwell and is hoping to be a freelance photographer. Victoria is doing 'A' levels at Cheltenham Ladies College and George is going to Harrow in September 2001. There are also 4 horses, 2 dogs, 2 cats, 10 ducks and 4 chickens at Aylworth House.

Ewart: English and Scots: 1) from *Ewart,* a Norman form of the given name EDWARD. 2) occupational name for a shepherd, from Middle English *ewehirde,* from Old English *eowu* ewe + *hierde* herdsman. 3) habitation name from a place in Northumbria, so called from Old English *ea* river + *woro* enclosure; it is enclosed on three sides by the rivers Glen and Till.
Ewart is the surname of a Galloway family, who probably migrated there from Roxburghs. They came originally from Northumbria and are not found in Scotland before the late 16th cent.
Perks: variant of **Park:** English: 1) metonymic occupational name for someone employed in a park or topographic name for someone who lived in or near a park. In the Middle Ages a park was a large enclosed area where the landowner could hunt game and a good local example was Sudeley Park at Winchcombe.

41. Rory and Lyn Fellowes are temporary residents who work away a lot, for whom this is a wonderfully peaceful refuge. The cottage is owned by Derrick and Mary James.

Fellowes: variant of **Fellow:** English: from Middle English *felagh, felaw*, late Old English *feolaga* partner, shareholder (Old Norse *felagi*, from *fe* fee, money + *legja* to lay (down). In Middle English the term was used in the general sense of a companion or comrade, and the surname thus probably denoted a (fellow) member of a trade guild.

42. Mary and Martin Fiveash moved from Chislehurst in Kent to Naunton in 1989 as a result of privatisation of the electricity supply industry, and have never looked back. The change in work location was a golden opportunity to move from London to the Cotswolds.

Mary originates from Great Driffield in East Yorkshire and is employed by British Nuclear Fuels Ltd as a Technical Publisher at Oldbury Nuclear Power Station. Martin originates from Southwark in London and is a Civil Engineer employed on the decommissioning of Nuclear Power Stations, currently at Berkeley, which is the last commercial nuclear power station to be decommissioned. Mary and Martin consider they are very fortunate to have found Naunton and can not imagine living anywhere else. The social life is constant and there are numerous people who work hard to keep the village alive and protected against pressures of the outside commercial world. Another asset of living in Naunton is being in the heart of the horse racing country and seeing the fine horses in and around the village on a daily basis.

Fiveash: Not in dictionary. Martin says that his family come from London's East End and although he doesn't know the origins of his surname, it is quite probably a habitation name from a place called Five Ashes, south of London in Kent.

43. John and Mary Foster moved from Putney to Naunton in 1993 and live in what was formerly the Cider Mill. John had retired in 1992 having spent most of his working life in the John Lewis Partnership. They have three children and one grandchild who all live in London. They love living in Naunton. 'It is such a friendly place with a marvellous sense of common purpose and we do what we can to help our village and those others who live here'.

Foster: 1) English: simplified variant of Forster, in any of its senses. 2) English: nickname from Middle English *foster* foster parent (Old English *foster*, a derivative of Old English *fostrian* to nourish, rear, from *foster* food)

44. Sophia and Richard Goldman are Swedish and they moved to London in 1993. After spending numerous weekends riding and walking in the Cotswolds, they found their new house in Naunton and moved here in 1997. The Goldmans have started an operation which they are running from home, working primarily with internet companies. They still find some time for riding and walking, as well as tennis and golf. Even Forbes, aged 2, has got his own riding gear and golf clubs. The Goldmans answer to the greatness of life in Naunton - sports of course!

Goldman variant of **Gold:** 1) English and German: metonymic occupational name for someone who worked in gold. A refiner, gilder or jeweller. 2) English and German: nickname for someone with bright yellow hair. 3) English: from the Old English personal name *Golda* (or female *Golde*) which persisted in the Middle Ages as a given name. The name was in part a byname from *gold* gold, and in part a short form of the various compound names with this first element. 4) Jewish: ornamental name from the modern German *Gold*. Yiddish *gold* gold. In the U.S. it is often a shortened form of almost 100 different compound names with gold as the first element.

45. David and Fiona Hallsworth were married in 1990. Fiona moved to Naunton from Bath and previously London where she had worked in the film industry as a Film Director, P.A. and Film Production Assistant. David moved to Naunton in 1980 from Guiting Power where he had lived for 7 years. He previously lived in the North of England. He retired in 1991 from being a director of a Multi-National Construction Company. David has two daughters both married with children; they both lived in Guiting Power and Naunton (Louise Smyth lives here now). David is presently Chairman of the Parish Council, Chairman of the Naunton Cricket and Sports Club. He was until recently Chairman of the Village Hall, prior to which he was a member of the sub-committee who raised the funds for the recent village hall development. He is the village Neighbourhood Watch Co-ordinator and a member of the North Cotswold Crime Prevention Panel. He was a founder member of both the Naunton Village Trust and also Naunton Dovecote Preservation Society. Both Fiona and David enjoy travel, swimming, reading and antiques. Fiona loves her garden where she does most of the work. David has been a keen game shooter all his life. They both support Village activities and fund raising for the many projects in the village. The photograph is taken in their garden adjacent to the Dovecote with their hard-working and loving Labrador - Teal.

Hallsworth: is a variant of **Hallworth.** English: habitation name from either of two places in W Yorks. Now called *Holdsworth*, both probably originally from an Old English byname *Halda* 'Bent' + *woro* enclosure.

46. Douglas and Penny Hanks (nee Harvey) both 48, together with sons Charles (21) and Gerard (19) and dog 'Samson' (10yrs) have lived together in Naunton for the past 14 years. Douglas' family have lived in

Naunton for many generations. His father was Gordon (Don) Hanks and his grandfather, Maurice Hanks of Longford. Douglas was born at Eyford, lived at The Rectory and then Summerhill Farm. He returned to Village Avenue (with Penny) in 1973 and converted Spring Barn in 1986/88. He attended school at St. Edward's, Oxford where he met Penny and they married in 1976, and worked as an agricultural storage erector (silos etc) in the UK and overseas. Hobbies include racing, shooting, and helping to revitalise Naunton Cricket Club in the 1980s, together with the new pitch on the site of the old allotments. Penny was brought up in Oxford, worked as a legal secretary in Stow, besides doing the accounts for Doug's business. Village interests include being Parish Clerk for 9 years (1980s), Secretary of Cricket Club, member of Naunton Dovecote Society Committee and related fundraising with her sister-in-law Donna Renney. Charles attended Bourton Primary and Cotswold Schools, Pates Grammar School and is now in his final year at Kent University, Canterbury. Gerard, who attended the same schools, is in his second year at the University of Liverpool and has spent a gap year travelling in India and Indonesia and both play cricket for Naunton. Their grandmother (Kay Harvey) lives in the village and their paternal grandmother lives at Swell Hill Farm, Lower Swell. Douglas' elder brother, Neil died in a car accident in 1972 aged 24 and his sister Donna lives nearby in Parkers Cottage.

47. Geoffrey Hanks was born at the Manor on 29 July 1916, living there with his mother Ruby Annie (1883-1973) and his father, George (1880-1942) and 2 sisters, Gwyneth (1912-1923), and Daphne, who grew up at Longford (1919-1980). Geoffrey's grandfather, also George (1843-1918) was the brother of William Bullock Hanks*, George also farmed 4 fields opposite the Manor, known as Humphries Barn, as well as the Manor Farm.

After attending school in Naunton, Geoffrey went to Northleach G.S. as a weekly boarder, living there with one of the masters. At 14 Geoffrey went to Wycliffe College, Stonehouse, Gloucestershire, as a full time boarder, leaving in 1932 to return home when he commenced taking over the running of the 545-acre farm from his father George. In his younger days Geoffery played rugby for Stow and Cricket for Naunton, once being a member of the village cricket team that was made up entirely of Hanks' from within the Parish. Geoffrey met his future wife, Joy Rendell (1921-1991) in 1943, during WW2, when she visited the village whilst nursing in Bristol. They married on 3 June 1945, just before 'D' Day and spent their honeymoon in Porthcawl. They had a daughter, Pamela (b1945) who lives with her husband near Burford. Geoffrey has 3 grandchildren, Gavin Collett, 35yrs who is a barrister, Clare, 32yrs who is in business and Andrew, 30yrs who is in I.T.

The Manor farm was a typical family–run Cotswold mixed-farm that once included Brockhill Stone and Slate Quarry, from which came much of the local Cotswold paving stone and roof tiles, some of the latter ending up on the roofs of Oxford colleges and some going as far as America. 5 or 6 local men worked in the quarry in Geoffrey's lifetime including Charlie Gleed, Sid Hill, Sam Weaving and Frank Staite, and these men also worked on the farm occasionally. Manor Farm once had 250 beef cattle and four 'milkers', which Frank Beames milked. The farm's sheep, like many others around the country were all lost in the severe winter of 1947 and were never replaced after that. Chickens were kept in the Dovecote, hence its concrete floor.

The Dove House Meadow (also known as Mill Hayes) was sometimes deliberately flooded in the winter and when frozen-over it became a popular skating rink. Geoffrey recalls that in his younger days his father was using some 8 to 10 cart-horses on the farm to draw the plough, carts, seed drills, binders and various other implements, and he recalls that Guiting Grange were still using teams of oxen for similar tasks. During WW1 his father bought an American International 10/20 tractor which gradually replaced much of the work undertaken by the horses, this being the first tractor in the Parish (an extremely significant advance after some 2000 years of nothing but draft animals).

Geoffrey's early farming experiences included using a threshing machine with a separate steam engine to power the threshing of corn (wheat, barley rye and oats). Subsequent farm mechanisation from the end of WW2 to the 1980s included the acquisition of a Fordson tractor and the marvellous little Ferguson T20 tractor with its multiple attachments that would have quite amazed the farmers of only 50 years before. He also had a Claas combine harvester. Parts of the village first saw electricity in 1925, being erratically generated by a water-powered turbine in a small 'power-house' building next to the Dovecote floodgates. This faltering supply was initially fed to the Manor, then to Longford, the Black Horse and finally to Reg Hooper's Cottage. During WW2 (1939-45), such was the up-stream extraction of water for the war-effort that it often caused the turbine to fail, resulting in seasoned old darts players at the Black Horse completely missing the board and (allegedly) attributing their inaccuracy to the weakness of the power supply; never to the power of the ale supply!

The village was connected to the National Grid just after WW2 (c1948) and was gradually extended to all houses who wanted it, or could afford it. Entering the 'electricity-age' proper, enabled Geoffrey to install the first corn-drier into the barn next to the Manor House in 1960, (now a private house called 'Barnhill'). The old Granary, between the house and the barn had been used as such for at least 2 or 3 hundred years. Malting barley was grown for Donnington Brewery, oats for feeding the horses. Hay, sainfoin grass** and vetches*** were grown for feeding horses, sheep and cattle.

A variety of old motor vehicles were used on Manor Farm over the years including a WW2 Dodge 4WD Command Car and numerous old Lorries for hauling grain back from the fields and bales of hay and straw for building ricks in the fields, or in and around the Manor yard. Geoffrey has been a keen golfer and fisherman most of his life. He joined Burford Golf Club at the end of WW2 in 1945 and has always fished the River Windrush. His 'fly-fishing' has been done on the Camel, Wye, Tweed and Tay. A keen shot, he used to breed pheasants at Hill Barn (top of Yarling Meadow) until about 5 years ago. His first car was a Standard 8 from Bourton-on-the-Water. Others were mainly Ford cars including the Zephyr, Zodiac and Consul Models. His 4WD off-road vehicles, unlike some of today's SUVs (or 'Chelsea Tractors') they were genuinely needed for rough-ground usage and included his first new Land Rover in 1953 and a number of others since. His current vehicle is an Isuzu Citation.

Geoffrey retired from farming in 1984 since which time most of the farm and outbuildings have been sold. The Dovecote was sold to the Naunton Village Trust in 1999, leaving him with some 5 acres adjacent to the Manor House. Geoffrey continues to enjoy his retirement years in Naunton but has been forced to give up sporting pastimes due to advancing years and declining mobility. Of the many changes he has witnessed in the village throughout his lifetime, he is particularly saddened by the decline in the farming industry. He also believes that the building of more new houses should be allowed to meet the chronic local demand, as a number of the old houses are now owned by 'weekenders' who snap up the occasional sale, depriving local people of homes due to cost and scarcity. Geoffrey firmly believes that planning permission is far too restrictive and that new, more affordable homes should be provided for young people within the village and not just bought up by wealthy people from outside.

He cites his own inability to build 4 new houses on Dovecote bank some years ago, an episode which he says resulted in the creation of the expression 'NIMBY' (not in my back yard) after the then Secretary of State for the Environment (the late Nicholas Ridley M.P.) who lived in the neighbouring Rectory, objected to the proposed development. Despite such differences of opinion, Geoffrey says he is of a time when plain speaking was appreciated and has always preferred to speak his mind about things. He has enjoyed living in Naunton and still enjoys a drive around the familiar tracks and fields that once formed part of Manor Farm.

Hanks: English (Gloucs.) patronymic from the Middle English given name *Hank,* a back formation from HANKIN (with the suffix taken to be *-in,* of Old French origin).

*A truncated version of the family lineage, compiled from surviving parts of the Registers of Naunton Parish Church and similar sources show a **Nick Hanks** in Naunton as early as 1568. Then a **Henry Hanks** 1st (who died in 1631) had a son called **Henry** 2nd (1631-1704) who had a son called **Henry** 3rd (1664-1729) who had a son called **John** 1st (1740-1782) who had a son **John** 2nd (1764-1846) who was the first known Hanks at the Manor. He had a son, **William Hanks**1st (d.1871) who had a son **William Bullock Hanks** (1852-1921), whose brother **George** (1843-1918) was **Geoffrey's** grandfather. One of **William Bullock Hanks'** sons was, **Horace Leslie Hanks** (1892-1969). One of his sons was, **Harold Douglas Hanks** (1917-1998) and one of his sons is, **David Roland Hanks** b.1948 (the author), but I doubt if this clarifies things very much!

****Sainfoin:*** From the 17th to the mid 20th century sainfoin, was a traditional forage legume, grown primarily as a source of high quality hay for fattening sheep and feeding heavy working horses, the demise of the latter no doubt contributing to its decline.

*****Vetches:*** any of the genusus *Vicia* of climbing herbaceous vines of the bean family, especially the common broad bean, grown for fodder.

---

48. Ian and Tracey Hanks, together with their 13 year old son William live at Dale Cottage. William attends the Cotswold School at Bourton-on-the-Water. Ian works for T H White at Andoversford as an Agricultural Machinery Sales Representative, visiting farms all over the North Cotswolds, and is a member of the Naunton Parish Council. Tracey (nee Pritchard) works as a florist for The Bay Tree flower shop in Chipping Campden. Tracey's home village was Broadwell near Stow-on-the-Wold, and she maintains her ties with the village as a member of the Broadwell Rifle Club. She is also a member of the North Cotswold Church Bell Ringers Association. Ian's parents, John and Sylvia (nee Miffling) also live in the village at 'Brookfield' from where they run a small farm. John was born at Waterloo Farm, which he ran with his brother Harold Hanks as a dairy unit, until the farm was split up and sold in 1977. He then continued to farm on his own with help from Sylvia. They keep a number of sheep and cattle and have a few geese which swim freely on the river. Sylvia was a member of the Village Parish Council for many years until 1999. Besides their son, Ian, they also have a daughter, Sandra, who is married and lives in North Wales with her husband and three children.

49. Joyce Hanks (nee Bainbridge) 84, moved from Bath to Longford (the house was built c1710) upon marrying Brian George Hanks (1920-1979) in 1966. Brian's father, Maurice Hanks (1877-1946) ran the farm before that and prior to that Brian's grandfather, George Hanks, (1843–1918) having bought the farm from John Gillett in 1872. George's younger brother, William Bullock Hanks, (1852-1921 and author's great grandfather). In Brian's time the 180 acre arable farm grew cereal crops, mostly barley, together with a little wheat. After Brian's death Joyce took over the running of the farm, growing only barley and leaving several fields to grass for grazing. After 1989 the 'farming crisis' meant that these cereal crops were no longer viable. The Government 'set-aside' scheme was introduced to help the ailing farming industry and this meant that the fields had to be 'topped' and the wild-life protected. By 2000 some 150 acres of good land was 'set-aside' in this way at Longford in return for compensation, with the remaining 30 acres now being rented by local people for grazing. Joyce was a qualified fitness instructor and started a branch of the Women's League of Health and Beauty (now the Fitness League) in Bourton-on-the-Water, which still continues.

50. Kevin and Gail Harding, 41 and 34yrs, (daughter of Joan and Arthur Mitchell) was born in Moreton-in-Marsh and raised in Naunton. She met Kevin, who lived in Northleach and they later married and lived on a farm in Northleach for a year. Kevin was made redundant as a farm stockman and they moved to Naunton, Gail's true home! They have two children, Luke, 6yrs and Jordan, 2yrs. Gail and Kevin would like to think that the boys will grow up to appreciate the friendly community and the beauty of the village, as much as their parents do.
Harding: English: from Old English personal name *Hearding*, formally a patronym for HARD.

51. David Harman and Jane Ford moved to Naunton in 1995 after living in Australia since the early 1970s. Jane, a journalist, and David, a former university academic, still own a publishing business in Australia, specialising in technical directories and newsletters. They moved to Naunton to be closer to Jane's mother who lives in Winchcombe and they now divide their time between Naunton and Canberra, Australia, running their business by the internet, fax and 'phone. Their twin daughters, Kathy and Sam, aged 32, live in Australia. Jane and David love walking, bird stalking, listening to classical music and enjoy the many music festivals in the Cotswolds during the summer, particularly the small Guiting and Hailes Festivals. They find Naunton a friendly and agreeable place to live, with its strong community spirit and rural atmosphere.
Harman: variant of **Hermann:** Germanic personal name composed of the elements *heri, hari* army + man. This is of very ancient origin, and the 1st century leader of the Cherusci (ancient Celtic tribe) recorded by the Latin historian Tacitus as *Arminius* has been claimed as the first known bearer. Name may also be a derivative of the element *Irmen, Ermen,* the name of a god.
Ford: 1) English: topographic name for someone who lived near a ford, Old English *ford*, or habitation name from one of the many places named with this word.

52. Kathleen (Kay) Harvey, 79yrs, grew up in Liverpool and on The Wirral. She trained as a nurse at Guy's Hospital. Married in June 1945, she has two children; Andrew (lives in Guiting Power) is a Zoologist, and Penny (Hanks) lives in Naunton. Kay has 2 grandsons, Charles and Gerard. She lived for many years in Oxford and came to live in Naunton in 1981. She enjoys playing the violin (orchestral and chamber music) and is a keen member of the Church. She has served on the P.C.C. and as a church warden for 1 year and also plays the violin in Church.
Harvey: English and Scots: from the Breton personal name *Aeruiu* or *Haerviu,,* composed of the elements *haer* battle, carnage + *vy* worthy, which was introduced into England by Breton followers of William the Conqueror, for the most part of the Gallicized form *Herve*. The surname is most common in Staffs,. Cornwall and S Devon, and E Anglia.

53. Megan and Nick Hayward, both aged 39, arrived at Aylworth in March 1991 when they bought the cottage from Ian and Mary Wilson (who at that time owned all of the Aylworth Estate). They married in August '91 and now have 3 children, Harriet (7) and Angus (5) both attend the local Primary School at Cold Aston, and Archie (4) goes to Guiting Play Group and Guiting Nursery School. They are expecting a 4th child in November 2000.* Nick works in Cheltenham as a Design Engineer for Spirax Sarco. He enjoys country

life very much together with golf at Naunton Downs Golf Club, which was opened in 1993, on land forming part of the Aylworth Estate at the time. Megan loves living in the country having always been involved in her parents farm Nr Dowdeswell, Cheltenham. Her interests are mainly bringing up her young family, cooking and running a small catering company. She also looks after various animals; mainly horses.
*STOP PRESS: late arrival, Theo William Hayward born 24 November 2000.

Haywood: English: occupational name for an official who was responsible for protecting land or enclosed forest from damage by animals, poachers or vandals. From Middle English *hay* enclosure + *ward* guardian.

54. William (Billy) Herbert was born at Notgrove on 29 April 1903. Billy initially attended school at Cold Aston (walking from Notgrove) and the family came over to Chapel at Naunton in a pony and trap. The family moved to a cottage at Lower Harford and his father went to work for Edgar Hanks at Roundhill Farm for £1 a week, having previously earned 15 shillings a week on Frank Perry's farm at Notgrove. His schooling then continued at Naunton, as did his attendance (85 years to date) at Naunton Chapel. Billy left school prematurely after Edgar Hanks obtained a dispensation for him to start work on the land because of a labour shortage caused by young men going off to war in 1914. Billy worked at Roundhill Farm for 11 years and when Edgar Hanks retired he went to Cheetham's Quarry at Eyeford as an apprentice stone worker (Cotswold tiles). This paid 11d (just under 5p) an hour, as long as it didn't rain, when you were paid nothing!

The family then moved into The Square, Naunton (now Brookside and Riverside Cottages), then owned by Edgar Hanks and which William Herbert (Snr) bought from Edgar. Billy also worked at Aylworth for several years for Will' Hanks, and was in charge of six of the thirty 'Aylworth horses' used for drawing the wagons and ploughs, working from 7am till 5pm 6 days a week. In 1923 he entered a ploughing competition with a team of these horses and won the Champions Prize of an engraved silver watch and chain (it doesn't work any more!) After Will Hanks retired from farming, Billy Worked for Mr Rand at Aylworth for a while. In about 1950 he started work for Lord Grey of Naunton at Overbrook. He worked for Lord and Lady Grey for the next 40 years, looking after the house and gardens before retiring in his eighties to look after his own splendid garden, which is a real credit to him. Billy married Dorothy Hobbs in 1927 at Naunton Chapel and they had 54 happy years together until Dorothy died in 1981. They bought Ashtree Cottage (then 3 small cottages) in 1927 for about £300 in total.

They had two sons, Robert and Dennis. Robert died in 1990 at the age of 60. Robert and his wife Kathleen had a daughter, Terri, who now lives next door with her husband, Oliver. Dennis lives at Gotherington. Billy has 3 grandchildren and 3 great grandchildren. He has without doubt seen more change in Naunton than anyone still living, recalling that life generally, as well as the winters, seemed a lot harder then than now. "In the 1920s the snowdrifts at 'Naunton Inn' cross-roads were so high you could stand on top and touch the telegraph wires. We had to go up the lane (Sheepwell) with a bucket to the pump for our water and we used oil lamps and candles before mains electricity came after the war, in about 1949, and we went down the garden to the privy until the early 1950s". Billy could also once name everyone from one end of the village to the other. He has never owned a motor-car, though he did have an Aerial 600cc motorcycle and sidecar in his younger days. Many of his memories stem from a time before the first motor car entered the village and he says things would now be far worse if Naunton didn't have the 'top road' which he says "is a natural old bypass that we should all be thankful for." "How life in the village has changed" he said wistfully, but still with a twinkle in his eye, because he just loves living in Naunton. (Billy passed away in 2001).

Herbert: English, French and German from a Germanic personal name composed of the elements *heri, hari* army + *berht* bright, famous. This Old French name, introduced to Britain by the Normans, reinforced the less common Old English cognate *Herebeorht*.

55. Christopher and Daphne Hickman, 75 and 71yrs came to Naunton in 1993 after 43 years at Home Farm, Kineton, Guiting Power. 'We have 4 married daughters and 9 grandchildren. We principally support the Church and the Voluntary Help Centre at Moreton-in-Marsh'.

Hickman: variant of **Hick:** English: from the medieval given name *Hicke*, a pet form of RICHARD. The substitution of *H-* as the initial resulted from the inability of the English to cope with the velar Norman *R-*

56. Robert and Caroline Hicks, 41yrs, and 40yrs, together with their two children, Charlotte, 18yrs and Sam, 15yrs have lived at Hill Farm, Aylworth since 1992. The farm (400 acres) is at present all arable, growing milling wheat, malting barley and bran for animal feeds. The farm's machinery consists of one Case MX 135 tractor, one Ford 774D SL Tractor, one Manston 626 Telescopic Loader, one Claas 108s 17-foot cut Combine Harvester. Road vehicles include a Range Rover and a Land Rover. They have three dogs, a Springer spaniel and 2 terriers (Paddy, Ollie and Digit). Robert and Caroline run the farm together and Sam helps out in the school holidays. Charlotte works full time for Nigel Twiston-Davies at Grange Hill. The Hicks family have been farming in this area since the end of World War Two.

Hicks: variant of **Hick:** English: from the medieval given name *Hicke,* a pet form of RICHARD. The substitution of *H-* as the initial resulted from the inability of the English to cope with the velar Norman *R-*

57. Eddie Higgins, son of John and Elizabeth Higgins, was born at Ash Tree Cottage, which then belonged to Guiting Grange. His father worked for the Bedwells at Summerhill Farm. They later moved to another cottage in Dale Street (since named 'Farmhouse') before moving further up Dale Terrace. After leaving the village school at age 14 (1939) Eddie worked at Guiting Grange for a few months. On 15 July 1940 he went to work for Horace and Hilda Hanks at Waterloo Farm where he worked alongside Horace's sons, Harold and John until the farm was sold on 5 October 1977. In the course of his working life on Waterloo Farm he saw them move from horses to tractors and from sheep to dairy and beef. Eddie continued to work for Tony Scrivens, who bought Waterloo House after the farm was sold. He later worked at Huntsmans Quarry followed by work for Mr Dalgetty at Ayleworth Farm and then Mr Parry at Roundhill Farm, where he did much dry-stone walling. Some of his last work before retirement in June 1990, included building the imposing stone gateposts at the entrance to Roundhill Fm. Eddie has been an indispensable companion-carer to Clarrie Collett for many years now, having lodged with the family throughout his working life. Eddie says "I am a country person and love living in Naunton where my roots are and I will always want to live here. We used to have several shops but they have gone and so much else has changed since the beer was 9d a pint and pipe tobacco was 9d an ounce (5p)."

Higgins: 1) English: patronymic from the medieval given name *Higgin,* a diminutive of HICK. 2) Irish: Anglicized form of Gaelic **O hUiginn** 'descendant of *Uiginn'* a byname meaning 'Viking', 'Sea-rover' (from Old Norse *vikingr*). 3) Irish: Anglicized form of Gaelic **O hAodhagain** 'descendant of *Aodhagan'* a personal name representing a double diminutive of *Aodh* 'Fire'.

57. Clara (Clarrie) Collett, nee Reeves, was born at Hampen, Nr Andoversford in 1914. She attended schools in Sevenhampton and Cheltenham before moving to Naunton as a teenager to go into service at Rockliffe (Eyeford). "I later moved to the Mill at Naunton to work for the rather eccentric owner, Miss Donisthorpe and that's where I met my future husband, Joe Collett. We were married in 1940 at Naunton Church and Joe worked on the Railway nearby. We had one son, Richard, born in 1943, who lives with his wife Ann at Hazleton. I've got two grand-sons, Darren is 27 and Steven is 23". Clara and her companion/helper, Eddie Higgins, have lived at Windrush View since 1987. Clara says she would prefer to have moved to Bourton-on-the-Water after Joe died in 1983 but Eddie always wanted to remain in Naunton. She reflects rather sadly: "it was better in the olden days when we all knew each other. People were friendlier and we all had so much more in common. We also had shops and a Post Office in the village". (Clarrie passed away in 2003)

Collett: is a variant of the surname **Coll;** 1) English: from the aphetic pet form of NICHOLAS. Forms of this name in which the first syllable is lost are found in several European languages. 2) Irish: variant of Cole. 3) Irish: Anglicized form of the Gaelic personal name *Colla,* which was borne by a warrior in Celtic mythology: it is of uncertain etymology. 4) Catalan: topographic name for someone who lived by a hill or mountain pass.

58. Graham and Elizabeth (Betty) Hill moved to the Cotswolds in 1975 with their two children, Alison and Andrew from Hemingford Grey in Huntingdonshire. Graham, after over 18yrs in the Royal Air Force, took up a Tutorship in Management at the Fire Service College and Betty a teaching post at Carterton County Primary School. Allison attended Oxford High School and Andrew (later) Westwoods in Northleach. The family moved to Windrush Vale Cottage the following year, having at last found their ideal home in which to settle: the children too remain committed to the Cotswolds. Both now married and each with two children of their own, Alison lives in Upper Oddington and Andrew in Lower Slaughter. Graham and Betty both retired in 1993 and after years of busy social life now relish the peace and tranquillity of Naunton. Graham is still working on the cottage; Betty spends as much time as possible painting and both enjoy the large garden that they have developed considerably over the years. They enjoy walking, travel and support the local Music and Dovecote Societies.

Hill: 1) English: extremely common and widely distributed topographic name for someone who lived on or by a hill, Old English *hyll.* The sound represented by Old English *y* developed in various ways in the different dialects of Middle English: in N England and in the E Midlands it became *i*, in SE England *e,* and in the W and central Midlands *u.* Traces of these regional differences may be found in the variants in spite of the influence of the standard English vocabulary word. 2) English: from the medieval given name *Hill,* a short form of HILARY or of one of the Germanic compound names with the first element *hild* battle, strife.

59. Bill and Madeleine Hindley, 74 and 69yrs moved to Naunton in 1986 after 50 and 30 years respectively spent living in Kenya, Bill farming and then engineering, Madeleine in the tourist business. They have seven children from former marriages and ten grandchildren, so a lot of time is spent travelling to keep in touch with them all, as until recently, four of the children and seven of the grandchildren lived in South Africa. Bill spends a lot of his time in the garden and repairing anything and everything that goes wrong in the house. Madeleine occupies her time doing the books for a local National Hunt racehorse trainer.

Hindley: English (Lancs): habitation name from a place near Manchester, so called from Old English *hind* female deer + *leah* wood, clearing. *Richard de* Hindele *was a substantial landowner in Lancs. c.1210-40. It seems likely that many modern bearers of the name are descended from him.*

---

60. Graham and Ann Hoult have been associated with Naunton since 1971. In that year they bought two (photo 51) derelict labourer's cottages and slowly converted them into a comfortable family home situated next to the Black Horse. At the time, they were both hospital consultants in Birmingham, but retired in the 1980s. Now in their eighties, Graham and Ann share the house with their own sons, Robin (married to Helen), Richard and David. Robin (52) is a scientist and lecturer and Helen (50), both work in London, as does Richard (49), whereas David (41), an engineer, runs a factory in Suffolk. The Hoult grandchildren, William (20) and Sophie (17) are also frequent visitors, with Sophie known to many horse lovers in the village. Ann and Graham are pictured here with 'Kim', the fourth 'Bledington' to bear that name, together with Sophie and her horse 'Kate', and Robin and Richard. We have all grown to love Naunton over the last thirty years and are pleased to have been able to support a diverse range of appeals and activities which demonstrate the vigour of this most welcoming and lively community. Naunton is a truly lovely English village.

Hoult: variant of **Holt:** English: topographic name for someone who lived by a wood or copse, from the Middle English, Old English *holt*, or habitation name from one of the many places named with this word. The surname is widely distributed, but rather more commonly in Lancs. than elsewhere.

---

61. Jean Hull, 67yrs, trained as a nurse and then lived and worked in and around London for the next ten years. She married, moved to Sussex and later trained as a social worker. Jean moved to Gloucestershire in 1976 having been offered a job as one of the Social Work Advisors to the area. "Moving to Naunton was one of the greatest blessings of my life", she says. Jean has now retired and lives with her dog Ben who was born at the village shop in 1989. "He is quite beyond my control, but I love him to bits!" Interests: "music, theatre and tending my 'pots'.
(Jean passed away in 2002).

Hull: English: 1) variant of **Hill.** 2) a pet form of HUGH.

---

62. Margaret and Graham Hunter moved to Naunton in 1998 from Buckinghamshire, having spent over 30 years in East and West Africa, where Graham was involved in the servicing of Caterpillar tractors through a branch of Unilever, as Parts and Service Director. Margaret was mainly a lady of leisure, resuming her love of flowers, cooking and the East African Women's League (akin to the Women's Institute) They have two children, Karen age 39 living with her partner in Berkshire, and Alastair, married with two little girls and also in Berkshire. Graham is now a man of leisure, enjoying golf, still giving advice to his former colleagues and helping Margaret with W.I. work and treasurer of her Flower Club. "We love Naunton and its community, the peace and the beauty of the Cotswolds".

Hunter: variant of **Hunt:** English: occupational name for a hunter, Old English *hunta* (a primary derivative of *huntian* to hunt). The term was used not only of hunters on horseback, of game such as stags and wild boars, which was in the Middle Ages a pursuit restricted to the ranks of the nobility, but also of much humbler bird catchers and poachers seeking food. The word seems to have been used as an Old English personal name and to have survived into the Middle Ages as an occasional given name.

---

63. Derrick James, 58yrs has always lived in Naunton. His wife Mary, 54yrs has lived in the village since they married in 1968, Mary was then living in Temple Guiting but she was born in Cutsdean. Derrick's grandfather, Tommy James lived at The Bakery and was a 'Carrier' with his own 'Ford T' lorry. Derrick's father, Ivor, was once the baker together with his wife Agnes and Derrick's early years were spent living at The Bakery and visiting his grandparents who lived at Littlesworth, where Derrick and Mary now live. He first attended school in the village and then went to Bourton Vale Secondary School. He worked for his father after leaving school as part of the family haulage business; I.T. James and Son, taking local livestock to markets in Andoversford, Cirencester, Kingham and Gloucester. Derrick and Mary have two children who also went to school in Bourton. Wendy, (27) is married and expecting twins and Peter (31) who is married and although living in a nearby village, works for his father as part of the ongoing father and son haulage business using two Volvo lorries (models FL6 and FL7) both of which are fitted with 'Bodycraft' cattle boxes, to carry livestock from local farms to slaughter-houses within a 25 mile radius of Naunton. Mary works at the nearby Cotswold Farm Park during the summer season.

James: English: from a given name that has the same origin as JACOB but that is now felt to be a separate name in its own right. This is largely because of the Authorised Version of the Bible (1611) the form *James* is used in the New Testament as the name of two of Christ's apostles (James the brother of John and James the brother of Andrew), whereas in the Old Testament the brother of Esau is called *Jacob*. The form *James* comes from Latin *Jacobus* via Late Latin *Jac(o)mus*, which also gave rise to *Jaime*, the regular form of the name in Spain (as opposed to the learned *Jacobo*).

64. Lesley and Harry Janssen, 54 and 60yrs came to Naunton in 1984. Harry was 4WD Manager for the Colt Car Company and retired in 1999. Lesley continued as Company Secretary for the Mitsubishi Motors Owner's Club, carried on to do freelance work. Lesley has a son, Dayne, and Harry has a son and two daughters, one being in Australia. Gladys Hartley (81) and her late husband, Cedric, who died in 1998, moved with Lesley and Harry to Naunton in 1984. In retirement, Cedric was Treasurer for the Naunton Baptist Church. After his death, Gladys has maintained a keen interest in the Church along with a very active life. Both Harry and Gladys are Vice Presidents of Naunton Cricket Club and support the club in every way.

Janssen: Flemish variant of **John**. English, from the Hebrew name *Yochanan* 'Jehova has favoured (me with a son)' or 'may Jehova favour (this child)', which was adopted into Latin (via Greek) as *Johannes* and has enjoyed enormous popularity in Europe throughout the Christian era, being given in honour of St John the Baptist, precursor of Christ, and of St John the Evangelist, one thousand saints of the name.

65. Paul Johnson and Pamela Stevenson moved to Naunton in March 1996. Paul is a G.P. at Bourton and Northleach and Pamela is Sister on the Coronary Care Unit at Cheltenham General Hospital.

Paul is originally from Surrey and went to medical school in London. Pamela was brought up in North Yorkshire. Their interests include following Manchester United, National Hunt Racing and music. They have both travelled extensively including South America, Africa and South East Asia.

Johnson: variant of **John**: English: from the Hebrew name *Yochanan* 'Jehovah has favoured (me with a son)' or 'may Jehovah favour (this child)', which was adopted into Latin (via Greek) as *Johannes* and has enjoyed enormous popularity in Europe throughout the Christian era, being given in honour of St John the Baptist, precursor of Christ, and of St John the Evangelist, author of the fourth gospel, as well as others of the nearly one thousand saints of the name.

66. Rob and Juliet Johnson, 54 and 52yrs moved to Naunton from Stroud in April 1981, with a desire to bring up their family in a small Cotswold Village and because Rob's family engineering business was relocating to Toddington. Juliet is a primary school teacher who has been employed in many of the local schools and currently works at Bourton-on-the-Water Primary School. Daughter Katy (26) teaches at an inner city Primary School in London. Daughter Lucy (23), after returning from 8 months voluntary teaching in Uganda is at Exeter University doing a P.G.C.E. and also hopes to teach in London in 2001. Son Timothy (16) is studying for 'A' levels at St. Edward's School in Cheltenham. All three children have enjoyed their childhood in Naunton and joined in various village activities. Rob and Juliet have also actively participated in many village organisations and continue to enjoy being part of this friendly and lively community.

67. Adrian and Heather Jones, 38 and 34yrs, together with Hannah, 4yrs, moved to Naunton in 1997 from Broadwell (Nr Stow) when Hannah was one. Lara was born in Naunton in July 1999. Heather produces travel brochures for an American company and works one day a week in Banbury. Adrian is Sales Director of a company, also based in Banbury, which manufactures sailing boats. We enjoy Naunton for its relaxed atmosphere; it has to be the perfect place to bring up young children and the pub is good too!

Jones: English and Welsh: patronymic from the Middle English given name *Jon(e)* JOHN. The surname is especially common in Wales.

68. Michael and Janet Jones, 59 and 58yrs live in Upper Harford House. They bought Upper Harford in 1987 when it comprised of two houses and a pair of cottages. All have since been tastefully renovated and the other three houses were sold by Mike and Janet to other flying enthusiasts, like themselves. There are two hangars and a 700 metre grass runway nearby set in about 70 acres, with magnificent views all round. Michael has been in Property Development all of his life. They have a daughter, Caroline, 35 who lives at Bradford on Avon with their one year daughter, Clara. They have a son, Warren, 33 who lives near Bath. Like everyone else at Upper Harford, Mike is a keen pilot and owns a 'Rallye' four-seater aircraft, this being his main hobby, as well as the general upkeep of the estate.

Jones: English and Welsh: patronymic from the Middle English given name *Jon(e)* JOHN. The surname is especially common in Wales.

68. David and Elizabeth Chalmers, 67 and 64yrs, moved to Upper Harford from Berkshire 10 years ago. Elizabeth is a professional watercolour artist and teacher. David is a retired military and civil professional pilot. The lure of Cotswold living was enhanced by the opportunity to join a small community of like minded aviation enthusiasts, sharing the grass airstrip at Upper Harford. Elizabeth established a studio at 'Upland House' to develop her art and to teach small groups of artists wishing to further their skills. David has taken advantage of the digital revolution to publish high class art prints for both Elizabeth and other artists working in the Cotswolds. They have two sons, Douglas (37) a career army officer and John (34) a marketing and sales executive.

Chalmers: Scots: variant of **Chambers**. The *-l-* was originally an orthographic device to indicate the length of the vowel after assimilation of *–mb-* to *–m(m)-*.

68. Mike and Phyl Harper bought their home in Upper Harford in 1991, mainly because of the Cotswold countryside, but also because as a private pilot, Bob was attracted by the Upper Harford airstrip. They retired from running their Cheshire based architectural metalwork business and came to live at 'The Cottages' Upper Harford on a permanent basis in 1999 and built a 'Ha-Ha' which affords them clear views across the valley. Bob also built an impressive workshop to house his collection of metal and woodworking machines. Bob and Phyl have three grown-up children and one grandson. Bob's interests are flying and model engineering, whilst Phyl enjoys wood-turning and spoiling their six year old grandson.

Harper: variant of **Harp**: English and Scots: occupational name for a player of the harp, from an agent derivative of Middle English *harp* harp (Old English *hearp*). The harper was one of the most important figures of a medieval baronial hall, especially in Scotland and N England, and the office of harper was sometimes hereditary. See also Crowther.

68. Paul and Helen Robinson, both 52yrs moved to 'Pooh Corner' Upper Harford in 1992; initially only part time due to Paul's job as a Boeing 747 pilot based in Hong Kong. In 1997 they moved permanently, along with their vintage (1941) Piper Cub airplane registration G-POOH, which is kept on the grass airstrip at Upper Harford. They enjoy exploring the beautiful Cotswolds from the air and then taking in the greater detail by car touring the country lanes and visiting the many lovely villages and other out of the way places.

Robinson: variant of **Rabin**: Jewish (E Ashkenazik) status name from Polish *rabin* rabbi (ultimately from Hebrew *rav*).

69. Philip and Anne Jones, 55 and 56yrs were both born in Newport, Monmouthshire. They have two children, Jeremy 32, who is married and living in Sydney and Matthew, 29, who is closer to home in Winchcombe.

Philip has always worked in the catering industry and before moving to Cheltenham to work at the Queens Hotel in 1978, ran a village pub in Llantrisant Major, Glamorgan, South Wales. "In 1996, being convinced that both children had left home, we decided to search for a small cottage and eventually found 3 Sunny Cottages Naunton. We have had four years in the village enjoying the friendliness, community spirit and various activities that are always taking place".

70. Philip and Robert Juggins have lived at 2 Rose Cottage for 3 years. Phil' was born in another beautiful village, called Chedworth, in 1954. He moved to Andoversford in 1985 and to Naunton in 1997. He was a farrier and blacksmith for 30 years but is now retired through injury and about to start an art and design course in Gloucester. Interests include motorcycles, gardening and art. Robert, son of Phil and Beverley (daughter of Lionel Beames) was born at Andoversford in 1988. Robert attended Guiting Power Primary School at the age of 4 to help bolster the numbers and prevent the school from closing (in vain). He later transferred to Cold Aston School. In 1999 Robert transferred to the Cotswold School at Bourton-on-the-Water. His interests include painting, drawing, computer games, nature and rugby.

Juggins: in its diminutive patronymic form, comes from the name **Jekyll**: English: of Breton or Cornish origin, from a Celtic personal name, OBret. *Indicael,* composed of elements meaning 'lord' + 'generous', 'bountiful', which was borne by a 7th century Saint, a king of Brittany who abdicated and spent the last part of his life in a monastery. Forms of this name (of which **Juggins** is one of about 35) are found in medieval records not only in Devon and Cornwall, where they are of native origin, but also in E Anglia and even Yorks., whither they were imported by Bretons after the Norman Conquest.

71. Kevin and Sue Kelleher, 58 and 49yrs moved to Naunton in the summer of 1991 and were married a few months later. They both work full-time in Cheltenham - Kevin as a purchasing manager for Dowty and Sue as a Journalist.

They have 5 daughters between them from previous marriages. Kevin's daughters are Clare (34) who is a nurse and lives in Cheltenham with her husband, and Fiona (33) who is single and works for the United Nations in Geneva, Switzerland. Sue's daughters are Tamsin (22) who is working in Lancaster as a statistician; Zoe (20) who is studying English at Oxford University, and Olivia (14) who is at Pate's Grammar School in Cheltenham.

The whole family enjoy living in the country, although the younger ones have occasionally yearned for the bright lights of Cheltenham! Naunton's secluded setting evokes tranquillity and it is possible to fully enjoy its peace and privacy while living in a friendly and extremely sociable community.

Kelleher: Irish: Anglicised form of Gaelic **O Ceileachair** 'descendant of *Ceileachar*', a byname meaning 'Uxorious'.
Variant: **Kelliher.**

---

72. Julia Kelly, 36 yrs moved to Naunton from Worcestershire in June 1998. Julia is the Head of Housing for a leading Midlands Housing Association, based in Cheltenham. She is involved in managing and developing new social housing throughout Gloucestershire and Wiltshire. She lives with her cat 'Ernie', 4 yrs. Asked to describe what she liked about Naunton she said 'village community life, the valley and surrounding area. I enjoy walking and running (I am an active member of the Bourton Road Runners Club) in and around the village and feel genuinely lucky to live in such beautiful surroundings', and well she might!

Kelly: 1) Irish: Anglicised form of Gaelic **O Ceallaigh** 'descendant of *Ceallach*', originally a byname meaning 'Troublesome', also said to mean 'Brightheaded'. There were several early Irish saints who bore this name, and *Kelly* is now the most common of all Irish surnames.
2) Scots: habitation name from any of the various places, such as *Kelly* near Arbroath, named with the Gaelic element *coille* wood, grove.
3) English: habitation name from *Kelly* in Devon, named with a Cornish cognate of 2. *There has been a family of this name at Kelly in Devon since Martin* de Kelly *was recorded there c.1100*

---

73. Val and Kevin Langley moved to Naunton in 1991 having previously lived in Hampshire and originating from East Sussex. They have two children, Vicki, 20yrs and Robert, 17 years. Vicki is at the University of Central England and Robert is Head Boy at the Cotswold School. Kevin joined the Cheltenham and Gloucester Building Society when moving to Naunton. The C&G is now part of Lloyds TSB PLC. Val is a Social Services Assistant dealing with the elderly in the North Cotswolds. Kevin and Robert enjoy regularly playing cricket for the village team and golf at Naunton Downs Golf Club. The village has been the perfect place for our family to grow into adulthood. Thank you.

Langley: English: 1) habitation name from any of the numerous places named with Old English *lang, long* LONG + *leah* wood, clearing. 2) from the Old Norse female personal name *Langlif*, composed of the elements *lang* long + *lif* life.

---

74. Adrian Loker, 44yrs and single. He moved to Naunton from Langport in Somerset in 1998. He has always worked in farming and joined Lower Harford Farm after being made redundant from a previous job. He is a keen roadrunner and a member of Bourton Road Runners Club. Other interests are cycling and playing darts. He also enjoys listening to music and especially musicals and opera.

Loker: variant of **Luker,** a habitation name from *Lucker* in Northumberland, so called from Old Norse *Lo* sandpiper + *kiarr* marsh, wetland (see Kerr). 2) occupational name for someone who had to watch or look after something, as for example a watchman or a keeper of animals, from Middle English *luk(en)* to look (OE *locian*). Also **Lo(o)ker.**

---

75. Bill (Mac) and Mary Macklin with their three sons, Mike aged 16, Miles 13 and Martin 10, built their home in Naunton (Greystones, Grange Hill) in 1969 and used it for holidays until 1975, when Bill took early retirement. He worked for BOAC and then BA for 25 years, initially as Public Relations Manager and after the merger, he set up B.A. News. After retirement he became a Cotswold District Councillor for 12 years and was a Parish Councillor for 22 years, part of this time as Chairman. He was on the Village Hall Committee for 23 years, and Chairman of the sub-committee organising the refurbishment of the hall in 1992. Bill was editor of Naunton News for 20 years when Mrs Higgs (from Littons) left the village. He was Chairman of the Cricket Club for 10 years and played a major part in organising the new ground. Meanwhile Mary was busy selling raffle tickets. Mary's mother, Mabel Hanks, was born at The Manor in 1886, so they had many relations in the village. They visited Australia seven times over the years to see other Hanks relations. Mike went into Journalism and became Assistant to the Editor on the Birmingham Mail. Miles went into the hotel business and worked at Stow Lodge Hotel. Sadly, he died from cancer in 1986, aged 30. Martin worked on the Australian Railways for a year and upon returning to the Cotswolds, became landlord of the Farmers Arms in Guiting Power and is now at the Black Horse. Bill Macklin died in February 2000 after a long illness and having seen in the new Millennium at the Black Horse.

Macklin: not listed in 'Oxford Dictionary of Surnames' and the family are unaware of its origins. In 'Dictionary of English and Welsh Surnames' by C.W.Bardsley, OUP 1901, **Macklin** and **Mackling**: Baptismal name, seemingly 'the son of Maculin'.

76. Martin and Helen Macklin moved to Naunton to run the Black Horse Inn in 1997, having previously run the Farmer's Arms pub in Guiting Power. Martin's parents have lived in the village since Martin was 13 yrs old. Martin and Helen (who comes from Chipping Norton) have a 10 year old son, James. Helen also has a daughter, Natasha Clifford, who lives in the village. They bought number 1 Village Avenue in 1999 and reside there, providing bed and breakfast from the house and the Black Horse.

In 2000 the following prices applied:
A pint of Donnington Best Bitter; £1.75
A Gin and Tonic: £2.20
A pint of Lager: £2.20
A tot of Whisky: £1.30

77. Julia Mangan and her mother Eileen Smith now live together. Eileen previously lived at Waterloo Farm with her husband Jack until his death in 1991. Julia and her daughters, Melissa and Isabelle moved to Summerhill in 1995 after the death of Roy Mangan, a former National Hunt Jockey for David Nicholson, and Saddler in Stow-on-the-Wold. Melissa is 17 years old and has recently finished at Secretarial College. Her ambition is to be a professional event rider. She has her own event horse and rides out for local racehorse trainers. Isabelle is 8 years old and attends Temple Guiting C of E School. She is also a keen rider and a member of Guiting Power Brownies.
Mangan: Irish: Anglicised form of Gaelic **O Mongain** 'descendant of *Mongan*', originally a byname for someone with a luxurious growth of hair (from *mong* hair, mane).

78. Will and Katy Manley, 40 and 36yrs moved to Aylworth in 1991. Will is a Principal Lecturer at the Royal Agricultural College in Cirencester and Katy is a partner in a firm of Solicitors in Bristol. Pippa is 4 and has just started school at Cold Aston this September. Annabel is 2. Will was born in Gloucestershire and moved with Katy to Aylworth just before getting married. We were fortunate to acquire some land and have a horse for hunting and a pony for the children. Will has been an active member of Naunton Social Committee and from 1999 is a Parish Councillor.
Manley: English: 1) habitation name from places in Devon and Cheshire, so called from Old English *(ge)moene* common, shared + *leah* wood, clearing. The surname is still chiefly found in the region around these villages. 2) Nickname from Middle English *manly*, manly, virile, brave (Old English *mannlic*, originally 'man-like').

79. Sue Marston and David Wintle say racing folk are in their element at 'Fox Hill' which stands at the junction of the B4068 with Tally Ho Lane, and a minor road leading to Guiting Power. Sue owns this splendid little 17th century building which she bought three years ago. It had previously been a pub (The Fox Hill Inn) on the old turnpike road to Stow. She has turned it into a very successful B&B base for race goers and the numerous other visitors who discover this lovely part of the wolds. Her son, Warren is a leading National Hunt rider and her partner, David Wintle, trains a successful string of horses at Lavender Hill Stud.
Marston: English: habitation name from any of the numerous places so called, of which there are examples in at least 16 counties. All get their names from Old English *mersc* MARSH + *tun* enclosure, settlement.
Wintle (English) is a variant of **Windle**, the latter being a habitation name from *Windhill* in W Yorks or *Windle* in Lancs., both so called from Old English *wind* wind + HILL, i.e, a mound exposed to fierce gusts. The variant name of **Wintle** appears to be exclusive to Gloucestershire.

80. Mollie Maughan, 78 yrs is a widow with 3 sons and nine grandchildren. She moved to Naunton in 1991 having previously lived in Suffolk and Australia. She was in the A.T.S. with SHAEF during the war, in France and Germany. She says "Naunton is a very friendly village but rapidly becoming a '2nd home' area".
Maughan: 1) Scots: habitation name from *Machan* (now also called *Dalserf*) in the former county of Lanarkshire, named with a diminutive form of Gaelic *machair* (river) plain. 2) Irish: Anglicised form of Gaelic *O Mochain;*; see Mohan. 3) Welsh: habitation name from either of two places in the former county of Monmouthshire, one of which is called *(St) Maughan* (an Anglicized form of Welsh *Llanfocha* 'Church of St. *Mochan*'), and the other *Machen* 'Place of *Cain*'.

81. Atalanti Meyer says, 'We raised our family of four children in Hertfordshire but we often took our holidays in Gloucestershire, where we grew to love and appreciate the Cotswolds. I was thrilled when my eldest daughter announced she was going to marry a young man from Stroud and planned to settle in

Cheltenham. Since then my youngest daughter has married a young man from Cirencester and they also live in Cheltenham. My other two children have settled in London where I have a flat. By dividing my time between Naunton and London I am able to enjoy all my children and my five grandchildren and I feel very lucky to be close to all of them. I also have a small antique business in Stow and this takes up any time I have left'.

Meyer is a variant of **Mayor.** 1) English: status name or occupational name for a mayor, Middle English, Old French *mair(e)* (from Latin *maior* greater, superior; cf. MAYOR). In France the title denoted various minor local officials, and the same is true of Scotland. In England, however, the term was normally restricted to the chief officer of a borough, and the surname may have been given not only to a citizen of some standing who had held this office, but also as a nickname to a pompous or officious person. 2) German: occupational name, originally for a village headman or similar official, from Middle High German *meier*. The German term also acquired the sense 'steward', 'bailiff', and later came to be used also to denote a (tenant) farmer.

82. James and Fiona Milton moved to Naunton in the autumn of 1989. Fiona is a minister of religion and came here to officiate at the Baptist Chapel. James is an advisory teacher and travels daily to Bromsgrove. During the past 10 years they have both put much time and energy into the upkeep and restoration of the Baptist Chapel at Naunton. James has made many alterations and improvements to the Manse (the Chapel House). They both enjoy walking in the lovely Cotswold area and love village life. Fiona likes to paint in watercolours in her spare time, though knowing how much she does I'm surprised she has any!

Milton: English: habitation name from any of the numerous places so called. The majority, with examples in at least fourteen counties, get the name from Old English *middle* middle + *tun* enclosure, settlement (cf. MIDDLETON); a smaller group, with examples in Cumberland, Kent, Northamptonshire, Northumberland, Nottinghamshire, and Staffordshire, have as their first element Old English *mylen* mill (cf. MILLINGTON). The surname is most common in Bedfordshire.

83. Joan and Arthur (Mitch) Mitchell, 60 and 62, have lived at 9 Millview for 33 years. Joan has lived in the village all her life and was born at Littlesworth where her parents (Bill and Margaret Gleed) moved to in about 1937. Joan's family have been in the village for some 200 years or more. Her mother (nee Lane) came from Little Rissington. Arthur has lived in the village for the past 40 years. Joan has one sister, Beryl who lives next door. Since getting married, Joan and Arthur previously lived at 5 Windrush View, after they were newly built in 1963, replacing the sub-standard housing known as 'The Yard' which previously occupied this location next to the church. Arthur is in the building trade and has been involved in building houses in the North Cotswolds since 1958. Joan does some part-time housework in the village. They have two married daughters, Karen who lives in Bourton and Gail who lives at 4 Sunny Cottages, Naunton. They have 4 grandchildren, Thomas, 14, Emma, 11, Luke, 6 and Jordan, 2 and see them as often as they can. Joan has seen much change in Naunton, a village she loves dearly. Whilst accepting that change is inevitable, Joan is reassured that the essence of the old community spirit has been maintained and built upon with the overwhelming majority of the 'new' villagers actively participating in and contributing towards a panoply of village events. Joan and Mitch, although they would not say so themselves have been stalwarts in ensuring the continuation of various traditional village functions and to this end they formed the 'Naunton Players' in about 1982. Their annual and professional stage productions have included Old Time Music Hall, The War Years, All Seasons, Nautical Themes and The Wild West, the success of which has now become a benchmark to others beyond this parish and which seems to epitomise the real face of community involvement here at the close of the 20th century. Joan and Mitch are reassured that the village has retained much of its old topographical layout and that it has so far been saved from major development or the insipid effects of mass tourism suffered by other nearby communities. At the same time, they recognise that the loss of the shop and post office was not helped by the relative isolation that adds to the attractiveness of living here.

Mitchell: English, Scots and Irish: from the Middle English, Old French given name *Michel*, the regular vernacular form of MICHAEL.
Gleed: Southern English: nickname from Middle English *glede* kite (Old English *Gleoda*), probably with reference to the bird's rapacious qualities.

84. Doug and Beryl Mitchell (nee Gleed) have lived in Naunton since they married in St. Andrew's Church here in 1963, though Beryl has lived here all of her 58 years. They have a son, Stuart, 33 years and a daughter, Sally, 30 years. Stuart and Sally were also married in St Andrew's Church. Doug works in Cheltenham as a Tool Setter Fitter and Beryl is a House carer in Naunton. 'There really isn't anywhere else we would prefer to live. Naunton is a very special village, with very special people'.

85. Peter and Jan Morton fell in love with Naunton after Jan had read Susan Hill's "Spirit of the Cotswolds" whilst house-hunting and they moved to Dale Street in the summer of 1989. Peter was being re-located by his, then, employer Eagle Star from London to Cheltenham and this presented them with the ideal opportunity for a move to the country. Jan managed to continue her career as a Chartered Librarian, latterly at Worcester Sixth Form College until 1993.

Their two children, Barnaby (6) and Eleanor (4) were born in Cheltenham and both were christened at St. Andrew's Church, Naunton in a joint ceremony that coincided with Peter's mother's 70th birthday, on August 18th 1996. In 1998 Peter left Eagle Star after 10 successful years and set up his own Management Consultancy business for the insurance sector with Jan. Its name was drawn from their love of the village, the valley and the river running through it: Windrush Consulting. And of Naunton! "Village life has its drawbacks and its riches. Facilities for food, education, recreation and entertainment are often a car's journey away; though Naunton does very well to compensate for this with an active social calendar that spans all age groups. There are few children of Barnaby's and Eleanor's peer group in the village, so social visits to friends usually involve a car ride of some description. However, we love our home, the wildlife and the access to the countryside. Naunton has all that - and more….."

Morton: English land Scots: habitation name from any of the many places called *Mor(e)ton*, from Old English *mor* marsh, fen moor + tun, enclosure, settlement.

86. Oliver and Judy Murphy, 49 and 56yrs, moved to Naunton in 1997 from Moreton-in-Marsh, where they were publicans. Judy has 4 children and 10 grandchildren, two of whom live locally (Bourton-on-the-Hill and Brailes) whilst one daughter lives in Potters Bar and the other has recently moved to Bridport, Dorset. Oliver cleans the Black Horse and during the summer mows the grass for people in the village. Judy cooks at the Black Horse and helps busy mums with their ironing. 'We love the peacefulness of this beautiful village and enjoy walking'.

Murphy: Irish: Anglicized form of Gaelic **O Murchadhab** 'descendant of **Murchadh'**, a personal name composed of the elements *muir* sea + *cadh* warrior. *Murphy is one of the commonest of all Irish names widely distributed throughout the English-speaking world, with some 6000 subscribers in the Irish telephone directories, 1,500 in London, some 900 in Chicago and 680 in Manhattan.*

87. Bob and Carol Newton moved to Naunton from London when they married in 1983. "Our first home was in Sunny Cottages, or Taterbury Row. We are now living in our third house in Naunton; on both occasions being reluctant to move outside the village. Our last move was a house swap, with Richard Tilbrook, which came about through talking together over dinner at one of Naunton's annual progressive suppers." Bob works for one of the electricity generating companies and is now lucky enough, thanks to modern technology, to work from home one day a week. Carol worked for Huntsmans Quarries in the old village school for 15 years before leaving the confines of the office to start a dog walking, cat sitting and house checking service in the village. The dog walking means that Carol, accompanied by her flat coated retriever Hamish, is regularly seen using the network of footpaths that criss-cross the Parish. Both Bob and Carol are keen skiers. They also took up golf enthusiastically when Naunton Downs opened in 1993. Carol was the Lady Captain quite early on with Bob following later as Club Captain, making it the first husband and wife team to fill the two roles. Both can now relax and enjoy their golf without these responsibilities. Carol, along with two other Nauntonians, Jane O'Malley and Liz Stevens, have all sung at the Royal Albert Hall and the Barbican as amateur singers. Bob would like to find more time to spend on his hobbies of woodworking and watercolour painting.

Newton: English: habitation name from any of the many places so called, from Old English *neowe* NEW + *tun* enclosure, settlement. According to Ekwall, this is the commonest English placename. For this reason, the surname has a highly fragmented origin.

88. Fergal O'Brien moved to Naunton in 1993 to work for Nigel Twiston-Davies's racing yard and has lived at 'Windrush View' ever since and says. 'I really like it here: I love the winter mornings with the frost, white on the gallops-field on the opposite side of the valley, which I can see from my kitchen window. Naunton is a particularly friendly village. I've even played cricket for the village (when they were really stuck), which isn't bad for an Irishman! Along with where I come from in Ireland, Naunton and The Cotswolds are the two most beautiful places in the world'!!

O'Brien: variant of **Bryan:** English: from the Celtic personal name *Brian*, which apparently contains the element *bre-* hill, probably with the transferred sense 'eminence'? Breton bearers of this name were among the Normans who invaded England in 1066, and they went on to invade and settle in Ireland in the 12th century where the name mingled with the native Irish version of it, born in particular by one of the greatest Irish septs, descendants of Brian Boru, who rose to the high kingship of Ireland in 1002. This native Irish name had been borrowed by Vikings, who introduced it independently in NW England before the Norman Conquest.

89. Ken and Sara Ogilvie, 59 and 41yrs have lived in Naunton for 31 years. They have two children, Hannah (14), Angus (11).They have a Paterdail Lakeland Terrier called Suzig age 7yrs. The family, together with Suzig love going for walks, especially to the pub! Suzig also enjoys the next door neighbour's chickens and cats! Hannah and Angus go to school in Bourton. Ken worked as a designer for a major Shower manufacturer in Cheltenham but now has his own design business which he runs from home. We all enjoy living in the village as it is a great place to live and the kids think so too. The children find plenty of things to do here and we all support the many village activities such as the cricket, the donkey-derby, fetes, flower-shows, progressive suppers and the super shows put on at the Village Hall, all of which can match anything seen in the surrounding villages. We have a great 'community spirit'. The household is connected to the internet and uses e-mail, a mobile telephone and runs two cars, a Ford Fiesta and a Peugeot. "We understand that the house was built in the 16th century.
Ogilvie: Scots habitation name from a place near Glamis in the former county of Angus, which was first recorded c.1205 in the form *Ogilvin*. It probably gets its name from British (pre-Gaelic) cognates of Old Welsh *ugl* high + *ma* plain, place (mutated to *fa*) or *ban* hill (mutated to *fan*).

90. Austin O'Malley was born in Coventry, Jane in Upminster, Essex. "We met whilst studying for our law degrees and married after qualifying, as solicitors in private practice in Essex, until moving to Naunton in 1988 - never looking back". Jane works for Kendal and Davies, Solicitors, in Stow. Austin works for the Law Society in Redditch. "We love living on the hill overlooking Naunton and Guiting Power. We couldn't believe it when the golf course was built next door". (Austin and Jane are both keen golfers). The other important member of the house is 'Tess' their beautiful golden retriever, who barks at everything that moves (including the photographer!)
O'Malley: is a variant of **Mally.** Irish: Anglicized form of Gaelic **O Maille** 'descendant of the nobleman', from *mal* prince, champion, poet.

91. John and Rose Outhwaite, 45 and 42yrs live at Sheepwell Cottage.
John is a Consultant Physician in Orthopaedic Medicine with practices in Oxford and London. Rose is an art dealer and horse coper. They moved to Naunton in 1998 following marriage although both had lived in the proximity before. They find Naunton delightful - friendly, peaceful and pretty. "It wasn't a conscious decision to move to Naunton - just the nearest to Oxford they could get at the time. Even though John finds the commuting to Oxford and on to London tiring it would be very hard to leave such a nice spot now we're here".
Outhwaite: Not in the dictionary but John believes it is an old habitation name, coming from (or *outside*) Thwaite in Yorkshire. In Old Norse *thwaite* was a piece of land cleared from the forest or reclaimed from wasteland: also a paddock.

92. Graham Owens, 57yrs has lived in and around Birmingham for the past 40 years. Divorced many years ago - now single, Graham has two children, a son, Christopher age 35, living in Bristol and a daughter, Charlotte age 30, living in Shrewsbury. Graham hopes to retire in 2/3 years time and plans to remain in Naunton. "I intend to work from my Naunton home from 2001 onwards. I am a Stockbroker with my own firm although this may be sold prior to continuing as a Consultant. Naunton attracts me as (A) a beautiful setting in a lovely part of the world and (B) it has a strong community spirit, with an excellent social calendar. I hope to participate more fully here when I retire. My interests are travelling, wine, horseracing and fishing".
Owen: Welsh: from the Welsh personal name *Owain*, the origin probably a borrowing from the Latin *Eugenius.*
Patronymic: **Bowen.** In 'Dictionary of English and Welsh Surnames' by C.W.Bardlsey, OUP 1901: **Owens:** 'the son of Owen; Owens is the genitive form'.

93. Sir Derek and Lady Shuna Palmar moved South in 1995 and came to live in the Cotswolds and are happy to have found a property in Naunton, nearer to many relatives and friends. There are facilities for Shuna to continue a lifelong involvement with horses and now Connemara ponies. There is a pleasing atmosphere in Naunton and activities in many spheres. Lady Palmar says "As chairman of the Village Trust which owns the Dovecote, I have been very glad to be involved with the restoration, now completed. I am also a member of the St. Andrews PCC". Sir Derek received his Knighthood in 1986 for services to Industry. He had been chairman of Bass for 12 years and Chairman of several other companies including Yorkshire Television. He first qualified as a Chartered accountant in 1947 after service as a Lt-Col on the staff of Headquarters ALFSEA during WW2.

Palmar: variant of **Palmer:** English: nickname for someone who has been on a pilgrimage to the Holy Land, Middle English, Old French *palmer, paumer* (from *palme, paume* palm tree, Latin *palma*). Such pilgrims generally brought back a palm branch as proof that they had actually made the journey, but there was a vigorous trade in false souvenirs, and the term also became applied to a cleric who sold false indulgences. Some of the European cognates may also be topographic names referring to dwellers near a palm tree or grove. *A family called* Palmer *trace their ancestry to Ralph Palmer(d.1559) who lived in Marston, Staffs. They had been earls of Selbourne since 1882.*
A Family of the name of Palmes *(Catalan variant) trace their ancestry to Manfred Palmes, who was granted lands in Somerset by Milo, Earl of Hereford, in the 12th century.*

---

94. Michael Parry (62 yrs) is a retired British Airways Pilot, who swapped flying Jumbo jets for the gentler pace of this beautiful Cotswold arable farm when he moved here from Surrey in 1986. Now a single man again, he bought the 456 acre farm from Hugh Dalgety for some £960,000 (the deal also involved a property exchange) when it was part of Mr Dalgety's 2000 acre Aylworth Farm, which was itself then an arable and dairy farm but is now purely arable. Roundhill farm employed five men in 1986, but just two now, (Jonathon Bowen-Jones who lives in the cottage and Jim Organ who travels to work from outside Naunton). Subsequent transactions involving both the sale and acquisition of land mean that today it is 601 acres in size. Michael grows mostly wheat, barley and oil seed rape on about 500 acres of this, the remainder being left to grass for hay and a little grazing. He currently has a 150hp Ford tractor and two smaller Ford tractors, all of which have cabs and CB radios, enabling him to maintain contact with Jonathon or Jim from the office/kitchen. He also has a New Holland TX34 Combine Harvester and a Matbro Materials Handler. He drives a Range Rover vogue around the farm and his road vehicles are a Mercedes Benz and a BMW. He rears pheasants and releases them each July, with friends and acquaintances coming for 'shoots' on the farm. Michael says 'the price of wheat and barley has halved since I bought Roundhill but I am fortunate in that I have some other income from a leather goods shop in Farnham. This is a most beautiful area to live and to work and I hope to stay here'.
Parry: 1) Welsh: Patronymic, with a reduced form of the Welsh element, apparently from the given name HARRY.
2) French: cognate of PARISH.

---

95. David and Jane Pickup, 48 and 44yrs have lived in Naunton since their marriage at St. Andrew's Church in October 1984. Their sons, James (13) and George (11) were born in Cheltenham and baptised at St. Andrew's Church. Both the boys attended Bourton-on-the-Water Primary School (where Jane is currently Chair of Governors) and are now at St. Edward's School, Charlton Kings, Cheltenham.

David is self-employed and Jane is the secretary at St. James' and Ebrington Primary School in Chipping Campden.

Naunton has provided a wonderful environment for the whole family and in turn the Pickups have become involved, over the years, with numerous activities and served on many committees concerned with various aspects of Naunton life including the church, the cricket club, the village show and numerous others.
Pickup: English: habitation name from a place in Lancashire, so called from Old English *pic* point + *copp* top, i.e. a hill with a sharp peak.

---

96. David and Lee Porter, after leaving London colleges were married in 1981 when living in Bourton on the Water. They moved to Naunton in 1986.

David is a Team Leader on a North Sea oil platform for British Petroleum in the Forties Field, regularly commuting to Aberdeen from Naunton. Lee is the Assistant Head Teacher of Temple Guiting village primary school. They have two sons who in the year 2000 are, Ben 17 and Matthew 15, along with a daughter Abigail who is 13. All who are studying at colleges and school respectively.

Most of David's and Lee's spare time is spent on improving their property by either renovating the building, which had suffered from neglect in the 1900's, or working in the garden, continually improving its vistas and planting. David practises falconry and flies his North American Red Tailed Hawk across local land, hunting rabbits. He drives his ex military Land Rover that saw action in the Gulf conflict. He wishes he had more time to attempt to catch the local trout in the Windrush.

Lee, as well as being a working mother likes to tend her garden, read and as a trained Graphic Designer still likes to be creative when time allows. All three children help out on a part time basis at the village pub, 'The Black Horse', serving tourists and locals alike, which they fit-in on a part time basis between their studies.
Porter: English: 1) occupational name for the gatekeeper of a town or the doorkeeper of a large house, Middle English *porter* (Old French *portier*, Late Latin *portarius*, an agent derivative of *porta* door, entrance; cf. PORT I).
2) Occupational name for a man who carried loads for a living, especially one who used his own muscle power rather than a beast of burden or a wheeled vehicle (see CARTER). This sense is from Old French *porteo(u)r* (Late Latin *portator,* from *portare* to carry, convey).

97. Graham and Corrinne Powell, 61 and 59yrs, moved to Naunton from Canada in 1969. Although Graham had lived in Cheltenham most of his life, he had never been to Naunton. Neither had his wife Corrinne, who is a Texan. 'House-hunting' and sheer good luck found them buying Kiftsgate cottage. Their children, Nicholas age 31 and Christiana age 29 both live in London. The lure of Naunton and the beautiful Cotswold countryside results in frequent visits 'home.' Graham and Nicholas share a love of vintage cars and Graham looks forward to sailing in his retirement. Graham, Nicholas and Christiana share the pleasures of walking and Corrinne, a typical Texan, has never developed this hobby. A pleasure shared by the whole family is being part of Naunton life. The Powells are a small family within an extended family that is Naunton. Corrinne and Graham's only anticipated move is from Kiftsgate Cottage to the churchyard

Powell: 1) Welsh: patronymic, with a reduced form of the Welsh element *ap*, from the given name *Hywel* (see HOWELL). 2) Variant of PAUL. *A welsh family bearing the name* Powell *claim descent from the Welsh chieftain known as Coel Hen Gotebauc 'the Old Protector', who probably ruled an area of Britain under the Romans around the year 400. The first recorded occurrence of the surname in its modern form is Roger ap* Howell, *alias* Powell, *named in a lawsuit in 1563. He was the grandson of Howell ap John (d.1535). Later members of the family include the novelist Anthony Powell (b.1905).*

98. Len, Nancy and Paul Quaranto, are 53, 51 and 10yrs old. "Having discovered Naunton during many previous visits to the Cotswolds, We bought Glebe House three and a half years ago for its beautiful view and 'edge of village' location". Len travels to London where he is Chief Legal Counsel for Kimberley-Clark Europe. Nancy manages two UK households and one in the States (we are all US citizens) and Paul is at Hill House International School, Chelsea. Nancy is a horsewoman who was raised hunting in Maryland and engages in show jumping in England. Len is into beating and shooting with the Temple Guiting shoot and walking the yellow 'labs' around Naunton; and young Paul enjoys riding his pony and playing with his many "village friends".

Quaranto: not in the dictionary. Len says, "the origin of the family name (correctly spelled Quaranta, meaning the number 40, but my name has an "o" at the end due to a US Navy snafu) is as follows: During the Second Crusade in around 1156 the Prince of Salerno sent for help as the gates of Salerno were being attacked by Saracens. A "cavalliere" (I think his name was Gaettano) from Cava dei Tirreni went to the docks at Amalfi and recruited 40 Norman soldiers who were in transit from the Holy Land. They went on to successfully defend the gates of Salerno. He was knighted and known from that time as Gaettano dei Quaranta and the family motto is "Pugnat et vincit con quadraginta" or "he fights and wins with the 40".

99. Patricia Quinn bought the farmhouse and 68 acres in 1974 from Stanley Clifford. At first the land was let to Aylworth Estate, and in the early days she was mainly occupied with 4 stepchildren and a son and daughter, Michael and Jane. When the family had grown up she decided to fulfil a life time ambition to farm the land herself. In 1977 she started the Harford herd of pedigree Longhorn cattle and a Flock of Rare Breed Cotswold Sheep. Over the years she made up the acreage to 155. The cattle and sheep won many championships at major agricultural Shows culminating in the millennium year of 2000 achieving the Champion Male, Female and Supreme Longhorn Champion at the Royal Show. Also in the same year gained the Reserve Interbreed Beef and Cotswold Sheep Breed Champion at the Three Counties Show. She entered the farm into the MAFF E.S.A. scheme and has received awards for conservation. About 8 hectares of woodland have been planted and the farm is now all grassland. Her life is devoted to this bit of the Windrush valley and her children all take a keen interest, although they all live out of the area at the moment. At 73 years she still has plans to go on improving the livestock and the property.

Quinn: Irish: Anglicized form of Gaelic **O Cuinn** 'descendant of *Conn*', a byname meaning 'Leader', 'Chief'.

100. Donna and David Renney have lived in Naunton since 1999, but Donna has a lifelong association with the village. When Donna was born in 1959, her parents Mr and Mrs Gordon S. Hanks, were living and farming in the village and she spent her early childhood here. David comes from the North of England, grew up in the Midlands and came to live in the Cotswolds in 1993. Donna has a son, Henry, from a previous marriage. Henry is now almost eighteen and lives away from home working as Second Whipper-in to the Portman Foxhounds. He comes home whenever he can, to visit his cousins, Charles and Gerard Hanks, and to ride out for Jack Smith, who trains steeplechasers in the village. Both Donna and David work at home, she is a part-time fundraiser for the Workers' Education Association; he is a marketing manager for an animal-health company, exploiting his veterinary training as well as his interest in marketing. Donna also keeps hunters at livery in a neighbouring village, and trains the family point-to-pointers. They both have interests in the local environment and rural life. Donna is a trustee of the Village Trust, which owns the dovecote next to the Manor and for which she tirelessly uses her fundraising skills. David is a passionate advocate for hunting and other country sports, knowing first-hand how important they are in the local economy and the life of the community. He is a volunteer worker for the Countryside Alliance, which defends the traditional way of life, and farming and country sports in particular.

Renney: variant of **Rainey:** Scots and Irish: from a diminutive of a short form of any of the various Germanic personal names with a first element *rand* (shield) rim (cf. RAND I) or *ragin* counsel. The given name was most frequently used as a form of RANDOLF and REYNOLD.

101. John and Valerie Ridge (nee Flanagan) have always lived in Naunton. Valerie's Great Grandfather, John Merrell moved from Birmingham on his marriage to a Bourton girl, Sarah Turner. John Merrell sold his two shops in Birmingham and bought and ran the village shop in Naunton called 'Merrell Stores', in Dale Street. In due course their son John married Beatrice Griffin from Winchcombe. Beatrice's father owned a bakery in Winchcombe. When John and Beatrice had a daughter (also named Beatrice) she joined them running the family business. Valerie is Beatrice's daughter by her marriage to Matthew Flanagan and has a sister called Hilary. John Ridge moved to Naunton aged two. He spent some time in the Army but later returned to Naunton. John and Valerie married and moved next door to the old shop twenty-three years ago. They have three sons; James (20) is in his last year at college taking a HND. David (17) and Paul (14) both attend the Cotswold School in Bourton-on-the-Water. John, Valerie and family enjoy living in Naunton and have no intention of moving because they know this is one of the most beautiful parts of the Cotswolds.

Ridge: English topographic name for someone who lived on or by a ridge, ME *rigge*, OE *hrcyg*.
Flanagan: Irish; Anglicized form of Gael. O'Flannagan, descendent of *Flannaghal*, a personal name composed of the elements *flann* red(dish), ruddy + *gal* valour.

102. Audrey Roome moved to Naunton from Birmingham in 1989. Audrey is a retired Primary School teacher with a special interest in art and ceramics. She has two children, Julie and David. Julie is single and lives in Birmingham and David lives in Badsey, Worcs, with his wife Elaine and their daughters Emma and Sarah. Audrey discovered 'Yew Tree Cottage' quite by chance after looking for some time for a cottage in the Cotswolds - she saw an advertisement in the Observer for a 17th century cottage in the Cotswolds and this turned out to be Yew Tree Cottage, Naunton. Not having visited Naunton before she describes finding a delightful village with a lovely church, a well stocked shop with a helpful owner and a village pub. Naunton has proved to be a friendly village that is welcoming to newcomers and has a good community spirit. There are many activities to participate in, some of them based in the now well equipped Village Hall.

Roome: Variant of **Roman:** 1) English, French, Catalan, Rumanian, Polish, Ukranian and Belorussian: from the Latin personal name *Romanus* (originally an ethnic byname from *Roma* Rome, of obscure, probably pre-Italic, origin), borne by several early saints, including the 7th century bishop of Rouen. It was also the baptismal name of St Boris. The name was popular in N France in the early Middle Ages and was introduced into England by the Normans, but did not become common. 2) English, French and Catalan: regional or ethnic name for someone from Rome or from Italy in general, or nickname for someone who had connection with Rome, as for example having been there on a pilgrimage.

103. Sophie and Edward Rugge-Price, 25 and 26yrs moved to Naunton in February 2000, when Edward's job brought him to the area. Their son, Thomas, was born on 7 April 2000. Edward managed and was the chef at a pub in Guiting Power and now helps manage another local pub, which keeps him busy. Sophie is a full-time mum but hopes to take up her place for teacher training in Cheltenham in September. They both love the peace of the countryside after London. They enjoy walking and are happy to be bringing up their son in such a pretty and friendly area.

Ruge [sic] is a variant of **Rauch:** German and Jewish (Ashkenazic): nickname for a shaggy or unkempt person, from German *rauch* rough, hairy. **Price:** Welsh: one of the commonest Welsh surnames, a patronymic with a reduced form of the Welsh element *ap*, from the given name RHYS. 2) English: the name is also found in very early parts of England far removed from Welsh influence and presumably derives from Middle English, Old French *pris* prize (Latin *pretium*; cf. PRECIOUS). 3): Jewish (Ashkenazic): Anglicized form of any of the Jewish surnames listed as PREUSS.

104. Christopher Samuels and Polly Hendry are young at heart (59 and 49yrs). Both are retired. Chris spent his life in the Oil Industry, travelling the world, with a particularly interesting spell in the Soviet Union, based in Moscow. Polly is a talented home maker with excellent skills in soft furnishings and colour co-ordination. "We both love walking and are for that reason fond of the Cotswolds". Chris comes originally from Birmingham whilst Polly comes from Coventry. "We both love our foreign holidays spent exploring the

Continent by car". Chris, as a chartered mechanical engineer has done most of the renovation of the cottage himself whilst Polly has used her skills at painting and decorating.

Chris and Polly are both divorced and both have two children.

Samuels: variant of **Samuel:** English, French, German and Jewish: from the biblical male given name *Samuel* (Hebrew *Shemuel* 'Name of God').

Hendry: variant of **Henry:** 1) English and French: from Germanic personal name composed of the elements *haim* home + *ric* power, introduced into England by the Normans in the form of *Henri*. During the Middle Ages this name became enormously popular in England and was borne by eight kings, a record not equalled until the 20th century when Edward caught up. In the period in which the majority of English surnames were formed, a common vernacular form of the name was HARRY.
2) Irish: Anglicized form of Gaelic O hInneirghe, 'descendant of IInneirghe', a byname meaning 'Abandonment', 'Elopement'.

105. Peter and Maralyn Scudamore, 42 and 46yrs both grew up in Herefordshire. They have lived at Grange Hill Farm (Racing Stables) for 14 years with their two sons, Tom 18yrs and Michael 16yrs.

Before buying Grange Hill (then 300 acres) in 1988, it had been a typical Cotswold mixed arable farm as far back as anyone knows!

Peter commenced his racing career with David Nicholson at Condicote and then with Martin Pipe in Devon and as a professional jockey he has ridden 1638 winners before establishing his own racing stables at Naunton in 1988. Here, in partnership with Nigel Twiston-Davies (Nigel and his family live across the road, just within the Parish of Guiting Power) they now train and stable some 90 race horses on the Grange Hill gallops. They can be seen almost daily walking out along the nearby roads and lanes and have now become a familiar part of the Naunton scenery. Between them they have trained some 700 winners, including Earth Summit in the 1998 Grand National. Tom, who has recently left Cheltenham College, is also an amateur jockey at Grange Hill who intends to continue the family tradition by establishing himself as a professional jockey. Michael, who is still at Cheltenham College, has recently joined the Gloucester Rugby Club Academy, hoping to become a professional rugby player and who knows, maybe one day to play for England!

Also in the photograph is Peter's father Michael Scudamore, (68yrs) who was himself a professional jockey from the 1940s to 1966. He and his wife live in nearby Mucky Cottage from where Michael (Snr) continues to play an active part in the business, riding out almost daily.

Scudamore: English (West Country): of uncertain origin, perhaps a habitation name from an unidentified place so called from Old English *scite* shit, dung + *mor* moor, fen.
A family of this name trace their descent from Ralph, who in 1086 held Opetone, Wilts, later known as Upton Scudamore. His son, who died before 1148, was known as Reginald Escudemor

106. Nick and Lotte Seal, 42 and 36yrs moved to Naunton in 1995. Brockhill Farm was the ideal place for the horse business and the location perfect for hunting, being on the border of the Heythrop, North Cotswold and Cotswold Hunts. Emily (2) and Jack (6) are both keen and capable riders and they attend Temple Guiting School. At present they have 45 head of cattle and some 35 horses and a few ponies. The majority of horses are liveries of various sorts, a few dressage horses, which is Lotte's passion, hunters, youngsters to break and school on and dealing horses. There are also some thoroughbred brood mares and young stock on the farm. "It's a busy life but we do manage to enjoy and take part in some of the many village activities".

Seal: English: 1) topographic name, variant of SALE. 2) Metonymic occupational name for a maker of seals or signet rings, from Middle English, Old French *seel* seal (Latin *sigillum* a diminutive of *signum* sign). 3) Metonymic occupational name for a maker of saddles, from Old French *seele* saddle. 4) nickname for a plump or ungainly person, from the aquatic mammal, Middle English *sele* (Old English *seolh*).

107. Lincoln and Tish Seligman have a barn of a place at Aylworth. After university, Lincoln worked as a shipping lawyer for seven years before becoming an artist in 1980. For the next ten years he worked on paintings and murals and had exhibitions, mainly in London and New York. His work now involves large-scale, three-dimensional pieces, usually in the form of mobiles and hanging sculptures for the atrium spaces of modern buildings. The majority of his commissions continue to come from Europe and Asia. He is able to use the converted barn as a studio and as a place to collect his thoughts. Tish studied history of art at university before going on to write numerous books on art subjects, the most prominent being a guide to murals and mural painting, which is still in print. Her current work involves the supervision of a large print collection housed near Oxford. They have three children, one at university, one about to go to university and one at school in Cheltenham.

Seligman: Variant of **Selig:** 1) German: cognitive of Sealey. 2) Jewish (Ashkenazic): from the Yiddish male given name *Zelik* 'Fortunate', 'Blessed' or from the modern German vocabulary word *selig* of the same meaning.

108. Mark and Andrea Seymour moved to Naunton in April 1997. Mark was a housemaster at Haileybury at that time and in 2000 moved to Edinburgh, as headmaster of Cargilfield School. Andrea, or Andy, had been a P.R. consultant in London before Tom (10) Ben (6) and Samantha (4) arrived. Number One Church Farm Barn is our home and we spend as much time there as Mark's job permits. We all love the Cotswolds, and particularly Naunton – the golf club, the cricket club, the 'Black Horse' have all become features of our holidays, along with the wonderful walks and the stunning view from our windows. The warm welcome we received on arrival, and the friendship we've experienced since then, makes us feel extremely fortunate to be living here.
Seymour: English: 1) Norman habitation name from *Saint-Maur*-des-Fossees in Seine, N France, so called from the dedication of the church there to St *Maur*. 2) habitation name from either of two places in N Yorks. Called *Seamer,* from Old English *soe* sea, 'the Lake' + *mere* lake, pond. There are also places called *Semer* in Norfolk, Suffolk and N Yorks, which have the same origin and may lie behind some instances of the surname.

109. Ralph (Jack) and Jayne Smith, 39 and 41yrs have lived in Naunton since 1994. Jack comes from Derbyshire and Jayne from Cheshire. They met whilst riding-out together from the stables of the local racehorse trainer, Nigel Twiston-Davies at Grange Hill. They have a 3 year old daughter, Ella, who attends Stepping-Stones day nursery near Upper Slaughter. Jack and Jayne now train horses at Mike Arnold's stables. They have trained a number of successful horses over the years, with winners at Fontwell and Fakenham and a fourth place at Cheltenham. Jayne says "we both love living in Naunton and we also believe it is a wonderful place in which to bring up our daughter".
Smith: English occupational name for a worker in metal, Middle English *smith,* Old English *smi?* (probably a derivative of *smitan* to strike, hammer) Metal working was one of the earliest occupations for which specialist skills were required, and its importance ensured that this term and its cognates and equivalents were perhaps the most widespread of all occupational surnames in Europe. Medieval smiths were important not only in making horseshoes, ploughshares, and other domestic articles, but above all for their skills in forging swords, other weapons and armour. Brett has calculated that there are about 187,000 subscribers named *Smith* in the British telephone directories; his regional study shows that the name is most common in the Aberdeen area, with a distribution of 184 per 10,000, and that it also common throughout the Midlands and again in East Anglia. It is least common in Wales and the West Country,

110. William and Theresa Smith bought Honeymans Cottage in 1987 and retired from a lifetime of farming in 1991 to come and live in Naunton. Both were associated with farming in various ways through the years and still look after farms for friends in Warwickshire, Wiltshire and Scotland. They enjoy walking and Theresa is an active W.I. member. They have a married daughter and two grand daughters who live near Tetbury. Both are very active in the Roman Catholic Parish Church at Stow-on-the-Wold.
Author's note: many of us say that we enjoy walking but I don't think I have yet been to Naunton without seeing Bill striding purposefully around the lanes. He has probably covered more miles along them than any other current Nauntonian!

111. David and Louise Smyth, 47 and 38yrs met in 2000 at a Village Hall function, once again proving the importance of this splendid social amenity. Since marrying they have lived at 'Sidelands' (built 1974) on the edge of Longford Farmyard. Louise was born in Lancashire but from the age of 13 she grew up in Guiting Power and attended Bourton Vale School. David was born in Devon and has lived in many different parts of the country, undergoing his secondary education at Cheltenham Boys College. He is now in partnership with a local man and together they are developing the old 'Happylands Quarry' at Springhill, near Broadway, into an Engineering based Industrial Estate. As for living in Naunton, the Smyths enjoy the local amenities such as Church, Societies, Pub, horse riding and the welcoming people, to the full.
Smyth: Variant of Smith – see above.

112. Philip Steele was born in Yorkshire and moved to the Cotswolds more than 20 years ago and to Naunton in 1989. Claire Walker joined Philip in Dale Street four years ago and is 'Cotswold' born and bred. Claire has a background in marketing and is now a buyer for the mail order company, Scotts of Stow. Philip lived in Africa for several years and then worked with the International Centre for Conservation Education (based in Guiting Power) from 1980 until it closed in 1998. He is now employed by the Guiting Manor Amenity Trust and works with the housing maintenance and renovation team.
Variant of **Steel:** English and Scots: nickname for someone considered as hard and durable as steel or metonymic occupational name for a foundry worker, from Middle English *stele* steel (Old English *style*).
Walker: English and Scots: 1) occupational name for a fuller, Middle English *walkere,* Old English *wealcere,* an agent derivative of *wealcan,* to walk, tread. 2) Habitation name from a place in Northumberland, so called from Middle English *wall* (Roman) wall + *kerr* marsh.

113. Bob and Barbara Steiner, 47 and 46yrs moved to Aylworth, just outside Naunton, in 1991. They had previously spent seven years in Cheltenham, after living in London and New York. Bob was born in Ashtead, Surrey, and Barbara was born in Birmingham. They have two children. Richard, aged 18, is currently in his last year at St. Edward's School in Cheltenham, studying English, History and French. He intends to go to the University of Toronto in Canada next year. Richard is very keen on sport and has played tennis, hockey and squash for Gloucestershire. Lolly, aged 16, is in her penultimate year at school, at The Cheltenham Ladies' College, studying English, French, Latin and Religious Studies. Bob and Barbara have had their own company for the past 14 years, running it first in Cheltenham and now from home. They run training courses for people involved in the financial markets and Bob is also the author of four books on financial maths and foreign exchange trading. Both are involved in various activities in Naunton: Bob is a Churchwarden at St. Andrew's church and Barbara runs the Naunton Music Society. Bob plays tennis and squash. Their house was originally two shepherds' cottages, built in the 18th century as part of the Aylworth estate. These were modernised and extended in 1991, to become a four-bedroom house, with a garden and paddock of just over two acres.

Steiner: variant of **Stone**: English: from Old English *stan* stone, in any of several uses. It is most commonly a topographic name, for someone who lived either on stony ground or by a notable outcrop of rock or a stone boundary-marker or monument, but it is also found as a metonymic occupational name for someone who worked in stone, a mason or stonecutter. There are various places in S and W England named with this word, for example in Bucks., Gloucs., Hants., Kent, Somerset, Staffs., and Worcs,. and the surname may also be a habitation name from any of these. The form *Stone* is also found in an Anglicization of various Jewish surnames, of which Steiner is but one.

114. Brian and Mary Stevens, built their house in 1986, having purchased and cultivated the land for the previous 12 years. Brian designed the house and spent a considerable time completing it and the garden layout, together with Mary. They previously lived in Redditch and both worked for the District Council, Brian as an architect and Mary in the Treasurer's Department. They have two sons and four grandchildren. Both sons are Biologists. Since being in Naunton, Brian has been involved in the design and construction of the extensions and refurbishments to the Village Hall. Mary is a W.I. member and both support the various village activities and enjoy the Community Spirit in Naunton. Their little dog Toppa ensures daily walks in the lovely Cotswold Countryside.

Stevens: a variant of **Stephen**: English: from the Middle English given name *Stephen, Steven* (Greek *Stephanos* 'Crown'). This was a popular name throughout Christendom in the Middle Ages, having been borne by the first Christian martyr, stoned to death at Jerusalem three years after the death of Christ.

115. John and Lizzie Stevens, 51 and 48yrs moved to Naunton in August 1981 from Oxfordshire. Lizzie was born in Lower Slaughter and is from a long line of Cotswold farming families. They have two daughters, Harriet (age 19) who is going to Art College in Cheltenham in September, and Freya (age 8) is at Cold Aston Primary School. John is a Stonemason and has a workshop in Vine House Yard where he runs a very successful business. His 'hobby' is restoring Vine House and making it look even more 'beautiful'! Lizzie is a partner in the business and works at a Classical Music Agency in Lower Swell. She enjoys walking, yoga and opera.

116. Ken Stonehewer says, "I moved to Naunton 34 years ago, spending a month or two as an assistant at Northleach Hospital and later being employed by Pates Grammar School in Cheltenham as a Groundsman, which I enjoyed very much for 10 years. My wife Kathleen was a professional artist, and I also painted. My wife had an exhibition at the Chapel which raised approximately £200. She died in March of this year. I am lonely but everyone in the village has been very supportive during this sad time. I love Naunton but may emigrate to Canada in the future".

Stonehewer: not in the dictionary but almost certainly an old occupational name for a hewer (cutter) of stone.

117. Doris Stratford, 77yrs was born at 2 Sunny Bank and believes that of the senior village residents, only she and Geoffrey Hanks can now claim to have been born here. Her father, Bert Stratford was born at Kiftsgate Cottage, her mother Elsie came from Donnington. Doris went to school in Naunton and recalls that Janet Griffin (sister of Hilda Hanks of Waterloo Farm) was a teacher, together with a Miss Herbert (no relations in village). Mr Smart was the headmaster, followed by Mr Pexton. Leaving school at 14yrs, Doris then had to look after her father and younger sister Iris (Porter) as their mother died when Doris was eleven. She later did some paid work for Mr and Mrs Victor Hayward at Windrush Cottage (now Windrush Vale) who did 'full-board' accommodation for visitors after the war. Doris recalls that Mrs Walker at Church House was the first person to offer such accommodation to visitors in about 1945 and some of her early visitors later bought Cromwell House. Doris has one son, Colin, 54yrs, who lives in Andoversford and one daughter, Jean, who lives in Winchcombe. She now has 6 grandchildren and 6 great grandchildren. Doris reflects that in her lifetime here there used to be a little shop at the Black Horse (Road end) in addition to Merrell's shop in Dale Street. Reg Morris (the cottage now called Rushdale) used to sell fruit and vegetables both in the village and surrounding villages from his van. Reg's parents used to do fish and chips 3 times a week and his father, who we called 'Wet Fish', sold fish around the villages from a pony and trap. They also made sweets which we loved as children. We all knew a little childhood ditty which went:

"Poor old Wet Fish, Lizzie is his wife
They fry fish and chips every Sat'dy night
Albert cuts the chips up, Lizzie frys the fish.
Along comes the ladies and takes them away in a dish"

"We also had a carpenter and an undertaker (Terry Muller) who also did building work. We had a petrol pump (where Honeyman's Ctg is now) where a gallon (4.5 litres) cost one shilling and 3d and later one shilling and 5d for a long time (12p and 13p compared with £4 a gallon today). We had Leonard Pritchard's shop (Parkers Cottage) where you could buy things like stationery, batteries and paraffin. Leonard did bicycle repairs and he collected the newspapers from Notgrove Railway Station each day with a motorcycle and sidecar in the 1930s (Billy Herbert later bought this machine). We Had Reynolds Bakehouse in The Quadrangle for lovely fresh bread and on Good Friday really hot-cross buns were put out on the steps on trays. We also had a Post Office (attached to what is now Littons) run by the two Misses Bedwell. We had Mr Painter the Blacksmith in Dale Street, and his services would still be in demand with all the riding stables we have round here now. We had Frank Bayliss in Sunny House doing general building. We had Waterloo Farm where we could get our milk and eggs from Horace Hanks, if you didn't have your own chickens. Hilda Hanks made butter and could even provide you with a cone of honey. You could get a haircut in the village for a few pennies and there was even a butcher here once. We had a travelling tailor from Stow, another from Moreton and Fosters from Bourton who would call once a month to see if any clothes were needed. Gilberts from Bourton would call on a Thursday, take your order for groceries and deliver them on Saturday without making any charge. The Tartaglias from Cheltenham brought us ice-cream. Colletts from Bourton brought the coal. Life was a little harder, the people were tougher and the kids were as mischievous as ever.
Stratford: English: habitation name from any of various places, for example in Greater London, Beds,. Bucks,. Northants,. Suffolk, Wilts., and Warwicks., so called from Old English *stroet* (Roman) road + *ford* FORD.

118. Laura Stutowicz, 43yrs moved to Naunton four years ago from Cornwall. Works for a Pharmaceutical Company; not married and no children. Also keeps two horses at Hill Farm, Aylworth, one of which was second at the Royal International Horse Show 2000, ridden and produced by Laura. Other hobbies are gardening, silver-smithing and jewellery making. Jake the whippet sleeps a lot and enjoys hurtling around the Brake and fields around the village. Orangina, the cat's favourite hobbies are mouse-murder and bird life (well, bird death actually!) Laura found the village when looking for somewhere to live and loved the way it cuddles down in the valley like a sleepy cat. **Stutowicz:** not listed in dictionary but Laura understands that it is a truncated version of a patronymic name from Poland.

119. Richard Tilbrook, 38yrs, moved to Naunton from Cheltenham in 1988 and was the first owner of Easter Cottage (since renamed 'Brambles'). A keen gardener, he enjoyed designing a small cottage garden there, which was one of a number opened to the public in aid of the Naunton Bells Appeal in 1991. Eventually it became impossible to cram any more plants in and so he did a house swap with Carol and Bob Newton, moving to Sunny House in 1997, where he is now developing a terraced garden stretching down to the River Windrush. Richard has been involved in most aspects of village life, performing with the Naunton Players, conducting the church choir, running a monthly Family Service, helping to organise the Music Society and serving on the PCC and Social Committee. He met Paul Warwick (43) in 1999. Paul also enjoys the strong Naunton community spirit. Paul's main interests are photography, cooking and transport, and he has created a beautiful flight of stone steps for the garden at Sunny House. Richard works in International Development and currently has responsibility for the British development programme in Ukraine, Maldova and Belarus. Paul is Company Secretary for a Publishing Company.

Tilbrook: English: habitation name from a place in the former county of Huntingdonshire (now part of Cambs.), so called from the Old English byname *Tila* (from *til* capable) + Old English *broc* BROOK.

Warwick: English: 1) habitation name from the county town of Warwicks., or regional name from the county itself. The town was originally named as the 'outlying settlement (see Wick) by the weir': cf. Warrington. 2) habitation name from a much smaller place of the same name in Cumberland, so called from Old English *warod* slope, bank + *wic*.

---

120. Joan Timmins, 50yrs and her two daughters, Hannah (10) and Beth (7), moved to Naunton from Wishaw, Warwicks in August 1999. Joan is a businesswoman. Hannah and Beth go to Rendcomb College, Cirencester. Hannah is a gifted artist and she would like to work with wild animals in Africa. Beth is a character and would like to become a comedienne. 'We all like walking, riding and travelling and doing things together. We enjoy living in Naunton and my mother tells me that when I was seven my grandpa brought me to the Cotswolds for a day trip and that on returning home to Birmingham I would not stop talking about how beautiful it all was and vowed that I would live there one day. Naunton is home to us now and we enjoy taking part in all the varied projects that people happen to put together'. 'Hooray for Naunton.'

Timmins: Variant of **Timm:** 1) English: probably from an otherwise unrecorded Old English personal name, cognate with the attested Continental Germanic form *Timmo*. This is of uncertain origin, perhaps a short form of DIETMAR. The given name *Timothy* was not in use in England until Tudor times, and is therefore not a likely source of this group of surnames. 2) Low German: from a short form of the medieval given name DIETMAR.

---

121. Derek and Margaret Tucker with their youngest daughter Claire moved from Bedfordshire to Naunton in May 1988 to take over the running of the Post Office and Village Store, which they ran until retirement in September 1999. They enjoy living in the village and share in the community spirit. Derek is a member of the Naunton Downs Golf Club, and plays the organ on two Sundays each month at the village chapel. He also acts as Musical Director and accompanies on the keyboards for the annual village variety show. Margaret is a keen gardener and loves to care for her animals (3 cats and a dog). Claire, having completed her drama course now lives in Cheltenham and the two older daughters, Corinne and Catherine, are in Nottingham and Douglas I.O.M.

Derek says that the following prices applied in the shop at the time of closure:

20 Silk Cut cigarettes £3.88	12 Large Free Range Eggs £1.50
20 Benson and Hedges cigarettes £3.88	1 Pint of Milk .42p
Daily Telegraph 45p (75p on Sat)	Kit Kat Bar, 4 Fingers .27p
Large Wholemeal Loaf 97p	Walkers Club (choc biscuit) .27p
Gordons Gin (70cl) £11.49	Heinz Baked Beans (415g) .39p
Bells Whisky (70cl) £12.49	Imperial Leather Soap (125g) .65p
1lb jar of Honey £1.90	Typhoo Tea Bags (80s) £1.49
Chunky Choc Ice Cream 55p	

Tucker: 1) English (chiefly West Country): occupational name for a fuller, from an agent derivative of Middle English *tuck*(en) to full cloth (Old English *tucian* to torment). This was the term used for the process in the Middle Ages in SW England, and the present-day distribution of the surname still reflects this (see also FULLER and WALKER). 2) English: occasionally perhaps a nickname for a brave or generous man, from Old French *tout* all (Latin *totus*) + *Coeur* heart (Latin *cor*).

---

122. David and Cathy Turton, 61 and 55yrs married in Naunton in 1984. Cathy, a Primary School Teacher came to live at Longford Farm in 1979, being just divorced. In November 1982 she bought the barns that had been used as offices by Huntsman's Quarries until the 1970s, from Mrs Joyce Hanks of Longford. David, a management consultant and qualified mechanical engineer, met Cathy through the Lansdown Hockey Club in Cheltenham and came to live in Naunton following his own divorce in 1984. David has a daughter, Sarah, and a son, Andrew, both in their 30s, who live in London and Brighton respectively. Since 1984 they have improved Bakehouse Cottage with notably in 1994, the addition of the conservatory and the nearby stable block for the horses that graze in the Brake behind Longford. They both enjoy sport. David plays cricket for the village, golf at Naunton Downs and Veterans hockey for Lansdown. Cathy, having retired early from teaching due to spondylosis has had her equestrian and other sporting activities temporarily curtailed. Both enjoy being closely involved in Village activities and have helped to raise funds for a number of projects over the years. Although they love the sea and sailing, the joy they derive from the countryside and rural life plus their love of Naunton and its inhabitants will keep them here forever!

Turton: English: habitation name from a place in Lancs. so called from Old Norse personal name *Pori* + Old English *tun* enclosure, settlement. The surname is now as common in the Midlands as it is in Lancs. and Yorks.

123. Neil and Lois Vincent (and their dog Wellington) moved to Naunton from the outskirts of Cheltenham in summer '98. In their early 40s (Wellington is 10) both are civil servants working locally in Cheltenham. Indeed, they met at work. They enjoy walking, although Wellington gives them no option. Both enjoy keeping fit. Neil still plays soccer on Saturdays and Lois has also started riding again. At home, Lois enjoys cooking whilst Neil struggles to keep pace with a large garden, including a productive vegetable plot. They always had more than half an eye on the village before they moved in. They had frequently walked through the delightful lanes and Lois had been singing for the church choir throughout the 1990s, so they were well aware that it was an active village with a strong "can-do" attitude. It has since proved to be all and more than they expected.

Vincent: English and French: from a medieval given name (Latin *Vincentius*, a derivative of *vincens*, genesis *vincentis*, present participle of *vincere* to conquer; cf. VICTOR). The name was borne by a 3rd-cent. Spanish martyr widely venerated in the Middle Ages and by a 5th-cent monk and writer of Lerins, as well as other early saints.

124. Cedric Virgin's 76th birthday coincided with the first day of the New Millennium. With his wife Vera, he moved to 'Cotswold House' from Cheltenham where he had been a Surveyor, Valuer and Auctioneer with Virgin and Richards of Montpellier for over 40 years. Vera lectured in Physical Education at St. Mary's Teacher Training College in Cheltenham. Sadly she died in February 2000 since when Cedric says "I'm frequently asked whether or not I'll move from the village - a thought which has never crossed my mind. This is a pleasant village set in beautiful countryside with a small but very friendly population. I'm in the Church Choir, a regular at our Black Horse pub and a Life Member at Naunton Downs Golf Club, three holes of which are visible from my house. There are plenty of social events and an outstanding annual Music Festival." Although involved in several activities in Cheltenham - Vice President of the Bach Choir, member of Lilley Brook Golf Club, Pockets Snooker Club and Gloucester County Cricket Club, Cedric has no desire to forsake rural for town life.

Virgin: variant of **Virgo:** English, of uncertain origin. The surname coincides in form with Latin *virgo*, genitive *virginis*, maiden, from which is derived (via Old French) modern English *virgin*. It is possible that the surname was originally a nickname for someone who had played the part of the Blessed Virgin Mary in a mystery play. This, and the vernacular variants (**Virgoe, Vergo; Virgin, Vergin(e)** may also have been nicknames for shy young men, or ironically for notorious lechers.

125. Fred Wardrop (66) was born in Scotland and has traveled widely, working in France, Australia, America and elsewhere in the building trade. The game of golf has always been in his blood and he played scratch 1, 2 and 3 for a number of years. He last played at scratch at Naunton Downs in about 1991, when the club opened. He has a son of 33 who lives in Scotland. Because of an industrial accident Fred has not worked since 1992 but enjoys living in the village and has no intention of moving. **(Fred passed away in 2003).**

Wardrop: English and Scots: metonymic occupational name for someone who was in charge of the garments worn by a feudal lord and his household, from Anglo Norman French *warde(r)* to keep, guard (cf. WARDEN and GUARD) + *robe* garment (cf. ROPERO).

126. Mark and Lorraine Webb, 40 and 38yrs live at 2 Hillcrest Cottages, Harford Hill. Mark is employed as a stockman by Mrs Heber-Percy, at nearby Hill Farm, Upper Slaughter, This is a mixed Cotswold farm of about 1000 acres, growing barley, wheat and oats and with some 700 head of beef cattle. Lorraine works part-time at Cold Aston School as a classroom assistant. Mark and Lorraine moved from another cottage on Hill Farm, at the far end of Penny Lane to 2 Hillcrest at the lower end, in 1986. They have three sons, Simon, 18yrs, who is doing his 'A' levels at the Cotswold School, Bourton-on-the-Water and hopes to go to university to study farm management. Adam, 15yrs, also attends the Cotswold School where he is doing his GCSEs. Daniel, 10yrs, attends Cold Aston School but will soon be transferring to the Cotswold School. Mark, who grew up in Bourton and went to Westwoods Grammar School at Northleach, enjoys shooting in his spare time. Lorraine grew up in Blockley until she was 10 and then moved and went to Bourton Vale Secondary School. They both love the Cotswolds, but particularly the peacefulness of where they are now living, which offers splendid views over most of the Parish of Naunton.

Webb: English occupational name for a weaver, early Middle English *webbe*, from Old English *webba* (a primary derivative of *wefan* to weave). This word survived into Middle English long enough to give rise to the surname, but was already obsolescent as an agent noun; hence the secondary forms with the (redundant) agent suffixes- *(st)er*.

127. Glenda and Mike Wells were both in advertising in London. They left for Mike to earn a living as a landscape painter. Both fell in love with the Cotswolds, particularly the villages, the towns and the way of life there. They love the countryside with its rivers and streams and for walking. They moved to Naunton to live on the River Windrush (their cottage is about as close to the river as any can be) and found the village to be a friendly and vibrant place - so they are staying! (Glenda died in March 2004)
Wells: variant of **Well:** English: topographic for someone who lived near a spring or stream, Middle English *well(e)* (Old English well(a)).

128. David Westall and Sarah Foulkes moved to Naunton from Oxfordshire in 1999. Both work in education, David as a school's inspector and Sarah as an education advisor. They both enjoy working on their cottage and in the garden when they can find time. David is also a vintage car enthusiast and Sarah is interested in ethnic textiles. They have thoroughly enjoyed getting involved in the wealth of village events and becoming part of the Naunton community.
Westall: not in Oxford Dictionary. In Penguin Dictionary of surnames; from the Western hall or retreat/enclosure. Old English
Foulkes: English: from a Norman given name, a short form of the various Germanic names with the first element *folk* people. See also VOLK.

129. Nicholas and Kathryn Wheeler moved to Waterloo Farm in 1992. Nicholas grew up in Lower Slaughter and is now MD of the family building firm, A.T.Wheeler, with offices on the Fosse-Way near Bourton. His grandfather once owned Church Farm, Naunton in the early part of the 20th century. Kathryn grew up in Newnham-on-Severn in the Forest of Dean. She is a housewife who also enjoys breeding and showing Australian terriers, and currently has 5 of them. They have two daughters, Elizabeth aged 7 and Victoria aged 2. They also have horses which can be safely ridden on the adjoining 40 acres of grassland, some of which abuts the river Windrush as it leaves the east end of the village.
Author's note: Nick and Katherine's house, 'Waterloo Farm' was built after 1977 from several of the old Waterloo Farm outbuildings, These included the dairy where some 60 cows were milked twice every day, together with several store sheds and a lean-to garage. One of them, a small stone building with a single room, was known as the 'flower house', complete with a long disused fireplace and old plastered walls where animal food was stored (the nearest building to Waterloo House in the old photographs). In the 1860s this is believed to have housed an early village school, referred to as the 'academy' in the Trade Directories.
Wheeler: English: occupational name for a maker of wheels (for vehicles or for use in spinning or various other manufacturing processes), from an agent derivative of Middle English *whele* WHEEL.

130. Frank and Jill White, 65 and 52yrs and their family have lived at Naunton Downs Cottage since they bought it in 1977. It was then a very run down pair of old farm cottages with overgrown gardens. Much work has been done since, and continues to be done to restore and extend the cottage and recover the one third of an acre gardens. Frank was born in Leckhampton, Cheltenham and Jill in Stow. He was a Design Draughtsman with Dowty Fuel Systems until redundancy in 1992. He remains busier than ever with ongoing building projects and various other activities such as being a swimming coach in Cheltenham and Gloucester. Jill has been involved with the catering business for most of her life and currently runs St. Edward's Café in The Square, Stow-on-the-Wold with her business partner. They have 3 daughters who have all grown up at Naunton Downs and attended the Cotswold School at Bourton. Katherine (22) graduated in Marine Biology from Bangor University and now works in a laboratory doing medical research work with serums. Susan (20) is in her final year at Swansea University studying mathematics and statistics. Jennifer (15) is still at the Cotswold School studying for her GCSEs and hopes to become an architect. Frank and Jill find Naunton a very attractive place to live, especially as they are literally on top of the Wolds at 800 feet above sea level, with the air and the views to go with it. They love living here on the periphery of the Parish and have no intention of moving.
White: English, Scots and Irish: nickname for someone with white hair or an unnaturally pale complexion, from Middle English *whit* white (Old English *hwit*). In some cases it may represent the Middle English use as a given name of an Old English byname, *Hwit(a),* of this origin. As a Scots and Irish surname it has been widely used as a translation of various Gaelic names derived from the elements *ban* white or *fionn* fair. There has also been some confusion with WIGHT.

131. Gill Wilkie age 46, has lived in Naunton for 22 years. She has two children, Julian age 24yrs and Josephine age 22 yrs. They both now live in Cheltenham but grew up in Naunton. Her late husband, Bob used to work on a farm in Upper Slaughter but was sadly killed in a road accident three years ago. Gill used to be a housekeeper in a local hotel but now works on a private shooting estate. She has two cats, and one dog. Gill enjoys gardening, running, tennis and the countryside. She was Clerk to Naunton Parish Council for eight years.

Wilkie: variant of **Wilk:** 1) English: from a medieval given name, a back-formation from WILKIN, as if that contained Anglo Norman French diminutive suffix –*in*. . 2) Polish from *wilk* WOLF probably from an Old Slavonic personal name containing this element.

132. Vera Williams was born in Skipton, West Yorkshire but grew up mostly overseas and mainly in India, when her father was in the Foreign Service. After a private education she met and married John T. Williams, when he was a barrister. John later became a Recorder and finally a Judge of Appeal in the Supreme Court. John and Vera spent many happy years overseas where his legal career took him to Hong Kong, Tonga, Gibraltar, Brunei, Australia, New Zealand, Tanzania and finally Fiji, before returning to England after the military coup there in 1987. Vera has been an artist throughout her life and she has painted in each of the countries where she and John have lived. A number of her paintings still grace the walls of various buildings in many of these countries. Vera continues to enjoy her painting, together with classical dancing and music, which she became familiar with early-on in life whilst in India. After John's retirement they moved to Naunton. When John died in 1993, Vera decided to remain here, in her 'little cottage,' as she likes to call it, situated on the edge of the village and commanding excellent views over Naunton and Lower Guiting. Vera has a studio where she continues to paint and write about her incredible life in Africa, no doubt being inspired as she looks up at a number of her beautiful paintings from the African continent and other parts of the world.

Vera has established a good number of new friends in the Cotswolds, whilst retaining contact with many old ones in Britain and abroad.

(The other young lady in the photograph is Miss Georgia Rose Dewar, 3yrs, the author's beautiful granddaughter).

Williams: variant of **William:** English, from the Norman form of an Old French personal name composed of the Germanic *wil* will, desire + *helm* helmet, protection. This was introduced into England at the time of the Norman Conquest (1066), and within a very short period it became the most popular given name in England, mainly no doubt in honour of the Conqueror himself. The given name has also enjoyed considerable popularity in Germany (as *Wilhelm*), France (as *Guillaume*), Spain (as *Guillermo*), and Italy (as *Guglielmo* with numerous diminutives).

133. Mike Wood (54) and Marion met in 1989 and married in 1990. Mike was born at nearby Clapton-on-the-Hill and his father used to attend the chapel at Naunton where many of Mike's ancestors were buried. Consequently, Mike feels that his roots are probably more firmly placed in Naunton than in Clapton They each have a son and a daughter from a previous marriage. Mike has 5 grandchildren and Marion has 2.

Eastern Hill Farm was built in 1979 and Michael bought it in 1985. It has 69 acres on which he has grown winter and spring barley and winter wheat - winning a National Malting Barley Competition in 1986. At that time barley was selling for £132 per ton whilst today it fetches only £70 per ton. This decline in grain prices set in during the early 1990s and has resulted in Mike having to take work at Farmington Stone Quarry for the past 3 years, whilst Marion runs a Bed and Breakfast business at Eastern Hill Farm. (Some 450 farmers/farm workers are leaving the land every month, which is currently referred to as the 'Farm Crisis'). They both love living in Naunton and have no plans to do anything but continue enjoying it for as long as they possibly can.

Wood: 1) It almost goes without saying that in the majority of cases, this English and Scots topographic name refers to someone who lived in or by a wood, or a metonymic occupational name for a woodcutter or forester, from Middle English *wode* wood (Old English *wudu*). 2) It was also a nickname for a mad, eccentric, or violent person, from Middle English *wod* mad, frenzied (Old English *wad*), as in Adam *le Wode* 'Adam the Mad', Worcs. 1221.

134. Diana Woolley (60), as with any good barrister, will be permitted the last word here, in defence of her flawless decision to move to Naunton. After qualifying as a barrister she worked for many years as Group Company Secretary for a multi-national advertising group. Then, one day much later in life, she walked down Grange Hill into Naunton one sunny afternoon (September 1992) and fell in love with the village, much as thousands have before her. After some twenty visits (and in 1996 having been appointed the first lady Vice-President of Naunton Cricket Club), in 1998 Diana gave into the inevitable and purchased Humphries Barn. At the end of April 2000, Diana finally severed her links with London to give herself up fully to Naunton village life although she retains a consultancy arrangement with her former employer.

Diana is now secretary of Naunton Village Trust and the PCC and has recently agreed to act as Naunton's Parish Clerk. She continues to support Naunton Cricket Club and also supports the Naunton Music Society, the Stow Music Club and the Cheltenham Bach Choir. She regularly attends Cheltenham Racecourse and can often be found lending a hand when there is something happening in the village. She continues to indulge in her passion for country walking whenever she can spare the time - particularly enjoying following the local Hunts.

Diana had always planned to retire to the Country and she considers herself exceptionally lucky to have found Naunton to live in, a village which she has found very welcoming and which has so much going on.

Woolley: English habitation name from any of various places so called. Most, including those in Berks., Cambs, (formerly Hunts.), and W. Yorks., get the name from Old English *wulf* wolf (or perhaps the personal name or byname *Wulf;* see WOLF) + *leah* wood, clearing; one example in Somerset, however, has as its first element Middle English *woll, wull* spring, stream.

194 *Naunton 2000*

1. John Fieldgate

2. Chris and Carole Adams

3. Ian Adcock and Vanessa Gatford

4. Andy and Zosha Anderson

5. Michael and Jane Arnold

6. Inger and Richard Ash

7. Jean Bacon

8. Mandy and Andy Barber

9. Leslie and Christine Barber

10. Neville 'Bart' and Ethel 'Niddy' Barton

11. Andrew and Judith Barwood

12. Alan and Edna Bayliss

13. Lionel Beames with Meg (dog) and daughter Bev'

14. Cecilia and David Bedford

15. James and Jeanne Beer

16. John and Lilian Bond

17. Pat and Ralph Boult

18. Edward and Victoria Bowen-Jones

19. Jonathon Bowen-Jones

20. Nora Brett

21. Elmar Bruening

22. Jonathan and Vanessa Cameron

23. Marie-Louise and Charlotte Chudleigh

24. Natasha Clifford

25. Dominic and Karen Collier

26. Matthew and Fiona Collins

27. Paul and Erica Cooper

28. Joan Cowan

29. Michael and Licia Crystal

30. Robin and Jane Davies

31. William, Jayne and Christian Davies

32. Terri (nee Herbert) and Oliver Davis

33. Connie Dearman

34. Thomas and Jeanette Donoghue

35. Jonny and Julia Duval

36. Jeff and Karen Dyer

37. John and Joan Egan

38. Marion and John Elliott

39. John and Maria Evans

40. Stephen and Jayne Ewart-Perks

41. Rory and Lyn Fellowes

42. Mary and Martin Fiveash

43. John and Mary Foster

44. Sophia and Richard Goldman

45. David and Fiona Hallsworth

46. Douglas and Penny Hanks

47. Geoffrey Hanks

48. Ian and Tracey Hanks

49. Joyce Hanks

50. Kevin and Gail Harding

51. David Harman and Jane Ford

52. Kathleen (Kay) Harvey

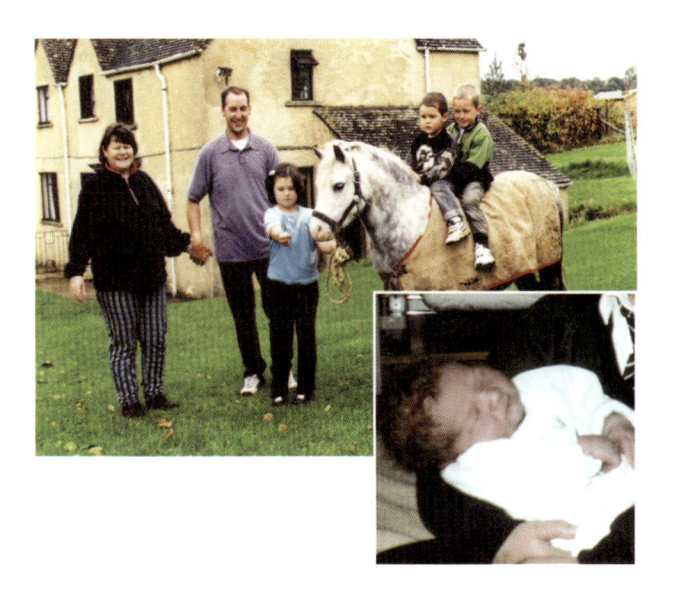

53. Megan and Nick Hayward

54. William (Billy) Herbert

55. Christopher and Daphne Hickman

56. Robert and Caroline Hicks

57. Eddie Higgins and Clara (Clarrie) Collett

58. Graham and Elizabeth (Betty) Hill

59. Bill and Madeleine Hindley

60. Graham and Ann Hoult

61. Jean Hull

62. Margaret and Graham Hunter

63. Derrick and Mary James

64. Lesley and Harry Janssen

65. Paul Johnson and Pamela Stevenson

66. Rob and Juliet Johnson

67. Adrian and Heather Jones

68. Philip and Anne Jones

69. Jones, Chalmers, Harper and Robinson families.

70. Philip and Robert Juggins

71. Kevin and Sue Kelleher

72. Julia Kelly

206 *Naunton 2000*

73. Val and Kevin Langley

74. Adrian Loker

75. Martin and Helen Macklin

76. Bill (Mac) and Mary Macklin

77. Julia Mangan and Eileen Smith

78. Will and Katy Manley

79. Sue Marston and David Wintle

80. Mollie Maughan

81. Atalanti Meyer

82. James and Fiona Milton

83. Joan and Arthur (Mitch) Mitchell

84. Doug and Beryl Mitchell

85. Peter and Jan Morton

86. Oliver and Judy Murphy

87. Bob and Carol Newton

88. Fergal O'Brien

89. Ken and Sara Ogilvie

90. Austin and Jane O'Malley

91. Graham Owens

92. John and Rose Outhwaite

93. Sir Derek and Lady Shuna Palmar

94. Michael Parry

95. David and Jane Pickup

96. David and Lee Porter

97. Graham and Corrinne Powell

98. Len and Nancy Quaranto

99. Patricia Quinn

100. Donna and David Renney

101. John and Valerie Ridge

102. Audrey Roome

103. Sophie and Edward Rugge-Price

104. Christopher Samuels and Polly Hendry

105. Peter and Maralyn Scudamore

106. Nick and Lotte Seal

107. Lincoln and Tish Seligman

108. Mark and Andrea Seymour

109. Ralph (Jack) and Jayne Smith

110. William and Theresa Smith

111. David and Louise Smyth

112. Philip Steele and Claire Walker

113. Bob and Barbara Steiner

114. Brian and Mary Stevens

Naunton 2000 213

115. John and Lizzie Stevens

116. Ken Stonehewer

117. Doris Stratford

118. Laura Stutowicz

119. Richard Tilbrook and Paul Warwick

120. Joan Timmins

214   *Naunton 2000*

121. Derek and Margaret Tucker

122. David and Cathy Turton

123. Neil and Lois Vincent

124. Cedric Virgin

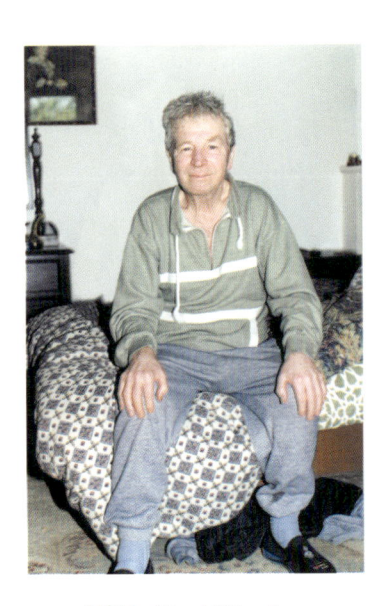

125. Fred Wardrop

126. Mark and Lorraine Webb

127. Glenda and Mike Wells

128. David Westall and Sarah Foulkes

129. Nicholas and Kathryn Wheeler

130. Frank and Jill White

131. Gill Wilkie

132. Vera Williams

133. Mike and Marion Wood

134. Diana Woolley

Naunton 2000 has moved us away from the anonymous residents of the past, such as these below.

Chapter 4

**A selection of old pictures of Naunton, entering from the east.
(includes exact year where known, or estimated decade if not)**

001 Lower Harford (10s)

002 Lower Harford & ancient ford (10s)

003 Lower Harford (10s)

004 Windrush 'Oxbows' through the meadows (20s)

005 Bowsing and dry stone bridge (50s)

006 Sheep dipping by Mill Coppice (50s)

218 *Naunton 2000*

007 View to west; old enclosure wall in Maggits Hays. (00s)

008 View to west; Waterloo & The Mill (20s)

009 View to west; cricket practice in Maggits Hays (20s)

010 View to west; Waterloo & The Mill (20s)

011 View to west; The Mill (20s)

012 First two Council houses in Maggits Hays (1943)

013 The Mill Race (10s)

014 Steam threshing at the Mill (10s)

015 William Bullock Hanks, Miller (1905)

016 Clara Hanks, family & workers, threshing at the Mill (10s)

017 The Mill House & front garden (10s)

018 Early motor transport at the Mill (20s)

019 The Mill (20s)

020 Hospital Sunday and the Mill (1913)

021 The Mill Stream (10s)

022 William, Clara & family, Mill garden (10s)

220 *Naunton 2000*

023 William, Clara & family, Mill garden (10s)

024 Waterloo House and garden (50s)

025 Mill Barn (50s)

026 Cromwell House (1900)

027 Cromwell House (20s)

028 Cromwell House (20s)

029 Cromwell House (00s)

030 Cromwell House (30s)

031 Kiftsgate House (00s)

032 Rose & Kiftsgate Cottages (10s)

033 A bicycle made for two (30s)

034 The Sheep Wash (50s)

035 The Sheep Wash (50s)

036 Taterbury Row (50s)

037 Abel Tom Smith (20s)

038 Centre of village from north (30s)

039 The Square and old cottage (00s)

040 Ivy Cottage and Longford House (30s)

041 Longford House (00s)

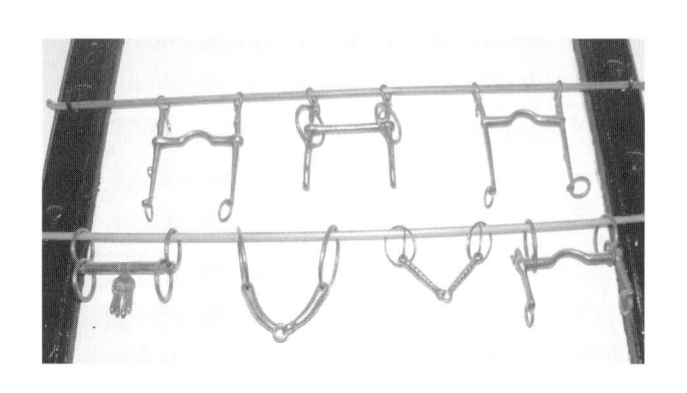

042 Old horse bits, Longford House (2000)

043 Longford yard (40s)

044 Longford House (20s)

045 Playing and posing (00s)

046 Black Horse Inn (00s)

047 A ride to the pub! (00s)

048 'Ole bwois' reminiscing! (00s)

049 Naunton Club (1913)

050 Dummer beagles at the Black Horse (50s)

051 The house before Northcote (50s)

052 Lost cottage on corner of North St (1954)

054 Lost cottages, corner of North St (10s)

053 Lost cottage and water pump (50s)

055 Carrying the water home (20s)

056 Flooded street (30s)

Naunton 2000   225

057 John Hurd's lower bridge (20s)

058 From Waterloo field, northwards (50s)

059 North-east view (20s)

060 North view (30s)

061 Northfield (30s)

062 North-west view (20s)

063 James Hooper (pre-1938)

064 Carol singers call at El Hogar (1954)

226 *Naunton 2000*

065 Cyril Tims - former postman (1988)

066 Paddock & cottages (30s)

067 John Stanley in paddock (50s)

068 Naunton Club in central paddock (1913)

069 Naunton Club (1913)

070 Caravan Mission (1917)

071 Yew Tree Cottage (30s)

072 Looking east (00s)

Naunton 2000 227

073 A young Mr Pulham (10s)

074 Edwardian children (1907)

075 David Pulham (1938)

076 Pulham's bus (30s)

077 Pulhams depot (50s)

078 Post Office & shop (00s)

079 Post Office & shop (00s)

080 Post Office & shop (00s)

081 Spring Cottage (40s)

082 Naunton Club (1920)

083 Hospital Sunday (1913)

084 Naunton Club (1914)

085 Naunton Club (1914)

086 Naunton Club (1914)

087 Central (opposite the Manor) (10s)

088 Central (opposite the Manor) (00s)

089 Central (opposite the Manor) (20s)

090 Looking N to Manor (00s)

091 Looking NW to Manor (00s)

092 Bird's eye view of Manor (50s)

093 Bird's eye view of Manor (50s)

094 Manor and ancient village track way (00s)

095 Manor, barns and dovecote (10s)

096 Manor gardener – one of the earliest village photographs (1890s)

097 Manor House (00s)

098 Manor view (00s)

099 Manor and ancient trackway (30s)

100 Manor cows return for milking (10s)

101 Dovecote view (20s)

102 Dovecote and hayricks (10s)

103 Dovecote view (10s)

104 Dovecote, Manor & Mill Hays (00s)

Naunton 2000 231

105 Floodgates & generator house (20s)

106 Manor floodgates (20s)

107 Dovecote & floodgates (30s)

108 North towards the School (10s)

109 Manor Hill (1905) Unknown, other than Irene Hanks on right

110 Manor Hill (2001) From L-R: Robert Juggins; Elizabeth Wheeler; James Macklin; George Pickup; James Pickup; Beth Timmins; Emily Palmer; Freya Stevens; Victoria Wheeler; Hannah Timmins.

111 Manor Hill & rickyard (20s)

232 *Naunton 2000*

112 Opening of new Village Hall (1937)

113 Young performers (50s)

114 Young performers (50s)

115 A village concert (50s)

116 Women's Institute (70)

117 Naunton Club (1905)

118 Naunton Club (1905)

119 Jasmine Cottage and the Pound (00s)

120 The School & Jasmine Cottage (30s)

121 Author's mother and sisters (1954)

122 The School (00s)

123 The School (10s)

124 The School (00s)

125 Naunton Club meeting W. B. Hanks on left (1912)

126 Naunton Club meeting (1912)

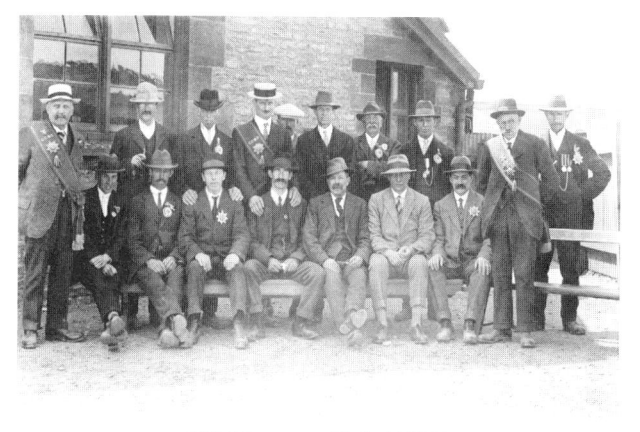

127 Naunton Club (1921)

234   *Naunton 2000*

128 The School (1926)

129 The School (30s)

130 School nativity play (1957)

131 School nativity play (1960)

132 School (1968)

133 The Manse (00s)

134 The Chapel (00s)

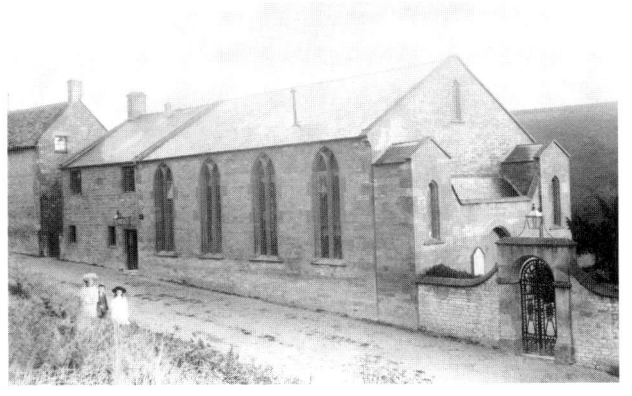

135 The Chapel (00s)

Naunton 2000 235

136 The Chapel (1939)

137 Chapel Sunday School (50s)

138 The Chapel (10s)

139 The Chapel (10s)

140 Chapel Hill from school bank (20s)

141 Naunton Club (1912)

142 Rock Cottage (20s)

143 West End towards Post Office (20s)

144 Windrush Cottage

145 The Quadrangle (00s)

146 The Bakery, Quadrangle (30s)

147 Cider Mill (30s)

148 Old Cider Mill undergoing conversion (1990)

149 Looking North across John Hurd's bridge (00s)

150 John Hurd's bridge (40s)

Naunton 2000   237

151 John Hurd's 1819 bridge (00s)

152 North across the bridge (00s)

153 Upstream side of bridge (00s)

154 Naunton Club (1912)

155 Naunton Club (1907)

156 Naunton Club (1907)

157 Naunton Club (1912)

158 Naunton Club (1920)

238   *Naunton 2000*

159 The Rectory (10s)

160 Rectory, sale of work (00s)

161 Rectory (00s)

162 Rectory, Naunton Club (10s)

163 Rectory, Naunton Club (10s)

164 Old cottage on the green (00s)

165 Old cottage on the green (00s)

166 Post Office on the green (20s)

Naunton 2000   239

167 Out for a ride (30s)

168 The Hunt meets on the green (1948)

169 Church House (00s)

170 Dale Street & Merrell's shop (00s)

171 Dale Street (00s)

172 Dale Street (00s)

173 Dale Street (00s)

174 Dale Street shop (60s)

240 *Naunton 2000*

175 Dale Street (00s)

176 Young cyclist (00s)

177 Dale Street Forge; Fred Higgs & Horace Fletcher (00s)

178 Maurice Hanks; farmer (30s)

179 Bill Parsons; shepherd (1953)

180 Dale Cottage (00s)

181 Dale House (20s)

182 Dale House (50s)

183 Cricket, Mill Hayes/Dove House Meadow (10s)

184 Naunton Club, Dove House Meadow (1919)

185 Naunton Club, Dove House Meadow (1919)

186 Mill Hayes and ancient village track way (20s)

187 West end view (20s)

188 Overbrook (30s)

189 St. Andrew's Church (00s)

190 St. Andrew's Church (20s)

242 *Naunton 2000*

191 St. Andrew's Church (20s)

192 St. Andrew's Church (20s)

193 St. Andrew's Church (00s)

194 West end view with tiny lost cottage in centre. (00s)

195 Looking north to Grange Hill/Sheepwell Lane (20s)

196 Looking N across the valley (20s)

197 Looking NE across the valley (20s)

198 Looking NE across the valley (30s)

199 Looking E down the valley (20s)

200 Naunton Band (10s)

201 Naunton Band (10s)

202 Naunton Club Committee (1919)

203 Coronation celebrations (1953)

204 Naunton cricket team (00s)

205 Up and coming cricketers (10s)

206 Cotswold League Cup winners (1923)

244   *Naunton 2000*

207 Cheltenham Challenge Cup winners (1938/9)

208 Hanks cricket team (40s)

209 Ayleworth harvesting (20s)

210 Aylworth hay cart (20s)

211 Aylworth Horses (20s)

212 Aylworth Horses (20s)

213 Ayleworth transport (20s)

214 Horse ploughing – Billy Herbert (20s)

215 Children's outing on Bedwell's wagon (10s)

216 Bedwell's wagon & team (10s)

217 Hay cart (20s)

218 Hay cart (30s)

219 Reaper-binder (20s)

220 Reaper-binder (30s)

221 Steam powered baling (10s)

222 The steam power (10s)

223 Stone cart (40s)

224 The Haulier (10s)

225 Water cart (20s)

226 Huntsmans steam lorry (20s)

227 Huntsmans diesel lorry (40s)

228 Huntsmans quarrymen (20s)

Naunton 2000 247

229 Huntsman's Tiler (40s)

230 Pulhams 'new' bus (1927)

231 Naunton motorcyclist (30s)

232 Naunton water dispute (1908)

233 Naunton water dispute (1908)

234 The Mill Floodgates (20s)

235 Manor Wedding group c1908

236 Earliest known colour view (Autochrome) c1914

236a Modern (Digital) view. Early C21

Naunton 2000 249

237 1954 photograph by Stu Russell

238 Representational view of farming scene (1940s)

Naunton in colour

Most images are from the author's collection of 35mm slides; hence some occasional variation in the colours.

Six Paintings

239 Cromwell House

240 Longford Yard

241 Longford Yard

242 Manor and Dovecote

243 Mill Hayes

244 Mill Barn

245 Early cottage; early transport (1995)

246 Ancient building; modern transport (90s)

247 Post Office (40s)

248 Post Office (50s)

249 Last shop and Post Office (1999)

250 Last orders at last shop (1999)

251 Ancient riverside track, eastward (1987)

252 Ancient riverside track, westward (1987)

253 'El Hogar' riverside cottage & garden (1954)

254 Flowers in the church (1990)

255 Chapel Row (1989)

256 Christmas Party (1992)

257 Comeley's Office Staff (1988)

258 Capturing change, Close Hill (1987)

259 Cider Mill conversion (1992)

260 Dovecote refurbishment (2001)

Naunton 2000   253

261 Dovecote refurbished (2001)

262 A Duck Race (2001)

263 A village game plays on (1988)

264 Up-Street v. Down-Street (1988)

265 Relaxed spectators (1988)

266 Generations of spectators (1988)

267 Some slashing (1988)

268 Some stone walling (70s)

269 Naunton Proms (2001)

270 Still treading the boards (1997)

271 Younger stars in the making (1990)

272 Play Group (1988)

273 Village Slide Show (1988)

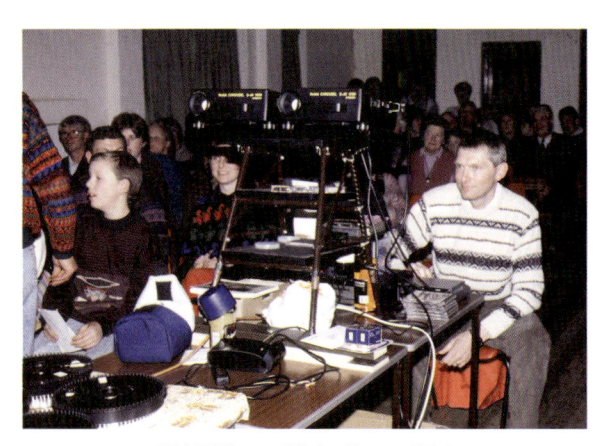

274 Village Slide Show (90s)

275 Trying to read; now attempting to write! (1954)

Naunton 2000   255

276 The great rural playground (1995)

277 Remember, remember; 5th of November!

278 Show stoppers (2001)

279 No longer roadworthy (1988)

280 Grazing on, from century to century.

281 Village line-up (early C21)

282 Sunday School (1988)

256 *Naunton 2000*

283 The Black Horse (1999)

284 Brothers chatting; Harold & John (1990)

285 Friends chatting – Harold & Ken (1989)

286 Friends chatting – Joan & Corinne (1988)

287 Harvesting; Eastern Hill (1995)

288 Another 'unprofitable' load of wheat (1995)

Naunton 2000   257

289 Another load of trouble (1995)

290 John the mason (1988)

291 Lord & Lady Gray; village show (1989)

292 Village shop (60s)

293 Service for new bells (1992)

294 A Chapel Wedding. Author's daughter Emma & Mr Brian Dewar (1998)

258 *Naunton 2000*

295 A Church Wedding Sally Mitchell & father Doug (1990)

296 Three happy faces (1989)

297 View from the Manor (90s)

298 View of the Manor (1988)

299 1 & 2 Millview (80s)

300 The former Water Corn Mill (C21)

Naunton 2000 259

301 An evening at Waterloo House (1991)

302 Sun setting on last hayrick! (90s)

303 Cornfield to Clubhouse (1995)

304 Racing into the future (2000)

305 The Windrush enters

306 The Windrush passes through

307 The Windrush leaves

308 Gazing and grazing, as ever (C21)

260   *Naunton 2000*

309 *Déjà vu* (dual-tone image, see also photo 110)

St. Andrews and the Moon (1987): Monuments in Earth, Space and Time
The Church, some 800 years after man placed his first footings in the ground here.
The Moon, some 18 years after man placed his first footings in the ground there.

William Mitchell's map of Naunton, 1838
Dwellings in red, workshops and farm buildings in black

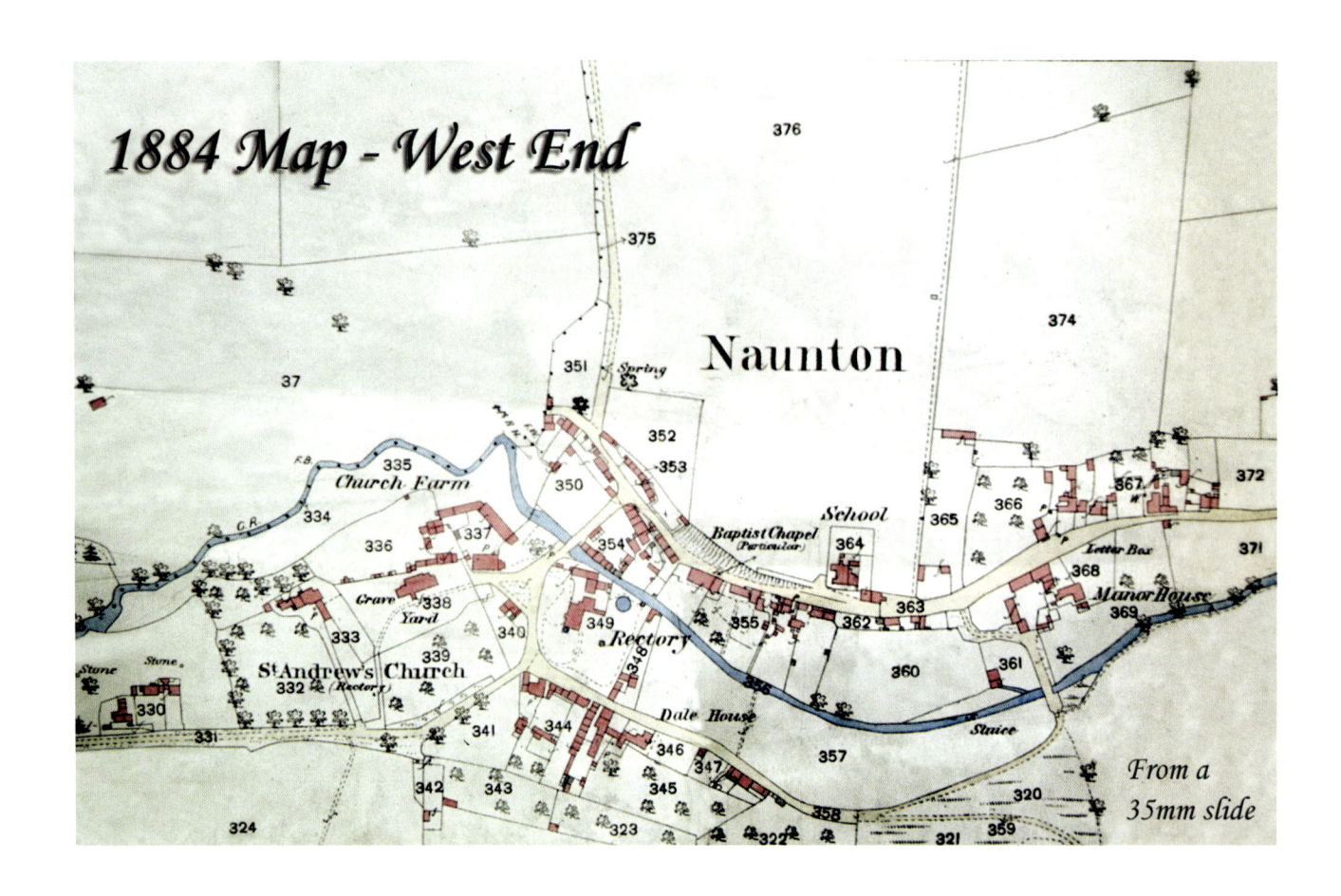

262 Naunton 2000

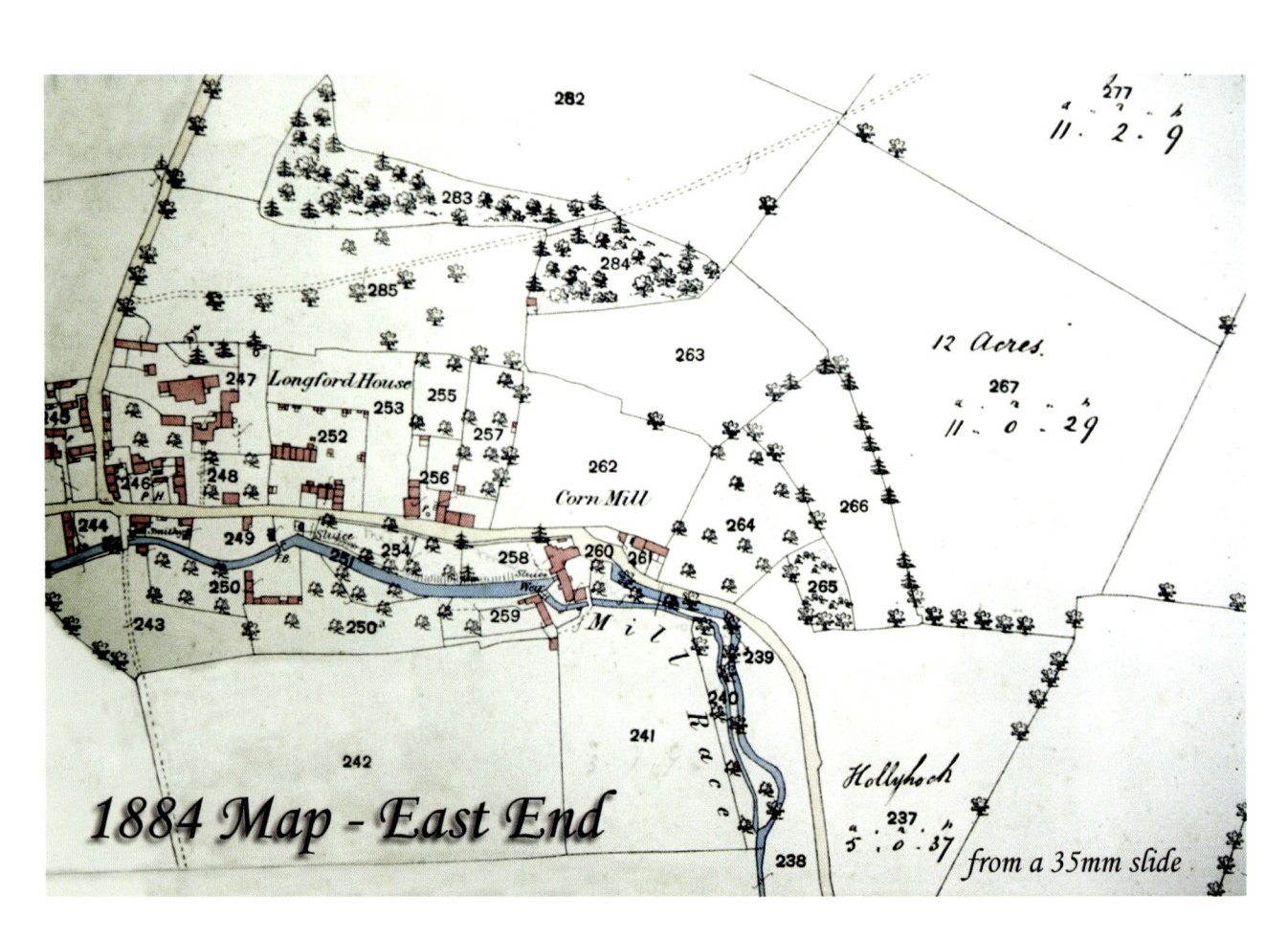

1884 Map - West End

From a 35mm slide

1884 Map - East End

from a 35mm slide

Part of Saxton's Map c1577

Geographical View of GLOUCESTERSHIRE during the CIVIL WAR.
WORCESTERSHIRE
HEREFORDSHIRE
WARWICKSHIRE
MONMOUTHSH.
OXFORDSHIRE
WILTSHIRE
SOMERSETSHIRE
BERKSH.
Pershore
Evesham stormed
Upton
Ledbury
Campden House burnt
Broadway
Mythe
Tewkesbury stormed
Snowshill
Dimmock
Rydmarley
Oxendon
Morton in Marsh
Corse Lawn
Winchcomb
Sudley Castle
Ross
Newent
Hartpury Court
Bodington House
Highleden House
Tainton
Cheltenham
Presbury
Naunton
Stow
Huntley
Vineyard
Highnam House
Ruerdean
Churcham
Badgworth
GLOUCESTER besieged
Andover's ford
Monmouth
Westbury
Matson House
Little Dean
Coberley
Newnham
Brockthorp
Northleach
Colford
Arlingham
Highmeadow House
Painswick
Burford
Sully House
Frampton
Eastington
Miserden House
Lidney House burnt
Stinbridge
Frocester
Stroud
Lypiat House
Nass
Saperton House
Llancaut
Wintour's leap
Berkeley Castle
Cirencester stormed
Dursley
Hampton road
Chepstow
Horsley
Fairford
Lechlade
River Severn
Beachley
Beverstone Castle
Wotton
Tetbury
Thornbury
Yate Court burnt
Malmsbury stormed
Badminton House
Tormarton House ruined
BRISTOL stormed
Tog Hill
Monument
Lansdown
BATH
EXPLANATION
Guards and Garrisons
Skirmishes and Battles
MARCHES
Kg. Charles to Gloucester, Augt. 1643
Do. from do. to Evesham,
Do. in pursuit of Essex,
E. of Essex to relieve Gloucester,
Do. on his return,
Septr. 1643
Kg. Charles from Evesham to Bath, July 1644
NB. The King's personal route, here laid down in every instance from Iter Carolinum, sometimes differed a little from that of the main body of his army.

Rudder's Map c1770

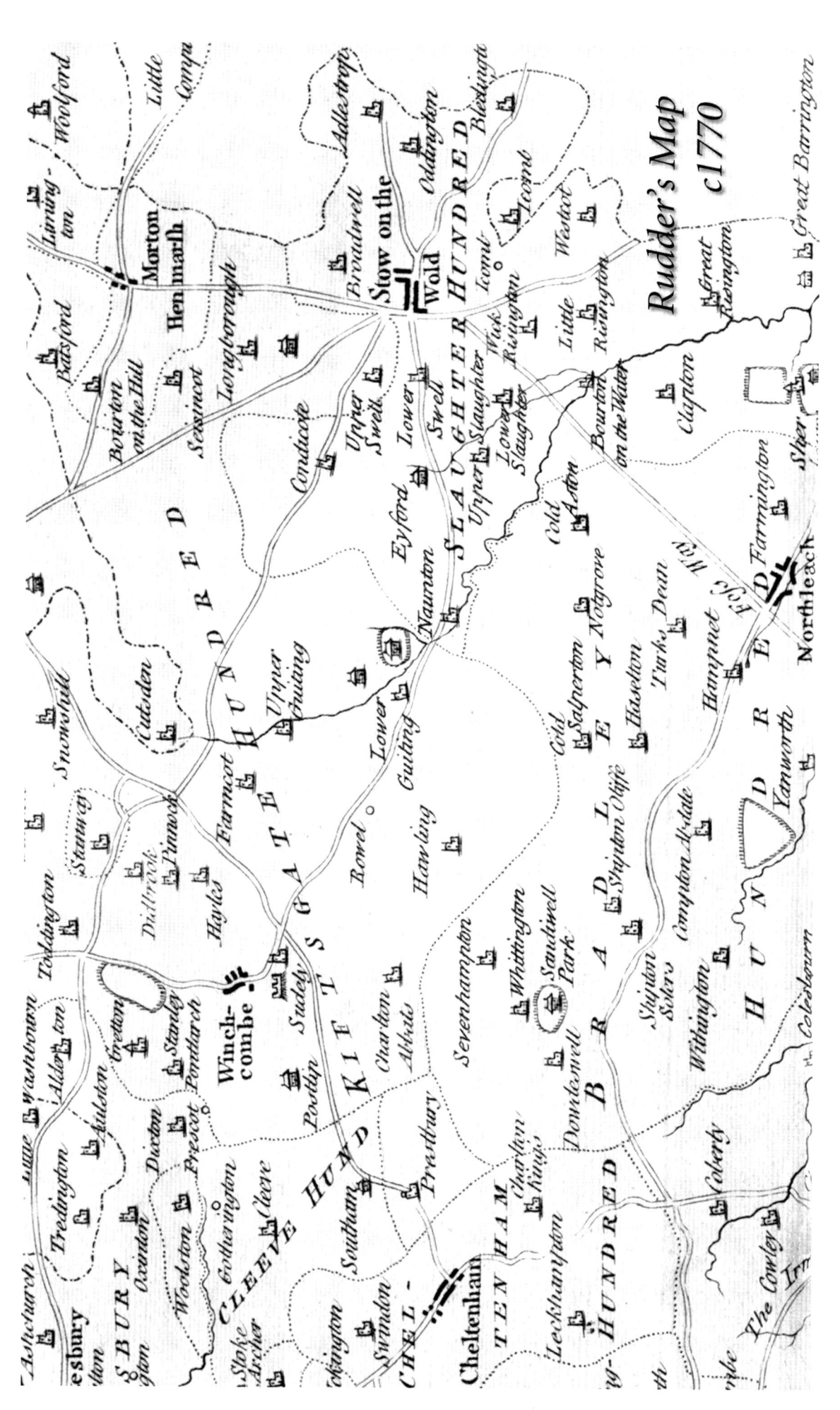

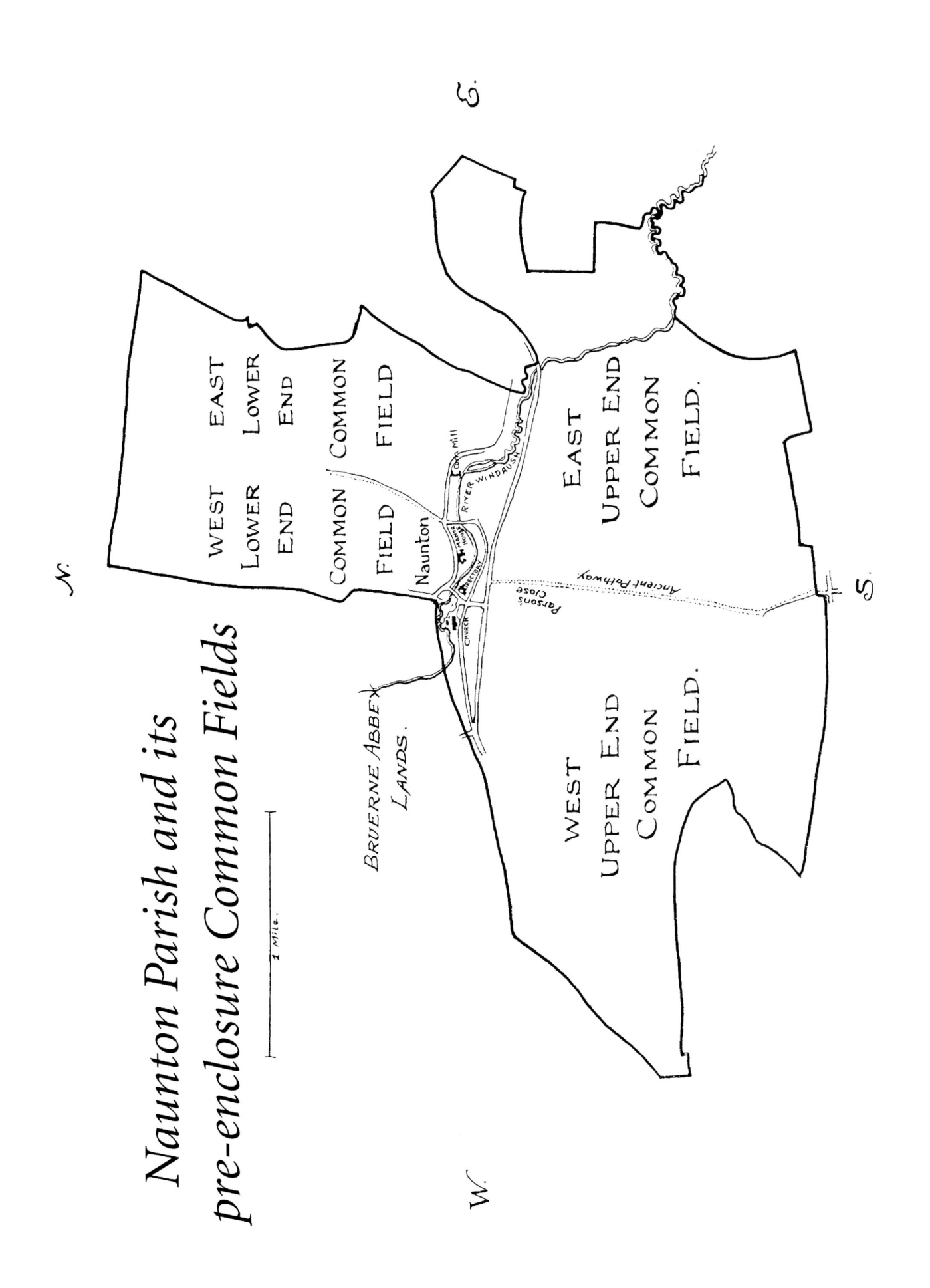

Naunton Parish and its pre-enclosure Common Fields

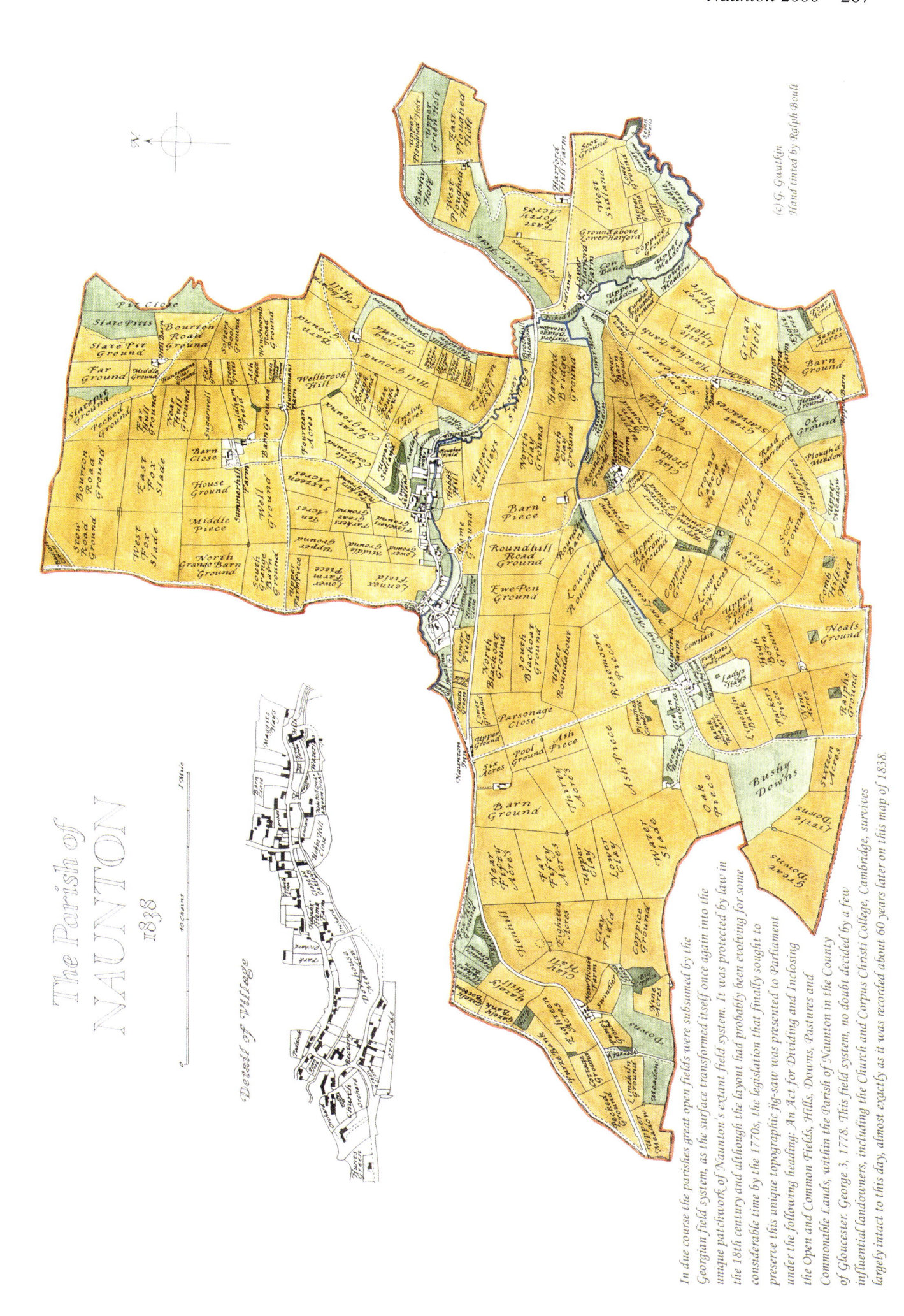

The Parish of NAUNTON 1838

In due course the parishes great open fields were subsumed by the Georgian field system, as the surface transformed itself once again into the unique patchwork of Naunton's extant field system. It was protected by law in the 18th century and although the layout had probably been evolving for some considerable time by the 1770s, the legislation that finally sought to preserve this unique topographic jig-saw was presented to Parliament under the following heading: An Act for Dividing and Inclosing the Open and Common Fields, Hills, Downs, Pastures and Commonable Lands, within the Parish of Naunton in the County of Gloucester. George 3, 1778. This field system, no doubt decided by a few influential landowners, including the Church and Corpus Christi College, Cambridge, survives largely intact to this day, almost exactly as it was recorded about 60 years later on this map of 1838.

(c) G. Gwatkin
Hand tinted by Ralph Boult

Pre-mechanised farming in The Cotswolds.

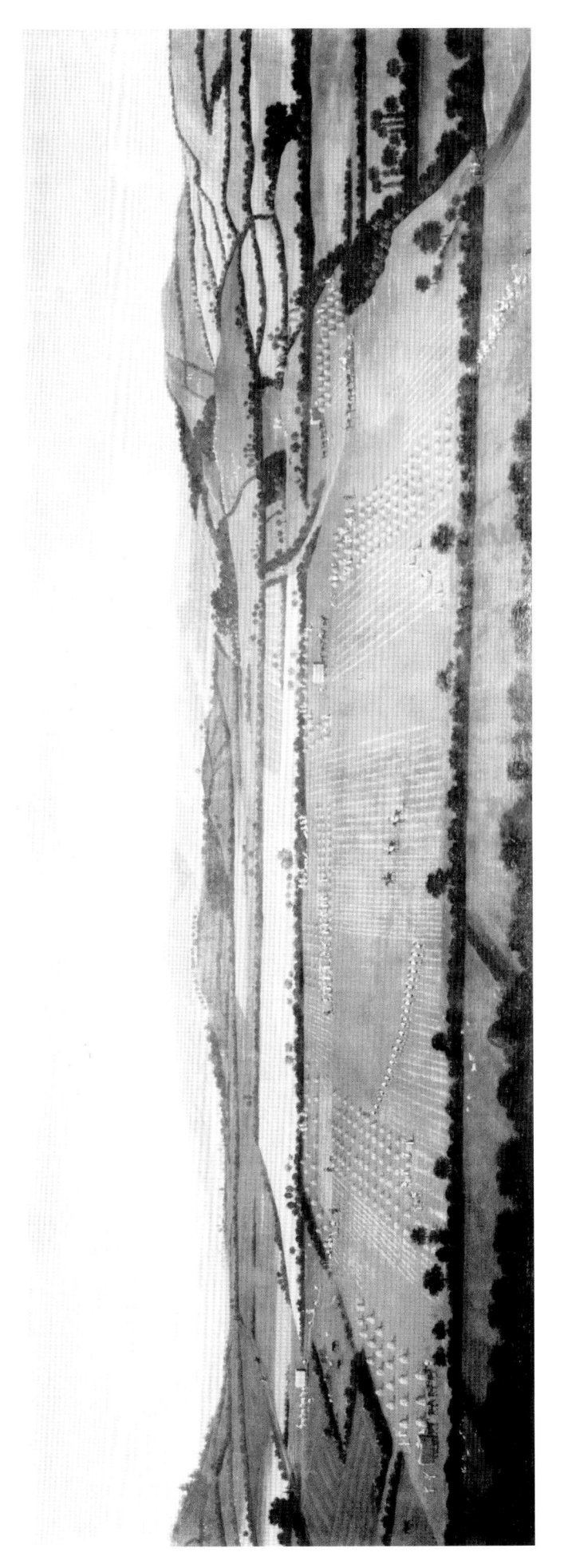

The Dixton Harvesters 1715
(Courtesy Cheltenham Museum and Art Gallery)

Appendix 1

What's in a name!

Various 'popular' meanings exist for places we are familiar with around here, including the District Name of *'Cotswolds'*. It has been suggested that it arose from the numerous small dry-stone *'Cots'* that once existed in the fields across the local *'Wolds'*, and there may be an element of truth in this or it could be just another myth. But it is no myth that the name was once linked with just a few local villages, of which **Naunton** was one, and not the much larger geographical area we now associate with the Cotswolds. I have added the more validated meanings for just a few of the relevant names. These include the years in which extant records support a particular name and its spelling. It does not mean that the name did not exist in that or similar form well before the dates shown, because as we now know, earlier documents that may have recorded the names have failed to survive.

Unless stated otherwise, details (plus abbreviated sources) are taken from 'The Place-Names of Gloucestershire' by A.H.Smith. Cambridge University Press, 1964, Part 1.

The Cotswolds

Montana de Codesuualt 12 Gir, *Coddeswold* 1269 Pat, 1294 Cl
Coteswaud 1250 Pat, *-wold* 1305 Cl, *-Wowlde* 1557 M, *-would* 1646 M, *Cotiswold* 1440 Pat, *Cotswold* 1592 Shakespeare (Ric 2)
Cottyswolde 1440, 1480 Cely, *Cottiswoldes* 1543 MinAcct, *Cotteswold, -wald* 1577 Harrison, 1590 Camd
Cottsold 1541 Roister Doister iv, 6, *Cotsall* 1602 Merry Wives I,i,92
'**Cod**'s high open land', *v.* **wald**. The personal name is an Old English *Cod* which appears in certain other names in this area, *Cutsdean*, *Codswell* and *Codesbyrig* are places in the hills between the head-waters of the Windrush and the Dikler, and it is possible that the same man gave his name to all four sites. The name may originally have referred to a stretch of hill country between the Cotswold escarpment east of Winchcombe and the Fosse Way in the neighbourhood of Blockley, Stow-on-the-Wold and **Naunton;** Giraldus Cambrensis passed through the Cotswolds between Blockley and Evesham, and in 1269 (Pat) Cotswold was described as 'towards Clapley'. The name Cotswold also occurs as an affix in the spellings of **Naunton,** a little to the east, but the term *wold* itself has a somewhat wider provenance in the earlier affixes of Withington, Stow-on-the-Wold and Westington. In recent times the name denotes the whole of this great upland region of Gloucestershire as far south as Northleach, Bibury, Cirencester, and Wotton under Edge.

Bourton On The Water

Burchtun 714, *-ton* 1206, Curr, 1221 *Ass to Burhtune* 949 BCS 882
to Burhtune 949 BCS 882
(into) *Burghtune* 949, *Burghton* 1221, *Ass,* 1375 Ipm, 1621 Inq, (*-juxta Sloughter*) 1496 AD ii (*-als. Bourton super aquam*). 1601 *FF,* (*-als Bowerton*) 1641 Inq, *Burghetone* 1428 AddRoll, *Burghton super Aquam als. Bowerton super Aquam,* 1610 GR 158
Bortune 1086 Domesday Book. *Borchton(e)* 1221 *Ass*
Burton 1195 P (p), 1221 Eyre, 1235 Cl, (*-super aquam*) 1535 VE, 1557, 1592 *FF,* 1610 M, (*-upon the water*)
Burgton 1251 Ch
Bourt(h)on 1291 Episc. Tax
Boruhton 1303 FA *Borouton* 1327 *SR*
Bourton super aquam 1575 *FF, -upon the water* 1605 *FF*

'Farmstead near the fortification', burh-tun. The 'fortification' is doubtless the encampment named Salmonsbury. The place called 'on the Water' (Latin *super aquam*) from the river Windrush which flows through the village, to distinguish it from Bourton on the Hill.

Burh 'fortified place or Stronghold'

ton or tun – the most common habitative element of Old English – originally meant enclosure, farmstead. Later it came to mean village or hamlet as well and in names formed after the Norman Conquest it could mean manor or estate, so it's meaning depends largely on its age.

Bereton essentially means barley farm or outlying part of an estate.

[from 'A Dictionary of English Place Names', by A.D.Mills, OUP 1991]

Bourton Bridge
Formerly *on Buruhford* 716-43 (11th) BCS 165, **'ford near the fortification'**, *v.* burh ford, and later *Burghtons Bridge, Fossebridge* c.1603, a bridge carrying the Fosse Way over the Windrush.

Salmonsbury
Sulmonnesburg 779 (Orig.) 230, *Salomonesbir'* 1276 RH, *Salemanburi* 1287 QW, *Salemonesbyri* 1293 Ipm, *Salmonysbury, -manis-* 1435 *MinAcct*. The name refers to a large four-sided 56 acre bivalate encampment, of which the north-east angle is best discernible (cf. Rudder 303) and which lies north-east of Bourton village. From this Salmonsbury Hundred took its name. The Old English from *Sulmonnes-* suggested to Ekwall and Anderson that the first element is an Old English *sulh-man* **'ploughman'** as the spelling is from a good original charter, and the place name would denote **'the encampment of a ploughman'**, that is, no doubt, 'one where he kept his oxen'; this interpretation would be paralleled by some examples of Old English *'stod-fald'* 'stud enclosure' as applied to prehistoric enclosures used by the English for their stud-horses; *v.* burh, which is also the first element of Bourton. The complete change of *Sul-* to *Sal(e)-, Salo-* from Domesday Book onwards is probably due to popular etymology when the rare Old English *sulh-man* was obviously confused with the Hebrew personal name *Salomon,* which seems to be found in Old German *Sul(u)man.* The lost *Salmondesleg* in the nearby Upper Slaughter may have a similar origin to the first element.

Naunton
Niwetone, -tune 1086 Domesday Book, 1185 Templar
Newynton, -in- J Monast, 13 Misc, 1287, 1375 Ipm, 1480 Pat, (-*super Codeswold*) J Monast, (-*on le Wolde*) 1378 AD iii, (-*de la Wolde*) 1379 FF, 1380 Ipm

Newenton(e) 1235 Fees, 1249 *Ass,* 1284 *Episc (p),* 1287 QW et freq to 1501 Ipm, (-*in Cotswold*) 1289 Episc, (-*super Coddeswolde*) 1303 Pat, (-*als. Nawnton super Cotteswold*) 1570 *FF*

Neweton 1303 FA, *Neuton on Coteswolde* 1304 Pat, *Newton als.*

Naunton 1591 *FF Niwenton super Coteswalde* 1307 Pat, *Niwenton* 1328 Misc

Newnton Hy 6 *AddCh*

Nawinton, -en- 1484 Rogers, 1545 LP, (-*upon Cotteswold*) 1544 ib, (-*upon Cottiswolde*) 1597 FF, (-*als. Nawneton on Cotteswoulde*)1625 Inq

Naun-, Nawnton 1476 IpmR, 1535 VE *et freq* to 1683 PR 4, (-*super Cott(e)swo(u)lde*) 1566, 1642 Inq

'**(At) the new farmstead'**, *v.* niwe tun. On the dialectal change of Middle English –*ewen*- to –*aun*-, which occurs in other Nauntons, Frampton, Brawne etc. For the affixes *v.* wald and Cotswold.

Windrush (affluent of the Thames)

fluvii....Uuenrisc, uuaenrisc 779, *on Wenrisc* 969 (*Wenrise, Wearisc, Wearise, Yearnisc*) *on Wenris* 949. *on Waenric* 949, *Wenricces* 969, *on, of, innon Wenric* 1016

Wen(e)rich(e), rych' 1247 Ass

Wynrysshe 1500-15 ECP, *Winruche, Wynderusch* c.1540

Windrush 1577

The village of Windrush is named from it. Eckwall has taken the name to be a compound of the older form of Welsh *gwyn* 'white' as in Welsh *Gwendraeth* **'white strand'** with a Celtic root *reisko*- which survived in Irish and Gaelic *riasg* 'moor, fen' and the early Welsh stream-name *nant ruisc*. The upper part of the river was called *Gytingbroc* 780.

People's names

Our 'modern' patronymic names, together with their meanings (if listed) are included for everyone who participated in 'Naunton 2000.' The reader will have to decide which ones, if any, reach back towards the earlier part of our 2000 year story. Whatever you know or don't know about your own name, there is little doubt that, change of spellings apart, surnames form one of the most convincing threads of continuity readily available to us today, tantalisingly linking us with our oldest paternal ancestry.

From very early times some people were linked with and then known by certain '*topographic*' features upon the landscape where they lived or worked. Examples abound and include many existing surnames, such as **Field, Paddock, Orchard**, **Hay**, **Lane**, **Fallow, Wood, Forrest**, **Hill**, **Barrow, Dale**, **Vale**, **Ridge**, **Pike**, **Pine**, **Peak**, **Fieldgate** and **Priestland**.[i]

In a similar way, as more settlements and manmade features appeared across the land, people began to be linked with them, before they and their family came to be identified by the name of that location. We refer to these as '*habitation*' names, and they seem to arise out of most places in Britain, from **Aylworth** to **Ambridge**; **Harford** to **Hannington**; **Naunton** to **Nancarrow,** and thousands of others.

In addition to '*topographic*' and '*habitation*' names, certain people within individual communities came to be known by what they did and many of these old '*occupational*' names live on with us today, even though the current name bearer is unlikely to be engaged in that particular occupation today. They include names like **Farmer**, **Wright, Ploughwright, Wheelwright, Shepherd**, **Horsman, Carter, Smith, Farrier, Straw, Weaver, Fuller, Tanner, Coulter, Carpenter, Joiner, Mason, Wheeler, Buckle, Butcher, Baker, Dyer, Skinner, Slatter, Kitchen, Hyde, Honey, Bacon** and of course **Salt,** to name just a few.

Most '*habitation*' name holders have also long since become detached from the places where the name originated. Some people with the surname of **Naunton** still live in Britain and Canada[ii]. Others like **Harford**[iii] survive around Britain whilst the **Aylworths**[iv] are all long gone from Britain, their descendants now live in Canada and the USA, leaving Naunton after the English Civil War. Emigration from Britain to the New World saw many *habitation* names going abroad, resulting in place names that are familiar to us on maps of other countries, especially the United States, Canada and Australia. Thank goodness for the continuity of the ancient patronymic naming system, because I for one would not wish to be named after some of our modern occupations or newer towns.

Forenames or Christian names are another story. Such 'given' names were once handed down from one generation to the next, more so in the past than today. They also tend to be influenced by what was fashionable at the time, particularly by religion or the monarchy. Many lovely old Naunton names such as **Cuthbert, Septimus, Jesse, Nelson, Eli, Lambert, Ezekiah, Reuben, Algernon, Moses Ada, Mona, Silas, Bessie** and **Blanch** have now slipped into the past, being considered unfashionable, whilst other equally old Naunton names have endured or been revived, such as **John, William, Henry, David, Thomas, Ellen, Debora, Elizabeth,** and **Jane.**

---

[i] Someone who farmed land held by the church. Old English *preost* Priest + *land* land.

[ii] Several people adopted the name in various forms such as John de Newnton (1288), Henry de Newynton (1301), Hugh de Newenton (1341). Sir Robert Naunton (1589-1635) was Secretary of State to James I. from 1618 to 1623, but had no son. One Sir Augustus Meredith Nanton KB was living in Winnipeg, Canada in the 20th century and his lady visited Naunton in the 1920s and was mentioned in E.F. Eeles book as a result. Lord Ralph Gray of Naunton (1910 - 2001) is one of the more recent people of note to be connected with the parish.

[iii] English: habitation name from places in Gloucs. and Devon. The former gets its name from Old English *heorot* HART + FORD, the latter has as its first element Old English *here* army.

[iv] See http://www.aylesworth.net/aylesmanor

Appendix 2

Domesday Book
(Verbatim text from 'Naunton Upon Cotswold' by E.F. Eeles, 1928)

Domesday Book is that great survey of English Lands and properties, which was made for taxation purposes by William the Conqueror, and deals with things as they were in the reign of Edward the Confessor (1042-1066) and of William (1066-1087). Its record concerning Naunton is clear and minute. Here, therefore we pass out of the twilight of uncertain imaginations into the clear light of facts. And as we study these facts we shall be amazed to find how little has changed here in the thousand years that are past.

It is the small things and not the great ones that have proved variable. And still we have the things that matter most – the men and the women, the river and the mill, the great plough lands of the four manors and the church. Take away the stone walls and the great county road and the parish will have very much the same appearance and perhaps the same fertility as it had in the Confessor's reign.
But Domesday Book is eloquent and this is what it tells us: (I quote from Taylor's Analysis of the Gloucestershire Domesday):

Name of the Parish	NIWETONE
Area	3106 Acres
Land cultivated	3060 Acres
No meadows and no woods	
Number of men with rights greater or less over the land (*villani* etc)	23
Number of men with no rights (*Servi*)	16
Number of working women (*Ancillae*)	9
Number of Plough Teams (8 oxen to the plough)	$25\frac{1}{2}$
Number of Corn Mills	2
Rateable value of the Parish	£12 15s 0d.

THE MANORS

NIWETONE(1)	(TURSTAN'S)
Rateable Value	£3
Area Cultivated	780 acres
Last Saxon Lord	TURSTAN
First Norman Lord	OSBERN FITZ RICARDI
Tenant (or Mesne Lord)	ROGER de OLGI
Plough Teams	
Of the (Mesne) Lord	2
Of the Tenant (Farmers)	$4\frac{1}{2}$

This is the upper village manor and contains the dovecote and the Church. Later it was for generations known as Baldwin's Fee and it retained the name of the Capital Manor after the next (Eilmer's) manor was separated from it in Saxon times.

NIWETONE (2) (EILMER'S)
Rateable Value | £5
Area Cultivated | 1200 acres
Last Saxon Lord | EILMER
First Norman Lord | The King
Tenant (? Mesne Lord) | QUINILD MONIALIS
Plough Teams
Of the Lord | 4
Of the Tenant (Farmers) | 6

Eilmer's is the lower village manor and contains the Naunton Mill of yearly value 5 shillings. (Author's note – this lower manor is believed to have been somewhere to the right of Sunny Cottages, or the rear of Kiftsgate House)

AILEWRDE
Rateable Value | 6 SHILLINGS
Area Cultivated | 120 acres
Last Saxon Lord | ALWIN
First Norman Lord | WILLIAM GOIZENBODED
Plough Team of the Lord | 1

This is the DEMESNE (Enclosed Land) round about the old manor house of Aylworth.

ELEURDE
Rateable Value | £2
Area Cultivated | 480 acres
Last Saxon Lord | ALWIN
First Norman Lord | GISLEBERT FITZ TUROLD
Tenant (or Mesne Lord) | WALTER
Plough Teams
Of the (Mesne) Lord | 2
Of the Tenant (Farmers) | 2

This is the manor farm or Common Field of Aylworth.

HURFORD
Rateable Value | £2
Area cultivated | 480 acres
Last Saxon Lord | ALSER
First Norman Lord | GISLEBERT FITZ TUROLD
Plough Teams
Of the Lord | 2
Of the Tenant (Farmers) | 2

This manor contained the Lower Harford mill of yearly value 5 shillings.

Certain things in the above extracts may be well noticed before we pass on, for they will help us to understand the condition of the parish not only in 1066 but for many years before that date and centuries after it. For instance the value of money at that time was so great that man or maid with 10/- or even 5/- a year *(50p or 25p in today's currency)* would be in the embarrassing position of being regarded as a matrimonial plum. Since that time money has been almost constantly diminishing in value.

Again, there were two mills here in 1066 and now there is only one – Naunton has gone back in this respect. All the milling was then done inside the parish whereas now it is almost all done outside and the money for it all goes outside, and we get less wholesome bread for it.

Again, it is amazing to find that in 1066 all the parish, except 46 acres was cultivated. This however is not really quite so amazing as it looks for the land lay mostly in the great Common Fields, and each Field was divided in such a way that the plough would not pass over more than half the ground in any given year, the rest being left fallow for rough pasture. The 46 acres of uncultivated land would represent the building sites and orchard gardens with perhaps some bog land by the brook side and some broken stone quarries chiefly in the Harford manor and on the border between Eilmer's manor and Eyford. Assuredly the great plough lands were then, as they still are, the chief feature of the parish – the source of its wealth, or shall we say, at least its salvation from bankruptcy.

In the case of each manor it should be noted that the number of ploughs belonging to the Lord is a fair indication of the acreage of the Demesne. Viz:-

Alwin: 120 acres.   Turstan: 240 acres.   Eilmer: 480 acres.   Alser: 240 acres

In each case the demesne would lie around the manor House, probably enclosed. In the case of Harford manor, its division (? from the old) into three separable farms may indicate that Lower Harford is the old demesne around the principal Mansion and that Upper Harford and Harford Hill are the two moieties of the ancient Common Field which were ploughed (or left fallow) in alternate years.

The parish boundaries remain unchanged these 1000 years in relation to the three original manors, but before 1087 Aylworth had been split into the demesne of 120 acres and the farm field of 480 acres. We cannot perhaps hope to fix the exact boundary of the demesne park. It must however have been round about the ancient manor house and such a plot of land as Lady's Hayes must surely have been inside the fence, and such a great field as Rosemore must have been in the farm. Before 1066 also the great manor of NIWETONE had been divided into TURSTON'S MANOR, 780 acres and EILMER'S MANOR, 1200 acres. The boundary between the two can only be guessed at, but we can guess it with probability which approaches certitude. The Capital Manor originally contained all the parish except Harford and Aylworth, viz., nearly 2000 acres. Turstan's portion of 780 acres contained the dovecote and the mill. And, if tradition is right in locating the site of EILMER'S house in the first block of cottages west of Cromwell House, then the dividing line must have been in the vicinity of the bridge opposite North Street westward of the present Black Horse Inn, and this is the likelier because the bridge is just above the millpool. Now from that point there is an ancient pathway (? Caswell's Path) running south west to Notgrove. We will assume that this was the line we seek from the brook to be the border with Aylworth manor. But both manor houses were on the north side of the brook, therefore both estates must have extended northwards across the water. It is at least probable that there was a continuation of the ancient (?Caswell's) path running northwards from the brook side in the fold of the ground towards summerhill where North Street now runs. For such a path would be needed in order to get to the ancient Saxon road from Lower Guiting to Bourton-on-the-Water and Slaughter (anciently called by the Naunton people Winchcombe Way, and by the Guiting folk, Slaughter Way). Indeed the North Street path may have been pre-Saxon for it leads up close to that field called '14 acres' where there are some indications of man's habitation of very great antiquity. We will assume once again that the boundary we are seeking ran up by North Street and doubled back by the Winchcombe Way to the parish border at Grange Hill Farm. This will give to Turstan's manor all the land from the top of Naunton down to Grange Hill and it is as near as possible to 780 acres. And it will give Eilmer's Manor all the land from the Temple Guiting border on the north to Roundhill farm (inclusive of the latter) on the south side and it is as near as possible 1200 acres. Judging by results it would seem no great folly for a sporting man to lay his shilling on the probable accuracy of this estimate of the boundary line required. The path itself, which we have ventured doubtfully to call 'Caswell's Path' was diverted a little eastwards between the brook and the blue stone road, no doubt for convenience when the great County Road was made in or near the year 1800. There was of course a ford over the stream, with stepping stones, above the mill pool before John Hurd, the old rector, built the present flat bridge in 1853.

Author's note:
It is worth comparing Naunton with Bourton here because in 1086 Bourton is listed as having, '10 Hides; In Lordship 6 Ploughs; 16 villagers, 8 smallholders and two free men with 7 ploughs. There is a Priest with half a plough. In total, value £8. Wulfric held 2 hides of this land as a manor, Tovi 5 virgates as a manor and Leofwin 1 virgate as a manor'. No mills are listed in Bourton and Naunton appears to be the larger of the two settlements, with two mills. In relation to acreage it also appears by then to have had more land under the plough ($25\frac{1}{2}$ plough teams compared with Bourton's $13\frac{1}{2}$ teams).

Appendix 3

The Ancient and Present State of Glostershire by Sir Robert Atkyns, 1712.

<u>Naunton</u>

This Parish lyes in the Hundred of *Slaughter*, 4 Miles distant South West from *Stow*, 4 Miles South East from *Winchcomb*, and 14 Miles North East from *Gloster*.

'The Church of St. *Mary de Winchcomb* held *Niwetone* in the Reigns of King *Edward* the Confessor, and King *William* the Conqueror: It was taxed at 3 Hides and a half ; there were 3 Plow-Tillages in Demean, and 2 Villains held another Plow-Tillage, and 6 more Plow-Tillages might be laid out. The Mannor yielded 40s yearly in both Reigns. *Domesday Book.*

This MANNOR continued in the Abbey of *Winchcomb* until its final Dissolution. It was then granted to *Thomas Culpeper* 33H.8. Livery of this Manor was granted to *Alexander Culpeper* 1 Eliz. It soon changed Owners; for *Giles Venfield* and *John Collet* were joint Lords of this Mannor in the Year 1608. It has since been divided amongst divers Freeholders.

John Lord *Clinton* of *Clinton* and *Say, John Smith* and *William Warburton,* levied a Fine of Lands in *Naunton* to *John Twineho* and *John Underhill* 1 R.3. A Lease of Lands in *Naunton*, lately belonging to *Winchcomb* Abbey, was granted to *Henry Tracy* 36H.8.

The Capital Messuage of *Naunton* was granted to *John Dalle,* who dyed 1E.6. and Livery thereof was granted the same year to *Thomas Dalle* Son of *John.* Another Grant was made to *Henry Tracy* and *Elizabeth* his *Wife* 7 E.6. *Robert Ashton* Levied a Fine of the Mannor of *Naunton* to *Henry Moody* 2 Mar.

The CHURCH is in the *Deanry* of *Stow:* It is a Rectory worth 120*l.* yearly; the Bishop of *Worster* is *Patron,* Mr. *Owen* is the present *Incumbent,* who hath a new built Parsonage House.

Clerks.	Patrons.
1570 *Ulpian Fulwell,*	Queen *Elizabeth*
Jos. Hunxman	
1660 *Clem. Barksdale,*	King *Charles* II
1687 *Henry Owen*	Bish, of *Worster,*

Clement Barksdale was born at *Winchcomb* in this County: He was of Loyal Principles, and presented to this Rectory by King *Charles* the Second, soon after the Restoration. He published many Treatises of various Subjects, and dyed at his Parsonage 1687.

Two Yard Lands belong to the Glebe: No Lands are exempted from Payment of Tithes. The Tithes in *Naunton* did formerly belong to the Abbey of *Winchcomb,* and were granted to Sir *Thomas Seymour* 1 E.6.

	l.	s.	d.
First Fruits	16	13	04½
Tenths	01	13	04½
Procurat	00	06	08
Synodals	00	02	00
Pentecost	00	00	11½

The Church is handsome, with a beautiful Tower adorned with Battlements and Pinnacles, and hath an Isle on the North Side belonging to the Family of the *Aleworths;* it is dedicated to St. *Andrew.*

The Images of the Apostles have been painted in full length in the Church Windows, and some do yet remain intire. In the North Windows are the Images of St. *Stephen* and St. *Catherine,* and in one Window is the Image of *John Bayle* in the Posture of Prayer, and in several Places is painted, to pray for the soul of *Ayleworth,* and for the soul of *John Bayle.*

There is an Inscription in the Chancel for *Joseph Hunxman* Rector of this Church. One Acre of meadow in upper *Slaughter,* and 4 Acres in the Common Fields, belong to the Repair of the Church.

The PARISH is 8 Miles in *compass;* It consists most of Arable. A Brook with very large Trouts, runs thro' this Parish into *Windrush* River.

There are several HAMLETS or smaller Divisions of this Parish. 1 *Ayleworth,* a Mile from the Church, where is the seat of the Family of that Name, who have a good Estate in the Place, and are of a very ancient Descent; they have continued here ever since the *Norman* Conquest.

"*Alwin* held *Ailewurde,* in the Reign of King Edward the Confessor, *William Gozenboded* held it in the Reign of King *William* the Conqueror. It was taxed at one Hide; there was 1 Plow's Tillage in Demean. It formerly paid a yearly Rent of *6s.* it paid *3s.* yearly in King *William's* Reign." *(Domesday Book).*

Petronella de la Mere dyed seized of *Elworth 47 H.3. Gilbert de Clare,* Earl of *Gloster* and *Hartford,* was seized of this Mannor, and of *Harford* in this Parish, in the Reign of King *Edward* the First, and his Claim to a *Court-Leet,* and other Privileges, was allowed in a *Quo Warranto* brought against him *15 E.1.*

This Mannor, at the dissolution of religious Foundations, did belong to the Priory of St. *Oswalds* in *Gloster,* and was granted to *Richard Andrews* and *Nicholas Temple,* in trust, *35 H.8.* A Farm in *Ayleworth* did belong to the Priory of *Lanthony,* and was granted to *Vincent Calmudee* and *Richard Calmudee 6 Eliz.*

Richard Aylworth had *Livery* of the Mannor and capital Messuage of *Ayleworth,* with Lands lately belonging to the Priory of St. *Oswalds,* and also of a Farm called *de Lantone 9 Eliz.* Other Lands in *Ayleworth,* and a Grove, did belong to the Chantry of St. *Mary* in *Westbury,* and were granted to *Anthony Cope 10 Jac. John Ayleworth* was seized of Lands in *Naunton, Calcut* and *Ayleworth 16 E.4.*

2. *Bail-Farm,* another *Hamlet,* which did heretofore belong to a family of the same Name, as appears by the Glass Windows in the Church.

3. Upper-Harford; *William de Clinton* Earl of *Huntington* was seized of the Mannor of *Harford 28 E.3. Richard,* Son of *John Browning,* was seized thereof *2 H.4.* The Prior of *Lanthony* was seized of Lands in *Harford* and *Ayleworth 15 H.4.*

4. Lower Harford, which has but one House. The Estate belongs to *Corpus Christi* College in *Oxford;* it is in Lease to Mr. *Oldish,* and is charged with *8s.* yearly towards the Repair of the Church. Mr. *Oldish* has a handsome Seat in this Place.

There are 34 *Houses* in this Parish and about 140 *inhabitants,* whereof 16 are *Freeholders.*

				l.	s.	d.
Yearly { births~5 deaths~4	Payments	{ 1692 To the Royal Aid		079	11	04
		1694 To the Land Tax		063	19	00
		1694 To the Poll-Tax		022	13	00

Appendix 4

Following on from Sir Robert Atkyns great tome:

'The Ancient And Present State Of Glostershire', published in 1710 came:
'A New History Of Gloucestershire' by Samuel Rudder, published in 1779.

Rudder's work, incorporating much of Atkyns', contains the following entry:-

Naunton lies in the hundred of Slaughter, and partly in that of Bradley. It is situated six miles south-westward of Stow, seven south-east from Winchcombe, and nineteen east from Gloucester, and the turnpike-road from Stow to Gloucester runs through the parish near four miles in length. The greater part of the parish is arable land. It has a little brook running thro' it from Guiting, which empties itself into the Windrush and serves as a nursery to supply that river with trout, for which it is so deservedly famous.

The present name of the village is so corrupted and altered from its original purity, by vulgar use, as not to bear the least resemblance to the antient[sic] and significant appellation. It was written *Niwetone* in *Domesday-book,* and was so called' because something later cultivated or inhabited than the other village in the neighbourhood, in comparison with which it was *New town.* It was afterwards written *Niuenton, Newinton,* and sometimes *Newinton in Cottswold,*[sic] probably to distinguish it from *Newinton* (now called *Naunton,* a hamlet) in the parish of Winchcombe, and *Newinton* or *Newton* in Ashchurch.

The parish is of middling size, situated in a fine open country, but has neither curious fossils, rare plants, nor other uncommon natural productions to distinguish it; and the only custom proper to the place seems to be, that of breaking a common called *Naunton-downs,* on the fourteenth day of May, for depasturing milch-cows, young heifers, and cow-calves only. Antiquities are matters of accident and curiosity, and tho' Naunton has none of them to boast of, yet in enjoys one blessing in a very eminent degree, which may well compensate for all its deficiencies. Whether from its open situation among the downs, free from woods, and far distant from marshy lands and large waters; or occasioned by what other cause I know not, but certain it is, that it enjoys a fine healthy air, scarcely to be equalled, not to be exceeded, by any spot in the kingdom.

Dr. Percival, in his curious inquiries concerning population, and the healthiness of many places in and about Lancashire, finds, that at a village called Estham, one in thirty-five inhabitants dies in a year; at Cokey, one forty-four; at Royston, one in fifty-two; at Edale, one in fifty-nine; and at Hale, which is the healthiest place of all the examples he produces, one dies annually out of sixty-nine: And the result of my own inquiries through this county is nearly the same. But how much more healthy than any of those is the parish of Naunton, where from the most authentic particulars given at the close of this account, it appears, that not one in a hundred dies in a year! The inhabitants are farmers and husbandmen, living remote from any market-town, and there is not a public house in the village.

Of the Manor and other Estates.

There were antiently three manors in this parish, reckoning Ayleworth for one.

'Roger de Olgi holds Niwetone in Salemananesberie hundred of Osbern the son of Richard. There are five hides taxed. Turstan held it. In demean are two plow-tillages, and eight villains, with four plow-tillages and a half. It is worth 3*l*' *(Domesday-book,* p.76)

'Cuenild the monk holds nine hides in Niwetone in Salemanesberie hundred of the king, four of which pay tax. Eslmer held them for a manor. In demean are four plow-tillages and seven villains, with five plow-tillages: And he has now one plow-tillage, and a mill of 5s. and thirteen among the *Servi* and *Ancillae*. It was worth 8*l*. now 5*l*.' *Domesday-book,* p.79.

In tracing the descent of the manor, Sir Robert Atkyns has fallen into the grossest of errors, by mingling and confounding the records, and appropriating to this parish the particulars which relate to Naunton in Winchcombe. He applies the same abstract from *Domesday-book* to both places, which serves to shew[sic] that this manor, or one of these manors, was held by the abbey of Winchcombe; and then asserts, that *this manor continued in the abbey of Winchcombe until its final dissolution; that a lease of lands in Naunton, lately belonging to Winchcombe abbey, was granted to Henry Tracy 36 H. 8. That another grant was made to Henry Tracy and Elizabeth his wife 7 E. 6.* and lastly, that *the tithes in Naunton did formerly belong to the abbey of Winchcombe, and were granted to Sir Thomas Seymour* 1 E. 6. Whereas it does not appear that the abbey of Winchcombe ever had any property in this parish, nor had the Tracies any 'till by purchase within a few years past. In short, the above particulars should have been applied to the hamlet of Naunton in Winchcombe.

King Edward the First commanded his sheriff of Gloucestershire to make a return of all the vills, &c. in the said county, with the several proprietors of them; and the sheriff returned, that the prior of St. Oswald in Gloucester, and the prior of the lesser Malvern were lords of Newenton in the hundred of Salmonesburye, 9 E. 1.

Giles Venfield and John Collett were joint lords of the manor in the year 1608, since which it has been divided between several freeholders. The late William Moore, esq; by his marriage with the heiress of Mr. Collett, claimed this manor; Powell Snell, esq; also claims it, who now pays a fee-farm rent for the crown; and Thomas Stone has some pretentions[sic] to it; but no court has been held within memory.

John lord Clinton, John Smith, and William Warburton, levied a fine of lands in Naunton to John Twineho and John Underhill I R. 3. The capital messuage of Naunton was granted to John Baile who died 1 E. 6. and Thomas Baile, son of John, had livery thereof the same year. Robert Ashton levied a fine of the manor of Naunton to Henry Moody 2 Mar.

HAMLETS. 1. *Ayleworth,* situated about a mile from the church. It lies in the hundred of Bradley, and gave name to a family who resided here from the time of the conquest 'till the beginning of the present century. In *Domesday-book* it is thus recorded:

'William Goizenboded holds Ailewrde in Salemanesberie hundred. Aluuin held it in the time of King Edward. There is one hide taxed, and one plow-tillage in demean, and two *servi*. It was worth 6s. now 3s.' p.74.

'Gislebert the son of Turold holds Elewrde in Salemanesberie hundred, and Walter holds it of him. Aluuin held it. There are four hides taxed, and two plow-tillages in demean, and three villains with two plow-tillages, and six between the *servi* and *ancillae*. It is and was worth 40s.' p.76.

The subsequent records shew, that Petronella de la Mere died seized of Elworth 47E.3. Gilbert de Clare, earl of Gloucester, proved his right to court leet and other privileges in this manor, and in Harford, in a *Quo warranto* brought against him 15E. 1. At the dissolution of religious houses, this manor belonged to the priory of St. Oswald in Gloucester, and was granted to Richard Andrews and Nicholas Temple, in trust, 35 H.8. But there was a farm in Ayleworth which belonged to the priory of Lanthony, and was granted to Vincent Calmudee and Richard Calmedee, 6 Eliz. Other lands in Ayleworth, and a grove, belonged formerly to the chantry of St. Mary in Westbury, and were granted to Anthony Cope 10 Jac.

Richard Ayleworth had livery of the manor and capital messuage of Ayleworth, with lands lately belonging to St. Oswald's priory; and of a farm called De Lantone, 9 Eliz. But John Ayleworth was seized of lands in Naunton, Calcut, and Ayleworth as early as 16 E. 4. Joshua Ayleworth, the last of this family, died in 1718, as did his widow the following year, aged ninety, as appears in the parish register, and both were buried in the church, without any memorial. Joshua Ayleworth, of Ayleworth esq; gave the interest of 100*l.* to be distributed yearly in bread to the poor of Stow. The manor and estate of Ayleworth were purchased by – Herring, esq; but Henry Blagg, of the county of Nottingham, is the present lord of the manor.

2. *Harford.*

'Gislebert the son of Turold holds Hurford in Salemanesberie hundred. Alfer held it. There is one hide taxed, and two plow-tillages in demean, and four villains, and one border, with two plow-tillages, and two *servi,* and a mill of 5s. It is worth and was worth 40s.' *Domesday-book,* p.76.

William de Clinton, earl of Huntingdon, was seized of the manor of Harford 28 E. 3. as was Richard the son of John Browning 2 H. 4. and the priory of Lanthony had lands in Harford and Ayleworth 13 H. 4. William Moore, esq; died seized of Harford, in right of his wife, about the year 1771.

Lower Harford is an estate belonging to Corpus Christi College in Oxford, now in the lease to Mrs Tracy, relict of Thomas Tracy, esq; deceased, and heiress of the late William Dodwell.

Bayle-farm is unworthily distinguished by Sir Robert Atkyns as a hamlet. It was so called from a family of that name, to whom it belonged, and from whom it went afterwards to the Ayleworths, and is now called *Round-hill farm.*

Of the Church, &c.

The church is a rectory, in the deanery of Stow, worth about 250*l.* a year. The bishop of Worcester is patron; Mr Anselm Jones the present incumbent. The whole parish is subject to tithes and two yard-lands belong to the glebe.

The church is dedicated to St. Andrew. It is a handsome building, with neat tower adorned with pinnacles and battlements. It has a small aile[sic] on the north side, which belonged to the Ayleworths, several of whom are buried there, but without any memorials. The whole church was formerly ornamented with painted glass, but time and mischievous hands have in great measure destroy'd it. In the south window, near the pulpit, is a large figure of a saint, [*Scs Philippus*] and in a scroll round his head.

Inde venturus ut iudicaret vivos & mortuos;

At his feet a man and woman praying, and under,

Orate p'bono statu.....bayle..........

On the next pane, round a saint's head, is written,

Credo in spiritu sanctu sanctam ecclesia cotholica;

At his feet a man and woman praying, and under,

Orate p' bono..........ayleworth et elsabeth.......

Then at the bottom of the next pane, where are several figures in a praying posture, it follows, *eius et oniu fidelu defunctor'*

In the south window of the chancel is the figure of Christ, round whose head is written,

Ascedit ad cellos fedit ad dexteram dei patris oipotentis;

And near it, St. John Baptist, with this mutilated legend in a scroll round his head,

........est de spiritu sancto in ereman.

In the north window are the figures of St. Catherine, with her wheel, and St. Stephen, in very good preservation.

First fruits £.16 13 4½ Synodals £.0 2 0 Tenths - 1 13 4½ Pentecostals 0 0 11½ Procurations 0 6 8

Monuments and Inscriptions.

On a small brass plate, against the north wall of the chancel,

Clemens Barksdalius atrium magister evangelii minister quotidieorans, quotidie moriens, iubet te viator coelestem cogitare patriam Ixb XXIII. MDCLXX AETAT LXI

On another plate against the same wall,

In memoriam Caroli Barksdale Cl. F hic depositi Jan I. 82. aet. 30. Clementis propeinhumati Jun. I. 68. aet. 24. Mariae virginis annorum 33 Deo redditae Lond. Ad S. Brig. 77. GulielmiOxon fepulti. Hos Liberos fuos (Ioanne et Charletona relictis)ex Maria Charletona conjuga pia (pridem defuncta et Winch. Juxta matrem condita) praemifit Cl.P moestus Ipfe fenex annorum 75 Christum expectat. Fiat voluntas Dei P.P. An. Dom. 1685.

Yong man lay to thy heart this sacred Truth
Remember thy Creator in thy Youth
Old man if pious do not thy death fear
Having Good hopes of better things so near.

On another brass plate, against the same wall,

Epitaphium in Iosephum Hanxman Hvivs Ecclesiae qui migravit ex hac vita primo die Augusti 1632.

Hic iacet in tumulo veri pastoris imago
Os verbum vitae mos verbi denoq; vita.
Perpende Lector.
Heere lies the paterne of a trew Diuine
His word and life were one would foe were thine.

On a marble table, within the communion rails,

Near this Place lieth the Body of Ambrose Oldys, Son of William Oldys, D.D. formerly V. of Adderbury in the County of Oxford, who for his Loyalty to his King, the Zeal for the established Church (tho' a Clergyman) was barbarously murthered[sic] by the rebels in the year 1645; whose unshaken loyalty to the Crown and constant Adherance to the established Religion was nevertheless perfectly imitated by his Son: But with better Fortune, for after he had escaped many and eminent Dangers, as well by Sea, as in Battles for the Honour and Service of the King and Country, (to which he frequently with undaunted Courage exposed himself) he ended his Days in Peace and Quiet, at his house called Harford in this parish, which at his Death he left to his Sister Cecilia Goad, who out of Gratitude to the Memory of so good a Man, and so kind a Brother, caused this Monumant to be erected.

Obijt 2do Die Maij Anno{Dom: 1710{AEtatis fuae 77

At top, *Azure, a chevron argent between three garbs Or.*

Benefactions.

An acre of hay-ground and an acre of tillage-land in the east upper-end field, and one acre of tillage in the west common field, in the lower end of this parish; and one acre of meadow-ground in the Brook-furlong, in the parish of Upper Slaughter; together with the yearly rent of 8s. charged on an estate at Harford in this Parish, are given for the repair of the church. And Thomas Freeman , of this parish, yeoman, in the year 1746, gave 30s. yearly to teach poor children to read.

Taxes   {The Royal Aid in 1692, £79 11s 4d
        {Poll-tax   —   in 1694, £22 13s 0d
        { Land Tax —   in 1694, £63 19s 0d
        { The same, at 3s. 1770, £47 16s 1½d

At the beginning of this century, there were 34 houses, and about 140 inhabitants in this parish, whereof 16 were freeholders; yearly births 5, burials 4. *Atkyns*. The old parish register being lost, I could not collect the numbers of baptisms and burials for ten years beginning with 1700, in my usual manner, but in ten years, commencing with 1760, the baptisms were 51, the burials 22; and in the year 1767, there were 52 houses, and 257 inhabitants, who were increased to 288 in the year 1776.

Appendix 5

The Dissenters' Document 1779

To the Right Reverend Father in God, William by Divine permission Lord Bishop of the Diocese of Gloucester.

We whose names are hereunto subscribed being His Majesty's Protestant Dissenting Subjects do hereby certify unto your Lordship that we intend to meet for the worship of Almighty God in the Dwelling House of Robert Rowland, Taylor, situate in the parish of Naunton in the County and Diocese of Gloucester and therefore pray that this Certificate may be registered in your Lordship's Registry according to an Act of Parliament made and passed in the first year of the Reign of their late Majesties King William and Queen Mary. As witness our hands this 2d day of January in the Year of our Lord 1779.

William Rowland
John Steel his mark X
Rich.d Reynolds
John Clarke
John Preston
Joseph Hitchman
Robert Hands
George Wood
Samuel Emery
W.m Fox

This Certificate was duly Registered in the Consistory Court of the Diocese of Gloucester this Ninth day of January 1779
by me Tho.s Rudge Dep.y Reg.r

This precious document has survived and is included here to represent the countless other priceless bits of Naunton History that may once have been created on bark, parchment, paper and other similar writing surfaces, before being lost or destroyed throughout some twenty centuries.

To the Right Reverend Father in God, William by Divine permiifsion Lord Bishop of the Bishops of Gloucester.

We Whose names are hereunto subscribed being his majesty's protestant Difsenting Subjects do hereby certify unto your Lordship that we intended to meet for the workship of almighty God in the Dwelling House of Robert Rowland Taylor situate in the parish of Naunton in the County and your Lordships Diocese of Gloucester and therefore pray that this certificate may be registered in your Lordships Registry according to an Act of Parliament made and pafsed in the first year of the Reign of their Late Majesties King William and Queen Mary. As Witness our hands this 2nd day of January in the year of our Lord 1779.

William Rowland
John Steel his mark . X
Rick Reynolds
John Hanks
John Preston
Joseph Hitchman
Robert Hanks
George Wood
James G perry
Wm Fox

This Certificate was duly registered in the Consistory Court of the Diocese of Gloucester this Ninth day of January 1779 by me Thos Rudge Deputy Registrar

Appendix 6

Trade Directories

Windows on the past

In the 1840s the larger centres of trade and commerce within the County such as Bristol, Cheltenham and Gloucester found themselves included in the newly emerging Trade Directories which listed a wealth of professionals and artisans throughout the county. By the 1850s these useful publications, the equivalent in the pre-telephone era of today's Yellow Pages, had expanded to include the other County towns, and a few years later the villages were included.

In the case of Naunton, a proportionately smaller range of occupations ranging from bakers to wheelwrights, together with a host of others, were all wrapped around the central core of Naunton's strong farming community.

At first glance, these short entries may be thought of as being unrepresentative of the village as a whole, consisting of some 400 people, but they were first and foremost *'trade'* directories. After further scrutiny, and a little reading between the lines, I believe their true historical value becomes apparent. They are another small insight into a thriving Naunton from Victorian times until the outbreak of WW2, including something of the class structure that pertained during that period. As you progress through them, in the village environment at least, you begin to see a steady progression of individuals engaged in the staple industry of farming, together with other mutually reliant trades and professions. You also see how various family businesses were handed down through generations, some of whom were here for centuries.

At the time the directories were printed, some of the occupations listed may have existed for less than a century, such as teaching or the Post Office, whilst others could have been around for one or two thousand years, such as the wheelwrights, blacksmiths & butchers; and as for farmers, well they were here since the land was cleared in Neolithic times.

In the relatively short period of time that has elapsed between the first directories being compiled and the second millennium, virtually all of these age-old occupations have disappeared from Naunton-in-the-Vale, with the exception of the ever-declining number of farmers, some quarrying and a mason.

A comparison between the old skills and the newer ones, as described by the residents in the Millennium part **'Naunton 2000',** again serves to indicate the enormous rate of change that has taken place during the last half of the 20th century. Whether you browse the directories for the purpose of family research or general interest matters not, but I believe that you are witnessing one of the greatest periods of change to have taken place here since the enclosure of the fields.

Initially, particularly in the towns, the 'Who's Who' type minority that ensured they were included in these County Directories were listed under the headings of ***'Nobility, Gentry & Clergy'.*** By 1856 this hierarchical type of presentation had given way to a slightly less divisive, more socio-economic style, after the town directories began listing all of the residents. This occurred some time around 1870, and they retained much the same layout over the next 70 years, until the outbreak of World War II when the directories reverted to the more limited style again, but without the villages.

Post 1870 listings were split between **'Private Residents'** and **'Commercial'**. Whilst some of us would now resent the unsubtle inferences or exclusionary nature of the original three headings, I don't believe many of us would object to such headings as **'Private'** and **'Commercial'** being used to describe us today.

Kelly's Directory 1856

NAUNTON or **NAUNTON-IN-THE-VALE** is a township, parish and long straggling village, pleasantly situated in a valley on the high road between Cheltenham and Stow-on-the-Wold, and is watered by the small river Windrush. The church is a neat stone building, covered with ivy, with well-proportioned tower containing 3 bells, in the early English and Norman styles.

The living is worth £500 yearly, with residence, in the gift of the Bishop of the diocese; the Rev. John Hurd, M.A. is the incumbent, and the Rev. Edmund H Haskins, M.A. is the curate. There is a newly-erected spacious and well-built Baptist chapel, also a village school for boys and girls. The acreage is 3210. The manorial rights are divided. Round Hill, Summer Hill, Harford and Aylworth are all farms. The population in 1851 was 568

Gentry:
Haskins Rev. Edmund H. M.A. [curate]
Hurd Rev. John, M.A. [rector]

Traders:
Buller Mary (Mrs) shopkeeper
Bullock John, farmer, Round Hill Farm
Burge Edward & James, saddlers
Charles Elizabeth (Mrs) farmer, Summer Hill Farm
Charles Sarah (Mrs) farmer, Harford farm
Comeley Robert, farmer, Naunton Downs farm
Cook Lawrence, farmer, Aylworth farm
Draper William, farmer
Fletcher George, carpenter
Fletcher Philip, carpenter
Gardiner George, wheelwright
Gillett John, farmer
Gorton William, baker
Hall Joseph, carpenter
Hanks William, farmer
Hyatt John, farmer
Jacques Stephen, carrier
Lodge Edmund, farmer
Mason Nathaniel, shoemaker & beer Retailer
Meadows Henry, blacksmith
Newman William, *'Naunton Inn'*
Phillips John, blacksmith
Restall Joseph, weaver & linen draper
Restall Michael, weaver & parish clerk
Smith Elizabeth, grocer
Thackwell Frederick, brick & tile maker
White Henry, grocer & draper

Wood Edward Thomas, miller & baker, Naunton Mill
Carrier- Stephen Jacques, to Cheltenham, Tuesday & Saturday, returning the same days.

Post Office Directory 1863

As above but with following additions:

Gentry:
Draper Miss
Heritage Rev. Alfred Wm [Baptist]

Traders:
Collett John, baker & miller, Naunton mill
Jacques Stephen, shopkeeper
Martin John, *'Naunton Inn'*
Smith William, farmer
Vann Joseph, academy, Waterloo house
National School- Miss Martha Elizabeth Turner, mistress

Morris & Co, Directory & Gazetteer 1866

NAUNTON or **NAUNTON-IN-THE-VALE**, is a long straggling village and parish in the Stow-on-the-Wold union, containing, by the census of 1861, 535 inhabitants, 3106 acres; in the deanery of Stow, archdeaconry of Gloucester, diocese of Gloucester and Bristol, lower division of Slaughter hundred, East Gloucestershire, near the small river Windrush; 5 miles west from Stow and 12 from Cheltenham. The rectory in the incumbency of the Rev. Edward Arthur Litton, M.A., is of the gross annual value of £630, with residence, in the patronage of the Bishop of Gloucester. The church, dedicated to Saint Andrew, is in the Norman and early English styles, and consists of nave, chancel and north aisle, with an embattled tower containing three bells. There is a British School for children of both sexes, and the Baptists have a place of worship here. A battle was fought in the neighbourhood between Prince Rupert and the Parliamentarians.

Clergy & Gentry:
Litton Rev. Edward Arthur M.A. Rectory.
Stevens, Rev. Mr. (Baptist)

Trades & Professions:
Buller Mrs. Mary, Shopkeeper
Bullock John, farmer & landowner, Round Hill Farm
Burge Mrs Ann, farmer
Burge James, saddler
Charles Mrs. Elizabeth, farmer, Summer-hill farm
Collett John, baker, miller & farmer, Naunton Mill.
Comeley Robert, farmer, Naunton Downs
Cook Lawrence, farmer, Aylworth farm
Fletcher George, carpenter
Fletcher Philip, carpenter

Gardiner George, wheelwright
Gillett John, farmer, maltster & landowner
Gorton William, baker
Hall Joseph, carpenter
Hanks John, butcher
Hanks William, farmer & landowner
Hyatt John, farmer
Hyatt William, farmer & landowner, Harford
Isherwood Richard, Inland Revenue Office *(N.B. possible erroneous entry)*
Jacques Stephen, Shopkeeper & carrier
Lodge Edmund, farmer
Martin John, Naunton Inn
Mason Nathaniel, shoemaker, Black Horse Inn
Mayne William E. road surveyor, Dale house
Meadows Henry, blacksmith
Phillips John, blacksmith
Pullam William & Edward, machine owners
Shillam Richard, grocer
Smith William, farmer
Vann Joseph, academy, Waterloo house
White Henry, grocer & draper

British School – Miss Martha Jane Reynolds

Post Office Directory 1870

NAUNTON or **NAUNTON-IN-THE-VALE** is a parish and straggling village, pleasantly situated in a valley, watered by the small river Windrush, and on the high road between Cheltenham and Stow-on-the-Wold, 3? miles north-east from Notgrove station on the Banbury and Cheltenham branch of the Great Western railway, 12 east from Cheltenham and 5 south-west from Stow-on-the-Wold, in the Eastern division of the county, lower division of Slaughter hundred, Stow-on-the-Wold union, petty sessional division and county court district, rural deanery of Stow, archdeaconry of Cirencester and diocese of Gloucester. The church of St. Andrew is a building of stone in the Early English and Perpendicular styles, consisting of chancel, nave and 2 bays, north aisle, south porch and an embattled western tower, with pinnacles, containing 3 bells: the church was repaired in 1878 at a cost of about £200 and completely restored in 1899 at a cost of £662, when it was entirely re-floored and re-seated, the walls underpinned and four new pinnacles placed on the tower: the church affords 200 sittings. The register dates from the year 1540. The living is a rectory, net yearly value £300, including 33 acres of allotment and 490 acres of glebe, with residence, in the gift of the Bishop of Gloucester, and held since 1897 by the Rev. Enoch Brooke Bradley.

There is a Baptist chapel, built in 1850 and seating 200 persons. There are two acres of land, the rent of which amounting to £1 10s, yearly, is applied to church purposes. The manorial rights are divided. The principal landowner is John Waddingham esq., of Guiting Grange. The soil is oolite and stone brash; subsoil light. The chief crops are wheat, turnips, oats and barley. The area is 3,173 acres of land and 4 of water; rateable value £2,277; the population in 1901 was 401. Parish Clerk, Charles Fletcher, Post & M.O.,S.B. & Annuity & Insurance Office - John William Hooper, sub-postmaster. Letters from

Cheltenham arrive at 8.25am; box cleared at 4.18pm. Lower Guiting is the nearest telegraph office, 1 mile distant. A School Board of 5 members was formed May 16 1873, James Hooper, clerk to the board, James Mills, Naunton, attendance officer. Board School (mixed), built with residence for master, in 1870, and enlarged in 1894, for 112 children; average attendance, 90; Frederick Nutt, master; Mrs Nutt, mistress.

Carriers to Cheltenham - William Pulham, jun. On thurs & sat. & Jesse Harris, on thurs; William Pulham, jun. To Bourton-on-the-Water & Slaughter, on Mon.

Private Residents:
Buller Mrs Mary
Gorton Mr William
Litton Rev. Edward Arthur, M.A. Rectory
Meadows Mr Henry
Stevens Rev. Mortimer (Baptist)
Walters Rev. Thomas, M.A.

Commercial:
Burge James, Saddler
Bullock John, Farmer & landowner
Round Hill Farm
Charles William, Farmer, Summerhill Farm
Collett John, Baker & Miller, Naunton Mill
Comely Robert, Farmer, Naunton Downs
Fletcher George, Carpenter
Fletcher Philip, Carpenter
Gardiner George, Wheelwright
Gillett William, Farmer
Godfrey William, Blacksmith
Hall Joseph, Carpenter
Hanks William, Farmer & landowner, Aylworth Farm
Harvey Ramond, Butcher
Martin John, *Naunton Inn*
Mason Nathaniel, *Black Horse Inn*
Matthews Frank, Farmer, Lower Harford
Mills James, Grocer
Moulder Elijah, Baker
Phillips John, Blacksmith
Shillam Richard, Grocer
Smith William, Farmer
Tidmarsh Thomas, Shoe maker
Vann Joseph, Grocer & Draper
White Henry, grocer & draper

The Population in 1871 was 538

Kelly's Post Office Directory 1879

Usual pre-amble for **Naunton** or **Naunton-in-the-Vale**…... The living is a rectory with 53 acres of glebe and 444 acres of allotment, tithe rent charge £130, gross estimated income £600 with a house in the gift of the Bishop of Gloucester and Bristol.

Private Residents:
Dickens Rev. Butler [Baptist]
Dunford, The Misses
Litton Rev. Edward Arthur M.A. Rectory

Commercial:
Bullock John, farmer & landowner
Round Hill Farm
Burge James, Saddler
Collett John, baker & miller, Naunton mill
Comeley Robert, farmer, Naunton Downs
Fletcher Philip, carpenter
Gardiner George, wheelwright
Godfrey William, blacksmith
Hanks George, farmer & landowner, Aylworth farm
Harris Henry, butcher
Hedgington George, Naunton Inn
Margetts Joseph, carpenter
Matthews Harold William, farmer, Lower Harford
Meadows John, farmer, Summerhill Farm
Mills James, grocer
Moulder Elijah, baker & farmer
Phillips William, blacksmith
Shillam Mary (Mrs) grocer
Smith George, farmer
Smith John, farmer, Church House Farm
Tims John, shoemaker
Wakefield Jane (Mrs) Black Horse Inn
White Henry, grocer & draper
Carriers to Cheltenham, William Pullen & George James

Kelly's Post Office Directory 1885

Usual pre-amble for **Naunton** or **Naunton-in-the-Vale**

Private Residents:
Dickens Rev. Butlin [Baptist]
Hanks Joseph
Hanks Mrs
Matthews George Fuller
Litton Rev. Edward Arthur M.A. Rectory
Insurance Agent, Henry White
Parish Clerk, William Phillips

Board School, William Swatman, Master,
(Average attendance 75)

Commercial
Burge James, saddler
Clarke John, farmer, Lower Harford
Collett Samuel George, baker & miller (water), seed merchant, Naunton mill
Comeley Robert, farmer, Naunton Downs
Fletcher Charles, carpenter
Gardiner George, wheelwright
Godfrey William, blacksmith
Hanks George, farmer
Hanks William, farmer & landowner, Aylworth farm
Hanks William Bullock, farmer
Harris Jesse, shopkeeper
Harter William, butcher
Harris Henry, butcher
Hooper John William, plumber
Margetts Joseph, carpenter
Meadows John, farmer, Summerhill farm
Mills James, grocer
Phillips William, blacksmith
Pulham William, baker
Pulham William (Jnr) carrier
Smith George, farmer
Waine James C, farmer, Round Hill Farm
Wakefield Jane (Mrs) grocer & draper
Withers Samuel, shopkeeper

Kelly's Post Office Directory 1889

Usual pre-amble for **Naunton** or **Naunton-in-the-Vale**
Post Office: John William Hooper, receiver, letters arrive from Cheltenham at 8.35am, box cleared at 4.55pm

Private Residents:
Dunford, The Misses
Goodman Rev. Frederick [Baptist]
Hanks Joseph
Matthews Mrs
Litton Rev. Edward Arthur M.A. Rectory

Commercial:
Burge James, saddler
Clarke John, farmer, Lower Harford
Collett Samuel George, baker & seed merchant & assistant overseer
Comeley Frederick, farmer, Naunton Downs
Fletcher Charles, carpenter
Gardiner Albert, wheelwright

Godfrey William, blacksmith
Griffin William George, baker & miller (water) Naunton mill
Hanks George, farmer
Hanks William, farmer & landowner, Aylworth farm
Hanks William Bullock, farmer
Harris Edwin, boot maker
Harris Henry, butcher
Harris Jesse, shopkeeper
Harter William, butcher
Hooper John William, plumber & school attendance office, Post Office
Margetts Joseph, carpenter
Merrell John, grocer
Phillips William, blacksmith
Pulham William, baker
Pulham William (Jnr) carrier
Smith George, farmer
Waine James C, farmer & bailiff to Mr J. Waddingham esq., Round Hill Farm
Wakefield Jane, Black Horse Inn

Kelly's Post Office Directory 1894

Usual pre-amble for **Naunton** or **Naunton-in-the-Vale**

Private Residents:
Dunford, The Misses
Goodman Rev. Frederick [Baptist]
Hanks Joseph
Litton Rev. Edward Arthur M.A. Rectory
Matthews Mrs

Commercial:
Bayliss John, plasterer
Brown William, farmer, Lower Harford
Burge James, saddler
Collett Samuel George, baker & seed merchant & assistant overseer
Fletcher Charles, carpenter
Gardiner brothers, wheelwrights
Godfrey George, blacksmith
Hanks George, farmer
Hanks William, farmer & landowner, Aylworth farm
Hanks William Bullock, farmer
Harris Edwin, boot maker
Harris Henry, butcher
Harris Jesse, shopkeeper, farmer & carrier
Hooper John William, plumber & school attendance officer, Post Office
Margetts Joseph, carpenter
Martin Benjamin J, baker & miller (water) Naunton mill
Merrell John, grocer
Phillips William, blacksmith & Parish Clerk

Pulham William, baker
Pulham William (Jnr) carrier
Smith George, farmer
Timms William, Naunton Inn
Waine James C, farm bailiff to J. Waddingham esq., Round Hill Farm
Wakefield Jane (Mrs) Black Horse Inn

Kelly's Post Office Directory 1897

Usual pre-amble for **Naunton** or **Naunton-in-the-Vale**

Private Residents:
Bradley Rev. Enock Brooke, Rectory
Dunford, The Misses
Hanks Joseph
Hanks Miss
Matthews Mrs
Spanton Rev. Emery [Baptist]

Commercial:
Bayliss John, plasterer
Bedwell Albert, farmer
Brown William, farmer, Lower Harford
Burge James Edward, saddler
Collett Samuel George, baker & seed merchant & clerk to the school board & assistant overseer
Cox Charles, Naunton Inn
Fletcher Charles, carpenter & Parish Clerk
Gardiner brothers, wheelwrights
Godfrey George William, blacksmith
Hanks George, farmer
Hanks William Wood, farmer & landowner, Aylworth farm
Hanks William Bullock, farmer, Manor House
Harris Edwin, boot maker
Harris Henry, butcher
Harris Jesse, shopkeeper, farmer & carrier
Hooper John William, plumber & school attendance officer, Post Office
James George, farmer
Margetts Joseph, carpenter
Martin Benjamin J, baker & miller (water) Naunton Mill
Merrell John, grocer
Phillips Rebecca (Mrs) shopkeeper
Pulham William, baker & farmer
Pulham William (Jnr) carrier
Smith George, farmer
Smith Raymond, blacksmith
Waine James C, farmer & bailiff to Mr J. Waddingham esq. Round Hill Farm
Williams George, Black Horse Inn

Kelly's Post Office Directory – 1902

Usual pre-amble for **Naunton** or **Naunton-in-the-Vale**

Private Residents:
Bradley Rev. Enoch Brooke, Rectory
Hanks Miss
Hanks Mrs
Matthews Mrs

Commercial:
Bayliss John, Plasterer
Bedwell Albert, Farmer
Brown Jsph Wm, Farmer, Lower Harford
Burge James Edward, Saddler
Collett Samuel George, Baker & seed merchant & assistant overseer & clerk to the Parish Council.
Cox Charles, Naunton Inn
Dunford Jane (Miss) Dress maker
Fletcher Chas. Carpenter & parish clerk
Gardener Brothers, Wheelwrights
Hanks George, Farmer
Hanks William, jun. Baker & Miller, Naunton Mill (water)
Hanks William Bullock, Farmer, Manor House
Hanks William Comely, Farmer & landowner, Aylworth Farm
Harris Henry, Butcher
Harris Jesse, Shopkeeper, farmer & carrier
Hooper John William, Builder & contractor, Post Office.
James George, Farmer
Margetts Joseph, Carpenter
Merrell John, Grocer
Phillips Rebecca (Mrs) Shopkeeper
Pulham William, Baker & farmer
Pulham William, jun. Carrier
Waine James C, Farm Bailiff to J Waddingham esq., Round Hill Farm
Williams George, Black Horse Inn

Kelly's Post Office Directory – 1906

Usual pre-amble for **Naunton** or **Naunton-in-the-Vale**; The living is a rectory, net yearly value £300 including 33 acres of allotment & 470 acres of glebe.

Private Residents:
The rector since 1902 is the Rev. Ernest Charles Eales M.A. of Corpus Christi College, Cambridge.
Hanks Miss
Hanks Mrs

Commercial:
Bayliss Henry & Frank, plasterers
Bedwell Albert, farmer

Bedwell William, farm bailiff to Mr J. Waddingham esq., Round Hill Farm
Betteridge Charles, Parish Clerk
Brown Joseph William, farmer, Lower Harford
Collett Samuel George, baker & seed merchant & assistant overseer & clerk to Parish Council
Cox Charles, Naunton Inn
Cox William, farmer
Dunford Jane (Miss) dress maker
Fletcher Charles, carpenter
Gardiner brothers, wheelwrights
Hanks George, farmer
Hanks Maurice, farmer
Hanks William (Jnr) baker & miller (water) Naunton mill
Hanks William Bullock, farmer, Manor House
Hanks William Comeley, farmer, Ayleworth farm
Harris Henry, butcher
Harris Jesse, shopkeeper, farmer & carrier
Hayward Thomas, saddler
Hooper John William, builder, Post Office
James George, farmer
Merrell John, grocer
Nutt Frederick, schoolmaster
Phillips Rebecca (Mrs) shopkeeper
Pulham William, baker
Pulham William (Jnr) farmer & carrier
Stait George, carrier
Williams George, Black Horse Inn

Kelly's Post Office Directory – 1910

Usual pre-amble for **Naunton** or **Naunton-in-the-Vale:**

Private Residents:
Eales Rev. Ernest Frederick, Rectory
Chipperfield Rev. Henry Francis [Baptist]
Hanks Miss
Hanks Mrs

Commercial:
Bayliss Henry & Frank, plasterers
Bedwell Albert, farmer
Bedwell William, farmer, Naunton Downs farm
Brown Joseph William, farmer, Lower Harford
Collett Samuel George (Mrs) baker
Cox Charles, Naunton Inn
Cox William, farmer
Dunford Jane (Miss) dress maker
Gardiner brothers, wheelwrights
Hanks Edgar, farmer

Hanks George, farmer
Hanks William Bullock, farmer, Manor House & miller (water)
Harris Henry, butcher
Harris Jesse, farmer & carrier
Hayward Thomas, saddler
Higgs Frederick Clarence, blacksmith
Hobbs Walter, boot repairer
Hooper John William, builder
James George, farmer
Merrell John, grocer
Phillips Rebecca (Mrs) shopkeeper
Pulham William, baker
Pulham William E, farmer, carrier & provisions dealer
Williams George, Black Horse Inn

Kelly's Post Office Directory – 1914

The usual geographical pre-amble commences: **Naunton** or **Naunton-upon-Cotswold.** (author's note -this interesting dual use of the village's name was reflected by the Reverend Eales, whose 1925 book was called **'Naunton upon Cotswold'**). The population in 1911 was 440.

Private Residents:
Eales Rev. Ernest, Rectory
Chipperfield Rev. Herbert [Baptist]
Hanks Miss
Hanks Mrs

Commercial:
Bayliss Henry & Frank, plasterers
Bedwell Albert, farmer
Bedwell William, farmer, Naunton Downs
Brown Joseph William, farmer, Lower Harford
Cox William, farmer
Dunford Jane (Miss) dress maker
Gardiner brothers, wheelwrights
Hanks Edgar, farmer
Hanks George, farmer
Hanks George (Jnr) farmer, Manor House
Hanks William Bullock, miller (water) Naunton mill
Hanks William Comeley, farmer, Aylworth farm
Harris Jesse, farmer & carrier
Harwood Wickliffe James, farmer
Hayward Thomas, Black Horse Inn
Higgs Frederick Clarence, blacksmith
Hobbs Walter, boot repairer
Hooper John William, builder
James George, farmer
Merrell John, grocer

Pulham William E, carrier
Young Charles, baker
Board School: Frederick Nutt, schoolmaster, average attendance 75.
Post Office: Henry Edward Hughes

Kelly's Post Office Directory – 1919 (End of WW1)

The usual geographical pre-amble for **Naunton** or **Naunton-upon-Cotswold.** The church contains 3 bells which were quarter-turned and re-hung in 1917. The church was repaired in 1878 and completely restored in 1899, when it was entirely re-floored and re-seated and the walls underpinned, and four new pinnacles placed on the tower and a new organ was provided in 1913. The church affords seating for 200 sittings. The churchyard was enlarged in 1910, the land being the gift of Mrs Waddingham of Guiting Grange. The living is a rectory, net yearly value £320, including 33 acres of allotments and 470 acres of glebe, with residence in the gift of the Bishop of Gloucester, and held since 1902 by the Reverend Ernest Frederick Eales M.A.. The manorial rights are divided and the principal land owner is Mrs Margaret Ann Waddingham. Post and M.O. office; Henry Edward Hughes. Lower Guiting is the nearest telegraph office. Public Elementary School (mixed) with residence for master 1870 & enlarged 1894 for 112 children. Miss Isobella Robb, Mistress.

Private Residents:
Eales Ernest Fredc. M.A. Rectory
Hanks Miss
Hanks Mrs
Wheatley Rev. William [Baptist]

Commercial;
Bayliss Henry & Frank, plasterers
Bedwell Albert, farmer
Bedwell William, farmer, Naunton Downs
Brown Joseph, farmer, Lower Harford
Cox William, farmer
Dunford Jane (Miss) dress maker
Gardner brothers, wheelwrights
Griffin Edward, dairyman & carrier
Hanks Edgar, farmer
Hanks George, farmer
Hanks George (Jnr) farmer, Manor House
Hanks William Bullock, miller (water)
Hanks William Comeley, farmer, Aylworth farm
Harris Edward, boot maker
Harris Jesse, farmer & carrier
Harwood Wickliffe James, farmer
Hayward Thomas, Black Horse Inn
Higgs Frederick Clarence, blacksmith
Hooper John William, builder
James George, farmer
Merrell John, grocer
Pulham William E., carrier
Young Charles, baker

Kelly's Post Office Directory – 1923

The usual geographical pre-amble for **Naunton** or **Naunton-upon-Cotswold,**
The living is a rectory, net yearly value £450. Deputy Parish Clerk, Albert Temple. Post & M.O. office – Henry Edward Hughes, sub-postmaster. Letters through Cheltenham, Lower Guiting is the nearest telegraph office. Carrier to Cheltenham by way of Andoversford & Hampen, William E. Pulham, on Thurs & Sat. To Bourton-on-the-Water by way of Slaughter, Rissington, Cold Aston & Notgrove on Mon & Wed, and to Swell & Stow-on-the-Wold occasionally.

Private Residents:
Eales Rev. Ernest Fredc. M.A. Rectory
Hanks Miss
Hanks Mrs
Thyne Rev. Arthur Victor [Bapist] The Manse

Commercial:
Bayliss Frank, plasterer
Bedwell Albert, farmer
Bedwell William, farmer, Naunton Downs
Bolter, Frederick Samuel, farmer, Lower Harford farm
Dunford Jane (Miss) dress maker
Gardner brothers, wheelwrights
Hanks George (Jnr) farmer, Manor House
Hanks Horace, dairyman
Hanks Maurice, farmer
Harris Edward, boot maker
Harwood, Wickliffe James, farmer
Hayward Thomas, Black Horse Inn
Hooper James, saddler & asst. overseer & Clerk to Parish Council
Hooper John William, builder
James George, farmer
Leworthy Frederick, blacksmith
Mason Charles, farmer
Merrell John Turner, grocer
Pulham, William E., carrier
Rand James Nicholas, farmer, Aylworth farm
Robinson J.R., farmer
Stevens Leslie, farmer
Young Charles George, baker

Kelly's Post Office Directory – 1927

The usual geographical pre-amble for **Naunton** or **Naunton-upon-Cotswold,**
The chief crops are wheat, turnips oats & barley. The area is 3,173 acres of land and 4 acres of water. Rateable value £2,929. Post & Telephone Call Office (available for calls within a limited distance) Mrs Laura Bedwell, sub-postmistress, Lower Guiting is the nearest Money Order & Telegraph office, 1 mile distant. Council School mixed, Miss Isabelle Robb, mistress. The population in 1921 was 404

Private Residents:
Banner Rev Alfred [rector] Rectory
Bibby William A
Hanks Miss
Hanks Mrs
Hanks William Comeley. J.P.
Holden Capt. George Henry [ret'd] Cromwell House
Savage Rev. Francis George, [Baptist], The Manse
Skirrow Geoffrey, Hill View

Commercial:
Marked thus # are farms of 150 (one hundred and fifty) acres or more

Bayliss Frank, plasterer
Bedwell Albert, farmer
Bloodworth Percival (Jnr) baker
Bolter Fredk. Saml. farmer, Lower Harford
Gardner Arthur, wheelwright
#Hanks George (Jnr) farmer, Manor House
Hanks Horace, dairyman
#Hanks Maurice, farmer
#Harwood Wickliffe Jas. Farmer
Hayward Florence (Mrs) Black Horse Inn
Hooper Jas. Saddler & assistant overseer, Official correspondent to Council School
James Raymond Thos. Haulier
Leworthy Frederick, blacksmith
Merrell John Turner, grocer
Pulham William E. carrier & farmer
#Rand Jas. Nicholas, farmer, Aylworth farm
#Robinson J.R. farmer
Stevens Leslie, farmer

Kelly's Post Office Directory – 1931

The usual geographical pre-amble for **Naunton** or **Naunton-upon-Cotswold,**
The living is a rectory, net yearly value £370, including 33 acres of allotments & 470 acres of glebe, held since 1926 by the Rev. Alfred Banner. Post and telephone call office (available for calls to places within a reasonable distance). Lower Guiting nearest M.O. & Telegraph Office. Conveyance: W.E. Pulham & Sons, to and from Cheltenham, Tues, Thurs & Sat.

Private Residents:
Ballantyne Arthur Oliver
Banner Rev. Alfred [rector] Rectory
Bibby William A.
Hanks William Comeley, J.P.
Savage Rev. Francis George [Baptist] The Manse
Skirrow Geoffrey, Hill View
Thompson Maj. Treffrey Owen M.D.

Commercial:
Marked thus # are farms of 150 (one hundred and fifty) acres or more
Bayliss Frank, plasterer
#Bedwell William, farmer, Naunton Downs
Bloodworth Percival (Jnr) baker
Bolter Fredk. Samuel, farmer, Lower Harford
Gardner Arthur, wheelwright
#Hanks George, farmer, Manor House
Hanks Horace, dairyman
#Hanks Maurice, farmer
#Harwood Wickliffe James, farmer
Hayward Florence (Mrs) Black Horse Inn
Heath George Thos. builder
Hooper Jas. saddler & rate collector, Clerk to Parish Council, correspondent to council school
James Raymond Thos. haulier
Merrell John Turner, grocer
Painter Albert, blacksmith
Pulham W.E. & Sons, omnibus proprietors. Telephone Guiting Power 35
Pulham William E. farmer
Pullin Allan Sidney, farmer
#Rand Jas. Nicholas, farmer, Aylworth Robinson J.R. farmer
Stevens Leslie, farmer

Kelly's Post Office Directory – 1935

The usual geographical pre-amble for **Naunton** or **Naunton-upon-Cotswold,**
The living is a rectory. £370 yearly, 33 acres of allotment & 470 acres of glebe, held since 1933 by the Rev. John Lister Coles of Gloucester Theological College. Post Office, Telegraph & Telephone Call Office (available for calls to places within a reasonable distance). Lower Guiting nearest M.O. Office. Conveyance: W.E. Pulham & Sons, to and from Cheltenham daily.

Private Residents:
Bibby William A.
Coles Rev. John Lister [rector]
Day Frederick John, Hill View
Donnisthorpe Miss, The Mill House
Hanks Mrs H.A.
Neal Rev. F [Baptist] The Manse
Walker Arthur Acock

Commercial
Marked thus # are farms of 150 (one hundred and fifty) acres or more
Bayliss Frank, plasterer
Bedwell L&F (Misses) drapers & Post Office
#Bedwell Wm, farmer, Naunton Downs
#Ford Alan Ferguson, farmer, Lower Harford
Gardner Arthur, wheelwright
#Hanks George, farmer, Manor House
Hanks Horace, dairyman

#Hanks Maurice, farmer
#Harwood Wickliffe James, farmer
Hayward Florence (Mrs) Black Horse Inn
Heath George Thos. builder
Hobbs A.W. boot & shoe repairer
Hooper Jas. Saddler & clerk to Parish Council & official correspondent to Council School
James Raymond Thos, haulier
Merrell John Turner, grocer
Painter Albert, blacksmith
Pritchard Leonard J. newsagent
Pulham W.E. & Sons, omnibus proprietors, Telephone Guiting Power 35
Pulham Wm E. farmer
#Rand Jas Nicholas, farmer, Aylworth farm
Reynolds George, baker
Roberts Bros, farmers
#Robinson J.R. farmer
Stevens Leslie, farmer

Kelly's Post Office Directory – 1939

The usual geographical pre-amble for **Naunton** or **Naunton-upon-Cotswold.** The principal landowners are Mr Arthur G. Walker and Messrs George & Maurice Hanks. The chief crops are wheat, turnips, oats & barley. By the County of Gloucester Review Order 1935, part of the parish was transferred to Temple Guiting. The area is 3,144 acres of land and inland water. The population in 1931 was 382. Post & Telegraph Office, Letters through Cheltenham, Lower Guiting nearest M.O. Office. Conveyance: W.E. Pulham & Sons, to and from Cheltenham daily.

Private Residents:
Coles Rev. John Lister [rector]
Day Frederick John, Hill View
Donisthorpe Miss, The Mill House
Foottit Cecil Carter, Cromwell House
Hanks Mrs H.A.
Rashdall Mrs, Overbrook
Walker Arthur G. Aylworth

Commercial:
Marked thus # are farms of 150 acres or more.
Bayliss Frank, plasterer
Bedwell L&F (Misses) drapers & Post Office, Telephone Guiting Power 37
#Dale William, farmer, Naunton Downs
#Ford Alan Ferguson, farmer, Lower Harford
#Hanks George, farmer, Manor House, Telephone Guiting Power 43
#Hanks Horace, dairy farmer
#Hanks Maurice, farmer, Telephone Guiting Power 34
#Harwood Wickliffe Jas, farmer
Hayward Aubrey Victor, saddler
Hayward Florence (Mrs) Black Horse Inn
Hooper Jas. Clerk to Parish Council & official correspondent to Council School

Merrell John Turner, grocer
Morris Eva Eliza (Mrs) grocer
Muller Terence Arthur, wheelwright
Painter Albert, blacksmith
Pritchard Leonard J. newsagent
Pulham W.E. & Sons. Omnibus proprietors, Telephone Guiting Power 35
Reynolds George, baker
#Saunders K.M. (Mrs) tea rooms, Spring Cottage
Stevens Leslie, farmer
Walker Arthur Acock, Guest House, Church House, Telephone Guiting Power 29
#Walker Arthur G. farmer, Aylworth farm, Telephone Guiting Power 38

Appendix 7

Naunton Board School

Memorandum of Arrangement made the 25th day of March 1890 between Edward Arthur Litton of Naunton in the County of Gloucestershire, Clerk in Holy Orders, James Burge of the same place, Farmer and Harness Maker, James Mills, also of the same place, Farmer . James Charles Waine, also of the same place, Farmer, The Managers of the Naunton National School, which said school is hereinafter called "The School" ……….. within the meaning of the Elementary Education Act 1870 ………… under an indenture bearing date - the Seventh day of June 1864 and made under the hands and seals of the Reverend Litton, Rector of Naunton, John Gillett and William Charles, Churchwardens.
Signed….E.A.Litton, Clerk of the Managers… S.G.Collett, Clerk of School Board
(The document goes on to detail the use to which the buildings can be put, the payment of rates, charges and taxes, insurance of the school, cleaning and repairs to same, etc).

Permanent (recorded) teaching staff from 1865 to 1969

Head - Mr William Swatman, from 1865 (no further details).
Head - Mr Fred Nutt. (b.10/07/1855) from 1898. £105p.a. Emoluments £8. Dwelling House - rent free.
Head - Mr George F.C. Wheeler (born 27/06/1894) £110 p.a. from Jan to Mar 1918.
Head - Alfred Leonard Smart (born 21/12/1897) £270p.a. from 1927 to 1932
Head - John Procter Pexton (b.03/03/1905) £238p.a. from 1933-1954. £238p.a. + War Allowance
Head - Mrs Frances F.L. Horton (b.04/09/1904) from 1955-1969 starting at £605p.a.

Teacher - Miss Flossie Grimes, from 1910 to1914 (mixed)
Teacher - Miss Louisa E Weston, from 1906, £35p.a. (mixed)
Teacher - Miss Janet Griffin from 1914 to 1935, £50p.a. (mixed)
Teacher - Miss Ellen Stratford, from 1904 to 1909 (mixed)
Teacher - Mrs Ellen Nutt, from 6 Jul 1898, £40 per annum (infants)
Teacher - Miss Isabella Robb, (born 08/09/1882) £ 130p.a. from 1918 to 1927, Mixed/infants (Later Head)
Teacher - Miss Lizzie Rosetta Betteridge, (b 04/05/1901) from 1918 to 1924 (infants) £35pa
Teacher - Miss Nellie Hurworth (B.26/04/1900) £90p.a. from 1924 to 1925
Teacher - Miss Gladys Elsie Maud Herbert (B.27/12/1906) £80p.a. from 1926 to 1929
Teacher - Miss Agness Haygarth Everness (b.06/02/1902) £190p.a. from 1922 to 1922
Teacher - Miss Frances Margaret Savage (b.16/08/1912) £65p.a. from 1931 to 1932
Teacher - Miss Hilda Forrester (b.04/07/1908) £81p.a. from 1932 to 1936
Teacher - Miss Kathlen Portlock (b.13.10.1918) £80p.a. 1937 to 1937
Teacher - Miss Winifred Catchpole (b.03/09/1919) no further details.
Teacher - Mrs Edith Mary Pexton (b.30/01/1899) from 1937-1952 (various dates)
Teacher - Miss Alice Brown (b.19/01/1913)1936.
Teacher - Miss Francis Allen (b.28/09/1918) from 1937-1940, £95p.a.
Teacher - Miss Charlotte Stewart (b.25/02/1891)1940. £258p.a.
Teacher - Miss Edith Robinson (b.15/09/1881) from 1940-1941. £156p.a. + War Allowance

Teacher - Miss Olive Blake (b.13/12/1912) from 1940-1941, £90p.a.
Teacher - Miss Margaret Long (b.01/05/1908) from 1942-1946, £144p.a. + War Allowance
Teacher - Miss Mair Evans (b.30/01/1928) from 1946-1949.
(all salaries shown are those applying on appointment)

School Management

The last two listed Parish Council Managers to be re-appointed for the school in 1967 were Mr W. Herbert, Ash Tree Cottage, Naunton, Gardener, and Mr H.L. Hanks, Waterloo Farm, Naunton, Farmer.

The Last County Council Managers were Mr Maurice G. Hanks, Northfield, Naunton. The Hon Mrs Nicholas Ridley, The Old Rectory, Naunton. Mr A.T. Williams, Church Farm, Naunton. Mr F.B. Pulham, Brookside, Station Road, Bourton-on-the-Water.

Appendix 8

Naunton National School Register Number One (1865 – 1923)

Names were originally in chronological order, as pupils entered the school. Now changed to alphabetical order for ease of searches

In	First & Surname	Birthday	Parent/Guardian/Address	Last School	Out	Remarks
1902	Abbott Frederick	25/08/1892	Henry Abbott, Naunton	Ascott-u-Wych	1902	Left the village
1873	Adams Florence	?	John Adams, Naunton		1877	
1898	Akers Albert	09/05/1894	James Akers, Naunton		1907	Labour certificate
1895	Akers Annie	23/05/1891	James Akers, Summerhill		1905	Exempt
1894	Akers Edmund J	02/04/1888	James Akers, Summerhill	Slaughter	1900	Exempt
1894	Akers Rhoda	28/01/1886	James Akers, Summerhill	Slaughter	1898	
1915	Alford Violet Phyllis	31/10/1911	Ernest Alford, Naunton	Evesham	1915	Back to Evesham
1898	Argent Corrisand	08/11/1894	Mrs Bayliss, Naunton		1899	To Oxford
1896	Argent Stephen Henry	12/03/1893	Harry Bayliss, Naunton		1899	To Oxford
1896	Armstrong Roderick	05/03/1885	Mrs Armstrong, Hawling		1896	
1880	Ash Albert Ed	03/03/1875	John Ash, Harford Hill			
1880	Ash Eleanor S	04/10/1873	John Ash, Harford Hill			
1880	Ash Elizabeth	20/10/1868	John Ash, Harford Hill		1881	
1880	Ash Richard J	23/05/1872	John Ash, Harford Hill			
1892	Ashwin Ernest J	31/12/1882	Mrs Ashwin, Guiting Villa	Miss Dunsfords	1898	
1919	Aston Kenneth	22/05/1914	Frank Aston, Naunton	Cold Aston	1928	Age
1917	Aston Kenneth Chas	22/05/1914	Frank Aston, Naunton		1919	Left for Aston
1875	Bailey Amelia	?	Richard Bailey, The Huts		1876	
1875	Bailey Fred	?	Richard Bailey, The Huts		1876	
1871	Barnes Jane	22/04/1868	Mary Barnes, Naunton		1877	
1903	Barnett Amy Gertrude	21/08/1898	Mrs Raymond Smith, Naunton	Beckford	1903	Back to Beckford
1911	Bartlett Fred'k Wm	24/12/1899	John (Grandfather) Hill Barn	Compton Abd'	1913	Gone to work
1911	Bartlett Reginald Alb'	07/01/1899	John Bartlett, Hill Barn	Compton Abd'	1912	Gone to work
1893	Bateman Esther	03/05/1889	Mrs Batemen, Naunton		1893	
1893	Bateman Esther M	03/05/1889	Mrs Bateman, Naunton		1902	Left the village
1913	Bayliss Bertram Victor	20/02/1910	Frank Bayliss, Naunton		1924	Left for work
1908	Bayliss Gertrude	29/04/1905	Frank Bayliss, Naunton		1919	Domestic Service

308 Naunton 2000

Appendix 8 (continued) Naunton National School Register Number One (1865 – 1923)

In	First & Surname	Birthday	Parent/Guardian/Address	Last School	Out	Remarks
1921	Bayliss Horace	29/09/1916	Frank Bayliss, Naunton		1930	Age
1910	Bayliss Jack	09/12/1906	Frank Bayliss, Naunton		1919	Left - baker's boy
1883	Bayliss Janet	08/11/1878	John Bayliss, Naunton		1890	Deceased 3 July 1897
1882	Beames Arthur	21/04/1876	?		1890	Deceased
1880	Beames Charles	23/10/1876	Sarah Beames, Naunton		1890	
1889	Beames Clara	08/02/1881	Wm Beames, Westfield		1889	
1895	Beames Ellen	13/05/1885	William Beames, Naunton	Bumford	1896	
1895	Beames Florence	25/10/1889	William Beames, Naunton	Bumford	1896	
1898	Beames Florence	25/09/1890	William Beames, Naunton	Hawling	1901	Labour certificate
1903	Beames Florence	25/09/1890	William Beames, Nosehill Fm	Slaughter	1904	To work
1882	Beames Frank	21/02/1878	William Beames, Summer Hill			
1898	Beames George	21/12/1892	William Beames, Naunton		1901	To Swell School
1903	Beames George	21/12/1892	William Beames, Nosehill Fm	Slaughter	1906	To work
1880	Beames Jane E	31/07/1871	William Beames, SummerHill		1890	
1885	Beames John	18/04/1880	William Beames, Summerhill			
1898	Beames Minnie	04/06/1888	William Beames, Naunton	Hawling	1901	Labour certificate
1880	Beames William	10/04/1874	William Beames, Summer Hill		1881	
1880	Beames, Mary Ellen	27/10/1869	William Beames, Summer Hill		1876	
1905	Beckingsale Reginald	17/08/1894	Mrs Hanks, Aylworth	Cheltenham	1905	Back to Cheltenham
1876	Beckley Jane	?	John Beckley, Naunton Downs		1876	
1875	Beckley Thomas	?	John Beckley, Naunton Downs		1883	
1876	Beckley William	?	John Beckley, Naunton Downs		1876	
1895	Bedwell Ada	21/12/1885	Noel Havard, Hawling Lodge	Tem' Guiting	1895	
1891	Bedwell Albert Jas	27/12/1887	Albert Bedwell, Naunton			
1895	Bedwell Alice A	30/07/1891	Henry Bedwell, Naunton		1905	Exempt
1876	Bedwell Caroline	02/01/1866	James Bedwell, Dale Terrace		1877	
1882	Bedwell Chas Ed	07/06/1879	Henry Bedwell, Naunton		1890	
1889	Bedwell Edward	20/04/1885	Albert Bedwell, Naunton		1898	Exempt
1888	Bedwell Ellen	02/09/1883	Harry Bedwell, Naunton			
1888	Bedwell Ellen A M	30/06/1885	John Bedwell, Summerhill			
1878	Bedwell Emily E	12/06/1874	James Bedwell, Naunton			
1891	Bedwell Fanny	28/09/1886	Henry Bedwell, Naunton		1899	Exempt
1886	Bedwell Florence	25/03/1883	Albert Bedwell, Naunton			

Naunton 2000   309

1896	Bedwell Florence A	30/12/1890	Henry Bedwell, Naunton		1896	Exempt
1899	Bedwell Francis Jane	02/01/1896	Albert Bedwell, Naunton		1904	Exempt
1874	Bedwell Frank	31/12/1869	James Bedwell, Naunton		1881	
1893	Bedwell Frank	19/02/1889	Harry Bedwell, Naunton		1902	Exempt
1905	Bedwell Fred' J H	17/02/1893	Henry Hunt (Grandfather)	Birmingham	1905	Back to Birmingham
1896	Bedwell Frederick	17/02/1893	Henry Bedwell, Naunton		1896	Exempt
1879	Bedwell Henry Albert	24/08/1876	Henry Bedwell, Naunton		1888	
1876	Bedwell James	24/10/1872	Henry Bedwell, New-town		1883	
1895	Bedwell Laura A	17/06/1890	Albert Bedwell, Naunton		1904	
1885	Bedwell Martha	10/05/1881	Henry Bedwell, Naunton		1894	
1874	Bedwell Mary A	24/06/1870	Henry Bedwell, Naunton		1883	
1873	Bedwell Millie	18/05/1868	James Bedwell, Naunton		1877	
1878	Bedwell Rosa	27/12/1874	Henry Bedwell, Naunton			
1912	Bedwell Stella Louise	23/06/1907	Wm Bedwell, Naunton Downs		1921	Exempt
1916	Bedwell Vera Frances	24/04/1911	Wm Bedwell, Naunton Downs		1923	Age
1881	Bedwell William	31/12/1876	Albert Bedwell, Naunton			
1892	Bedwell William J	10/09/1887	John Bedwell, B'ham			
1886	Bellamy Annie	?	?		1886	
1912	Benfield Algernon C	31/07/1907	Charles Benfield, Naunton		1921	Exempt
1907	Benfield Leslie Ernest	01/06/1899	Charles Benfield, The Yard	Slaughter	1913	To work
1907	Benfield Mabel Lizzie	12/07/1901	Charles Benfield, The Yard	Slaughter	1915	Exempt
1923	Benfield Margery	05/09/1918	Mrs Benfield, Dale Street		1932	Age
1907	Benfield Mervyn W C	11/10/1902	Charles Benfield, The Yard	Slaughter	1915	To work
1914	Berry Beatrice Martha	13/02/1904	Joseph Thos Berry, Grange Hill	Rodmarton	1916	Left the village
1914	Berry Wm Geo	07/06/1905	Joseph Thos Berry, Grange Hill	Rodmarton	1916	Left the village
1904	Betteridge Lizzie R	04/05/1901	Charles Betteridge, Naunton		1915	Exempt
1898	Bettridge Alice May	27/05/1892	Charles Bettridge, Naunton	Slaughter	1906	Exempt
1898	Bettridge Florence Chr	05/01/1894	Charles Bettridge, Naunton	Slaughter	1908	Exempt
1876	Black Arthur	?	Samuel Black, Harford		1876	
1876	Black Lizzie	?	Samuel Black, Harford		1876	
1876	Black Samuel	?	Samuel Black, Harford		1876	
1922	Blowing Albert	19/02/1910	Frank Day, Aylworth Cottages	Aston Blank	1923	Return to Aston Blank
1922	Blowing Cecil	23/10/1916	Frank Day, Aylworth Cottages		1923	Return to Aston Blank
1901	Blowing Wm Edw'd	?	Edward Blowing, Naunton		1901	Left the village
1876	Bond Edward	?	Robert Bond, Little London		1876	
1876	Bond Mary	?	Robert Bond, Little London		1876	
1876	Bond Sarah	?	Robert Bond, Little London		1876	

310 *Naunton 2000*

Appendix 8 (continued) Naunton National School Register Number One (1865 – 1923)

In	First & Surname	Birthday	Parent/Guardian/Address	Last School	Out	Remarks
1923	Bosher Alice	02/02/1912	James Bosher, Roundhill	Eynsham	1925	Left for Yanworth
1923	Bosher Annie	22/02/1913	James Bosher, Roundhill	Eynsham	1925	Left for Yanworth
1923	Bosher Frederick	12/03/1915	James Bosher, Roundhill	Eynsham	1925	Left for Yanworth
1923	Bosher Thomas	11/06/1910	James Bosher, Roundhill	Eynsham	1925	Left for Yanworth
1877	Branch B	17/03/1871	Sarah Ann Branch, Naunton	this	1877	
1884	Branch Rosa Jane	08/09/1875	Mra Williams, Naunton			
1892	Brawn Florence P	19/04/1889	George Williams, Naunton		1902	Exempt
1907	Broadway Charles	28/05/1901	George Broadway, Summerhill		1907	To Cutsdean
1889	Brodrick Rosa	25/06/1878	John Brodrick, Naunton Downs	Churchill		
1903	Brooks Grace S	27/05/1896	Samuel Brooks, Naunton	T Guiting	1904	Left the village
1903	Brooks Joan Lamont S	29/06/1899	Samuel Brooks, Naunton	T Guiting	1904	Left the village
1903	Brooks Thos Philip S	01/01/1898	Samuel Brooks, Naunton	T Guiting	1904	Left the village
1911	Brunsdon Beatrice M	08/08/1906	Richard Brunsdon, Aylworth		1916	Left the village
1912	Brunsdon Birtha	05/01/1908	Richard Brunsdon, Aylworth		1916	Left the village
1902	Brunsdon Ernest Geo	12/11/1898	Richard Brunsdon, Naunton		1902	Left for the winter
1903	Brunsdon Ernest Geo'	12/11/1898	Richard Brunsdon, Naunton		1911	Gone to work
1909	Brunsdon Sibyl Gladys	14/06/1905	Richard Brunsdon, Aylworth		1916	Left the village
1901	Brunsdon Walter Fred	12/05/1897	Richard Brunsdon, Naunton		1910	Gone to work
1898	Brunsdon William	14/04/1894	?		1899	Labour certificate
1876	Bryan Charles	21/02/1871	John Bryan, Naunton		1883	
1915	Bryan Helen Eliz	04/10/1910	Charles Bryan, Naunton		1924	Age
1909	Bryan Lambert Tho	06/11/1904	Charles Bryan, Naunton		1918	Agricultural labourer
1876	Bullock John R	?	John Bullock, Round Hill Farm		1876	
1879	Burdock Harry T	13/07/1872	Edward Burdock, Naunton	Rissington		
1880	Burdock Ruth	07/05/1876	Edward Burdock, Naunton			
1879	Burdock Walter S	26/12/1873	Edward Burdock, Naunton			
1914	Burgess Albert Frank	20/08/1903	Frank Burgess, Dale House	Swell	1917	Exempt
1914	Burgess Joyce Marie	04/06/1910	Frank Burgess, Dale House		1915	Deceased
1914	Burgess Muriel Dorothy	15/10/1901	Frank Burgess, Dale House	Swell	1916	Exempt
1907	Chadband Amy	06/10/1898	Charles Chadband, Naunton	Lower Swell	1908	To Guiting
1907	Chadband Edgar Chas	15/12/1894	Charles Chadband, Naunton	Lower Swell	1908	To Guiting
1907	Chadband Minnie Ada	20/04/1901	Charles Chadband, Naunton	Lower Swell	1908	To Guiting
1887	Chamberlain A Jane	10/01/1882	Edwin Turner, Summerhill			

1887	Chamberlain Gertrude	01/05/1880	Edwin Turner, Summerhill		
1887	Chamberlain T E	29/09/1878	Edwin Turner, Summerhill		
1919	Chessington Ernest Jas	19/10/1908	James Chessington, Naunton	Chr' Chu' Chelt	1890	Left for Salperton
1907	Chipperfield Mabel G	25/06/1902	H F Chipperfield, The Manse		1921	To Private School
1892	Clarke Beatrice E	05/02/1884	John Clark, Naunton		1914	
1892	Clarke Nellie	12/05/1886	John Clark, Naunton		1892	
1892	Clarke Sarah A	14/07/1882	John Clark, Naunton	Malvern	1891	
1901	Clayton Albert Hy	09/02/1897	James Clayton, Naunton	Stanton	1892	
1901	Clayton Elizabeth	16/03/1894	James Clayton, Naunton	Stanton	1901	Left the village
1901	Clayton Norah G	05/01/1893	James Clayton, Naunton	Stanton	1901	Left the village
1901	Clayton Thomas	18/05/1895	James Clayton, Naunton	Stanton	1901	Left the village
1916	Cleevely Alb't Hy	11/05/1909	Geo Hy Cleevely, Naunton	U Slaughter	1901	Left the village
1916	Cleevely Ellen Eliz	13/12/1911	Geo Hy Cleevely, Naunton	U Slaughter	1917	Left - work
1916	Cleevely George Hy	20/08/1907	Geo Hy Cleevely, Naunton	U Slaughter	1917	Left district
1916	Cleevely Jas Fred'k	14.12.1904	Geo Hy Cleevely, Naunton	U Slaughter	1917	Left district
1923	Clifford George	04/12/1910	William Clifford, The Yard		1917	Left - work
1885	Clifford Kate	08/05/????	?		1924	Left for work
1923	Clifford Mona	19/06/1918	William Clifford, The Yard		1926	Left for Aston Blank
1876	Clifford William	?	John Townsend, The Square		1876	
1882	Collett Ada	30/11/1872	Richard Collett, Naunton			
1902	Collett Elizabeth Mary	13/02/1898	Samuel Geo Collett, Naunton		1912	Exempt
1893	Collett Flossie	17/08/1887	Frank Collett, Naunton		1893	Exempt
1908	Collett Henrietta	10/02/1904	Annie R Collett, Naunton		1914	Gone to Chelt
1903	Collett John Geo	23/08/1899	Samuel Geo Collett, Naunton		1913	To work in Chelt'
1915	Collins Muriel Francis	02/09/1910	Martha Collins (mother)	Sevenhampton	1915	Left the village
1882	Comely Bertie	19/06/1876	Thos Comely, Westfield		1890	
1883	Comely Chas C	27/08/1877	Thomas Comely, Westfield			
1877	Comely Frank	06/06/1864	Mr Robert Comely, Naunton	Miss Dunford's		
1886	Comely Norman	20/06/1880	Thomas Comely, Westfield			
1880	Comely Raymond	04/09/1874	Thos Comely, Westfield		1888	
1880	Comely Robert	05/03/1871	Thos Comely, Westfield			
1880	Comely Thos George	01/04/1872	Thos Comely, Westfield			
1886	Comely William	05/05/1878	Aldon W Comely, Guiting Grange		1886	
1911	Cook Dorothy	15/09/1905	Fred'k Cook, Summerhill	Stow	1918	Domestic Service
1919	Cook Evelyn	25/08/1915	Fred Cook, Naunton		1927	Left for Slaughter
1901	Cook George	17/03/1888	Richard Cook, Guiting	Lower Guiting	1902	Work
1911	Cook Hubert	22/12/1907	Fred'k Cook, Summerhill	Stow	1920	Agricultural Work

Naunton 2000   311

312 Naunton 2000

1895	Corson Archie	01/09/1882	Thomas Corson, Hawling	Sevenhampton	1896	To Hawling
1895	Corson George	08/10/1890	Thomas Corson, Hawling	Hawling	1899	To Hawling
1894	Corson Janet	12/12/1885	Thomas Corson, Hawling		1899	To Hawling
1895	Corson William	27/11/1889	Thomas Corson, Hawling		1908	To Cheltenham
1908	Cosnett Muriel F	15/04/1902	Wm Bullock Hanks, Naunton	Cheltenham	1904	Deceased
1901	Cox Alaricc Wm	09/09/1897	Charles Cox, Naunton Inn		1915	Back to Nottingham
1915	Cox Albert	23/08/1903	Wm Cox (Grandfather)	Nottingham	1916	Visitor
1916	Cox Albert	23/08/1903	George Cox, Naunton	London	1883	
1876	Cox Alfred	06/02/1873	William Cox, Back Lane			
1895	Cox Arthur Henry	15/05/1890	Geo Wm Cox, Naunton		1899	Left the village
1897	Cox Arthur Henry	15/05/1890	George W Cox, Naunton	Nottingham	1899	Back to Nottingham
1899	Cox Arthur Hy	15/05/1891	Charles Cox, Naunton Inn	Nottingham Bd	1901	To Nottingham
1901	Cox Arthur Hy	15/05/1891	Geo Wm Cox, Naunton		1877	
1870	Cox Charles	21/01/1868	William Cox, Naunton		1876	
1868	Cox George	28/12/1865	William Cox, Back Lane		1909	Exempt
1900	Cox Helen Lizette	22/11/1896	Charles Cox, Naunton Inn			
1878	Cox Lambert	02/03/1875	William Cox, Naunton	Nottingham Bd	1901	To Nottingham
1901	Cox Lambert	06/10/1894	Geo Wm Cox, Naunton		1904	Deceased
1899	Cox Lionel Chas	21/08/1894	Charles Cox, Naunton Inn			
1887	Cox Nellie	09/02/1884	Wm Cox, Naunton	Birmingham	1919	Return to Birmingham
1919	Cox Winifred	07/03/1908	Tom Davis, (Guardian) Naunton			
1878	Crook Alfred	03/12/1874	John Crook, Naunton		1881	
1880	Crook Jesse	?	?	Birmingham	1876	To Condicote
1917	Crump William	02/07/1910	Wm Crump, Chalk Hill Lodge			
1875	Cummings Ellen	?	?			
1884	Davies Abert	15/05/1887	Alfred Davies, Naunton		1906	Exempt
1895	Davis Alice May	24/05/1892	George Davis, Naunton		1917	Land Work
1908	Davis Bert	20/10/1904	George Davis, Naunton			
1888	Davis Charles	22/08/1885	Alfred Davis, Naunton		1907	Exempt
1901	Davis Edith	11/02/1897	Alfred Davis, Westfield		1906	Exempt
1902	Davis Edith	11/02/1897	Alfred Davis, Westfield		1910	Mother's help
1907	Davis Edith	11/02/1897	Alfred Davis, Naunton	Longborough	1895	
1886	Davis Emily	01/04/1884	Alfred Davis, Naunton		1914	Deceased
1911	Davis Ernest Albert	27/07/1906	Albert Davis, Eyford		1917	Domestic Service
1908	Davis Esther Gwend'	22/11/1903	John Davis, Notgrove Station		1911	Mother's Help
1900	Davis Florence Win	28/11/1897	George Davis, Naunton		1904	
1894	Davis Frederick	04/12/1890	Alfred Davis, Naunton			

1899	Davis Gladys	16/04/1895	George Davis, Naunton		1908	Labour Certificate
1921	Davis Hilda	31/05/1916	Frederick Davis, Naunton		1928	Left for Cheltenham
1919	Davis Ivy	23/02/1919	Tom Davis, Naunton		1922	Left for Stroud
1904	Davis James Hy	18/10/1899	John Davis, Railway Hut		1913	To work
1919	Davis Leslie	09/02/1915	Mrs Emily Davis, Naunton		1926	Northleach Gr School
1918	Davis Leslie Charles	09/02/1915	Mrs Emily Davis, Naunton		1919	
1903	Davis Nelly Priscilla	20/07/1900	George Davis, Naunton		1914	Gone to service
1911	Davis Raymond Geo	03/06/1907	George Davis, Naunton		1920	Agricultural Work
1913	Davis Reginald Walter	17/02/1910	George Davis, Naunton		1923	Left for work
1903	Davis William	11/03/1898	John Davis, Notgrove Station		1912	Gone to work
1923	Dawson James	22/10/1913	Edward Hughes, The Huntsman	Lowestoft	1923	Return to Lowestoft
1887	Day David	21/02/1883	Thomas Day, Summerhill		1890	
1887	Day Emily	03/06/1880	Thomas Day, Summerhill			
1887	Day Mary A	11/05/1877	Thomas Day, Summerhill		1890	
1896	Dean Alice B	23/09/1890	John Dean, Naunton	Hampnett		
1904	Dean Ernest	04/02/1896	John Dean, Naunton	Cutsdean	1904	To work
1904	Dean Ethel	27/07/1898	John Dean, Naunton	Cutsdean	1912	Exempt
1896	Dean Frank	01/08/1887	John Dean, Naunton	Hampnett		
1916	Dean Gladys Mary	22/06/1911	John Dean (Grandfather)	Barnwood		Back to Barnwood
1896	Dean William	12/07/1885	John Dean, Naunton	Hampnett		
1879	Denfall Maud	18/01/1872	Henry Denfall, Naunton			
1915	Deverson Albert	14/02/1908	Mrs Winter, Naunton	London	1915	Back to London
1877	Dickens Butlin V	20/07/1866	Rev Butlin Dickens, Naunton	Guiting	1879	
1877	Dickens Ernest M	24/10/1867	Rev Butlin Dickens, Naunton		1881	
1883	Dickins Evelyn	08/04/1877	Butlin Dickens, Naunton			
1879	Dickins Laurence S	08/08/1871	Rev Butlin Dickins, Naunton		1879	
1880	Dickins Leonna Amelia	06/07/1873	Butlin Dickins, Naunton			
1920	Dix Arthur	25/01/1913	Hubert Dix, Naunton	Sherborne	1922	Left for Shipton Oliffe
1920	Dix Ernest	29/04/1909	Hubert Dix, Naunton	Sherborne	1922	Left for Shipton Oliffe
1920	Dix Violet	25/03/1915	Hubert Dix, Naunton	Sherborne	1922	Left for Shipton Oliffe
1895	Dixey Elsie	10/08/1891	James Dixey, Summerhill	Gt Barrington	1896	
1895	Dixey William	28/12/1885	James Dixey, Summerhill	Gt Barrington	1895	
1896	Dixey Wm	23/12/1885	Jas Dixey, Naunton	Longborough	1896	re-admitted 689
1889	Dixon Bessie	27/03/1880	Wm Dixon, Naunton	Bourton	1895	
1889	Dixon Emma	21/04/1884	Wm Dixon, Naunton	Bourton	1895	
1891	Dixon Henry	22/04/1888	William Dixon, Naunton		1900	Exempt
1889	Dixon Septimus	10/04/1878	Wm Dixon, Naunton	Bourton	1890	

Naunton 2000 313

314 Naunton 2000

Appendix 8 (continued) Naunton National School Register Number One (1865 – 1923)

In	First & Surname	Birthday	Parent/Guardian/Address	Last School	Out	Remarks
1889	Dixon William	11/04/1882	Wm Dixon, Naunton	Bourton	1895	
1879	Doughty Fanny G	01/07/1876	John Doughty, Naunton		1879	
1917	Dovaston Marjorie Ell'	18/06/1913	Henry Dovaston, Naunton		1919	Left for South Wales
1878	Dove Annie	16/08/1868	Benj Dove, Summerhill			
1878	Dove Florence	14/11/1870	Benj Dove, Summerhill			
1876	Dowler Albert	22/04/1873	James Dowler, Jaques Lane		1883	
1876	Dowler Annie	22/02/1864	James Dowler, Jaques Lane	this	1877	
1882	Dowler Arthur	15/10/1877	James Dowler, Naunton			
1894	Dowler Arthur	24/11/1886	James Dowler, Notgrove Station	Salperton	1899	Exempt
1871	Dowler Charles	5/12/1868	James Dowler, Naunton		1877	
1895	Dowler Elsie Mary	17/02/1888	James Dowler, Notgrove Station	Salperton	1900	Left the village
1873	Dowler Emily	17/02/1871	James Dowler, Naunton		1881	
1866	Dowler James	5/10/1863	Samuel Dowler, Naunton		1876	
1878	Dowler Kate	06/06/1875	James Dowler, Naunton		1879	
1886	Dowler Nellie	?	James Dowler, Naunton			
1899	Dowler Nora	17/10/1893	James Dowler, Notgrove Station		1900	Gone to Stow
1868	Dowler Walter	?	James Dowler, Naunton		1876	
1892	Drake William	?	Harry Neal, Naunton		1892	
1878	Draper Alice Blanch	11/04/1873	George Draper, Naunton			
1878	Draper Clara Eveline	27/06/1875	Mr George Draper, Naunton			
1876	Draper George	26/12/1870	George Draper, Back lane		1883	
1875	Draper Ralph	25/06/1865	George Draper, Naunton		1876	
1875	Draper William	25/11/1867	George Draper, Naunton		1876	
1916	Eakets Leslie Harry	19/12/1910	Harry Eakets, Tally Hoo (sic)		1916	Left the village
1922	Eaketts Elsie	21/04/1912	Mrs R Willis, Naunton	C' Kings	1922	Return to Ch' Kings
1921	Eaketts Leslie	19/12/1910	Minnie Eaketts, Naunton	Charlton Kings	1921	Return to Ch' Kings
1921	Eaketts William	02/04/1914	Minnie Eaketts, Naunton	Charlton Kings	1921	Return to Ch' Kings
1915	East Alice Muriel	31/07/1911	Walter East, Naunton	L Guiting	1925	Age
1878	Edginton Adela E	10/01/1871	Chas W Edginton, Naunton Inn			
1885	Edginton Albert	??/01/1881	?			
1884	Edginton Bessie	03/06/1874	Return to Ch' Kings			
1884	Edginton Charles F	26/03/1876	Joseph Edginton, Aylworth			
1878	Edginton Edwin	03/03/1872	Chas W Edginton, Naunton Inn			

1884	Edginton Frederick	16/01/1878	Joseph Edginton, Aylworth		
1878	Edginton Ivor E	13/08/1868	Chas W Edginton, Naunton Inn		
1878	Edginton Mabel B	25/08/1873	Chas W Edginton, Naunton Inn		
1899	Eeles Eva	02/04/1890	David Eeles, Naunton	Condicote	1903	To T Guiting
1899	Eeles Jennie	09/12/1891	David Eeles, Naunton	Condicote	1903	To T Guiting
1899	Eeles Robert	19/04/1895	David Eeles, Naunton	Condicote	1903	To T Guiting
1911	Elvin Lilian	28/08/1907	William Elvin, Naunton		1912	Gone to Stow
1876	Evans Sarah	?	William Glede, Near the Mill		1876	
1916	Eyles Dorothy Beatrice	26/05/1910	Fred'k Geo Eyles, Naunton		1918	Return to Reading
1882	Farley William	17/03/1875	William Farley, Harford Hill			
1876	Farmer Albert Geo	?	James Farmer, Harford		1881	
1877	Farmer Eunice Eliza	11/03/1874	James Farmer, Harford Hill		1877	
1873	Farmer Kate	8/03/1868	James Farmer, Harford		1877	
1876	Farmer Millie	?	James Farmer, Harford		1881	
1873	Farmer William	25/01/1870	James Farmer, Harford		1877	
1902	Fathers John	04/03/1891	Joshua Fathers, Naunton	Lower Swell	1904	Left for Notgrove
1902	Fathers Thomas	18/12/1893	Joshua Fathers, Naunton	Lower Swell	1904	Left for Notgrove
1876	Feebry Harry	27/04/1867	James Feebry, Aylworth		1877	
1876	Feebry Jessie	22/05/1871	James Feebry, Aylworth		1881	
1877	Finch Elizabeth	06/05/1869	Thomas Finch, Naunton		1877	
1877	Finch George	02/04/1872	Thomas Finch, Tally Ho	none	1877	
1877	Finch John	15/01/1870	Thomas Finch, Naunton		1877	
1877	Finch Sarah Jane	?	Thomas Finch, Naunton		1877	
1891	Fisher Bernard	04/02/1887	John Fisher, Cheltenham	Cheltenham		
1891	Fisher Harold	01/03/1885	John Fisher, Cheltenham	Cheltenham		
1885	Fletcher Alice Sophia	31/08/1881	Charles Fletcher, Naunton			
1896	Fletcher Chas Wm	09/12/1893	Thomas Fletcher, Naunton		1900	Left the village
1891	Fletcher Christopher	01/03/1888	Charles Fletcher, Naunton		1900	Exempt
1879	Fletcher E Eliz	27/09/1875	Joseph Fletcher, Naunton			
1899	Fletcher Ellen	26/11/1895	Charles Fletcher, Naunton		1903	Deceased
1900	Fletcher Elsie Agnes	15/09/1896	Thomas Fletcher, Naunton		1900	Left the village
1898	Fletcher Frank	19/11/1894	Thomas Fletcher, Naunton		1900	Left the village
1874	Fletcher Geo	06/03/1872	Joseph Fletcher, Naunton		1881	Killed by cart Nov 1882
1889	Fletcher George	27/12/1886	Charles Fletcher, Naunton			
1894	Fletcher Horace A	18/10/1890	Charles Fletcher, Naunton		1903	Exempt
1887	Fletcher Lizzie	08/01/1884	Charles Fletcher, Naunton		1895	
1896	Fletcher Marjorie E	05/05/1892	Charles Fletcher, Naunton		1906	Exempt

316 Naunton 2000

Appendix 8 (continued) Naunton National School Register Number One (1865 – 1923)

In	First & Surname	Birthday	Parent/Guardian/Address	Last School	Out	Remarks
1912	Fluck Alfred Hy	02/07/1907	Alfred Fluck, Naunton		1921	Exempt
1917	Fluck Winifred Ed'	11/08/1903	Edward(Mrs Alf' Fluck)Naunton		1917	Left for Notgrove
1907	Forth Lillian Ellen	27/06/1903	Eustace Bertram, Naunton		1917	Domestic Service
1919	Fox Cyril	17/02/1911	Ernest Fox, Naunton	Gt Barrington	1919	Left for Milton
1919	Fox Evelyn	24/12/1912	Ernest Fox, Naunton	Gt Barrington	1919	Left for Milton
1886	Freeman Ellen	05/04/1877	John Freeman, Westfield		1888	
1888	Freeman Fanny	21/07/1881	John Freeman, Westfield	Turkdean	1888	
1887	Freeman Fanny	21/07/1881	John Freeman, Westfield			
1886	Freeman Thos	22/08/1874	John Freeman, Westfield			
1878	French Jemima	27/041969	John French, Naunton	Tadmarton		
1884	Gardner Edith M	02/01/1880	Albert Gardner, Naunton			
1876	Gardner Emma	12/07/1864	George Gardner, Naunton	Highbury Chelt	1877	
1877	Gardner George Ed	04/02/1873	?			
1901	Gardner Hy Walter	14/04/1898	Walter Gardner, Naunton		1905	To Guiting
1880	Gardner Lambert	19/12/1876	Albert Gardner, Naunton		1888	
1919	Gleed Albert	31/05/1915	Frederik Gleed, Naunton		1929	Age
1893	Gleed Charles	07/03/1889	John Gleed, Naunton		1902	Exempt
1876	Gleed Frank	08/08/1869	Adam Gleed, Near the Church	this	1877	
1899	Gleed Frank	11/03/1896	John Gleed, Naunton		1909	Labour Certificate
1888	Gleed Fred William	23.01/1884	Adam Gleed, Near the Church			
1876	Gleed George	10/09/1867	John Gleed, Naunton		1877	
1889	Gleed Rosa	26/07/1885	John Gleed, Naunton			
1915	Gleed Wm Chas	30/04/1911	Fred'k Gleed, Naunton		1925	Age Exempt
1876	Goddard Jane	?	Adam Goddard, Gristfield		1876	
1876	Goddard Joseph	?	Adam Goddard, Gristfield		1876	
1872	Godfrey George	11/05/1865	William Godfrey, Naunton		1877	
1876	Godfrey Harry	31/12/1868	William Godfrey, Back Lane	none	1877	
1893	Godwin Edith	09/081883	John Godwin, Naunton	Sevenhampton	1894	
1879	Godwin Ellen	?	?			
1879	Godwin Enos	?	?			
1876	Grallon Mary	02/11/1869	John Grallon, Fox Hill		1877	
1893	Green Albert	15/01/1886	Thomas Green, Aylworth	Yanworth	1894	
1898	Green Albert	?	Thomas Green, Naunton	Kemerton	1898	Left the village

Naunton 2000   317

1898	Green Bessie	?	Thomas Green, Naunton	Kemerton	1898	Left the village
1898	Green Jesse	?	Thomas Green, Naunton	Kemerton	1898	Left the village
1893	Green Josia	15/12/1883	Thomas Green, Aylworth	Yanworth	1894	
1891	Green Morgan	?	? Green, Nosehill Farm			Left
1898	Green Rose	?	Thomas Green, Naunton	Kemerton	1898	Left the village
1877	Greenaway Eliza	11/03/1874	Thomas Greenaway, Harford Hill		1877	
1896	Greenaway Emily	02/10/1885	Thos Greenaway, Naunton Downs	Hawling		
1879	Greenaway Rebecca	23/06/1875	Thos Greenaway, Harford Hill		1879	
1888	Griffin Beatrice Ann	15/04/1876	Wm George Griffin, Naunton	Flyford Flavel	1889	
1888	Griffin Delia	23/05/1882	Wm George Griffin, Naunton	Flyford Flavel	1889	
1888	Griffin George Chas	26/12/1879	Wm George Griffin, Naunton	Flyford Flavel	1889	
1922	Griffin John	15/01/1918	Walter Griffin, Naunton		1924	Left for Cold Aston
1910	Griffin Phyllis	31/07/1907	Walter Griffin, Naunton		1920	Domestic Service
1916	Griffin Victor Tho	10/11/1913	Walter Griffin, Naunton		1924	Left for Cold Aston
1913	Griffin Wm Walter	30/05/1909	Walter Griffin, Naunton		1923	Left for work
1878	Groves Emily	27/06/1871	James Groves, Naunton Downs			
1877	Groves Frederick	04/04/1868	J Groves, Naunton Downs	this	1877	Left the village
1909	Guest Florence Clara	08/06/1904	Joseph Guest, Lower Harford		1911	Gone to service
1909	Guest Mary Frances	18/07/1896	Joseph Guest, Lower Harford	Didbrook	1910	Left district
1916	Habgood Hedley Edw'd	16/08/1908	Wm Habgood, Grange Hill		1918	
1882	Hailey Thomas	?	? Broderick, Nan House?		1893	
1916	Haines Albert Charles	02/08/1911	George Haines, Kineton Hill		1917	Left for Condicote
1912	Haines Annie B	21/04/1907	George Haines, Kineton Hill		1917	Left the village
1915	Haines Edith Kate	20/12/1909	George Haines, Kineton Hill		1917	Left the village
1903	Haines Florence	09/02/1899	George Haines, Kineton		1912	Gone to Service
1907	Haines Frank	22/03/1902	George Haines, Kineton		1915	Gone to work
1909	Haines Harold Geo	16/08/1903	George Haines, Kineton		1916	To work
1902	Haines Sarah Eliz	16/01/1897	George Haines, Kineton		1910	Gone to service
1888	Hall Charles	12/10/1876	Charles Hall, Lower Harford		1888	
1888	Hall Kate	14/03/1879	Charles Hall, Lower Harford		1888	
1888	Hall William	16/08/1884	Charles Hall, Lower Harford		1888	
1878	Hamblett Charlotte	22/09/1871	John Hamblett, Naunton			
1878	Hamblett Eliz A	12/02/1866	John Hamblett, Naunton	Notgrove		
1879	Hamblett Florence	?	?			
1878	Hamblett Sydney Jas	20/11/1868	John Hamblett, Naunton			
1875	Hamlett Mary	?	James hamlett, Naunton		1876	
1875	Hamlett William	?	James hamlett, Naunton		1876	

318 *Naunton 2000*

Appendix 8 (continued) Naunton National School Register Number One (1865 – 1923)

In	First & Surname	Birthday	Parent/Guardian/Address	Last School	Out	Remarks
1898	Hanks Augusta G F	25/03/1889	Thomas Hanks, Salperton	Salperton	1901	To Salperton School
1891	Hanks Beatrice E	14/02/1882	Wm Bullock Hanks, Naunton		1927	Northleach G. School
1887	Hanks Edgar	01/04/1881	William Wood Hanks, Aylworth		1899	Exempt
1921	Hanks Edward Leslie	17/01/1916	Horace L Hanks, Waterloo Fm		1927	Northleach G. School
1891	Hanks F Mary	13/12/1885	George Hanks, Naunton		1900	Exempt
1921	Hanks Geoffrey	28/07/1916	George Hanks, The Manor		1928	Cirencester G.S.
1887	Hanks George	11/07/1880	George Hanks, Naunton		1922	To Private School
1891	Hanks Gerald	04/03/1887	George Hanks, Naunton		1929	Northleach G. School
1922	Hanks Gordon	31/01/1915	Maurice Hanks, Naunton		1876	
1917	Hanks Gwyneth Eleanor	21/02/1912	George Hanks, Manor House	U Slaughter	1901	To Salperton School
1880	Hanks Harold C	16/03/1872	William Wood Hanks, Aylworth		1907	Exempt
1921	Hanks Harold Douglas	19/03/1917	Horace L Hanks, Waterloo Fm		1901	Exempt
1876	Hanks Harry	?	Ellen Hanks, Gristfield		1911	Private School Stow
1898	Hanks Henry Albert	30/03/1892	Thomas Hanks, Salperton	Salperton	1908	To Chelt-Private Sch
1896	Hanks Horace Leslie	18/10/1892	Wm Bullock Hanks, Naunton		1901	To Salperton School
1891	Hanks Hubert Rowland	30/10/1887	Wm Bullock Hanks, Naunton		1908	Middle Class, Chelt'
1902	Hanks Irene	26/10/1898	Wm Bullock Hanks, Manor Hse		1900	To Chelt-Private Sch
1898	Hanks Irene	11/03/1894	William Hanks, Naunton		1889	Exempt
1898	Hanks James Thos	15/12/1890	Thomas Hanks, Salperton	Salperton	1915	Taught at home
1880	Hanks John	10/10/1868	William Wood Hanks, Aylworth	1882	1894	
1898	Hanks Kathleen Hilda	11/03/1894	William Hanks, Naunton		1925	To Private School
1891	Hanks Mabel F	15/07/1886	Wm Bullock Hanks, Naunton		1882	
1883	Hanks Maurice	14/05/1877	Mr George Hanks, Naunton		1893	
1915	Hanks Maurice Gerald	23/05/1909	Maurice Hanks, Eyford		1901	Salperton School
1891	Hanks Muriel	22/10/1881	George Hanks, Naunton		1883	
1880	Hanks Muriel	28/03/1870	William Wood Hanks, Aylworth	1890	1883	
1883	Hanks Reg' Graham	22/12/1877	Wm Wood Hanks, Aylworth			
1922	Hanks Roger	17/06/1913	Maurice Hanks, Naunton	U Slaughter		
1891	Hanks Ruby A	20/01/1884	Wm Bullock Hanks, Naunton			
1880	Hanks William C	28/03/1870	William Wood Hanks, Aylworth			
1887	Hanks Willie	19/10/1880	Wm Bullock Hanks, Naunton			
1900	Hanks Winifred Maud	28/09/1894	Thomas Hanks, Salperton			
1876	Hansford Henry	?	Robert Hansford, The Huts			

1876	Hansford John	?	Robert Hansford, The Huts		1908	Left the village
1912	Hardiman Charles	23/02/1903	Frank Hardiman, Harford Hill		1916	Left the village
1914	Hardiman Florence Ed'	05/11/1908	Frank Hardiman, Harford Hill		1919	To Little Compton
1910	Harding Florence Maud	13/12/1902	Geo Harding, Naunton Downs	Lower Swell	1912	To Guiting
1898	Harris Albert Shotton	08/04/1895	James Harris, Naunton	Rissington	1877	
1876	Harris Alfred	31/07/1866	William Harris, Naunton		1877	
1889	Harris Amelia	24/10/1885	Jas Harris, Naunton		1890	
1870	Harris Annie	14/04/1866	Henry Harris, Naunton		1881	
1883	Harris Charles	20/11/11879	William Harris, Naunton		1894	
1876	Harris Clara	06/08/1872	Wm Harris, Naunton		1896	
1886	Harris Edith M	17/08/1882	Edwin Harris, Naunton		1890	
1889	Harris Eliz Florence	04/12/1884	Edwin Harris, Naunton		1911	Gone to service
1882	Harris Ellen	16/08/1878	Henry Harris, Naunton		1896	
1902	Harris Elsie May	06/01/1898	Henry Harris, Naunton		1902	Exempt
1889	Harris Emily	14/08/1884	Henry Harris, Naunton		1899	Left the village
1892	Harris Emily E	13/09/1888	James Harris, Naunton		1899	Left the village
1893	Harris Evelyn A	02/08/1889	Edwin Harris, Naunton		1906	Exempt
1891	Harris Frank	09/05/1887	Edwin Harris, Naunton		1881	
1895	Harris Geo Jas	03/12/1892	James Harris, Naunton		1899	Exempt
1878	Harris George	21/07/1874	Henry Harris, Naunton		1883	
1890	Harris Herbert	06/06/1887	Henry Harris, Naunton		1903	Exempt
1872	Harris Kate	19/02.1870	William Harris, Naunton		1877	
1892	Harris Leah R	29/08/1889	James Harris, Naunton		1879	
1877	Harris Lottie	25/02/1874	William Harris, Naunton		1900	Exempt
1873	Harris Mary	12/01/1867	Henry Harris, Naunton		1914	Left the village
1890	Harris Mary	29/04/1887	James Harris, Naunton		1888	
1914	Harris Norman Victor	24/05/1911	William Harris, Naunton		1886	
1885	Harris Oliver	01/10/1880	Henry Harris, Naunton	Upper Guiting	1877	
1879	Harris Rosa	04/06/1876	William Harris, Naunton		1914	Left the village
1886	Harris Tom	21/09/1873	Elizabeth East, Kineton		1914	Left the village
1871	Harris Walter	12/07/1868	William Harris, Naunton		1914	Left the village
1913	Harris Wm Hy Jas	23/04/1910	Wm Harris, Naunton	Bourton	1914	Left the village
1912	Harrison Evaline M	20/12/1907	George Harrison, Naunton	Bourton	1911	Gone to work
1911	Harrison Gladys	01/12/1905	George Harrison, Naunton	Condicote	1917	Left the village
1910	Harrison Violet	19/01/1902	George Harrison, Naunton			
1910	Harrison Wm Geo	23/02/1897	George Harrison, Naunton			
1915	Hart Phyllis	30/09/1907	Mrs Higgins, Naunton			

320 *Naunton 2000*

Appendix 8 (continued) Naunton National School Register Number One (1865 – 1923)

In	First & Surname	Birthday	Parent/Guardian/Address	Last School	Out	Remarks
1894	Harvey Alice	16/09/1882	Frank Harvey, Westfield		1889	
1886	Harvey Annie	22/08/1878	Wm Harvey, Naunton Downs		1889	
1886	Harvey Emma	01/09/1881	Wm Harvey, Naunton Downs		1889	
1886	Harvey Emma	25/07/1876	Frank Harvey, Westfield	Coln St Aldwins		
1884	Harvey Emma E	02/10/1879	Priscilla Harvey, Aylworth			
1885	Harvey Frederick	24/12/1875	William Harvey, Naunton Downs			
1889	Harvey Lucy	28/10/1884	Wm Harvey, Naunton Downs			
1882	Harvey Sarah Ann	25/07/1876	Priscilla Harvey, Aylworth			
1882	Harvey Thomas	07/07/1876	Priscilla Harvey, Aylworth			
1887	Harvey William	01/06/1883	Wm Harvey, The Downs			
1908	Hathaway Albert Hy	12/11/1899	George Hathaway, Naunton	Hasleton	1912	To work
1894	Hathaway Alfred W	25/02/1888	Alfred Hathaway, Summerhill	L Swell	1895	
1908	Hathaway Eva Matilda	13/01/1904	George Hathaway, Naunton	Hasleton	1917	Domestic Service
1894	Hathaway Frank Ed'	19/09/1890	Alfred Hathaway, Summerhill	L Swell	1889	
1908	Hathaway Lily Hilda M	29/12/1897	George Hathaway, Naunton	Sneedslad?	1911	To work
1888	Hathaway Mahay1	14/07/1880	Edward Hathaway, Aylworth	Sneedslad?	1889	
1908	Hathaway Margaret E	21/01/1902	George Hathaway, Naunton	L Swell	1915	Gone to service
1908	Hathaway Percy Victor	05/11/1895	George Hathaway, Naunton	L Swell	1908	To work
1888	Hathaway Wm	22/05/1878	Edward Hathaway, Aylworth			
1908	Hawker Emily Maud	13/07/1904	Wm Hawker, Naunton		1917	Domestic Service
1920	Hayward Joyce	14/06/1916	Tom Hayward, Black Horse		1927	Northleach Gr School
1891	Heath John	21/10/1882	Sarah Ann Heath, Naunton	Evesham	1899	Back to Evesham
1899	Hedges Albert	?	Mr Stratford, Naunton	Blockley Rd	1877	
1877	Hedges Algur	11/01/1870	Wm Henry Hedges, Naunton			
1897	Hedges Alice Mary	?	John Stratford, Summerhill	Evesham	1901	To Evesham
1901	Hedges Beatrice	16/09/1891	Mr Stratford, Naunton		1888	
1885	Hedges George	11/02/1882	?	Blockley Rd	1877	
1877	Hedges Matilda C	20/03/1864	Wm Henry Hedges, Naunton	Evesham	1906	To Evesham
1901	Hedges May Alice	?	Mr Stratford, Summerhill			
1904	Hedges William	15/03/1897	John Stratford, Summerhill	Evesham	1905	Back to Evesham
1880	Heels Mary Ellen	24/08/1870	Ann Heels, Naunton	Badsey Bd	1906	To T Guiting
1903	Hemming Flo' May	14/08/1893	Charles Hemming, Hill Barn	Slaughter		
1886	Hemming Fred	18/04/1875	Thos Hemming, Eyford	Badsey Bd	1904	To T Guiting

1902	Hemming Thomas	31/03/1890	Charles Hemming, Hill Barn	Badsey Bd	1906	To T Guiting
1902	Hemming William	06/07/1895	Charles Hemming, Hill Barn		1881	
1882	Hemmings Henry	16/06/1875	James Hemmings, Naunton		1881	
1882	Hemmings William	24/01/1874	Richard Good, Naunton			
1877	Henry Neal	?	John Mifflin, Naunton			
1914	Herbert Alec	31/05/1909	Mr Jas Hunt, Naunton	Condicote	1914	Back to Condicote
1910	Herbert Elsie	01/09/1904	John Wm Herbert, Roundhill		1910	Left the village
1908	Herbert Harry	01/05/1896	Jms Wm Herbert, Roundhill	Down Ampney	1910	To Condicote
1908	Herbert Maud	23/01/1903	Jms Wm Herbert, Roundhill	Down Ampney	1910	To Condicote
1908	Herbert Reginald Rob't	28/06/1898	Jms Wm Herbert, Roundhill	Down Ampney	1910	To Condicote
1912	Herbert William Geo	29/04/1903	William Herbert, Naunton	Cold Aston	1912	Back to Aston
1908	Herbert Winifred J	21/04/1900	Jms Wm Herbert, Roundhill	Down Ampney	1910	To Condicote
1915	Herbert Wm George	29/04/1903	Wm Herbert, Lower Harford	Cold Aston	1916	Gone to work
1879	Herman Eliza	13/05/1872	John Herman, Naunton	Slaughter		
1886	Herrer James Henry	21/12/1874	James Herrer, Eyford		1902	To Cutsdean
1902	Hickman Annie	20/02/1899	George Hickman, Naunton	Guiting	1902	To Cutsdean
1912	Hickman Frederick Ed'	06/09/1909	Wm John Hickman, Naunton		1913	Left the village
1910	Hickman Geo Edw'd	15/05/1907	Wm Tho, Naunton		1913	Left the village
1912	Hickman Harry	08/07/1908	Wm John Hickman, Naunton		1913	Left the village
1907	Hickman Ruth Mary	30/05/1897	William T Hickman, Naunton	Farmington	1911	Exempt
1901	Hickman Wm Jms	09/09/1897	George Hickman, Naunton			
1907	Hickman Wm Tho	15/12/1899	William T Hickman, Naunton	Farmington	1912	To work
1882	Hicks Annie	16/01/1873	John Hicks, Naunton			
1882	Hicks George	16/12/1876	John Hicks, Naunton			
1882	Hicks Jane	?	John Hicks, Naunton			
1920	Higginbottom Cath' M	15/02/1910	Alice Smith, Naunton	Leeds	1920	Return to Leeds
1884	Higgins Edith	09/03/1879	? Higgins, Naunton		1905	To L Guiting
1916	Higgins George	18/02/1911	Henry Higgins, Grange Hill		1925	Age
1904	Higgins James	21/12/1897	James Higgins, Naunton	Swell	1911	To Work
1922	Higgins Nellie	16/03/1918	Henry Higgins, Grange Hill		1925	Left for Bibury
1923	Hill Elsie	13/01/1919	Ernest Hill, Dale Streeet		1933	Age
1918	Hill Henry	02/08/1906	Wenel Hill, Fox Hill Inn	Oddington	1918	Return to Oddington
1908	Hobbs Alfred Walter	14/05/1905	Walter Geo Hobbs, Naunton		1918	Agricultural Exemption
1910	Hobbs Algernon Wm	18/05/1907	Walter Geo Hobbs, Naunton		1919	Gone to Slaughter
1901	Hobbs Dorothy Gladys	06/08/1898	William Hobbs, Naunton	Hawling	1900	To L Guiting
1917	Hobbs Edna Gwenith	22/08/1914	Walter Hobbs, Naunton		1918	Left for Slaughter
1899	Hobbs Herbert W	29/12/1888	William Hobbs, Naunton	Hawling	1904	To L Guiting

322 *Naunton 2000*

Appendix 8 (continued) Naunton National School Register Number One (1865 – 1923)

In	First & Surname	Birthday	Parent/Guardian/Address	Last School	Out	Remarks
1899	Hobbs Jane E	27/08/1890	William Hobbs, Naunton		1905	To Guiting
1903	Hobbs Mabel Lilian	25/09/1899	William Hobbs, Naunton		1905	To Guiting
1904	Hobbs Nelly	17/07/1901	Wm Hobbs, Naunton		1905	To Lower Guiting
1913	Hobbs Rhoda Ellen	10/01/1910	Walter Hobbs, Naunton	L Slaughter	1918	To Slaughter
1876	Holloway George	12/03/1865	William Holloway, Dale St		1876	
1876	Holtom Charles	?	?		1876	
1876	Holtom William	?	?			
1886	Hooper Edgar	03/03/1882	James Hooper, Naunton		1876	
1876	Hooper James	21/12/1864	Jane Wakefield, The Black Horse		1876	
1897	Hooper James Wynn	06/02/1894	James Hooper, Naunton		1897	
1888	Hooper Laura M J	02/09/1883	James Hooper, Naunton		1901	Exempt
1891	Hooper Reginald Fred	28/01/1888	James Hooper, Naunton		1902	Exempt
1892	Hooper Sydney J W	18/10/1889	James Hooper, Naunton	Condicote	1903	To Swell
1915	Hopkins Clara Eliz	15/09/1910	James Hopkins, Naunton Downs			To Salperton
1914	Hovard Albert Edw	06/05/1910	Geo Hy Hovard, L Harford	Left the village		
1913	Hovard Arthur Geo	05/10/1903	Geo Hy Hovard, L Harford	Hawling	1914	Left the village
1913	Hovard Edith Lydia A	21/05/1902	Geo Hy Hovard, L Harford	Hawling	1914	Left the village
1905	Hughes Archibald V	26/11/1895	Frederick Hughes, Huntsman	L Swell	1909	To work
1905	Hughes Dora Ellen	04/04/1897	Frederick Hughes, Huntsman	L Swell	1910	To Cold Aston
1902	Hughes Edith Annie	18/04/1890	Edward Hughes, Swell Wold	this	1876	
1876	Hughes Edward	13/07/1863	Charles Hughes, Nosehill Farm		1900	Left the village
1893	Hughes Edward	05/12/1888	Edward Hughes, Naunton		1891	
1905	Hughes Frederick Jas	09/04/1900	Frederick Hughes, Huntsman		1910	To work
1891	Hughes Gertrude	21/03/1886	Wm James, Summer Hill		1876	
1912	Hughes Gertrude Eliz	04/09/1907	Elizabeth Hughes, Naunton	Clapton	1913	Gone to Northleach
1914	Hughes Gertrude Eliz	04/09/1907	Mrs Midwinter, Naunton	Clapton	1914	To Northleach
1908	Hughes Ida Maud C	11/07/1902	Lambert Hughes, Naunton	Compton	1910	Left the village
1912	Hughes Ida Maud E	11/07/1902	Mrs Midwinter, Naunton	Northleach	1913	To Northleach
1876	Hughes Lambert	20/05/1870	George Hughes, New-town	Guiting	1902	Left the village
1908	Hughes Lucy Mary	12/11/1897	Mrs Midwinter (Grandmother)	Clapton	1911	Exempt
1908	Hughes Margaret Mary	28/08/1903	Hy Edward Hughes, Naunton		1916	Exempt
1905	Hughes May	05/11/1898	Frederick Hughes, Huntsman		1909	To Cold Aston
1901	Hughes Norah May	14/03/1893	Lambert Hughes, Naunton	Condicote	1903	To Swell

1908	Hughes Olive	06/03/1903	Fred'k Jas Hughes, Tally Ho	Cold Aston	1917	To Cheltenham
1902	Hughes Percival A	25/06/1891	Edward Hughes, Swell Wold	Condicote	1903	To Swell
1913	Hughes Phyllis	26/10/1908	Edward Hughes, Naunton		1922	Age Exemption
1902	Hughes Ruby May	21/08/1895	Edward Hughes, Swell Wold	Swell	1909	To Condicote
1908	Hughes Ruby May	21/08/1895	Hy Edward Hughes, Naunton	L Swell	1909	Exempt
1916	Hughes Victor	14/06/1910	Fred'k Hughes, Tally Hoo (sic)		1917	Left district
1905	Hughes Walter Ernest	16/05/1894	Frederick Hughes, Huntsman	L Swell	1908	To work
1917	Humphries Ivy	19/06/1911	Bertram Humphries, U Harford	Bristol	1917	Back to Bristol
1917	Humphries Lily	22/10/1905	Bertram Humphries, U Harford	Bristol	1917	Back to Bristol
1917	Humphries Ray	29/05/1912	Bertram Humphries, U Harford	Bristol	1917	Back to Bristol
1887	Hunt Albert	14/12/1875	James Hunt, Naunton		1902	Exempt
1891	Hunt Alice Mary	29/06/1887	James Hunt, Naunton			
1882	Hunt Bessie	07/05/1878	James Hunt, Naunton			
1884	Hunt Edith Emily	11/12/1880	James Hunt, Naunton		1881	
1876	Hunt Eliza	16/08/1872	Joseph Hunt, Spring Villas		1908	Exempt
1898	Hunt Ethel	10/06/1894	Joseph Hunt, Naunton		1901	Exempt
1890	Hunt Florence	02/11/1887	Joseph Hunt, Naunton		1905	Exempt
1894	Hunt Frank	22/06/1890	James Hunt, Naunton		1907	Exempt
1897	Hunt George	?	?		1877	
1867	Hunt Gertrude	28/08/1864	Henry Hunt, Naunton		1901	Exempt
1895	Hunt John Henry	17/05/1888	William Hunt, Naunton		1879	
1868	Hunt Kate	27/10/1866	Henry Hunt, Naunton		1877	
1877	Hunt Laura Emily	09/08/1874	Joseph Hunt, Naunton			
1882	Hunt Mary	19/10/1875	John Hunt, Naunton			
1880	Hunt Mary Eliz	17/03/1877	Joseph Hunt, Naunton			
1920	Hunt Mollie	10/01/1916	Miss Rose Hunt, Naunton		1930	Age
1884	Hunt Rosa Ellen	21/04/1881	Joseph Hunt, Naunton			
1921	Hunt Rose	13/11/1916	Frank Hunt, Naunton			
1882	Hunt William	18/07/1874	John Hunt, Naunton			
1888	Hunt William	21/11/1884	James Hunt, Naunton	Chester	1902	Back to Chester
1902	Hyde Thomas	?	Charles Fletcher, Naunton		1877	
1916	Iles Ada May	08/07/1911	Fred'k Slade, Aylworth	Winchcombe	1922	L Guiting
1916	Iles Florence Annie	03/10/1909	Fred'k Slade, Aylworth	Winchcombe	1922	L Guiting
1920	Iles Frank	19/06/1916	Frederick Iles, Aylworth		1922	To Lower Guiting
1916	Iles Fred'k Arthur	23/03/1908	Fred' Slade, Aylworth	Winchcombe	1921	Agriculture
1877	Iles Pollie	?	Joseph Iles, Naunton		1903	Exempt
1917	Iles Reginald John	13/08/1913	Ellen Iles, Naunton		1927	Age

324　Naunton 2000

Appendix 8 (continued) Naunton National School Register Number One (1865 – 1923)

In	First & Surname	Birthday	Parent/Guardian/Address	Last School	Out	Remarks
1916	Iles Reginald Tho	13/08/1913	Ellen Iles, Naunton		1916	Left the village
1918	Iles Winifred	05/03/1914	Fred'k Iles, Aylworth		1922	
1907	Ivins Alfred F	19/11/1896	George Ivins, Naunton	Trafalgar	1908	To Ford
1907	Ivins Elenour	16/07/1902	George Ivins, Naunton	Trafalgar	1908	To Ford
1907	Ivins Eliza	19/11/1904	George Ivins, Naunton	T Guiting	1908	To Ford
1907	Ivins Georgina May	27/07/1893	George Ivins, Naunton	Trafalgar	1908	To Ford
1907	Ivins Reginald J	24/06/1900	George Ivins, Naunton	Trafalgar	1908	To Ford
1907	Ivins Rob't Emmanuel	04/10/1898	George Ivins, Naunton	Trafalgar	1908	To Ford
1896	Jacobs William C	24/03/1890	George Locky, Hafrord Hill		1899	Exempt
1890	James Albert	09/07/1887	Charles James, Naunton			
1914	James Albert Chas	02/02/1911	Oliver James, Naunton		1921	Cheltenham G.Sch
1882	James Albert Ed	06/04/1877	George James, Back lane		1902	Left the village
1901	James Albert Geo	27/11/1896	George James, Naunton Downs	Upper Guiting	1896	
1882	James Alfred	12/01/1885	Thomas James, Naunton			
1920	James Arthur	04/04/1907	Ernest R James, Naunton	Bishops Cleeve	1921	Age
1904	James Charles	13/02/1892	George James (Guardian)	London	1904	Back to London
1882	James Charlie	08/03/1879	Thomas James, Naunton	Guiting	1894	
1909	James Cuthbert F J	22/10/1899	Frank Cuthbert, Tally Ho	L Guiting	1913	Gone to work
1920	James Doris	16/01/1916	Edward James, Naunton		1925	Left for Cold Aston
1923	James Dorothy	22/07/1918	Thomas James, Littlesworth		1932	Age
1923	James Dorothy	30/11/1918	Richard James, Tally Ho		1927	To Bibury
1893	James Edith	08/05/1888	David James, Naunton		1903	Exempt
1893	James Emily	20/08/1890	Charles James, Naunton			
1884	James Emma	10/06/1880	George James, Back lane		1894	
1885	James Etta	13/06/1882	Charles James, Naunton		1909	Exempt
1898	James Florence Eliz	05/07/1895	Charles James, Naunton			
1917	James Frances Grace	23/03/1914	Walter James, Naunton			
1872	James Frank	25/11/1867	George James, Naunton		1877	
1920	James Frank	31/03/1913	Ernest R James, Naunton	Bishops Cleeve	1927	Age exempt
1910	James Geo Wm	17/02/1901	Frank James, Tally Ho	L Guiting	1913	To Guiting
1886	James George	14/03/1883	George James, Back lane		1894	
1886	James George	26/09/1876	Thos James, Naunton Downs	Upper Guiting	1916	Left the village
1908	James George	27/10/1905	Wm James, Littlesworth			

1886	James Hannah	12/05/1881	Thos James, Naunton Downs		1898	Exempt
1916	James Hilda Florence	05/07/1913	Oliver James, Naunton		1927	Age
1921	James Ivor	10/02/1917	Thomas James, Naunton		1931	Age
1915	James Joan Louise	27/09/1912	Walter James, Naunton		1922	Age
1909	James Leslie Mark	21/11/1905	Mark James, Naunton		1918	Agriculture
1889	James Mark	05/10/1885	George James, Naunton			
1886	James Mary	22/02/1878	Thos James, Naunton Downs		1876	
1878	James Millie	04/08/1874	George James, Naunton		1890	
1876	James Minnie	?	Sarah James, Domino Lane			
1882	James Oliver Chas	22/02/1878	Charles James, Naunton		1900	Exempt
1891	James Raymond Thos	19/01/1888	George James, Back lane	Guiting	1894	Left for work
1912	James Reginald Walter	22/08/1909	Mark James, Littlesworth		1913	
1921	James Richard	26/02/1917	Oliver James, Naunton		1930	Age
1893	James Sarah A	25/03/1887	David James, Naunton	Upper Guiting	1895	
1882	James Thomas	06/04/1883	Thomas James, Naunton		1902	To Guiting
1902	James Vera R E	?	Geo' (Grandfather) Naunton		1889	
1912	James Vera R E	22/11/1898	Frank James, Tally Ho	Lower Guiting	1912	Exempt
1922	James Victor Stanley	26/08/1917	Beatrice James, Dale Street		1927	Left for Birdlip
1887	James Walter	19/07/1884	Charles James, Naunton		1894	
1920	James Walter	20/10/1909	Ernest R James, Naunton	Bishops Cleeve	1923	Age exempt
1894	James William	26/12/1890	David James, Naunton		1877	
1865	Jaques Fred	04/02/1905	Stephen Jaques, Naunton		1877	
1876	Jeffries Sarah	09/05/1873	? Jeffries, Naunton			
1884	Jennings Thomas	24/12/1874	John Jennings, Naunton			
1884	Jennings William	17/12/1878	John Jennings, Naunton		1892	Left the village
1892	Johnson Hilda	01/01/1889	Jesse Williams, Naunton	London		To America
1898	Johnson Hilda	21/12/1889	A visitor from London			
1878	Jones Arthur	11/02/1870	Thomas Jones, Tally Ho	Newport G.S.	1899	Back to Newport
1899	Jones Geoffrey L	09/05/1887	Mr Brown, Naunton		1895	
1892	Jones Walter	14/03/1883	Arthur Thomas Jones, Naunton		1893	Deceased
1908	Keen Blanche	24/07/1901	John Keen, Hill Barn	Oddington	1912	Left the village
1908	Keen Ciciley Alice	09/05/1904	John Keen, Hill Barn	Oddington	1912	Left the village
1911	Keen Dorothy Violet	21/04/1906	John Keen, Hill Barn		1912	Left the village
1908	Keen Marjorie M	12/09/1897	John Keen, Hill Barn	Oddington	1911	Left School 14yrs
1912	Kilbey Elsie E	01/08/1900	Walter Kilbey, Fox Hill Inn	Hawling	1914	Exempt
1912	Kilbey Hilda Emily	04/09/1902	Walter Kilbey, Fox Hill Inn	Hawling	1915	To Broadwell
1912	Kilbey, Walter Tho	06/12/1906	Walter Kilbey, Fox Hill Inn	Hawling	1915	To Broadwell

326　Naunton 2000

Appendix 8 (continued) Naunton National School Register Number One (1865 – 1923)

In	First & Surname	Birthday	Parent/Guardian/Address	Last School	Out	Remarks
1873	Kilby Alice	23/09/1867	Edward Kilby, Naunton		1883	
1875	Kilby Emily	16/08/1871	Edward Kilby, Naunton		1876	
1876	Kilby Gertie	?	William Kilby, Domino Lane		1876	
1876	Kilby Laura	?	William Kilby, Domino Lane			
1886	Kilby Sally	24/12/1874	Edward Kilby, Naunton			
1878	Kilby Sarah Ann	24/12/1874	Edward Kilby, Naunton			
1882	Kine Edith	07/03/1872	George Kine, Naunton		1877	
1921	King Henry	09/02/1911	Mrs Leworthy, Naunton	Cookham	1921	Back to Cookham Berks
1903	Kingston Violet	23/12/1896	Mr Privett, Naunton	London Bd	1903	To London
1876	Lainchbury Basil	06/04/1870	? Beecham, Sheepwell Lane		1876	
1909	Lambert Mary Selyva	15/10/1903	Alfred E Lambert, Littlesworth		1909	To Notgrove
1875	Large Augustas	14/07/1871	Richard Large, Near the Chapel		1876	
1876	Large Edward	24/01/1865	Richard Large, Chapel Hill		1876	
1876	Large Emily	30/01/1867	Richard Large, Chapel Hill	none	1877	
1876	Large Ernest	15/08/1874	Richard Large, Chapel Hill		1877	
1872	Large Frank	2/11/1869	Richard Large, Naunton		1900	Left the village
1900	Large Lily B	?	Raymond Large, Naunton	Salperton	1900	Left the village
1899	Large Margaret	18/05/1891	Raymond Large, Naunton	Salperton	1900	Left the village
1899	Large William	03/06/1891	Raymond Large, Naunton			
1885	Laurence Frank	16/09/1887	Lambert Laurence, Harford		1886	
1885	Laurence Frederick	15/09/1875	Lambert Laurence, Harford			
1885	Laurence Leah	22/12/1878	Lambert Laurence, Harford			
1914	Lawrence Edward	06/06/1908	Fred'k Lawrence, Naunton	Salperton	1915	Left the village
1914	Lawrence Fred'k Jesse	09/04/1905	Fred'k Lawrence, Naunton	Salperton	1915	Left the village
1914	Lawrence Irene	27/05/1903	Fred'k Lawrence, Naunton	Salperton	1915	Left the village
1886	Lawrence Jesse T	22/06/1880	Lambert Laurence, Harford		1896	
1894	Leach Chas Edward	31/08/1890	John Leach, Aylworth	Northleach	1896	
1894	Leach Jesse R	17/05/1887	John Leach, Aylworth		1896	
1896	Leach John	11/04/1892	John Leach, Aylworth	Brookthorpe	1896	
1896	Leach Lucy	06/04/1886	John Leach, Aylworth			
1885	Lewis A Bertie	26/09/1881	Thomas Lewis, Naunton		1909	Labour Certificate
1920	Lewis Basil	17/06/1916	Bert Lewis, The Yard		1924	Stow Workhouse
1899	Lewis Elsie May	03/01/1896	Thomas Lewis, Naunton		1901	Exempt

Naunton 2000   327

1892	Lewis George Ernest	23/07/1888	Thomas Lewis, Naunton	Birmingham	1890	Back to B'ham
1908	Lewis Hector George	04/11/1900	Joseph Hunt, Naunton		1908	
1885	Lewis I Thomas	20/02/1879	Thomas Lewis, Naunton		1896	Back to B'ham
1908	Lewis Laura A	19/06/1902	Joseph Hunt, Naunton	Birmingham	1908	Stow Workhouse
1917	Lewis Mary Kath' Eliz'	29/03/1914	Alfred Lewis, Naunton		1924	Exempt
1887	Lewis Minnie	03/07/1883	Thomas Lewis, Naunton		1904	
1895	Lewis Nellie M	30/07/1890	Thomas Lewis, Naunton		1896	Stow Union
1923	Lewis Wilfred	16/05/1919	Bert Lewis, The Yard		1924	
1889	Lewis William	25/01/1886	Thomas Lewis, Naunton		1896	
1919	Leworthy Elsie	12/06/1910	Fred'k Wm Leworthy, Naunton	Colesbourne	1924	Age
1920	Leworthy Ethel	20/10/1915	Fred Wm Leworthy		1927	fonet Ilfacante
1919	Leworthy Phyllis	25/07/1912	Fred'k Wm Leworthy, Naunton	Colesbourne	1926	Age
1896	Locke Alice Rose	26/12/1892	Henry Locke, Naunton	Snowshill		
1895	Locke Frederick	07/11/1888	Henry Locke, Naunton	Snowshill	1896	
1895	Locke George	02/12/1890	Henry Locke, Naunton	Snowshill	1896	
1895	Locke Mary	17/01/1887	Henry Locke, Naunton		1901	Left the village
1912	Locket Elizabeth	05/09/1902	Henry Lockey, Lower Harford	Hawling	1913	Gone to Eyford
1900	Lockey Blanche	07/11/1895	Denis Lockey		1901	To L Guiting
1904	Lockey Christopher Ed	15/05/1899	George Lockey, Harford Hill		1904	To Swell
1915	Lockey Edith	19/09/1909	Henry Lockey, Harford Hill	Hawling	1923	Age
1917	Lockey Ellen Kate	04/12/1912	Henry Lockey, Harford Hill		1926	Over age
1901	Lockey Esther L	28/03/1897	Denis Lockey, Naunton		1901	To Guiting
1897	Lockey Nora	04/09/1892	Dennis Lockey, Naunton		1904	To Swell
1902	Lockey Stanley	23/10/1896	George Lockey, Naunton		1901	To Guiting
1897	Lockey Susie	30/03/1894	Dennis Lockey, Naunton		1881	
1880	Locky Edward	02/08/1874	Edward Locky, Naunton		1879	
1878	Luckett Annie	30/05/1871	Ruben Luckett, Naunton		1879	
1878	Luckett Rosa	13/03/1873	Ruben Luckett, Naunton	U-Slaughter	1899	
1895	Mace Edith Amy	19/04/1890	George Buckle, Naunton		1879	
1904	Mace Percival Chas	26/04/1894	Wm Albert Mace, Notgrove Stn	Salperton	1907	To Leamington
1904	Mace Wm Albert	05/05/1892	Wm Albert Mace, Notgrove Stn	Birmingham	1907	To Leamington
1869	Maisey Millie	6/04/1867	Charles Maisey, Naunton	Sherborne	1900	Back to Birmingham
1899	Maisy Wm Arthur	10/07/1894	Mr F Bayliss, Naunton			
1904	Mallard Chas Haddon	04/09/1899	Joseph Geo Mallard, Aylworth		1911	To Swell
1890	Mallard George	08/07/1881	Joseph G Mallard, Westfield	Bourton	1908	Labour Certificate
1901	Mallard J Llewellyn	12/07/1896	Joseph Mallard, Aylworth		1898	
1907	Mallard Jas Arthur P	19/07/1903	Joseph Mallard, Aylworth		1911	To Swell

328 Naunton 2000

Appendix 8 (continued) Naunton National School Register Number One (1865 – 1923)

In	First & Surname	Birthday	Parent/Guardian/Address	Last School	Out	Remarks
1893	Mallard Joseph	26/05/1888	Joseph Mallard, Westfield	Sherborne	1896	
1890	Mallard Rose	01/07/1883	Joseph G Mallard, Westfield	Sherborne		
1890	Mallard Sarah	25/08/1878	Joseph G Mallard, Westfield		1876	
1891	Mallard Thomas	13/10/1885	Joseph G Mallard, Westfield		1876	
1875	Manning Angelina	?	Elizah Manning, Little London		1876	
1875	Manning Ellen	?	Elizah Manning, Little London		1876	
1876	Manning John	?	Elijah Manning, Little London		1876	
1875	Margetts George	?	Joseph Margetts, Naunton		1888	
1887	Marse Frank	04/11/1879	W W Hanks, Aylworth		1901	Left the village
1898	Martin Hannah M	07/11/1894	Benjamin Martin, Naunton		1901	Left the village
1891	Martin John	31/08/1887	Benjamin Martin, Naunton		1899	Left the village
1891	Martin Mabel	09/06/1887	Benjamin Martin, Naunton		1901	Left the village
1895	Martin Ruby B	17/05/1890	Benjamin Martin, Naunton		1876	
1913	Mason Barbara Alice	06/07/1908	Charles Harris Nosehill		1922	Exempt
1875	Mason Charles	17/02/1871	Elizabeth Mason, Naunton		1881	
1923	Mattock James	08/05/1919	Lucy Mattock, Chapel Hill	T Guiting	1933	Age
1878	Meadows Edwin	18/07/1872	Mr J Meadows, Summer Hill	B Sch, Moreton		Died Good Friday 1882
1877	Meadows Harry A	17/03/1869	Mr John Meadows, Summer Hill	B Sch, Moreton		
1877	Meadows Thomas	26/04/1870	Mr John Meadows, Summer Hill	B Sch, Moreton		
1877	Meadows William H	09/01/1867	Mr John Meadows, Summer Hill		1881	
1880	Merchant Henry John	02/01/1875	Henry Merchant, Aylworth			
1915	Merrell Beatrice M	24/01/1911	John Merrell, Naunton		1925	Age - Home
1887	Merrell John T	08/09/1874	John Merrell, Naunton		1891	
1887	Merrell Walter	15/03/1876	John Merrell, Naunton		1889	
1896	Mial Daisy	01/01/1893	John Smith, Naunton	Lower Guiting		
1888	Midwinter Alice M	30/03/1876	Wm Midwinter, Naunton	Lower Guiting		
1888	Midwinter Ida	23/06/1882	Wm Midwinter, Naunton	Lower Guiting		
1888	Midwinter Lucy	31/01/1880	Wm Midwinter, Naunton		1899	Exempt
1890	Midwinter Walter J	06/11/1885	Wm Midwinter, Naunton			
1888	Miffling Annie	24/10/1889	William Miffling, Roundhouse		1890	
1889	Miffling Caroline	26/03/1881	Wm Miffling, Roundhouse		1890	
1903	Miffling Harry	16/09/1898	Mrs Miffling (Grandmother)		1911	To work
1888	Miffling Mary Jane	02/02/1877	William Miffling, Roundhouse		1900	Left the village

1905	Miffling Wm	08/01/1901	Mrs Miffling (Grandmother)	1914	To work
1895	Miles Geoffrey H	29/07/1891	James Miles, Naunton	1900	Left the village
1897	Miles Hubert W J	01/08/1893	James Miles, Naunton		
1896	Millerson Frank	11/05/1891	Tom Midwinter, Naunton	1883	
1908	Mills Ada Harriet	25/01/1902	John Mills, Summerhill	Cold Aston	1909	To Notgrove
1908	Mills Annie C	07/07/1897	John Mills, Summerhill	Cold Aston	1909	To Notgrove
1908	Mills Ethelbert	08/07/1895	John Mills, Summerhill	Cold Aston	1908	To Notgrove
1908	Mills Henry	16/06/1900	John Mills, Summerhill	Cold Aston	1909	To Notgrove
1883	Mills Martha	21/04/1874	George Mills, Naunton		
1908	Mills Nellie	25/04/1904	John Mills, Summerhill		1909	To Notgrove
1896	Mitchell Margaret	13/08/1892	Joseph Mitchell, Naunton		
1915	Monk Edith Annie	23/08/1909	John Monk, Grange Hill	U Swell	1923	Domestic Service
1915	Monk Eliz' Grace	17/08/1907	John Monk, Grange Hill	U Swell	1920	Domestic Service
1915	Monk Florence	11/10/1910	John Monk, Grange Hill		1924	Age
1885	Morehouse Percy	22/07/1881	Wm Morehouse, Naunton	Cutsdean	1901	Exempt
1896	Morris Ellen	19/10/1888	John Morris, Naunton	Cutsdean	1899	Exempt
1896	Morris John Walter	19/05/1886	John Morris, Naunton		1908	Labour Certificate
1899	Morris Minnie Miriam	14/03/1895	John Morris, Naunton	Cutsdean	1906	Exempt
1922	Morris Reginald W	09/06/1918	Albert Morris, Naunton		1932	Age
1896	Morris Walter Chas	15/04/1892	John Morris, Naunton		
1880	Moulder Annie E	06/08/1870	Elija Moulder, Naunton		
1880	Moulder Christopher	13/02/1877	Elija Moulder, Naunton	Private Sch	
1878	Moulder Ernest	21/01/1869	Mr Elijah Moulder, Naunton		
1878	Moulder Florence F	16/07/1874	Mr Elijah Moulder, Naunton		
1880	Moulder Mary S	16/02/1872	Elija Moulder, Naunton		1892	
1907	Muller Bertha Lucy	28/07/1900	Mrs Smith, Naunton	London	1909	A home in London
1907	Muller Henry George	15/08/1901	Arthur Gardner, Naunton		1909	A home in London
1910	Muller Hy Geo	15/08/1901	Mrs Muller, Naunton	Swanley, L'don	1915	To work
1909	Muller Terence Arthur	17/09/1905	Mrs Muller, Naunton		1919	Left School 14yrs
1882	Munn Harry Jas	28/07/1887	Henry Munn, Naunton			
1884	Mustoe George W	11/07/1872	James Mustoe, Naunton			re admitted
1908	Mustoe Albert	19/09/1903	James Mustoe, Eyford	U Slaughter	1916	Horticultural Labourer
1889	Mustoe Emily	01/07/1882	James Mustoe, Naunton		1890	
1884	Mustoe Emily S	04/06/1877	James Mustoe, Naunton			Left
1885	Mustoe Minnie	01/07/1882	James Mustoe, Naunton		1920	Domestic Cook
1911	Mustoe Muriel Gert'	09/11/1906	James Mustoe, Eyford	U Slaughter		
1908	Mustoe Reuben	21/06/1901	James Mustoe, Eyford		1914	Horticultural Labourer

Naunton 2000 329

330   Naunton 2000

Appendix 8 (continued) Naunton National School Register Number One (1865 – 1923)

In	First & Surname	Birthday	Parent/Guardian/Address	Last School	Out	Remarks
1891	Mustoe Wm Thos	?	Henry Mustoe, Naunton		1877	
1876	Neal Henry	12/04/1868	? Neal, Naunton Hill		1877	
1876	Neal Sarah	13/11/1865	? Neal, Naunton Hill	Guiting		Left the village
1911	Niblett Alice Violet	30/06/1899	George Niblett, Summerhill	Lower Guiting	1912	To Guiting
1908	Norris Margaret Flo	10/02/1905	George Norris, Naunton		1908	To Lower Guiting
1907	Norris Thomas L	17/04/1899	George Norris, Naunton	Sevenhampton	1908	To Lower Guiting
1907	Norris Wm George	10/01/1901	George Norris, Naunton	Sevenhampton	1908	To Lower Guiting
1889	Palmer Dora	12/08/1883	Joseph Palmer, Naunton	Guiting		
1889	Palmer Frank	11/02/1881	Joseph Palmer, Naunton	Guiting		
1883	Palmer Joseph	22/09/1878	Joseph Palmer, Naunton Downs	Guiting		
1889	Palmer Lucy	18/05/1882	Joseph Palmer, Naunton	Guiting		
1889	Palmer Nellie	29/09/1884	Joseph Palmer, Naunton			
1891	Palmer Oliver	26/02/1887	Joseph Palmer, Naunton		1892	
1892	Palmer Oliver	26/02/1888	Joseph Palmer, Naunton			
1884	Palmer Sarah Ann	08/11/1879	Joseph Palmer, Naunton Downs			
1883	Palmer Walter	06/03/1875	Joseph Palmer, Naunton Downs			
1890	Palmer William	09/01/1886	Joseph Palmer, Naunton			
1919	Parker Cyril Bruce	23/05/1913	Mrs Parker, Ivy Cottage	Lower Swell	1920	Left for Cheltenham
1919	Parsons Albert	05/07/1911	Wm Tho Parsons, The Terrace	Farmington	1925	Age
1919	Parsons Charles	05/05/1915	Wm Tho Parsons, The Terrace		1929	Age
1919	Parsons Edith	15/07/1906	Wm Tho Parsons, The Terrace	Farmington	1918	Domestic Service
1919	Parsons Frederick	05/08/1907	Wm Tho Parsons, The Terrace	Farmington	1920	Agricultural Work
1919	Parsons George	13/09/1919	Wm Tho Parsons, The Terrace	Farmington	1923	Agricultural Work
1921	Parsons Vera	07/09/1916	William Parsons, Naunton		1930	Age
1922	Parsons Victor	18/04/1918	Wm John Parsons, Naunton		1932	Age
1919	Parsons Wm Tho	05/11/1912	Wm Tho Parsons, The Terrace	Farmington	1926	Agricultural Work
1878	Partlow Emma	31/08/1873	James Partlow, Naunton			
1878	Partlow James	27/01/1869	James Partlow, Naunton			
1879	Partlow Thomas	22/02/1875	James Partlow, Naunton			
1878	Partlow William	04/06/1871	James Partlow, Naunton	Sherborne Bd	1904	Left the village
1902	Pittaway Flo' Rose	19/12/1895	Horace Ed Pittaway, Naunton			
1917	Pawley Ethel Doris	30/09/1905	Florence Pawley, London	Tottenham Rd	1919	Moved to Stow
1917	Pawley Gladys Kate	18/02/1908	Florence Pawley, London	Tottenham Rd	1919	Moved to Stow

Naunton 2000   331

1917	Pawley Grace Louise	07/10/1910	Florence Pawley, London	Tottenham Rd	1919	Moved to Stow
1896	Pawley Kate	??/12/1891	Martha Hunt, Naunton	London Bd	1901	To London
1901	Pawley Kate Mary M	11/12/1890	Mrs Pawley, Naunton		1877	Moved to Stow
1917	Pawley Marjorie Ellen	01/11/1907	George Pawley, Naunton	London	1917	To Slaughter
1912	Peachey Harry	08/10/1901	John Peachey, Eyeford	Icomb	1912	To Slaughter
1912	Peachey Hubert	29/08/1899	John Peachey, Eyeford	Icomb	1912	
1872	Pembridge Ellen	29/10/1864	Annie M Pembridge, Naunton		1877	
1879	Perry Mortimer	?	Mr Reuben Perry, Notgrove			Visitor
1916	Petch Roland Samuel	19/04/1910	Mrs Petch (Visitor) Naunton	Smethwick	1916	
1876	Phillips Lily Maude	31/04/1871	William Phillips, Naunton			
1912	Piddington Gertrude A	23/12/1902	Mrs Iles (Aunt) Naunton	London	1912	Gone to London
1878	Pratley Francis	10/06/1868	David Pratley, Naunton			
1878	Pratley Laura	21/12/1866	David Pratley, Naunton			
1879	Pratley Mary Ann	16/06/1872	David Pratley, Naunton		1904	Exempt
1908	Preston Edith Eleanor	30/01/1904	? Hill Barn		1908	To Cold Aston
1920	Preston Percy	28/02/1911	Benjamin Preston, Harford Hill	U Slaughter	1924	Left for Sherborne
1920	Preston Phyllis	28/03/1915	Benjamin Preston, Harford Hill	U Slaughter	1924	Left for Sherborne
1920	Preston Reginald	28/09/1913	Benjamin Preston, Harford Hill	U Slaughter	1924	Left for Sherborne
1893	Privett Alice Priscilla	26/03/1890	William Privett, Naunton		1899	Exempt
1911	Privett Cecil	25/10/1907	Mrs Privett (Guardian)		1911	Left the village
1891	Privett J Frank	18/11/1887	William Privett, Naunton		1881	
1876	Puffit Eli	?	William Puffit, Sheepwell Lane		1876	
1875	Puffit Harban	?	William Puffit, Naunton	Gretton	1900	Back to Gretton
1900	Pulham Annie M	14/06/1888	Mrs Pulham, Naunton			
1878	Pulham Clara Jane	06/12/1868	William Ed Pullam (sic)		1906	Exempt
1878	Pulham Edward	17/07/1875	William Ed Pullam (sic)		1910	Labour Certificate
1896	Pulham Edward E	03/06/1893	William Pulham, Naunton		1921	
1899	Pulham Elen Eliz	05/09/1896	William Pulham, Naunton		1931	Age
1921	Pulham Ernest	16/10/1917	Edward Pulham, Naunton		1904	Exempt
1903	Pulham Florence Mary	23/04/1900	Wm Pulham, Naunton		1920	Agriculture
1909	Pulham Fred'k Bertram	22/04/1906	Wm Edw'd Pulham, Naunton		1915	To work
1905	Pulham John Wm	30/05/1902	Wm Edward Pulham, Naunton		1908	Left the village
1895	Pulham Lilian	09/09/1891	William Pulham, Naunton		1917	Left for home
1907	Pulham May Clara	18/05/1904	Wm Pulham, Naunton			
1898	Pulham Wilfred Wiltsh'	12/02/1895	William Pulham, Naunton			
1921	Pulham William	08/02/1911	Wm Ed' Pulham, Naunton	Broadwell	1925	Left - age
1878	Pulham William Ed	08/12/1866	William Ed Pullam (sic)		1879	

332 Naunton 2000

Appendix 8 (continued) Naunton National School Register Number One (1865 – 1923)

In	First & Surname	Birthday	Parent/Guardian/Address	Last School	Out	Remarks
1893	Smith Alice	09/02/1890	John Smith, Naunton	Coberley		
1892	Smith Amelia	18/02/1884	Thomas Smith, Naunton		1898	Left the village
1878	Smith Ann C	14/03/1872	George Smith, Naunton	Swainswick	1889	
1897	Smith Arthur	08/08/1894	Wm Jas Smith, School House		1927	Age
1916	Smith Cuthbert Hy	20/05/1913	Tom Smith, Naunton		1912	Exempt
1888	Smith Edith	20/05/1882	Sarah Smith, Naunton		1883	
1902	Smith Elsie Rebecca	26/08/1898	Abel Tom Smith, Huntsman's		1907	To T Guiting
1907	Smith Frances Marie C	15/08/1900	Mrs Lane, Church House		1877	
1876	Smith Frank	16/06/1873	Isaac Smith, Naunton		1881	Sent to Reformatory
1870	Smith Fred	9/11/1867	John Smith, Naunton		1898	Left the village
1882	Smith George	05/07/1874	Joseph Smith, Chapel Hill	Swainswick	1881	
1897	Smith Gertrude	16/02/1888	Wm Jas Smith, School House			
1882	Smith Harriet	08/09/1870	Joseph Smith, Naunton	Farmington	1883	
1889	Smith Harry	12/10/1882	Wm Smith, Naunton		1898	Left the village
1876	Smith Helen	06/07/1871	John Smith, Dale Terrace	Swainswick		
1897	Smith Horace E E	01/07/1889	Wm Jas Smith, School House		1924	Left for work
1913	Smith Ivy Caroline	18/02/1910	Abel Tom Smith, Naunton		1920	Service
1909	Smith Lily Francis	14/05/1906	Abel Tom Smith, Naunton			
1880	Smith Lydia	19/09/1874	George Smith, Naunton		1881	
1891	Smith Mabel	11/12/1887	John Smith, Naunton		1883	
1873	Smith Margaret	21/09/1869	John Smith Naunton		1914	Gone to service
1903	Smith Matilda A	26/08/1900	Tom Smith, Naunton		1933	Age
1873	Smith Millie	31/10/1866	Isaac Smith, Naunton		1894	
1923	Smith Monica	18/02/1919	Elsie Smith, North Street		1881	
1877	Smith Raymond	26/03/1868	?	Farmington	1876	
1879	Smith Thomas	02/08/1876	Joseph Smith, Naunton		1910	Work
1889	Smith Walter	28/03/1884	Wm Smith, Naunton		1877	
1882	Smith Walter J H	17/10/1872	John Smith, Naunton		1899	Left the village
1876	Smith William	30/03/1865	Joseph Smith, Chapel Hill		1883	
1900	Smith William	20/04/1896	Abel Tom Smith, Naunton			
1876	Smith Wm Raymond	26/03/1868	George Smith, Naunton	Modbury		
1896	Spanton Chas Graham	17/05/1885	Emery Spanton, Naunton	Modbury		
1896	Spanton Tom Hen'	08/12/1883	Emery Spanton, Naunton			

Naunton 2000   333

1914	Pulham Wm Edw	16/02/1911	Wm Pulham, Naunton		1920	To Broadwell
1870	Pullam Annie	31/07/1867	Daniel Pullam, Naunton		1876	
1876	Pullam Eliza	04/02/1905	William Pullam, 2 Mt Pleasant	Brenood Nat?	1877	
1878	Pullam Eliza Ellen	18/10/1871	William Pullam, Naunton		1879	
1868	Pullam Frank	27/07/1865	William Pullam, Naunton		1877	
1870	Pullam Fred	6/09/1867	William Pullam, Naunton			
1880	Pullam Mary Ann	20/10/1874	Daniel Pullam, Naunton	Swainswick	1898	Left the village
1897	Raymond Noel	26/12/1885	Wm Jas Smith, School House		1898	Left the village
1898	Reason Albert	?	John Reason, Naunton		1898	Left the village
1893	Reason Annie M	30/05/1890	John Reason, Naunton		1898	Left the village
1896	Reason Louisa	12/06/1892	John Reason, Naunton		1899	Left the village
1899	Risnell William	16/04/1894	Ivor Risnell, Nose Hill Farm		1881	
1882	Robertson Elsie Alice	08/01/1877	Sarah Ann Smith, Naunton		1889	
1887	Rogers Jane	13/10/1877	John Rogers, Naunton		1876	
1876	Rogers Mary	08/03/1871	George Rogers, Nr the Washpool	Turkdean	1896	
1895	Rogers Mary	06/09/1885	George Rogers, Westfield		1888	
1887	Ruck Austin	10/01/1878	Wm Ruck, Upper Slaughter			
1886	Ruck Eva	28/12/1879	James Ruck, Aylworth			
1914	Ruck Harold Jas	24/04/1903	William Ruck, Naunton	Charlton Kings	1914	To Cheltenham
1886	Ruck Sarah A	28/09/1876	James Ruck, Aylworth	Stow	1901	Private School Stow
1900	Sands Edith	09/11/1889	Mr Smith, Guiting	Chedworth	1902	Left the village
1901	Scotford Sophia Edith	14/02/1889	Wm Joseph Scotford, Naunton	Fifield		
1890	Shepherd Alice	27/07/1881	Joshua Shepherd, Aylworth	Fifield		
1890	Shepherd Harry	25/12/1884	Joshua Shepherd, Aylworth	Pershore		
1916	Slade Wm Rob't	25/03/1905	Fred'k Slade, Aylworth	Winchcombe	1918	Agriculture
1891	Smart Amy	28/07/1887	Charlie Smart, Aylworth	Pershore	1895	
1891	Smart Annie	16/01/1884	Charlie Smart, Aylworth		1902	Left the village
1895	Smart Edward C	11/10/1891	Charles Smart, Grange Hill		1902	Left the village
1899	Smart Isaac Fred Nelson	28/03/1895	Charles Smart, Grange Hill Farm		1902	Exempt
1892	Smart James	27/12/1888	?	Pershore	1899	Left the village
1898	Smart Minnie	01/01/1886	Charles Smart, Grange Hill		1909	Exempt
1898	Smart Nelson	28/03/1895	Charles Smart, Naunton		1902	Work at home
1902	Smart Ruby	03/03/1897	Charles Smart, Grange Hill Farm			
1877	Smith A Tom	03/02/1871	George Smith, Naunton		1894	
1890	Smith Agnes	13/09/1887	William Smith, Naunton		1904	Exempt
1917	Smith Alfred	01/04/1906	Fred'k Cook, Summerhill	Birmingham	1917	Return to B'ham
1893	Smith Alice	27/11/1889	Wm Smith, Naunton			

Appendix 8 (continued) Naunton National School Register Number One (1865 – 1923)

In	First & Surname	Birthday	Parent/Guardian/Address	Last School	Out	Remarks
1890	Sparrow Alfred Robert	05/02/1884	John Hooper, Naunton			
1882	Spencer Eliz	01/11/1869	Daniel Spencer, Naunton Inn		1883	
1883	Spencer Ernest John	22/04/1879	Daniel Spencer, Naunton Inn		1883	
1882	Spencer Kate	28/05/1874	Daniel Spencer, Naunton Inn		1883	
1882	Spencer William	07/09/1876	Daniel Spencer, Naunton Inn		1877	
1871	Stait Annie	2/11/1867	Fred Stait, Naunton		1881	
1874	Stait Fred	14/01/1871	Fred Stait, Naunton		1877	
1872	Stait Mary	17/05/1869	Fred Stait, Naunton			
1886	Staite Alice	20/07/1882	Fred Staite, Naunton		1888	
1888	Staite Ellen	16/06/1884	Fred Staite, Lower Harford		1906	Exempt
1896	Staite Frank	31/05/1893	Ann Staite, Naunton		1888	
1882	Staite George	10/02/1877	Fred Staite, Naunton			
1877	Staite Jane	22/02/1873	Fred Staite, Naunton			
1878	Staite William	17/02/1875	Fred Stait, Naunton	Liverpool Bd	1903	To Liverpool
1910	Staite William	15/02/1903	William Staite, Naunton	Bolsover	1911	Gone to India
1904	Stanley Minnie	?	Joseph Stanley, Naunton		1905	Left the village
1902	Stant Ernest	05/09/1893	Hy Bedwell, Naunton	Liverpool Bd	1908	Back to Liverpool
1901	Stant Rosie May	13/11/1895	Charles L Stant, Naunton	Liverpool Bd	1908	Back to Liverpool
1905	Stanton Dorothy Esth'	19/03/1899	Elizabeth Stanton, The Square	London	1906	Back to London
1910	Steptoe Doris L Emily	09/04/1902	Mrs Collins, Naunton	Brit: Chelt	1910	Gone to Cheltenham
1918	Steptoe Freda C	20/11/1905	Collins, Naunton	Dunalley St	1918	Return to Chelt
1910	Stickley Edith Fanny	13/07/1901	Miss Pulham, Naunton	Lower Swell	1910	To Lower Swell
1914	Stratford Albert Jas B	19/04/1911	Ellen Stratford, Naunton			
1896	Stratford Bertie	27/03/1893	John Stratford, Naunton	Charlton Kings	1906	Exempt
1900	Stratford Bertie	20/03/1893	John Stratford, Naunton	Bd School	1901	Exempt
1915	Stratford Cora Christina	25/03/1912	Wm Stratford, Naunton		1926	Age
1909	Stratford Daisy Elen'	22/12/1904	John Stratford, Naunton		1918	Age Exemption
1920	Stratford Evelyn	12/09/1915	William Stratford, Naunton		1929	Age
1900	Stratford George Wm	27/12/1888	John Stratford, Naunton		1900	Exempt
1920	Stratford Joseph	25/05/1914	John Stratford (Grandfather)		1928	Age
1917	Stratford Joseph Wm E	25/05/1914	John (Grandfather) Naunton	Sully, Barry	1919	Left for Barry
1922	Stratford Leslie	10/03/1911	Thomas Higgins, Grange Hill	Ampney	1925	Left for work
1895	Stratford Nellie	10/10/1889	John Stratford, Naunton		1895	

1919	Stratford Stanley	11/05/1915	Hy Higgins, Grange Hill		1925	Left for Bibury
1894	Stratman Cecil M	16/02/1890	Wm Stratman, Naunton			
1888	Stratman Daisy P H	28/10/1883	W Stratman, Naunton			
1893	Stratman Ethel May	15/01/1889	Wm Stratman, Naunton			
1882	Stratman Harold W	20/06/1876	W Stratman, Naunton			
1886	Stratman Wilfred W	12/06/1880	W Stratman, Naunton	Moreton British		
1888	Strong Robert Wm	06/11/1877	Richard Strong, Moteron			
1882	Styles Frank	12/06/1876	? Styles, Naunton		1888	
1887	Styles Frank	17/06/1884	Ezekiah Styles, Naunton		1888	
1887	Styles Fred	22/07/1882	Ezekiah Styles, Naunton		1888	
1887	Tame Annie	14/05/1880	George Hy Tame, Aylworth		1888	
1887	Tame Emily Maria	20/03/1879	George Hy Tame, Aylworth		1888	
1887	Tame George Henry	03/10/1881	George Hy Tame, Aylworth		1888	
1887	Tame Wm Thomas	14/06/1887	George Hy Tame, Aylworth	Hawling	1905	To L Guiting
1900	Tandy John	19/04/1891	Wm Hobbs, Naunton	none	1877	
1876	Taylor Edith	06/08/1873	Charles Taylor, Chapel Hill		1877	
1870	Taylor George	28/07/1867	Charles Taylor, Naunton			
1878	Taylor George	28/07/1867	Charles Taylor, Naunton	Guiting	1902	Back to L Guiting
1910	Temple Arthur	03/05/1899	Joseph Temple, Grange Hill		1912	To work
1910	Temple Geo Ernest	15/03/1901	Joseph Temple, Grange Hill		1914	To work
1923	Temple Harold	15/04/1919	Albert Temple, The Yard		1933	Age
1910	Temple Henry Victor	20/05/1897	Joseph Temple, Grange Hill	L Guiting	1911	To work
1921	Temple Vera	20/02/1917	Albert Temple, Naunton		1931	Age
1900	Thiele Cart Wm Emil	28/09/1890	Henry Dyer, Guiting	London Bd	1902	To Guiting
1900	Thiele Irene	08/11/1891	Henry Dyer, Guiting			
1888	Thornton William	12/09/1879	Harry Bayliss, Naunton			
1921	Thynne John	12/08/1916	Arthur V Thynne, The Manse	Br'n City Ferry	1929	Left for London
1920	Thynne Margaret	23/12/1912	Arthur V Thynne, The Manse	Br'n City Ferry	1924	Left for London
1920	Thynne Theodora	19/06/1914	Arthur V Thynne, The Manse	Br'n City Ferry	1924	Left for London
1912	Tibbetts Jms Thos	13/01/1905	Edward Tibbetts, Upper Harford	Farmington	1913	Left the village
1912	Tibbetts Lizzie A M	06/09/1907	Edward Tibbetts, Upper Harford		1913	Left the village
1909	Tibbetts Wm Edw'd	21/05/1903	Mrs Midwinter, Naunton	Lechlade	1910	Left the village
1912	Tibbetts Wm Edw'd	20/05/1903	Edward Tibbetts, Upper Harford	Farmington	1913	Left the village
1886	Timbrell Harry	06/06/1880	John Timbrell, Harford Hill			
1880	Timbrell James	16/02/1874	Thos Timbrell, Naunton			
1887	Timbrell Jas	16/06/1873	John Timbrell, Harford Hill		1899	Left the village
1896	Timbrell John	04/04/1891	John Timbrell, Naunton Downs			

Naunton 2000   335

336   Naunton 2000

Appendix 8 (continued) Naunton National School Register Number One (1865 – 1923)

In	First & Surname	Birthday	Parent/Guardian/Address	Last School	Out	Remarks
1884	Timbrell Richard	27/07/1878	Jms Timbrell, Naunton			
1891	Timbrell Richard	27/07/1880	John Timbrell, Harford Hill			
1880	Timbrell Thos W	16/06/1873	John Timbrell, Harford Hill			
1888	Timbrell William	??/01/1882	John Timbrell, Harford Hill			
1916	Timms Cyril Merrell	07/05/1911	Fred'k Jas Timms, Naunton		1925	Age
1914	Timms Decima Lucy	04/12/1910	Charles Timms, Aylworth	Cold Aston	1917	Left the village
1908	Timms Dorothy Fanny	25/10/1902	George Timms, Fox Hill Inn		1912	Left the village
1914	Timms Eric John	17/04/1908	Charles Timms, Aylworth	Cold Aston	1917	Left the village
1909	Timms Hubert George	15/08/1904	George Timms, Foxhill Inn		1912	Gone to Cheltenham
1914	Timms Ivy Annie	24/06/1903	Charles Timms, Aylworth	Cold Aston	1917	Exempt
1908	Timms Jms Thomas	23/04/1904	Fred'k Timms, Naunton		1918	Grocery Assistant
1914	Timms Maud Alice	26/08/1901	Charles Timms, Aylworth	Cold Aston	1915	Gone to service
1912	Timms Oscar Herbert	10/01/1908	Fredk Timms, Littlesworth		1922	Exempt
1880	Tims Adaline Mary	09/11/1876	John Tims, Naunton		1877	
1873	Tims Alban	22/10/1869	William Tims, Naunton			
1884	Tims Alberta	20/10/1879	Jesse Tims, Naunton			Deceased
1878	Tims Anne E S	02/05/1875	John Tims, Naunton			
1880	Tims Cuthbert	13/08/1872	William Tims, Tally Ho			
1882	Tims Eliz A	28/02/1879	John Tims, Naunton			
1884	Tims Florie	31/12/1880	John Tims, Naunton		1876	
1867	Tims Frank	16/10/1864	Ann Tims, Naunton			
1880	Tims George	28/03/1871	William Tims, Tally Ho		1881	
1874	Tims John	18/11/1870	William Tims, Naunton		1883	
1880	Tims Leonard	29/06/1875	William Tims, Tally Ho		1881	
1876	Tims Lucy	22/04/1873	William Tims, Jaques Lane	Guiting	1877	
1877	Tite Elizabeth	02/05/1867	William Tite, Tally Ho		1877	
1877	Tite Walter	06/08/1871	William Tite, Tally Ho		1876	
1866	Townsen Thirza	5/10/1863	Thomas Townsen, Newtown			
1880	Townsend Alice	?	?			
1888	Townsend Annie	31/10/1884	John Townsend, Naunton		1902	
1892	Townsend Arthur	24/06/1889	John Townsend, Naunton			Exempt

Naunton 2000   337

1904	Townsend Cecil Geo	?	James Townsend (Grandfather)	Swindon	Back to Swindon
1894	Townsend Cuthbert F	09/12/1891	John Townsend, Naunton		
1885	Townsend Dulcie	13/03/1882	John Townsend, Naunton		
1875	Townsend Edward	12/05/1872	James Townsend, Naunton		
1875	Townsend Elizabeth	19/05/1872	John Townsend, Naunton		
1879	Townsend Elizabeth	26/08/1873	Henry Townsend, Naunton		To Cold Aston
1901	Townsend Elsie Alice	04/02/1898	Reuben Townsend, Naunton		
1882	Townsend Emily M	17/07/1878	John Townsend, Naunton		Exempt
1890	Townsend Ethel	30/03/1887	John Townsend, Naunton		
1910	Townsend Fred Sidney	24/01/1907	Ethel Townsend, Naunton		Agricultural Work
1871	Townsend Geo	5/03/1869	James Townsend, Naunton		
1870	Townsend Henry	27/07/1867	James Townsend, Naunton	Broadway	
1877	Townsend Jane	17/02/1867	John Townsend, Naunton		To Cold Aston
1921	Townsend John	19/05/1916	Cuthbert Townsend, Naunton		Left for Sevenhampton
1903	Townsend Nelly M	06/04/1900	Reuben Townsend, Naunton		
1916	Townsend Percy Fr	06/09/1911	Cuthbert Townsend, Naunton	this	To Sevenhampton
1914	Townsend Percy N	06/09/1911	Cuthbert Townsend, Naunton		Distance - too far
1876	Townsend Priscilla	?	Joseph Townsend, New-town		
1877	Townsend Ruben	12/02/1874	Tho Townsend, Naunton		
1874	Townsend S A	18/05/1870	John Townsend, Naunton		
1879	Townsend William	20/01/1876	John Townsend, Naunton		
1914	Tracey Dorothy Maud	24/01/1906	James S Tracey, Huntsman	Churchdown	Left for Puckham
1914	Tracey Fred'k James	12/05/1908	James S Tracey, Huntsman	Churchdown	Left fro Puckham
1917	Tracey Kathleen Mary	13/03/1912	James S Tracey, Huntsman		Left for Puckham
1894	Tranter Ellen	20/02/1884	George Townsend, Naunton	Clapton	
1879	Tye Alice	?	John Tye, Naunton		
1914	Tye Edith Alice	27/06/1901	R Buckham, Naunton	Moreton-in-M	To Moreton
1879	Tye Mary Jane	?	John Tye, Naunton		Left the village
1896	Waine Albert James	28/05/1891	Jas E Waine, Roundhill		
1887	Waine Alice	29/11/1879	James Waine, Roundhill		Exempt
1891	Waine Edith Jane	23/01/1886	James C Wain, Roundhill		
1896	Waine Frank	07/12/1887	James E Wain, Roundhill	Miss Dunsfords	
1888	Waine John Edwin	31/10/1883	James C Wain, Roundhill		
1880	Waine Kate Sus	18/05/1875	James Waine, Naunton		Exempt
1893	Waine Lucy	19/07/1888	James E Wain, Roundhill		

338 Naunton 2000

Appendix 8 (continued) Naunton National School Register Number One (1865 – 1923)

In	First & Surname	Birthday	Parent/Guardian/Address	Last School	Out	Remarks
1893	Waite Florence E E	17/09/1888	Fred'k Waite, Summerhill		1881	
1876	Wakefield M J	?	Hannah Harvey, Little London		1889	
1905	Walters Alec	05/11/1893	Joseph Walters, Naunton	Blockley	1905	To Notgrove
1905	Walters Beatrice	07/02/1897	Joseph Walters, Naunton	G Power	1905	To Notgrove
1889	Webb Emma	18/07/1877	George Webb, Naunton Inn	G Power	1889	
1889	Webb Ethel	16/09/1882	George Webb, Naunton Inn	Blockley	1889	
1888	Webb Frederick	24/05/1880	Geo Wm Webb, Naunton Inn		1889	
1889	Webb Geo Henry	20/03/1876	George Webb, Naunton Inn		1879	
1878	Webley Alice	16/10/1869	Thomas Webley, Naunton	Bristol	1876	
1876	Wescott George	?	Thomas Wescott. The Hutts	Bristol	1876	
1876	Wescott Richard	??/01/1867	Thomas Wescott. The Hutts		1876	
1876	Wescott Thomas	?	Thomas Wescott. The Hutts		1883	
1918	Wheatley Eileen D	25/01/1913	Wm Wheatley, The Manse		1918	Taught by father
1917	Wheeler Daisy Idris	03/12/1907	Charles Wheeler, Naunton	Duckington	1919	Left for Whittington
1917	Wheeler Doris Evelyn	13/05/1905	Charles Wheeler, Naunton	Duckington	1918	Domestic Service
1917	Wheeler Dorothy Ivy	24/04/1911	Charles Wheeler, Naunton	Duckington	1919	Left for Whittington
1919	Wheeler Stanley	11/05/1915	Charles Wheeler, Naunton		1919	Left for Whittington
1917	Wheeler Violet Con'	20/06/1913	Charles Wheeler, Naunton		1919	Left for Whittington
1883	White Rt Rowland	23/02/1879	A M White, Naunton		1881	
1876	Whitfield Willie	09.08/1872	George James, Back lane	Stow	1901	Left the village
1908	Wiggins Florence	17/11/1901	Frank Wiggins, Roundhill		1908	Left the village
1900	Wiggins Harriett M H	28/04/1892	Richard Wiggins, Naunton		1901	Left the village
1901	Wiggins Herbert	31/03/1898	Richard Wiggins, Naunton	Stow	1901	Left the village
1900	Wiggins Sydney	06/03/1896	Richard Wiggins, Naunton		1876	
1908	Wilks Joseph Truby	24/03/1903	Joseph Wilks, The Yard		1917	Exempt
1873	Williams Arthur	?	Thomas Williams, Naunton		1881	
1880	Williams Edith	18/12/1874	David Williams, Aylworth		1879	
1869	Williams Eliza	23/03/1867	Charles Williams, Naunton			
1877	Williams Emma	23/02/1871	David Williams, Aylworth		1903	
1894	Williams Ernest Chas	27/12/1889	Richard Williams, Naunton		1876	
1873	Williams Florence	?	Thomas Williams, Naunton		1899	Exempt

1890	Williams George	22/10/1885	Richard Williams, Naunton		1881
1874	Williams Lionel	?	Thomas Williams, Naunton		
1885	Williams Louisa	17/08/1880	David Williams, Harford Hill		
1877	Williams Mary A	02/11/1866	David Williams, Aylworth		
1878	Williams Matthew	12/04/1870	David Williams, Aylworth		1908	Exempt
1898	Williams Minnie	14/12/1893	Richard Williams, Naunton		
1887	Williams Nellie	24/05/1883	Richard Williams, Naunton		
1885	Williams Percy F	17/11/1881	Richard Williams, Naunton		1877
1865	Williams Priscilla	6/11/1862	Charles Williams, Naunton		1889
1917	Williams Stanley	29/05/1909	John Williams, Fox Hill	Dunsford	1918	Returned home
1884	Willis Agnes	25/01/1877	John Willis, Naunton		
1891	Willis Alice	31/12/1886	John Willis, Hill Barn		1910	To work
1902	Willis Arthur Wm	02/06/1897	John Willis, Naunton Downs		1909	Labour Certificate
1899	Willis Edith Mary	04/01/1895	John Willis, Hill Barn		
1886	Willis Elen	21/05/1887	John Willis, Naunton		1903
1884	Willis Eliza	25/07/1879	John Willis, Naunton		1895
1895	Willis Ernest J	11/10/1890	John Willis, Naunton		1907	Gone to service
1905	Willis Flo Kate	03/06/1893	John Hunt, Naunton Downs		1904	Exempt
1887	Willis George	13/03/1883	John Willis, Hill Barn		1896
1898	Willis Kate	02/06/1894	John Willis, Hill Farm		1888
1889	Willis Robert	03/02/1885	John Willis, Hill Barn		1931	Age
1922	Willis Ronald	29/11/1917	Robert Willis, Naunton		1910	Gone to service
1884	Willis Sarah	20/05/1875	John Willis, Naunton		1881
1900	Willis Winifred May	07/10/1896	John Willis, Hill Barn		
1874	Withers Albert	28/08/1871	Samuel Withers, Naunton		1876
1878	Withers Ernest Ed	08/04/1873	Samuel Withers, Naunton		
1871	Withers Harry	2/01/1869	Samuel Withers, Naunton		1888
1884	Withers Nellie	08/06/1881	Samuel Withers, Naunton		1910	Left the village
1910	Wooler John Wm	24/01/1906	Arthur Wooler, Naunton Downs		1876
1887	World Annie	24/09/1882	John World, Harford		
1875	World Eliza	18/10/1869	John World, Harford		1876
1878	World George	08/01/1875	John World, Harford		1888
1875	World Jane	10/03/1867	John World, Harford		
1887	World John	01/07/1877	John World, Harford		
1877	World Mary	09/05/1872	?		

340 *Naunton 2000*

Appendix 8 (continued) Naunton National School Register Number One (1865 – 1923)

In	First & Surname	Birthday	Parent/Guardian/Address	Last School	Out	Remarks
1888	World Sarah A	08/07/1884	William World, Naunton		1876	
1875	World William	?	John World, Harford			
1886	Wragg Ada	02/03/1882	George Wragg, Naunton		1893	
1891	Wragg Florence	09/07/1887	George Wragg, Naunton		1893	
1893	Wragg Mabel	26/10/1889	George Wragg, Naunton		1893	
1887	Wragg Walter	10/10/1883	George Wragg, Naunton		1882	
1920	Wright Donald	01/10/1916	Wm Pill, Naunton		1927	Left for Bibury
1923	Wright Dora	28/01/1919	Blance Wright, Ivy Cottage		1927	Left for Bibury
1923	Young Barbara	05/05/1919	Charles Young, The Bakery		1925	Left for Northleach
1922	Young Noah	16/05/1917	Charles Young, The Bakery		1925	Left for Northleach

Naunton Primary School, 1958

Left to right, back row: Robin Muller, Hilary Flanagan, Myra Bond, Mrs. Horton, John Parker, Valerie Flanagan.

Front row: Paul Staite, Joy Muller, Janet Hunt, Monica Lockey, Patricia Hanks, Valerie Jones, Mary Lockey, David Hanks.

Appendix 9

Naunton National School Register Number Two, 1924 - 1969

The actual entries in the registers were recorded in chronological under the pupil's name
To facilitate your search the pupils have been presented in alphabetical order.

In	Christian & Surname	Birthday	Parent/Guardian & Address	Last School	Out	Remarks
1949	Abram Martin	12/02/1942	Graham Abram, The Mill House	Pinner, Middx	1949	Left for Campden G.S.
1949	Abram Stella	07/04/1939	Graham Abram, The Mill House	Pinner, Middx	1949	Left for Campden G.S.
1943	Alcock Elizabeth Anne	10/03/1938	William Alcock, Yew Tree Cottage		1948	Northleach G.S.
1929	Alcock John	06/09/1924	William Alcock, Naunton		1938	Over age
1959	Alcock Linda	19/01/1955	Naunton			
1961	Arkell Nicholas	06/05/1955	Sheepwell Cottage			
1926	Aston Margaret	08/07/1922	Frank Aston, Sunny Row	Rhodesia	1929	Left for Northleach
1954	Atkin Hilary	11/02/1947	Cecil Henry Atkin, 2 Spring Ctgs	Sleaford Lincs	1955	Gone to RAF Little Rissington
1939	Bartlett Daphne	18/11/1930	Church Square		1940	To Cold Aston
1939	Bartlett Evelyn May	04/04/1926	Church Square		1940	Over age
1926	Bartlett John	06/01/1922	Reginald Bartlett, Chapel Hill		1933	Awarded free place Northleach G.S.
1939	Bartlett Kenneth	25/08/1934	Reginald Davis, Hillside		1949	Left for work
1939	Bartlett Pamela	25/06/1927	Church Square		1940	To Cold Aston
1939	Bartlett William	23/11/1929	Church Square		1940	To Cold Aston
1925	Bateman Betty	27/04/1912	Fred'k Bateman, Kineton Thorns	U Slaughter	1926	Over age
1926	Bateman Winifred	31/01/1921	Fred'k Bateman, Kineton Thorns		1934	Over age
1945	Bayliss Alan Frederick	21/09/1940	Horace Bayliss, Sunny Cottages		1947	Transferred to Bourton
1944	Bayliss Patricia	14/12/1938	Horace Bayliss, Sunny Cottages		1945	Over age
1947	Bayliss Peggy	08/10/1942	Horace Bayliss, Parker's Cottage		1954	Transferred to Bourton
1958	Bayliss Sheila G	28/09/1951	Mrs Harker, Spring Cottage			
1958	Bayliss Stephen J	15/05/1953	Mrs Harker, Spring Cottage			
1933	Beames Alan Edward	05/01/1930	Frank Beames, Maida Vale, North St		1943	To work
1966	Beames Beverley Carolanne	14/03/1962	Lionel Beames, Naunton			
1931	Beames Ernest	19/09/1918	Peter Beames, Windrush Row	Ashington	1933	Northleach G.S. (awarded free place)
1943	Beames Ivy	20/07/1938	Frank Beames, North Street		1950	Special Place Award Northleach G.S.
1931	Beames Lionel Frank	02/06/1927	Frank Beames, The Lane	Longlevens	1932	Gone to Cheddar
1965	Beames Malcolm	23/04/1960	Lionel Beames, Elm Tree Ctg			To Bourton Primary

342 Naunton 2000

Appendix 9 (continued) Naunton National School Register Number Two, 1924 - 1969

In	Christian & Surname	Birthday	Parent/Guardian & Address	Last School	Out	Remarks
1941	Beard Dorothy	17/08/1928	C/o Mrs Dean, Harford	Broughton Green	1941	Returned to Broughton Green
1941	Beard Margaret	03/01/1932	C/o Mrs Dean, Harford	Broughton Green	1941	Returned to Broughton Green
1946	Bedwell Robert	27/02/1932	Harford	Bourton	1946	Over age
1946	Bedwell Sidney	15/06/1934	Harford		1946	Left for Tewkesbury
1928	Benfield Claude Edwin	21/09/1923	Wm Charles Benfield, Dale Street		1937	Over age
1932	Benfield Dennis Mervyn	17/06/1928	Mervyn Benfield, Dale Street		1937	Over age
1929	Bennett Alice May	23/06/1920	Arthur Bennett, Lower Harford	Kelmscott Oxon	1929	Left for Cold Aston
1929	Bennett Dorothy Gladys L	12/07/1917	Arthur Bennett, Lower Harford	Kelmscott Oxon	1929	Left for Cold Aston
1929	Bennett Margaret Gwend'	15/09/1918	Arthur Bennett, Lower Harford	Kelmscott Oxon	1929	Left for Cold Aston
1931	Bibby Ruth Shirley	09/07/1925	Wm Ashcroft Bibby, El Hogar	Charlton Kings	1931	To Charlton Kings
1939	Bissell Margaret	14/06/1934	Henry Bissell, The Post Office	Birmingham	1939	Returned home
1926	Blackwell Albert	10/11/1913	Albert Jas Blackwell, Roundhill	Bisley	1927	Left for Northleach District
1926	Blackwell Alfred	26/08/1915	Albert Jas Blackwell, Roundhill	Bisley	1927	Left for Northleach District
1926	Blackwell Edna	15/01/1920	Albert Jas Blackwell, Roundhill	Bisley	1927	Left for Northleach District
1926	Blackwell Rose	07/10/1917	Albert Jas Blackwell, Roundhill	Bisley	1927	Left for Northleach District
1926	Bloodworth Betty	12/07/1920	Percy Bloodworth, The Bakery		1929	Private School, Stow
1959	Bloxham Matthew	20/05/1954	The Old Mill			
1959	Bloxham Sefton	26/04/1952	The Old Mill			
1930	Bolter Denys Perry	02/03/1925	Fred'k Bolter, Lower Harford Fm		1932	To Whichford, Warwicks
1959	Bond Alan John	01/04/1954	Kenneth Bond, The Square			
1952	Bond Myra Kathryn	22/06/1947	Kenneth Bond, Cherry Cottage		1958	Transferred to Bourton
1928	Bosworth Brenda Eliz'	07/10/1921	Walter Storey Bosworth, Chalk Hill	Chapel Brampton	1928	Left for Chapel Brampton
1927	Bosworth Mabel	03/09/1915	Walter Storey Bosworth, Chalk Hill	Colesbourne	1929	Age 14
1940	Brooksbank Josephine	27/06/1933	C/o Mrs Roberts, Cherry Cottage		1940	Returned to London
1948	Butterworth Rosaline	17/12/1942	Charles E Butterworth, Lower Harford		1948	Left for Cheltenham
1961	Cambridge Margaret	05/11/1952	The Caravan, Naunton	Harlow		
1924	Carter Dorothy	21/03/1912	George Carter, Roundhill	Churchill C	1925	Over age
1924	Carter Harold	23/03/1914	George Carter, Roundhill	Churchill C	1925	To Condicote
1924	Carter Percy	21/03/1916	George Carter, Roundhill	Churchill C	1925	To Condicote
1925	Clifford Pamela	11/01/1921	William Clifford, The Yard		1926	Cold Aston School
1942	Cole Victor	12/10/1937	Fred'k Kear, El Hogar	St Pauls, Chelt	1943	Returned to Cheltenham
1949	Collett Richard Truby	13/10/1943	Joseph Collett, Dale Terrace		1955	Transferred to Bourton
1938	Collicutt Evelyn May	18/07/1926	Edgar W Collicutt, The Square	Bourton	1940	Over age

1938	Collicutt Miriam Joyce	04/10/1929	Edgar W Collicutt, The Square	U Slaughter	1943	Over age. Employment
1940	Collins Patricia	27/04/1930	The Forge, Naunton	Acton	1940	Return to London
1935	Cooper John Percy	16/04/1926	? Cooper, Roundhills(*sic*) Naunton		1937	Left the district
1939	Cooper Kenneth	23/01/1929	?	Finchley	1940	Evacuee - returned to London
1935	Cooper Leslie Walter	25/02/1923	? Cooper, Roundhills(*sic*)Naunton	Andoversford	1936	Attending Aldsworth
1949	Cotterell Kathleen May	22/06/1939	Wm Cotterell, 2 Council Houses	Deerhurst	1949	Left district
1949	Cotterell Mary Elizabeth	18/10/1943	Wm Cotterell, 2 Council Houses	Deerhurst	1949	Left district
1957	Cove Christine Lois	17/02/1952	Herbert J Cove, Grange Hill			
1965	Cowle John Brian	30/12/1957	Fred'k Cowle, Upper Harford			
1966	Cowle Richard Andrew	21/06/1961	Fred'k Cowle, Upper Harford			
1924	Cox Frederick	05/04/1915	Mrs Taylor, Aylworth Cottages	Bristol, St Giles	1925	Left for Bibury
1941	Cox Joan	12/09/1927	George Cox, Aylworth	Berkeley	1941	Over age
1941	Coxhead Doreen	21/07/1933	Douglas Coxhead, Aylworth	Ham, Stone	1943	Left for Eyford
1943	Coxhead Shirley	25/12/1937	Douglas Coxhead, Aylworth		1943	Left for Eyford
1941	Crayden Betty	26/08/1930	Dale Street		1944	
1944	Crayden Doreen Marian	24/10/1939	Dale Street		1945	Returned to London
1941	Crayden John	22/10/1932	Dale Street		1945	
1941	Crayden Roy	13/11/1934	Dale Street		1945	
1945	Crellin Alex	31/03/1939	El Hogar	Charlton Kings	1950	Special Place Award Northleach G.S.
1948	Crellin Edward Henry	27/04/1943	Tom Crellin, Meadow Vale		1954	Transferred to Bourton
1945	Crellin Winifred	21/10/1937	El Hogar	Charlton Kings	1951	Transferred to Bourton
1940	Cumming Charles	02/09/1933	Charles Cumming, Aylworth	Wootton	1943	To Blagdon, Somerset
1940	Cumming Helen	09/07/1932	Charles Cumming, Aylworth	Wootton	1943	To Blagdon, Somerset
1940	Cumming Marian	29/05/1935	Charles Cumming, Aylworth	Wootton	1943	To Blagdon, Somerset
1966	Cumming Michael Ian	21/02/1956	Ronald Cumming, 1 Harford Ctgs	Moreton		
1966	Cumming Paul	?	Ronald Cumming, 1 Harford Ctgs			
1966	Cumming Wendy	?	Ronald Cumming, 1 Harford Ctgs			
1942	Cummings James Gray	06/08/1937	Charles Cummings, Aylworth		1943	To Blagden, Somerset
1956	Curtis Christopher	18/07/1951	Joseph Curtis, 1 Mill View			
1955	Curtis David Royston	02/04/1950	Joseph Curtis, 1 Mill View			
1963	Curtis Graham	28/02/1958	Joseph Curtis, Aylworth			
1957	Curtis Valerie Jean	07/08/1952	Joseph Curtis, 1 Mill View			
1940	Daniels Ronald	07/05/1932	Horace Daniels, Dale Street	Fulham	1941	Gone to Liverpool
1939	Davis Doreen	18/04/1935	Raymond G Davis, Church Square		1950	Left for work
1926	Davis Kathleen	16/10/1921	Mrs Ruby Davis, Parker's House		1928	Cheltenham
1939	Davis Kathleen	18/07/1929	Raymond G Davis, Church Square	Cold Aston	1943	Over age
1947	Davis Maureen	11/12/1941	Raymond Davis, The Yard		1954	Transferred to Bourton

Naunton 2000 343

344   *Naunton 2000*

Appendix 9 (continued) Naunton National School Register Number Two, 1924 - 1969

In	Christian & Surname	Birthday	Parent/Guardian & Address	Last School	Out	Remarks
1952	Davis Pauline	06/02/1944	John Stanley, Grange Hill	Plymouth	1955	Transferred to Bourton
1926	Dawson Betty	04/02/1916	Mrs E Hughes, The Huntsman	Lowestoft	1927	Left for Lowestoft
1940	Dawson Kenneth	?	C/o Mrs Merrell	Private	1940	Gone to Canada
1932	Dean Albert James	28/05/1920	Henry Dean, Lower Harford		1937	To Gotherington
1939	Dean Amy	15/08/1934	Ethel Dean, Church Square		1947	Arts & Crafts Sch, Cheltenham
1928	Dean Arthur	19/12/1924	William Fletcher, The Yard		1938	Over age
1935	Dean Beryl Margaret	10/01/1931	Henry Dean, Lower Harford	Naunton Pk Chelt	1942	To Wormington, Worcs
1937	Dean Freddie	30/04/1933	Violet Dean, Harford		1948	Left for work
1932	Dean Frederick Thomas	27/08/1927	Henry Dean, Lower Harford		1941	Over age
1932	Dean George Henry	24/03/1923	Henry Dean, Lower Harford		1939	Left to Bourton
1932	Dean Jeffrey Francis W	15/07/1928	Edith Dean, Roundhill Cottages		1932	Left the district
1940	Dean Margaret	25/08/1935	Ethel Dean, Church Square		1950	Left for work
1924	Dean Violet	04/11/1914	Wm John Dean, The Yard		1928	Over age
1963	Dearman Mandy Jacqueline	02/07/1958	William Dearman, 1 Mill View	Donnington	1969	
1957	Dearman Roger	27/02/1952	William Dearman, Naunton		1963	Northleach G.S.
1953	Duncan Rodney	13/07/1944	The Quadrangle	Hull, Yorks	1953	Moved to Scotland
1929	Dunn Cyril	30/11/1920	Albert Dunn, Grange Hill	Bousfield L.C.C.	1929	Left for London
1969	Edwards Jill	02/04/1963	Doreen Edwards, 4 Windrush View			
1969	Edwards Nicola	14/09/1960	Doreen Edwards, 4 Windrush View			
1946	Evans Margaret	17/05/1938	Walter R Evans, Church Farm	Oakridge Lynch	1946	Official Evacuee, now resident.
1946	Evans Richard John	25/11/1933	Walter R Evans, Church Farm	Oakridge Lynch	1946	Left the village
1956	Ferris David	27/04/1951	Robert W Ferris, The Manse			
1959	Ferris Margaret	11/01/1955	Robert W Ferris, The Manse			
1937	Field Geoffrey	22/05/1928	Lionel Field, Chalk Hill	Stanford Bridge	1937	Returned home
1927	Finlay Barbara	29/08/1920	Mrs Hathaway, Naunton	Neath	1927	Gone to Gloucester
1940	Fisher Daphne Margaret	11/03/1935	Arthur James, The Quadrangle	LCC	1942	Evacuee - returned to London
1940	Fisher Donald James	05/01/1933	Arthur James, The Quadrangle	LCC	1942	Evacuee - returned to London
1932	Fisher Ernest Albert	22/10/1927	Frank Reeves, Dale Street		1932	To Charlton Kings
1946	Fisher Joan Peggy	18/02/1936	Ernest G Fisher, Farm Cottages	Alcester	1947	Left for Dorchester, Oxon
1951	Flanagan Hilary	05/08/1946	Matthew Flanagan, The Stores, Dale St			
1953	Flanagan Valerie	14/01/1948	Matthew Flanagan, The Gables		1959	Transferred to Bourton
1928	Fletcher Charles John	07/04/1923	George Fletcher, Dale Street		1934	
1928	Fletcher Mary Isabelle	21/12/1924	Mrs Ellen Fletcher, Sunnyside		1936	Northleach G.S. (free place)

1951	Forsyth Miranda	02/09/1946	Alistair Forsyth, Church House	Salop	1951	Now living at Prestbury
1944	Freeman Graham	?	Miss Read, Sunny Cottages		1944	Returned to Cheltenham
1944	Freeman Jennifer	?	Miss Read, Sunny Cottages		1944	Returned to Cheltenham
1937	Freeman Kenneth	?	?		1937	Returned home
1937	Freeman Pamela	09/12/1930	? Freeman, Brookdale		1938	Returned home
1945	Fulham Fred'k Roger	31/07/1940	Fred B Fulham, Wayside	New Market	1947	Transferred to Bourton
1960	Gardiner Andrew	22/06/1954	Wm Gardiner, The Manse			
1964	Gardiner Joy	08/10/1959	Wm Gardiner, The Manse			
1943	Gardner Irene	29/01/1930	Robert J Gardner, The Yard	Stow	1944	Over age
1943	Gardner Peter	10/10/1931	Robert J Gardner, The Yard	Stow	1945	Over age
1947	Gay Barbara Rose	06/11/1939	Henry Gay, Sunny Cottages	Northleach CofE	1951	Left for Gt Rissington
1947	Gay Henry Lewis	18/06/1936	Henry Gay, Sunny Cottages	Northleach CofE	1950	Transferred to Bourton
1926	Gilbert Percy	10/01/1922	Fred'k Gilbert, Hill Barn		1936	Over age
1926	Gleed Audrey	23/02/1922	Frank Gleed, Naunton		1932	Left for Guiting
1947	Gleed Beryl	02/02/1942	William Gleed, Littlesworth		1954	Transferred to Bourton
1933	Gleed Denis	14/05/1929	Frank Gleed, School Cottages		1943	Over age
1943	Gleed Joan Margaret	22/10/1938	William Gleed, Littlesworth		1952	Transfer to Bourton
1924	Gleed Reginald John	05/04/1919			1925	Over age
1963	Goodall Robin	23/01/1955	The Square		1953	
1953	Gorganus Linda Lee	07/06/1947	Spring Cottages		1947	To Convent School, Cheltenham
1942	Gorman Marjorie	22/02/1937	William Gorman, The Bakery			
1959	Grant Kathleen	04/12/1954	Thomas Grant, The Square			
1956	Grant Keith Thomas	04/05/1950	Henry Grant, Spring Ctgs			
1958	Grant Shirley	?	? The Yard, Naunton			
1940	Greaves Thos Wm Fred'k	08/11/1928	Black Horse Cottages	Birmingham	1942	Evacuee - Returned home
1958	Grey Amanda Mary	23/01/1950	Sir Ralph Grey, Overbrook	Nigeria		
1938	Groves Aldwyn John	31/08/1932	? Groves, Naunton	Salperton	1938	Returned home
1967	Groves April Margaret	07/04/1962	John Wm Groves, Aylworth			
1967	Groves Michael John	14/08/1958	John Wm Groves, Aylworth	G Power		
1929	Habgood Peggy Barton	09/02/1924	Wm Habgood, Grange Hill Farm		1934	Left for Guiting
1946	Hanks Anthony	01/04/1941	Maurice G Hanks, Northfield		1948	Private School at Stow
1925	Hanks Brian George	09/09/1920	Maurice Hanks, Longford		1932	Cirencester G.S.
1924	Hanks Daphne	20/10/1919	George Hanks, Manor Farm		1927	Private School, Stow
1953	Hanks David	31/05/1948	Harold Hanks, 2 Council Houses		1959	Transferred to Bourton
1936	Hanks Doreen	08/12/1931	Horace Leslie Hanks, Waterloo		1941	Left for Northleach G.S.
1961	Hanks Ian	19/01/1957	John Hanks, Brookfield			
1956	Hanks Jacqueline	21/12/1951	Brian Hanks, Longford		1968	Transferred to Bourton

346 *Naunton 2000*

Appendix 9 (continued) Naunton National School Register Number Two, 1924 - 1969

In	Christian & Surname	Birthday	Parent/Guardian & Address	Last School	Out	Remarks
1961	Hanks Janet	02/03/1957	Harold Hanks, 2 Mill View		1968	Transferred to Bourton
1929	Hanks John Aubrey	22/10/1924	Horace Hanks, Waterloo		1938	Over age
1963	Hanks Nigel	11/11/1958	Harold Hanks, 2 Mill View		1969	To Bourton Primary
1955	Hanks Patricia Hilda	18/07/1950	Harold Hanks, 2 Mill View		1961	Northleach G.S.
1960	Hanks Rachel	01/03/1956	Brian Hanks, Longford			
1964	Hanks Sandra	12/12/1959	John Hanks, Brookfield		1969	To Bourton Primary
1958	Hanks Susan	24/04/1953	Harold Hanks, 2 Mill View		1964	Transferred to Bourton
1925	Hanks Violet Kathleen	26/11/1921	Horace Hanks, Waterloo		1932	Awarded half place Northleach G.S.
1933	Hannam Ronald	31/08/1925	Percy Hannam, Dale Terrace	Shipton	1934	To Cheltenham G.S.
1960	Harker David	18/01/1956	Philip Harker, Spring Cottage			
1968	Harker Deborah	28/04/1958	Mill View	Bovington		
1955	Harkness Yvonne	25/06/1950	Harold Harkness, Dale Street			
1963	Harper Deborah	28/11/1958	Mill View			
1929	Harris Harold George	11/02/1925	Herbert Harris, The Lane		1939	Over age
1925	Harris Irene	30/11/1920	Herbert Harris, North Street		1934	Over age
1937	Harris Roy Cecil	30/01/1930	Cecil Harris, El Hogar	Portsmouth	1940	Return to Portsmouth
1930	Harrison Arthur Thomas	15/04/1921	William Harrison, Roundhill	Kingsholme	1930	Return to Gloucester
1941	Hart Brian	?/10/1929	Dale Cottage	Bristol	1938	Official Evacuee - left for work
1941	Hart Murray	12/08/1927	Dale Cottage	Bristol		Official Evacuee - returned home
1941	Hart Shirley	09/11/1933	Dale Cottage	Bristol		Official Evacuee - returned home
1929	Harwood Kenneth Jms	07/08/1924	Roy Harwood, Ash Tree Cottage		1938	Over age
1926	Hathaway Betty	11/06/1922	Frank Hathaway, Sunny Row		1934	Left for Cold Aston
1929	Hathaway Gerald	17/10/1925	Frank Hathaway, Sunny Cottages		1934	Left for Cold Aston
1925	Hathaway Reginald	18/10/1920	Frank Hathaway, Naunton		1931	Scholarship to Northleach G.S.
1932	Hathaway Sheila Doris Ann	07/02/1928	Frank Hathaway, Washpool Cottages		1932	Left the district
1926	Hawker Cecil	14/04/1920	Mrs Gleed, Naunton		1934	Over age
1927	Hawker Kathleen	14/04/1922	Mrs Gleed, Naunton		1936	Over age
1929	Hayward Ian	20/12/1925	Victor Hayward, Windrush Villa	Birmingham	1936	Northleach Sec School (free place)
1931	Hayward Ralph	01/04/1927	Victor Hayward, Ash Tree House		1934	Left district
1938	Haywood Rosemary	14/10/1933	George Haywood, Cromwell House	Holy Apostles	1939	Gone to Cheltenham
1934	Herbert Dennis George	14/06/1929	William Herbert, Ash Tree Cottage		1943	Over age
1933	Herbert Robert William	26/12/1927	William Herbert, Ash Tree Cottage		1941	Over age
1968	Herbert Theresa	18/11/1963	Robert Herbert, Ash Tree Cottage		1969	To Bourton Primary

Naunton 2000 347

1956	Herring David	16/08/1950	John Herring, Overbrook			Left for Cirencester
1956	Herring Robert	13/07/1950	Mr Herring, The Mill			Left for London
1929	Heyden Joyce	16/06/1924	Wm Heyden, Lower Harford		1929	Left for Cheltenham
1930	Higgins Edward Russell	15/06/1925	John Higgins, Dale Terrace		1939	Over age
1932	Hill Betty	07/03/1928	Ernest Hill, Dale Terrace	T Guiting	1934	Over age
1944	Hill David	13/07/1939	Ernest Hill, The Terrace		1952	Transfer to Bourton
1926	Hill Doris	28/12/1920	Ernest Hill, Dale Street		1934	Over age
1927	Hill Vera Winifred	09/06/1917	Mrs Miles, Fox Hill	Oddington	1928	Return to Oddington
1933	Hill William John	26/04/1929	Ernest Hill, Dale Street		1943	Over age
1959	Hopkins Pamela Joyce	09/03/1951	Harold Hopkins, Grange Hill			
1939	Howard Donald	12/11/1930	Cherry Cottage	London	1942	Cheltenham Central Sch.
1956	Howard Janette Anne	13/08/1950	Michael F Howard, Naunton	Ombersley		Returned to Droitwich
1938	Howard Michael Fred'k	04/09/1927	Mrs Bedwell, Holmleigh	London	1938	Returned home
1956	Howard Stephen Michael	13/01/1949	Michael F Howard, Naunton	Ombersley		Returned to Droitwich
1940	Hudson Joan	12/04/1928	C/o Miss Duester, Grange Hill	Liverpool	1941	Gone to Sussex
1953	Hughes Christine	15/02/1948	Betty Hughes, Mount Pleasant		1954	Left village
1929	Hughes Grace Mary	24/02/1924	Percy Hughes, Oxford Villa	Brockhampton	1932	Gone to Lechlade
1943	Hughes Joyce Mabel	30/07/1931	Joseph Hughes, Ash Tree Cottage	Oare, Wilts	1944	Left for Wokingham
1928	Hughes Norman John	16/11/1922	Charles Edward Hughes, Huntsmans Fm	Co Sch, Stroud	1936	Over age
1943	Hughes Sybil Ida	27/11/1933	Joseph Hughes, Ash Tree Cottage	Oare, Wilts	1944	Special Place Northleach G.S.
1955	Hunt Janet	04/04/1950	Leslie Hunt, Littlesworth			
1924	Hunt Walter George	07/01/1920	Frank Hunt, The Yard, Naunton		1928	Left for Cheltenham
1950	James Ann	15/07/1945	Arthur James, Littlesworth	G Power		
1948	James Derrick	14/10/1942	Ivor T James, The Quadrant (*sic*)		1954	Transferred to Bourton
1931	James Dorothy Ruth	26/08/1926	Walter James, Sunny Cottages		1941	Over age
1953	James Hugh	?	The Quadrangle	Hereford	1953	To Weston-under-Penyard
1926	James Muriel	10/05/1921	Raymond James, Littlesworth		1935	Over age
1963	Jones Alison	29/09/1957	The Square			
1963	Jones Kevin	16/09/1956	The Square			
1955	Jones Valerie	14/06/1949	Stanley Jones, Naunton	Roman Rd, Chelt		
1931	Joynes Hubert Leslie	25/08/1925	Ernest Joynes, Kineton Thorns	Charlton Kings		
1942	Kear Arthur Douglas	17/07/1937	Fred'k Kear, El Hogar	Bibury	1944	Moved to Cheltenham
1944	Kear Quentin	05/05/1939	Fred Kear, El Hogar		1944	Moved to Cheltenham
1938	Lane John Evelyn	12/02/1929	Wm Gleed, Littlesworth	L Rissington	1938	Returned home
1941	Lawrence Michael	08/03/1935	Sidney Walter Lawrence, Roundhill	Privately	1941	Left for Worthing
1953	Leeke William John R	11/08/1943	The Quadrangle	Private	1954	Left village
1944	Lockey Amelia Dian	07/09/1939	Leslie Lockey, The Forge		1951	Left for Taunton

348 *Naunton 2000*

Appendix 9 (continued) Naunton National School Register Number Two, 1924 - 1969

In	Christian & Surname	Birthday	Parent/Guardian & Address	Last School	Out	Remarks
1942	Lockey Derek	?/02/1937	Leslie Lockey, Harford		1950	Transferred to Bourton
1953	Lockey Mary	01/02/1948	Claude Lockey, 5 Dale Street			
1955	Lockey Monica	27/06/1950	Claud Lockey, 3 Mill View			
1939	Lockey Noreen	02/11/1933	Lower Harford		1946	Left for School of Art
1940	Lodemore Minnie	30/01/1927	C/o Miss Fry, Cromwell House	New Malden	1940	Returned to London
1939	Lynott Janet	?	The Bakery	Birmingham	1942	Evacuee - returned home
1957	Macpherson Wendy	24/01/1949	Colin Macpherson, El Hogar	G Power		
1940	Manchester Elizabeth	19/01/1936	Spring Cottage	LCC	1945	Evacuee - returned to London
1925	Mann Emily	13/03/1913	Arthur Mann, Roundhill	Tortworth	1926	To Long Newnton
1925	Mann Eva	04/05/1917	Arthur Mann, Roundhill	Tortworth	1926	To Long Newnton
1940	Marks Judith Ann	21/06/1933	C/o Mrs Roberts, Cherry Cottage		1940	Returned to London
1926	Miffling Ernest	21/10/1920	Amelia Miffling, Harford Hill		1934	Over age
1936	Miffling Sylvia Doreen	25/07/1932	Harry Miffling, Ivy Cottage		1946	Left for employment
1943	Miles Anthony Wm	31/10/1938	Arthur Miles, Spring Cottage		1949	Special Award Northleach G.S.
1949	Miles Gordon Arthur	09/03/1944	Arthur Miles, Spring Cottage		1953	Left for Stow Hill
1941	Miles Stanley Graham	30/07/1936	Arthur Miles, Spring Cottage		1947	Northleach G.S.
1968	Milne James	01/01/1964	Aylworth			
1968	Mitchell Karen	03/06/1963	Windrush View		1969	To Boarton Primary
1928	Monk Eileen Gwenneth	16/07/1923	Wm Arthur Monk, Naunton		1928	Left for Condicote
1939	Montague Cynthia Marie	22/03/1934	Sunny Cottages	Slough	1939	Returned home
1955	Moreton Penelope	22/01/1946	? Old Mill, Naunton	Nigeria		To Boarding Sch
1958	Morris Rowena	12/07/1953	Reg Morris, Rushdale			
1928	Morse Doris	16/04/1917	Albert Morse, Harford Hill	North Cerney	1930	Left for Taunton
1928	Morse Ernest	10/02/1916	Albert Morse, Harford Hill	North Cerney	1930	Over age
1928	Morse Nora	22/09/1918	Albert Morse, Harford Hill	North Cerney	1930	Over age
1944	Muller Arthur John	27/02/1939	Terence A Muller, Rose Cottage		1952	Transfer to Bourton
1953	Muller Joy Elizabeth	25/06/1948	Terence Muller, Kiftsgate		1959	Transferred to Bourton
1948	Muller Michael George	?/02/1943	Terence A Muller, Rose Cottage		1954	Transferred to Bourton
1952	Muller Robin	21/01/1947	Terence Muller, Kiftsgate		1958	Transferred to Bourton
1937	Neal Peggy	23/04/1927	Charles Neale, Rushdale	Tewkesbury	1937	Return to Tewkesbury
1931	Neale Joan	05/05/1920	Charles Neale, Rushdale		1932	Gone hop picking in Worcs
1927	Nunney Jack	19/10/1915	George Nunney, New Town	Chelt	1927	Return to Chelt'
1928	Oakey Frances Ruth	08/01/1916	George Oakey, Naunton Downs	Condicote	1928	Left for Condicote

Naunton 2000   349

1961	Osborne Lesley A	27/04/1957	Kiftsgate		
1961	Osborne Susan	06/10/1955	Kiftsgate		
1927	Painter Mabel Joyce	17/09/1922	Albert Painter, The Forge	1936	Over age
1939	Palmer Constance	08/03/1927	Mrs Painter, The Smithy	Chiswick 1939	Returned home
1942	Palmer David Michael eo G	31/08/1934	Aylworth	Aston Blank 1942	Returned to Cold Aston
1940	Parker Derrick	09/10/1933	Harford Hill	Whaddon Chelt 1940	Returned home
1954	Parker John	26/11/1948	Lionel Parker, Black Horse Cottages		
1947	Parker Roger Anthony Lewis	14/01/1942	Lionel J Parker, Black Horse Cottages	Stow 1954	Transferred to Bourton
1934	Parsone Fred'k Wm Dennis	28/12/1928	Fred'k Parsons, Naunton	L Slaughter 1937	Left the district
1945	Parsons Bryan	18/07/1933	Mrs Collett, The Terrace	Shipton Oliffe 1947	Returned home
1928	Parsons Margaret Ethel	11/04/1923	Wm Parsons, Aylworth	1937	Over age
1933	Parsons Mary	26/03/1928	William Parsons, Aylworth	1937	Left the district
1952	Paterson Doris	23/12/1946	Summerhill	G Rissington 1954	Left village
1953	Paterson George	?/06/1948	Summerhill	1954	Left village
1944	Pates David	28/02/1935	Mrs Parsons, Ash Tree Cottage	Naunton Park 1944	Returned to Cheltenham
1927	Pawley Joyce Daphne	14/03/1920	Mrs Kate Pawley, Naunton	Tottenham Rd 1927	Return to London
1924	Payne Dorothy	16/04/1913	Ernest Payne, Dale Street	T Guiting 1927	To Tetbury
1926	Payne Violet Daisy	25/09/1921	Ernest Payne, Dale Street	1927	Tetbury
1924	Payne Winifred	29/05/1918	Ernest Payne, Dale Street	T Guiting 1927	To Tetbury
1940	Pexton Brian	?	Dudley F Pexton, School House	Bentley Hse Sch 1940	Returned home
1940	Pexton David	?	Dudley F Pexton, School House	ditto - Surrey 1940	Returned home
1933	Pexton Frank William	06/03/1929	John Pexton, School House	1938	Cheltenham Grammar Sch
1935	Pexton Margaret Mary	27/04/1931	John Pexton, School House	1935	Left for Ventnor I.O.W.
1931	Philpots William	28/12/1922	Mrs Harrison, Roundhill	1938	Northleach G.S.
1959	Pineott Carole F	30/12/1953	Spring Cottage	Germany	
1959	Pineott Kay E	13/02/1957	Spring Cottage	Germany	
1939	Pocock Glenda	??/06/1934	Cherry Cottage	London 1939	Returned home
1939	Porter Fred	?	Naunton	L.C.C. 1941	Official Evacuee
1959	Porter Judith	27/10/1954	Fred'k Porter, Sunny Bank	1946	Left for Folkestone
1941	Pritchard Patricia	24/07/1936	Leanard Pritchard. Parker's House	1951	Transfer to Bourton
1943	Pulham David William	19/07/1938	William E Pulham, Sunnyside	1934	To Lower Swell
1933	Pulham Elizabeth Valeria	25/04/1929	John Pulham, Yew Tree Cottages	1943	Left for Northleach Sec.
1936	Pulham Gladys Ethel	10/09/1931	Fred Pulham, Wayside	Bourton	Returned to Bourton
1941	Pulham Jean	18/11/1934	Miss E Fletcher, Yew Tree Ctg	Bourton Ccl 1937	Left to live at Bourton
1934	Pulham John Albert	13/08/1930	John Pulham, Yew Tree Cottages		
1957	Pulham Keith	31/12/1952	Ernest Walter Pulham, Naunton		
1937	Pulham Michael	?	John Pulham, Sunnyside	Bourton Ccl 1937	Returned home

350 *Naunton 2000*

Appendix 9 (continued) Naunton National School Register Number Two, 1924 - 1969

In	Christian & Surname	Birthday	Parent/Guardian & Address	Last School	Out	Remarks
1938	Pulham Peggy May	10/05/1933	Fred'k Pulham, Wayside		1944	To Northleach G.S.
1948	Pulham Peter	04/03/1943	William E Pulham, Sunnyside		1954	Transferred to Bourton
1924	Pulham Ronald Wm	22/02/1920	Edward Pulham, Dale Street		1934	Over age
1949	Pulham Sally	13/09/1944	William E Pulham, Sunnyside		1954	Left for Bourton
1940	Rachael Kenneth Graham	13/03/1930	Joseph Rachael, Aylworth	Bibury C.E.	1941	To Sherborne
1940	Rachael Maurice Graham	09/04/1927	Joseph Rachael, Aylworth	Bibury C.E.	1941	To Sherborne
1940	Rachael Stanley Donald	15/08/1928	Joseph Rachael, Aylworth	Bibury C.E.	1941	To Sherborne
1963	Raftery Brigid	26/03/1957	Kiftsgate			
1963	Raftery Frances	31/01/1959	Kiftsgate			
1960	Ralph Carol	31/12/1952	Joseph Ralph, Tuppeny Cottage	Withington		
1960	Ralph Linda	12/06/1954	Joseph Ralph, Tuppeny Cottage	Withington		
1960	Ralph Susan	12/06/1954	Joseph Ralph, Tuppeny Cottage	Withington		
1926	Rea Alfred	31/08/1918	Mrs Smith, Harford Hill (mother)	Charlton	1927	Destination unknown
1926	Rea Dorothy May	19/08/1912	Mrs Smith, Harford Hill (mother)	Charlton	1927	Destination unknown
1926	Rea Harry	06/05/1916	Mrs Smith, Harford Hill (mother)	Charlton	1927	Destination unknown
1944	Read Josephine	30/04/1939	Charles Read, Sunny Cottages		1945	Gone to Stroud
1952	Reed Keith	25/03/1947	Fred'k Reed, Sunny Cottages	Cold Aston	1953	Transferred to Bourton
1959	Revers Mary Elizabeth	26/01/1955	Tho's Henry Revers, Dale Street			
1947	Revers Michael Henry	09/01/1942	Henry Revers, Dale Street		1954	Transferred to Bourton
1939	Reynolds Michael	03/07/1930	Mrs Reynolds, High Fm, T Guiting	T Guiting	1939	Cheltenham Grammar Sch
1935	Rhind Duncan	27/08/1922	? Rhind, El Hogar, Naunton		1939	Left for Ventnor I.O.W.
1939	Riches Coral	18/01/1924	?	London	1940	Evacuee - Pates G.S. Cheltenham
1939	Riches Joyce	18/01/1924	?	London	1940	Evacuee - Pates G.S. Cheltenham
1943	Ridge John	21/08/1938	Mrs Ridge, Yew Tree Cottage		1951	Transfer to Bourton
1947	Ridge Michael	14/02/1942	Herbert Ridge, Dale Terrace		1947	Killed on the road
1945	Ridge Patricia	31/03/1940	Herbert Ridge, Yew Tree Cottage		1953	Transferred to Bourton
1960	Ridley Jane	15/05/1953	Nicholas Ridley, The Old Rectory	Private tuition	1962	Berkhampsted, Cheltenham
1962	Ridley Jessica	05/09/1957	Nicholas Ridley, The Old Rectory		1965	Berkhampsted, Cheltenham
1960	Ridley Susanna	19/05/1955	Nicholas Ridley, The Old Rectory		1964	Berkhampsted, Cheltenham
1939	Ridoutt Naomi	12/01/1932	Cherry Cottage	London	1939	Returned home
1940	Robbins Dulcie	13/08/1928	Roundhills(*sic*) Farm	Llanelly	1940	To Stratford on Avon
1940	Robbins Lucy	04/01/1932	Roundhills(*sic*) Farm	Llanelly	1940	To Stratford on Avon
1940	Robbins Marie	13/02/1934	Roundhills(*sic*) Farm	Llanelly	1940	To Stratford on Avon

1938	Robbins Sylvia	03/11/1932	James Robbins, Harford		1938	To Cold Aston
1939	Roberts David	14/06/1929	Cherry Cottage	London	1940	Northleach G.S.
1940	Robles Maria	09/01/1928	C/o Miss Fry, Cromwell House		1940	Returned to London
1938	Rooke Arthur John	03/07/1928	Arthur Rooke, Hill Fm Ctgs, Slaughter	U Slaughter	1942	Over age
1941	Rooke David Norman	24/03/1936	Arthur Rooke, Hill Farm Cottages	Bristol	1950	Transferred to Bourton
1938	Rooke Gwendoline Olive	12/01/1927	Arthur Rooke, Hill Fm Ctgs, Slaughter	U Slaughter	1941	Over age
1944	Rowberry Kathleen Rose	30/07/1936	Edmund Rowberry, Naunton Inn	Rodmarton	1944	Moved to Tally Ho
1937	Rooke Norah	26/05/1925	Arthur Rooke, Hill Fm, Slaughter	Kempsford	1939	Over age
1944	Rowberry Kenneth Ed' Geo'	14/02/1935	Edmund Rowberry, Naunton Inn	Rodmarton	1944	Moved to Tally Ho
1944	Rowberry Lillian Ann M	28/02/1931	Edmund Rowberry, Naunton Inn	Rodmarton	1944	Moved to Tally Ho
1930	Ruck Cecil Frank	28/06/1920	Henry Wm Ruck, Lower Harford	Leckhampton	1930	Left for Cheltenham
1930	Ruck Gerald Wm	19/02/1919	Henry Wm Ruck, Lower Harford	Leckhampton	1930	Left for Cheltenham
1930	Ruck Phyllis Evelyn	12/03/1924	Henry Wm Ruck, Lower Harford	Leckhampton	1930	Left for Cheltenham
1966	Rudd Francis Mary	01/12/1962	Francis Rudd, Aylworth			
1965	Rudd Margaret	07/06/1957	Francis Rudd, Aylworth			
1954	Russell Gregg	08/08/1948	Stuart Russell, El Hogar	Charlton Kings	1955	Gone to Germany
1955	Russell Scott	23/11/1949	Stuart Russell, El Hogar	Charlton Kings	1955	Gone to Germany
1939	Saunders Alan	31/12/1926	North Street	Birmingham	1939	Returned home
1939	Saunders Sheila	30/06/1930	North Street	Birmingham	1939	Returned home
1939	Saunders Victor	24/04/1929	North Street	Birmingham	1939	Returned home
1925	Savage Alban	21/06/1914	George Savage, The Manse	Cambridge	1926	Gloucester,Tredworth Rd School
1925	Savage Betty	27/05/1920	George Savage, The Manse	Cambridge	1927	Left for Tenby
1928	Savage David John	02/09/1923	George Savage, The Manse		1929	Left for Longlevens
1925	Savage Dorothy Ruth	26/05/1918	George Savage, The Manse	Cambridge	1928	Left for Tenby
1925	Savage Humphrey	06/12/1915	George Savage, The Manse	Cambridge	1929	Northleach G.S.
1925	Savage Irene Helen	11/02/1917	George Savage, The Manse	Cambridge	1927	Left for Tenby
1925	Savage Margaret	16/08/1912	George Savage, The Manse	Cambridge	1925	Glos High Sch, passed exam
1960	Scales Richard	21/09/1950	Spring Cottage	St Albans		
1960	Scales Roland	21/02/1954	Spring Cottage	St Albans		
1933	Scrivens Audrey	07/04/1923	Mrs Bedwell, Holmleigh	Ada St, B'ham	1934	Returned home
1960	Scrivens Gillian Elizabeth	20/06/1952	Lower Slaughter	L Slaughter		
1960	Scrivens Wendy Jane	27/08/1953	Lower Slaughter	L Slaughter		
1933	Sell Doris Maud	11/03/1920	Herbert Sell, Roundhill		1934	Over age
1934	Sell Douglas	25/08/1929	Herbert Sell, Roundhill		1943	Over age
1940	Sell Edward	17/07/1929	Cherry Cottage	Belmont	1940	Returned home
1938	Sell Peter	29/10/1932	Herbert Sell, Roundhill		1946	Left for employment
1953	Shelley Patricia Anne	16/03/1947	2 Spring Cottages	Private	1954	Moved to Scotland

352   Naunton 2000

Appendix 9 (continued) Naunton National School Register Number Two, 1924 - 1969

In	Christian & Surname	Birthday	Parent/Guardian & Address	Last School	Out	Remarks
1940	Slater Derrick	10/08/1932	C/o Miss Fry, Cromwell House	Aylesbury	1940	Returned to London
1940	Slater Paul	10/08/1932	C/o Miss Fry, Cromwell House	LCC Shoreditch	1940	Returned to London
1929	Smart Francis Beryl	15/03/1926	Alfred L Smart, School House		1932	Left for Coleford
1926	Smith Cecil	03/02/1922	Elsie Beames, Naunton		1936	Over age
1961	Smith Gwenda	26/06/1953	Grange Hill			
1943	Snape Derek	01/10/1932	Harold W Snape, Aylworth Cottages	Alvechurch	1943	Attending Aston Blank
1943	Snape Ernest	27/07/1929	Harold W Snape, Aylworth Cottages	Alvechurch	1943	Over age
1943	Snape Harold	09/03/1931	Harold W Snape, Aylworth Cottages	Alvechurch	1943	Attending Aston Blank
1943	Snape Raymond	02/12/1933	Harold W Snape, Aylworth Cottages	Alvechurch	1943	Attending Aston Blank
1940	Snow Barbara	18/11/1929	Cornelius, The Yard	Birmingham	1941	Returned home
1940	Snow Eileen	18/04/1931	Cornelius, The Yard	Birmingham	1940	Returned home
1932	Staite Constance	10/09/1928	Frank Staite, Washpool Cottages	Gloucester	1943	Over age
1937	Staite George	06/05/1931	Wm Staite, Harford	Cropthorne	1937	Returned home
1930	Staite Marjorie	15/01/1927	Frank Staite, Black Horse Cottages		1938	To Northleach G.S.
1937	Staite Mary	25/02/1929	Wm Staite, Harford	Cropthorne	1937	Returned home
1952	Staite Paul	04/12/1947	Constance Staite, Rose Cottage		1959	Transferred to Bourton
1960	Stallabrass David	24/10/1954	Thos Stallabrass, Grange Hill			
1960	Stallabrass John	27/03/1953	Thos Stallabrass, Grange Hill			
1931	Stamp Dorothy	08/07/1922	Thomas Stamp, Roundhill		1940	Over age
1931	Stamp Mary	29/10/1920	Thomas Stamp, Roundhill		1933	Return to Northumberlad
1946	Stanbridge Beryl	07/04/1935	Tom Stanbridge, Dale Street		1946	Northleach G.S.
1944	Stanbridge Janet	04/03/1934	Fred Stanbridge, Dale Street	Leckhampton	1944	Returned to Cheltenham
1955	Stanley Catherine Ann	17/06/1950	Arthur Stanley, Grange Hill			
1954	Stanley Doreen Mary	10/12/1946	Arthur Wm Stanley, Hill Grange Ctg	Tewkesbury		
1954	Stanley Patricia Lilian	07/09/1948	Arthur Wm Stanley, Hill Grange Ctg	Tewkesbury		
1927	Stanley William	19/06/1913	Mrs Stanley, Naunton	Prac Sch, Chelt	1927	Return to Chelt'
1937	Stephens Fred	29/09/1925	Arthur Stephens, Wayside	Heythrop C.E.	1937	To Cheltenham
1937	Stephens Nancy	13/07/1923	Arthur Stephens, Wayside	Heythrop C.E.	1937	Over age
1939	Stephens Raymond John	11/11/1930	Sunny Cottages	Slough	1939	Returned home
1950	Stratford Colin	30/01/1945	Doris Stratford, Sunny Bank		1956	Left for Bourton
1927	Stratford Doris Eileen	09/04/1923	Albert Stratford, Sunnybank		1937	Over age
1931	Stratford Eric Wm	16/03/1927	William Stratford, Chapel Hill		1941	Over age
1926	Stratford Freda?	11/09/1922	William Stratford, Naunton		1931	Left for Stonehouse

1931	Stratford Iris May	03/02/1927	Bertram Stratford, Chapel Hill		1931	Gone to Stonehouse
1947	Stratford Jean Marion	27/08/1942	Doris Stratford, Sunny Bank		1954	Transferred to Bourton
1961	Sutton Edward	15/05/1955	Edward J Sutton, The Caravan	Tuffley		
1961	Sutton Shaun	09/06/1956	Edward J Sutton, The Caravan	Tuffley		
1955	Swarbrick Richard	15/01/1947	Harold Swarbrick, El Hogar	Kettering		
1955	Swarbrick Stephen	31/12/1948	Harold Swarbrick, El Hogar	Kettering		
1959	Tabor Jean Alison	17/02/1950	Albert Tabor, The Stores, Dale St			
1969	Taylor Alison	23/07/1964	John Taylor, Dale Terrace			
1967	Taylor Kathrin	09/01/1963	Dale Street			
1940	Taylor Maureen Wray	20/04/1934	GE Taylor, 5 The Quadrangle	Pitsea Essex	1949	Left for Ilfracombe
1934	Temple Albert Vernon	06/03/1931	Albert Temple, The Yard	Longborough	1942	Left for Gainsborough, Moreton
1925	Temple Edward Wm	24/04/1921	Albert Temple, The Yard		1935	Over age
1940	Temple Shirley Ann	07/08/1925	Albert Temple, Grange Hill		1948	Arts & Crafts Sch, Cheltenham
1945	Timms Doris Muriel	30/10/1930	Clement Timms, Chalk Hill Fm		1947	Left for Condicote
1941	Timms Joan	28/05/1931	C/o Mrs Merrell	Fishponds, B'tol	1942	Evacuee - returned home
1942	Timms Raymond Walter	16/02/1936	Clement Timms, Chalk Hill Fm		1947	Left for Condicote
1954	Tomalin Ann Gwendoline	16/03/1949	Ernest J Tomalin, West View		1954	Gone to Chipping Norton
1955	Tonge Andrew	29/06/1949	Geoffrey Tonge, 2 Spring Ctgs			
1925	Townsend John	19/05/1916	Cuthbert Townsend, Dale Street	Sevenhampton	1927	To Bishops Cleeve
1925	Townsend Percy	06/10/1911	Cuthbert Townsend, Dale Street	Sevenhampton	1925	Over age
1940	Townshend Robert Edward	09/03/1929	GE Taylor, 5 The Quadrangle	Pitsea Essex	1943	Over age
1939	Trickey Alec	?	Edward Trickey, Harford	London	1939	Returned home
1939	Trickey Ethel	?	Edward Trickey, Harford	London	1939	Returned home
1934	Tuley Audrey	16/11/1924	Albert Tuley, Roundhill	Brafferton	1935	Return to Yorkshire
1946	Turk Anne	?/09/1940	Mrs Pritchard, Parker's House	Cheltenham	1946	Returned to Cheltenham
1953	Vyner Dennis	27/11/1948	Rex Vyner, Roundhills (sic)			
1939	Waters Anthony Bernard	06/04/1929	Windrush Ctg	Birmingham	1941	Northleach G.S.
1924	Watson Reginald	22/10/1916	Reg Bartlett, Naunton	L Slaughter	1924	Return to L Slaughter
1926	Weller Edna Margaret	24/06/1920	Nellie Weller, Fox Hill Inn	Hanley Castle	1927	Left for London
1926	Weller Gladys Lusty	17/11/1915	Nellie Weller, Fox Hill Inn	Hanley Castle	1927	Left for London
1952	Wells Stewart	10/08/1946	Eric Wells, The Caravan, Huntsmans	Oxford	1952	Transferred to Bourton
1952	Wells Trevor	13/05/1939	Eric Wells, The Caravan, Huntsmans	Oxford	1952	Transferred to Bourton
1932	Wheeler Joyce	17/01/1928	Harry Wheeler, The Yard			
1935	Wheeler Margaret	26/03/1931	Harry Wheeler, The Yard		1939	Left for Bourton
1955	White Susan	07/06/1949	Richard White, Spring Cottages			Left for Bishops Cleeve
1931	Williams Edward	11/10/1921	George Williams, Parkers House	Slaughter	1931	Return to Slaughter
1937	Williamson Daphne	28/10/1927	George Ed' Williamson, Naunton	Charlton Kings	1937	Return to C' Kings

Naunton 2000   353

Appendix 9 (continued) Naunton National School Register Number Two, 1924 - 1969

In	Christian & Surname	Birthday	Parent/Guardian & Address	Last School	Out	Remarks
1925	Willis Norman	14/04/1920	Robert Willis, Chapel Hill		1934	Over age
1944	Wilsdon Joan	25/04/1939	Upper Harford		1947	Left for Kingham
1947	Wilsdon Margaret Lilian	14/02/1942	Edward Wilsdon, Harford Hill		1947	Left for Kingham
1943	Wilsdon Peter Edward	11/06/1937	Edward Wilsdon, Harford Hill		1947	Left for Kingham
1932	Wright Violet May	31/01/1927	Fred Wright, Cromwell House		1942	Over age
1937	Young George	21/11/1929	Wm Young, Aylworth	Brosbeck Yorks	1938	Return to Yorkshire
1937	Young William	24/11/1923	Wm Young, Aylworth	Brosbeck Yorks	1937	Over age

Naunton County Primary School closed in 1969 leaving Naunton children to embark on genuine School-runs to the displacement Primary Schools in Cold Aston, The Guitings and Bourton-on-the-Water. Bourton Vale Secondary School became Comprehensive in 1988 and was renamed The Cotswold School. Westwoods Grammar School at Northleach closed in the same year.

Below are some 145 Naunton school children (under 11 years of age) who between 1969 & 2000 attended the nearby Primary Schools. Botw = Bourton-on-the-Water. GP = Guiting Power. TG = Temple Guiting. CA = Cold Aston

1972	Ainousa Tariz Aziz	14/03/1965	Aziz, 5 Bungalow	Saudia Arabia		(Botw)
1982	Allard Simon Alistair	01/05/1973	Sunny House		1982	Cairo (Botw)
1983	Andrews Beverly Selina	29/09/1978	Eddie & Pauline, Roundhill Farmhouse		1986	To Frome (CA)
1986	Andrews Christopher R	11/05/1982	Eddie & Pauline, Roundhill Farmhouse		1986	To Frome (CA)
1984	Andrews Vicky Jane	22/03/1980	Eddie & Pauline, Roundhill Farmhouse		1986	To Frome(CA)
1983	Armstrong Matthew Peter	30/10/1978	Peter & Julie, 1 Aylworth Cottage			(CA)
1984	Armstrong Natalie	06/11/1979	Peter & Julie, 1 Aylworth Cottage			(CA)
1980	Arthur John Leighton	03/03/1975	Denise, 1 School House Flats	USA	1982	Longborough (Botw)
1980	Arthur Lorraine Marie	17/10/1971	Denise, 1 School House Flats	USA	1982	Longborough (Botw)
1991	Barber Helen Claire	27/04/1987	Mr/Mrs A.K. Barber 3 Mill View		1998	Cotswold School (Botw)
1989	Barber Kevin Francis	10/05/1985	Mr/Mrs A.K. Barber 3 Mill View		1996	Cotswold School (Botw)
1970	Barrell James William	04/08/1962	Geoffrey Roger, 3 The Quadrangle	Marham	1970	Oakington (Botw)
1970	Barrell Naomi Karen	18/05/1964	Geoffrey Roger, 3 The Quadrangle	Kings Lynn	1970	Oakington (Botw)
1977	Bartoloni Justin Marc	13/03/1973	Susan, Shepherds Ctg Aylworth		1984	Bourton Vale (CA)

1974	Bayliss Marcella	03/12/1969	Alan Frederick, Jasmine Cottage		1971	Bourton Vale (Botw)
1982	Bayliss Neil	28/03/1978	Alan Bayliss, Glebe House, Grange Hill		1989	Cotswold School (TG)
1973	Boscombe Jacqueline	03/03/1963	Robert, Longford	Kenya	1973	Left area (Botw)
1983	Bovett Emma Sophie	06/07/1977	Mr/Mrs G., The Gables	Minchinhampton	1986	Churchdown (Botw)
1979	Bowen-Jones Jonathan	01/03/1979	Jennifer & Adrian, Black Horse Inn		1980	Bourton Vale (CA)
2000	Bowen-Jones Rowland	07/01/1996	Edward & Victoria, Rosemary Cottage	Stepping Stones		(TG)
1990	Boyer Charles William David	23/04/1982	Mr/Mrs N Buser, Mill House	USA	1991	USA (Botw)
1977	Brook Lucy Jane	14/03/1971	John Edward, Sunnyside Cottage	Candover		(Botw)
1977	Brook Mark Alexander	29/05/1969	John Edward, Sunnyside Cottage	Preston		(Botw)
1972	Brown Andrew Watson	06/08/1965	R.E.Brown, Grange Hill Cottage	Kingsclere		(Botw)
1972	Brown Angela Lorraine	08/02/1962	R.E.Brown, Grange Hill Cottage	Kingsclere		(Botw)
1972	Brown Mark Andrew	18/01/1963	R.E.Brown, Grange Hill Cottage	Kingsclere		(Botw)
1970	Brown Michael Anthony	12/10/1959	Naunton		1970	(GP)
1978	Collett Andrew	28/08/1973	Ian, Manor House		1979	Private School (Botw)
1976	Curtis Deborah Jane	03/03/1972	Christopher & Pamela, 2 Aylworth Ctgs		1983	Bourton Vale (CA)
1978	Curtis Mark Christopher	30/04/1973	Christopher & Pamela, 2 Aylworth Ctgs		1984	Bourton Vale (CA)
1981	Curtis Stephen	18/06/1977	Christopher & Pamela, 2 Aylworth Ctgs		1988	Cotswold School (CA)
1994	Davies Christian	13/12/1988	Wm & Jayne Davies, Sunnydale	Guiting Power	1998	Dean Close Jnr (TG)
1979	Davis Andrew	10/03/1974	Philip William, Valley View		1985	Bourton Vale (Botw)
1994	Davis Henry	18/11/1987	Mr/Mrs R., Summerhill Farmhouse		1996	USA (Botw)
1997	Davis Henry John	18/11/1987	Mr/Mrs R., Summerhill Farmhouse	Readmitted	1999	St Edwards (Botw)
1977	Davis James Richard	20/06/1972	Philip William, Valley View		1983	Bourton Vale (Botw)
1994	Davis Joseph	26/02/1986	Mr/Mrs R., Summerhill Farmhouse		1996	USA (Botw)
1969	Dindinto Rosemary	19/09/1963	Lisa, The Old Rectory	Naunton		(Botw)
1976	Eddlestone Mary Kathleen	13/03/1969	J Eddlestone, Mill Barn House	U. Slaughter	1980	Bourton Vale (Botw)
1984	Edgeworth Jason	17/12/1979	The Council Houses			(GP)
1970	Edmonds Timothy	20/04/1963	A.R.Edmonds, 3 The Quadrangle	Anton?	1970	Temp' 3 weeks (Botw)
1978	Ellis Bryan Christopher	10/03/1967	c/o Ogilvie, 2 Dale Street			(GP)
1978	Ellis Edniss Elizabeth	27/04/1972	c/o Ogilvie, 2 Dale Street			(GP)
1980	Evans Anna	07/07/1976	Mary Evans, 8 Windrush View			(GP)
1984	Everitt Michael	26/04/1977	Sally Everitt, Grange Hill Cottage	Guiting Power	1985	To Suffolk (TG)
1982	Everitt Michael Peter Geoffrey	26/04/1977	Mrs B.E. Everitt, 2 Grange Hill Cottage			(GP)
1970	Eves Michelle	20/11/1965	A.K. Eves, Sundeala Cottage		1970	To Germany (GP)
1970	Eves Nichole	20/11/1965	A.K. Eves, Sundeala Cottage		1970	To Germany (GP)
1978	Farquhar Alexandra Elizabeth	04/08/1971	Elizabeth & Anthony, Harford Fm house		1982	To Banbury (CA)
1971	Freeman Nigel	06/09/1964	Huntsmans Cottage		1973	To Somerset (GP)
1994	Gayton (Dyer) Robert	08/02/1987	Mrs K., 3 Millview		1998	Cotswold School (Botw)

356 Naunton 2000

Appendix 9 (continued) Children in nearby Primary Schools, 1969 - 2000

In	Christian & Surname	Birthday	Parent/Guardian & Address	Last School	Out	Remarks
1994	Gayton (Dyer) Ryan	08/02/1987	Mrs K., 3 Millview		1998	Cotswold School (Botw)
1992	Gullen Olivia	08/08/1984	Kevin & Susan, The Old Forge		1995	Pates, Cheltenham (CA)
1994	Hammond Alexander	24/10/1988	Summerhill Farm	St Marys, Tetbury	1997	To Surrey (TG)
1994	Hammond Georgina	06/04/1990	Summerhill Farm		1997	To Surrey (TG)
1964	Hanks Donna Teresa	26/03/1959	Gordon Hanks, Summer Hill Farm		1970	To Boarding School (GP)
1985	Hanks Gerard Alistair James	01/03/1981	Mr/Mrs D. 5 Village Ave		1992	Cotswold School (Botw)
1992	Hanks William	19/01/1988	Ian & Tracey Hanks, Dale Cottage		1999	Cotswold School (CA)
1998	Harding Luke McLennan	26/06/1994	Mr/Mrs K., 4 Sunny Cottages			(Botw)
1979	Harris Darren Michael	24/12/1971	Cyril Harris, Huntsmans Farm Cottage			(GP)
1979	Harris Tracy Ann	24/01/1973	Cyril Harris, Huntsmans Farm Cottage			(GP)
1999	Hayward Angus	25/04/1995	Nick & Megan, 1 Aylworth Cottage			(CA)
1997	Hayward Harriet	22/07/1993	Nick & Megan, 1 Aylworth Cottage			(CA)
2000	Houldsworth Matthew	12/11/1992	Richard & Catherine, Lower Harford			(TG)
1999	Houldsworth Matthew James	12/11/1992	Mr/Mrs H, Lower Harford Cottage	Cold Aston	1999	To T Guiting (CA)
1974	James Peter Clive	19/11/1969	Derrick, Littleworth		1981	Bourton Vale (Botw)
1978	James Wendy	01/02/1973	Derrick, Littleworth	Guiting Power	1984	Bourton Vale (Botw)
1981	Johnson Katy Marie	12/10/1974	Mr/Mrs R., Waterloo House	Upfield Prep	1986	Westwoods (Botw)
1981	Johnson Lucy Charlotte	26/04/1977	Mr/Mrs R., Waterloo House		1988	St Edwards (Botw)
1987	Johnson Ricky	03/10/1980	Margaret & Clifford, Roundhill Farm		1990	Moved to Kent (CA)
1988	Johnson Timothy James	14/05/1984	Mr/Mrs R., Waterloo House		1995	St Edwards (Botw)
2000	Jones Hannah	16/04/1996	Adrian & Heather, Dale End			(CA)
1975	Keevil Louise Joan	21/01/1970	Brian James, Upper Dale Terrace	Guiting Power	1981	Westwoods (Botw)
1975	Keevil Sarah Katherine	04/12/1967	Brian James, Upper Dale Terrace	Guiting Power	1979	Westwoods (Botw)
1992	Kington John Robert	25/09/1986	Mr R., Weavings, Sunny Cottages	Hereford	1994	Unknown (Botw)
1982	Kosmala Amy	21/05/1978	Mr/Mrs J., Farm House, Dale Street		1989	Cotswold School (Botw)
1980	Kosmala Sebastian	12/11/1975	Jan, Farmhouse, Dale Street		1987	Westwoods (Botw)
1976	Lootes Dion	03/11/1971	David, High Dale		1983	Westwoods (Botw)
1995	Macklin James	17/04/1991	Helen & Martin, The Black Horse			(TG)
1995	Mangan Isabelle	20/08/1992	Julia, Summerhill House	Stepping Stones		(TG)
2000	Manley Phillipa Clara	29/12/1995	Will & Katy, Ashpiece, Aylworth			(CA)
1994	Miles Tamsin Hannah	08/09/1986	Mr/Mrs A., Brockhill Farm	Christchurch	1994	Bledington (Botw)
1998	Miranda Emily	07/08/1994	Ms D Everitt, 8 Windrush View			(Botw)
1970	Mitchell Gail Suzanne	08/01/1966	Arthur, 9 Mill View			(Botw)

1974	Mitchell Sally Victoria	16/12/1969	Douglas Anderson, 2 Rose Cottage	1971	Bourton Vale (Botw)
1971	Mitchell Stuart Anderson	07/02/1967	Douglas, Rose Tree Cottage	1978	Westwoods (Botw)
1998	Morton Barnaby	25/12/1993	Peter & Janet, Lower Dale Cottage	St Edwards Kind'n	1994 St Edwards Kindergarten (TG)
1969	Moss Graham	03/07/1963	H.F.Moss, Shepherds Ctg, Aylworth	Wilmslow	1970 To Cheshire (Botw)
1969	Moss Steven	28/05/1961	H.F.Moss, Shepherds Ctg, Aylworth	Wilmslow	1970 To Cheshire (Botw)
1980	Mosson Neil	21/04/1976	Mr/Mrs S.V., 2 Grange Hill Cottages		1987 Westwoods (Botw)
1994	Ogilvie Angus	04/10/1989	Mr/Mrs K., 2 Dale Street		(Botw)
1991	Ogilvie Hannah Francesca	02/11/1986	Mr/Mrs K., 2 Dale Street		1998 Cotswold School (Botw)
1980	Perry Danielle	29/10/1975	Jane Davies, Sunny Dale	C/Kings Convent	(TG)
1993	Pickup George Frederick	20/07/1989	Mr/Mrs D., Farthing Green		2000 St Edwards (Botw)
1991	Pickup James David Ludlow	01/03/1987	Mr/Mrs D., Farthing Green		1998 St Edwards (Botw)
1995	Porter Abigail	10/12/1987	Lee & David, The Gables	Cold Aston	1999 Cotswold School (TG)
1987	Porter Benjamin David	12/02/1983	David & Lee, The Gables		1994 Cotswold School (CA)
1995	Porter Matthew	08/03/1985	Lee & David, The Gables	Cold Aston	1996 Cotswold School (TG)
1976	Powell Christina Marie	05/10/1971	Graham & Corrinne, Kifts Gate House		1983 Charrton Park Convent (CA)
1974	Powell Nicholas Powell	22/05/1969	Graham & Corrinne, Kifts Gate House		1980 To Whitefriars, Chelt (CA)
1988	Ridge David Alexander Scott	30/03/1984	Mr/Mrs J., Ferndale, Dale Street		1995 Cotswold School (Botw)
1985	Ridge James Matthew John	28/03/1981	Mr/Mrs J., Ferndale, Dale Street		1992 Cotswold School (Botw)
1991	Ridge Paul Andrew Jordon	26/11/1986	Mr/Mrs J., Dale Street		1998 Cotswold School (Botw)
1979	Rozier Julia Della	04/07/1975	Huntsmans Farm Cottage		1979 To Naunton Park (GP)
1977	Saunders Nadine Je'al	01/09/1972	Colin Saunders, Sunnyside		(GP)
1976	Saunders Wayne Lee Marcus	11/06/1971	Colin Saunders, Sunnyside		(GP)
1995	Seal Emily	07/05/1991	Lotte & Nicholas, Brockhill Farm		(TG)
1998	Seal Jack	15/04/1994	Lotte & Nicholas, Brockhill Farm		(TG)
1982	Seminti Amalia Elizabeth	13/03/1973	Mrs H.M. Cotswold Cottage, Dale St.	Charlton Park	1982 USA (Botw)
1970	Shurgold Alison Jane	07/03/1966	William, 10 Dale Street		(Botw)
1972	Shurgold Angela Mary	29/07/1967	William, 10 Dale Street		1978 Bourton Vale (Botw)
1972	Shurgold Christine Ann	11/07/1968	William, 10 Dale Street		1979 Bourton Vale (Botw)
1969	Shurgold Ian William	06/09/1964	William, 10 Dale Street		(Botw)
1996	Stevens Freya	19/09/1991	John & Elizabeth, Vine House		(CA)
1985	Stevens Harriet Elizabeth	06/01/1981	John & Elizabeth, Vine House		1992 Cotswold School (Botw)
1982	Stockwell Martina	12/04/1978	Christopher & Philadelphia, Dale House		1983 Moved to Kingham (CA)
1969	Taylor Allison Louise	23/07/1964	John Taylor, Dale Terrace		1975 (GP)
1969	Taylor Katherine Louise	09/01/1963	John Taylor, Dale Terrace		1974 (GP)
1977	Taylor Sarah	17/04/1972	T.F. Taylor, Windrush View		Bourton C.P. (GP)
1999	Timmins Hannah Leah	15/11/1990	Joan Timmins, Littons		(CA)

358 *Naunton 2000*

Appendix 9 (continued) Children in nearby Primary Schools, 1969 - 2000

In	Christian & Surname	Birthday	Parent/Guardian & Address	Last School	Out	Remarks
1997	Twiston-Davies Sam	15/10/1992	Nigel & Cathy, Grange Hill Farm	Stepping Stones		(TG)
1999	Twiston-Davies William	01/12/1994	Nigel & Cathy, Grange Hill Farm	Stepping Stones		(TG)
1994	Tyack Samuel Jeremy	12/11/1989	Mr/Mrs Tyack, 7 Windrush View		1994	Bledington (Botw)
1981	Urry Jonathan Wavel	29/03/1977	Wavel J. Urry, Littons		1986	Whitefriars (GP)
1979	Urry Rowan Jo	23/08/1974	W.J. Urry, Littons			(GP)
1990	Webb Adam	22/10/1985			1997	Cotswold School (CA)
1994	Webb David	29/05/1990	Mark & Lorraine, 2 Hillcrest Cottage			(CA)
1987	Webb Simon Mark	27/12/1982	Mark & Lorraine, 2 Hillcrest Cottage		1994	Cotswold School (CA)
1982	Wilkie Josephine Helen	05/05/1978	Robert & Gillian, 1 Harford Hill Cottage		1989	Westonbirt School (CA)
1980	Wilkie Julian	18/03/1976	Robert & Gillian, 1 Harford Hill Cottage		1987	Rendcombe College (CA)
1993	Williams Emma Margaret	03/08/1989	Mr/Mrs Williams, 4 Mill View		1996	(Botw)
1990	Williams Thomas Edward	10/04/1986	Mr/Mrs Williams, 4 Mill View		1997	Cotswold School (Botw)
1994	Wilson Hugo	11/11/1989	Mrs M Wilson, Aylworth		1998	Independent Education (CA)

N.B. The Guiting Power School Register from November 1989 to 1994, when the School closed could not be located so several Naunton children may be missing. We have since resurrected Naunton County Primary School by creating an entry within the new (July 2000) website known as: **www.friendsreunited.co.uk**

Appendix 10

1901 Census (200 males, 201 females)

Earlier census details for Naunton are available on www.genuki.org.uk (Geneology UK & Ireland) and are omitted to save space in this book

Recorded by enumerator John W.R. Buffin on 8 April 1901 and being the most recent census available for public viewing under the 100 year closure rule

(H) = Head of household. (W) = wife. (S) = son. daur = daughter. nei = niece. nep = nephew. wid = widow. widr = widower. Serv = servant.

(e.& o.e. due to Mr Buffin's handwriting being difficult to decipher at times)

Road, Street, number or name of House	Name & Surname of each person, relation to head of family, age last birthday	Profession or Occupation	Employer, Worker or Own account	Where born
1 Harford Hill Ctg	Lockey George (H) 46 Lockey Constance Helen (W) 35, Jacobs William Chas (stepson) 11 Lockey Stanley (S) 4 Lockey Christopher Edward (S)1	Stone slate maker	Own acc.	L Swell Gravely, Herts Jersey,C.I Naunton Naunton
2 Harford Hill Ctg	Workman Henry Francis (H) 38 Workman Sarah Ann (W) 35 Butler Madeline (nei) 3	Carter on farm(horse)	Worker	Lt. Rissington Tallyho Edgbaston, B'ham
3 Harford Holt	Barrett Henry (H) 64 Barret Ellen (W) 63	Shepherd	Worker	Eastleach, Glos Rodmarton, Glos
4 Harford	Brown John Wm (H) 37 Elsie Annie Brown (W) 27	Farmer	Employer	Minsterworth Glos Naunton
5 Harford	Akers James (H) 36 Akers Elizabeth Sarah (W) 40 Akers Edmund John (S) 12 Akers Annie (D) 9 Akers Albert (S) 6	Cattleman on farm	Worker	Ramsden, Oxon Condicote Condicote Eyford Eyford
6 Roundhill	Waine James Charles (H) 51 Waine Susan Sarah (W) 50 Waine Alice (D) 21 Waine Edwin (S) 17 Waine Edith (D) 15 Waine Lucy (D) 13 Waine Albert (S) 9 Edward Williams (single) 35	Farm Bailiff School teacher Fm Bailiff's Asst Worker Carter & groom	Employer	Aldsworth Glos Gt Rissington Naunton Naunton Naunton Naunton Naunton Notgrove
7 Naunton Ctg	Martin Benjamin John (H) 45 Martin Hannah (W) 50 Martin Mabel (D) 19 Martin John (S) 13 Martin Ruby (D) 10 Martin Hannah (D) 6 Lodge Charles (bro-in law) 61 Lodge Mary (sis-in-law) 57	Miller & baker Dressmaker Agr/labourer Living on own means	Own acc. (home) Own acc. (home) Worker	Chadlington, Oxon Chadlington, Oxon Cherrington, Warwicks Wickford Mill, do Cherrington, Warwick Naunton Mill Naunton Shipton Olliffe

Road, Street, number or name of House	Name & Surname of each person, relation to head of family, age last birthday	Profession or Occupation	Employer, Worker or Own account	Where born
8 Waterloo House	Harris Henry (H) 58 Harris Martha (W) 58 Harris Oliver (S) 20 Harris Emily (D) 17 Harris Bert (S) 14	Butcher Agr/labourer Agr/labourer	Own acc. (home) Worker Worker	Naunton Naunton Naunton Naunton Naunton
9 Naunton Ctg	Gardener Albert George (H) 53 Gardener Jane (W) 57 Pulham Eliza (m-in-law/wid) 81	Master wheelwright Dressmaker	Own acc. (home) Own acc. (home)	Lower Guiting Notgrove Lower Guiting
10 Naunton Ctg	Phillips Rebecca (H) (wid) 55	Shopkeeper/draper	Own acc. (home)	Naunton
11 Cromwell Ctg	Mills James (H) 59 Mills Harriet (W) 54	Mason & farmer	Own acc. (home)	Naunton Lower Guiting
12 Naunton Ctg	Gleed John (H) 48 Gleed Emily (W) 41 Gleed Frederick Wm (S) 17 Gleed Rosa (D) 15 Gleed Frank (S) 5	Agr/labourer Cattleman on farm Domestic servant	Worker Worker Worker	Naunton Burford Naunton Naunton Naunton
13 Naunton Ctg	Miffling Ann (H) (wid) 64 Miffling Harry George (grandson)			Evenlode Cheltenham
14 Naunton Ctg	Mustoe James (H) 32 Mustoe Sarah Ann (W) 30	Agr/labourer	Worker	Stowell, Northleach Naunton
15 Naunton Ctg	Williams Laura (H) (wid) 42 Williams George (S) 15 Williams Ernest (S) 11 Williams Minnie (D) 7	Agr/labourer	Worker	Hawling Naunton Naunton Naunton
16 Naunton Ctg	Townsend James (H) 63 Townsend Elizabeth (W) 62	Road contractor	Own acc.	Naunton Naunton
17 Naunton Ctg	Barnes William (H) (widr) 69 Barnes Mary Ann (sister) 65 Barnes Jane (niece) 32	Plate layer	Worker	Broadway, Worcs Naunton Naunton
18 Naunton Ctg	Bayliss Frederick (H) 42 Bayliss Selina (W) 32 Axtell George (boarder) 40 Jones Edwin (boarder) 1	Slater Haulier Haulier	Worker Worker Worker	Bourton on the Water Naunton Yarnton, Oxon Yarnton, Oxon
19 Naunton Ctg	Kite Martha (H) (wid) 64			Hodnet, Salop
20 Naunton Ctg	Beecham Richard (H) 63 Beecham Louisa (W) 61	Agr/labourer	Worker	Nether Swell Gt Rissington
21 Naunton Ctg	Bryan John (H) 59 Bryan Jane (W) 59	Agr/labourer	Worker	Naunton Naunton
22 Naunton Ctg	Townsend John (H) 58 Townsend Mary Ann (W) 50 Townsend Arthur Jesey (S) 11 Townsend Cuthbert Frank (S) 9	Road labourer	Worker	Naunton Bourton-on-the-Hill Naunton Naunton
23 Naunton Ctg	Hughes Charles (H) 67 Hughes Mary (W) 65	Cattleman on farm	Worker	Winchcombe Childswickham
24 Naunton Ctg	Harris Joseph (head-widr) 75	Agr/labourer	Worker	Naunton
25 Naunton Ctg	Wiggins? Richard? (H) 36 Wiggins? Sarah (W) 37 Wiggins? Harriett M (D) 9 Wiggins Sidney (S) 9	Agr/labourer	Worker	Hazelton London Birmingham Birmingham
26 Naunton Ctg	Clayton James Henry (H) 27 Clayton Ruth (W) 28 Clayton Nora Gladys (D) 8 Clayton Annie Elizabeth (D) 7 Clayton Thomas (S) 5 Clayton Albert Henry (S) 4 Clayton Alfred William (S) 1	Agr/labourer	Worker	Winchcombe London Winchcombe Stanway Stanway Stanway Stanway

Road, Street, number or name of House	Name & Surname of each person, relation to head of family, age last birthday	Profession or Occupation	Employer, Worker or Own account	Where born
27 Naunton Ctg	Townsend Reuben John (H) 27	Carter on farm	Worker	Naunton
	Townsend Sarah Ann (W) 26			Naunton
	Townsend Elsie Alice (D) 3			Naunton
	Townsend Nellie Maud (D) 11 mths			Naunton
	Kilby Edmund (f-in-law/widr) 73	Cattleman on farm	Worker	Naunton
28 Longford House	Hanks George (H) 56	Farmer	Employer	Naunton
	Hanks Eleanor (W) 46	Farmer	Employer	L. Rissington
	Hanks Maurice (S) 23	Engineer (Own acc.)	at home	Naunton
	Hanks George (S) 20	General dealer (Own acc.)		Naunton
	Hanks Mary (D) 15			Naunton
	Hanks Gerald (S) 14			Naunton
	Ennats Albert (visitor) 54			Lt. Haughton, Beds
	Ennats Mary (visitor) 53			Lt. Rissington
	Johnson Jane Ellen (servant) 29	Nurse (Own acc.)		Newcastle-u-Tyne
	Hopkins Harriet (servant) 18	Domestic servant		Blockley
29 Black Horse Inn	Williams George (H) 54	Coal agent	Worker	Naunton
	Williams Hannah Elizabeth (W) 54			Naunton
	Beame Florence Penelope (niece) 11			Cheltenham
30 Naunton Ctg	Smith Amy (H) wid. 73			Notgrove
	Hunt Alice (visitor) 13			Naunton
31 Naunton Ctg	Hunt Martha (H) 54			Stantonhavercourt Oxon
	Hunt Rosa (D) 19			Naunton
	Hunt Florence (D) 13			Naunton
	Hunt Ethel (D) 5			Naunton
32 Naunton Ctg	Bedwell Henry (H) 52	General labourer	Worker	Gt. Barrington
	Bedwell Elizabeth (W) 50			Naunton
	Bedwell Martha Jane (D) 19			Naunton
	Bedwell Frank (S) 12			Naunton
	Bedwell Alice Amelia (D) 9			Naunton
33 Shop	Harris Jesse (H) 50	Farmer/carrier/grocer	employer	Naunton
	Harris Elizabeth (W) 51			Icomb
	Harris Charles Mason (stepson) 30	Farmer's son	Worker	Icomb
34 Naunton Ctg	Oliver William (H) 38	Shepherd	Worker	Woodstock Oxon
	Oliver Emma (W) 41			Ely, Cambs
35 Naunton Ctg	Smith Raymond Wm (H) 32	Blacksmith (Own acc)	Worker	Naunton
	Smith Alice (W) 36			Conderton
	Barnett George (S of wife) 15	Blacksmith	Worker	Conderton
36 Naunton Ctg	Huckin Charles (H) widr. 66	Agr/labourer	Worker	Chadlington, Oxon
37 Naunton Ctg	Gardener Walter (H) 39	Wheelwright Own acc.	(at home)	Naunton
	Gardener Annie (W) 37			St. Awain, Mon
	Gardener Henry Walter (S) 2			Naunton
38 Naunton Ctg	Blowing Edward (H) 28	Shepherd	Worker	Dilkes, Glos
	Blowing Ada (W) 26			Fifield, Glos
	Blowing William (S) 3			Fairford
	Blowing Mary Ann (D) 1			Naunton
39 Naunton Ctg	Smith George (H) 58	Platelayer	Worker	Naunton
	Smith Ann (W) 49			Naunton
	Stait Frank (grandson) 7			Naunton
40 Naunton Ctg	Hunt James (H) 50	Shepherd	Worker	Condicote
	Hunt Harriet (W) 47			Naunton
	Hunt Albert (S) 25	Horseman on farm	Worker	Naunton
	Hunt William (S) 16	Horseman on farm	Worker	Naunton
	Hunt Frank (S) 10			Naunton
	Hunt George (S) 7			Naunton
41 Naunton Ctg	Pulham William (H) 80	Road labourer	Worker	Naunton
	Pulham Ann (W) 76	Dressmaker (own/cc)	(at home)	Naunton
	Pulham Joseph (S) 50			Naunton
	Pulham Clara (D) 41			Naunton

Road, Street, number or name of House	Name & Surname of each person, relation to head of family, age last birthday	Profession or Occupation	Employer, Worker or Own account	Where born
42 Naunton Ctg	Sidman Joseph (H) 72 Sidman Hannah (W) 78	Farm labourer		Westcote Lt. Rissington
43 Naunton Ctg	Pulham Daniel (H) 63 Pulham Sarah (W) 64 Pulham Mary Ann (D) 26	Stone Mason	Worker	Guiting Power Naunton Naunton
44 Naunton Ctg	Oakey James (H) 74 Oakey Elizabeth (W) 75	Stone Mason	Worker	Naunton Naunton
45 Naunton Ctg	Gardener Arthur M. (H) 42	Wheelwright	(Own acc. at home)	Naunton
46 Naunton Private House	Pulham William E. (H) 33 Pulham Mary E. (W) 34 Pulham Lilian (D) 9 Pulham Edward E. (S) 7 Pulham Wilfred W. (S) 6 Pulham Ellen E. (D) 5 Pulham Florence M (D) 11mths	Carrier & farmer	employer (at home)	Winchcombe Hatherly, Glos Naunton Naunton Naunton Naunton Naunton
47 Naunton Private House	Comeley Raymond E. (H) 26	Farmer (Own acc.)		Westfield Farm
48 Springfield Ctg	Matthews Elizabeth (H) wid. 92 Oakey Sarah (servant) 75	Living on own means Domestic servant		Naunton Naunton
49 Naunton Ctg	Hanks Rosa (H) 40 Millard Emily (companion) 26	Living on own means Companion/help		Naunton Wells, Som
50 Naunton Ctg	Hanks William Bullock (H) 48 Hanks Clara Maria (W) 46 Hanks William (S) 20 Hanks Horace Leslie (S) 8 Hanks Kathleen Hilda (daur) 7 Hanks Rene (daur) 2 Eeles Minnie (Serv) 16	Farmer Farmer's Son Domestic Servant	(Employer) at home Worker, at home	Naunton Naunton Naunton Naunton Naunton Naunton Burford, Oxon
51 Round House Huntsmans	Smith Abel Tom (H) 30 Smith Sarah (W) 28 Smith William (S) 4 Smith Elsie (daur) 2 Smith Matilda (daur) 7mths	Farm Bailiff	Worker	Greenham Fm, N'bury, Berks Greenham Fm, N'bury, Berks Naunton Naunton Naunton
52 Summerhill Farm Do Cottage	Stratford John (H) 53 Stratford Emma (W) 52 Stratford Mary (grand-daur) 11	Carter on farm	Worker	Gt. Barrington Northleach Eyford Hill
53 Naunton Ctg	Margetts Joseph (H) 74 Margetts Sarah (W) 67	Carpenter (house)	Own acc (at home)	Withington Westwall
54 Naunton Ctg	Hunt Henry (H) 63 Hunt Martha (W) 63 Bedwell Nellie (grand-daur) 16 Hunt Harry (grand-son) 13	General labourer	Own acc (at home)	Naunton Naunton Naunton Pontypridd, Wales
55 Naunton Ctg	Baylis John (H) 66 Baylis Janet (W) 71	Slate merchant	Employer (at home)	Naunton Scotland
56 Naunton Ctg	Baylis Henry (H) 40 Bayliss Elizabeth (W) 41 Argent Corisand (neice) 6	Slater	Worker	BOTW Oxford Oxford
57 School House	Nutt Frederick (H) 45 Nutt Ellen (W)	School master (certified teacher) Schoolmistress		Barnstaple, Devon Barnstaple, Devon
58 Naunton (cottage)	Privett Lucy (H) 37 Privett Frank (S) 14 Privett Alice (daur) 11	Farm labourer	Worker	SOTW(Stow on the Wold) Naunton Naunton
59 Naunton (cottage)	Lapper Richard (H) 65 Lapper Emma (W) 53	Agri/labourer	Worker	Bledington Naunton

Road, Street, number or name of House	Name & Surname of each person, relation to head of family, age last birthday	Profession or Occupation	Employer, Worker or Own account	Where born
60 Naunton (cottage)	Mitchell Joseph (H) 65 Mitchell Emma (W) 40	Slate maker Dress maker	Own acc (at home)	Cutsdean, Worcs Inkpen, Berks
61 Naunton (cottage)	Harris James (H) 39 Harris Ellen (W) 35 Harris Mary (daur) 13 Harris Emily Elizabeth (daur) 12 Harris Leah Rachel (daur) 11 Harris George James (S) 8	Agri/labourer	Worker	Naunton Preston Naunton Naunton Naunton Naunton
62 Naunton (cottage)	Hooper James (H) 37 Hooper Emily (W) 40 Hooper Reginald Fred' (S) 13 Hooper Sidney John Wakefield(S)11 Hooper James Wynn (S) 7	Postman	Worker	Northleach Naunton Naunton Naunton Naunton
63 Naunton (Post Office)	Hooper John William (H) 43 Wakefield Jane (Aunt-Wid) 77	Builder	Own acc (at home)	Northleach Sherborne
64 Naunton (cottage)	Gardon Walter (H) 26 Gardon Sarah (W) 29	Journey Baker	Worker	Coleman, Glos Ford, Glos
65 Naunton (cottage)	James George (H) 55 James Mary (W) 55 James William (S) 26 James Edward (S) 23 James Emma (daur) 20 James George (S) 18 James Mark (S) 15 James Raymond (S) 13 James Vera (grand-daur) 2	Farmer	Own acc	Moreton-in-Marsh BOTW Naunton Naunton Naunton Naunton Naunton Naunton Naunton
66 Naunton (cottage)	Midwinter William (H) 52 Midwinter Ann (W) 56 Midwinter Ada (daur) 18 Midwinter John (S) 15	Cattleman on farm Undercarter on farm	Worker Worker	Naunton Aldsworth Sherborne Turkdean
67 Naunton (cottage)	Organ James (H) 53 Organ Charlotte (W) 40	Carter on farm	Worker	Naunton Crawley, Oxon
68 Naunton (cottage)	Pulham Mary (H) wid 71 Dowler Mary (neice) 44	Dressmaker	Own acc (at home)	Naunton Naunton
69 Naunton (cottage)	Pulham Joseph (H) 72 Pulham Rebecca (W) 69	Plasterer		Naunton Naunton
70 Naunton (cottage)	James Charles (H) 45 James Emily (W) 46 James Walter (S) 16 James Albert (S) 13 James Emily (daur) 10 James Florence (daur) 5	Labourer Roadman Labourer Roadman Carter on farm	Worker	Naunton Naunton Naunton Naunton Naunton Naunton
71 Naunton (cottage)	Forth Eustace Bertram (H) 26 Forth Elizah Ellen (W) 30	Baker, bread	Worker	Lt. Rissington Brewood, Staffs
72 Naunton (cottage)	Pulham William (H) 58 Pulham Ellen (W) 58	Baker, bread	Own acc (at home)	Notgrove Winchcombe
73 Naunton (cottage)	Wheeler Jane (H) Wid 70			Barrington, Oxon
74 Naunton (cottage)	Dunford Jane (H) 59 Dunford Esther (sister) 58	Dressmaker Do	Own acc (at home) Do	Barrington, Oxon Barrington, Oxon
75 St. Andrew's Rectory, St. Andrew's Church	Bradley Enoch Brook (H) 46 Bradley Laura Midelton (W) 33 Pulham Annie (Serv) 33 Clements Mabel (Serv) 22 Wiggins Lily Elizabeth (Serv) 14	Clergyman (C of E) Cook/domestic Parlour maid/domestic General/domestic		Sedgley, Staffs Stapleton, Glos Naunton Itchington, Glos Birmingham
76 Naunton (cottage)	Wilks John (H) Widr 53	Agri/labourer	Worker	Milton-U-Wychwood
77 Naunton (cottage)	Hughes George (H) Widr 75	General labourer	Worker	BOTW
78 Naunton (cottage)	Mustoe George (H) widr 28 Mustoe Elizabeth Ann (mother-wid) 51	Cattleman on farm	Worker	Stowell, Northleach Oddington

Road, Street, number or name of House	Name & Surname of each person, relation to head of family, age last birthday	Profession or Occupation	Employer, Worker or Own account	Where born
79 Naunton (cottage)	Packer Mary (H) Wid. 61			Naunton
80 Naunton (cottage)	Davis Peter (H) 71	General labourer	Worker	Upper Swell
	David Mary (W) 70			Naunton
	David Albert (grandson) 19	Agr/labourer		Naunton
	Morris Albert Edward (grandson) 26	Agr/labourer		Naunton
81 Naunton (cottage)	Hobbs William (H) 39	Stonemason's labourer	Worker	Guiting Power
	Hobbs Mary Jane (W) 33			BOTW
	Hobbs Herbert William (S) 13	Errand Boy		Guiting Power
	Hobbs Jane Elizabeth (daur) 10			Guiting Power
	Tandy John (stepson) 9			Guiting Power
	Hobbs Gladys Dorothy May (daur) 2			Hawling
	Hobbs Mabel Lillian (daur) 1			Hawling
82 Naunton (cottage)	Davis Emily (H) 29			Naunton
	Davis Alice May (daur) 8			Naunton
	Davis Gladys Mary (daur) 5			Naunton
	Davis Florence Winnie (daur) 3			Naunton
	David Nellie Priscilla (daur) 9mths			Naunton
83 Naunton (cottage)	Bedwell Albert (H) 46	Farmer	Own acc (at home)	Maisey Hampton
	Bedwell Fanny Jane (W) 44			Naunton
	Bedwell William George (S) 24	Farmer's son		Naunton
	Bedwell Edward Arthur (S) 15	Farmer's son		Naunton
	Bedwell Albert Joseph (S) 15	Farmer's son		Naunton
	Bedwell Laura Annie (daur) 10			Naunton
	Bedwell Francis Jane (daur) 5			Naunton
84 Shop	Merrell John, (H) 54	Grocer	Employer (own acc)	Upton-on-Severn
	Merrell Sarah Elizabeth (W) 56			BOTW
	Merrell John Turner (S) 26		At home	Birmingham
85 Naunton (cottage)	Midwinter Thomas (H) 30	Agr/labourer	Worker	Naunton
	Midwinter Agnes (W) 40			Naunton
	Lane Herbert (boarder) 25	Baker, bread		Trowbridge
86 Naunton (cottage)	James Charles (H) 57	Agr/labourer		Guiting Power
	Reynolds George (lodger) 38	Agr/labourer		Kempsford
87 Naunton (cottage)	Lewis Elizabeth (H) 50			Chipping Norton
	Lewis Alfred Bertie (S) 19	Cattleman on farm	Worker	do
	Lewis Charles William (S) 15	Undercarter on farm	Worker	do
	Lewis George Ernest (S) 11			do
	Lewis Nellie Maria (daur) 9			do
	Lewis Elsie May (daur) 5			do
88 Naunton (cottage)	Smith Frank (H) 27	Cattleman on farm	Worker	Naunton
	Smith Emma (mother-wid) 66			Compton Abdale
89 Naunton (cottage)	Fletcher Charles (H) 56	Carpenter	Worker	Naunton
	Fletcher Sarah Ann (W) 44			Bledington
	Fletcher George (S) 15	Carpenter	Worker	Naunton
	Fletcher Christopher Chas (S) 13	Farm labourer	Do	Naunton
	Fletcher Horace Albert (S) 10			Naunton
	Fletcher Marjorie Emma (daur) 8			Naunton
	Fletcher Ellen Mary (daur) 5			Naunton
90 Naunton (cottage)	Smith John (H) 58	Machine minder (threshing)	Worker	Winchcombe
	Smith Matilda (W) 50			Naunton
	Smith Mabel (daur) 13			Naunton
	Smith Alice (daur) 11			Naunton
91 Naunton (cottage)	Heath Sarah Ann (H) 49	Agr/labourer	Worker	Naunton
	Heath John Haxley (S) 19			Lancashire
92 Naunton (cottage)	Maisey Mary Ann (H) 76			Calne, Wilts

Road, Street, number or name of House	Name & Surname of each person, relation to head of family, age last birthday	Profession or Occupation	Employer, Worker or Own account	Where born
93 Naunton (cottage)	Morris John (H) 46	Building Thatcher	Worker	Cold Aston
	Morris Elizabeth (W) 46			Naunton
	Morris John Walton (S) 15	Letter carrier		BOTW
	Morris Ellen (daur) 12			Chedworth
	Morris William Chas. (S) 8			Condicote
	Morris Minnie Mirriam (daur) 6			Sezingcote
94 Naunton (cottage)	Godfrey Charlotte (H) wid 65			Naunton
95 Naunton (cottage)	Collett (?) Samuel Geo. (H) 56	Baker	Employer (at home)	Guiting
	Collett Ann? Rebecca (W) 32			Whitchurch, Warwicks
	Collett Elizabeth Mary (daur) 3			Naunton
	Collett John George (S) 1			Naunton
	Millard Alice (Serv) 20	Asst' housekeeper		SOTW
96 Naunton (cottage)	Betteridge Charles (H) 31	Gardener domestic	Worker	Burford, Oxon
	Betteridge Sarah (W) 30			BOTW
	Betteridge Alice May (daur) 8			Naunton
	Betteridge Florence Christiana (daur) 7			Upper Slaughter
97 Naunton (cottage)	Cox William (H) 56	Farrier & coal agent	Employer (at home)	Finstock, Oxon
	Cox Jane (W) 54			Naunton
	Cox Lambert (S) 26	Farm labourer		Naunton
	Cox Ellen Selina (daur-in-law) 29			Handsworth, B'ham
	Cox Alfred (grandson) 3			Vauxhall, B'ham
98 Naunton (cottage)	Burge James Edward (H) 74	Sadler	Own acc (at home)	Naunton
	Burge Emily (W) 73			Cheltenham
	Burge George (S) 40	Sadler	Worker	Naunton
99 Naunton (cottage)	Hanks Eliza (H) wid 58	Living on own means		SOTW
	Hanks Alice Rosa (daur) 30			Naunton
100 Naunton (cottage)	Lockey Dennis (H) 31	General labourer	Worker	Lower Swell
	Lockey Ada (W) 28			Guiting
	Lockey Susie (daur) 7			Naunton
	Lockey Blanche (daur) 5			Naunton
	Lockey Hester Lavinia (daur) 4			Naunton
	Lockey Fred. William (S) 1			Naunton
101 Naunton (cottage)	Hopcroft James (H) 68	Dairyman (milk)	Own acc (at home)	Banbury, Oxon
	Hopcroft Mary Ann (W) 70			Naunton
	Collett Charlotte Lavinia (daur-in-law) 32			Shipton Oliffe
	Lockey Nora (grand-daur) 8			Naunton
102 Naunton Inn	Cox Charles (H) 33	Farmer	Employer (at home)	Naunton
	Cox Jane (W) 31			Northleach
	Cox Lionel (S) 6			SOTW
	Cox Suzett (daur) 4			SOTW
	Cox Alaric (S) 3			Naunton
	Cox Margaret (daur) 10mths			Naunton
103 Naunton (Down Farm)	Willis John (H) 49	Carter on farm	Worker	Filkins, Oxon
	Willis Elizabeth (W) 46			Chedworth
	Willis George (S) 18	Carter on farm	Worker	Fulbrook, Oxon
	Willis Robert (S) 16	Farm labourer	Worker	Naunton
	Willis Alice (daur) 14			Naunton
	Willis Ernest (S) 10			Naunton
	Willis Kate (daur) 8			Naunton
	Willis Edith (daur) 6			Naunton
	Willis Winnie (daur) 4			Naunton
	Willis Arthur (S) 3			Naunton
	Willis Frederick (S) 4mths			Naunton
104 Naunton Down Cottage	James George (H) 54	Shepherd	Worker	Greenham, Berks
	James Emma (W) 52			BOTW
	Cross Albert George (nephew of S) 4			Naunton

Road, Street, number or name of House	Name & Surname of each person, relation to head of family, age last birthday	Profession or Occupation	Employer, Worker or Own account	Where born
105 Aylworth Farm House	Hanks Ann (H) Wid 61		Employer (at home)	Tipton, Staffs
	Hanks William Comeley (S) 31	Farmer		Aylworth, Naunton
	Hanks Harold Charles (S) 29	Farmer	Do	Aylworth, Naunton
	Hughes Samuel William (guest) 26	Baptist Minister		Far Cotton, Northants
	Williams Beatrice (Serv) 22	General servant	Worker	Aylworth, Naunton
106 Naunton (Aylworth cottage)	Brunsdon Richard (H) 33	Shepherd on farm	Worker	Coln swire, Glos
	Brunsdon Matilda (W) 31			Hazelton
	Brunsdon William (S) 7			Longborough
	Brunsdon Fred (S) 4			Eyford Hill
	Brunsdon Ernest (S) 2			Aylworth, Naunton
	Wiggins Richard (fath'-in-law) Widr 67	Cattleman on farm		Northleach
107 Naunton (Aylworth cottage)	Green Thomas Wm. (H) 27	Carter on farm	Worker	Brockhampton
	Green Edith (W) 26			Aylworth, Naunton
	Green Thomas Wm (S) 3			Aylworth, Naunton
	Green John (S) 1			Aylworth, Naunton
	Weaving Wm Henry (boarder) 23	Under carter on farm	Worker	Coln St. Aldwyn
	Smith Harry (boarder) 18	Groom on farm	Worker	Notgrove
108 Harford Cottage	Tubb Henry (H) 61	Carter on farm	Worker	Southrop
	Tubb Mary Ann (W) 59			Baunton
109 Harford Cottage	Williams David (H) Widr 58	Shepherd on farm	Worker	Lower Swell
	Williams Louisa (daur) 20			Aylworth, Naunton
110 Hill Barn	Beames William (H) 55	Carter on farm	Worker	Arlington Glos
	Beames Eliza (W) 57			Northleach
	Beames Frank (S) 22	Agr/labourer	Worker	Turkdean
	Beames Charles (S) 18	Agr/labourer		Naunton
	Beames Minnie (daur) 12			Hawling
	Beames Florence (daur) 10			Hawling
	Beames George (S) 8			Gt. Barrington

Appendix 11

The 1914 Domesday Record of Naunton Properties (Finance Act 1909/10)

Details are extrapolated from 'Form 37' completed for each property by the District Valuer for the Commissioner Of Inland Revenue to determine duties on land values. The number on the left is the 'Hereditament' No (legal term). Letters in the Notes column, 'v' = valuation, and 'Edc' is believed to be the certification of the owners death.

Sale details in the Notes column do not necessarily indicate that the whole of the property was sold, as occasionally only a portion of the whole was sold.

Where the present location of these largely unnamed properties is not immediately apparent, I have tried to add the location (in brackets) but some errors are possible.

Acre = 4840 square yards   A Rood = a quarter of an acre or 1210 sq yds   . A Perch = one fortieth of a Rood or 30½ square yards.

No	Description	Owner	Occupier	O.G.V.	Area	Notes
1	House & Cottages, buildings & land Roundhill Farm	Mrs Margaret A. Waddingham Guiting Grange, Lower Guiting	Mr Edgar Hanks	£7980	562 acres 2 roods 13 perches	v.20749 Edc. Margaret A Waddingham 19/11/1918 £4500 PD. Sale to Bellow 1936 £5000 (563 acres) PD. Sale to Bellow 1937 £4500
3	Floodlands, Naunton	Mrs Margaret A. Waddingham Guiting Grange, Lower Guiting	Mrs Waddingham	£630	29½ acres	Edc. Margaret Waddingham 19/11/1918, £100. Sale to Kilmer, 1936 £7200 (see 23) Sale to Dale 1937 £3100 (283 acres)
6	Building & land, Church Farm (West side of Aylworth Road)	Mrs Margaret A. Waddingham Guiting Grange, Lower Guiting	Harwood (late Hooper)	£2425	172 acres 21 perches	Edc. Margaret Waddingham £2900 To Kennard (See GP 30)
10	House & cottages, buildings & land Naunton Downs	Mrs Margaret A. Waddingham Guiting Grange, Lower Guiting	Mr Albert Bedwell	£3835	260 acres 2 roods 31 perches	Edc. Margaret Waddingham 1918 £3379 Sale to Killmer 1936 £7200 (845 acres) see 23 Sale to Dale 1937 £3100 (283 acres)
13	Cottage & Garden (Ash Tree Cottage)	Mrs Margaret A. Waddingham Guiting Grange, Lower Guiting	Mrs Pulham	£80	9 perches	Edc. Margaret Waddingham 1918, £50 To Kennard
14	Cottage & Garden (Ash Tree Cottage)	Mrs Margaret A. Waddingham Guiting Grange, Lower Guiting	Harry Higgins	£60	7 perches	Edc. Margaret Waddingham 1918, part of £14000 To Kennard (See GP 30)
15	Cottage & Garden (Ash Tree Cottage)	Mrs Margaret A. Waddingham Guiting Grange, Lower Guiting	George Higgins	£60	7 perches	Edc. Margaret Waddingham 1918, part of £11000. To Kennard (see GP 30)

368 Naunton 2000

No	Description	Owner	Occupier	O.G.V.	Area	Notes
18	House & Paddock (Church House)	Mrs Margaret A. Waddingham Guiting Grange, Lower Guiting	Mrs Dunford	£650	1 rood 39 perches	Edc. Margaret Waddingham 1918, part of £11000 To Kennard (See GP 30)
19	Land, orchard & garden near Church (rear of Littons)	Mrs Margaret A. Waddingham Guiting Grange, Lower Guiting	Mr Albert Bedwell Naunton	£90	1 acre 23 perches	Edc. Margaret Waddingham 1918 £60 To Kennard (see GP 30)
20	Land, Mill Ham (Meadow North of Windrush View)	Mrs Margaret A. Waddingham Guiting Grange, Lower Guiting	Mr Pulham	£70	1 acre 2 roods 27 perches	Edc. Margaret Waddingham 1918 part of £1400 To Kennard (see GP 30)
21	House, buildings & land Naunton Inn Farm (East side of Aylworth Road)	Mrs Margaret A Waddingham Guiting Grange, Lower Guiting	Mr C Cox (now Harwood)	£960	26 acres 2 roods 31 perches	Edc. Margaret Waddingham 1918 £2900 To Kennard (see GP 30)
23	House & cottages, buildings & land, Aylworth	Mrs Margaret A. Waddingham Guiting Grange, Lower Guiting	Mr William Comely Hanks	£7650	565 acres 3 roods 2 perches	Edc. Margaret Waddingham 1918 £7000 Sale to Killmer 1936 (845 acres) £7200 Sale to Layland 1936 (562 acres) £6800
27	Land, garden & shed "The Oven" (Garden down to the river; Windrush Vale)	Mrs Margaret A. Waddingham Guiting Grange, Lower Guiting	Mr E James	£38	2 roods 6 perches	Edc. Margaret Waddingham 1918 £35 To Kennard (see GP 30)
28	House, buildings & land, Summerhill	Rev Ernest Frederick Eales The Rectory, Naunton	Albert Bedwell	£2575	201 acres 2 roods 15 perches	Sale to Hanks 31/12/1935 £2200 Sch A, 14.01.1937 £95 (200 acres)
30	Land, Summerhill	Rev Ernest Frederick Eales The Rectory, Naunton	Harris	£585	65 acres 3 roods 29 perches	Sale to Hanks 1935 £2200 (see 280)
31	Buildings & land, Hill Farm (Part of Golf Course)	Rev Ernest Frederick Eales The Rectory, Naunton	Chas Cox	£1080	78 acres 1 rood 4 perches	Sale to Hanks 1936 £1780 (with 35, 49 & 33)
33	Buildings & land, Hill Farm (Part of Golf Course)	Rev Ernest Frederick Eales The Rectory, Naunton	Mr W Pulham	£800	58 acres 3 roods 33 perches	Sale to Hanks 1936 £1780 (see 31)

No	Description	Owner	Occupier	O.G.V.	Area	Notes
35	Buildings & land (Part of Golf Course)	Rev Ernest Frederick Eales The Rectory, Naunton	Wm Cox	£1140	81 acres 3 roods	Sale to Hanks 1936, £1780 (see 31)
39	House, buildings & land, The Rectory	Rev Ernest Frederick Eales The Rectory, Naunton	Rev Ernest F Eales	£1575	1 acrs 3 perches	
40	Allotment land & buildings (Most of the cricket ground)	Rev Ernest F Eales The Rectory, Naunton	Various	£700	25 acres 6 perches	
41	2 houses, buildings & orchard (Overbrook)	Mrs Eliza Hanks Oxford Villa, Naunton (Overbrook)	W Cox & void	£400	2 acres 29 perches	Sale Mrs E Hanks to Mrs Helen Fowler, South Shields 1912, £400. Sale, Fowler to Perry 1916, £450 Death, Chas Perry 1918, v.£450 Edc. Lucy Perry 1921 £625 Edc Philip Brook 1928 £360 (Oxford Villa) Sale to Hodson 1934 £1750 Sale to Buckley 1936 £2850 Sale to Rashdall 1937 £3500
44	Land, shed, Grange Hill (Old Well Cottage)	Rev E.F. Eales	Mr Albert Bedwell	£45	1 rood 31 perches	
45	House & premises (Waterstone Cottage)	Thomas Wm Hooper Naunton	F Timms (now Davis)	£135	22 perches	Sale, Hooper to Heath 1918 Sale, Hooper to Pulham & Sons 1919 £115 Edc. G.J.Heath £825
46	Storehouse & Cottage near Chapel (South-West of Waterstone Cottage)	James Hooper Naunton	J Hooper & Privett, (now James)	£80	12 perches	Sale, Hooper to Heath 1918, with No 45 Sale, Hooper to Pulham 1919, £115 Edc. G.J.Heath (dec'd) £100
48	Land, Aylworth Road	As Trustees: Rev E.J. Eales, Mr F Nutt & Mr A Bedwell	Wm Cox	£30	1 acre 3 roods 20 perches	
49	Land, pasture, meadows, Harford Bridge	Rev E.J. Eales Naunton Rectory	James Mills (now Griffin)	£180	5 acres 3 roods 33 perches	Sale to Hanks in 1936, £1780 (see 31)
50	House, buildings & land Waterloo (Waterloo House & field)	Trustees: Mr W.C. Hanks, Edgar Hanks & Mrs Wm Brown (all of Naunton) & Mr Reginald Hanks (of Charlton Abbots)	Mr Gardener	£400	8 acres 14 perches	v. W.C.Hanks (dec'd) 1932 £400 Sale, Hanks to Hanks H.L. 1935 £550 (includes part 51 & 56)

370 Naunton 2000

No	Description	Owner	Occupier	O.G.V.	Area	Notes
51	Land, Waterloo (Between Waterloo Hse & Brookfield)	William Comely Hanks, Aylworth Farm	R.N. Smith	£45	3 roods 26 perches	v.Wm C Hanks (dec'd) 1932 £40 (in No 50) Sale Hanks to Hanks H.L. 14/10/1935 £550 (in No 50)
54	Cottage, buildings & land, Huntsmans Barn (Lavender Hill Stud)	*Trustees*: W.C. Hanks, Aylworth Farm Reginald Hanks, Charlton Abbots Edgar Hanks, Roundhill Farm Mrs Wm Brown, Lower Harford	William Brown & Jas Harris	£340	25 acres 14 perches	Sale, Hanks & others to Hanks 1918, £415 Sale to Huntsmans Quarries, £400
56	House, Mill, buildings & land (The Mill)	Mr William B. Hanks Naunton Mill	Mr WB Hanks, Harris & Townsend now the owner	£510	9 acres 2 roods 8 perches	v. Wm B. Hanks (dec'd) 1921, £600 Sale, Hanks to Hanks H.L. 14/10/1935, £550, (included in part 50)
58	Longford Farm, Buildings and land	Mr G Hanks, Snr Longford Farm	Mr G Hanks	£3775	238 acres 2 roods 8 perches	v. G Hanks, 1918, £4315 58/1 sale, Freeman & another to Hanks 1919, £3270. 58/2 Hanks & others to Hanks, 1919, £895. 58/3 sale Hanks & others to Fluck 1920 £85. Sale, Hanks to Huntsmans Quarries 1941 £400 (see 54)
62	3 cottages & gardens (Elm Tree Cottage, Hope Cottage & Cherry Tree Cottage)	Mr Geo Hanks	Smith, Hill & Stratford	£150	1 rood 5 perches	Sale, Freeman & another to Hanks 1919, £150
64	Cottage (Northcote)	Mr Geo Hanks	J Hunt	£50	14 perches	
69	House, Bakery, buildings & land (Yew Tree House & The Bakehouse)	A.J. Smith Naunton	A.J. Smith	£340	1 acre 3 roods 33 perches	v. death S.C.Smith 1917 £430 Sale, Spiers to Butler 1917 £? Sale, Butler to Hooper 1918 £170 Sale, Butler to Hayward 1918 £295 v. Thomas Hayward 1924 £295
70	House, premises & orchard, Dale House	Annie Rebecca Collett Dale House, Naunton (deceased)	Mrs A R Collett (deceased)	£440	4 acres	Mr Wilkins, Slaughter Mill, as trustee to the children of Mrs Collett. Mr W C Hanks, 1932 £250
72	House & garden (11 Dale Street)	Annie Rebecca Collett Dale House, Naunton (dec'd)	Alfred Fluck	£80	12 perches	Mr Wilkins, Slaughter Mill, as trustee to the children of Mrs Collett

Naunton 2000 371

No	Description	Owner	Occupier	O.G.V.	Area	Notes
73	House & garden (10 Dale Street)	Annie Rebecca Collett Dale House, Naunton (dec'd)	L Cox	£65	21 perches	Mr Wilkins, Slaughter Mill, as trustee to the children of Mrs Collett
74	House & garden (Dale Cottage)	Annie Rebecca Collett Dale House, Naunton (dec'd)	Betteridge	£100	33 perches	Mr Wilkins, Slaughter Mill, as trustee to the children of Mrs Collett
77	4 cottages, buildings & land, Dale Terrace	J Dean and others	Mr J Dean & others	£435	4 acres 32 perches	Vendor, Joseph Thos Wilkins, L Slaughter, purchaser, Edgar Hanks, Aylworth. Sale 1910 £435. Sale to Hilda Hanks 1932 £300 Sale to Pulham 1934 £15. Sale, Hanks to Pulham 1934 £25
83	House, Shop & garden, Dale Terrace	Annie Rebecca Collett, Dale House, Naunton & Mr Wilkins, Slaughter Mill, Lower Slaughter	Clarence Higgs	£100	26 perches	Mr Wilkins, as trustee to the children of Mrs Collett (dec'd). WC Hanks (dec'd) 1932 £160 (inc No 70)
84	House & cottage, buildings & land; Manor Farm	William Thos Garne, Esq Aldsworth, Northleach	W.B. Hanks (now G Hanks Jun'r)	£4955	286 acres 28 perches	Sale Garne to Hanks 1920 £4,400
88	3 cottages & gardens (Hatters Cottage)	William B. Hanks Naunton Mill	Jesse Woods; void; W.J.Hobbs	£110	28 perches	v. WB Hanks (dec'd) £66 v. WA Bibby 1939 £225
91	House, 5 cottages, buildings & land at Lower Harford	H le Blanc Lightfoot Esq, Bursar, Corpus Christi College, Oxford	William Brown	£4370	266 acres 2 roods 37 perches	
100	4 cottages & bakery (The Quadrangle)	Mr W Williams Birmingham	Messrs W Pulham, now Hawker, Midwinter & Forth	£400	1 rood 5 perches	
104	House & premises (The Pound)	James William Hooper Naunton	James Wm Hooper	£250	32 perches	Sale to Brain 1922 £600 v. Brain (dec'd) 1926 £550 Sale to Timms £200. v. Hooper J 1938 £260
105	Smithy	Mary Rebecca Phillips Naunton		£15	2 perches	

372 *Naunton 2000*

No	Description	Owner	Occupier	O.G.V.	Area	Notes
106	2 cottages adjoining Black Horse Inn (Black Horse Inn)	Various Shareholders of the Brewery	Mrs Phillips Mrs Higgins	£121	11 perches	Sale to A.B Green, Stow Brewery (20/21 shares) 1913, £114. 5s 9d. Sale 1914 Freeman (mortgagee) to Cheltenham Original Brewery Co, £140
107	Land, Naunton (Opp' Brambling Cottage, Summer Hill Lane)	William C. Hanks Aylworth, Naunton	Void	£5	6 perches	
108	Cottage (Behind water pump, west of Black Horse Inn - now gone)	William C. Hanks Aylworth, Naunton	Griffin	£50	12 perches	v. W.C. Hanks 1932 £45
109	Cottage (North end of Black Horse Inn)	Mrs Eliza Coleman Grafton Farm, Pendock, Tewkesbury	Mrs Higgins	£60	3 perches	Sale, Coleman to Arkell 1913 £45
110	Land – Littlesworth (West & North of Littlesworth)	Geo James Naunton	G James	£50	2 acres 3 roods 2 perches	v. Geo James 1925 £390 (includes 111)
111	House & buildings (1 Littlesworth)	Geo James Naunton	Larway	£100	1 rood 4 perches	v. Geo James 1924 £390 (includes 110)
112	Cottage & garden (3 Littlesworth)	Geo James Naunton	William James	£50	8 perches	v. Geo James 1924 £100 (includes 113)
113	Cottage & garden (2 Littlesworth)	Mr George James Naunton	Mark James	£50	8 perches	Geo James 1924 £100, includes 112
114	Cottage & garden (Rushdale)	Mrs Julia Ann Bayliss	Jas Hunt	£56	20 perches	Sale, Bayliss to Morris 1920 £68
115	House & land (orchard) (Grays Orchard)	Mrs J.A.Bayliss, Cheltenham Rd Winchcombe	Mr A Gardner	£130	2 roods 29 perches	v. J Bedwell 1925 £200 v. Julia A Bayliss 1925 £20 sale to Muller 1936 £350
116	3 cottages & gardens (1&2 Rose Ctg & Kiftsgate Ctg)	Mr Henry Bayliss Naunton	Townsend, Williams & Fletcher	£180	26 perches	Sale: Bayliss to James 1919 £160 v. Lescelles 1934 £165 v. Muller 1937 £150

Naunton 2000   373

No	Description	Owner	Occupier	O.G.V.	Area	Notes
117	1&2 Sunny Bank	Unknown - Form 37 is missing	Unknown	Unknown	Unknown	Unknown
118	2 cottages & gardens (1&2 Jasmine Cottage)	Mr Henry Bayliss Naunton	Bayliss & Beacham	£140		
123	4 cottages & gardens (Kiftsgate House)	Frank Bayliss Naunton	Williams, Gleed, Miffling & Davis	£210	36 perches	
124	Cottage & garden (Sunny House)?	Frank Bayliss Naunton	Beames	£35	5 perches	v. Bayliss 1938 £50 with 125 v. Fluck & Bayliss to BV Bayliss all (126)
125	Cottage & garden (Sunny House)?	Frank Bayliss Naunton	J Mitchell (now F Gleed)	£40	5 perches	v. E.Bayliss 1938 £50 with 124 (see 126) v. Fluck & Bayliss to BV Bayliss all (126)
126	House & Harness Shop (Garden of Sunny House)?	Frank Bayliss Naunton	James, Hooper & Bayliss	£170	1 rood 6 perches	
131	7 cottages & gardens (Sunnydale & 2, 3 and 4 Sunny Cottages)	Fred'k J Bayliss Naunton	Owner + Hughes, Daws, Townsend, Bryan, Brasham & Harris	£360	1 rood 33 perches	Sale to James 1921, (2 cottages) £123. Sale to Aston 1921, £62. v. F Bayliss 1923 £200
138	2 cottages & gardens (Windrush Vale)	G Williams Naunton	C James & Oliver James (now void)	£180	?	v. G Williams dec'd 1915 £165
140	House & garden (Rock Cottage)	John Stratford Naunton	J Stratford	£150	20 perches	
141	House & land (Farthing Green)	Jas Mills Naunton	James Mills	£160	2 roods 12 perches	v. 1923 £225
142	House & land (Cromwell House)	Jas Mills Naunton	Mr Merrett (late Phillips)	£90	8 perches	Sale + 141, 1923 £225
143	House & land (Vine House)	Arthur Gardner c/o Mr L Gardner, Shipton Oliffe	Oliver James; formerly A Gardner	£120	2 roods 29 perches	
144	Cottage, buildings & land (Spring Cottage)	Mr Maurice Hanks, Eyford	Mr Geo Hanks (now W.B.Hanks)	£800	27 acres 3 roods 4 perches	Owner Maurice Hanks, Eyford. Sale to M.R.Hanks 1932 £100 for No 1 Spring Cottages
145	Cottage (used as Saddler's Shop) (Spring Barn)	Maurice Hanks, Eyford	J Hayward	£80	14 perches	

No	Description	Owner	Occupier	O.G.V.	Area	Notes
146	4 cottages & gardens (Windrush View)	Wm Buttle, Ford, Broadway	Davis, Benfield, M Davis, Packer	£210	1 rood 29 perches	1.1.1929 Hannah Buttle, v.£240
150	4 cottages & gardens (Windrush View)	George James Naunton	Organ, Hughes, Dowler & Wilkes	£150	1 rood 24 perches	v. Geo James 1924 £115
154	House & land (The Gables & Cotswold Cottage)	J Merrell Naunton	J Merrell	£230	3 roods 29 perches	v. death J Merrell 7.9.1918, £225
155	5 cottages & gardens (2&5 Dale Street & Farmhouse)	Florence E Cosnett 'Clifton' Severn Stoke, Worcs	Lewis; James; Midwinter; (void) F.Smith	£165	25 perches	Sale 1912, £110 26.10.1912 28.10.1918 Ellis to Williams £200 e.d. Williams £300
160	Cottage & garden (Sheepwell Cottage?)	John Wood, Notgrove	Geo James	£150	17 perches	
161	2 cottages & shed (Yew Tree Cottages)	James Oakey Naunton	Oakey & Pulham	£85	15 perches	OAP file No 504, Jas Oakey (Claimant) £45
164	The Manse	Trustees: Basil Wood, Stow. Thos Comely, Notgrove Station. Geo Hanks, Longford Hse. Frank Perry, Notgrove.	Rev' H.F. Chipperfield	£250		
165	House & garden (Sunnyside)	Mrs Jane Shotton Winchcombe	W.E. Pulham	£260	1 rood 3 perches	Sale, Shotton to Pulham & Sons 1919, £275
166	Cottage & garden (Rosemary Cottage)	Mr J Pulham Naunton	J Silman	£40	8 perches	v.Clara Pulham, dec'd 1925 £120
167	Cottage & garden (Rosemary Cottage)	Mr J Pulham Naunton	Mr J Pulham	£40	8 perches	v.Clara Pulham, dec'd 1925 ££120
169	Building, land Parkers Barn Summerhill Lane	Mr George Hanks Now William B. Hanks Naunton	Miss Rosa Hanks Spring Cottage	£500	20 acres 3 roods 16 perches	Sale 1929 £500 V 1930 £350 Miss R Hanks
170	House (Parkers Cottage)	Miss Rosa Hanks, Spring Cottage	E Hughes	£180	24 perches	Sale 1930 £320

No	Description	Owner	Occupier	O.G.V.	Area	Notes
171	House & Paddock (Brambling Cottage)	Mr Jesse Harris Naunton	Mr J Harris	£280	2 rood 17 perches	Sale 1922 £302 Sale 1928 £302
172	House & premises The Black Horse	Mrs C.S.Freeman, 236 St James Ct London	Mr George Williams	£1000	12 perches	Vendor 1915: Mrs CS Freeman, London Purchaser: Cheltenham Original Brewery Co Ltd
173	House (Cherry Cottage)	Mr Walter Gardner Naunton	Mr Walter Gardner	£100	25 perches	
176	School, Schoolhouse & land	*Trustees:* Rev E.F.Eales, The Rectory. F. Nutt, Schoolhouse. A. Bedwell, Naunton		£1085	1 rood 6 perches	
177	Church of St Andrews	Rev E.F.Eales The Rectory, Naunton		£3900	2 roods 39 perches	
178	The Baptist Chapel	*Trustees:* Basil Wood, Stow Thos Comely, Notgrove Station Geo Hanks, Longford House Frank Perry, Notgrove		£900	20 perches	
180	The Parish Pound (Garden adjoining The Manor side of house called 'The Pound')	Edward Francis Stow-on-the-Wold		£5	6 perches	

Appendix 12

Victoria History of Gloucestershire, vol. VI (1965), pp. 76–87; the history of Naunton.

NOTE: This article is reproduced by permission of the General Editor of the Victoria History of the Counties of England. Although the text has not been altered to take account of 2003 V.C.H. punctuation conventions, a few misprints have been silently corrected.

Information in the glossary and in the alphabetically-keyed notes has been supplied by the author. Words marked on their first occurrence with an asterisk are explained in the glossary.

The Parish of **Naunton** lies on the west border of the hundred, 12 miles east of Cheltenham and 5 miles west of Stow-on-the-Wold, crossed by the River Windrush and the main road from Cheltenham to Stow. The southern part of the parish includes the hamlet of Aylworth, which though forming part of Slaughter hundred in the Middle Ages[1] was from 1608 considered to be in Bradley hundred,[2] and the hamlet of Harford. Both had small villages in the early Middle Ages which later shrank to become single farms. The parish, which is irregular in shape, comprised 3,177 a.,[3] of which 33 a. were transferred to Temple Guiting in 1935.[4]

The River Windrush, which forms the boundary for a short distance on both the east and west sides, runs through the middle of the parish. Above Harford Bridge the course of the river has been straightened, and the old course, which can be traced in the meadows, remains the parish boundary. A stream runs from Aylworth into the river at Lower Harford. The land rises steeply on both sides of the river valley at 500 ft. to a height of 650 ft. in the south and 750 ft. in the north at Summer Hill. The parish, which is mainly on the Great and Inferior Oolite, has fault lines running across the middle of it and along its north and south boundaries.[5] A number of quarries, some still in use, could be seen in 1962 particularly on the Great Oolite in the north. The lower slopes on each side of the river have long been used mainly for arable farming, and it was there that the open fields lay before inclusure in 1778.[6] Aylworth and Harford have provided extensive sheep-pastures from the 14th century, and Naunton Downs on the west side of the parish was used always as pasture. The river valley contains alluvial deposits which make good meadows. The parish has little woodland and in the 18th century it was suggested that this fact with the absence of marshland and its situation on the downs accounted for the healthy climate of Naunton, where the death-rate was said to be unusually low.[7]

The parish has a number of antiquities, including round barrows, Roman burial sites, and Romano-British occupation sites.[8]

The earliest village in the parish is traditionally said to have been at Lower Harford,[9] on the gravel[10] beside the ford from which the hamlet derives its name, at the point where Harford Bridge was later built. The tradition is perhaps supported by the name Naunton, suggesting a new settlement. The population of Harford was still relatively high, in proportion to its hidage, in 1086[11] compared with the rest of the parish, but before that date Naunton village, almost a mile and a half farther up the river valley from Harford, had probably become the main centre of population. The village, which stretches for about a mile along the river valley, probably began as a more compact settlement in the hollow at the west end of the village where the church stands, a small area of grass perhaps being all that remains of a green around which houses were grouped. A small 16th-century house close to the church is thought to have been the rectory before a new one was built, slightly east of it, in 1694,[12] and Church House, beside the churchyard, though built in the 18th century, may be the ancient site of the manor.[13] A group of cottages, called Little Worth, north of the church was built in the 17th and 18th centuries, but tradition associates the cottages with Little Malvern Priory[14] and they may be on a site built over in the Middle Ages. The village extended, probably at an early date, across the river (where the bridge known as Hurd Bridge is traditionally said to mark the position of an ancient ford), and eastwards along the river valley, perhaps as far as the manor house.

The village expanded farther east in the 16th and 17th centuries towards the site of the mill at the extreme east end of the village. Three large houses, Cromwell House, Kiftsgate, and Longford House, were built at the east end of the village in the 16th, 17th, and 18th centuries respectively. During the 19th century the number of houses increased considerably with the rise in population. Cottages were built on the hill, leading up from the west end of the village, which was cut away *c.* 1850 when the Baptist chapel was rebuilt.[15] The village extended, in the 18th and 19th centuries, along Dale Street (the name possibly derives from the Dale family which held land in the parish in the 16th century), formerly a track leading south from the west end of the village towards Roundhill Farm. Dale Terrace, leading off Dale Street, was built in 1871[16] and at the east end of the village nine council houses were built between 1943 and 1960.[17; a] Outside the village, at Naunton Downs and Summer Hill, two post-inclosure farm-houses were built *c.* 1800.

The settlement at Harford, where seven people were enumerated in 1086[18] and two people paid subsidy in 1327,[19] was largely deserted by 1341[20] and by 1381 it was no longer distinguished from Naunton.[21] In the 16th century Llanthony Priory had a house at Harford[22] and in the 17th century the only house in the hamlet was Lower Harford Farm.[23] A farm was built at Upper Harford, about a mile south of Lower Harford, probably in the 18th century[24] and in the early 20th century it was replaced by two cottages. During the 19th century a few cottages were built at Upper and Lower Harford and at Harford Hill[25] where the cottages were converted into a farm-house *c.* 1960.[26]

The settlement at Aylworth lay in a hollow surrounded by springs, south-west of Naunton village. In 1086 eleven people were mentioned there[27] and in 1327 three were assessed for subsidy.[28] By 1341 Aylworth, like Harford, had been partially deserted,[29] and in 1381 only six people paid poll tax.[30] By the 17th century Aylworth formed one estate with a single large house[31] and perhaps a few cottages, as in 1962. Roundhill Farm, which became part of Aylworth[32] although it may not always have been, was possibly built in the 17th century or earlier and rebuilt in the 18th century; a cottage at Roundhill was built in 1886.[33]

Forty-six people in all were mentioned in 1086 in Naunton, Harford, and Aylworth;[34] although the population may have decreased by the 14th century it is also possible that the desertion of the two hamlets resulted in a redistribution rather than a decline of population. Fifty-three people from the whole parish

Victoria History of Gloucestershire, vol. VI (1965), pp. 76–87; the history of Naunton.

paid poll tax in 1381.[35] In the late 16th century and early 17th the population almost doubled, from 18 families in 1563[36] to 35 in 1650,[37] and it continued to rise during the 18th century; the number of families had increased to 40 by the late 17th century[38] and to 44 by 1735.[39] The population, which was 433 in 1801, rose steadily during the earlier 19th century to 568 in 1851; by 1881 there was a slight decrease and thereafter the population declined rapidly until 1951 when it had dropped to 340.[40]

A road referred to in the 10th century as the 'way of the people of Bourton'[41] was the ancient road, Buckle Street,[42] which crossed the north-east corner of the parish, and the minor road leading from Harford Bridge towards Upper Slaughter was, at the same date, called the ridgeway.[43] The road running across the north of the parish was called Slaughter Way in the 14th century[44] and apparently was later known as Winchcombe Way;[45] Sheepwell Lane running from it to the village divided Naunton fields from those of Guiting Power.[46] Since Harford Bridge is by the site of the ford from which Harford took its name, the Gloucester–Stow road, turnpiked in 1775,[47] may follow the course of an ancient road, possibly pre-dating Naunton village. The fact that Harford Bridge was made by the 16th century[48] supports the suggestion that the road (called the Gloucester way in the 16th century)[49] passed the village on the south side of the river by that time. Before 1778 roads ran from the turnpike road to the village, to Aylworth Farm, and to Guiting Power.[50] The bridge at the west end of the village was built by the rector, John Hurd, c. 1819, and in 1851 the same rector was responsible for building the bridge at the other end of the village.[51] The Banbury and Cheltenham Railway was built in 1881[52] across the southern part of the parish, with Notgrove station about three miles from Naunton village.

The water supply for the village was drawn from the river and from springs on the high ground above the village; in the late 19th and early 20th century the parish council was much occupied with schemes for improving the water supply,[53] and pumps could be seen in many parts of the village in 1962. Aylworth had a good supply of water from the several springs on the hills around it. Main water was supplied to Naunton in the early 1950's. Electricity was provided only by private supplies[54] until 1948 when the main supply was made available.[55] A main sewage disposal system was introduced in 1962. A small village hall, built on land conveyed in trust for that purpose in 1937, was managed by trustees appointed by the parish council.[56;b]

All the buildings in Naunton, except the council houses, are of stone and most have Cotswold stone roofs. A notable feature of the village is the large number of buildings, including the church and many of the cottages, in which *ashlar has been used. A considerable amount of rebuilding took place in the 19th century, and in a number of the houses sash or casement windows have replaced stone mullioned windows. Naunton village is unusual because the most dominant building is the large 19th-century Baptist chapel built in a prominent position on a hill.

The Manor House, a large 17th-century farm-house, was almost entirely rebuilt in the late 19th century though the back of the house retained the 17th-century windows with mullions and transoms. The house is of ashlar, two-storied with dormers and a Cotswold stone roof; the front entrance has a pointed arched porch and the windows at the front have sashes. To the west of the house stands a large dovehouse, reputedly built in the 15th century, of rubble with a stone roof, four gables, and a small central turret which apparently was a lantern. The windows have stone mullions and a continuous dripmould, and the doorway has a four-centered arch. The dovehouse had fallen into disrepair and was restored c. 1949.[57] The oldest surviving house in the village probably is Cromwell House, at the east end, built c. 1600 of rubble partly roughcast with a stone roof and two gables. It was originally **L**-shaped on plan. The windows have mullions, dripmoulds, and leaded lights, and the side elevation has a four-centered arched doorway with imposts, keystone, and moulded jambs and arch. There is no apparent foundation for the tradition that Cromwell House was so called because Oliver Cromwell stayed there, but it may have belonged to the Aylworth family, one member of which was an active supporter of Parliament during the Civil War.[58] The rectory, built in 1694, is a square two-storied house of ashlar with mullioned and transomed windows, and has hipped roofs with dormers.

Aylworth Farm was rebuilt in the late 17th century[59] and rebuilt again, supposedly on a slightly different site, in the 18th century.[60] It is three-storied, of ashlar with a Cotswold stone roof and sash windows which, on the south-west side, are in round-headed recesses. One of the large 18th-century barns has a small reset 15th-century window. Lower Harford Farm was also a 16th- or 17th-century house rebuilt in the 18th century, and a vaulted cellar, found during alterations to the house in the mid-20th century,[61] probably belongs to an earlier building. The house is of ashlar with a Welsh slate roof, two-storied with dormers. The windows at the front have segmental heads, and those at the side of the house, with dripmoulds and mullions, are of an earlier date.

With the exception of the Aylworth family and the rectors, none of the principal landowners lived in the parish until the mid-19th century, a fact which perhaps accounts for the influential position that the rectors enjoyed. Most of the rectors, from the 16th century, were resident[62] and took an active part in parish affairs, and rectors were responsible, among other things, for building the school and the bridges in the village. The rectory is the largest house in the village and at inclosure the rector received the largest allotment.[63] Two of the rectors, Ulpian Fulwell (d. 1585)[64] and Clement Barksdale (d. 1687),[65] were noted poets and writers. A 19th-century rector, Edward Litton, was a friend of 'Lewis Carroll', who is said to have often visited Naunton Rectory.[66] The Aylworth family held land and lived in the parish from the 14th century to the 18th. Captain Richard Aylworth (d. 1661) was with the Parliamentary army at the siege of Malmesbury (Wilts.) in 1644,[67] and took a prominent part in stopping the king's army at Stow. In 1646 he claimed that he had spent a large sum in the service of Parliament[68] and in 1656 his financial difficulties were said to have ruined his family.[69] The Hanks family, one of the principal landowners in 1962, also has a long association with the parish. A Nicholas Hanks was living there in 1568,[70] and members of the family afterwards became lessees and, later, owners of the manor. The only event of national importance which has touched the parish was in 1643 when the Earl of Essex and his army

Victoria History of Gloucestershire, vol. VI (1965), pp. 76–87; the history of Naunton.

passed through Naunton on the way from Stow to Gloucester.[71]

Manors And Other Estates. The manor held by Aylmer in NAUNTON in 1066 was held in 1086 by a nun, Quenild.[72] It was probably part of Quenild's estate that was sold by the Abbess of Lisieux (Eure) in the 13th century to Little Malvern Priory[73] which held it of the Crown as a third of a fee.[74] The monks evidently attached the estate to their other manor in Naunton and there seems to be no further reference to it as a separate manor.

The manor of NAUNTON held by Turstan in 1066 was held in 1086 by Osbern son of Richard, whose under-tenant was Roger Doyly.[75] The manor passed, with the rest of Osbern's land, by marriage to the Mortimer family of Richards Castle (Herefs.) in the early 13th century,[76] and presumably in the early 14th century it passed to Richard Talbot (d. 1328), whose wife Joan was daughter and heir of Hugh Mortimer.[77] Richard's grandson, John Talbot, died seised of the manor in 1374[78] and was succeeded in turn by his sons, Richard (d. 1382) and John (d. 1388), and his daughter Elizabeth, wife of Sir Warin L'Arcedekne;[79] on her death in 1407 the estates were divided between her daughters,[80] and no further evidence has been found of the over-lordship of Naunton manor. Members of the Doyly family continued as under-tenants during the 12th and early 13th centuries, Ralph Doyly holding the manor in the mid-12th century, Hugh Doyly towards the end of the century,[81] and Roger Doyly c. 1211.[82] In 1235 the manor was held as half a fee by Baldwin,[83] perhaps the same as the Baldwin of Harford who was lord of Harford. Little Malvern Priory had acquired the manor by 1287[84] and retained it until the Dissolution[85] when the priory held it in chief.

In 1544 the manor was granted to Richard Andrews,[86] who in the same year sold it to John Dale (d. 1547),[87] the lessee from 1530.[88] It passed to John Dale's brother Thomas in 1548,[89] and in 1551 he granted it to Thomas Dale the younger.[90] The manor may have reverted to John Dale's wife, Margaret, who had married Edward Baskerville in 1547,[91] for Sir Thomas Baskerville died seised of it in 1572.[92] In 1591 the manor passed to John Talbot, who married Eleanor, daughter and heir of Thomas Baskerville,[93] and he sold it to Giles Venfield and others[94] before 1608, when Venfield and John Collett were lords of the manor.[95]

Collett's half of the manor passed to his brother Henry in 1642[96] and afterwards to Anthony Collett (d. 1719), then to Anthony's brother Henry (d. 1731),[97] and then to William Moore[98] (d. 1768), whose wife Elizabeth was Henry Collett's daughter. After the death of Moore's second wife c. 1795 the estate passed to Hill Dawe, an illegitimate son of William Moore,[99] and William Dawe was the owner from c. 1807 to 1826.[100] It was probably this estate, with the reputed manor, centered on the Manor House with the large dovecot,[101] which William Hanks[c] purchased from James Clark in 1857.[102] In 1962 it was owned by Mr. G. Hanks,[d] the great-grandson of William Hanks.

Giles Venfield's *moiety of the manor passed to his son Thomas in 1612,[103] and by 1650 it had been sold to William Rogers.[104] In 1720 John Rogers sold to John Snell of Guiting Grange,[105] and the estate, called Naunton farm and later Church farm,[106] remained part of the Guiting Grange estate until the 20th century. It was owned successively by John Snell's son, Powell (d. 1767), Powell's son, also Powell, the Revd. Reginald Winniat[107] and, from 1848, by John Waddingham and later by his son John[108] and John's daughter Margaret. Most of the land, which by 1936 was no longer part of the Guiting Grange estate,[109] became attached to the house, formerly the Naunton Inn,[110] which was then called Church Farm, and in 1962 there was little land belonging to the former site of the Venfield moiety of the manor, then called Church House.

The land in Aylworth held as a manor by Alvin in 1066 was, by 1086, divided into two estates, held by Gilbert son of Turold and William Goizenboded;[111] neither part seems to have been separately called a manor before the 14th century. Gilbert's holding, which became attached to his manor of Rendcomb, passed with the rest of his estate to the Earl of Gloucester in the mid-12th century and descended with the earldom until it became extinct in 1347.[112] Aylworth then passed by marriage to Ralph, Earl of Stafford, and descended with that earldom until 1444 when Humphrey, Earl of Stafford and Duke of Buckingham, was attainted and his lands passed to the Crown.[113] In the 16th century the over lordship of Aylworth seems to have passed successively to the lords of Rendcomb manor, John Tame, his son Edmund, (d. 1544), Edmund's wife Katherine, and his sister Margaret, wife of Sir Humphrey Stafford.[114] The association with Rendcomb manor persisted until the 17th century,[115] but by 1640 Edward Aylworth was said to hold in chief.[116]

The tenant of the manor in 1086 was Walter,[117] and from the 12th century to the late 13th the mesne tenants were members of the Delamare family, who were lords of Rendcomb also.[118] Towards the end of the 12th century William Delamare granted his land in Aylworth to Llanthony Priory[119] whose estate, called the manor of AYLWORTH from the mid-14th century,[120] passed to the Crown at the Dissolution.[121] Land in Harford also belonging to the priory was treated as part of Aylworth manor.[122] Small grants of land in Harford were made to the priory in 1395 and 1411,[123] but in 1538 Llanthony Priory's estate was said to include only one messuage in Harford.[124] In 1564 the manor of Aylworth was granted to Vincent and Richard Calmudy,[125] who in the same year sold it to Anthony Aylworth[126] whose family were holding land in Aylworth by the early 14th century.[127]

By 1566 Anthony Aylworth also owned the estate in Aylworth[128] that was held by St. Oswald's Priory, Gloucester, from the mid-13th century.[129] The estate, probably deriving from the land held by William Goizenboded in 1086,[130] was in the 16th century called the manor of AYLWORTH or ROSE COURT.[131] It passed to the Crown at the Dissolution[132] and was granted in 1543 to Richard Andrews and Nicholas Temple, who sold it to John Stafford in the same year.[133] After the manor had passed to Anthony Aylworth (d. 1566) the two parts of Aylworth were treated as one manor. It passed successively to Richard Aylworth[134] (d. 1578), Richard's son Edward (d. 1640), Edward's son Bray[135] (d. 1640), Bray's son Richard (d. 1661), and Richard's son Joshua,[136] after whose death in 1718 the manor was sold to John Herring of London.[137] The manor then passed successively to Herring's sister, Mary Blagg of Gunthorpe (Notts.) in 1742, to her son Henry, and in 1764 to Henry's six children jointly.[138] In 1801 it was purchased by

Victoria History of Gloucestershire, vol. VI (1965), pp. 76–87; the history of Naunton.

Thomas Vernon Dolphin of Eyford and in 1803 passed to his son Vernon Dolphin.[139] In 1854 it was sold[140] to John Waddingham of Guiting Grange and was subsequently owned by his son John, and then in turn by John's daughters, Margaret Waddingham[141] and Mrs. Richardson,[142] who sold it in 1936 to Mr. A. G. Walker. The estate was sold by Mr. Walker in 1959 to Mr. G. E. Mavroleon,[143] the owner in 1962.[144]

It is suggested that the manor of Herfortin given by Denebeorht, Bishop of Worcester, to the see of Worcester in 822 was HARFORD manor;[145] a grant of 963 by Oswald, Bishop of Worcester, to his *thegn Ethelnoth of land in Harford[146] may support the theory. In 1066 the manor was held by Alfer and in 1086 by Gilbert son of Turold,[147] from whom it passed, with Aylworth, to the Earls of Gloucester and, after 1347, to the Earls of Stafford.[148] In the mid-13th century the manor was held by Baldwin of Harford, who alienated half the manor to the Templars, and his heirs held of the honor of Gloucester in 1328.[149] By 1359 it was held by Thomas of Rodborough (d. 1367) and seems to have been attached to Rodborough Manor.[150] It is unlikely that there were any real manorial rights associated with the small estate in Harford which Thomas of Rodborough held and it was not often called a manor. The estate passed in 1392 to the great-nephew and heir of Thomas of Rodborough, Richard Browning,[151] who died in 1400, when it passed to his sister Cecily[152] and afterwards to her husband Guy Whittington of Pauntley (d. 1441).[153] John Whittington, Guy's grandson or great-grandson, died seised of the manor in 1525 when it passed to his son Thomas[154] (d. 1546). John Whittington, possibly Thomas's step-brother, was dealing with the manor in 1588,[155] and in 1640 Edmund Whittington, perhaps the great-grandson of Alexander, another step-brother of John Whittington, sold the manor to Henry and John Collett and John Taylor.[156]

In the 18th century, under the name of Upper Harford farm, Harford manor belonged to the owners of the Collett moiety of Naunton manor.[157] In 1857 Upper Harford was sold,[158] probably to John Waddingham, who owned it in 1869,[159] and in 1936 it was sold with Roundhill farm[160] to Mr. A. G. Walker, becoming part of the Aylworth estate. By the early 20th century a ruined house and a few cottages were the only indications of the possible site of the manor at Harford.[161]

Eynsham Abbey, to which Ralph Doyly had given the *tithes of his *demesne in Naunton by the mid-12th century, was granted a small estate there in the late 12th century by Hugh Doyly.[162] The abbey was receiving rent from the land, describing it as a messuage and *yardland, up to 1465, and it was probably included with the abbey's land in Wick Rissington in 1535.[163]

By 1185 the Templars had half a hide in Naunton, given to them by Roger Doyly,[164] and during the 13th century they acquired half the hamlet of Harford from Baldwin of Harford.[165] The land became attached to the manor of Temple Guiting with which it passed to Hugh Despenser and, in 1328, to Pancius de Controne,[166] who sold it to William de Clinton, Earl of Huntingdon, before 1354.[167] The estate was granted in the late 15th century to John Huddleston of Sudeley,[168] whose wife sold it in 1517 to the Bishop of Winchester,[169] from whom Corpus Christi College, Oxford, received it in 1518.[170] Land in Naunton held of the College in 1612 by Giles Venfield[171] may later have been sold, but the estate in Harford, including c. 250 a., which in the 17th century was divided into two farms,[172] called by the 18th century Lower Harford and Harford Hill,[173] was retained by Corpus Christi College until 1958. In that year both farms were bought by the lessee, Mr. S. J. Clifford, who sold Harford Hill Farm a few years later.[174]

St. Oswald's Priory, Gloucester, had been granted an estate in Naunton (possibly part of the land held by Quenild in 1086)[175] by 1316, when the prior was said to be one of the lords of Naunton.[176] The estate was leased by John Dale from 1532[177] and it may have been the farm said to have been called Bale Farm[178] and later Roundhill Farm. It was granted in 1543 to Richard Andrews and Nicholas Temple,[179] who sold it in the same year to John Stratford,[180] and afterwards it passed to the Aylworth family,[181] becoming part of the Aylworth estate until the mid-18th century.[182] In 1796 Roundhill was owned by members of a family called Ruck and was sold in or before 1826 to John Bullock[183] whose family owned it until 1880,[184] when it was bought by John Waddingham and became part of the Aylworth estate again.[185]

Economic History. The larger of the two estates in Naunton, which had decreased in value from £8 to £5 in 1086, had five demesne ploughs and five shared by seven *villani*. The smaller estate had a smaller demesne with two ploughs and no *servi* and eight *villani* with four and a half ploughs. The five hides in Aylworth, where there was possibly more land to a plough and fewer tenants than at Naunton, had three demesne ploughs (the estate of one hide being all demesne), and two ploughs shared by three *villani*. Harford, though including only one hide, was of the same value as the estate of four hides in Aylworth, and, with two demesne ploughs and two held by four *villani* and one bordar, had proportionately a considerably higher number of ploughs and tenants than the rest of the parish.[186]

There seems to be no evidence of the amount of land kept in demesne in Naunton by Little Malvern Priory, and in 1535 almost the whole value of the priory's estate there came from assized rents and rents of tenants at will.[187] St. Oswald's Priory in 1291 had two *carucates in demesne in Aylworth and Aston Blank,[188] and in the 16th century probably most of the priory's estate in Aylworth was demesne land. Llanthony Priory's estate included one carucate in demesne in 1279,[189] and demesne pasture was presumably increased especially after the mid-14th century when some land in Aylworth and Harford ceased to be cultivated.[190] In the 15th century and early 16th, when Aylworth manor with the arable demesne was leased, the pasture seems to have been kept for the priory's sheep.[191] In 1535 the arable land held by Llanthony Priory was valued at 36s.^{e} and the pasture at £7 16s.[192] The three yardlands attached to Harford manor in the 14th century[193] were probably all held in demesne.

Some small freeholders held land in Naunton parish in the 13th century.[194] In 1260 the tenants of the Mortimer manor were holding 14 yardlands,[195] and in 1535 the rents of free tenants and tenants at will of the same manor amounted to £4 15s. 6d.[196] Of ten landholders who paid subsidy in 1327 in Naunton township two paid respectively 10s. and 6s. and the others less than 2s.[197] The estate of St. Oswald's Priory

Victoria History of Gloucestershire, vol. VI (1965), pp. 76–87; the history of Naunton.

in Naunton had at one time six tenants each holding a messuage and yardland,[198] and, in 1536, one free tenement.[199] By 1568 the same estate included four tenants.[200] Tenants of the priory in Aylworth and Aston Blank paid 77s. rent in 1291; a lay fee from which the priory received 6 marks may have been entirely in Aston Blank.[201] There seems to be no evidence of tenants on St. Oswald's Priory's land in Aylworth in 1536, apart from the farmer of the manor.[202] Llanthony Priory's estate in Aylworth included free and customary tenants in the 12th century,[203] and in 1291 tenants' rents amounted to 20s.[204] Customary tenants evidently owed *heriots[205] and *bedrips, though a tenement where labour service had been commuted for money payment by the 14th century may have been typical of the other customary holdings.[206] The number of tenants at Aylworth had decreased by the mid-14th century[207] but there were still some freeholders, as well as the farmer of the demesne, towards the end of the century.[208] In 1540 Llanthony Priory's estate apparently included only one tenant.[209] In the Templars' estate, where there was at least one tenant holding a yardland in 1185,[210] 14 yardlands were held by tenants in 1260.[211] The estate included four yardlands in the early 14th century[212] and at least one free tenant in 1507.[213]

Although no direct evidence has been found of separate open fields for Aylworth and Harford it is probable that both places had their own fields at one time. The names Upper and Lower Aylworth field, used in the 17th century to describe inclosures of c. 600 a.,[214] suggest a former open field divided into two parts, with perhaps common pasture on Aylworth Downs. Aylworth and especially Harford supported a large number of ploughs in 1086,[215] and up to 1220 when they were said to include seven and five ploughs respectively,[216] but by 1341 both places had been largely deserted and allowed to go out of cultivation.[217] By that time it was presumably no longer economic to cultivate the infertile uplands that formed the greater part of Aylworth and Harford and it is probable that the 14th and 15th centuries saw an extensive change from arable to sheep farming in those places.

Some land remained arable in Harford in the 14th century[218] and in Aylworth in the 16th,[219] but sheep farming was important on Llanthony Priory's estate by the mid-14th century when the prior's shepherd was paid an annual stipend by the farmer of part of the demesne.[220] In 1385 the Prior of Llanthony claimed 200 a. of pasture from John Aylworth,[221] and in the 16th century the Aylworth family had 600 sheep at Aylworth.[222] In 1535 pasture was much the most valuable part of Llanthony Priory's estate.[223] The increase in pasture was probably accompanied by inclosure by Llanthony Priory and St. Oswald's Priory. The Templars' land in Harford was also probably inclosed by the 16th century and though there was still common pasture in Harford in 1545[224] and in Aylworth in 1538,[225] by the late 16th century probably both places were wholly inclosed.

Most of the land in Naunton manor remained arable during the Middle Ages, although sheep farming was generally important in the parish by the 16th century. Nearly half the rector's tithes in 1535 came from wool[226] and in the early 17th century there were four shepherds in Naunton.[227] The common fields of Naunton lay north and south of the village, stretching from the common pasture land called Naunton Downs on the west, to Harford on the east and including most of the parish north of the village. The land around Summer Hill in the north also provided common pasture and the land beside the river was meadow. A hedge divided the land into an East and West field in the 16th century and, probably, earlier. The two fields were later distinguished as the Upper and Lower fields and in the early 16th century they seem to have been subdivided into the east and west Upper and Lower End fields. Both fields were divided into *furlongs and, if the rector's *glebe was typical, land was held in scattered pieces of one or often half a field acre, with c. 30 field acres to a yardland.[228] Fifty sheep-pastures to a yardland was the usual stint in the 17th century.[229] At inclosure in 1778 more than half the parish was included in the open fields.[230]

In 1608 five people in Naunton and Harford, including a *yeoman and three *husbandmen, probably had large farms.[231] In the mid-17th century Edward Aylworth's land in Naunton included a number of tenants.[232] By the late 17th century the manor was divided among freeholders,[233] and it is unlikely that any *copyhold tenure persisted. Of nine people holding land in the open fields of Naunton in the late 17th century, three seem to have had large farms.[234] Harford in the 17th century included two farms of c. 200 a. and one smaller one.[235] Aylworth apparently formed one large farm in the early 17th century[236] though later Roundhill was farmed separately.[237] During the 17th and 18th centuries the number of landholders probably increased and just before inclosure in 1778 some 20 people were holding land in the parish. In Naunton itself there was one large farm and another six substantial holdings, with about eight smaller holdings. Harford was still divided into three farms at that time and Aylworth included one farm of c. 600 a., another of 200 a., and two small farms.[238]

In 1778 all the remaining open land in Naunton, including 1,699 a. of arable and pasture, was inclosed. The two fields, then called the Upper and Lower End fields, were of almost equal size, the Upper field being slightly larger, and Naunton Downs included c. 150. a. Fourteen landholders received allotments, the largest being that of the rector who received 496 a. in lieu of glebe and tithe; two other people received allotments of more than 200 a., three between 100 a. and 200 a., and eight less than 50 a. The land was allotted, on the whole, in scattered pieces, though most of the larger estates included about half their land in single large allotments, and the inclosure award also provided for some exchange of land to consolidate estates.[239] During the 19th century the number and size of the farms underwent little change, and in the late 19th century the number of substantial farms was about eight, with some 20 small holdings.[240] Although during the 19th century several farms were bought by the owners of the Guiting Grange estate, they continued to be farmed separately. By 1962 Aylworth, Upper Harford, and Roundhill were farmed as one estate of 1,100 a.,[241] Manor Farm was c. 500 a.,[242] and four other farms were more than 200 a.

Arable farming may have increased at Aylworth during the 17th century: in 1686 Aylworth Farm included 350 a. arable and 125 a. pasture,[243] and in the late 18th century it was mostly arable land.[244] At Harford farming was mixed arable and pasture in the 17th and 18th centuries.[245] The parish was said to be mainly arable in the late 17th century,[246] but after

Victoria History of Gloucestershire, vol. VI (1965), pp. 76–87; the history of Naunton.

inclosure there may have been an increase in sheep farming again and in 1801 less than half the parish was returned as sown.[247] During the 19th century sheep-and-corn farming continued, with a predominance of arable land on most of the farms. In 1936 when the Aylworth estate was sold only a small part of it was under cultivation,[248] but by 1962 more than half the land was arable and the rest was used for sheep and cattle. On the other farms also farming was mixed, with beef and dairy cattle replacing sheep to some extent.

Quarries at Harford may have been in use by the late 13th century when one of the principal masons employed by the Crown was a Walter of Harford,[249] and the property of Corpus Christi College at Harford included a quarry in 1541.[250] By the 17th century quarries were in use in Naunton manor also[251] but it was possibly not until the 19th century that quarrying became an important source of employment in the parish.[252] The most extensive quarrying was carried out in the north-east part of the parish, at Huntsman's Quarries, and smaller quarries in various parts of the parish were in use in the 19th century,[253] especially for providing stone slates for roofing. Although there were still builders and slaters in Naunton in the early 20th century several of the quarries had closed.[254] Brockhill Quarry, on the east side of the parish, was in use until the 1950's and in 1962 Huntsman's Quarry and the building company associated with it were an important source of employment in the parish.[255; f]

There was a butcher in the parish in the 16th century,[256] and in 1608 two tailors, a carpenter, and a smith were working in Naunton; 18 people were employed as servants at that date, but the figure apparently includes agricultural labourers working on the Aylworth estate.[257] The parish had tailors in the mid-17th century[258] and in 1779,[259] a shoemaker in 1735,[260] and a cordwainer in the late 18th century.[261] There were smiths in Naunton during the 17th century[262] and, probably continuously, until the first half of the 20th century.[263] In 1811 26 families were occupied in trade, manufacture, or industry, compared with 63 families employed in agriculture.[264] Towards the end of the 19th century Naunton had 2 carpenters, a wheelwright, a bootmaker, 3 bakers, 2 butchers, and 2 shops.[265] There was no inn in the parish[266] until the early 19th century when the Naunton Inn was built on the turnpike road to Stow. By 1910 it had become a farm-house,[267] and another inn in the village, opened by 1870,[268; g] was the only one in 1962. A cider-press, said to have been in use for c. 150 years, could be seen there in 1962, although it had not been used since 1940. In 1962 there were two shops, a bakery, and a petrol station in the village. The greater part of the population worked on the land or in quarrying in 1962, but several worked outside the parish. The village had several residents who had retired there from other parts of the country.

Mills. The mill in Naunton belonging to the estate of Quenild in 1086, when it was valued at 5s.,[269] may have passed to either Little Malvern or St. Oswald's Priory. In 1590 Naunton manor included at least one mill;[270] Naunton Mill, at the east end of the village, built in the 17th century, probably on the site of the earlier mill, was presumably one of the two mills belonging to John Charles of Naunton in 1788.[271] By 1867 it belonged to William Hanks[272] and members of that family held the mill, which included a bakery in the late 19th century, until the 1930's when it was sold[273] and ceased to be used as a mill. The range of buildings was apparently built in the 18th century, and the mill machinery, still almost intact in 1962, was made largely of wood in the late 19th century, though some parts were probably earlier.

It is suggested that a track called Mill Way in 743 ran from the north boundary of Notgrove to a mill at Lower Harford, and there was a mill below Lower Harford in 963.[274] It was probably the mill that belonged to the estate of Gilbert son of Turold in 1086, when it was worth 5s.,[275] but no later evidence of Harford Mill has been found.

Local Government. In 1286 view of *frank-pledge was claimed by the Abbot of Fécamp in Naunton and Aylworth as part of Salmonsbury hundred, by the Templars in their land in Naunton and Harford, and by the Earl of Gloucester in Aylworth and Harford.[276] The hamlet of Aylworth, which attended the court at Rendcomb of the Earls of Gloucester[277] and, subsequently, of the Earls of Stafford, until the 16th century,[278] had by the early 17th century apparently become part of Bradley hundred. In the late 16th century Naunton and Aylworth each had a constable and tithingman,[279] but there seems to be no evidence that Harford was a separate tithing at that time.

Little Malvern Priory and Llanthony Priory held courts in Naunton[280] and Aylworth,[281] but no court rolls are known to have survived for any of the manors in the parish. Naunton manor court had ceased to function long before the mid-18th century.[282]

Churchwardens' accounts survive from 1776; a vestry minute book for the years 1540 to 1776 was apparently lost in the late 19th century.[283] Expenditure on poor-relief increased fivefold between 1776 and 1803, when parish expenditure in lawsuits was high. In that year 34 people received regular relief and 10 occasional relief,[284] and although there was a decrease in the numbers relieved in 1813, expenditure had increased. From 1813 expenditure fell.[285] Naunton became part of the Stow-on-the-Wold Poor Law Union in 1835, and of the Stow-on-the-Wold Rural Sanitary District in 1872, being transferred in 1935 to the newly formed North Cotswold Rural District.[286] The parish council, formed in 1894,[287] met regularly in 1962.

Church. There seems to be no evidence for the tradition that the earliest church in the parish was at Lower Harford.[288] The church at Naunton was probably built by the mid-12th century when there was a dispute about the tithes of Naunton between the Abbot of Eynsham (Oxon.) and Alan of Slaughter, priest;[289] the building includes some 12th-century work.[290] The earliest known documentary reference to the church is of 1260, when the cure was served by a rector. In that year the tithes were confirmed by the Bishop of Worcester to Little Malvern Priory,[291] to which also the advowson was granted by the Abbess of Lisieux during the 13th century.[292] In 1281 the prior granted the advowson and the tithes to the bishop for an annual pension of 8s.[293] In 1286 the living was held by the chaplain of the mortuary chapel of Worcester Cathedral[294] and the following year, during the absence of the chaplain, the bishop annexed the church to the mortuary chapel.[295] A vicar was apparently officiating in 1291[296] but a

Victoria History of Gloucestershire, vol. VI (1965), pp. 76–87; the history of Naunton.

vicarage was not endowed. The next chaplain of the mortuary chapel, given administration of Naunton church in 1292,[297] seems to have assumed the revenue without presentation[298] and a dispute arose when in 1301, during a vacancy of the bishopric, the Prior of Little Malvern tried to present.[299] Thereafter the association with the chapel ceased, the church retained its original status as a rectory, and the bishop retained the patronage.[300] No later evidence of the 8s. pension has been found. In 1962 the benefice was still a rectory. The bishops of Worcester retained the patronage until 1852 when it was transferred to the Bishop of Gloucester,[301] who was the patron in 1962.[302]

The church was valued at £6 13s. 4d. in 1291 when the vicar's portion was £4 6s. 8d. and Little Malvern Priory's portion was 8s.[303] By 1535 the value had increased to £15[304] and it continued to rise, to £90 in 1650[305] and £140 in 1750.[306] In 1535 the rector had all the tithes, which were valued at £14 19s. 7d.[307] Until inclosure in 1778 all the land in the parish was subject to tithe.[308] A messuage and half a yardland which belonged to the rector in the late 13th century[309] may have been the glebe, which in 1535 included 35½ a. of arable and 1 a. of meadow.[310] In 1584 and during the 17th and 18th centuries the glebe consisted of two yardlands with 100 sheep-commons and 8 cow-commons and a house,[311] rebuilt in 1694.[312] At inclosure the rector received 53 a. for his glebe and 443 a. for tithe from the land inclosed and from c. 1000 a. of old inclosures.[313] In 1841 the tithes still payable from 563 a. of old inclosures were commuted for a corn-rent.[314] During the 19th century and early 20th the rector's estate was one of the largest in the parish and the rectory was valued at c. £450. Most of the rectory estate was sold between 1935 and 1939[315] and in 1961 the glebe amounted to 40 a.[316] The rectory house[317] was sold in the mid-20th century,[h] since when there has been no residence in the parish.

In 1303 the Crown presented to the rectory a man who was not even in minor orders, and the following year this rector was licensed to go to Rome with the Archbishop of York[318] and to study for seven years, during which he was to receive the order of subdeacon.[319] The next rector, a subdeacon when he was instituted, was given leave of absence to serve the Bishop of Bath and Wells,[320] and the rector in 1317 was chaplain to Aymer of Valence and a pluralist.[321] His successor, a clerk of the Bishop of Worcester, did not receive priest's orders for two years after his institution.[322] John Whittington, whose tenure of the rectory for 13 years in the late 14th century[323] seems to have been longer than most, was probably a member of the family that held Harford manor.[324] In the late 15th century and early 16th, when there were curates at Naunton, the rectors probably did not reside.[325] One of the 14th-century and two of the 15th-century rectors were graduates.[326]

In 1551 the rector was not resident but the curate was said to be satisfactory.[327] The rector instituted in 1559 was deprived of the living two years later.[328] In 1570 Ulpian Fulwell, the poet, became rector and, though he was a pluralist, he seems to have lived at Naunton.[329] His successor Joseph Hanxman, a graduate and preacher,[330] rector for 46 years, also lived at Naunton, and the lessee of the rectory estate at this time was called Hanxman.[331] Thomas Freeman, who became rector in 1632, was related to a family of that name holding land in Naunton.[332] He was ejected from his living in 1651 but continued to live in the parish, probably carrying on a private ministry, and was buried at Naunton in 1660.[333] Two ministers served the cure during the Interregnum and one of them was ejected in 1660 when Clement Barksdale became rector.[334] A royalist and a noted preacher, scholar, and poet, Barksdale held two other benefices in 1660, but he lived at Naunton and died there in 1687.[335]

The glebe house was rebuilt in 1694[336] and during the 18th and 19th centuries the rectors continued to live at Naunton, serving the cure themselves, often with the assistance of a curate.[337] Between 1764 and 1860 two men, Anselm Jones and John Hurd, held the rectory, for 43 and 53 years respectively.[338] Edward Litton, a noted theological writer, was rector in the late 19th century.[339] From the 16th century Naunton appears to have been unusually well served by its rectors, and it is perhaps surprising that by the mid-19th century the congregation of the parish church was apparently very much smaller than that of the Baptist chapel.[340] In the mid-20th century the rectory was vacant for 10 years, being served by a retired priest and then by the Vicar of Guiting Power, who in 1962 was instituted to the rectory.[341]

Several small benefactions by unknown donors for the repair of the church amounted to c. 5 a. in the 17th century,[342] and an estate in Harford, about which there had been a dispute settled in Chancery in the late 17th century, produced 8s. in 1736.[343] By the early 19th century 2 a. allotted at inclosure were let for 30s.; the 5 a. and the 8s. had been lost by that time.[344] In 1953 1 a., called Church Bell Rope Land, produced 15s. which was used for maintaining the bells.[345]

The church of *ST. ANDREW*, built of ashlar with a Cotswold stone roof, comprises chancel and nave undivided by a chancel arch, short north aisle, north vestry, west tower, and south porch. The church was probably built in the 12th century and before 1878 the south door retained a rounded arch with toothed mouldings of that date.[346] A corbel head reset over the east window of the vestry is thought to be of the 12th century, and a Saxon cross found under the nave during the rebuilding in 1878[347] was reset in the north-west wall of the nave. The masonry used to block a window at the south-east end of the nave bears markings possibly of the 12th century. The eastern of the north windows of the aisle, square-headed of three lights with tracery, was built c. 1400. The west tower, embattled and pinnacled, of three stages with carved heads and gargoyles, was built in the 15th century. The west windows of the tower and aisle, of three lights with hoods and corbel heads, are of the same period. In the 16th century some windows in the church contained painted glass, including representations of the apostles and other saints,[348] fragments of which were still visible in the late 18th century.[349] The east end of the aisle was a Lady Chapel, used in the 16th century as a burial place by the Aylworth family.[350]

In the 16th century the church was largely rebuilt, the new work including the chancel, the nave, and the north aisle. The north aisle does not reach to the west end of the nave, on which it opens through two wide flat arches supported on an octagonal pillar with concave sides. The roof of the nave was lowered and the weathering of the former roof can be seen on the east side of the tower. In 1962 some of the timbers

Victoria History of Gloucestershire, vol. VI (1965), pp. 76–87; the history of Naunton.

appeared to survive from the 16th century. The round-headed windows of the aisle, nave, and chancel are probably of the same period.

In 1878 the south porch was rebuilt and a new east window was inserted in the chancel. In 1899 the church was restored and the floor level altered.[351]

The stone pulpit attached to the south wall of the nave is of c. 1500;[352] the octagonal bowl of the font is 15th-century.[353] A scratch-dial can be seen on the south wall of the tower,[354] and it is said that two more were visible on the south wall of the nave;[355] two sundials on the south and west walls of the tower were placed there by the rector in 1743.[356]

Three small 17th-century memorial brasses commemorate Clement Barksdale and members of his family. On the north wall of the chancel is a marble wall tablet to Ambrose Oldys (d. 1710), of Harford. A table of charitable gifts to the parish is on the north wall of the nave. In the early 19th century there was a tomb for members of the Aylworth family,[357] of which no later evidence has been found.[i]

One of the bells is dated 1684 and the other two are of 1775.[358; j] A new organ was installed, in what was formerly the Lady Chapel, in 1912.[359] The church plate includes a 17th-century credence paten, and a chalice, paten cover, and salver of the 18th century.[360] The registers begin in 1540 and are virtually complete.

Nonconformity. In 1676 there were said to be six nonconformists in Naunton[361] and by 1735 the number had increased to 11; six were described as Presbyterians, three as Anabaptists, and two as Sabbatarians.[362] A Seventh Day Baptist began to preach in Naunton in 1737,[363] and a few years later the Baptist community there was being served from Bourton-on-the-Water Baptist church.[364] Private houses were used for worship until 1797 when a Baptist chapel was built at Naunton,[365] in the main village street. In 1800 the Baptists at Naunton had had their own pastor for about two years and in 1812 their independence of Bourton-on-the-Water was recognized;[366] the community was later united with Stow Baptist church, but by 1821 was independent again.[367] In 1827 Lower Guiting chapel was united with Naunton chapel.[368; k]

By the mid-19th century when the number of members was 69[369] the chapel was too small for the increasing congregation, and a new chapel, on the same site, was built in 1850. The work, which involved lowering the hill on which the chapel stands, was financed largely by the Baptist community at Naunton,[370] and the chapel, a large building of stone with a Welsh slate roof and lit by tall round-headed windows, had seating accommodation for c. 300, a lecture room, and two vestries. In 1851 when two services were held the average congregation was said to be 260, with 30 attending the Sunday school.[371] The chapel, which had a burial ground before 1850,[372] was in 1855 registered for marriages[373] and in 1861 the premises adjacent to the chapel were bought as a house for the minister.[374] The chapel was reseated and the schoolroom enlarged in 1903.[375] There were 31 members in the mid-20th century,[376] and in 1962, when the chapel still had a resident minister and regular services, the congregation was c. 15.[377]

In 1830, 1841, and 1846 private houses were being used as places of worship by a nonconformist community which was probably Methodist.[378] In 1851 the Wesleyan minister of Chipping Norton was in charge of a congregation of c. 20 at Naunton meeting in a building not used solely as a chapel but known as Naunton Hill Wesleyan Chapel.[379; l] No evidence of later Methodist meetings in Naunton has been found.

Schools. In the early 18th century a church school for poor children was supported by voluntary subscription,[380] and in 1746 Thomas Freeman gave 30s. annually from his estate in Naunton for a teacher, to be appointed by the rector and churchwardens, to teach poor children to read. Before the end of the 18th century Freeman's charity had been lost.[381]

While John Hurd was rector a school was housed in some of the rectory buildings[382] and in 1864 the rector gave part of the glebe land for the erection of Naunton National school,[383] a large stone building with a stone roof and gables standing on the main village street, opposite the Baptist chapel. The school, supported mainly by voluntary contributions in 1864, received a grant from 1866. The average attendance in that year was 36.[384]

A British school was held in the Baptist chapel from 1860. It had an average attendance of 25 in 1870.[385]

In 1873 the National and British schools were replaced by a board school,[386] held in the building of the former National school, which, however, remained church property.[387] In 1905, when the attendance had risen to c. 77, a separate infants' department was formed.[388] In 1962, when the older children attended schools at Bourton-on-the-Water and Northleach, the number of pupils was c. 35.[389; m]

Charities. No *eleemosynary charities are known.

GLOSSARY

ashlar: in masonry, a rough-hewn block of stone or a thin dressed square stone used for facing a wall.

bedrip: a service which some tenants had to perform to their lord, at his request or bidding, to reap his corn at harvest time.

caruca: a plough or a plough team.

carucate: the amount of land that could be ploughed in a year by one plough.

copyhold: tenure evidenced by a copy of the manor court roll.

demesne: part of an estate held by its owner and not by freehold or copyhold tenants.

eleemosynary: pertaining to charity or alms; existing for the relief of the poor.

frankpledge: in Anglo Saxon times the term was ***frithborhs*** or peace-pledges which the Normans later mistranslated. It was a custom whereby a man's

Victoria History of Gloucestershire, vol. VI (1965), pp. 76–87; the history of Naunton.

relations were responsible for his behavior. This evolved into a system by which each member of a tithing (notionally a group of ten men) was responsible at law for every other member.

furlong: a measure of length, one eighth of a mile, 220 yards or 201.168 meters.

glebe: a portion of land attached to an ecclesiastical benefice as part of its endowment.

heriot: payment to the lord of the manor on the death of a customary tenant.

husbandman: a farmer.

moiety: one of two shares in something which has been divided. Usually taken to mean half.

thegn: originally, a warrior companion of the king. After the Norman Conquest, a man who ranked above an ordinary freeman (or ceorl/churl; being a freeman of the lowest rank) but below an earl or nobleman.

tithe(s): a tax or assessment of one tenth, especially when paid in kind, e.g. wool, corn or other agricultural or farm produce. Generally, a tenth part of the yearly proceeds arising from lands or the personal industry of the inhabitants, for the support of the clergy and the church.

yardland: the amount of land deemed adequate to sustain a household for a year. Yardlands therefore varied in size depending on the quality of the land. About 4 yardlands made up a carucate or ploughland (see above).

yeoman: a freeholder next under the rank of a gentleman. In earlier times, one who owned a small landed estate.

AUTHOR'S NOTES

[a] Numbers 1 and 2 were built in 1943 and the remainder in 1960.

[b] The village hall was modernized and extended in 1995 at a cost of £84,000, the funds being met by the village community and grant aid.

[c] His full name was William Bullock Hanks.

[d] Full name, Geoffrey Hanks.

[e] 36 shillings is approximately £1.80p.

[f] Brockhill Quarry was re-opened in 1984 by Mr. Julian Palmer. The offices of Huntsman's Quarry were moved into the old village school buildings after the school closed in 1969.

[g] The Black Horse.

[h] It was bought in 1960 for £11,000 by the Rt. Hon. Nicholas Ridley M.P.

[i] No trace of this notable family name can now be found in Britain and all post English Civil War descendants are now believed to be in Canada. See http://www.aylesworth.net/index.

[j] Three new bells, making a total of 6, together with their new steel supporting frame (replacing the old wooden structure) were installed in 1991, being paid for by the village at a cost of £30,000. Inf. from Mr. Rob. Johnson, Waterloo Ho

[k] In 1835 a member of Naunton chapel bought a parcel of land in Lower Guiting upon which the Guiting chapel was built, the latter becoming the 'daughter' chapel of Naunton chapel. Ex inf. Fiona Milton, Baptist Minister for Naunton & Guiting, and D. Hanks (the author).

[l] In 1998 the chapel was refurbished and re-roofed at a cost of £40,000, as a result of various fund-raising events, grants, and donations, under the auspices of the minister and the village.

[m] The school closed in 1969 due to declining pupil numbers and children thereafter attended primary schools in Cold Aston, Guiting Power (whose school itself closed in 1994), Temple Guiting, and Bourton-on-the-Water.

V.C.H. Notes

The footnotes of the original V.C.H. text have been renumbered into one consolidated sequence and slightly modified and expanded. The first citation of a printed work gives its full title; subsequent citations use an abbreviated title. Unless otherwise stated, the place of publication is London. To assist the reader, some notes have been updated, but citations and abbreviations follow the conventions used by the V.C.H. before 2002. The following abbreviations may be useful:

bk.	book
c.	approximately (Latin: *circa*)
BL	British Library
Bodl.	Bodleian Library, Oxford
Char. Com.	Charity Commission
D.N.B.	*Dictionary of National Biography*
episc.	episcopal
G.D.R.	Gloucester Diocesan Records, in Glos. R.O.
Glos. Colln.	The Gloucester Collection, in Gloucester Library. Some material has been transferred to Glos. R.O.
Glos. R.O.	Gloucestershire Record Office
Hockaday Abs.	The 'Hockaday Abstracts', being abstracts of ecclesiastical records relating to Gloucestershire, compiled by F. S. Hockaday mainly from diocesan records, in Glos. R.O.
Ibid.	In the same place as the previous reference.
Libr.	Library
MS(S)	Manuscript(s)
P.R.O.	Public Record Office, now part of the National Archive
Par. reg.	Parish register(s)
R.O.	Record Office
R.S.	Rolls Series
Rec. Com.	Record Commission
Soc.	Society
S.P.	State Papers
Trans. B.G.A.S.	*Transactions of the Bristol and Gloucestershire Archaeological Society*
visit.	visitation by the bishop
Warws.	Warwickshire
Worcs.	Worcestershire

Victoria History of Gloucestershire, vol. VI (1965), pp. 76–87; the history of Naunton.

[1] e.g. *Gloucestershire Subsidy Roll, 1Ed. III, 1327* (privately printed by Sir Thos. Phillipps n.d. [? 1856], 18.

[2] *The Names and Surnames of All the Able and Sufficient Men in Body Fit for His Majesty's Service in the Wars, within the County of Gloucester*, compiled by John Smith (1902), 268.

[3] *O.S. Area Bk.* (1884).

[4] *Census*, 1951.

[5] Geological Survey Map (drift edn., revised), sheet 217.

[6] Glos. R.O., Q/RI, 105; below, economic history.

[7] S. Rudder, *A New History of Gloucestershire* (Cirencester, 1779), 559.

[8] 'Finds near Stow', *Trans. B.G.A.S.* vii. 70–72; 'Glos. Barrows', *Trans. B.G.A.S.* lxxix. 125; 'A Roman burial on Summerhill', *Trans. B.G.A.S.* lvi. 129–31; G. B. Grundy, *Saxon Charters and Field Names of Gloucestershire* (B.G.A.S. 1935), 173–4.

[9] E. F. Eales, *Naunton upon Cotswold* (Oxford, 1928),The place called Iorotlaforda where a Mercian Council was held in 779 is apparently identified as Harford in F. M. Stenton, *Anglo-Saxon England* (1947), 200, and the same identification is given by Eales, *Naunton upon Cotswold*. The form suggests, however, that its identification as Hartleford in Hartlebury (Worcs.), given in Stubbs and Hadden, *Councils and Eccl. Documents*, iii. 437, is more probable.

[10] Geol. Surv. Map (drift edn., revised), sheet 217.

[11] *Domesday Book* (Rec. Com.), i. 168*b*.

[12] Par. reg.

[13] Below, Manors and other estates.

[14] Eales, *Naunton upon Cotswold*, 106.

[15] Baptist min. bk. *penes* the minister.

[16] Date on bldg.

[17] Local information.

[18] *Dom. Bk.* (Rec. Com.), i. 168*b*.

[19] *Glos. Subsidy Roll, 1327*, 18.

[20] *Nonarum Inquisitiones in Curia Scaccarii*, ed. G. Vandersee (Rec. Com., 1807), 412.

[21] P.R.O., E 179/113/31 m. 1.

[22] Ibid. S.C. 6/Henry VIII/ 1224 m. 9.

[23] Bodl. MS. Rawl. B. 323, f. 249*b*.

[24] Glos. R.O., D 77/T 1.

[25] Ibid. P 224A/OV 8/1; G.D.R. Naunton tithe award, 1841.

[26] Local information.

[27] *Dom. Bk.* (Rec. Com.), i. 167, 168*b*.

[28] *Glos. Subsidy Roll, 1327*, 18.

[29] *Non. Inq.* (Rec. Com.), 412.

[30] P.R.O., E 179/113/31 m. 1d.

[31] Ibid. E 179/247/14 m. 23.

[32] Glos. R.O., Q/REl.

[33] Date on bldg.

[34] *Dom. Bk.* (Rec. Com.), i. 167, 168*b*, 170*b*.

[35] P.R.O., E 179/113/31 m. 1d.

[36] Hockaday Abs. xlii, 1563 visit. f. 32.

[37] P.R.O., C 94/1 f. 29.

[38] Bodl. MS. Rawl. B. 323, f. 249*b*.

[39] G.D.R. vol. 285B.

[40] *Census*, 1801–1951.

[41] Grundy, *Saxon Charters*, 174.

[42] For Buckle Street, *Victoria History of Gloucestershire*, vi. 128 and n.

[43] Grundy, *Saxon Charters*, 275.

[44] *Calendar of the Patent Rolls preserved in the Public Record Office* (H.M.S.O., 1891 to date), 1364–7, 345.

[45] Glos. R.O., Q/RI 205.

[46] *Cal. Pat.* 1364–7, 345.

[47] Glos. and Warws. Roads Act, 28 Geo. II, c. 47.

[48] G.D.R. Naunton terrier, 1584.

[49] Ibid.

[50] Glos. R.O., Q/RI 105.

[51] Eales, *Naunton upon Cotswold*, 123.

[52] Ex inf. British Railways (Western Region).

[53] Glos. R.O., P 224A/PC 1/1.

[54] G. E. Payne, *Gloucestershire: a Survey* (Gloucester, n.d. [1946]), 204.

[55] Local information.

[56] Char. Com. files.

[57] *Gloucestershire Countryside* (Glos. Rural Community Council) vi. 242–4.

[58] *Calendar of State Papers, Domestic Series* (H.M.S.O., 1856–1972), 1656–7, 12.

[59] P.R.O., E 179/247/14 m. 23.

[60] Eales, *Naunton upon Cotswold*, 105.

[61] Ex inf. Mr. S. J. Clifford, of Lower Harford.

[62] Below, Church.

[63] Glos. R.O., Q/RI 105.

[64] *D. N. B.*

[65] Ibid.

[66] *Glos. Countryside*, vii. 500.

[67] *Bibliotheca Gloucestrensis; a Collection of Scarce and Curious Tracts ... Illustrative of and Published during the Civil War ...* (2 vols. Gloucester, 1825, privately printed), ii. 333.

[68] Glos. R.O., EL 140, MSS. of the Civil War and Commonwealth.

[69] *Cal. S.P. Dom.* 1656–7, 12.

[70] P.R.O., C 142/146/135.

[71] Eales, *Naunton upon Cotswold*, 116.

[72] *Dom. Bk.* (Rec. Com.), i. 170*b*.

[73] *Calendar of Inquisitions Miscellaneous (Chancery) preserved in the Public Record Office* (H.M.S.O. 1916–68), i. 139.

[74] *Inquisitions and Assessments relating to Feudal Aids preserved in the Public Record Office* (H.M.S.O. 1899–1920), ii. 252.

[75] *Dom. Bk.* (Rec. Com.), i. i68*b*.

[76] *Book of Fees* (H.M.S.O. 1920–31), 40.

[77] *Complete Peerage*, ix. 266.

[78] *Calendar of Inquisitiones post mortem preserved in the Public Record Office* (H.M.S.O. 1904–92), xiv, p. 229.

[79] *Complete Peerage*, xii (1), 631.

[80] *Abstracts of Inquisitiones post mortem for Gloucestershire* (6 vols. issued jointly by the British Record Soc., Index Library vols. xxx, xl, xlviii, and ix, xxi, xlvii, and the B.G.A.S. 1893–1914) 1359–1413, 250.

[81] H. E. Salter (ed.), *Eynsham Cartulary,* i (Oxford Hist. Soc. xlix, 1907), pp. 62, 75.

[82] H. Hall (ed.), *Red. Book of the Exchequer* (R.S. ic, 3 vols., 1896), 604.

[83] *Bk. of Fees*, 440.

[84] *Cal. Inq. p.m.* ii, p. 395.

[85] *Valor Ecclesiasticus temp. Hen. VIII auctoritate regia institutus*, eds. J. Caley and J. Hunter (Rec. Com., 1810–34), iii. 244.

[86] *Letters and Papers, Foreign and Domestic, of the Reign of Henry VIII*, (H.M.S.O. 1864–1932), xix (1), p. 629.

[87] Ibid. p. 641.

[88] P.R.O., S.C. 6/Henry VIII/4034 m. 18.

[89] Ibid. C 142/86/92.

[90] *Cal. Pat.* 1550, 3, 87.

[91] Par. reg.

[92] P.R.O., C 142/160/66.

[93] Ibid. C.P. 25(2)/145/1885/15; *V.C.H. Glos.* vi. 51.

[94] P.R.O., C 142/336/55.

[95] Smith, *Men and Armour*, 141.

[96] *Inq. p.m. Glos.* 1625–42, iii. 32.

Victoria History of Gloucestershire, vol. VI (1965), pp. 76–87; the history of Naunton.

[97] Notes by A. G. Fort *penes* Mrs. H. E. O'Neil, of Bourton-on-the-Water.
[98] Rudder, *Glos.* 559.
[99] Notes by A. G. Fort.
[100] Glos. R.O., Q/REl.
[101] Above, Introduction.
[102] Will of W. Hanks *penes* Mr. G. Hanks, of Manor House, Naunton; papers *penes* Capt. H. J. Kennard, of Guiting Grange.
[103] P.R.O., C 142/336/55.
[104] Ibid. C.P. 25(2)/553/1650 East./32.
[105] Ibid. C.P. 25(2)/1016/7 Geo. I Mich./12; Rudder, *Glos.* 464.
[106] Papers *penes* Capt. H. J. Kennard; Glos. R.O., P 224A, par. rate bks.
[107] Glos. R.O., Q/REl.
[108] Ibid. D 1388, bound sales partics. 1848, no. 121; ibid. P 224A, par. rate bks.
[109] Glos. R.O., SL 169.
[110] Ex inf. Capt. H. J. Kennard.
[111] *Dom. Bk.* (Rec. Com.), i. 167, 168*b*.
[112] *Complete Peerage*, v. 685–715; e.g. *Bk. of Fees*, 311; P.R.O., C 115/A 12 f. 29b.
[113] e.g. ibid. C 115/A 7 ff. 5-6; *Complete Peerage*, xii (1), 177–81.
[114] Rudder, *Glos.* 622; P.R.O., E 150/350/1; C 142/142/83.
[115] P.R.O., C.P. 25(2)/297/8 Jas. I Trin./28.
[116] *Inq. p.m. Glos.* 1625–42, ii. 117.
[117] *Dom. Bk.* (Rec. Com.), i. 168*b*.
[118] P.R.O., C 115/A 2/22.
[119] Ibid.
[120] Ibid. C 115/A 12 f. 15.
[121] Ibid. S.C. 6/Henry VIII/1224 m. 9.
[122] Ibid. C 115/A 7 f. 4.
[123] Ibid. C 115/A 2/22; C 47/59/6/261.
[124] Ibid. S.C. 6/Henry VIII/1224 m. 9.
[125] B.G.A.S. Libr., Royce MS. VV, Aylworth.
[126] Deeds *penes* Mr. L. W. Hill, of Bourton-on-the-Water.
[127] *Glos. Subsidy Roll, 1327*, 18.
[128] P.R.O., C 142/142/83.
[129] Ibid. C.P. 25(1)/13/15/296.
[130] *Dom. Bk.* (Rec. Com.), i. 167.
[131] P.R.O., C 142/142/83.
[132] Ibid. S.C. 6/Henry VIII/1212 m. 10d.
[133] *L. & P. Henry VIII*, xviii (2), pp. 53, 59.
[134] J. Maclean and W. C. Heane (eds.), *Visitation of the county of Gloucester, 1623* (Harleian Soc. xxi, 1885), 7.
[135] *Inq. p.m. Glos.* 1625–42, ii. 117.
[136] P.R.O., C 78/1454/4.
[137] Rudder, *Glos.* 560.
[138] Glos. R.O., D 1395/II 4/E 3.
[139] B.G.A.S. Libr., Royce MS. VV, Aylworth.
[140] Diary of F. E. Witts, of Upper Slaughter *(penes* Maj. Gen. Witts, Chesterton), 30 June 1854.
[141] Ex inf. Capt. H. J. Kennard.
[142] *Kelly's Directory of Gloucestershire* (1927), 274.
[143] Ex inf. Mr. A. G. Walker, of High Beeches, Prestbury.
[144] For the house, above, Introduction.
[145] W. Dugdale, *Monasticon Anglicanum*, ed. J. Caley and others (6 vols. 1817–30) i. 568.
[146] Grundy, *Saxon Charters*, 173–5.
[147] *Dom. Bk.* (Rec. Com.), i. 168*b*.
[148] e.g. P.R.O., C 115/A 7 ff. 5-6.
[149] *Cal. Inq. Misc.* ii. 253; see below.
[150] B.L. Sloane Ch. xxxiii. 40.
[151] *Inq. p.m. Glos.* 1359–1413, 183.
[152] Ibid. 225.
[153] *Cal. Close* 1405–9, 17.
[154] P.R.O., C 142/44/156; Bodl. MS. Willis 16, p. 328.
[155] P.R.O., C.P. 25(2)/144/1871/4.
[156] Ibid. 423/15 Charles I Hil./I4.
[157] Rudder, *Glos.* 560.
[158] Papers *penes* Capt. H. J. Kennard.
[159] Glos. R.O., P 224A, par. rate bk. 1869.
[160] Ibid. SL 169.
[161] Eales, *Naunton upon Cotswold*, 106.
[162] *Eynsham Cartulary*, i (Oxford Hist. Soc. xlix), pp. 62, 75.
[163] Ibid. ii (Oxford Hist. Soc. li), p. lv.
[164] Dugdale, *Mon.* vii. 823.
[165] *Cal. Inq. Misc.* ii, p. 253.
[166] *Cal. Pat.* 1327–30, 321.
[167] *Cal. Inq. p.m.* x, p. 173.
[168] Corpus Christi Coll. Oxford, mun. F. 1, Cap. 1 (1) 10.
[169] Ibid. 21.
[170] Ibid. Cap. 2. 5.
[171] P.R.O., C 142/336/55.
[172] Corpus Christi Coll. Oxford, mun. F. 6, 46.
[173] Glos. R.O., Q/REl. For the farm-house at Lower Harford, above, Introduction.
[174] Ex inf. Mr. S. J. Clifford.
[175] *Dom. Bk.* (Rec. Com.), i. 170*b*.
[176] *Feud. Aids*, ii. 252.
[177] P.R.O., S.C. 6/Henry VIII/1212 m. 10d.
[178] Atkyns, *Glos.* 566; the name Bale Farm, said by Atkyns to be taken from a family of that name, may be a misreading for Dale Farm.
[179] *L. & P. Henry VIII*, xviii (1), p. 53.
[180] Ibid. p. 59.
[181] Rudder, *Glos.* 560.
[182] Eales, *Naunton upon Cotswold*, 78.
[183] Glos. R.O., Q/REl.
[184] Ibid. D 1388, bound sale partics. 1880, no. 69.
[185] Ibid. SL 169.
[186] *Dom. Bk.* (Rec. Com.), i. 167, 168*b*, 170*b*.
[187] *Valor Eccl.* (Rec. Com), iii. 244.
[188] *Taxatio Ecclesiastica Angliae et Walliae auctoritate P. Nicholai IV circa A.D. 1291*, eds. S. Ayscough and J. Caley (Rec. Com., 1802), 233.
[189] P.R.O., C 115/A 2/22.
[190] *Non. Inq.* (Rec. Com.), 412.
[191] P.R.O., C 115/A 12 f. 15.
[192] *Valor Eccl.* (Rec. Com.), ii. 427.
[193] *Calendar of the Close Rolls preserved in the Public Record Office* (H.M.S.O. 1892–1963), 1399–1402, 235.
[194] P.R.O., C.P. 25(1)/73/11/182.
[195] Worcs. R.O. 704:24/259.
[196] *Valor Eccl.* (Rec. Com.), iii. 244.
[197] *Glos. Subsidy Roll, 1327*, 18.
[198] P.R.O., S.C. 6/Henry VIII/1212 m. 10d.
[199] Ibid.
[200] P.R.O., C 142/146/135.
[201] *Tax. Eccl.* (Rec. Com.), 233.
[202] P.R.O., S.C. 6/Henry VIII/1212 m. 10d.
[203] Ibid. C 115/A 2/22.
[204] *Tax. Eccl.* (Rec. Com.), 233.
[205] P.R.O., C 115/A 12 f. 15.
[206] Ibid. C 115/A 2/22.
[207] *Non. Inq.* (Rec. Com.), 412.

Victoria History of Gloucestershire, vol. VI (1965), pp. 76–87; the history of Naunton.

[208] P.R.O., C 115/A 2/22; ibid. C 115/A 7 f. 48; *Year Bk.* 1313 (Selden Soc.), 200.
[209] P.R.O., S.C. 6/Henry VIII/1225 m. 11B.
[210] Dugdale, *Mon.* vii. 823.
[211] Worcs. R.O. 704: 24/259.
[212] Corpus Christi Coll. Oxford, mun. F.1 vol. xxi, p. 3.
[213] *Calendar of Inquisitiones post mortem, Henry VII* (H.M.S.O. 1898–1955), iii, p. 267.
[214] B.G.A.S. Libr., Royce MS. VV, Aylworth.
[215] *Dom. Bk.* (Rec. Com.), i. 168*b*.
[216] *Bk. of Fees*, 311.
[217] *Non. Inq.* (Rec. Com.), 412.
[218] P.R.O., C 115/A 7 f. 4.
[219] Ibid. C 115/A 14 f. 73.
[220] Ibid. C 115/A 12 f. 15.
[221] Ibid. C 47/59/1/22.
[222] Ibid. STAC 2/2/277.
[223] *Valor Eccl.* (Rec. Com.), ii. 427.
[224] *L. & P. Henry VIII*, xx (1), p. 662.
[225] P.R.O., S.C. 6/Henry VIII/1225 m.. 11B.
[226] *Valor Eccl.* (Rec. Com.), ii. 439.
[227] Smith, *Men and Armour*, 141.
[228] G.D.R. Naunton terriers, 1584, 1683, 1736.
[229] Glos. R.O., D 45/M 19/S. 100.
[230] Ibid. Q/RI 105.
[231] Smith, *Men and Armour*, 141.
[232] *Inq. p.m. Glos. 1625–42*, ii. 117.
[233] R. Atkyns, *Ancient and Present State of Glostershire* (1712), 565.
[234] G.D.R. Naunton terrier, 1683.
[235] Corpus Christi Coll. Oxford, mun. F. 6, 46.
[236] Smith, *Men and Armour*, 268.
[237] Glos. R.O., Q/RE1.
[238] Ibid.
[239] Ibid. Q/RI 105.
[240] Ibid. P 224A, poor-rate bks.
[241] Ex inf. Mr. B. Stanley, Manager of Aylworth Farm.
[242] Ex inf. Mr. G. G. Hanks, of Manor Farm.
[243] B.G.A.S. Libr., Royce MS. VV, Aylworth.
[244] Survey of Aylworth Estate *penes* Mr. A. G. Walker.
[245] Corpus Christi Coll. Oxford, mun. F. 6, 46.
[246] Bodl. MS. Rawl. B. 323, f. 249*b*.
[247] Acreage Returns, 1801, *Trans. B.G.A.S.* lxviii. 179.
[248] Ex inf. Mr. A. G. Walker.
[249] J. Harvey (with contributions from A. Oswald), *English Medieval Architects. A biographical dictionary ...*(1911), 126.
[250] Corpus Christi Coll. Oxford, Leases Naunton, i. Harford.
[251] e.g. *Inq. p.m. Glos.* 1625–42, iii. 32.
[252] Eales, *Naunton upon Cotswold*, 125.
[253] O.S. Map 6", Glos. XXI. SW. and SE., XXVIII. NW. and NE. (1st edn.).
[254] Ibid. (2nd and 3rd edns.).
[255] Ex inf. Mr. G. G. Hanks, of Manor Farm. Cf. W. J. Arkell, *Oxford Stone* (1947), 143–6.
[256] Eales, *Naunton upon Cotswold*, 125.
[257] Smith, *Men and Armour*, 141, 208.
[258] Glos. Colln. deeds 211.1.
[259] Hockaday Abs. ccxci.
[260] G.D.R. vol. 285B.
[261] Glos. R.O., Q/RI 105.
[262] P.R.O., E 179/247/14 m. 23.
[263] *Kelly's Dir. Glos.* (1870 and later edns.).
[264] *Census*.
[265] *Kelly's Dir. Glos.* (1870 and later edns.).
[266] Rudder, *Glos.* 560.
[267] Eales, *Naunton upon Cotswold*, 107.
[268] *Kelly's Dir. Glos.* (1870), 603.
[269] *Dom. Bk.* (Rec. Com.), i. 170b.
[270] P.R.O., C.P. 25(2)/145/1885/15.
[271] B.G.A.S. Libr., Royce MS. VV, Naunton.
[272] Glos. R.O., P 224A.
[273] Ex inf. Mr. H. Hanks, of Waterloo Farm, Naunton.
[274] Grundy, *Saxon Charters*, 178, 175.
[275] *Dom. Bk.* (Rec. Com.), i. 168*b*.
[276] *Placita de Quo Warranto ... in Curia Receptae Scaccarii Westm. asservata*, eds. W. Illingworth and J. Caley (Rec. Com. 1818), 258, 245, 253.
[277] P.R.O., C 115/A 2/22.
[278] Ibid. C 115/A 14 f. 73.
[279] Glos. R.O., D 678/ct. roll/20; P.R.O., STAC 2/2/227.
[280] *Valor Eccl.* (Rec. Com.), iii. 244.
[281] P.R.O., C 115/A 2/22.
[282] Rudder, *Glos.* 539.
[283] Eales, *Naunton upon Cotswold*, 126.
[284] *Abstract of Returns Relative to the Expense and Maintenance of the Poor* (Parl. Papers 1804), 182.
[285] *Abstract of Returns to Orders of the House of Commons Relative to Assessments for Relief of the Poor* (Parl. Papers 1820 (294), XII), 154.
[286] *Census*, 1881, 1931.
[287] Glos. R.O., P 224A/PC 1/1.
[288] Eales, *Naunton upon Cotswold*, 22.
[289] *Eynsham Cartulary*, 1. (Oxford Hist. Soc. xlix), 62.
[290] Cf. S. R. Glynne, *Gloucestershire Church Notes*, eds. W. P. W. Phillimore and J. Melland Hall (1902), 150.
[291] Worcs. R.O., 704:24/259.
[292] *Cal. Inq. Misc.* i. 139.
[293] Dugdale, *Mon.* iv. 452.
[294] J. W. W. Bund (ed.), *Register of Bishop Godfrey Giffard, 1268–1302* (Worcs. Hist. Soc. 1902), 285.
[295] Ibid. 336.
[296] *Tax. Eccl.* (Rec. Com.), 222.
[297] *Reg. Giffard* (Worcs. Hist. Soc), 424.
[298] J. W. W. Bund (ed.), *Register of the Diocese of Worcester during the Vacancy of the See* (abb. as *Reg. Sede Vacante*). (Worcs. Hist. Soc.), 28.
[299] Ibid. 64.
[300] e.g. Worc. Episc. Reg., Reg. Wakefield, f. 76; Hockaday Abs. ccxci.
[301] *London Gazette* 1852, p. 1578.
[302] *Gloucester Diocesan Year Book* (1962–3), 63.
[303] *Tax. Eccl.* (Rec. Com.), 222.
[304] *Valor Eccl.* (Rec. Com.), ii. 439.
[305] P.R.O., C 94/1 f. 29.
[306] G.D.R. vol. 393.
[307] *Valor Eccl.* (Rec. Com.), ii. 439.
[308] Rudder, *Glos.* 560.
[309] Dugdale, *Mon.* iv. 452.
[310] *Valor Eccl.* (Rec. Com.), ii. 439.
[311] G.D.R. Naunton terriers, 1584, 1683, 1705.
[312] Eales, *Naunton upon Cotswold*, 79.
[313] Glos. R.O., Q/RI 105.
[314] G.D.R. Naunton tithe award, 1841.
[315] *Kelly's Dir. Glos.* (1870 and later edns.).
[316] Ex inf. the rector, the Revd. L. P. Mills.
[317] For the house, above, Introduction.

Victoria History of Gloucestershire, vol. VI (1965), pp. 76–87; the history of Naunton.

[318] *Reg. Sede Vacante*; 37; Hockaday Abs. ccxci.

[319] J. W. W. Bund (ed.), *Register of Bishop William Ginsborough, 1303–7* (Worcs. Hist. Soc. 1907), 134.

[320] R. A. Wilson (ed.), *Register of Bishop Walter Reynolds, 1308–13* (Worcs. Hist. Soc. 1927), 86.

[321] *Calendar of Entries in the Papal Registers relating to Great Britain and Ireland* (H.M.S.O. 1893–1961), ii. 141.

[322] *Reg. Cobham* (Worcs. Hist. Soc.), 80, 118.

[323] Worc. Episc. Reg., Reg. Wakefield, f. 16b.

[324] Above, Manors and other estates.

[325] Hockaday Abs. xxii, 1498 visit. f. 44; ibid. ccxci.

[326] E. H. Pearce (ed.), *Register of Bishop Thomas de Cobham, 1317–27* (Worcs. Hist. Soc. 1930), 80; Worc. Episc. Reg., Reg. Peverell, f. 28b.; Hockaday Abs. xxii, 1498 visit. f. 44.

[327] 'Bp. Hooper's Visit. 1551', *English Historical Review* xix. 110.

[328] Hockaday Abs. ccxci.

[329] *D.N.B.*

[330] Hockaday Abs. lii, state of clergy 1593, f. 4.

[331] G.D.R. Naunton terrier, 1584.

[332] Hockaday Abs. ccxci.

[333] *Walker Revised*, ed. Matthews, 173.

[334] Eales, *Naunton upon Cotswold*, 61; E.A. Matthews (ed.), *Calamy Revised, being a revision of Edmund Calamy's Account ... of the Ministers and others ejected and silenced, 1660–2* (Oxford, 1934) 273.

[335] *D.N.B.*

[336] Atkyns, *Glos.* 505.

[337] G.D.R. vols. 382, 384, 385; Hockaday Abs. ccxci.

[338] Hockaday Abs. ccxci.

[339] Eales, *Naunton upon Cotswold*.

[340] P.R.O., H.O. 129/14/342/1/7.

[341] Ex inf. the rector.

[342] G.D.R. Naunton terrier, 1699.

[343] Ibid. 1736.

[344] *21st Report of the Commissioners Appointed to Enquire Concerning Charities* (Lord Brougham's Commission) (Parl. Papers 1829 (349), VIII), 173.

[345] Char. Com. files.

[346] *Glos. Ch. Notes*, 150.

[347] U. Daubeny, *Ancient Cotswold Churches* (Cheltenham and London, 1921), 72.

[348] Hockaday Abs. ccxci, 1524.

[349] Rudder, *Glos.* 560.

[350] Hockaday Abs. ccxci, 1524.

[351] Eales, *Naunton upon Cotswold*, 25–26.

[352] 'Glos. churches', *Trans. B.G.A.S.* lxxii. 11.

[353] 'Glos. fonts', *Trans. B.G.A.S.* xlvi. 127.

[354] 'Scratch dials in Glos.', *Trans. B.G.A.S.* xlvi. 183.

[355] Eales, *Naunton upon Cotswold*, 27.

[356] Ibid.

[357] *Historical, Monumental, and Genealogical Collections Relative to the County of Gloucester, Printed from the Original Papers of Ralph Bigland* (3 vols. 1791–1889, issued in parts: vol. iii is unpaginated), ii. 235.

[358] H. T. Ellacombe, *The Church Bells of Gloucestershire* (Exeter, 1881), 57.

[359] Eales, *Naunton upon Cotswold*, 33.

[360] *Glos. Ch. Plate*, 152.

[361] Compton Census.

[362] G.D.R. vol. 285B.

[363] *Cheltenham Chronicle* 23 Nov. 1903.

[364] Thomas Brooks, *Pictures of the Past; the History of Bourton Baptist Church* (1861) 68.

[365] Hockaday Abs. ccxci.

[366] Brooks, *Pictures of the Past*, 68, 93.

[367] T. E. Blackaby, *Past and Present History of Stow Baptist Church* (Stow-on-the-Wold, 1892),19–20.

[368] Eales, *Naunton upon Cotswold*, 121.

[369] *Cheltenham Chron.* 23 Nov. 1903.

[370] Baptist min. bk. *penes* the minister.

[371] P.R.O., H.O. 129/14/342/1/7.

[372] Baptist min bk.

[373] *Lond. Gaz.* 1855, p. 4045.

[374] Baptist min. bk.

[375] *Cheltenham Chron.* 23 Nov. 1903.

[376] *Baptist Handbook* (1959).

[377] Ex inf. the minister, the Revd. T. Gardiner.

[378] Hockaday Abs. ccxci.

[379] P.R.O., H.O. 129/14/342/1/7.

[380] G.D.R. vol. 285B.

[381] *21st Rep. Com. Char.* 173.

[382] Eales, *Naunton upon Cotswold*, 120.

[383] P.R.O., E.D. 7/35/228.

[384] *Report of the Education Committee of Council, 1866–7* (Parl. Papers 1867 (3883), XXII), p. 575.

[385] P.R.O., E.D. 7/37.

[386] *Report of the Education Committee of Council, 1877–8* (Parl. Papers 1878 (2048–I), XXVIII), p. 15; correspondence *penes* the rector.

[387] Ex inf. the rector.

[388] *Public Elementary Schools, 1906* (Parl. Papers 1906 [3182], LXXXVI), p. 187.

[389] Ex inf. the rector.

Appendix 13

The Lost Dialect

A fraction of the rich vocabulary once heard in Naunton is included here to give a flavour of the local (Cotswold) dialect. Some words were peculiar to Naunton but most had a wider geographical spread, varying slightly in pronunciation between parishes. Most are now obsolete but a few have crept through into common parlance today; some as modern slang. It could be said that it represents a purer form of English than many of the imported words now in common usage. I believe that most of it was only ever spoken, and rarely, if ever written down, other than by researchers (as here). A little practice is required to make it role off the tongue as naturally as it once did round here. The way some of the words and phrases are now reduced into print does not help us to enunciate them as authentically as we might, if we could have heard it *'spo'k praper leik'*.

A, used in place of he, as "yunt a," isn't he. Aater, after. Abear, to endure. A-brimin, brimming, on heat; of a sow. A-bullin, bulling, on heat; of a cow. Aileo, Aylworth. Aimekin, haymaking. Auturds, afterwards. Afore or avore, before. Agin, against. Aakard, awkward. Allus or ollus, always. Anks, Hanks. A's, A'sis, horse and horses. At: If anything had not been accomplished properly, instead of saying "It is only half-done," it used to be said "It is done at," great stress being put upon the 'at'.

Backen, retard. Bailis, Bayliss. Baltn, bolting. Barrer, wheelbarrow. Baint, am not. Bark, fat trimmings of mutton. Bazzled or sucked in, have been taken advantage of. Bekes, bakehouse. Bested or sucked in, "he bested I over that." Be, am, "I be bad," I am ill. Beuns, beans. Beunt, am not, "I beunt agoin," I am not going. Bilan, belong. Bittle, Iron bound wooden wedge or stake driver (beetle). Bit, gimlet. Bist, contraction of beest though? Bissent, contraction of beest though not? Blakbriz, blackberries. Blarm, a mild oath, "Blarm the kid." Blow, to blossom or bloom. Blowens, blossoms. Blaarin, crying or howling; possibly derived from Danish *blaren*, to cry. Bousing, bowsen, bowzin, cow-shed with open front. Bone dry, very dry. Brevet, poking about. Bread and cheese, young shoots of white thorn. Breeds, the rim of a hat. Bry, cow fly. Bury: from an early British word meaning earth thrown up for defence; from same word comes *burrow*, meaning shelter, hence "In the burrow," "the burrow side of the hedge or wall," etc., meaning the side sheltered from the wind; Roots such as potatoes, mangolds and swedes etc, are put in a 'bury' for winter use, by heaping them upon straw laid on the ground and then covering them over with straw, with a covering of earth over that. Burning daylight away, lighting a lamp before it is necessary. Bush-house; an unlicensed house for the sale of intoxicants on special days. They were identified by a bush hanging on the door, from which a saying arose, "Good ale needs no bush."

Cart, carted, to carry, such as carrying or 'carting' mud about on ones boots. Canst, can; possibly a contraction of canest. Casnt, a contraction of "canst not," but is used as can you not, i.e. "Casnt go?" Can you not go? Cavinz, cavings, straw refuse after threshing. Chawn, crack in wall or ground. Chits, shoots on potatoes when in store in a dark place. Chog, clog for securing headstall chain. Chop, exchange; used also with change, i.e. "chopin an changing about." Cherrycurds, the first milk from a cow after calving, considered by some to be a great delicacy when made into a pudding. Chitlinz, chitterlings, pig's innards. Chubby-heads, young frogs in early stage consisting of head and tail only. Chuck, throw, as in "chucking stuns," i.e. throwing stones. Chimbley or chimmuck, chimney. Clutter or clitter, things lying about in an untidy state. Clapt, saw, as in "as sun as I clapt on'n I knowed 'n," as soon as I saw him I knew him. Climin, climbing. Coppy, coppice. Cotch, catch and cotched, caught. Cratch, rack for sheep killing. Critter, creature. Cruel, intense, such as "a cruel pain." Cubby-house or hole, a snug place. Cull, a freshwater fish 2" to 3" long, sometimes known as a miller's thumb. Cus'd, cussid, awkward or uncooperative.

Daaz, Dall, Dang, Darn & Dallnation, a mild form of oath. Deman, dayman, general farm worker. Dinksin, jumping a baby up and down is said to be "dinksin it about." Dodment, old black grease from wheel axle. Dollop, lump, as in "her gied I a dollop o' puddi'n." Drill, machine for sowing seeds. Drum, threshing machine. Dust, a contraction of doest. Dusn't, a contraction of doest not. Downdashious, audacious. Dowle, feathers' down, also first appearance of hair on a boy's face. Dress, decorate, such as decorating the church. Drip out, to draw last drops of milk from a cow. D'snow? doest thou know? Dub, throw, "dubbin stwuns," throwing stones. Dustered, dusted. Dzardz, George.

Ed, along, as in "cum ed you," come along. Emmut, ant or Et, all used to a horse to turn it towards the right, appending the horse's name, "Et Blackbird." [also see waw]. Edike'shn, education. Eriwig, earwig. E't, hate

Faggot, an indolent woman; also smallish wood for "stickin peas." Fart, a fussy person. Fit, fet. Ferrikin, poking about. Feow, few. Forrard, forward. Fut, foot. Fuz, furze. Furrin, foreign. Fun, found. Furrer, furrow.

Gawk, ungainly person. Gawkin, staring. Gallus, rather doubtful, used in several ways, "Cum yer, you young gallus," also "I'll gie thee a gallus good hiding." Gaffer, the master. Gabbern, empty and cheerless. Gaapin, staring with open mouth. Gez, gaze. Gie, give, as in "Gie I sum." Gied, gave. Gis, give, as in "Gis a bit, you." Gin, gave, as in "He gin I sum." Gobble or Gollopin, swallowing quickly. Gret, great, as in " a gret big un." Gris, grinding with ones teeth. Gramp or Grampy, grandfather. Grindstun, grindstone. Grum, groom. Gwain, going. N.B. in all the above words the 'g' has a hard sound.

Hadt, contraction of had it. Hadst, had. Harp or arp, long for, as in "allus arpin ater what thee casn't git." Hocketin, clearing the throat. Head and race: head, windpipe, liver and lights of a pig. Hern, hers. Hisn, his. Hize, as in "a hize of a job." Ows, house. Hooet, wilt, or will you? Avl, hovel (shed). Huds, pea or bean shells. Hunk, a large piece of food, "a hunk o' bread." Hunt or oont, a mole or fox.

Insight, a slight knowledge of. Inion, onion. Innards: inwards, intestines, as "pig's innards."

Jer, here. Jonnuck, straightforward. Jumbles, sweets of any kind.

Kak, cock, heap of hay. Keck, wild parsley. Klatkauld, quite cold. Klag, clog, wooden-soled shoe. Kleninz, cleanings, afterbirth of cow. Klo's, close, enclosed piece of pasture near farmhouse. Knowed, knew. Knowdst, knew. Kalimeker, colley-maker or saddler. Koomers, combers, coping stones on dry stone wall.

Larum, alarm clock. Lap, wrap, as in "thee hadst better lap up well." Leben, eleven. Leazin, gleaning. Lissum, active. Littler, smaller. Licker, a mystery. Livelastic, a water vermin, having appearance of a piece of elastic.

Ma'ket, market Marnin, good morning. Med, may. Medst, mayest. Mesh-tub, a tub used in brewing.

Messed, squandered. Meowt, newt. Miskin, ash-heap. Mistek, mistake. Moithered, distracted. Mossel, morsel.

Nat'n, Naunton. Nation, used as "A nation good thing," etc. Nerrum, not one. Nern, neither. Never didn't: one negative strengthening another. Nighish, near.

Offer, try, as in "Offer the key to the lock." Okard, awkward. Ole, old. Ommer, hammer. On, of, as in "he's no good on." On't, of it, as in "I don't know on't." Ooman, woman. Ool, wool. Oot, will you? Orn't, ought not. Ortnst, oughtest not. Owrn, ours. Owzn, housing.

Paason, parson. Pantney, pantry or larder. Paasnip, parsnip. Piece, allotment. Patch, allotment. Pecker, a bird's bill. Pester, annoy. Pidzin, pigeon. Praize, to take care of, value. Pussy, a hare. Pwostes, posts.

Quaar, quarry. Quine, coin.

Raddle or riddle, red earth for colouring. Rattling, an expression denoting force. Reaves, top rails of a wagon. Ronk, offensive or rank. Rozum, resin. Rown, round, as in "rown ows" or 'round house'. Rowndl, Roundhill. Roxy: a pear is roxy when it is sleepy or in first stages of rotting. Rummy, funny. Runners, sheep's inwards.

Sag, to droop, cf. A.S. sigan. Saaternun, this afternoon. Scwosh, plunge into water. Scruff of neck, back of neck. Scrat, scratch. Scratchins, the remains of pigs' 'leaf' after the lard has been extracted. Screggin or scrumpin, gleaning apples. Scamberin or scamblin, scrambling. Sebn, seven. Seed, saw, as in "I seed 'n," I saw him. Ship, sheep. Shup, shepherd. Shatn't? shall you not? Shalst? shall you? Shik-shak, oak apple and leaf. Shuppic, pitchfork. Sight, a great deal, as in "a sight better." Sidlin, allotment on side of hill or ridge along end of other ridges. Skiddy, bird. Skew-bald, piebald (brown and white). Slat, stone roof tile. Slommack, untidy or slattern. Slibberin, slipping. Slibbery or slippy, slippery. Slicky, smooth. Smornin, this morning. Smaam or smaum, make a mess. Spreed, soreness from winds. Sturs, stairs. Stillurds, weighing instrument, steelyard. Staddle, raised foundation of a rick. Straddle, astride or standing with legs wide apart. Summat, something. Swig, to drink. Swill, was, as in "I swilled the yard," "I had a swill." Sneedge, sneeze. Spager. sparrow. Sod, as in "you silly sod." Squitch, couch grass. Squeedge, squez or squedge, squeeze. Stank, a water dam. Stju:pid, stupid.

Tallot, loft or room over a stable. Talents, talons. Tarmined, determined. Tack, almost anything but generally horse's saddle, bridle, martingale etc. Ten-o'-clock, a small meal taken at 10am. Telled, told. Teunt, it is not. This'n, this one. Thic, this. Thuc, that. Thern or thayern, theirs. Thay thur, those. "Be thay thur ship [sheep] thine?" Thee, you. Thine, yours. Thenky, thank you. Tisn, it is his. Tisn't, it is not. Tother'n, the other one. Trow, trough. Tush, one of the front teeth of a fox. Tundish, funnel. Tuer, an alley. Turmot, turnip. Twern't, it was not.

Ummux, treat roughly. Us, me: the plural invariably being used for the singular. i.e. tellus, tell me.

Varge, crab-apple. Var, very. Vour, four. Vittals, food. Vor't, for it.

Watty-handed, left handed. Waw, used to a horse to turn it to the left. Whack, share. Whinnock or whinnick, to whimper. Withy, willow. Wolst, wilt thou.

Yaard, heard. Yaew, ewe. Yeut, eat. Yeurt, here it, as in "yeurt be," here it is.

A poem and a song are included here to help contextualize some of this linguistic puzzle:

THE TURMOT HOWER

I be a turmot hower,
Vram Glarstershur I cum.
My parents be hard workin fokes:
Dan Whipstraw be my name.
    Th' vly, th'vly!
    Th'vly be on the turmot,
    As it be aal me eye, an no use to try
    To kip um off th' turmots.

Zum be vond o' haaymakin,
An zum be vond o' mowin,
But of aal th' trades that I likes best
Gie I th' turmut howin,*Th'vly, th'vly! etc.*

'Twas on a summer marnin,
Aal at th' brek o' day,
When I tuk up me turmut hower'
An trudged it far away.
    Th'vly, th'vly! etc.

Th' next pleace I got wark at,
'Twer by th' day,
Var one ole Varmer Vlower,
Who sed I wur a rippin turmut hower,
    Th'vly, th'vly! etc.
Sumtimes I be a mowin,
Sumtimes I be a plowin,
Gettin th' furrers aal bright an clur
Aal ready vor turmut sowin
    Th'vly, th'vly! etc.

An now me song be ended,
I ope you wunt call encore
But if you'll kum hur another night'
I'll sing it ye once more.
    Th'vly, th'vly! etc.

(*Untitled*)
If thee true Glarstershur would know
I'll tell thee how us always zays un:
Put "I" for "me" and "a" for "o"
On every possible occasion

When in doubt squeeze in "w";
"Stwuns" not "stones" and don't forget "zur,"
That "thee" must stand for "thou" and "you,"
"Her" for "she," and *vice versa*.

Put "v" for "f," for "s" put "z,"
"Th" and "t" we change to "d,"
So dry and kip this in thine yead,
An thou wilt talk as plain as we.

Appendix 14

We shall remember them

1914-1919
In memory of the men of Naunton who fell in the Great War:

Fletcher Christopher C
Hathaway Frederick C
Iles James
Lockey Albert
Munday William C A
Dean Ernest
Davis Charles
Higgins James
Bartlett John
Timms William F
Gardner Henry W
Smith William
East Walter R J

Men who enlisted from Naunton for the Great War & returned.

Aston Frank
Bartlet Fred
Bartlett Reginald
Beames Frank
Benfield Leslie
Burgiss Jack
Davis Albert
Davis Fred
Davis Tom
Elvin William
Fletcher George
Fletcher Joseph A
Fluck Alfred
Gleed Charles
Gleed Frank
Griffin Fred
Harris Albert
Harris Charles T
Harris Herbert
Harris James

Harwood Roy
Hathaway Albert H
Hathaway Alfred
Hathaway Frank
Hathaway Percy V
Hawker William
Hayward Victor
Hill Ernest
Hill Sidney
Hobbs Herbert W
Hobbs Walter J
Hooper James W
Hooper Sidney
Hughes Edward
Hughes Percy
James Mark
James Raymond
Leacey Stanley
Lockey Frank
Lockey Walter
Midwinter John
Miffling Harry
Pulham Edward
Pulham Wilfred
Scott Charles J
Staite Frank
Stratford Bert
Stratford William
Temple Albert
Timms Fred
Townsend Arthur
Tucker William
Williams Ernest

1939-1945
In memory of the men of Naunton who fell in the Second World War:

Aston Kenneth
Saunders Cyril A
Storey Gilbert L

Men and women who enlisted from Naunton in the Second World War & returned:

Arkell Muriel Francis
Bayliss Ernest Horace
Benfield Algernon C
Benfield Claude E
Crayden Ernest
Day Geoffrey R
Dean Leslie
Dean Frank
Dean George H
Fletcher Charles J
Fletcher Cuthbert
Gleed Albert
Gleed Reginald
Hanks Edward L
Hanks Roger R
Hanks Daphne M
Harwood Kenneth J
Hawker Cecil J
Hobbs Alfred L
James Ivor T
James Richard
Jones Hermas
Kenneally Thomas
Lister-Coles Theodore
Mattock James W
Miffling Ernest
Morris Reginald W
Neale George
Perry Ernest E
Read Charles G
Ridge Gilbert G
Ridout Charles
Sell Gladys
Smith Monica M
Smith Cecil J
Stanbridge Thomas J
Temple Harold W
Watson Lionel
Willis Ronald A
Willis Norman H
Wright Muriel

Epilogue – from little acorns.....

Taking some old village values forward into the twenty-first century.

By 1775 the people of Naunton had the following words cast into
the treble bell of St. Andrew's Church, and proudly rang them out over the parish:

'Peace and good neighbourhood'

By the twentieth century they were carrying banners through the street emblazoned with the words:

'Peace and Unity'

Ever since crafting his words and swords of some 2000 years ago, man has consistently lost sight of such flawlessly simple phrases as these. The last century alone saw his technologically improved armoury used with such deadly efficiency that stone memorials are all that now remain to many young men from this and other parishes, after war cut them down in their prime. Once again, history taught us nothing, as mankind continued to develop sophisticated weapons of mass destruction, as well as more efficient 'conventional' ones. Their use, or misuse, again threatens world peace, as they fall into the hands of war-mongers who espouse terror, genocide, and even total-war all over again.

I believe that such simple words as once fell easily from the lips of the good folk of Naunton; with a few taking them into the virgin fields of the British Commonwealth, and more sadly, the killing fields of Europe and beyond, remain as valid today as ever. Occasionally they were heard and even heeded, making the world a better place as a result, as key-players drew back from the brink of heaven knows what. At other times they were ignored, at terrible human cost, with individual communities and whole countries suffering as a consequence. From the time of the first bronze swords to these ultra-modern times, in which we find ourselves saddled with expertly crafted metal bombs of enriched uranium, high explosives and deadly chemicals, simple cautionary words such as these, were, and possibly always will be the only ones that may cause some men to hesitate. Almost everyone in the world craves 'Peace and Unity' and I believe that places like Naunton are as historically entitled as anywhere else in the world to take a lead in preserving it for future generations; possibly acting as a non-political catalyst, by nailing these beautifully simple words to its modern electronic mast.

In this seemingly much smaller world, where irksome data (e.g. spam, chain-letters, viruses, et al) flash around the globe in an instant, I would like to suggest another, more beneficial way of using the immense power of this 'Superhighway' of words and images. If Naunton were now to 'headline' these fine old words onto the front page of its two websites, which almost the whole world now has access to; it could do very little harm, and maybe a little unknown good. We have come a long way from the days when Naunton men and women first set off for various parts of the New World, taking their mother tongue and Christian values with them. I believe we could now (at no financial cost) electronically re-export a few of the same faultless values. If they impacted beneficially on just one or two 'modern' but still aggressive individuals, tribes or countries, it would have proved worthwhile.

Perhaps Naunton might now consider taking this pioneering electronic initiative, sending its user-friendly message to the ever increasing number of people and places in the world with their own website. The 'Peace and Good Neighbourhood' bulletin boards within www.ngbc.org and www.Naunton.org could be partitioned into other countries, to collect equally peaceful feedback from them, as electronic signatures in a digital 'Visitor's Book'. Who knows, one day Naunton's miniscule electronic banner of 'Peace and Unity', originating from just one small Cotswold community in the heart of rural England, may once again begin to have some noticeably beneficial global effect.

Bibliography, together with some further reading and web-browsing

Prehistoric Gloucestershire, Timothy Darvill, Alan Sutton, 1987
Food & Cooking in Prehistoric Britain, Jane Renfrew, English Heritage, 1985
Farming in the Iron Age, Peter Reynolds, Cambridge University Press, 1976
Celtic Coinage in Britain, Philip De Jersey, Shire Publications Ltd, 1996
The Coinage of the Dobunni, R.D. Van Arsdell, Oxbow Books, 1994
Roman Gloucestershire, Alan McWhirr, Alan Sutton, 1981
The Place Names of Gloucestershire, A.H. Smith, Cambridge University Press 1964.
The Place Names of Roman Britain, A.L.F. Rivet & Colin Smith, BCA, 1979
Saxon Charters and Field Names of Gloucestershire, G.B. Grundy, Bristol & Gloucestershire Archaeological Society, 1935/6
Bibliotheca Gloucestrensis, John Washbourn, 1825, A Collection of Scarce & Curious Tracts of the County & City published during the Civil War.
Bourton-on-the-Water, Harry Clifford, J.H. Alden, Stow-on-the-Wold, 1916
Bourton-on-the-Water Roman Settlement, Colin Renfrew, 1974
Naunton Upon Cotswold, Ernest F. Eales, (self-published) The Alden Press, Oxford, 1928
The Dialect Of Naunton, Ernst Barth, V.P.G. Keller, Zurich, 1968 (a study made in Naunton in 1952/3)
Memories of a Cotswold Childhood, James Mattock (Pigman Poet of Naunton, 1920-1983) The Delahaye Gallery, Cirencester, 1990
Stow-on-the-Wold, Joan Johnson, Alan Sutton, 1980
A Dictionary of English Place Names, A.D.Mills, OUP 1991
A Dictionary of Surnames, Patrick Hanks & Flavia Hodges, OUP 1988
Glevensis, Issue 34, The Dobunni, Tom Moore & Richard Reece 2001
Mother Tongue, Bill Bryson, Penguin Books, 1990
Meet The Ancestors, Julian Richards, BBC Wordlwide Ltd, 1999
Excavations at Kingscote and Wycombe: A Roman Estate Centre and Small Town in the Cotswolds & Related Settlements including Salmonsbury. J.R. Timby, Cotswold Archaeological Trust Ltd, 1968

■ *Some websites to browse:*

www.naunton.org (the village website)
www.ngbc.org.uk (Naunton & Guiting Baptist Chapels)
www.cotswold.gov.uk/museum (A wealth of local material at Corinium Museum)
www.cheltenhammuseum.org.uk (Salmonsbury collection & much more)
www.gloucestershire.gov.uk (GRO – the local Record Office and related areas)
www.writer2001.com (to Celtic Coin Index) www.gallica.co.uk (Celtic gods etc)
www.roman-britain.org (to Salmonsbury & Corinium)
www.genuki.org.uk (for pre-1801 censuses)
www.butser.org.uk (Iron Age farm life in Hampshire)
www.cinderbury.co.uk (Iron Age farm life in Gloucestershire)
www.finds.org.uk (Portable Antiquities Scheme and finder's obligations)
www.bbc.co.uk/history (TV trail into history and pre-history)
www.uktv.co.uk/uktvHistory (TV history trail and related programmes)
www.stonepages.com (if you wish to step back even further)

Thanks and acknowledgements

Public Record Office (The National Archive), Kew, for 1901 Census (PRO Ref: RG13 2453). Gloucester Record Office, for several things, particularly the School Registers, Financial Domesday and 1838 map by William Mitchell. Geoff Gwatkin for repro' 1838 Map. Cheltenham Library for Trade Directories. The Corinium Museum, Cirencester and the Ashmolean, Oxford (Salmonsbury artefacts and validation). Dr Carrie Smith, for her unstinting help as County Editor, Victoria County History of Gloucestershire. Tim Grubb, SMR Officer, Gloucestershire County Council Archaeology Service. Richard Bryant (Salmonsbury painting). Dr Steven Blake, Keeper of Collections, Cheltenham Museum & Art Gallery (Dixton Harvesters painting and Salmonsbury Collection). Robert Juggins, (that young man will go far) and Peter Hodge (who already has) for their front-cover paintings. Philip Juggins, for his rear-cover aerial photo. Stu Russell from Florida for all 1954 photos. Tony Huggard - Bourton-on-the-Water Primary School; Ian Rushin - Temple Guiting Primary School; Marianne Campbell - Cold Aston Primary School, and Guiting Power Amenity Trust, for access to School Registers (1970-2000). Fiona Milton, for Dissenters' Document. Peter Renfrew, ©1999, for colour 'Autochrome' photograph c1914, by Broadway veterinarian, Archibald Renfrew (1861-1930) M.R.C.V.S. Joan Johnson, Roger Box and Rosemary Aitken, for advice on matters historical. Bruton Knowles Land Agents for Waterloo Farm sale map. To numerous Nauntonians, both past and present, who over the years I have been privileged to know, many allowing me to copy their pictures; especially my Cousin Ian for his help and advice. To the Village Hall Millennium Committee, later the Social Committee, who were unequivocally supportive, particularly David and Cathy Turton, without whose positive and unwavering encouragement the unpublished manuscript might now be languishing in the Church tower. To my sister Pat and brother-in-law Ralph Boult, who assisted in so many ways, especially in delivering numerous missives around the parish. And of course to all of you who kept faith by pre-purchasing 300 copies of the book, thereby enabling things to advance to the printing stage; with apologies to anyone who is disappointed, because there can be no refunds! One or two others are akin to discreet puppeteers; desiring to remain anonymous, but genuinely supportive by pulling several silent strings to make it happen. My heartfelt thanks go to them, without needing to breach any confidences.

All of this coupled with a little personal doggedness, resulted in the manuscript reaching the Alden Press in the Spring of 2004. This is the same printer that produced Eales' book in 1928; representing just one more historical stitch amongst the countless threads of continuity that still hold the ancient fabric of this fine old place together.

That just leaves me to thank Steve Neville and Brian Talmage of Alden Press, who faced with a rank amateur and his first book on a CD, as opposed to the customary package they might normally expect from a professional Publisher, remained unfazed and equally enthusiastic to see it roll off their modern (Heidelberg) press.

To all the above, and a good few others, I am indebted beyond mere words.

David Hanks – 2004AD